Pro SQL Server 2022 Administration

A Guide for the Modern DBA

Third Edition

Peter A. Carter

Apress®

Pro SQL Server 2022 Administration: A Guide for the Modern DBA

Peter A. Carter
SOUTHAMPTON, UK

ISBN-13 (pbk): 978-1-4842-8863-4
https://doi.org/10.1007/978-1-4842-8864-1

ISBN-13 (electronic): 978-1-4842-8864-1

Managing Director, Apress Media LLC: Welmoed Spahr
Acquisitions Editor: Jonathan Gennick
Development Editor: Laura Berendson
Coordinating Editor: Jill Balzano

Cover designed by eStudioCalamar

Cover Photo by Anton Maksimov 5642.su on Unsplash

Distributed to the book trade worldwide by Springer Science+Business Media New York, 1 New York Plaza, Suite 4600, New York, NY 10004-1562, USA. Phone 1-800-SPRINGER, fax (201) 348-4505, e-mail orders-ny@ springer-sbm.com, or visit www.springeronline.com. Apress Media, LLC is a California LLC and the sole member (owner) is Springer Science + Business Media Finance Inc (SSBM Finance Inc). SSBM Finance Inc is a **Delaware** corporation.

For information on translations, please e-mail booktranslations@springernature.com; for reprint, paperback, or audio rights, please e-mail bookpermissions@springernature.com.

Apress titles may be purchased in bulk for academic, corporate, or promotional use. eBook versions and licenses are also available for most titles. For more information, reference our Print and eBook Bulk Sales web page at http://www.apress.com/bulk-sales.

Any source code or other supplementary material referenced by the author in this book is available to readers on GitHub (https://github.com/Apress). For more detailed information, please visit http://www.apress.com/source-code.

Printed on acid-free paper

For Terri. My inspiration, my rock.

Table of Contents

About the Author

 **Peter Carter** is a SQL Server expert with over 15 years of experience in developing, administering, and architecting SQL Server platforms and data-tier applications. He was awarded an MCC by Microsoft in 2011 to sit alongside his array of MCTS, MCITP, MCSA, and MCSE certifications in SQL Server from version 2005 onward. Peter has written a number of books across a variety of SQL Server topics, including security, high availability, and automation.

About the Technical Reviewer

Ian Stirk is a freelance SQL Server consultant based in London. In addition to his day job, he is an author, creator of software utilities, and technical reviewer who regularly writes book reviews for www.i-programmer.info.

He covers every aspect of SQL Server/Azure SQL and has special interest in performance and scalability. If you require help with your SQL Server systems, feel free to contact him at ian_stirk@yahoo.com or www.linkedin.com/in/ian-stirk-bb9a31.

Acknowledgments

I want to say a big thank you to Ian Stirk for a great tech review. As always, the quality of this book is better because of his contribution to the project.

I would also like to thank Jonathan Gennick for the continued support and partnerial attitude that he has shown through this, and all of the projects that we have worked on together.

Credit goes to Chris Dent, who has helped me improve some of the PowerShell scripts within this book.

Finally, I need to thank Terri, without whom this edition of the book would probably never have been written. She has provided constant motivation and support through what has been a rather grueling schedule this year.

PART I

Installation and Configuration

CHAPTER 1

Planning the Deployment

Planning a deployment of SQL Server 2022, in order to best support the business's needs, can be a complicated task. You should make sure to consider many areas, including edition, licensing requirements, on-premises vs. cloud hosting, hardware considerations, software configuration, and even if Windows is the best platform. For example, if your new instance will be supporting a PHP Web App, hosted on Linux, then maybe your instance should also be hosted on Linux? And all of this is before you even start to consider which features of SQL Server you may need to install to support the application.

This chapter will guide you through the key decisions that you should make when you are planning your deployment. You will also learn how to perform some essential operating system configurations, should you decide to host your instance on Windows Server. This chapter will also give you an overview of the top-level features that you can choose to install and discuss why selecting the appropriate features is important.

Editions and License Models

Choosing the edition of SQL Server 2022 to support your data-tier application may sound like a simple task, but in fact, you should spend time thinking about this decision and consulting with both business stakeholders and other IT departments to bring their opinions into this decision. The first thing to consider is that there are five editions of SQL Server. These editions not only have different levels of functionality, but they also have different license considerations. Additionally, from an operational support perspective, you may find that the TCO (total cost of ownership) of the estate increases if you allow data-tier applications to be hosted on versions of SQL Server that are not deployed strategically within your estate.

A full discussion of feature and licensing considerations is beyond the scope of this book; however, Table 1-1 details the available licensing models for each edition of SQL Server, whereas Table 1-2 highlights the primary purpose of each edition.

3

© Peter A. Carter 2023
P. A. Carter, *Pro SQL Server 2022 Administration*, https://doi.org/10.1007/978-1-4842-8864-1_1

Table 1-1. *SQL Server Edition License Models*

Edition	License Model(s)	Comments
Enterprise	Per-core	–
Standard	• Per-core • Server + CAL	–
Web	Third-party hosting only	–
Developer	Free for noncommercial use	Not for use in a production environment
Express	Free edition of SQL Server	Limited functionality and small capacity limits, such as a 10GB database size, a 1GB limit on RAM, and a CPU limit of one socket, or four cores

A CAL is a client access license, where a client can refer to either a user or a device. You can choose whether to purchase user or device licenses based on which will be cheapest for your environment.

For example, if your organization had a SQL server that was supporting a call center that had 100 computers, and it ran 24/7 with three eight-hour shifts, then you would have 100 devices and 300 users, so device CALs would be the most sensible option for you to choose.

On the flip side, if your organization had a SQL server that was supporting a sales team of 25 who all connected to the sales application not only via their laptops, but also via their iPads, then you would have 25 users, but 50 devices, and therefore choosing user CALs would be the more sensible option.

To summarize, if you have more users than devices, then you should choose device CALs. If you have more devices than users, on the other hand, you should choose user CALs. Microsoft also supplies a tool called Microsoft Assessment and Planning (MAP) Toolkit for SQL Server, which will help you plan your licensing requirements.

Table 1-2. *SQL Server Edition Overview*

Edition	Edition Overview
Enterprise	Fully featured edition of SQL Server for Enterprise systems and critical apps
Standard	Core database and BI functionality, aimed at departmental-level systems and noncritical apps
Web	Is only available for service providers hosting public websites that use SQL Server
Developer	A fully featured edition, to the level of Enterprise edition, but meant for development use and not allowed for use on production systems
Express	A free, entry-level version of SQL Server geared toward small applications with local data requirements

The version(s) of SQL Server that you choose to support in your Enterprise applications will vary depending on the project's requirements, your organization's requirements, and the underlying infrastructure. For example, if your organization hosts its entire SQL Server estate within a private cloud, then you are likely to only support the Enterprise edition, since you will be licensing the underlying infrastructure.

Alternatively, if your organization is predominantly utilizing physical boxes, then you most likely need to support a mix of SQL Server versions, such as Enterprise and Standard editions. This will give projects the flexibility to reduce their costs if they only require a subset of features and are not expecting high-volume workloads, and hence can live with the limits that Standard edition imposes on RAM and CPU.

The next thing you should consider before choosing which edition you will use is whether or not you will use a Windows Server Core installation of SQL Server. Installations on Server Core can help improve security by reducing the attack surface of your server. Server Core is a minimal installation, so there is less surface to attack and fewer security vulnerabilities. It can also improve performance, because you do not have the overhead of the graphical user interface (GUI) and because many resource-intensive applications cannot be installed. If you do decide to use Server Core, then it is also important to understand the impacts of doing so.

From the SQL Server perspective, the following features cannot be used:

- Reporting Services

- SQL Server Data Tools (SSDT)

- Client Tools Backward Compatibility

- Client Tools SDK

- SQL Server Books Online

- Distributed Replay Controller

- Master Data Services (MDS)

- Data Quality Services (DQS)

The following features can be used, but only from a remote server:

- Management Tools

- Distributed Replay Client

From the broader perspective of operational support, you will need to ensure that all of your operational teams (DBAs, Windows Operations, etc.) are in a position to support Server Core. For example, if your DBA team relies heavily on a third-party graphical tool for interrogating execution plans, does this need to be installed locally on the server? Is there an alternative tool that would meet their needs? From a Windows operations perspective, does the team have the tools in place for remotely monitoring and managing the server? Are there any third-party tools they rely on that would need to be replaced?

You should also consider if your operations team has the skill set to manage systems using predominantly command-line processes. If it does not, then you should consider what training or upskilling may be required.

Hardware Considerations

When you are planning the hardware requirements for your server, ideally, you will implement a full capacity planning exercise so you can estimate the hardware requirements of the application(s) that the server will support. When conducting this exercise, make sure you take your company's standard hardware life cycle into account, rather than planning just for today. Depending on your organization, this could be between one and five years, but will generally be three years.

This is important in order to avoid undersizing or oversizing your server. Project teams will generally want to oversize their servers in order to ensure performance. Not only is this approach costly when scaled through the enterprise, but in some environments, it can actually have a detrimental effect on performance. An example of this would be a private cloud infrastructure with shared resources. In this scenario, oversizing servers can have a negative impact on the entire environment, including the oversized server itself.

Specifying Strategic Minimum Requirements

When specifying the minimum hardware requirements for SQL Server within your environment, you may choose to specify the minimum requirements for installing SQL Server—4GB RAM and a single 2GHz CPU (based on Enterprise edition). However, you may be better served to think about operational supportability within your enterprise.

For example, if your environment consists predominantly of a private cloud infrastructure, then you may wish to specify a minimum of 2 vCores and 4GB RAM + (number of cores * 1GB) since this may be in line with your enterprise standards.

On the other hand, if you have a highly dispersed enterprise, which has grown organically, and you wish to help persuade projects to use a shared SQL Server farm, you may choose to enforce much higher minimum specifications, such as 32GB RAM and 2 sockets/4 cores. The reasoning here is that any projects without large throughput requirements would be "forced" to use your shared farm to avoid the heavy costs associated with an unnecessarily large system.

Storage

Storage is a very important consideration for any SQL Server installation. The following sections will discuss locally attached storage and SAN storage, as well as considerations for file placement.

Locally Attached Storage

If your server will use locally attached storage, then you should carefully consider file layout. By its very nature, SQL Server is often input/output (I/O) bound, and therefore, configuring the I/O subsystem is one of the critical aspects for performance. You first need to separate your user databases' data files and log files onto separate disks or arrays and also to separate TempDB, which is the most heavily used system database. If all of these files reside on a single volume, then you are likely to experience disk contention while SQL Server attempts to write to all of them at the same time.

Typically, locally attached storage will be presented to your server as RAID (redundant array of inexpensive disks) arrays and various RAID levels are available. There are many RAID levels available, but the most common are outlined in the following pages.

RAID 0

A RAID 0 volume consists of between two and n spindles, and the data bits are striped across all of the disks within the array. This provides excellent performance; however, it provides no fault tolerance. The loss of any disk within the array means that the whole array will fail. This is illustrated in Figure 1-1.

Tip   In the diagrams in this section, the red X denotes a disk failure.

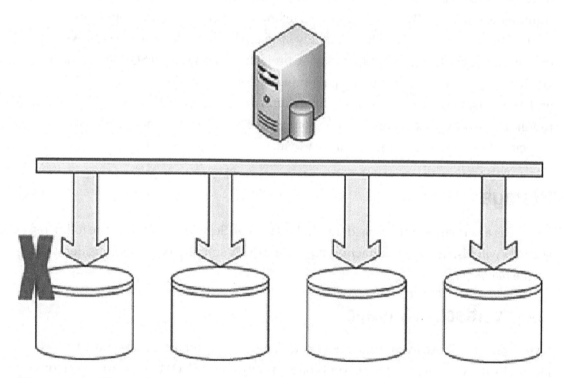

Figure 1-1.   *The RAID 0 array provides no redundancy*

Caution   Because RAID 0 provides no redundancy, it should not be used for production systems.

RAID 1

A RAID 1 volume will consist of two spindles, working together as a mirrored pair. This provides redundancy in the event of failure of one of the spindles, but it comes at the expense of write performance, because every write to the volume needs to be made twice. This method of redundancy is illustrated in Figure 1-2.

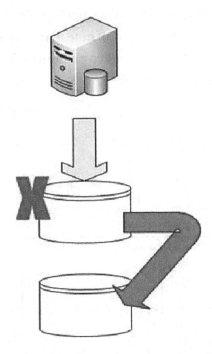

Figure 1-2. *RAID 1 provides redundancy by mirroring the disk*

Note   The formula for calculating the total IOPS (input/output per second) against a RAID 1 array is as follows: IOPS = Reads + (Writes * 2).

RAID 5

A RAID 5 volume will consist of between three and *n* spindles and provides redundancy of exactly one disk within the array. Because the blocks of data are striped across multiple spindles, read performance of the volume will be very good, but again, this is at the expense of write performance. Write performance is impaired because redundancy is achieved by distributing parity bits across all spindles in the array. This means that there is a performance penalty of four writes for every one write to the volume. This is regardless of the number of disks in the array. The reason for this arbitrary penalty is because the parity bits are striped in the same way the data is. The controller will read the original data and the original parity and then write the new data and the new parity, without needing to read all of the other disks in the array. This method of redundancy is illustrated in Figure 1-3.

It is worthy of note, however, that should a spindle within the array fail, performance will be noticeably impaired. It is also worthy of note that rebuilding a disk from the parity bits contained on its peers can take an extended amount of time, especially for a disk with a large capacity.

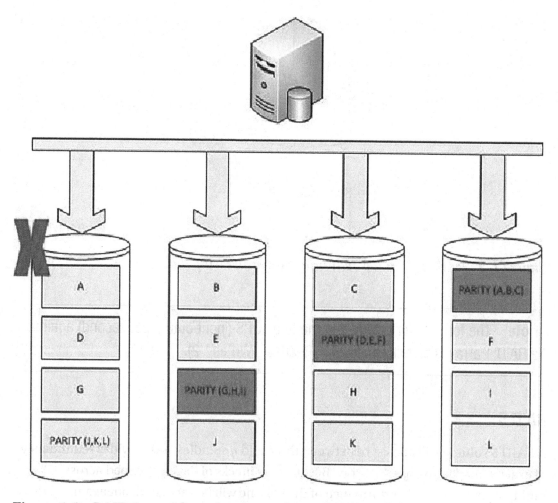

Figure 1-3. *RAID 5 provides redundancy through parity bits*

Note   The formula for calculating total IOPS against a RAID 5 array is as follows: IOPS = Read + (Writes * 4). To calculate the expected IOPS per spindle, you can divide this value for IOPS by the number of disks in the array. This can help you calculate the minimum number of disks that should be in the array to achieve your performance goals.

RAID 10

A RAID 10 volume will consist of four to n disks, but it will always be an even number. It provides the best combination of redundancy and performance. It works by creating a stripe of mirrors. The bits are striped, without parity, across half of the disks within the array, as they are for RAID 0, but they are then mirrored to the other half of the disks in the array. It is a combination of RAID 1 and RAID 0.

This is known as a nested, or hybrid RAID level, and it means that half of the disks within the array can be lost, providing that none of the failed disks are within the same mirrored pair. This is illustrated in Figure 1-4.

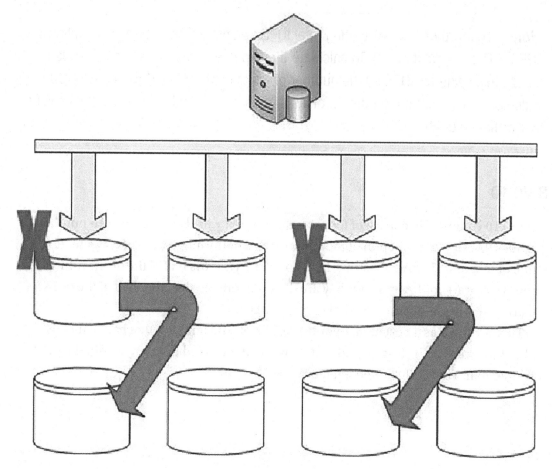

Figure 1-4. *RAID 10 provides redundancy by mirroring each disk within the stripe*

Note   The formula for calculating total IOPS against a RAID 10 array is as follows: IOPS = Read + (Writes * 2). In the same way as for RAID 5, in order to calculate the expected IOPS per spindle, you can divide the value for IOPS by the number of disks in the array. This can help you calculate the minimum number of disks that should be in the array to achieve your performance goals.

File Placement

It is generally accepted that RAID 0 should not be used for any SQL Server files. I have known people to suggest that RAID 0 may be acceptable for TempDB files. The rational here is that a heavily used TempDB often requires very fast performance, and because it is re-created every time the instance restarts, it does not require redundancy. This sounds perfectly reasonable, but if you think in terms of uptime, you may realize why I disagree with this opinion.

Your SQL Server instance requires TempDB in order to function. If you lose TempDB, then your instance will go down, and if TempDB cannot be re-created, then you will not be able to bring your instance back up. Therefore, if you host TempDB on a RAID 0 array and one of the disks within that array fails, you will not be able to bring the instance back up until you have performed one of the following actions:

1. Wait for the storage team to bring the RAID 0 array back online.

2. Start the instance in "minimal configuration mode" and use SQLCMD to change the location of TempDB.

By the time either of these steps is complete, you may find that stakeholders are jumping up and down, so you may find it best to avoid this option. For this reason, TempDB is generally best placed on a RAID 10 array, whenever possible. This will provide the best level of performance for the database, and because its size is significantly smaller than the user database files, you do not have the same level of cost implication.

In an ideal world, where money is no object, the data files of your user databases will be stored on RAID 10 arrays, since RAID 10 provides the best combination of redundancy and performance. In the real world, however, if the applications you are supporting are not mission critical, this may not be justifiable. If this is the situation, then RAID 5 can be a good choice, as long as your applications have a fairly high ratio of reads to writes. I would normally use a ratio of three to one in favor of reads as being a good baseline, but of course, it can vary in every scenario.

If your databases are only using basic features of SQL Server, then you will likely find that RAID 1 is a good choice for your log files. RAID 5 is not generally suitable, because of the write-intensive nature of the transaction log. In some cases, I have even known RAID 1 to perform better than RAID 10 for the transaction log. This is because of the sequential nature of the write activity.

However, some features of SQL Server can generate substantial read activity from the transaction log. If this is the case, then you may find that RAID 10 is a requirement for your transaction log as well as your data files. Features that cause transaction log reads include the following:

- AlwaysOn availability groups

- Database mirroring

- Snapshot creation

- Backups

- DBCC CHECKDB

- Change data capture

- Log shipping (both backups, and also if restoring logs WITH STANDBY)

Solid-State Drives (SSDs)

One common reason to use locally attached storage, as opposed to a storage area network (SAN), is to optimize the performance of SQL Server components, which require extremely fast I/O. These components include TempDB and buffer cache extensions. It is not uncommon to find that a database's data and log files are stored on a SAN, but TempDB and buffer cache extensions are stored on locally attached storage.

In this example, it would make good sense to use SSDs in the locally attached array. Solid-state drives (SSDs) can offer very high I/O rates, but at a higher cost, compared to traditional disks. SSDs are also not a "magic bullet." Although they offer a very high number of IOPS for random disk access, they can be less efficient for sequential scan activities, which are common in certain database workload profiles, such as data warehouses. SSDs are also prone to sudden failure, as opposed to the gradual decline of a traditional disk. Therefore, having a fault-tolerant RAID level and hot spares in the array is a very good idea.

Working with a SAN

Storage area network are three words that can strike fear into the heart of a database administrator (DBA). The modern DBA must embrace concepts such as SAN and virtualization; however, although they pose fundamental change, they also ease the overall manageability of the estate and reduce the total cost of ownership (TCO).

The most important thing for a DBA to remember about a SAN is that it changes the fundamental principles of the I/O subsystem, and DBAs must change their thinking accordingly. For example, in the world of locally attached storage, the most fundamental principle is to separate your data files, log files, and TempDB, and to ensure that they are all hosted on the most appropriate RAID level.

In the world of the SAN, however, you may initially be alarmed to find that your SAN administrators do not offer a choice of RAID level, and if they do, they may not offer RAID 10. If you find this to be the case, it is likely because the SAN is, behind the scenes, actually stripping the data across every disk in the array. This means that although the RAID level can still have some impact on throughput, the more important consideration is which storage tier to choose.

Many organizations choose to tier the storage on their SAN, offering three or more tiers. Tier 1 will be the highest tier and may well consist of a combination of SSDs and small, highly performing Fiber Channel drives. Tier 2 will normally consist of larger drives—potentially SATA (serial advanced technology attachment)—and Tier 3 will often use near-line storage. Near-line storage consists of a large number of inexpensive disks, such as SATA disks, which are usually stopped. The disks only spin up when there is a requirement to access the data that they contain. As you have probably guessed, you will want to ensure that any applications that require good performance will need to be located on Tier 1 of your SAN. Tier 2 could possibly be an option for small, rarely used databases with little or no concurrency, and Tier 3 should rarely, if ever, be used to store SQL Server databases or logs.

Your real throughput will be determined by these factors, but also many others, such as the number of network paths between your server and the SAN, how many servers are concurrently accessing the SAN, and so on. Another interesting quirk of a SAN is that you will often find that your write performance is far superior to your read performance. This is because some SANs use a battery-backed write cache, but when reading, they need to retrieve the data from the spindles.

Next, consider that because all of your data may well be striped across all of the spindles in the array—and even if it isn't, the likelihood is that all files on a single server will probably all reside on the same CPG (common provisioning group)—you should not expect to see an instant performance improvement from separating your data, log, and TempDB files. Many DBAs, however, still choose to place their data, log, and TempDB files on separate volumes for logical separation and consistency with other servers that use locally attached storage. In some cases, however, if you are using SAN snapshots or SAN replication for redundancy, you may be required to have the data and log files of a database on the same volume. You should check this with your storage team.

Disk Block Size

Another thing to consider for disk configuration, whether it is locally attached or on a SAN, is the disk block size. Depending on your storage, it is likely that the default NTFS (New Technology File System) allocation unit size will be set as 4KB. The issue is that SQL Server organizes data into eight continuous 8KB pages, known as an *extent*. To get optimum performance for SQL Server, the block sizes of the volumes hosting data, logs, and TempDB should be aligned with this and set to 64KB.

You can check the disk block size by running the Windows PowerShell script in Listing 1-1, which uses fsutil to gather the NTFS properties of the volume. The script assumes that f: is the volume whose block size you wish to determine. Be sure to change this to the drive letter that you wish to check. Also ensure that the script is run as Administrator.

Listing 1-1. Determine Disk Block Size

```
# Populate the drive letter you want to check

$drive = "f:"

# Initialize outputarray

$outputarray = new-object PSObject

$outputarray | add-member NoteProperty Drive $drive

# Initialize output

$output = (fsutil fsinfo ntfsinfo $drive)

# Split each line of fsutil into a separate array value

foreach ($line in $output) {

    $info = $line.split(':')
```

```
$outputarray | add-member NoteProperty $info[0].trim().Replace(' ','_')
$info[1].trim()

    $info = $null

}

# Format and display results

$results = 'Disk Block Size for ' + $drive + ' ' + $outputarray.Bytes_Per_
Cluster/1024 + 'KB'

$results
```

Cloud Storage

When building IaaS (infrastructure as a service) in a cloud platform, in order to host SQL Server, careful consideration should be given to the storage requirements of the data-tier application. Storage options in cloud are complex and ever changing. They also vary between cloud providers. Therefore, you should consult with your Cloud architect or DevOps engineer. However, this section will provide a brief overview of the main points of consideration.

The first consideration is shared storage. If you are building a stand-alone SQL Server instance, or indeed an AlwaysOn Availability Group topology, with no shared storage, then this is not a worry. If you intend to deploy a SQL Server failover clustered instance, however, then the type of storage you use is important. In AWS, then instead of using standard EBS (Elastic Block Storage) for your data disks, you will need to use Amazon FSx file share, which can be shared between multiple EC2 (Elastic Compute Cloud) instances. In Azure, you will still use Azure managed disks for your VMs, but you will need to implement S2D (Storage Spaces Direct) and Cluster Shared Volumes, which can be configured within Windows Server.

You will also need to consider storage performance. There are two separate components to this. Firstly, you will need to ensure that the storage you choose is fast enough to meet the requirements of the use case.

In Azure, Microsoft recommends using Premium SSDs, which are no larger than 2048 GiB for the data volume, to optimize cache support. A P40 disk (2048 GiB) provides 7500 maximum nonbursting IOPS (input/output per second) with a maximum 250

MB/s nonbursting throughput. If you step down in size to a P30 disk (1024 GiB), then the maximum nonbursting IOPS reduces to 5000 with the maximum nonbursting throughput at 200 MB/s.

If you require higher IOPS, then you would need to consider using Azure ultra disks instead. These disks can provide submillisecond latency with up to 160,000 IOPS and 4000 Mbps, depending on the size of the disk.

In AWS, the storage options (at the time of writing) are GP2 (General Purpose 2), GP3 and Provisioned IOPS SSD (io1 and io2). GP2 storage is a predecessor to GP3 and generally shouldn't be considered for SQL Server. Its performance is tied to its size, which means you may end up needing to buy more larger disks than you require. GP3 also has a maximum throughput four times higher than GP2 and is less expensive.

GP3 has a baseline performance of 3000 IOPS and 125 MiB/s throughput. For an additional fee, however, performance can be increased to a maximum of 16,000 IOPS and 1000 MiB/s throughput. If additional IOPS are required, then you can move to a Provisioned IOPS volume. The io2 type is available at the same price point as io1 and has improved performance, so io1 generally should not be considered for SQL Server. Io2 volumes provide 500 IOPS per GiB, with a maximum of 64,000 IOPS.

In AWS, when considering storage performance, it is important to consider the size of the EC2 instance, as well as the performance of the disk itself. Different instance types and sizes have storage throttled at different levels. This means that you need to be careful that you do not buy fast, expensive storage, but then throttle that performance by using the wrong instance type. For example, a m4.xlarge instance has an EBS bandwidth of 750 Mbps (715 MiB/s). Therefore, if you have purchased a GP3 volume with 1000 MiB/s throughput, then you will only actually get 715 MiB/s.

Operating Systems Considerations

SQL Server has support for many operating systems, including many versions of Windows. It is unlikely, however, that you will want to allow SQL Server to be installed on any version of any operating system that is supported. For example, within your Windows estate, it is advisable to align a version of SQL Server with a specific version of Windows. This gives you two benefits.

First, it drastically reduces the amount of testing that you need to perform to sign off your build. For example, imagine that you decide you will only allow Enterprise edition within your environment. In theory, you would still need to gain operational sign-off on more than a dozen versions of Windows. In contrast, if you allow both SQL Server Enterprise and Standard editions of SQL Server, but you align both editions with Windows Server 2022 Standard edition, then you would only require sign-off once for each of your supported editions of SQL Server.

The second benefit is related to end of life cycle (EOL) for your platforms. If you allow SQL Server 2019 to be installed on Windows Server 2016, the end of mainstream support for Windows is January 2022, as opposed to January 2025 for SQL. At best, this will cause complexity and outage while you upgrade Windows, and at worst, it could lead to extended support costs that you could have avoided.

Tip   It is a good idea to run the latest version of Windows Server and SQL Server, as they provide the most benefit in terms of features, security, and performance. If your organization is risk adverse, however, and does not like to run the latest version of software, in case there are any early life stability issues, then I recommend trying to adhere to a current version − 1 policy, if possible.

Configuring the Operating System

Do your Windows administration team have a "gold build" for Windows Server 2022? Even if they do, is it optimized for SQL Server? Unless they have produced a separate build just for the purposes of hosting SQL Server, then the chances are that it will not be. The exact customizations that you will need to make are dependent on how the Windows build is configured, your environmental requirements, and the requirements of the data-tier application that your server will be hosting. The following sections highlight some of the changes that are often required.

Note   A *gold build* is a predefined template for the operating system that can be easily installed on new servers to reduce deployment time and enforce consistency.

Setting the Power Plan

It is important that you set your server to use the High Performance power plan. This is because if the balanced power plan is used, then your CPU may be throttled back during a period of inactivity. When activity on the server kicks in again, you may experience a performance issue.

You can set the power plan through the Windows GUI by opening the Power Options console in Control Panel and selecting the High Performance or you can use PowerShell or the command line. Listing 1-2 illustrates this by passing in the GUID of the High Performance power plan as a value for the -setactive parameter of the powercfg executable.

Listing 1-2. Set High Performance Power Plan with PowerShell

```
powercfg -setactive 8c5e7fda-e8bf-4a96-9a85-a6e23a8c635c
```

Optimizing for Background Services

It is good practice to ensure that your server is configured to prioritize background services over foreground applications. In practice, this means that Windows will adapt its context-switching algorithm to allow background services, including those used by SQL Server, to have more time on the processor than foreground applications have.

To ensure that Optimize for Background Service is turned on, enter the System console in Control Panel and choose Advanced System Settings. In the System Properties dialog box, select Settings within the Performance section.

Optimizing for background services can also be set by using PowerShell. Listing 1-3 demonstrates using the set-property command to update the Win32PrioritySeperation key in the Registry. The script must be run as Administrator.

Listing 1-3. Setting Optimize for Background Services with PowerShell

```
Set-ItemProperty -path HKLM:\SYSTEM\CurrentControlSet\Control\
PriorityControl -name Win32PrioritySeparation -Type DWORD -Value 24
```

Assigning User Rights

Depending on the features of SQL Server that you wish to use, you may need to grant the service account that will be running the SQL Server service user rights assignments. These assignments allow security principles to perform tasks on a computer. In the case of the SQL Server service account, they provide the permissions for enabling some SQL Server functionality where that functionality interacts with the operating system. The three most common user rights assignments, which are not automatically granted to the service account during installation, are discussed in the following pages.

Initializing the Instant File

If you have not enabled Instant File Initialization during the installation of the SQL Server instance, then when you create or expand a file, the file is filled with 0s. This is a process known as "zeroing out" the file, and it overwrites any data that previously occupied the same disk space. The issue with this is that it can take some time, especially for large files.

It is possible to override this behavior, however, so that the files are not zeroed out. This introduces a very small security risk, in the respect that the data that previously existed within that disk location could still theoretically be discovered, but this risk is so small that it is generally thought to be far outweighed by the performance benefits.

In order to use instant file initialization, the Perform Volume Maintenance Tasks User Rights Assignment must be granted to the service account that is running the SQL Server Database Engine. Once this has been granted, SQL Server will automatically use instant file initialization. No other configuration is required.

To grant the assignment through Windows GUI, open the local security policy from Control Panel ➤ System and Security ➤ Administrative Tools, before drilling through Local Policies ➤ User Rights Assignment. This will display a full list of assignments. Scroll down until you find Perform Volume Maintenance Tasks. This is illustrated in Figure 1-5.

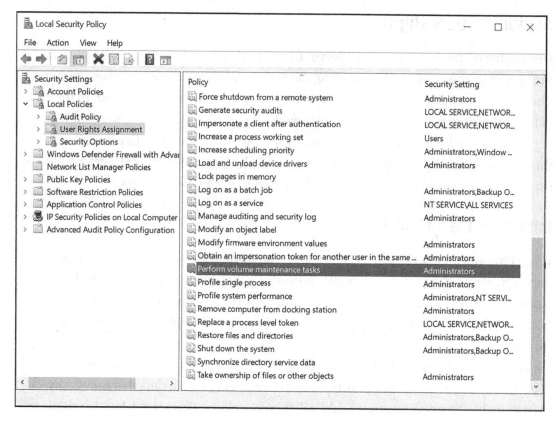

Figure 1-5. *Local Security Policy*

Right-clicking the assignment and entering its properties will allow you to add your service account.

Tip   Instant File Initialization can also be configured during SQL Server installation. This will be discussed in Chapter 2.

Locking Pages in Memory

If Windows is experiencing memory pressure, it will attempt to page data from RAM into virtual memory on disk. This can cause an issue within SQL Server. In order to provide acceptable performance, SQL Server caches recently used data pages in the buffer cache, which is an area of memory reserved by the Database Engine. In fact, all data pages are read from the buffer cache, even if they need to be read from disk first. If Windows decides to move pages from the buffer cache out to disk, the performance of your instance will be severely impaired.

In order to avoid this occurrence, it is possible to lock the pages of the buffer cache in memory, as long as you are using the Enterprise, or Standard, edition of SQL Server 2022. To do this, you simply need to grant the service account that is running the Database Engine the Lock Pages In Memory assignment using the same method as for Perform Volume Maintenance Tasks.

Caution   If you are installing SQL Server on a virtual machine, depending on the configuration of your virtual platform, you may not be able to set Lock Pages In Memory, because it may interfere with the balloon driver. The balloon driver is used by the virtualization platform to reclaim memory from the guest operating system. You should discuss this with your virtual platform administrator.

SQL Audit to the Event Log

If you are planning to use SQL Audit to capture activity within your instance, you will have the option of saving the generated events to a file, to the security log, or to the application log. The security log will be the most appropriate location if your enterprise has high security requirements.

In order to allow generated events to be written to the security log, the service account that runs the Database Engine must be granted the Generate Security Audits User Rights Assignment. This can be achieved through the Local Security Policy console.

An additional step, in order for SQL Server to be able to write audit events to the security log, is to configure the Audit Application Generated setting. This can be located in the Local Security Policy console, by drilling through Advanced Audit Policy Configuration ➤ System Audit Policies ➤ Object Access. The properties of the Audit Application Generated event can then be modified as illustrated in Figure 1-6.

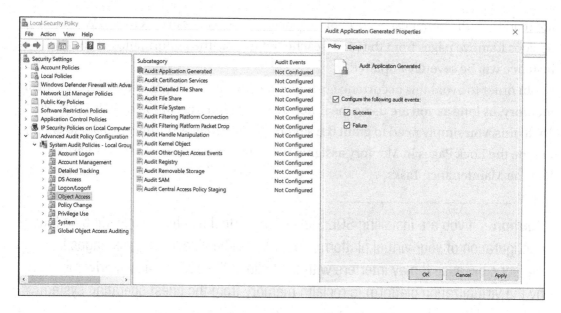

Figure 1-6. *Audit Application Generated Properties*

Caution   You need to ensure that your policies are not overridden by policies implemented at the GPO level. If this is the case, you should ask your AD (Active Directory) administrator to move your servers into a separate OU (organizational unit) with a less restrictive policy.

Selecting Features

When installing SQL Server, it may be tempting to install every feature in case you need it at some point. For the performance, manageability, and security of your environment, however, you should always adhere to the YAGNI (you aren't going to need it) principle. The YAGNI principle derives from extreme programming methodology, but it also holds true for the platform. The premise is that you do the simplest thing that will work. This will save you from issues related to complexity. Remember that additional features can be installed later. The following sections provide an overview of the main features you can select during an installation of SQL Server 2022 Enterprise edition.

The features are split into two categories, namely, instance features and shared features. Features within the instance features category can be installed multiple times on the server, associated to different instances. This is opposed to features within the shared features category, which can only be installed once on a server and are shared between all instances. The following sections will discuss the features available within each of these sections.

Instance Features

The following sections discuss each of the features that can be installed for each SQL Server instance on the server.

Database Engine Service

The Database Engine is the core service within the SQL Server suite. It contains the SQLOS, the Storage Engine, and the Relational Engine, as illustrated in Figure 1-7. It is responsible for securing, processing, and optimizing access to relational data.

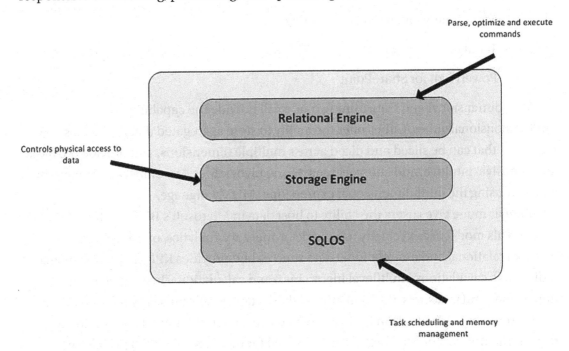

Figure 1-7. *Database Engine architecture*

It also contains replication components, in-database machine learning services and language extensions, full-text and semantic extractions for search, the PolyBase query service, and the DQS Server features, which can be selected optionally.

Replication is a set of tools that allows you to disperse data. In-database machine learning services provide Python and R integration, while sematic extractions allow you to use full text to search for the meaning of words rather than just keywords themselves. PolyBase query service allows you to run T-SQL against Hadoop data sources. DQS Server is a tool that allows you to easily find and cleanse inconsistent data. The machine learning services provide support for the R and Python languages, providing the ability to create both data science and machine learning solutions. These solutions can then import, explore, and analyze heterogeneous datasets. This book focuses primarily on core Database Engine functionality.

Analysis Services

SSAS (SQL Server Analysis Services) is a set of tools that can be harnessed for the analytical processing and data mining of data. It can be installed in one of three modes:

- Multidimensional and Data Mining

- Tabular

- PowerPivot for SharePoint

Multidimensional and Data Mining mode will provide the capability to host multidimensional cubes. Cubes offer the ability to store aggregated data, known as *measures*, that can be sliced and diced across multiple dimensions, and provide the basis of responsive, intuitive, and complex reports and pivot tables. Developers can query the cubes by using the multidimensional expressions (MDX) language.

Tabular mode gives users the ability to host data in Microsoft's BI semantic model. This model uses xVelocity to provide in-memory analytics, offering integration between relational and nonrelational data sources and provides KPIs (key performance indicators), calculations, multilevel hierarchies, and calculations. Instead of using dimensions and measures, the tabular model uses tables, columns, and relationships.

PowerPivot is an extension for Excel, which like the tabular model uses xVelocity to perform in-memory analytics and can be used for datasets up to 2GB in size. The PowerPivot for SharePoint installation expands on this by running Analysis Services in SharePoint mode, and it offers both server-side processing and browser-based interaction with PowerPivot workbooks; it also supports Power View reports and Excel workbooks through SharePoint Excel Services.

Shared Features

The following sections describe the features that can only be installed once on a server and are shared between all SQL Server instances.

Data Quality Client

The Data Quality Server is installed as an optional component of the Database Engine, as mentioned earlier. The Data Quality Client, however, can be installed as a shared feature. A shared feature is installed only once on a server and is shared by all instances of SQL Server on that machine. The Client is a GUI that allows you to administer DQS, as well as perform data-matching and data-cleansing activities.

Integration Services

Integration Services is a very powerful, graphical ETL (extract, transform, and load) tool provided with SQL Server. For the last decade, Integration Services is incorporated into the Database Engine. Despite this, the Integration Services option still needs to be installed for the functionality to work correctly, because it includes binaries that the functionality relies on.

Integration Services packages comprise a *control flow*, which is responsible for management and flow operations, including bulk inserts, loops, and transactions. The control flow also contains zero or more data flows. A *data flow* is a set of data sources, transformations, and destinations, which provides a powerful framework for merging, dispersing, and transforming data.

Integration Services can be horizontally scaled out across multiple servers, with a master and n workers. Therefore, in recent versions of SQL Server, you have the option to install classic, stand-alone Integration Services or install a scale out master, or scale out worker, on the server.

SQL Client Connectivity SDK

The Client Connectivity SDK provides a SDK for SQL Native Client to support application development. It also provides other interfaces, such as support for stack tracing in client applications.

Master Data Services

Master Data Services is a tool for managing master data within the enterprise. It allows you to model data domains that map to business entities, and it helps you manage these with hierarchies, business rules, and data versioning. When you select this feature, several components are installed:

- A web console to provide administrative capability

- A configuration tool to allow you to configure your MDM databases and the web console

- A web service, which provides extensibility for developers

- An Excel add-in, for creating new entities and attributes

SQL Server Extension for Azure

The SQL Server Extension for Azure provides out-of-the-box functionality to allow your on-premises SQL Server instances to be managed using Azure tooling, as if they were within your Azure environment. This is achieved by using an Azure Arc agent. This will be discussed in more detail in Chapter 21.

Note   In SQL Server 2022, Distributed Replay Controller and Distributed Replay Client are no longer included with the SQL Server setup media. Instead, they need to be downloaded separately.

Additionally, the runtimes for Python, R, and Java are no longer installed during setup. Instead, the required runtime packages should be installed manually, as required.

Summary

Planning a deployment can be a complicated task that involves discussions with business and technical stakeholders to ensure that your platform will meet the applications requirements, and ultimately the business needs. There are many factors that you should take into account.

Make sure you consider which is the appropriate version of SQL Server to install and the associated licensing considerations for that version. You should consider the holistic supportability of the estate when making this decision and not just the needs of the specific application. You should also consider if an Azure hosting option may be right for your application, or potentially even a hybrid approach, involving both on-premises and cloud hosting.

When planning a deployment, make sure to carry out thorough capacity planning. Also think about the hardware requirements of the application. How much RAM and how many processor cores you will need are important considerations, but perhaps the main consideration is storage. SQL Server is often an I/O-bound application, so storage can often prove to be the bottleneck.

You should also consider requirements for the operating system. This should not be limited to the most appropriate version of Windows, but also to the configuration of the operating system. Just because there is a Windows gold build available, does this mean that it is configured optimally for your SQL Server installation?

Finally, consider which features you should select to install. Most applications require only a small subset of features, and by carefully selecting which features you require, you can reduce the security footprint of the installation and also reduce management overheads.

CHAPTER 2

GUI Installation

You can invoke SQL Server's Installation Center by running SQL Server's `setup.exe` application. The Installation Center provides many utilities that will help you install an instance; these include links and tools to assist you with planning your deployment, stand-alone and clustered installation capability, and advanced tools, which will allow you to build instances using configuration files or based upon prepared images.

This chapter will provide an overview of the options available to you in the Installation Center before guiding you through the process of installing SQL Server using the graphical user interface (GUI). It will also offer real-world advice on decisions that are critical to the ongoing supportability of your instance.

Obtaining SQL Server Media

If you work within a large organization, then the SQL Server media will usually be made available by your licensing team, where it will have been downloaded from Microsoft's volume licensing portal. Alternatively, if you are a developer, then you may obtain the media from the MSDN portal. When you obtain media in this way, it is usually pre-pidded, which means that a license key is embedded within the media.

If you work for a smaller organization, however, then you may need to download the installation application from Microsoft's website. When you do this, a simple install helper is available, instead of the full media being immediately downloaded. This helper app will give you the option of a very basic installation of SQL Server that installs all features, on the current server. This should usually be avoided, as it maximizes the attack surface. You will also have the option of performing a customized installation on the current server. Finally, you have the option of simply downloading the media, which will allow you to copy the media to a different server, to perform an offline install. This installation application can be seen in Figure 2-1.

© Peter A. Carter 2023
P. A. Carter, *Pro SQL Server 2022 Administration*, https://doi.org/10.1007/978-1-4842-8864-1_2

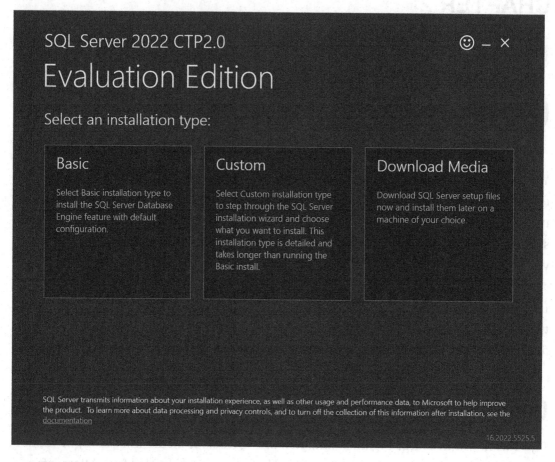

Figure 2-1. *Installation helper*

From this point forward, I will assume that you have access to the downloaded media and the installation helper application will not be mentioned again.

Installation Center

The SQL Server Installation Center is a one-stop shop for all activity that relates to planning, installing, and upgrading a SQL Server instance. It is the application that you are greeted with when you run the SQL Server installation media. Installation Center consists of seven tabs, and the following sections will describe the content of those tabs.

The Planning Tab

The Planning tab is illustrated in Figure 2-2 and consists of numerous links to MSDN (Microsoft Developer Network) pages, which provide you with important documentation on SQL Server, such as a complete set of hardware and software requirements and documentation for SQL Server's security model.

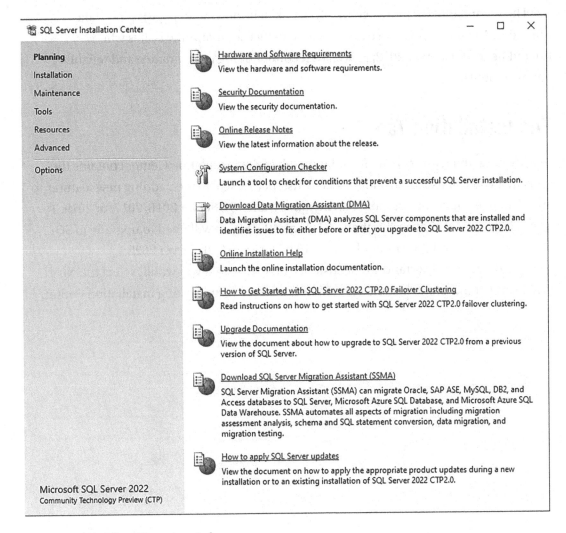

Figure 2-2. *The Planning tab*

In addition to accessing documentation with the links provided, you can also access two tools. The first of these is the System Configuration Checker. This tool runs during the installation process to determine if there are any conditions that will prevent SQL

Server from being installed. These checks include ensuring that the server is not already configured as a domain controller and checking that the WMI (Windows Management Instrumentation) service is running. When you run this tool before you begin installing SQL Server, it can prewarn you of any issues that may cause the installation to fail so that you can fix them before you begin installation. The System Configuration Checker is also available on the Tools tab on the Installation Center.

The second tool (or more accurately, a link to its download page) is the Data Migration Assistant. This tool can be used to detect compatibility issues when upgrading to SQL Server 2022, as well as recommending performance and reliability enhancements.

The Installation Tab

As illustrated in Figure 2-3, the Installation tab of the Installation Center contains the tools that you will use for installing a new instance of SQL Server, adding new features to an existing instance, or upgrading an instance from SQL Server 2016, 2017, or 2019. To upgrade from a version earlier than SQL Server 2016, you will need to upgrade to SQL Server 2016 first and then upgrade the 2016 instance to SQL Server 2022.

In order to install a stand-alone instance of SQL Server, you would select the New SQL Server stand-alone instance or add new features to an existing installation option.

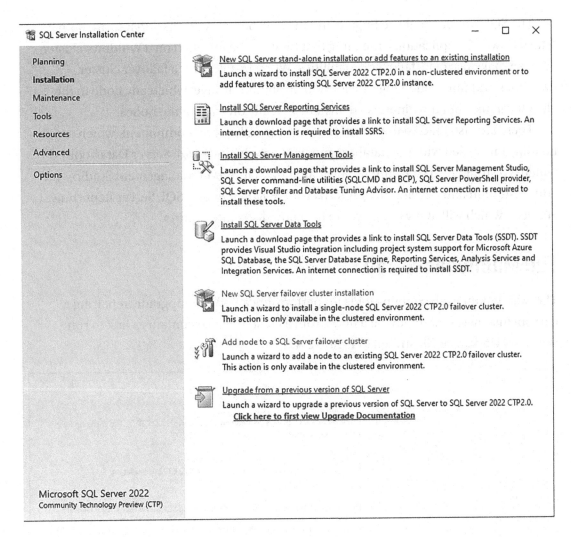

Figure 2-3. *The Installation tab*

In addition to installing a stand-alone instance, adding new features to an instance, and upgrading an existing instance to the latest version, there are also options on this screen for installing a SQL Server failover clustered instance and for adding a new node to an existing failover cluster. A *failover cluster* is a system where between 2 and 64 servers work together to provide redundancy and protect against a failure that stops one or more of the servers from functioning. Each server that participates in the cluster is known as a *node*.

The SQL Server Database Engine and the SQL Server Analysis Services are both "cluster-aware" applications, meaning that they can be installed on a Windows cluster and can make use of its failover capabilities. When installed on a failover cluster, databases and transaction logs are located on shared storage, which any node in the cluster can use, but the binaries are installed locally on each of the nodes.

There are also links to the download pages of SQL Server component, which are no longer included with the database media. These include SQL Server Data Tools, which is a studio for T-SQL and BI development, SQL Server Management Studio—an administration and development interface for SQL Server and SQL Server Reporting Services, which will allow the server to host and distribute reports.

The Maintenance Tab

The Maintenance tab contains tools for performing an edition upgrade, repairing a corrupt instance, and removing a node from a cluster; it also contains a link to run Windows Update, as illustrated in Figure 2-4.

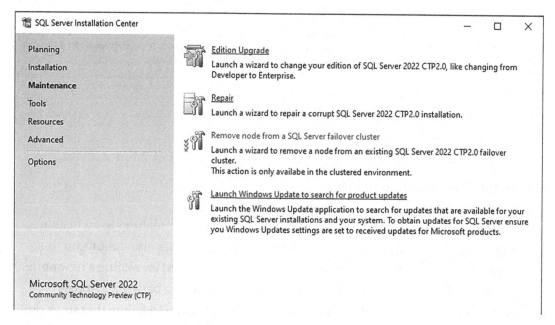

Figure 2-4. *The Maintenance tab*

You can use the Edition Upgrade option to upgrade an existing SQL Server 2022 instance from one edition to another, so, for example, you may wish to upgrade an instance installed as Developer edition to Enterprise edition.

You can use the Repair option to attempt to resolve issues with a corrupt installation of SQL Server. For example, you can use this tool if the Registry entries or binaries are corrupt, preventing the instance from starting.

Tip   This Repair option won't help if the Master database is corrupt and preventing the instance from starting. In this instance, you should use setup. exe from the command line, or PowerShell, with the `ACTION` parameter set to `REBUILDDATABASE`.

Use the Remove node from a SQL Server Failover cluster option to remove SQL Server from a node within a failover cluster. You can use this option as part of the process for evicting a node. Unfortunately, the Installation Center has no functionality for uninstalling an instance. You must do this through the Control Panel.

Not surprisingly, you can use the Launch Windows Update to search for product updates option to launch Windows Update. You can then choose to install the updates and fixes that are available for SQL Server.

The Tools Tab

The Tools tab contains a selection of tools that will assist you in installing SQL Server, as illustrated in Figure 2-5. This includes the System Configuration Checker, which I introduced earlier in this chapter, a discovery tool for SQL Server components already installed on the local server, and the Microsoft Assessment and Planning (MAP) tool.

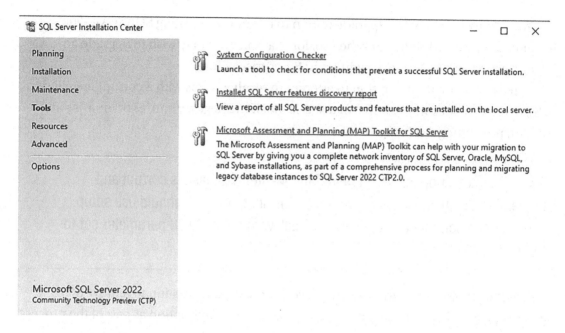

Figure 2-5. *The Tools tab*

Choose the Installed SQL Server features discovery report option to analyze the local server and return a list of all SQL Server features and components that are installed. This will include features from all versions, from SQL Server 2000 and on.

The Microsoft Assessment and Planning (MAP) Toolkit For SQL Server option will provide you with a link from which you can download the MAP for SQL Server tool. When you run this tool, it will perform a network-wide search for SQL Server, Oracle, and MySQL installations. It will produce a detailed report, which, for SQL Server, will include the name, version, and edition of the component. For Oracle, it will include the size and usage of each schema, including complexity estimates for migration. You can also use this tool to plan migration and consolidation strategies and to audit license requirements across the enterprise.

The Resources Tab

As illustrated in Figure 2-6, the Resources tab contains links to useful information regarding SQL Server. This includes a link to SQL Server Books Online, the Developer Center, and the SQL Server product evaluation site. Additionally, on this tab, you will also find links to Microsoft's privacy statement and the full SQL Server license agreement. Another very useful link is one that directs you to the SQL samples site. From this site, you can download the WideWorldImporters databases, which will aid you in testing features of SQL Server with a precreated database.

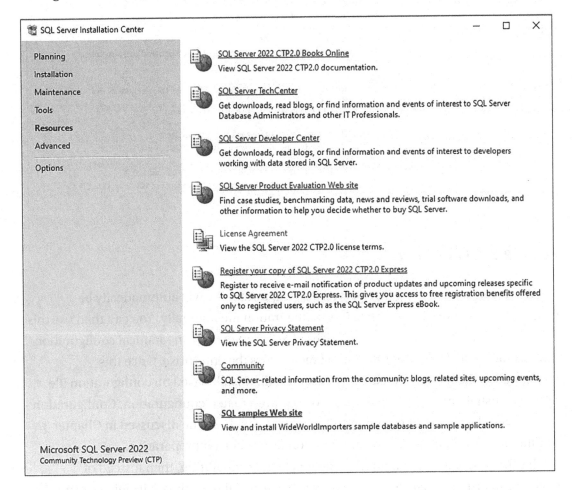

Figure 2-6. *The Resources tab*

The Advanced Tab

On the Advanced tab, illustrated in Figure 2-7, you will find tools for performing advanced installations of SQL Server, both as a stand-alone instance and also as a cluster. These tools include Install based on configuration file, Advanced cluster preparation, Advanced cluster completion, Image preparation of a stand-alone instance of SQL Server, and Image completion of a stand-alone instance of SQL Server.

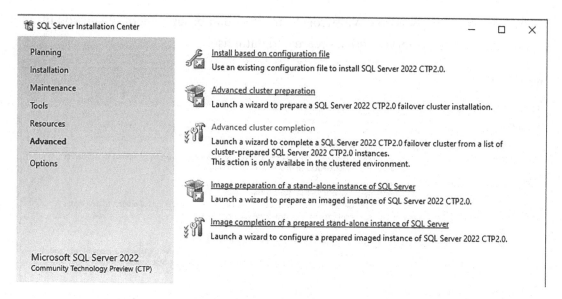

Figure 2-7. *The Advanced tab*

When you are installing SQL Server, a configuration file will automatically be created. It is also possible to create this configuration file manually. You can then use this configuration file to install other instances of SQL Server with an identical configuration. This can be useful for promoting consistency across the enterprise. Once this configuration file has been created, you can use the Install based on configuration file option to install further instances based on the pre-created configuration. Configuration files can also be useful for command-line installs, which will be discussed in Chapter 3. Additionally, you can also use a configuration file for cluster preparation.

If you wish to use a configuration file for cluster preparation, then instead of choosing to install the cluster via the New SQL Server failover cluster installation and Add node to a SQL Server failover cluster wizards, which are available on the Installation tab, you should choose the Advanced cluster preparation option on the Advanced tab. You will initially run this on one of the cluster nodes that can be a possible owner of the SQL Server instance, and a configuration file will be generated. Subsequently running the Advanced cluster preparation wizard on all other nodes of the cluster that can be possible owners will result in the configuration file being used to ensure consistency of installation across the cluster. This approach will even work for multi-subnet clusters (also known as geoclusters), since SQL Server will automatically detect the relationship between the subnets and you will be prompted to select an IP address for each subnet. The installation will then add each of the IP addresses as dependencies to the cluster role, using the OR constraint, where each node cannot be the possible owner of every IP address. Alternatively, it will use the AND constraint, where each node can be the possible owner of every IP address.

Once you have run the Advanced cluster preparation wizard on every node that is a possible owner of the clustered instance, you can run the Advanced cluster completion wizard. You only have to run this wizard once and you can run it on any of the nodes that are possible owners. After this wizard has completed successfully, the clustered instance will be fully functioning.

The Image preparation of a stand-alone instance of SQL Server option will use Sysprep for SQL Server to install a vanilla instance of SQL Server, which is not configured with account-, computer-, or network-specific information. It can be used in conjunction with Windows Sysprep to build a complete template of Windows with prepared SQL Server instances, which can then be used for deployments across the enterprise. This helps enforce consistency. In SQL Server 2022, all features of a stand-alone instance are supported by Sysprep; however, repairing an installation is not supported. This means that if an installation fails during either the prepare phase or the complete phase of the process, the instance must be uninstalled.

To finish the installation of a prepared image, you can use the Image completion of a prepared stand-alone instance of SQL Server option. This option will allow you to complete the configuration of the instance by inputting the account-, computer-, and network-specific information.

The Options Tab

As illustrated in Figure 2-8, the Options tab of the SQL Server Installation Center allows you to specify a path to the installation media. This can be useful if you have a copy of the media stored locally on the server.

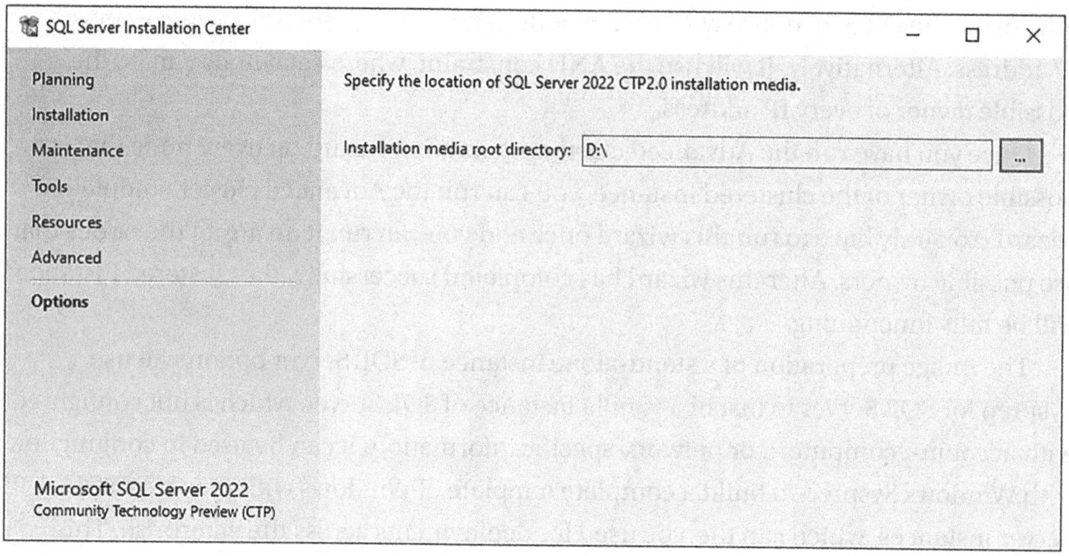

Figure 2-8. *The Options tab*

Installing a Stand-Alone Database Engine Instance

As discussed in the preceding section, an instance of SQL Server can be installed in various ways, including via the command line, by using Sysprep with an advanced installation using a configuration file, or by using the New SQL Server stand-alone installation or add features to an existing installation option on the Installation tab. It is the last of these options that we will use to install SQL Server in the following demonstration. In the following sections, we will install a Database Engine instance with features that will be examined in further detail throughout this book. We will also take an in-depth look at choosing the correct collation and service account for the instance.

Preparation Steps

When you choose to install a new instance of SQL Server, the first screen of the wizard that you are presented with will prompt you to enter the product key for SQL Server, as illustrated in Figure 2-9.

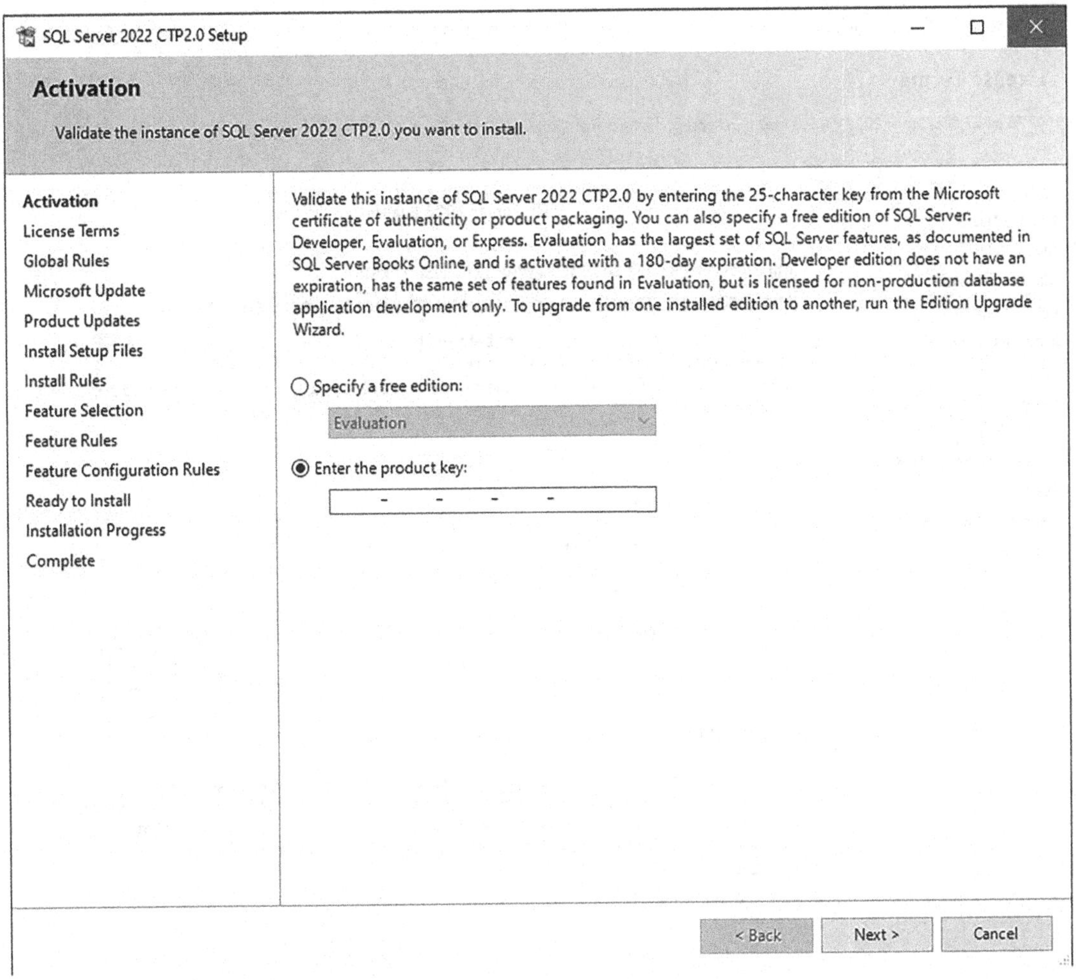

Figure 2-9. *Product Key page*

If you do not enter a product key on this screen, you will only be able to install either the Express edition of SQL Server, the Developer edition, or the Evaluation edition. Express edition provides a free, but cutdown edition of SQL Server with a reduced feature set and limits on database size. The Developer edition provides the same level of functionality as Enterprise but is not licensed for production use. The Evaluation edition has the same level of functionality as the Enterprise edition, but it expires after 180 days.

The next screen of the wizard will ask you to read and accept the license terms of SQL Server, as illustrated in Figure 2-10. A link provided on this screen will give you further details of Microsoft's privacy policy.

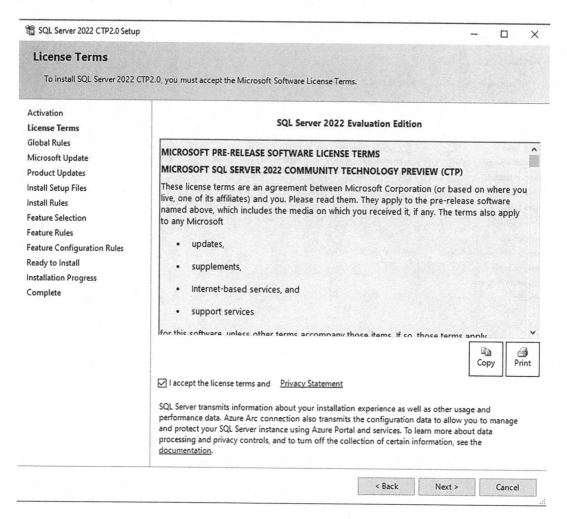

Figure 2-10. *License Terms page*

After you accept the license terms, SQL Server setup will run a rules check to ensure that it can continue with the installation, as illustrated in Figure 2-11. This is the same configuration check that you can run independently from the Planning tab of SQL Server Installation Center, as discussed earlier in this chapter.

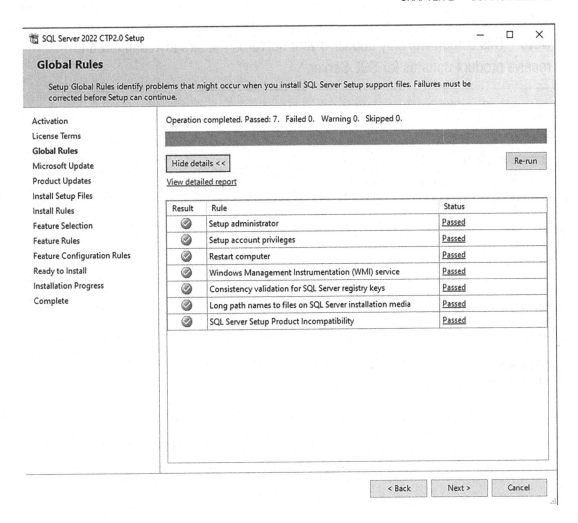

Figure 2-11. *Global Rules page*

Assuming that all checks pass successfully, the screen of the wizard illustrated
in Figure 2-12 will prompt you to choose if you want Microsoft Update to check for
SQL Server patches and hotfixes. The choice here will depend on your organization's
patching policy. Some organizations implement a ridged patching regime for the testing
and acceptance of patches, followed by a patching cycle, which is often supported with
software such as WSUS (Windows Server Update Services). If such a regime exists in your
organization, then you should not select this option.

Note   This screen will only appear if your server is not already configured to receive product updates for SQL Server.

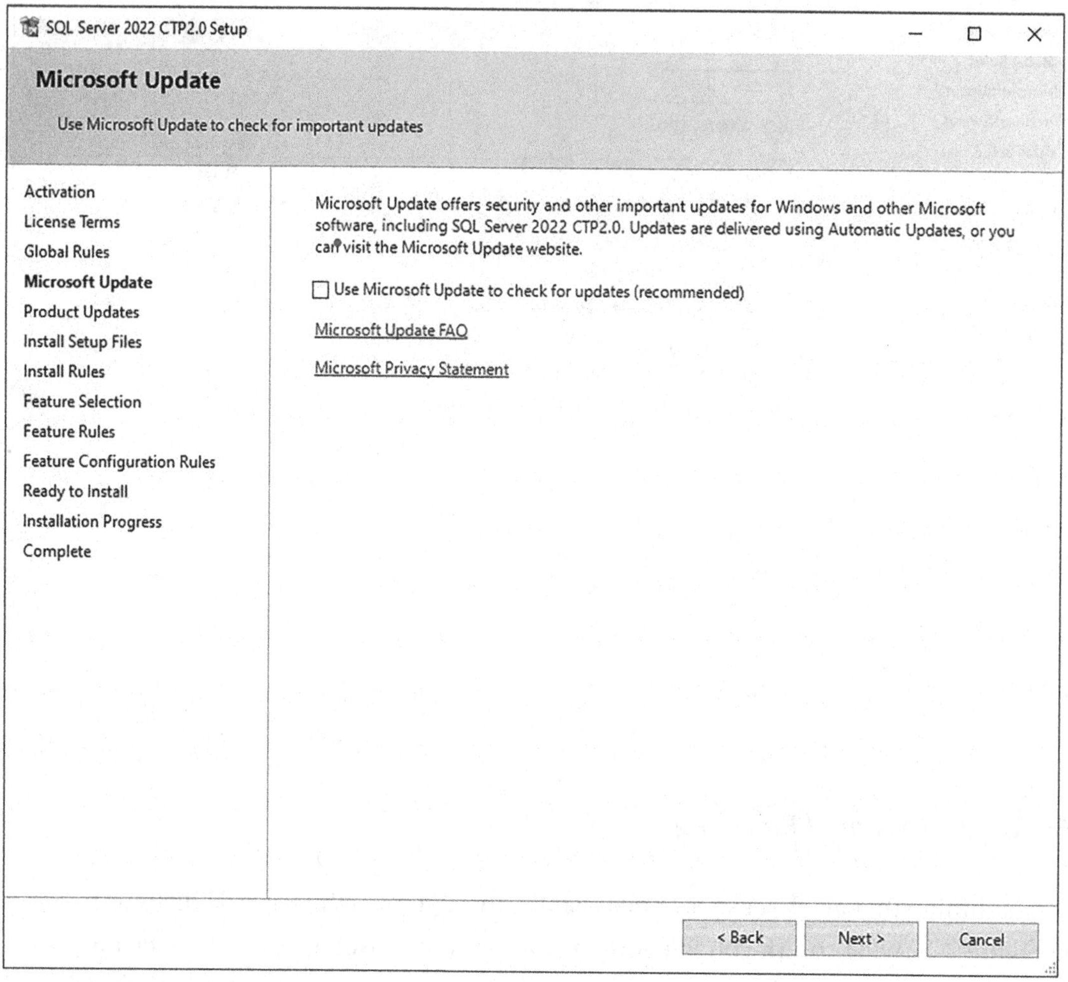

Figure 2-12. *Microsoft Update page*

The next screen of the wizard will attempt to scan for SQL Server updates to ensure that you install the latest CUs (cumulative updates) and SPs (service packs) with your installation. It will check the Microsoft Update service on the local server for these updates and list any that are available. This is an extension of slipstream installation functionality, which allows you to install updates at the same time as the installation of the base binaries by specifying their location for setup, but it has now been deprecated. The Product Updates page can also be configured to look for updates in local folders or network locations. This functionality will be discussed in further detail in Chapter 3.

Note   This screen will not appear if product updates are not found.

As setup moves to the next page of the wizard, the extraction and installation of the files required for SQL Server setup begin, and the progress displays. This screen also displays the progress of the download and extraction of any update packages that were found by Product Updates.

As illustrated in Figure 2-13, the next screen of the wizard runs an installation rule check and displays and errors or warnings that you may need to address before installation begins.

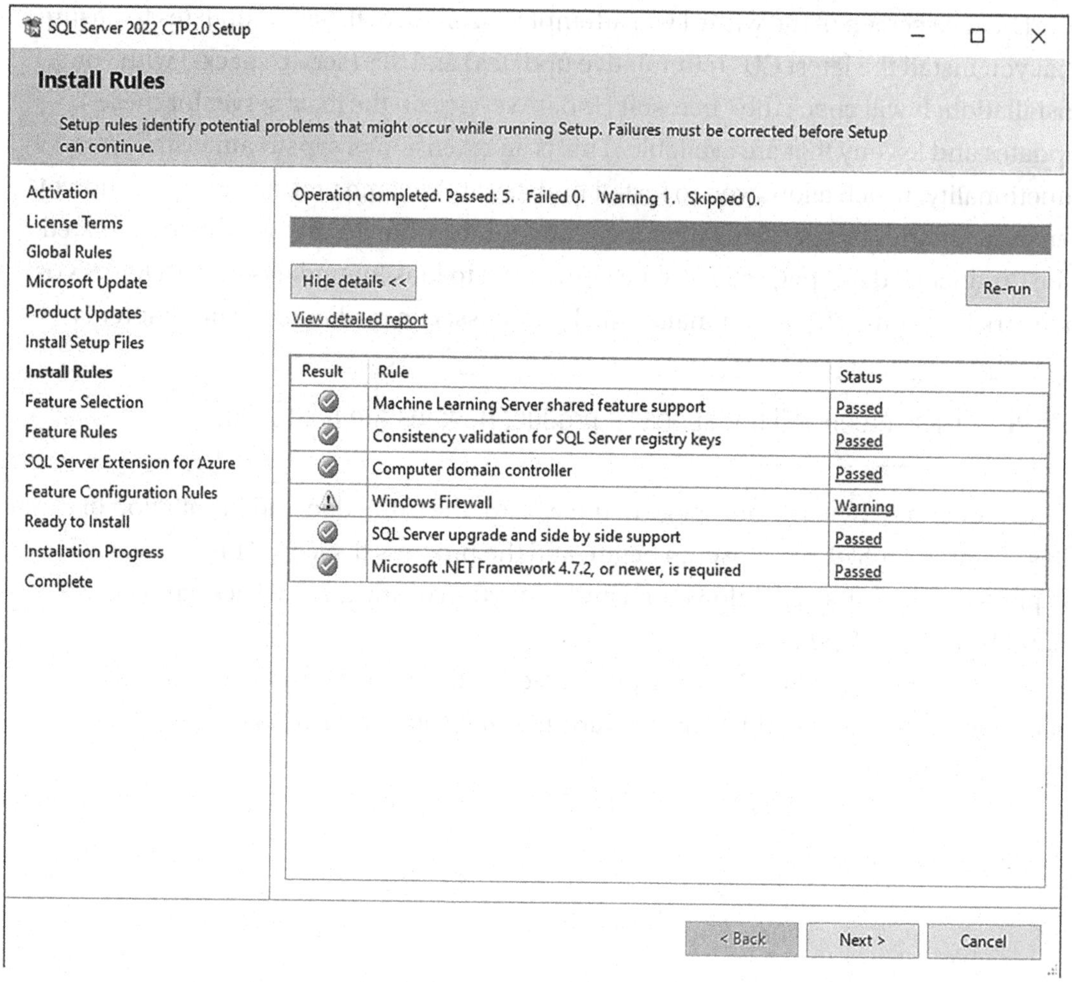

Figure 2-13. *Install Rules page*

In Figure 2-13, notice the warning being displayed for Windows Firewall. This will not stop the installation from proceeding, but it does warn you that the server has Windows Firewall switched on. By default, Windows Firewall is not configured to allow SQL Server traffic, so rules must be created in order for client applications to be able to communicate with the instance that you are installing. We will discuss SQL Server ports and Firewall configuration in detail in Chapter 5.

Assuming no errors are discovered that need to be addressed before you continue, the next page of the wizard will allow you to choose the feature that should be installed. This is discussed in detail in the next section.

The Feature Selection Page

The Feature Selection page of the setup wizard allows you to select the options that you wish to install. An overview of each of the available options can be found in Chapter 1. The Feature Selection page is illustrated in Figure 2-14.

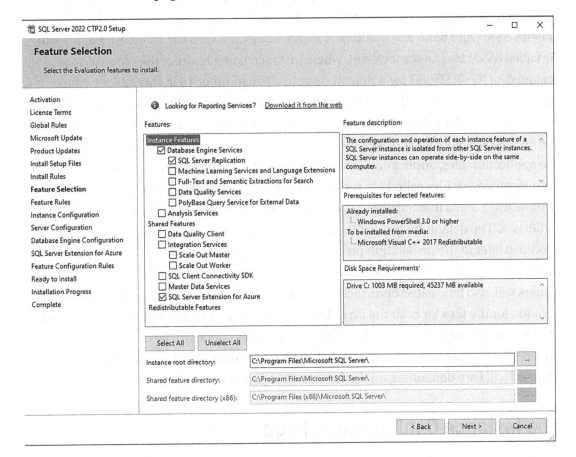

Figure 2-14. *Feature Selection page*

We will select the following features, since they will be used for demonstrations and discussions throughout this book:

- Database Engine Services

  - SQL Server Replication

- SQL Server Extension for Azure

Additionally, this page of the wizard requires you to specify folder locations for the instance root directory and the shared features directory. You may want to move these to a different drive in order to leave the C:\ drive for the operating system. You may want to do this for space reasons, or just to isolate the SQL Server binaries from other applications. The instance root directory will typically contain a folder for each instance that you create on the server, and there will be separate folders for the Database Engine, SSAS, and SSRS installations. A folder associated with the Database Engine will be called MSSQL16.[InstanceName], where instance name is either the name of your instance, or MSSQLSERVER for a default instance. The number 16 in this folder name relates to the version of SQL Server, which is 16 for SQL Server 2022. This folder will contain a subfolder called MSSQL, which in turn will contain folders that will be home to the files associated with your instance, including a folder called Binn, which will contain the application files, application extensions, and XML configurations associated with your instance; a folder called Backup, which will be the default location for backups of databases; and a folder called Data, which will be the default location of the system databases. The default folders for TempDB, user databases, and backups can be modified later in the installation process, and splitting these databases onto separate volumes is a good practice in many environments, as discussed in Chapter 1. Other folders will also be created here, including a folder called LOGS, which will be the default location for the files for both the Error Logs and the default Extended Event health trace.

On the next page of the wizard, an additional rules check will be carried out to ensure that the features that you have selected can be installed. The rules that are checked will vary depending on the features that you have selected.

The Instance Configuration Page

After successful completion of the rules check, the following screen of the wizard will allow you to specify if you would like to install a default instance or a named instance, as illustrated in Figure 2-15. The box in the lower half of the screen will give you details of any other instances or shared features that are already installed on the server.

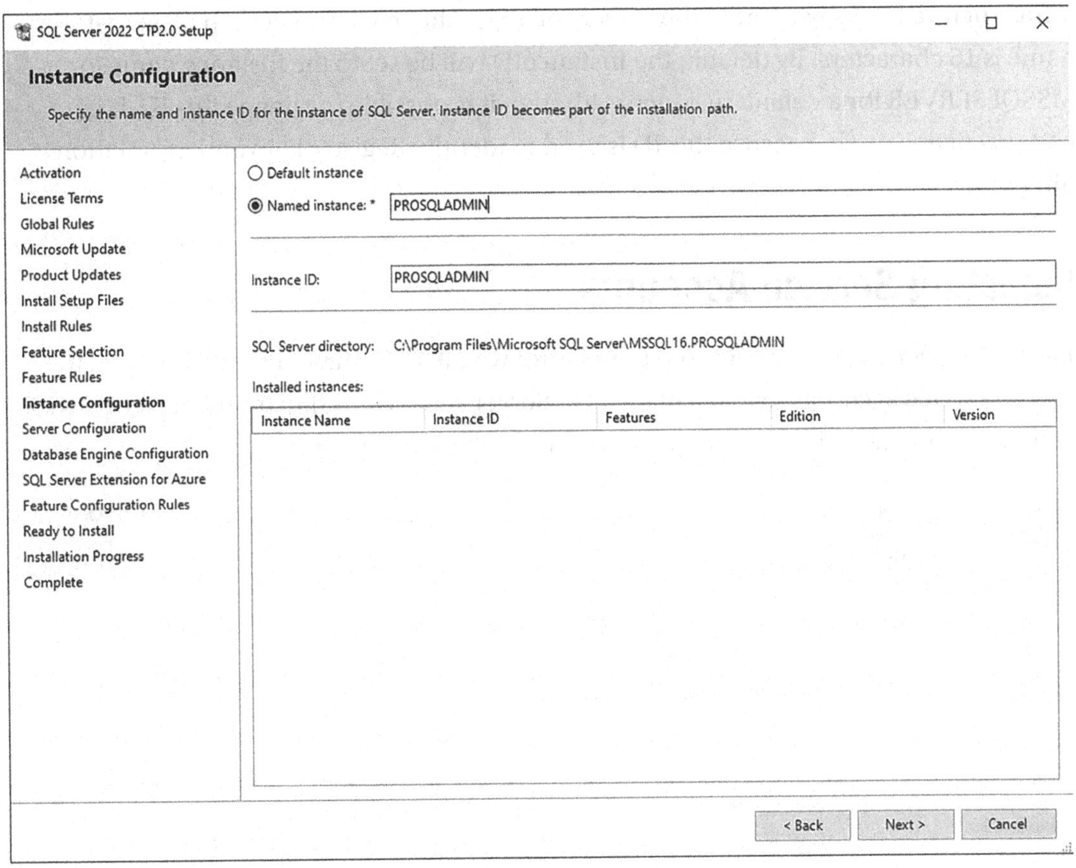

Figure 2-15. *Instance Configuration page*

The difference between a default instance and a named instance is that a default instance takes the name of the server that it is installed on, whereas a named instance is given an extended name. This has the obvious side effect that it is only possible to have a single default instance of SQL Server on a server, but you can have multiple named instances. With SQL Server 2022, up to 50 stand-alone instances can be hosted on a single server. Naturally, these instances will share the server's physical resources. For failover clusters, this number stays the same if your data is hosted on an SMB file share, but it reduces to 25 if you use a shared cluster disk for storage.

You are not required to install a default instance before installing a named instance. It is a perfectly valid configuration to have only named instances on a server with no default instance. Many DBA teams choose to only support named instances in their environments so that they can enforce naming conventions that are meaningful at the SQL Server layer, as opposed to relying on the naming conventions imposed by the infrastructure teams who build the servers or VMs. The maximum length of an instance name is 16 characters. By default, the InstanceID will be set to the instance name, or MSSQLSERVER for a default instance. Although it is possible to change this ID, it is bad practice to do so, because this ID is used to identify Registry keys and installation directories.

Selecting Service Accounts

The next screen of the wizard is separated into two tabs. The first tab will allow you to specify service accounts for each of the SQL Server services, as illustrated in Figure 2-16, and the second tab will allow you to specify the collation of your instance.

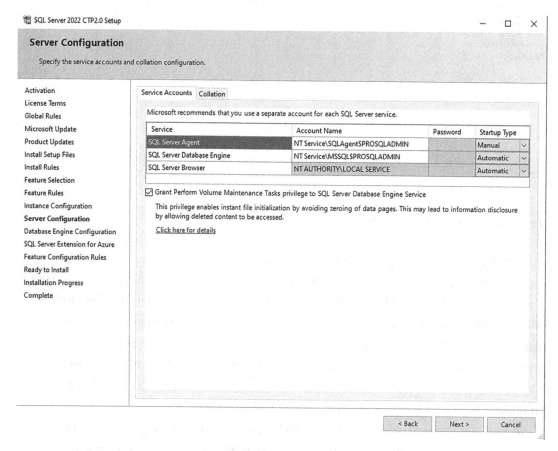

Figure 2-16. *Service Accounts Configuration page*

SQL Server 2022 supports the use of local and domain accounts, built-in accounts, virtual accounts, MSAs (managed service accounts), and gMSAs (group managed service accounts) as the security context used to run a service. The service account model that you choose is key to both the security and manageability of your environment.

Different organizations have different requirements for service account models, and you may be constrained by compliance requirements and many other factors. Essentially, the choice that you make is a trade-off between the security and operational supportability of your environment. For example, the Microsoft best practice is to use a separate service account for every service and to ensure that every server in your environment uses a discrete set of service accounts, since this fully enforces the principle of least privilege. The *principle of least privilege* states that each security context will be granted the minimum set of permissions required for it to carry out its day-to-day activities.

In reality, however, you will find that this approach introduces significant complexity into your SQL Server estate, and it can increase the cost of operational support while also risking increasing outage windows in disaster scenarios. On the flip side, I have worked in organizations where the service account model is very coarse, to the point where there is only a single set of SQL Server service accounts for each region. This approach can also cause significant issues. Imagine that you have a large estate and the whole estate uses the same service account. Now imagine that you have a compliance requirement to change service account passwords on a 90-day basis. This means that you would cause an outage to your entire SQL Server estate at the same time. This simply is not practical.

There is no right or wrong answer to this problem, and the solution will depend on the requirements and constraints of individual organizations. For organizations that use domain accounts as service accounts, however, I tend to recommend a distinct set of service accounts for each data-tier application. So if you imagine an environment, as shown in Figure 2-17, where your data-tier application consists of a two-node cluster and an ETL server in a primary site, and two disaster recovery (DR) servers in a secondary site, this design would involve a common set of service accounts used by all of these instances, but other data-tier applications would not be allowed to use these accounts and would require their own set.

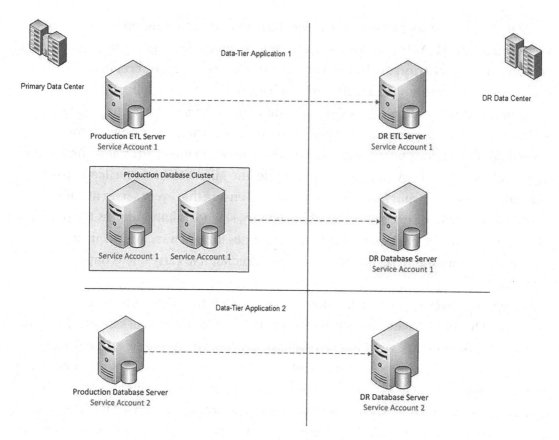

Figure 2-17. *Service account model by data-tier application*

Of course, this model poses its own challenges. For example, you would need to review and amend this policy if you were to start a process of consolidation. Because of the challenges surrounding service account management, Microsoft introduced virtual accounts and MSAs. *Virtual accounts* are local accounts that have no password management requirements. They can access the domain by using the computer identity of the server on which they have been created. *Managed service accounts*, on the other hand, are domain-level accounts. They provide automatic password management within AD (Active Directory) and also automatically maintain their Kerberos SPNs (service principal names), as long as your domain is running at the functional level of Windows Server 2008 R2 or higher.

Both of these types of account have a limitation, however. They can only be used on a single server. As discussed earlier, this can introduce complexity into your SQL Server estate, especially for highly available, multiserver applications. This issue has been resolved by the introduction of group MSAs, which give you the ability to associate an

MSA with multiple servers within the domain. In order to use this functionality, however, your forest needs to be running at the functional level of Windows Server 2012 or higher.

Additionally, on this page of the wizard, you can choose to grant the Perform Volume Maintenance Tasks user rights assignment to the SQL Server service account. If you select this option, then SQL Server will have the ability to create database files and grow database files without the need to fill the empty space with zeros. This significantly improves the performance of file creation and growth operations.

The trade-off is that it opens a very small security hole. If any data was stored on the same area of the disk, that the database file is created on, then with specialized tooling, it is possible to retrieve that data, as it has not been overwritten. The chance of exploitation of this security hole is so remote, however, that I always recommend granting this privilege, in all but the most secure environments.

Note   This functionality only applies to database files. The free space in transaction log files always have to be filled with zeros when they are created, or when they grow.

Choosing the Collation

The second tab of the Server Configuration page will allow you to customize your collation, as illustrated in Figure 2-18.

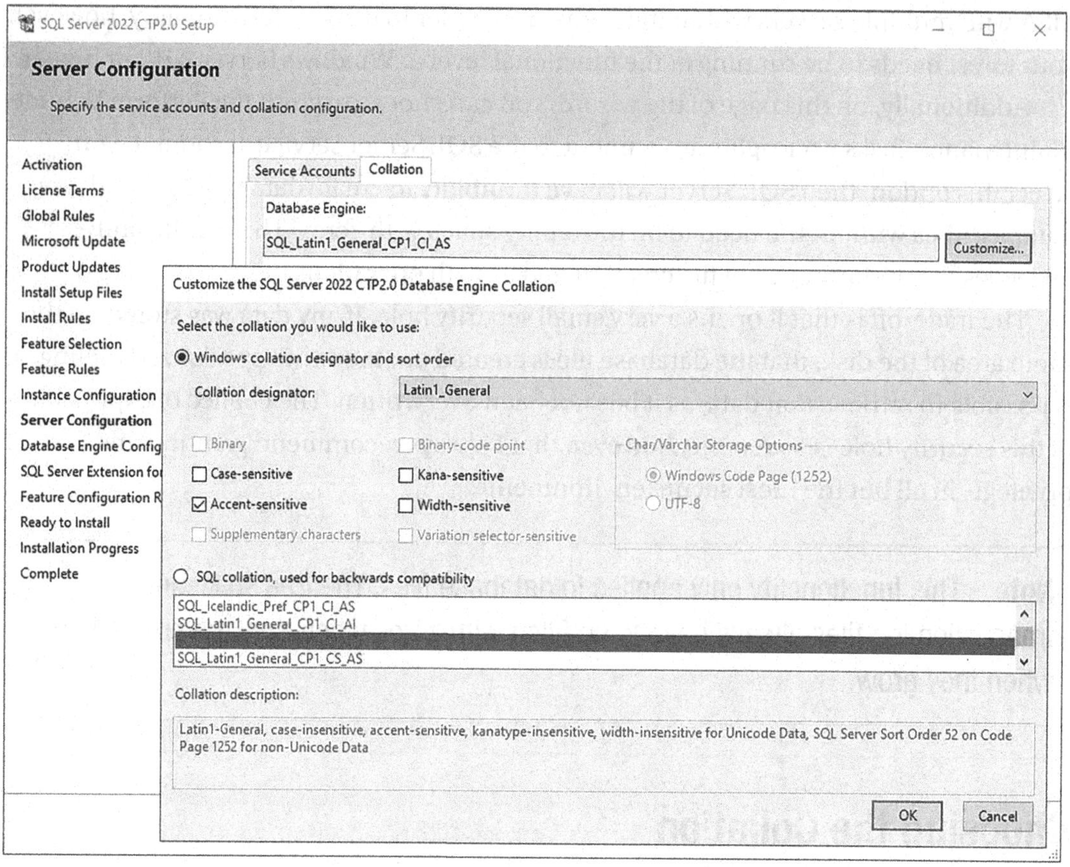

Figure 2-18. *Collation Configuration page*

Collations determine how SQL Server will sort data and also define SQL Server's matching behavior, with regard to accents, kana, width, and case. You can also specify that sorting and matching should be carried out on the binary or binary code point representations.

If your collation is accent sensitive, then in comparisons, SQL Server does not regard è as the same character as e, whereas it will treat these characters as equal, if accent insensitivity is specified. Kana sensitivity defines if the Japanese Hiragana character set is equal to the Katakana character set. Width sensitivity defines if a single byte representation of a character is equal to its two-byte equivalent.

Case sensitivity defines if a capital letter is equal to its lowercase equivalent during comparison. For example, the code in Listing 2-1 will create and populate a temporary table and then run the same query, but using two different collations.

Listing 2-1. Effect of Case Sensitivity of Matching

```
--Create a local temporary table

CREATE TABLE #CaseExample
(
        Name            VARCHAR(20)
)

--Populate values

INSERT INTO #CaseExample
        VALUES('James'), ('james'), ('John'), ('john')

--Count the number of entries for James, with case-sensitive collation

SELECT COUNT(*) AS 'Case Sensitive'
FROM #CaseExample
WHERE Name = 'John' COLLATE Latin1_General_CS_AI

--Count the number of entries for James, with case-insensitive collation

SELECT COUNT(*) AS 'Case Insensitive'
FROM #CaseExample
WHERE Name = 'John' COLLATE Latin1_General_CI_AI

--DROP temporary table

DROP TABLE #CaseExample
```

You can see from the results in Figure 2-19 that the first query only found one example of the word John, because it used a case-sensitive collation, but because the second query uses a case-insensitive collation, it matched two results.

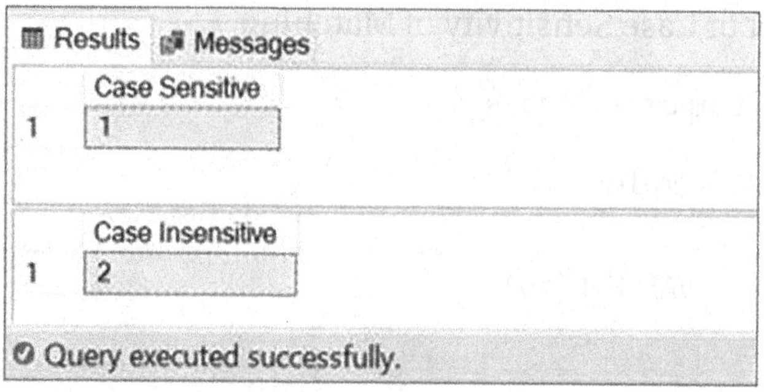

Figure 2-19. *Results of case sensitivity example*

Although the effects of the various collation sensitivities may be fairly straightforward, a slightly more confusing aspect is how collations can affect sort order. Surely there is only one correct way to order data? Well, the answer to this question is no. There are various ways that data can be correctly ordered. For example, while some collations order data alphabetically, other collations may use nonalphabetic writing systems, such as Chinese, which can be ordered using a method called radical and stroke sorting. This system will identify common character components and then order them by the number of strokes. An example of how collations can affect sort order is demonstrated in Listing 2-2.

Listing 2-2. Effect of Collations on Sort Order

```
--Create a temporary table

CREATE TABLE #SortOrderExample
(
        Food        VARCHAR(20)
)

--Populate the table

INSERT INTO #SortOrderExample
VALUES ('Coke'), ('Chips'), ('Crisps'), ('Cake')

--Select food using Latin1_General collation
```

```
SELECT Food AS 'Latin1_General collation'
FROM #SortOrderExample
ORDER BY Food
COLLATE Latin1_General_CI_AI

--Select food using Traditional_Spanish collation

SELECT Food AS 'Traditional_Spanish collation'
FROM #SortOrderExample
ORDER BY Food
COLLATE Traditional_Spanish_CI_AI
```

The results in Figure 2-20 show that the value Chips has been sorted differently using the two collations. This is because in traditional Spanish, ch is regarded as a separate character and is sorted after cz.

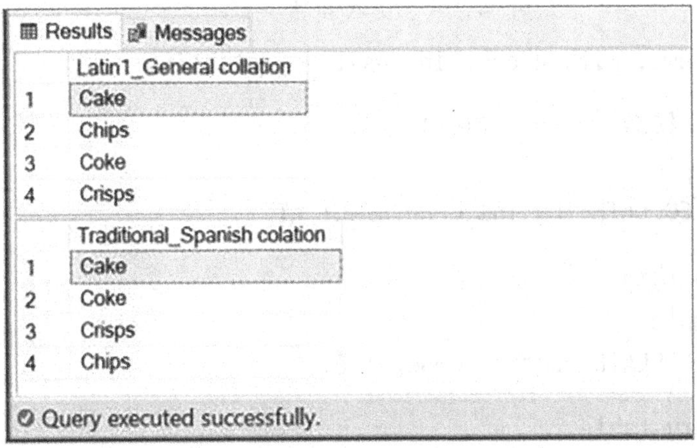

Figure 2-20. *Results of sort order example*

There are two types of binary collation to choose from. The older style binary collations are included for backward compatibility only and are identified with the BIN suffix. If you choose to choose this type of binary collation, then characters will be matched and sorted based on the bit patterns of each character. If you choose the modern binary collations, which can be identified with a BIN2 suffix, then data will be sorted and matched based on Unicode code points for Unicode data and the code point of the relevant ANSI code page, for non-Unicode data. The example in Listing 2-3 demonstrates the behavior of a binary (BIN2) collation, compared to case-sensitive and case-insensitive collations.

Listing 2-3. Binary Collation Sort Order

```
CREATE TABLE #CaseExample
(
        Name            VARCHAR(20)
)

--Populate values

INSERT INTO #CaseExample
        VALUES('James'), ('james'), ('John'), ('john')

--Select all rows with a case-sensitive collation

SELECT name as [Case Sensitive]
FROM #CaseExample
Order by Name COLLATE Latin1_General_CS_AI

--Select all rows, with a case-insensitive collation

SELECT name as [Case Insensitive]
FROM #CaseExample
Order by Name COLLATE  Latin1_General_CI_AI

SELECT name as [binary]
FROM #CaseExample
Order by Name COLLATE  Latin1_General_BIN2

--DROP temporary table

DROP TABLE #CaseExample
```

The results in Figure 2-21 show that because the data is ordered by code point rather than alphabetically, the values beginning with capital letters are ordered before those beginning with lowercase letters, since this matches the code points of the characters.

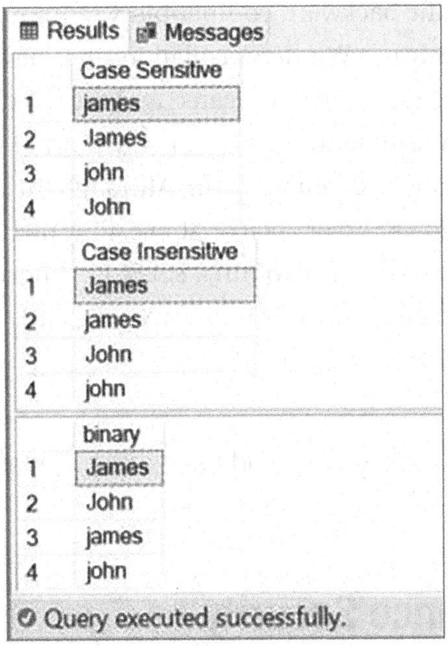

Figure 2-21. *Binary collation sort order*

Collations can be challenging, and ideally you will maintain consistent collations across the enterprise. This is not always possible in today's global organizations, but you should aspire to it. You should also be careful to select the correct collation for the instance at the point of installation. Changing the collation afterward can be challenging, because databases and columns within tables have their own collations, and a collation cannot be changed if other objects depend on it. At a high level, a worst-case scenario will involve the following actions to change your collation at a later date:

1. Re-create all databases.

2. Export all data into the newly created copies of the databases.

3. Drop the original databases.

4. Rebuild the Master database with the desired collation.

5. Re-create the databases.

6. Import the data back into your database from the copies that you created.

7. Drop the copies of the databases.

Unless you have a specific backward compatibility requirement, you should avoid using SQL collations and only use Windows collations. It is best practice to use Windows collations because SQL collations are deprecated and are not all fully compatible with Windows collations. Additionally, you should be mindful when selecting newer collations, such as Norwegian or Bosnian_Latin. Although this new family of collations map to code pages in Windows Server 2008 or above, they do not map to code pages in older operating systems. So if you were to run a SELECT * query, against your instance from an older operating system, such as Windows XP, the code page would not match, and an exception would be thrown.

Note   Examples in this book, you should use Latin1_General_CI_AS.

Provisioning Instance Security

The next page of the setup wizard allows you to configure the Database Engine. It consists of six tabs. In the first tab, you can specify the authentication mode of the instance and instance administrators, as illustrated in Figure 2-22. The second tab allows you to specify the folder that will be used as the default data directory, as well as specific locations for user databases and TempDB. The third tab provides configuration options for TempDB, while the fourth allows you to configure the maximum degree of parallelism for the instance, the fifth allows for instance memory settings to be configured, and the final tab will allow you to configure FILESTREAM.

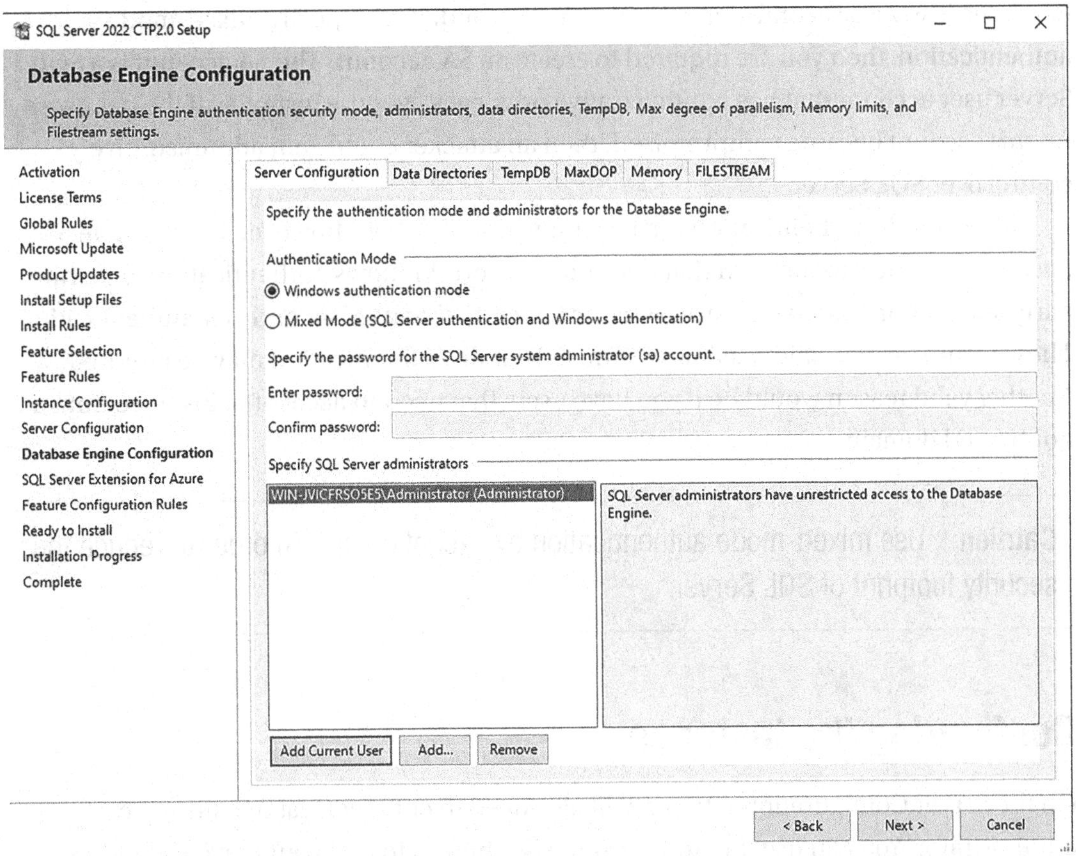

Figure 2-22. *The Server Configuration tab*

Windows authentication mode means that the credentials that a user supplies when logging into Windows will be passed to SQL Server, and the user does not require any additional credentials to gain access to the instance. With Mixed Mode, although Windows credentials can still be used to access the instance, users can also be given second-tier credentials. If this option is selected, then SQL Server will hold its own usernames and passwords for users inside the instance, and users can supply these in order to gain access, even if their Windows identity does not have permissions.

For security best practice, it is a good idea to only allow Windows authentication to your instance. This is for two reasons. First, with Windows authentication only, if an attacker were to gain access to your network, then they would still not be able to access SQL Server, since they would not have a valid Windows account with the correct permissions. With mixed-mode authentication, however, once inside the network, attackers could use brute-force attacks or other hacking methodologies to attempt to gain access via a second-tier user account. Second, if you specify mixed-mode authentication, then you are required to create an SA account. The SA account is a SQL Server user account that has administrative privileges over the instance. If the password for this account became compromised, then an attacker could gain administrative control over SQL Server.

Mixed-mode authentication is a necessity in some cases, however. For example, you may have a legacy application that does not support Windows authentication, or a third-party application that has a hard-coded connection that uses second-tier authentication. These would be two valid reasons why mixed-mode authentication may be required. Another valid reason would be if you have users that need to access the instance from a nontrusted domain.

Caution   Use mixed-mode authentication by exception only in order to reduce the security footprint of SQL Server.

Configuring the Instance

On the Server Configuration tab, you will also need to enter at least one instance administrator. You can use the Add Current User button to add your current Windows security context, or the Add button to search for Windows security principles, such as users or groups. Ideally, you should select a Windows group, which contains all DBAs that will require administrative access to the instance, since this simplifies security.

The Data Directories tab of Database Engine Configuration page is illustrated in Figure 2-23.

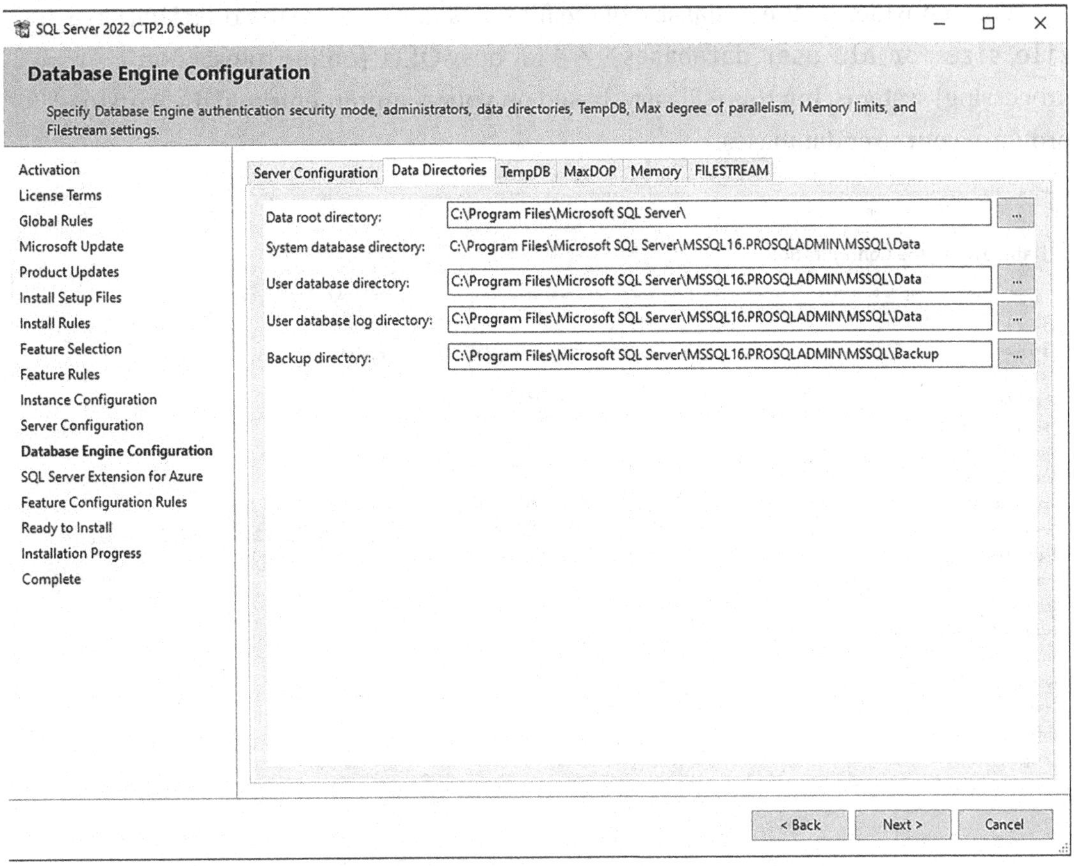

Figure 2-23. *The Data Directories tab*

The Data Directories tab allows you to alter the default location of the data root directory. On this screen, you can also change the default location for user databases and their log files, as well as specify where TempDB data and log files should be created. As you may recall from Chapter 1, this is particularly important, because you will probably wish to separate user data files from their logs and also from TempDB. Finally, this tab allows you to specify a default location for backups of databases that will be taken.

The TempDB tab (Figure 2-24) allows you to configure file options for TempDB. The number of files required for TempDB is important, as too few files can cause contention on system pages, such as GAM (Global Allocation Map) and SGAM (Shared Global Allocation Map). The optimal number of files can be calculated using the formula: SMALLEST(Number of logical cores, 8). If your server has hyper-threading turned on, then the number of logical cores will be the number of physical cores multiplied by two. On VMWare, the number of logical cores will be equal to the number of virtual cores.

When considering the initial size of the files, I usually work to the rule: SUM(Data file size for all user databases) / 3 for busy OLTP (online transaction processing) systems, but this will vary, based on your requirements and the workload profile of your user databases.

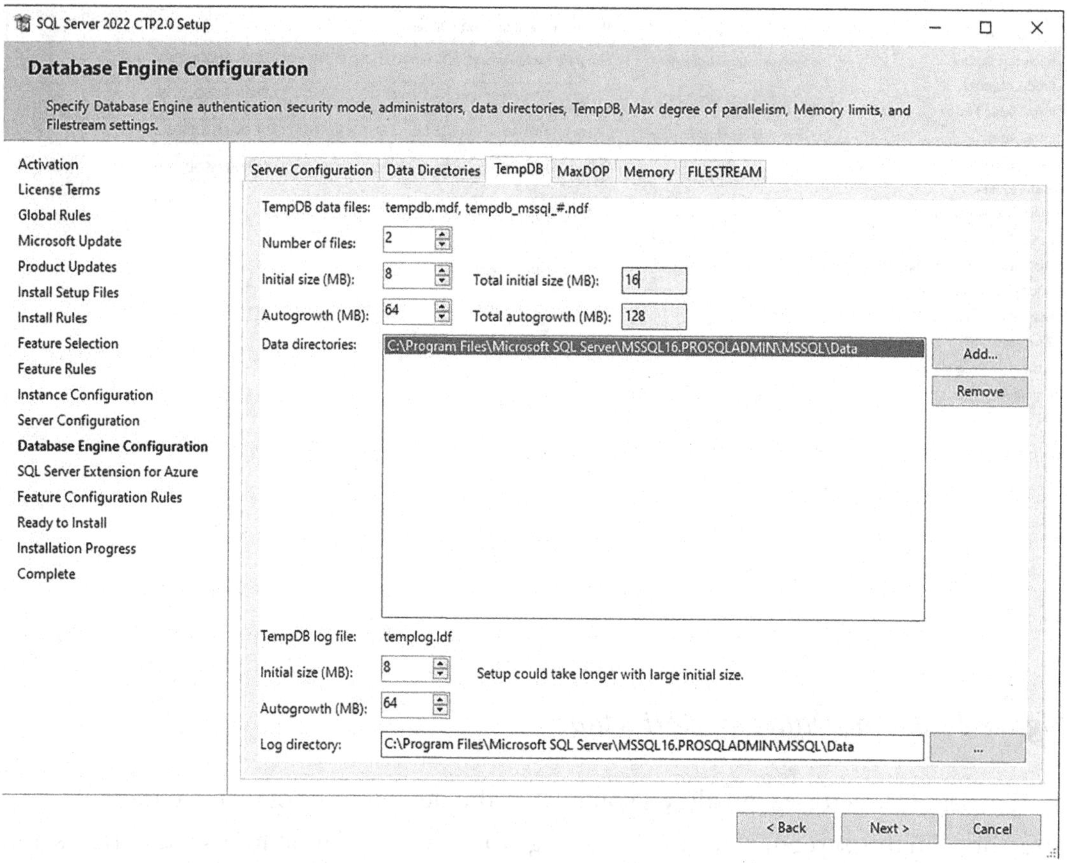

Figure 2-24. *TempDB tab*

The MaxDOP tab of the wizard, illustrated in Figure 2-25, allows you to configure the maximum number of CPU cores that can be used by any single query. The setup program calculates a default recommended value, but you can override this if required. Please see Chapter 5 of this book for a detailed discussion of how MaxDOP should be configured.

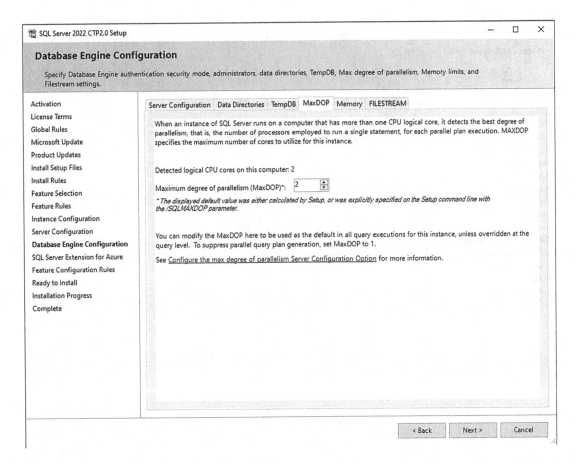

Figure 2-25. *MaxDOP tab*

Figure 2-26 illustrates the Memory tab. Here, you are able to specify if you would like to use the default configuration, for the minimum and maximum amount of memory that can be allocated to the instance, use the recommended values, calculated by the setup wizard, or specify your own values. To specify your own preferred values, choose the recommended option, enter your values, and check the Click here to accept the recommended memory configurations for the SQL Server database engine check box. This check box must also be used, if you wish to adhere to the setup program's recommendations. A detailed discussion of how best to configure minimum and maximum memory settings for the database engine can be found in Chapter 5 of this book.

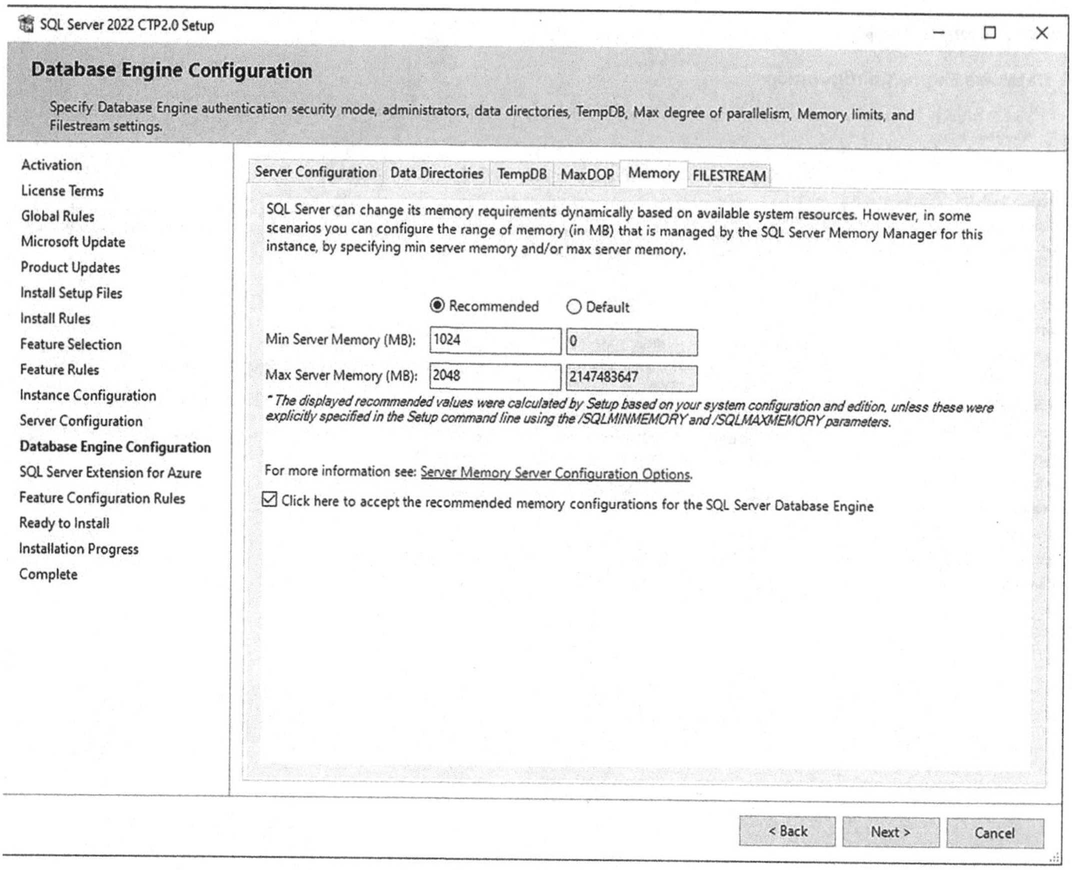

Figure 2-26. *Memory tab*

The FILESTREAM tab of the Database Engine Configuration page allows you to enable and configure the level of access for SQL Server FILESTREAM functionality, as illustrated in Figure 2-27. FILESTREAM must also be enabled if you wish to use the FileTable feature of SQL Server. FILESTREAM and FileTable provide the ability to store data in an unstructured manner within the Windows folder structure while retaining the ability to manage and interrogate this data from SQL Server.

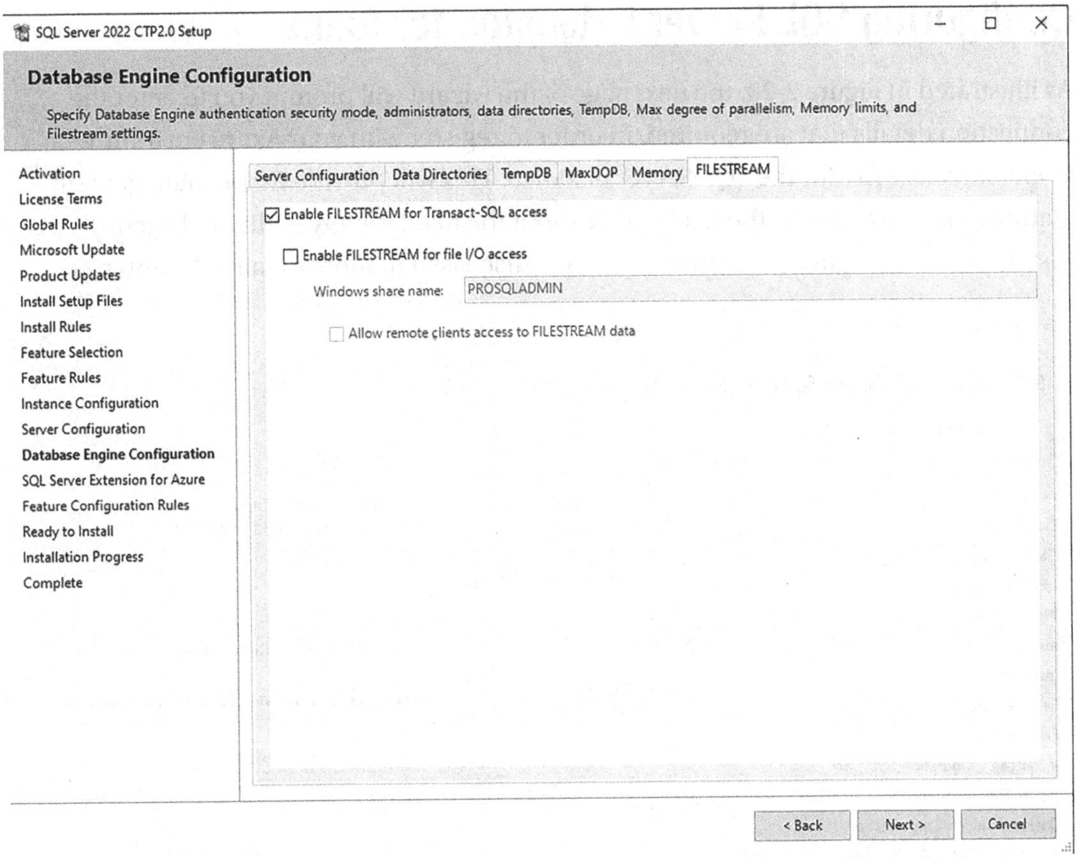

Figure 2-27. *The FILESTREAM tab*

Selecting Enable FILESTREAM for Transact-SQL access will enable FILESTREAM, but the data can only be accessed from inside SQL Server. Additionally, selecting Enable FILESTREAM for file I/O access enables applications to access the data directly from the operating system, bypassing SQL Server. If this option is selected, then you will also need to provide the name of a preexisting file share, which will be used for direct application access. The Allow remote clients access to FILESTREAM data option makes the data available to remote applications. The three options build on top of each other, so it is not possible to select Enable FILESTREAM for file I/O access without fist selecting Enable FILESTREAM for Transact-SQL access, for example. FILESTREAM and FileTable will be discussed further in Chapter 6.

Configuring SQL Server Extension for Azure

As illustrated in Figure 2-28, the next page of the wizard will prompt you to enter the connection details that are required, in order to register with your Azure environment, to enable Azure Arc for the SQL Server instance. This will provide Azure management features, via Azure Arc, to the instance, without the need for any additional agent installations. Configuring this functionality is discussed in more detail in Chapter 21.

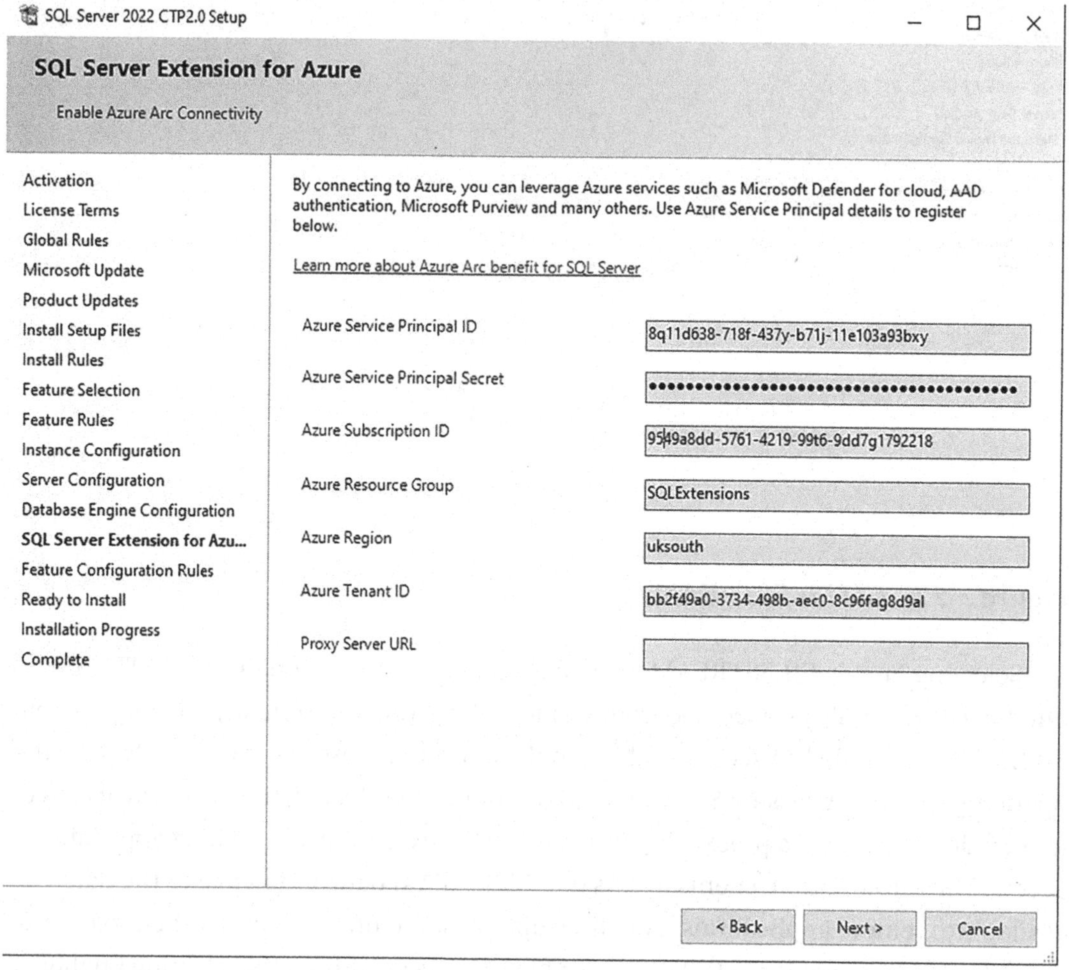

Figure 2-28. *The SQL Server Extension for Azure page*

Completing the Installation

After a final rules check, the Ready to Install page of the wizard is displayed. This is the final page before installation commences, and it is illustrated in Figure 2-29. This screen gives you a summary of the features that will be installed, but possibly the most interesting component of this page is the Configuration file path section. This gives you the path to a configuration file that you can reuse to install further instances with an identical configuration. Configuration files will be discussed further in Chapter 3.

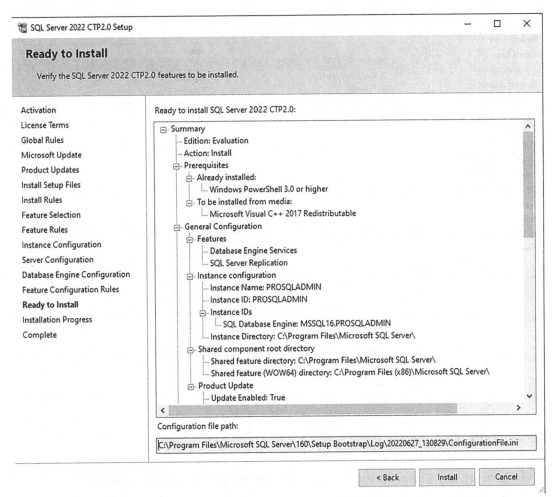

Figure 2-29. *The Ready to Install page*

The setup wizard will display a progress bar during the installation. When installation is complete, a summary screen will be displayed, as shown in Figure 2-30. You should check to ensure that each of the components being installed has a status of Succeeded. The SQL Server installation is then complete.

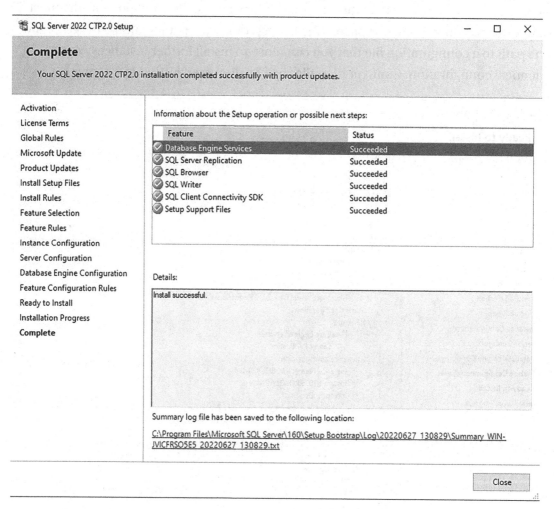

Figure 2-30. *Completion page*

If there are any issues during installation and one or more component fail, then a useful point to start troubleshooting is the installation Summary log. A URI to this log can be found at the bottom of the screen. We will discuss installation logs in Chapter 3.

Summary

SQL Server's Installation Center provides many useful tools and links for guiding and assisting you in the installation process. You can use the Installation Center to install failover clustered instances as well as stand-alone instances of SQL Server. There are also tools to assist in advanced installation requirements, such as prepared images of SQL Server and installations based on configuration files.

In addition to using the SQL Server 2022 Setup wizard to install an instance of the Database Engine, you can also use the same tool to install the tools within the BI and ETL suite, such as Analysis Services, Integration Service, Data Quality Services, and Master Data Services. If you use the wizard to install Analysis Services, then the tool can be configured with the multidimensional model or tabular model.

Although you can install SQL Server successfully using default values, for the ongoing supportability of your instance, and indeed your estate, make sure you consider many aspects of the installation. This applies especially to collations, service accounts, and other security considerations, such as the most appropriate administrators group to add and the authentication model to implement.

CHAPTER 3

Server Core Installation

Because SQL Server does not support remote installations and because Windows Server Core provides only a command-line interface (CLI) and no graphical user interface (GUI), you must perform installation of SQL Server on Windows Server Core as a command-line operation. You can also use a configuration file to produce consistent, repeatable installations.

In this chapter, we will review the considerations for installing SQL Server on Windows Server Core before demonstrating how to perform an installation on this platform. We will also discuss using configuration files and how you can use them to simplify future installations and enforce consistency.

In Chapter 1, you may remember that we discussed the limitations of SQL Server on Windows Server Core and how some features, such as Reporting Services, Master Data Services, and Data Quality Services, are not supported, whereas other features, such as Management Tools and Distributed Replay Client, are only supported remotely. You should also ensure that you have operational supportability across various competencies within your organization, including proficiency in PowerShell and the compatibility of operational tooling.

Installing an Instance

Installing SQL Server in Windows Server Core involves running setup.exe from the PowerShell terminal. Setup.exe can be found in the root directory of the SQL Server installation media. When running setup.exe from the PowerShell terminal, you can use switches and parameters to pass in values, which will be used to configure the instance.

Note You can follow the same process to install SQL Server on a GUI-based version of Windows, if required.

75

© Peter A. Carter 2023
P. A. Carter, *Pro SQL Server 2022 Administration*, https://doi.org/10.1007/978-1-4842-8864-1_3

Required Parameters

Although many switches and parameters are optional, some must always be included. When you are installing a stand-alone instance of the Database Engine, the parameters listed in Table 3-1 are always required.

Table 3-1. *Required Parameters*

Parameter	Usage
/IACCEPTSQLSERVERLICENSETERMS	Confirms that you accept the SQL Server license terms.
/ACTION	Specifies the action that you want to perform, such as Install or Upgrade.
/FEATURES or /ROLE	Specifies the features that you wish to install.
/INSTANCENAME	The name to be assigned to the instance.
/SQLSYSADMINACCOUNTS	The Windows security context(s) that will be given administrative permissions in the instance of the Database Engine.
/AGTSVCACCOUNT	The account that will be used to run the SQL Server Agent service.
/SQLSVCACCOUNT	The account that will be used to run the Database Engine service.
/qs	Performs an unattended install. This is required on Windows Server Core since the installation wizard is not supported.

Tip   If you plan to use the /Q or /QS switch to perform an unattended installation, then the /SUPPRESSPRIVACYSTATEMENTNOTICE should also be used.

IACCEPTSQLSERVERLICENSETERMS Switch

Because /IACCEPTSQLSERVERLICENSETERMS is a simple switch that indicates your acceptance of the license terms, it does not require any parameter value be passed.

Additional License Terms Parameters

Depending on the Database Engine features that you select to install, other switches, denoting your acceptance of license terms, may become applicable. /IACCEPTPYTHONLICENSETERMS is required if you plan to plan to install the Python package and /IACCEPTROPENLICENSETERMS is required to install the R package. You should note, however, that this only applies if you are installing SQL Server 2019, as these packages are no longer shipped with SQL Server 2022 and should be installed separately.

ACTION Parameter

When you perform a basic installation of a stand-alone instance, the value passed to the /ACTION parameter will be install; however, a complete list of possible values for the /ACTION parameter is listed in Table 3-2.

Table 3-2. *Values Accepted by the /ACTION Parameter*

Value	Usage
install	Installs a stand-alone instance
PrepareImage	Prepares a vanilla stand-alone image, with no account-, computer-, or network-specific details
CompleteImage	Completes the installation of a prepared stand-alone image by adding account, computer, and network details
Upgrade	Upgrades an instance from SQL Server 2016, 2017, or 2019
EditionUpgrade	Upgrades a SQL Server 2022 from a lower edition (such as Developer edition) to a higher edition (such as Enterprise)
Repair	Repairs a corrupt instance
RebuildDatabase	Rebuilds corrupted system databases
Uninstall	Uninstalls a stand-alone instance
InstallFailoverCluster	Installs a failover clustered instance
PrepareFailoverCluster	Prepares a vanilla clustered image with no account-, computer-, or network-specific details

(continued)

Table 3-2. (*continued*)

Value	Usage
CompleteFailoverCluster	Completes the installation of a prepared clustered image by adding account, computer, and network details
AddNode	Adds a node to a failover cluster
RemoveNode	Removes a node from a failover cluster

FEATURES Parameter

As shown in Table 3-3, the /FEATURES parameter is used to specify a comma-delimited list of features that will be installed by setup, but not all features can be used on Windows Server Core.

Table 3-3. *Acceptable Values of the /FEATURES Parameter*

Parameter Value	Use on Windows Core	Description
SQL	NO	Full SQL Engine, including Full Text, Replication, Data Quality Server, in-database machine learning, and PolyBase core components
SQLEngine	YES	Database Engine
FullText	YES	Full Text search
Replication	YES	Replication components
DQ	NO	Data Quality Server
PolyBaseCore	YES	PolyBase components
AdvancedAnalytics	YES	In-database machine learning services
AS	YES	Analysis Services
DQC	NO	Data Quality Client
IS	YES	All Integration Services components
IS_Master	YES	Integration Services scale-out master

(*continued*)

Table 3-3. (*continued*)

Parameter Value	Use on Windows Core	Description
IS_Worker	YES	Integration Services scale-out worker
MDS	NO	Master Data Services
Tools	NO	All client tools
SNAC_SDK	NO	Client connectivity SDK
Arc	YES	Installs the Arc connectivity that allows you to manage workloads in data centers or in AWS as if they were in Azure, allowing you to unify management of your SQL Server enterprise
LocalDB	YES	An execution mode of SQL Server express, which is used by application developers

Note   If you choose to install other SQL Server features, such as Analysis Services or Integration Services, then other parameters, such as service accounts for these services, will also become required.

Role Parameter

Instead of specifying a list of features to install, with the /FEATURES parameter, it is possible to install SQL Server in a predefined role, using the /ROLE parameter. The roles supported by the /ROLE parameter are detailed in Table 3-4.

Table 3-4. *Available Values for the /ROLE Parameter*

Parameter Value	Description
SPI_AS_ExistingFarm	Installs SSAS as a PowerPivot instance in an existing SharePoint farm.
SPI_AS_NewFarm	Installs the Database Engine and SSAS as a PowerPivot instance in a new and unconfigured SharePoint farm.
AllFeatures_WithDefaults	Installs all features of SQL Server and its components. I do not recommend using this option, except in the most occasional circumstances, as installing more features than are actually required increases the security and resource utilization footprints of SQL Server.

Basic Installation

When you are working with command-line parameters for setup.exe, you should observe the rules outlined in Table 3-5 with regard to syntax.

Table 3-5. *Syntax Rules for Command-Line Parameters*

Parameter Type	Syntax
Simple switch	/SWITCH
True/False	/PARAMETER=true/false
Boolean	/PARAMETER=0/1
Text	/PARAMETER="Value"
Multivalued text	/PARAMETER="Value1" "Value2"
/FEATURES parameter	/FEATURES=Feature1,Feature2

Tip   For text parameters, the quotation marks are only required if the value contains spaces. However, it is considered good practice to always include them.

Assuming that you have already navigated to the root directory of the installation media, then the command in Listing 3-1 provides PowerShell syntax for installing the Database Engine, Replication, and client connectivity components. It uses default values for all optional parameters, with the exception of the collation, which we will set to the Windows collation Latin1_General_CI_AS.

Tip   When Windows Server core boots, the interface you see is the command prompt, not the PowerShell prompt. Type powershell to enter a PowerShell prompt.

Listing 3-1. Installing SQL Server from PowerShell

```
.\SETUP.EXE /IACCEPTSQLSERVERLICENSETERMS /ACTION="Install"
/FEATURES=SQLEngine,Replication,Conn /INSTANCENAME="PROSQLADMINCORE2"
/SQLSYSADMINACCOUNTS="Administrator" /SQLCOLLATION="Latin1_General_CI_AS"
/qs
```

Note   If using the command prompt, instead of PowerShell, the leading . \ characters are not required.

In this example, a SQL Server instance named PROSQLADMINCORE2 will be installed. Both the Database Engine and the SQL Agent services will run under the SQLServiceAccount1 account, and the Windows group called SQLDBA will be made administrator. When installation begins, a pared-down, noninteractive version of the installation wizard will appear to keep you updated on progress.

Smoke Tests

After installing an instance on Windows Server Core, where you have no summary screen at the end of installation, it is always a good idea to perform some smoke tests. In this context, *smoke tests* refer to quick, high-level tests that ensure that the services are running and the instance is accessible.

The code in Listing 3-2 will use the PowerShell Get-Service cmdlet to ensure that the services relating to the PROSQLADMINCORE instance exist and to check their status. This script uses asterisks as wildcards to return all services that contain our instance name. This, of course, means that services such as SQL Browser will not be returned.

Listing 3-2. Checking Status of Services

```
Get-Service -displayname *PROSQLADMINCORE* | Select-Object name,
displayname, status
```

The results are displayed in Figure 3-1. You can see that both the SQL Server and SQL
Agent services have been installed. You can also see that the SQL Server service is started
and the SQL Agent service is stopped. This aligns with our expectations, because we did
not use the startup mode parameters for either service. The default startup mode for the
SQL Server service is automatic, whereas the default startup mode for the SQL Agent
service is manual.

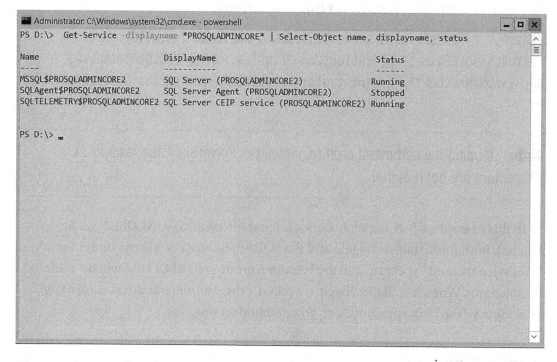

Figure 3-1. *Results of check service status smoke test*

The second recommended smoke test is to use `invoke-sqlcmd` to run a T-SQL
statement which returns the instance name. To use the invoke-sqlcmd cmdlet (or any
other SQL Server PowerShell cmdlets), the sqlserver PowerShell module needs to be
installed. This module replaces the deprecated SQLPS module and contains many more
cmdlets.

If you are running Windows Server with Desktop Experience, then the sqlserver module is included when you install SQL Server Management Studio, which can be downloaded from https://docs.microsoft.com/en-us/sql/ssms/download-sql-server-management-studio-ssms. If you are using Windows Server in core mode, however (or if you simply don't choose to install SSMS), then the sqlserver module can be downloaded from the PowerShell Gallery. Alternatively, if your server has Internet access, the script in Listing 3-3 will firstly find the latest version of the module, before downloading and installing it.

Listing 3-3. Install the sqlserver Module

```
#Locate and list the current version of the sqlserver module
Find-Module sqlserver

#Download and install the sqlserver module
Install-Module sqlserver
```

Tip   The first time you run Find-Module you will be prompted to install the NuGet provider.

Once the sqlserver module has been installed, the script in Listing 3-4 can be used to return the name of the instance.

Note   This is also the query that is used by the IsAlive test, which is performed by a cluster. It has little system impact and just checks that the instance is accessible.

Listing 3-4. Checking If Instance Is Accessible

```
Invoke-Sqlcmd –serverinstance "localhost\PROSQLADMINCORE2" -query "SELECT
@@SERVERNAME"
```

In this example, the -serverinstance switch is used to specify the instance name that you will connect to, and the -query switch specifies the query that will be run. The results of this smoke test are illustrated in Figure 3-2. As you can see, the query resolved successfully and returned the name of the instance.

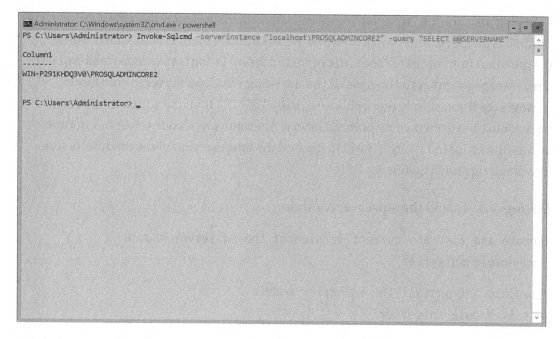

Figure 3-2. *Results of check instance accessible smoke test*

Troubleshooting the Installation

If an error occurs during the installation of the instance, or if your smoke tests fail, then you will need to troubleshoot the installation. With no GUI, this may seem like a daunting task, but luckily the SQL Server installation process provides a full set of verbose logs, which you can use to identify the issue. The most useful of these logs are listed in Table 3-6.

Table 3-6. *SQL Server Installation Logs*

Log File	Location
Summary.txt	`%programfiles%\Microsoft SQL Server\160\` `Setup Bootstrap\Log\`
Detail.txt	`%programfiles%\Microsoft SQL Server\160\` `Setup\Bootstrap\Log\<YYYYMMDD_HHMMSS>\`
SystemConfigurationCheck_Report.htm	`%programfiles%\Microsoft SQL Server\160\` `Setup Bootstrap\Log\<YYYYMMDD_HHMMSS>\`

Summary.txt

Summary.txt will normally be your first point of call when you troubleshoot SQL Server installation issues. It provides basic information regarding the installation and can often be used to determine the issue. The sample in Figure 3-3, for example, clearly shows in Exit Message that the installation of an instance failed because the instance name specified was too long.

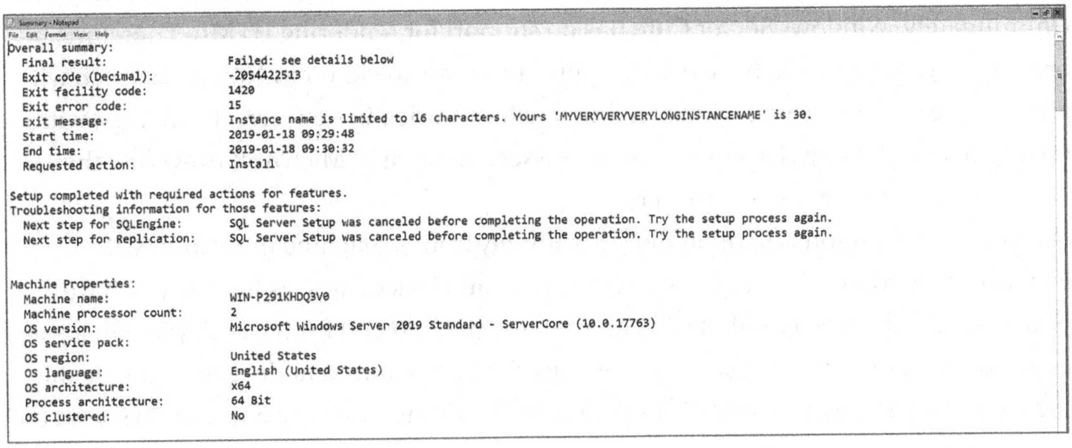

Figure 3-3. *Summary.txt*

In addition to returning high-level information, such as the exit code, exit message, and start and end time of the installation, summary.txt will also provide you with details about the OS environment. Additionally, it will detail the components that setup tried to install with the status of each MSI (Microsoft Installer) that was executed, and it will list any command-line parameters that were specified. At the end of the file, you will also find an exception summary, which includes a stack trace.

You can use Notepad to open a text file in Windows Server Core. So, assuming that you had already navigated to the `%programfiles%\Microsoft SQL Server\160\Setup Bootstrap\Log\` folder, you could use the command `notepad summary.txt` to open this file.

Detail.txt

If summary.txt does not provide the granular detail that you need, then your next stop will be detail.txt. This is a verbose log of actions performed by the installation, which are organized by the time at which the execution occurred, rather than by the component that executed them. To find errors in this log, you should search for the strings *error* and *exception*. The Detail.txt file can be found in `%programfiles%\Microsoft SQL Server\160\Setup Bootstrap\Log\<YYYYMMDD_HHMMSS>\`.

SystemConfigurationCheck_Report.htm

The SystemConfigurationCheck_Report.htm file provides a description and the status of each of the rule checks that happened during the installation in a web page format. Unfortunately, Windows Server Core has no support for rendering HTML. Therefore, in order to view this file, you have two options. The first is to view it in Notepad, which will give you the detail you are looking for, but it will be buried in between HTML tags, with no intuitive formatting. This pretty much misses the point of Microsoft providing the information in a user-friendly format.

The second option is to open the file remotely from a machine that has a GUI installed. This sounds like a much better option, and indeed it is, as long as you have a share created on the server that you can drop the file into and from which you can access it quickly. If this is not the case, however, and if your environment does not provide the capability to quickly move this file onto another machine, you may not want to spend too much time on this—especially since the only reason you would normally be accessing it is because your installation has just failed and you are likely to have project teams requesting that you resolve the issue quickly.

Other Log Files

Many additional log files are produced by the SQL Server setup routine, including a folder named Datastore, which contains a series of XML files, each of which represents individual settings that have been configured. Also of interest, you will find a copy on the configuration file that setup generated and a file called settings.xml. This file defines the metadata for the configuration options, including the source of where the value of the configuration was contained, such as a default value, or user specified.

A verbose log will also be created for every MSI that was run during the setup process. The quantity of these logs will of course depend on the features that you have chosen to install. On Windows Server Core, as long as you are not performing an SSAS-only installation, at a minimum, there will be a .log file relating to the SQL Engine. These .log files can provide even more granular detail regarding their specific MSI, which can assist you in troubleshooting.

Using the MSI logs is not totally straightforward, however, since you may find many errors that are caused by a preceding error, as opposed to being the root cause of the issue. To use these log files, you should order them by the time that they were created. You can then work through them backward. The last error that you find will be the root cause issue. To search these files for errors, search for the string *Return value 3*. It can get even more complicated, however, because not all *Return value 3* occurrences will relate to unexpected errors. Some of them may be expected results.

Optional Parameters

There are many switches and parameters that can optionally be used to customize the configuration of the instance that you are installing. The optional switches and parameters that you can use for the installation of the Database Engine are listed in Table 3-7.

Tip   Account passwords should not be specified if the account being used is a MSA/gMSA. This includes the accounts for the Database Engine and SQL Server Agent services, which are otherwise mandatory.

Table 3-7. *Optional Parameters*

Parameter	Usage
/AGTSVCSTARTUPTYPE	Specifies the startup mode of the SQL Agent Service. This can be set to Automatic, Manual, or Disabled.
/BROWSERSVCSTARTUPTYPE	Specifies the startup mode of the SQL Browser Service. This can be set to Automatic, Manual, or Disabled.
/CONFIGURATIONFILE	Specifies the path to a configuration file, which contains a list of switches and parameters so that they do not have to be specified inline, when running setup.

(*continued*)

Table 3-7. (*continued*)

Parameter	Usage
/ENU	Dictates that the English version of SQL Server will be used. Use this switch if you are installing the English version of SQL Server on a server with localized settings and the media contains language packs for both English and the localized operating system.
/FILESTREAMLEVEL	Used to enable FILESTREAM and set the required level of access. This can be set to 0 to disable FIESTREAM, 1 to allow connections via SQL Server only, 2 to allow I/O streaming, or 3 to allow remote streaming. The options from 1 to 3 build on each other, so by specifying level 3, you are implicitly specifying levels 1 and 2 as well.
/FILESTREAMSHARENAME	Specify the name of the Windows file share where FILESTREAM data will be stored. This parameter becomes required, when /FILESTREAMLEVEL is set to a value of 2 or 3.
/FTSVCACCOUNT	The account used to run the Full-Text filter launcher service.
/FTSVCPASSWORD	The password of the account used to run the Full-Text filter launcher service.
/HIDECONSOLE	Specifies that the console should be hidden.
/INDICATEPROGRESS	When this switch is used, the setup log is piped to the screen during installation.
/INSTANCEDIR	Specifies a folder location for the instance.
/INSTANCEID	Specifies an ID for the instance. It is considered bad practice to use this parameter, as discussed in Chapter 2.
/INSTALLSHAREDDIR	Specifies a folder location for 64-bit components that are shared between instances.
/INSTALLSQLDATADIR	Specifies the default folder location for instance data.
/NPENABLED	Specifies if Named Pipes should be enabled. This can be set to 0 for disabled or 1 for enabled.

(*continued*)

Table 3-7. (*continued*)

Parameter	Usage
/PID	Specifies the PID for SQL Server. Unless the media is pre-pidded, failure to specify this parameter will cause Evaluation edition to be installed.
/PBENGSVCACCOUNT	Specifies the account that will be used to run the PolyBase service.
/PBDMSSVCPASSWORD	Specifies the password for the account that will run the PolyBase service.
/PBENGSVCSTARTUPTYPE	Specifies the startup mode of the PolyBase. This can be set to Automatic, Manual, or Disabled.
/PBPORTRANGE	Specifies a range of ports for the PolyBase service to listen on. Must contain a minimum of six ports.
/PBSCALEOUT	Specifies if the Database Engine is part of a PolyBase scale-out group.
/SAPWD	Specifies the password for the SA account. This parameter is used when /SECURITYMODE is used to configure the instance as mixed-mode authentication. This parameter becomes required if /SECURITYMODE is set to SQL.
/SECURITYMODE	Use this parameter, with a value of SQL, to specify mixed mode. If you do not use this parameter, then Windows authentication will be used.
/SQLBACKUPDIR	Specifies the default location for SQL Server backups.
/SQLCOLLATION	Specifies the collation the instance will use.
/SQLMAXDOP	Specifies a maximum degree of parallelism for queries run against the instance.
/SQLMAXMEMORY	Specifies the maximum amount of RAM that should ever be allocated to the database engine.

(*continued*)

Table 3-7. (*continued*)

Parameter	Usage
/SQLMINMEMORY	Specifies the minimum amount of memory that should ever be allocated to the database engine. When the instance starts, the database engine will immediately consume this amount of memory.
/SQLSVCSTARTUPTYPE	Specifies the startup mode of the Database Engine Service. This can be set to Automatic, Manual, or Disabled.
/SQLTEMPDBDIR	Specifies a folder location for TempDB data files.
/SQLTEMPDBLOGDIR	Specifies a folder location for TempDB Log files.
/SQLTEMPDBFILECOUNT	Specifies the number of TempDB data files that should be created.
/SQLTEMPDBFILESIZE	Specifies the size of each TempDB data file.
/SQLTEMPDBFILEGROWTH	Specifies the growth increment for TempDB data files.
/SQLTEMPDBLOGFILESIZE	Specifies the initial size for the TempDB log file.
/SQLTEMPDBLOGFILEGROWTH	Specifies the growth increment for TempDB log files.
/SQLUSERDBDIR	Specifies a default location for the data files or user databases.
/SQLUSERDBLOGDIR	Specifies the default folder location for log files or user databases.
/SQMREPORTING	Specifies if SQL Reporting will be enabled. Use a value of 0 to disable or 1 to enable.
/SQLSVCINSTANTFILEINIT	Specifies that the Database Engine service account should be granted the Perform Volume Maintenance Tasks privilege. Acceptable values are **true** or **false**.
/TCPENABLED	Specifies if TCP will be enabled. Use a value of 0 to disable or 1 to enable.
/UPDATEENABLED	Specifies if Product Update functionality will be used. Pass a value of 0 to disable or 1 to enable.
/UPDATESOURCE	Specify a location for Product Update to search for updates. A value of MU will search Windows Update, but you can also pass a file share or UNC.

Product Update

The Product Update functionality replaces the deprecated slipstream installation functionality of SQL Server and provides you with the ability to install the latest CU (cumulative update) or GDR (General Distribution Release—a hotfix for security issues) at the same time you are installing the SQL Server base binaries. This functionality can save DBAs the time and effort associated with installing the latest update immediately after installing a SQL Server instance and can also help provide consistent patching levels across new builds.

Tip   From SQL Server 2017 onward, service packs are no longer released. All updates are either CUs or GDRs.

In order to use this functionality, you must use two parameters during the command-line install. The first of these is the /UPDATEENABLED parameter. You should specify this parameter with a value of 1 or True. The second is the /UPDATESOURCE parameter. This parameter will tell setup where to look for the product update. If you pass a value of MU into this parameter, then setup will check Microsoft Update, or a WSUS service, or alternatively, you can supply a relative path to a folder or the UNC (Uniform Naming Convention) of a network share.

In the following example, we will examine how to use this functionality to install SQL Server 2022, with CU1 included, which will be located in a network share. When you download a GDR or CU, they will arrive wrapped in a self-extracting executable. This is extremely useful, because even if WSUS is not in use in your environment, once you have signed off on a new patching level, you can simply replace the CU within your network share; when you do, all new builds can receive the latest update, without you needing to change the PowerShell script that you use for building new instances.

The PowerShell command in Listing 3-5 will install an instance of SQL Server, named PROSQLADMINCU1, and install CU1 at the same time, which is located on a file server.

Note   The account that you are using to run the installation will require permissions to the file share.

Listing 3-5. Installing CU During Setup

```
.\SETUP.EXE / IACCEPTSQLSERVERLICENSETERMS /ACTION="Install"
/FEATURES=SQLEngine,Replication,Conn /INSTANCENAME="PROSQLADMINCU1"
/SQLSVCACCOUNT="MyDomain\SQLServiceAccount1" /SQLSVCPASSWORD="Pa$$w0rd"
/AGTSVCACCOUNT="MyDomain\SQLServiceAccount1" /AGTSVCPASSWORD="Pa$$w0rd"
/SQLSYSADMINACCOUNTS="MyDomain\SQLDBA" /UPDATEENABLED=1
/UPDATESOURCE="\\10.0.0.3\SQL2022_CU1\" /qs
```

The code in Listing 3-6 demonstrates how you can interrogate the instance metadata. The code uses invoke-sqlcmd to connect to the PROSQLADMINCORE2 instance and return the systems variable that contains the full version details of the instance, including the build number. The name of the instance is also included to help us easily identify the results.

Listing 3-6. Determining Build Version of Each Instance

```
$parameters = @{
    ServerInstance = 'localhost\PROSQLADMINCORE2'
    Query          = "
        SELECT
            @@SERVERNAME
          , @@VERSION
    "
}

Invoke-sqlcmd @parameters
```

In this example, we have used a PowerShell technique called splatting. This allows us to make our code more readable, by defining the parameters in advance. Because we can use multiple splatting groups in our invoke-sqlcmd statement, we could also use splatting to make our code reusable. For example, we could have our query in a separate splatting group to the other parameters, meaning that each invocation of invoke-sqlcmd could use the same parameter set. The results are shown in Figure 3-4.

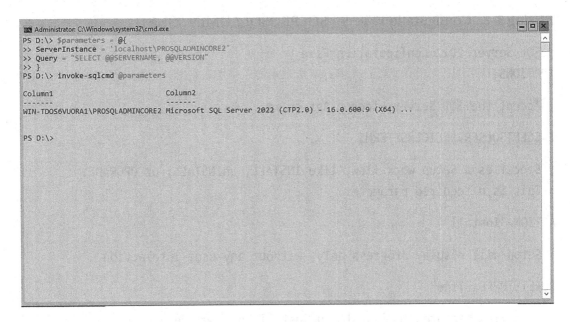

```
Administrator: C:\Windows\system32\cmd.exe
PS D:\> $parameters = @{
>> ServerInstance = 'localhost\PROSQLADMINCORE2'
>> Query = "SELECT @@SERVERNAME, @@VERSION"
>> }
PS D:\> invoke-sqlcmd @parameters

Column1                         Column2
-------                         -------
WIN-TDOS6VUORA1\PROSQLADMINCORE2 Microsoft SQL Server 2022 (CTP2.0) - 16.0.600.9 (X64) ...


PS D:\>
```

Figure 3-4. *PROSQLADMINCORE2 version details*

We can see from the results that PROSQLADMINCORE2 is running on SQL Server build version 16.0.600.9, which is the build number of SQL Server 2022 CTP 2.0.

Using a Config File

We have touched on using configuration files to produce consistent builds at several points already in this book. The sample in Listing 3-7 is the content of a configuration file, which has been populated with all of the required parameters that are needed to install an instance named PROSQLADMINCONF1 on Windows Server Core. It also contains the optional parameters to enable named pipes and TCP/IP, enables FILESTREAM at the access level where it can only be accessed via T-SQL, sets the SQL Agent service to start automatically, and configures the collation to be Latin1_General_CI_AS. In this .ini file, comments are defined with a semicolon at the beginning of the line.

Listing 3-7. Configuration File for SQLPROSQLADMINCONF1

```
; SQL Server 2022 Configuration File
[OPTIONS]

; Accept the SQL Server License Agreement

IACCEPTSQLSERVERLICENSETERMS

; Specifies a Setup work flow, like INSTALL, UNINSTALL, or UPGRADE.
; This is a required parameter.

ACTION="Install"

; Setup will display progress only, without any user interaction.

QUIETSIMPLE="True"

; Specifies features to install, uninstall, or upgrade.

FEATURES=SQLENGINE,REPLICATION,CONN

; Specify a default or named instance. MSSQLSERVER is the default
instance for
; non-Express editions and SQLExpress is for Express editions. This
parameter is
; required when installing the SQL Server Database Engine (SQL), Analysis
; Services (AS)

INSTANCENAME="PROSQLADMINCONF1"

; Agent account name

AGTSVCACCOUNT="MyDomain\SQLServiceAccount1"

; Agent account password

AGTSVCPASSWORD="Pa$$w0rd"

; Auto-start service after installation.

AGTSVCSTARTUPTYPE="Automatic"

; Level to enable FILESTREAM feature at (0, 1, 2 or 3).
```

```
FILESTREAMLEVEL="1"

; Specifies a Windows collation or an SQL collation to use for the Database
; Engine.

SQLCOLLATION="Latin1_General_CI_AS"

; Account for SQL Server service: Domain\User or system account.

SQLSVCACCOUNT="MyDomain\SQLServiceAccount1"

; Password for the SQL Server service account.

SQLSVCPASSWORD="Pa$$w0rd"

; Windows account(s) to provision as SQL Server system administrators.

SQLSYSADMINACCOUNTS="MyDomain\SQLDBA"

; Specify 0 to disable or 1 to enable the TCP/IP protocol.

TCPENABLED="1"

; Specify 0 to disable or 1 to enable the Named Pipes protocol.

NPENABLED="1"
```

Tip   If you use a configuration file created by a previous SQL Server installation as a template for your own config file, you will notice that the following parameters are specified: MATRIXCMBRICKCOMMPORT, MATRIXCMSERVERNAME, MATRIXNAME, COMMFABRICENCRYPTION, COMMFABRICNETWORKLEVEL, and COMMFABRICPORT. These parameters are intended for internal use by Microsoft only and should be ignored. They have no effect on the build.

Assuming that this configuration file had been saved as c:\SQL2022\configuration1. ini, then the code in Listing 3-8 could be used to run setup.exe from PowerShell.

Listing 3-8. Installing SQL Server Using a Configuration File

```
.\setup.exe /CONFIGURATIONFILE="c:\SQL2022\Configuration1.ini"
```

Although this is a perfectly valid use of a configuration file, you can actually be a little bit more sophisticated and use this approach to create a reusable script, which can be run on any server, to help you introduce a consistent build process. Essentially, you are using a scripted version of a prepared stand-alone image for Windows Server Core. This is particularly useful if your Windows operational teams have not adopted the use of Sysprep or use other methods to build servers.

In Listing 3-9, you will see another configuration file. This time, however, it only includes the static parameters that you expect to be consistent across your estate. Parameters that will vary for each installation, such as instance name and service account details, have been omitted.

Listing 3-9. Configuration File for PROSQLADMINCONF2

```
;SQL Server 2022 Configuration File
[OPTIONS]

; Accept the SQL Server License Agreement

IACCEPTSQLSERVERLICENSETERMS

; Specifies a Setup work flow, like INSTALL, UNINSTALL, or UPGRADE.
; This is a required parameter.

ACTION="Install"

; Setup will display progress only, without any user interaction.

QUIETSIMPLE="True"

; Specifies features to install, uninstall, or upgrade.

FEATURES=SQLENGINE,REPLICATION,CONN

; Auto-start service after installation.

AGTSVCSTARTUPTYPE="Automatic"

; Level to enable FILESTREAM feature at (0, 1, 2 or 3).
```

```
FILESTREAMLEVEL="1"
```

; Specifies a Windows collation or an SQL collation to use for the Database Engine.

```
SQLCOLLATION="Latin1_General_CI_AS"
```

; Windows account(s) to provision as SQL Server system administrators.

```
SQLSYSADMINACCOUNTS="MyDomain\SQLDBA"
```

; Specify 0 to disable or 1 to enable the TCP/IP protocol.

```
TCPENABLED="1"
```

; Specify 0 to disable or 1 to enable the Named Pipes protocol.

```
NPENABLED="1"
```

This means that to successfully install the instance, you will need to use a mix of parameters from the configuration file and also in line with the command that runs setup.exe, as demonstrated in Listing 3-10. This example assumes that the configuration in Listing 3-9 has been saved as C:\SQL2022\Configuration2.ini and will install an instance named PROSQLADMINCONF2.

Listing 3-10. Installing SQL Server Using a Mix of Parameters and a Configuration File

```
.\SETUP.EXE /INSTANCENAME="PROSQLADMINCONF2" /SQLSVCACCOUNT="MyDomain\
SQLServiceAccount1" /SQLSVCPASSWORD="Pa$$w0rd" /AGTSVCACCOUNT="MyDomain\
SQLServiceAccount1" /AGTSVCPASSWORD="Pa$$w0rd" /CONFIGURATIONFILE="C:\
SQL2022\Configuration2.ini"
```

Automatic Installation Routines

This approach gives us the benefit of having a consistent configuration file that we do not need to modify every time we build out a new instance. This idea can be taken even further, however. If we were to save our PowerShell command as a PowerShell script, then we could run the script and pass in parameters, rather than rewrite the command each time. This will give a consistent script for building new instances, which we can place under change control. The code in Listing 3-11 demonstrates how to construct a parameterized PowerShell script, which will use the same configuration file. The script assumes D:\ is the root folder of the installation media.

Listing 3-11. PowerShell Script for Autoinstall

```
param(
[string] $InstanceName,
[string] $SQLServiceAccount,
[string] $SQLServiceAccountPassword,
[string] $AgentServiceAccount,
[string] $AgentServiceAccountPassword
)

D:\SETUP.EXE /INSTANCENAME=$InstanceName /SQLSVCACCOUNT=$SQLServiceAccount
/SQLSVCPASSWORD=$SQLServiceAccountPassword /AGTSVCACCOUNT=$AgentService
Account /AGTSVCPASSWORD=$AgentServiceAccountPassword /CONFIGURATIONFILE=
"C:\SQL2022\Configuration2.ini"
```

Assuming that this script is saved as SQLAutoInstall1.ps1, the command in Listing 3-12 can be used to build an instance named PROSQLADMINAUTO1. This command runs the PowerShell script, passing in parameters, which are then used in the setup.exe command.

Listing 3-12. Running SQLAutoInstall.ps1

```
./SQLAutoInstall.ps1 -InstanceName 'PROSQLADMIN1' -SQLServiceAccount
'MyDomain\SQLServiceAccount1' -SQLServiceAccountPassword
'Pa$$wOrd' -AgentServiceAccount 'MyDomain\SQLServiceAccount1'
-AgentServiceAccountPassword 'Pa$$wOrd'
```

Tip   Because I have specified the parameter's names, they do not need to be specified in the order they are declared in the script. It also makes the code more readable.

Enhancing the Installation Routine

You could also extend the SQLAutoInstall.ps1 script further and use it to incorporate the techniques that you learned in Chapter 1 for the configuration of operating system components and the techniques that you learned earlier in this chapter for performing smoke tests.

After installing an instance, the amended script in Listing 3-13, which we will refer to as SQLAutoInstall2.ps1, uses powercfg to set the High Performance power plan and set-ItemProperty to prioritize background services over foreground applications. It then runs smoke tests to ensure that the SQL Server and SQL Agent services are both running and that the instance is accessible.

Listing 3-13. Enhanced PowerShell Autoinstall Script

```
param(
[string] $InstanceName,
[string] $SQLServiceAccount,
[string] $SQLServiceAccountPassword,
[string] $AgentServiceAccount,
[string] $AgentServiceAccountPassword
)

# Initialize ConnectionString variable

$ServerName = $env:computername
$ConnectionString = $ServerName + '\' + $InstanceName

#Install the instance

./SETUP.EXE /INSTANCENAME=$InstanceName /SQLSVCACCOUNT=$SQLServiceAccount
/SQLSVCPASSWORD=$SQLServiceAccountPassword /AGTSVCACCOUNT=$AgentService
Account /AGTSVCPASSWORD=$AgentServiceAccountPassword /CONFIGURATIONFILE=
"C:\SQL2022\Configuration2.ini"

# Configure OS settings

powercfg -setactive 8c5e7fda-e8bf-4a96-9a85-a6e23a8c635c

Set-ItemProperty -path HKLM:\SYSTEM\CurrentControlSet\Control\
PriorityControl -name Win32PrioritySeparation -Type DWORD -Value 24
```

```
# Run smoke tests

Get-service -displayname *$InstanceName*

Invoke-sqlcmd -Serverinstance $ConnectionString -Query "SELECT
@@SERVERNAME"
```

As well as passing variables into the setup.exe command, this script also uses the $InstanceName parameter as input for the smoke tests. The parameter can be passed straight into to get-service cmdlet, with wildcards on either side. For invoke-sqlcmd, however, we need to do a little extra work. Invoke-sqlcmd requires the full name of the instance, including the server name, or local, assuming that the script is always run locally. The script pulls the name of the server from the ComputerName environmental variable and then concatenates this with the $InstanceName variable, placing a \ between the two. This concatenated value populates the $ConnectionString variable, which can then be passed into the -Serverinstance switch.

Production Readiness

Finally, you may wish to add some defensive coding to your script in order to make it production ready. Although PowerShell has try/catch functionality due to setup.exe being an external application, which will generate its own messages and errors, the most effective technique for ensuring the smooth running of this script is to enforce mandatory parameters.

The code in Listing 3-14 is a modified version of the script, which we will refer to as SQLAutoInstall3.ps1. This version of the script uses the Parameter keyword to set the Mandatory attribute to true, using [Parameter(Mandatory=$true)], for each of the parameters. This is important because if the person running this script were to omit any of the parameters, or if there was a typo in the parameter name, the installation would fail. This provides a fail-safe by ensuring that all of the parameters have been entered before allowing the script to run. The additional change that we have made in this script is to add annotations before and after each step, so that if the script does fail, we can easily see where the error occurred.

Listing 3-14. Autoinstall Script with Defensive Code

```
param(
[Parameter(Mandatory=$true)]
[string] $InstanceName,
[Parameter(Mandatory=$true)]
[string] $SQLServiceAccount,
[Parameter(Mandatory=$true)]
[string] $SQLServiceAccountPassword,
[Parameter(Mandatory=$true)]
[string] $AgentServiceAccount,
[Parameter(Mandatory=$true)]
[string] $AgentServiceAccountPassword
)

# Initialize ConnectionString variable

$ServerName = $env:computername
$ConnectionString = $ServerName + '\' + $InstanceName

"Initialize variables complete..."

#Install the instance

./SETUP.EXE /INSTANCENAME=$InstanceName
/SQLSVCACCOUNT=$SQLServiceAccount        /SQLSVCPASSWORD=$SQLServiceAccount
Password /AGTSVCACCOUNT=$AgentServiceAccount /AGTSVCPASSWORD=$AgentService
AccountPassword /CONFIGURATIONFILE="C:\SQL2022\Configuration2.ini"

"Instance installation complete..."

# Configure OS settings

powercfg -setactive 8c5e7fda-e8bf-4a96-9a85-a6e23a8c635c

"High Performance power plan configured..."

Set-ItemProperty -path HKLM:\SYSTEM\CurrentControlSet\Control\
PriorityControl -name Win32PrioritySeparation -Type DWORD -Value 24
```

```
"Optimize for background services configured..."

# Run smoke tests

Get-service -displayname *$InstanceName* -ErrorAction Stop

"Service running check complete..."

Invoke-sqlcmd -Serverinstance $ConnectionString -Query "SELECT
@@SERVERNAME"

"Instance accessibility check complete..."
```

The SQLAutoInstall3.ps1 script has been run, but without any parameters specified. In previous versions of the script, PowerShell would have gone ahead and executed the code, only for setup.exe to fail, since no values were specified for the required parameters. In this version, however, you can see that you will be prompted to enter a value for each parameter in turn.

When running the script, you will notice that after each phase of the script execution, our annotations are shown. This can aid you in responding to errors because you can easily see which command caused an issue before you even begin to decipher any error messages that may be displayed.

Summary

Installing SQL Server on Windows Server Core can be as simple as running a single command from PowerShell and passing in the appropriate parameters. However, for consistency across the enterprise and to reduce manual effort, you may wish to automate your build process. You can do this by using a configuration file, but you can also expand this process out to fully automate the installation, including OS configuration. You will then be able to keep a PowerShell script under change control and simply run it, passing parameters, every time you wish to build a new instance.

After installing an instance, you should run smoke tests to ensure that the services are running and that the instance is accessible. This will highlight any show-stopping issues. If you do need to troubleshoot a build, then your starting point should be to check the Summary.txt log file and, if you need to, the Detail.txt log file.

In addition to installing the base binaries, you can use SQL Server's Product Update functionality to install the latest cumulative update at the same time. Product Update can be configured to check Microsoft Update, a folder location, or network folder. If you store the latest fully tested update on a network share, then you can use this when installing any instance on the network, and when you wish to increase the level of update that you support, you can simply replace the update file on the network share.

CHAPTER 4

Installation on Heterogeneous Operating Systems

The last two major releases of SQL Server have focused heavily on providing capability to install SQL Server in a variety of nontraditional environments. In this chapter, we will explore how to install SQL Server on Linux and how to build and run Docker images and containers that include SQL Server.

Tip   The commands used to install and configure SQL Server on Linux vary slightly between distributions. This chapter focused on Ubuntu, as it is arguably the friendliest, for Windows-based DBAs, and this chapter's intent is to familiarize you with the concepts and process. Microsoft provides quick start guides for each distribution, at docs.microsoft.com/en-us/sql/linux/sql-server-linux-setup?view=sql-server-2022.

Installing SQL Server on Linux

Table 4-1 details the distributions and versions of Linux, on which SQL Server 2022 is supported. If you choose to install SQL Server 2022 on a nonsupported distribution of Linux, then you may not receive full support.

© Peter A. Carter 2023
P. A. Carter, *Pro SQL Server 2022 Administration*, https://doi.org/10.1007/978-1-4842-8864-1_4

Tip   At the time of writing, the supported versions of SUSE Linux had not been announced. Additionally, supported versions can change with CUs (cumulative updates). The following link will provide an up-to-date list of version support for each of the three supported distributions: docs.microsoft.com/en-us/sql/linux/sql-server-linux-setup-2022.

Table 4-1. *Supported Linux Distributions and Versions*

Distribution	Supported Version(s)
Red Hat Enterprise	8.0–8.5
SUSE Enterprise Server	N/A at time of writing
Ubuntu	20.04

In the following sections, we will look at how to install SQL Server manually on Linux and how to create an unattended install.

Installing SQL Server Manually

Unlike the installation of SQL Server on Windows, where you specify the way in which you would like your instance to be configured, prior to the installation, on Linux, the reverse is true. You initially install a base version of SQL Server and then configure the instance, post deployment. In this section, we will review the process of manually installing SQL Server on a Linux platform. For this demonstration, we will use Ubuntu 20.04.4.

The first step in installing SQL Server is to import the public gpg keys, which will give us access to the SQL Server repo (repository). This can be achieved using the bash command in Listing 4-1.

Listing 4-1. Import the Public GPG Key

```
wget -qO- https://packages.microsoft.com/keys/microsoft.asc | sudo apt-
key add -
```

If we break this command down, we are using the wget command to pull the keys from the Microsoft website. wget is a command that is used to get web content. We then use the | operator to pass the key into the apt-key command, which is a key management tool. The add command adds the key to a list of trusted keys. Once the SQL Server package is authenticated using the trusted key, the package will become trusted. Using sudo is similar to the principle of Run As Administrator on a Windows platform. It is used to elevate the user's permissions to that of root (which is the equivalent of the Windows Administrator).

The next step is to register the SQL Server repository. This can be done using the bash command in Listing 4-2. This command uses the add-apt-repository script to add an external repository. The embedded wget command pulls the package from Microsoft's website.

Listing 4-2. Register the SQL Server Repository

```
sudo add-apt-repository "$(wget -qO- https://packages.microsoft.com/config/
ubuntu/20.04/mssql-server-2022.list)"
```

Next, we will use the apt-get, which is the Linux package manager, to pull a list of packages from the package repos and update these lists, with the most recent versions of the packages. Listing 4-3 demonstrates this.

Listing 4-3. Update Repo Package Lists

```
sudo apt-get update
```

In Listing 4-4, we will use apt-get again, this time with the install command, to install the SQL Server package. The -y switch is used to provide automatic acceptance on user prompts.

Listing 4-4. Install the SQL Server Package

```
sudo apt-get install -y mssql-server
```

When package installation is complete, the output will prompt you to run sudo /opt/mssql/bin/mssql-conf setup, which is the SQL Server configuration tool that will allow you to configure the instance. Running mssql-conf setup tool will be prompted to select the edition of SQL Server that you wish to use, as illustrated in Figure 4-1. Use number 1 through to 8 to make your selection.

```
pete@sql20221inux:~$ sudo /opt/mssql/bin/mssql-conf setup
Locale en_GB not supported. Using en_US.
Choose an edition of SQL Server:
  1) Evaluation (free, no production use rights, 180-day limit)
  2) Developer (free, no production use rights)
  3) Express (free)
  4) Web (PAID)
  5) Standard (PAID)
  6) Enterprise (PAID) - CPU Core utilization restricted to 20 physical/40 hyperthreaded
  7) Enterprise Core (PAID) - CPU Core utilization up to Operating System Maximum
  8) I bought a license through a retail sales channel and have a product key to enter.

Details about editions can be found at
https://go.microsoft.com/fwlink/?LinkId=2109348

Use of PAID editions of this software requires separate licensing through a
Microsoft Volume Licensing program.
By choosing a PAID edition, you are verifying that you have the appropriate
number of licenses in place to install and run this software.

Enter your edition(1-8): _
```

Figure 4-1. *Selecting the edition*

Next, you will be asked to accept the SQL Server license terms, as illustrated in Figure 4-2. They can be accepted by typing Yes.

```
Enter your edition(1-8): 1
The license terms for this product can be found in
/usr/share/doc/mssql-server or downloaded from:
https://go.microsoft.com/fwlink/?LinkId=2104078

The privacy statement can be viewed at:
https://go.microsoft.com/fwlink/?LinkId=853010

Do you accept the license terms? [Yes/No]:_
```

Figure 4-2. *Accept license terms*

As illustrated in Figure 4-3, you will next need to select your language, using numbers 1 through to 11.

```
Choose the language for SQL Server:
(1) English
(2) Deutsch
(3) Español
(4) Français
(5) Italiano
(6) ✦ ✦ ✦
(7) ✦ ✦ ✦
(8) Português
(9) Руййкий
(10) ✦ ✦  -  ✦ ✦
(11) ✦ ✦  ✦ ✦ ✦ ✦
Enter Option 1-11:
```

Figure 4-3. *Language selection*

> **Tip**   The languages that have not rendered correctly in Figure 4-3 are multicharacter languages, such as Chinese.

You will now be prompted to enter and confirm the password for the sa account, as shown in Figure 4-4.

```
Enter the SQL Server system administrator password:
Confirm the SQL Server system administrator password:
```

Figure 4-4. *Adding the sa password*

Your instance is now configured and you can connect to it, either using sqlcmd (which is installed on the Linux server as part of the SQL Server Tools package— discussed in the "Unattended Installation" section of this chapter) or remotely, by using SSMS (SQL Server Management Studio).

Configuring SQL Server

Although SQL Server is now installed and basic configuration has been performed, there are many configuration aspects that may need to be addressed, at both the operating system and instance levels, to make the instance fully functional, for your requirements. In this section, we will explore some of the common configuration requirements that may need to be performed in a Linux environment.

The main tool for configuring the SQL Server instance is mssql-conf. This is the same tool that we used during the installation process to configure the edition and language, as well as to set the password for the sa account. This tool also offers many other parameters that can be configured, and these parameters are detailed in Table 4-2.

Table 4-2. *mssql-conf Parameters*

Parameter	Description
Active Directory authentication	Creates a keytab to allow AD authentication. Note that the user and SPN (service principal name) must be prestaged.
Agent	Enable or disable SQL Server Agent.
Collation	Sets the instance collation.
Customer feedback	Specifies if customer feedback is sent to Microsoft. This is on by default and cannot be turned off for free editions.
Database Mail profile	Sets the Database Mail profile that is used for e-mail alerts.
Default data directory	Sets the default directory for user database files.
Default log directory	Sets the default directory for user database's transaction log files.
Default master database directory	Sets the directory for Master database data and log files.
Default master database file name	Changes the name of the database files for the Master database.
Default dump directory	Sets the directory to be used for memory dump files.
Default error log directory	Sets the directory to be used for new SQL Server ErrorLog, Default Profiler Trace, System Health Session XE, and Hekaton Session XE files.
Default backup directory	Sets the directory to be used for new backups.
Dump type	Specify the type of memory dump file to capture. Allows full dumps to be captured in addition to mini dumps. Also allows you to specify the type of dump file (mini, miniplus, filtered, and full).

(*continued*)

Table 4-2. (*continued*)

Parameter	Description
Edition	Changes the edition of SQL Server. For example, if you wish to upgrade from Developer edition to Enterprise edition.
High availability	Enables or disables AlwaysOn Availability Groups.
Local Audit directory	Sets the directory to be used for Local Audit files.
Locale	Sets the locale for the SQL Server instance.
Memory limit	Set the amount of physical memory available to the SQL Server instance.
Microsoft Distributed Transaction Coordinator	Configures MSDTC to allow distributed transactions.
Network settings	Configures SQL Server network settings, such as IP Addresses for inbound connections and which privileged accounts can use AD authentication.
Outbound Network Access	Enables outbound connectivity for machine learning services.
TCP port	Sets the port, on which SQL Server will listen for connections.
TLS	Used to configure various networking aspects of the SQL Server instance, including forceencryption, tlscert, tlskey, tlsprotocols, tlsciphers, and the kerberoskeytabfile.
Traceflags	Sets global trace flags on the instance.

Probably the most common configuration requirement is to start SQL Server Agent. This can be achieved using the Agent parameter, as shown in Listing 4-5.

Listing 4-5. Start Server Agent

```
sudo /opt/mssql/bin/mssql-conf set sqlagent.enabled true
```

Another good example of how to use the tool is the TCP port parameter. Just as in a Windows environment, TCP 1433 is used as the default port number for SQL Server. There are reasons why you would want to change this, however, such as in high security environments, to avoid a well-known port number that can be attacked.

The command in Listing 4-6 will configure the SQL Server instance to listen on Port 50001. 50001-500xx is a port range I often use, as it is not reserved.

Listing 4-6. Configure the Port

```
sudo /opt/mssql/bin/mssql-conf set network.tcpport 50001
```

For the setting to take effect, we will first need to restart the SQL Server service. This can be achieved using the systemctl, which is a Linux tool for managing services. The command in Listing 4-7 will restart the SQL Server service.

Listing 4-7. Restart the SQL Server Service

```
sudo systemctl restart mssql-server
```

The systemctl tool can also be used to check if a service is running, as demonstrated in Listing 4-8.

Listing 4-8. Check a Service Is Running

```
sudo systemctl status mssql-server
```

Now that we have configured SQL Server to listen on Port 50001, we also need to configure the local Firewall to allow traffic through this port. The local Firewall is managed using a tool called ufw (Uncomplicated Firewall). The script in Listing 4-9 illustrates how to install ufw, set default rules, allow traffic through port 50001, and then reset it for the rules to take effect. Finally, the script will display the configured rules.

Listing 4-9. Working with ufw

```
#Install ufw
sudo apt-get install ufw

#Start ufw
sudo systemctl start ufw

#Enable ufw
sudo systemctl enable ufw

#Set default Firewall Rules
sudo ufw default allow outgoing
sudo ufw default deny incoming
```

```
#Add A Rule For SQL
sudo ufw allow 50001/tcp

#Restart ufw
sudo ufw reload

#Show ufw Status
sudo ufw status
```

Note   In SQL Server 2019 and above, TempDB will automatically be configured with one data file per core, to a maximum of eight files. For previous versions, however, only a single data file will be created during setup.

Unattended Installation

Because Bash is a scripting language, the SQL Server installation can be scripted in the same way that you can use PowerShell to script installation in a Windows environment. To do this, we will first create a text file, with the text editor, vi. The command in Listing 4-10 will create and open a file called sqlconfig.sh. sh is a commonly used extension for bash scripts.

Listing 4-10. Create a Bash Script with VI

```
vi sqlconfig.sh
```

A full discussion of vi commands is beyond the scope of this book. To insert text, however, use the i command. When finished, use ESC to return to command mode. Here, :q! will exit vi without saving, or :wq will save and exit.

The script in Listing 4-11 can be added to the bash script. The first line of the file indicates that it is executable. You will also notice that we are installing full-text indexing for this instance and configuring both a trace flag and a maximum memory limit for SQL Server.

Possibly the most interesting thing to note, however, is that we are also installing a package called mssql-tools. This package contains the command-line tools for SQL Server on Linux, including sqlcmd. We will use this to create a new user, and add them to the sysadmins fixed server role, at the end of the script.

Tip   Microsoft are working on a new multi-platform command-line interface for SQL Server, called mssql-cli. This tool can be used on Linux Windows and Mac. At the time of writing, the tool was in preview, but further information can be found at github.com/dbcli/mssql-cli.

Listing 4-11. Scripted SQL Server Installation

```bash
#! /bin/bash

# Set environment variables

MSSQL_SA_PASSWORD='Pa££w0rd'

MSSQL_PID='developer'

SQL_USER='SQLAdmin'
SQL_USER_PASSWORD='Pa££w0rd'

# Configure keys and add repository

wget -q0- https://packages.microsoft.com/keys/microsoft.asc | sudo apt-
key add -

sudo add-apt-repository "$(wget -q0- https://packages.microsoft.com/config/
ubuntu/20.04/mssql-server-2022.list)"

sudo add-apt-repository "$(wget -q0- https://packages.microsoft.com/config/
ubuntu/20.04/prod.list)"

sudo apt-get update -y

# Install SQL Tools

sudo apt-get install -y mssql-server

# Install ODBC Driver

sudo ACCEPT_EULA=Y apt-get install -y mssql-tools unixodbc-dev

# Install SQL Server Instance
```

```
sudo MSSQL_SA_PASSWORD=$MSSQL_SA_PASSWORD \
    MSSQL_PID=$MSSQL_PID \
    /opt/mssql/bin/mssql-conf -n setup accept-eula

#Enable SQL Agent

sudo /opt/mssql/bin/mssql-conf set sqlagent.enabled true

#Configure Max Memory

sudo /opt/mssql/bin/mssql-conf set memory.memorylimitmb 2048

# Configure Trace Flags

sudo /opt/mssql/bin/mssql-conf traceflag 3226 on

# Install Full Text Search

sudo apt-get install -y mssql-server-fts

# Restart SQL Server

sudo systemctl restart mssql-server

# Create a SQL Server Login

/opt/mssql-tools/bin/sqlcmd \
  -S localhost \
  -U SA \
  -P $MSSQL_SA_PASSWORD \
  -Q "CREATE LOGIN [$SQL_USER] WITH PASSWORD=N'$SQL_INSTALL_PASSWORD';
ALTER SERVER ROLE [sysadmin] ADD MEMBER [$SQL_USER]"
```

The command in Listing 4-12 will grant the execute permission on the script.

Listing 4-12. Grant Execute Permissions

```
chmod +x sqlconfig.sh
```

The script can be executed using the command in Listing 4-13.

Listing 4-13. Execute the Installation

```
sh sqlconfig.sh
```

Installing and Managing SQL Server in a Docker Container

Containers are isolated, lightweight units, which can be used to run applications. Unlike virtual machines, which emulate hardware, containers sit on top of an operating system and emulate the kernel. Kernel emulation with containers is referred to as containerization. Containers are becoming popular in organizations of all sizes, because they are efficient and portable. The portability of containers also simplifies deployment processes and makes them very popular in DevOps environments.

Docker is the application platform that is used to run containers. It was originally developed for Linux but is now also supported on Windows. This means that SQL Server can utilize containers, regardless of the required base operating system.

A docker image is a single file, which contains a fully packaged application. So, in terms of SQL Server, a Docker image may be built on an operating system such as Windows Server 2022 Core and the SQL Server binaries. Your instance would be fully configured, following your best practices, so that every time you create a container from your image, it will be ready to use.

Caution   An important consideration, when containerizing SQL Server, is that containers are stateless. One of their advantages is that you can drop a container and spin it up again, very quickly and easily, and it will be exactly the same as it was originally. A side effect of this is that if you have data files inside a container, when you drop the container, the data files are also destroyed. For this reason, user data files and msdb data files should be stored outside of the container. I usually recommend keeping the data files for master inside the container, as this database stores many of your instance configuration details, but in certain circumstances, you may wish to store these outside of the container as well.

Running a Microsoft-Supplied Docker Image

Microsoft supply a small number of docker images for SQL Server. For example, at the time of writing, there is a SQL Server 2022 for Ubuntu 20.04 image. Microsoft's Beta program for SQL Server on Windows containers has been suspended. Therefore, if you wish to run a Windows Server Core container running SQL Server, then you will need to build the container image yourself.

Note Using SQL Server on Windows containers is not officially supported at the time of writing.

Our first step will be to import the public keys for the docker repo. This can be achieved with the script in Listing 4-14.

Listing 4-14. Import GPG Public Keys

```
wget -q0- https://download.docker.com/linux/ubuntu/gpg -- | sudo apt-
key add -
```

Next, we will add the docker repo to our list of repositories and update the apt cache policy to ensure we install from the correct repo, using the script in Listing 4-15.

Listing 4-15. Add Docker Repository

```
sudo add-apt-repository "deb [arch=amd64] https://download.docker.com/
linux/ubuntu focal stable" I apt-cache policy docker-ce
```

The final step is to perform the Docker installation itself with the command in Listing 4-16. During the install, you will be prompted to accept the amount of disk space that will be used.

Listing 4-16. Start the Docker Service

```
sudo apt install docker-ce
```

We can now pull the image from the Microsoft Container Registry (MCR). This is a repository of base Windows containers. The Docker Hub is the default repository for container images, but even though Windows images are listed on Docker Hub, they are stored on the MCR. We can pull the image using the command in Listing 4-17.

Listing 4-17. Pull the Docker Image

```
sudo docker pull mcr.microsoft.com/mssql/server:2022-latest
```

Finally, we will need to start the container. We can start out container using the command in Listing 4-18. In this example, the -d switch is used to denote that the container should be run as a daemon, meaning that the container will run as a background process, as opposed to interactively. We are also using -p to publish the containers port to the host. In this example, we are mapping port 1433 inside the container to port 50001 on the host. We are configuring the container name with the --name parameter and the container host name with the –hostname parameter. -e is used to set the environment variables. Here, we are setting the password for the sa account and accepting the SQL Server license terms.

Listing 4-18. Run the Container

```
sudo docker run -e "ACCEPT_EULA=Y" \
    -e "SA_PASSWORD=Passw0rd" \
    -p 50001:1433 \
    --name pro-sql-admin-container \
    --hostname pro-sql-admin-container-host \
    -d \
    mcr.microsoft.com/mssql/server:2022-latest
```

Working with Containers

Once your container is running, there will be times when you need to interact with it. Docker provides numerous subcommands that allow you to do this. For example, the ps and image subcommands, shown in Listing 4-19, can be used to list containers and images, respectively.

Listing 4-19. Listing Containers

```
sudo docker ps

sudo docker images
```

You can connect to a SQL Server instance installed within a container, locally from the container itself, by using sqlcmd. Listing 4-20 demonstrates this by using the exec subcommand to run bash within the container. The -i option opens an interactive bash session. If this option was omitted, then exec would simply run the command that you specify (in this case bash) and then exit the session.

Listing 4-20. Use exec to Open an Interactive Bash Session

```
sudo docker exec -i pro-sql-admin-container "bash"
```

Once an interactive bash session is open, we can use the command in Listing 4-21 to run sqlcmd against the instance. In this example, we simply return a list of database names from the instance.

Listing 4-21. Use sqlcmd Inside the Container

```
/opt/mssql-tools/bin/sqlcmd -S localhost -U sa -P Password -Q "SELECT *
FROM sys.databases"
```

Once we have finished with our interactive bash session, we can use the exit command to return to the terminal.

Alternatively, we can connect to the SQL Server instance from the host, or from anywhere else on the network, using sqlcmd, SQL Server Management Studio, or Azure Data Tools, just as we would any other instance.

The command in Listing 4-22 demonstrates running the same query from a remote Linux server, using sqlcmd. The command assumes that the server on which the container is hosted is called ubuntusql and that port 50001 on the server is mapped to the port (probably 1433) that SQL Server is listening on, inside the container. The command also assumes that mssql-tools is installed on the server, from which you are running the command.

Listing 4-22. Connect to the SQL Server Instance Remotely

```
/opt/mssql-tools/bin/sqlcmd -S ubuntusql,50001 -S sa -P Password
```

A container can be stopped by using the stop subcommand and be destroyed by using the rm subcommand, as shown in Listing 4-23. In this example, we will stop the pro-sql-admin-container container. A container must be stopped before it can be removed.

Listing 4-23. Stop and Remove a Container

```
sudo docker stop pro-sql-admin-container

sudo docker rm pro-sql-admin-container
```

Creating Custom SQL Server Containers

In the following sections, we will discuss how to create a custom Windows container that runs SQL Server. We will then explore how we can make the image configurable by using a startup script. It is important to note that SQL Server in Windows containers is not officially supported at this time. Therefore, you should not look to implement them in a production environment. However, their usefulness for development and testing scenarios means that they are still worth seriously considering for nonproduction environments.

Caution   SQL Server on Windows containers is not supported at this time.

Although this section demonstrates how to build a custom Windows container, the same techniques can also be used to create customized Linux containers. Customized containers always start from a base image, so you could start from a CentOS base image, and create a SQL Server container, that like SQL Server on Windows containers is not supported. Alternatively, you could use the supported SQL Server RedHat container and install additional management tools that you require.

Tip   You may wish to use CentOS containers instead of RedHat containers for development and testing purposes, as CentOS shared a kernel with RedHat, but does not have a license fee.

Creating a Simple Docker Image for SQL Server

While Microsoft do not currently supply Windows-based Docker images with SQL Server installed, you can create your own Docker image with your own desired operating system and required configuration. In this section, we will explore how to use a Docker file to create an image that will install SQL Server 2022 and SQL Server command-line tools on Windows Server Core.

Tip   In this section, we will use a Windows Server 2019 host, which has had the containers feature, Docker module, and Microsoft Docker provider installed. Details of how to perform these preparation steps can be found in the "Running a Microsoft Supplied Docker Image" section of this chapter.

The first step in creating our own container image is to pull the Windows Server 2019 Core image from the MCR. This is the image that we will use as a base for our image. We can do this with PowerShell, by using the command in Listing 4-24.

Listing 4-24. Pull the Base Image

```
docker pull mcr.microsoft.com/windows/servercore:ltsc2019
```

Our next step will be to create a simple folder structure on the host. Firstly, we will create a folder called C:\DockerBuild. This folder will store our build scripts. We will also create a folder underneath, called C:\DockerBuild\SQL2022. This folder should contain the SQL Server 2022 installation media.

A Docker file is a deployment script, which specifies how the container image should be built. We can use this Dockerfile to customize and configure a container. The file consists of a set of instructions. The instructions that are most relevant to creating SQL Server containers are detailed in Table 4-3.

Table 4-3. *Docker File Instructions*

Instruction	Description
FROM	The container image, on which your new image should be based
RUN	Specifies a command that should be run
COPY	Copies files from the host to the container image
ADD	Similar to COPY, but allows files to be copied from a remote source
WORKDIR	Specifies the working directory, for other Docker instructions
CMD	Sets a default command to run, when an instance of the container image is deployed
VOLUME	Creates a mount point
LABEL	Allows you to add comments to the dockerfile

We will now need to create two scripts, both of which we will place in the C:\ DockerBuild folder. The first of these files is the docker file. This file must be called Dockerfile and have no extension.

Tip   When saving dockerfile, ensure that your text/code editor has not automatically appended a default file extension to the file. If it has, then the build of the image will fail.

The script in Listing 4-25 contains the contents of the docker file we will use.

Listing 4-25. Dockerfile

```
#Use the Server Core base image

FROM mcr.microsoft.com/windows/servercore:ltsc2019

#Make temp folders for the SQL Server and SQL Command Line Utilities media

RUN powershell -Command (mkdir C:\SQL2022)

#Copy the SQL Server media into the container

COPY \SQL2022 C:/SQL2022

#Install SQL Server
```

```
RUN C:/SQL2022/SETUP.exe /Q /ACTION=INSTALL /FEATURES=SQLENGINE /
INSTANCENAME=MSSQLSERVER \
/SECURITYMODE=SQL /SAPWD="Passw0rd" /SQLSVCACCOUNT="NT AUTHORITY\System" \
/AGTSVCACCOUNT="NT AUTHORITY\System" /SQLSYSADMINACCOUNTS="BUILTIN\
Administrators" \
/IACCEPTSQLSERVERLICENSETERMS=1 /TCPENABLED=1 /UPDATEENABLED=False

#Install Chocolatey and SQL Server Command-Line Utilities

RUN @"%SystemRoot%\System32\WindowsPowerShell\v1.0\powershell.exe"
-NoProfile -InputFormat None -ExecutionPolicy Bypass -Command "iex ((New-
Object System.Net.WebClient).DownloadString('https://chocolatey.org/
install.ps1'))" && SET "PATH=%PATH%;%ALLUSERSPROFILE%\chocolatey\bin"

RUN choco install sqlserver-cmdlineutils -y

#Set SQL Server to start automatically

RUN powershell -Command (Set-Service MSSQLSERVER -StartupType Automatic)

#Remove the installation media

RUN powershell -Command (Remove-Item -Path C:/SQL2022 -Recurse -Force)

#Create a mountpoint for data files

VOLUME C:/datafiles

#Copy start.ps1 to container

COPY \start.ps1 /

WORKDIR /

CMD powershell -Command (.\start.ps1)
```

Working through the contents of the file, even without experience of Docker, it is fairly easy to see what is happening. Our first statement indicates that our build will be based upon the Windows Server 2019 Core build, supplied by Microsoft. We then use the RUN and COPY instructions to copy the SQL Server media to the container.

After this, we move straight into the installation of SQL Server. Installing SQL Server via PowerShell is discussed in Chapter 3. There is no difference in this code, as to when you install SQL Server on a traditional server running Windows Server Core. The only interesting thing to note is that because the command spans multiple lines, we have used the \ at the end of each line to let Docker know that it is a single instruction.

The next part of the script is quite interesting. We are installing Chocolatey. Chocolatey is a package manager for Windows, which has a large gallery of prepackaged applications. In this case, it is helpful, because it allows us to easily install SQL Server Command-Line Utilities, which is available on the Chocolatey gallery.

Tip   Chocolatey can also be used to package your own SQL Server builds. I did this for a client recently, and it fits very nicely into a DevOps/Configuration Management style of operations.

Next, we use the RUN instruction to run PowerShell commands, which will clean up our installation files and ensure that the Database Engine service is started. Our next step is to use the VOLUME instruction to create a mount point for datafiles. When we run an instance of the container, we will be able to map this to a folder on our host, to allow our data to be persisted.

Finally, we copy a file called Start.ps1 to our container and run it. The contents of Start.ps1 are shown in Listing 4-26. This script is used to run an infinite loop. If we did not do this, then the container would stop, as soon as the last instruction was sent.

Listing 4-26. Start.ps1

```
$lastCheck = (Get-Date).AddSeconds(-2)
while ($true)
{
    $lastCheck = Get-Date
    Start-Sleep -Seconds 2
}
```

After saving both of these files in the C:\DockerBuild folder of the host, we can build the image by running the command in Listing 4-27. We use the -t switch to tag the build. I have used the major.minor notation to indicate a build version.

Tip   Make sure you are in the C:\DockerBuild folder before running the command.

Listing 4-27. Build the Image

```
docker build -t sql2022:1.0 .
```

Once the build has completed, we can create an instance of the container by using the command in Listing 4-28.

Listing 4-28. Run a Docker Container

```
docker run -p 1433:1433 --name sql-2022 -d --volume c:\datafiles:c:\
datafiles sql2022:1.0
```

In this command, we are using -p to expose a port to the host machine and -d to run the container as a background process. We are also using --name to identify the container. Most interestingly, we are using --volume to map the mount point in the container to a folder on our host. This takes the format source:target.

We have not specified an IP Address for the container, so we can check the IP Address that it has been assigned by using the command in Listing 4-29. This is using the docker inspect command to pull out a specific node from the JSON-based configuration, followed by the name of the container that you are interested in.

Listing 4-29. Obtain the Container's IP Address

```
docker inspect --format "{{ .NetworkSettings.Networks.nat.IPAddress }}"
sql-2022
```

We can now connect to the instance, from outside of the container, using SSMS (or other SQL client) using the IP Address.

Let's use the script in Listing 4-30 to create a database on the mounted volume.

Listing 4-30. Create a Database

```
CREATE DATABASE PersistedData
ON  PRIMARY
( NAME = N'PersistedData', FILENAME = N'C:\datafiles\PersistedData.mdf' ,
SIZE = 8192KB , FILEGROWTH = 65536KB )
```

```
  LOG ON
( NAME = N'PersistedData_log', FILENAME = N'C:\datafiles\PersistedData.ldf'
, SIZE = 8192KB , FILEGROWTH = 65536KB )
GO
```

If we now destroy the container, then the data will persist. We can drop the container using the script in Listing 4-31. This script first stops the container and then removes it.

Listing 4-31. Remove the Container

```
docker stop sql-2022
```

```
docker rm sql-2022
```

If you now re-create the container using the script in Listing 4-28 and obtain the new IP Address by using the script in Listing 4-29, you will notice, when you connect to the instance, that the PersistedData database is no longer on the instance. This is because the database is not attached during the build. Because the files are stored on the host, however, then you can simply reattach the database using the command in Listing 4-32.

Listing 4-32. Reattach the Database

```
CREATE DATABASE PersistedData ON
( FILENAME = N'C:\datafiles\PersistedData.mdf' ),
( FILENAME = N'C:\datafiles\PersistedData.ldf' )
 FOR ATTACH
```

```
GO
```

Create a Configurable Docker Image for SQL Server

While the build discussed in the "Creating a Simple Docker Image for SQL Server" was easy to follow, it was also rather inflexible. Everything was hard-coded and there was no means of attaching databases during the build process. Therefore, in the following demonstration, we will make a major change to our build, which allows us to parameterize it, making the build a lot more useable, in real-world scenarios.

Following the same process as before and using the same folder structure on the host, let's first create a new Docker file. The contents of Dockerfile that we will use can be found in Listing 4-33. The file is similar, but you will notice a few changes. Firstly, we have removed the code which installs SQL Server Command Utilities. This is because we will be using the sqlserver PowerShell provider instead.

We have also changed the hard-coded sa password in the SQL Server installation step to be TempPassw0rd. This is because when we run an instance of the container, we will pass in the password that we want to use.

Most significantly, you will notice that the call to Start.ps1 has been expanded, to pass in parameters. In this build, Start.ps1 is where all of the magic happens. You will notice that we are passing environment variables to each of the script's parameters.

Listing 4-33. Dockerfile

```
#Use the Server Core base image
FROM mcr.microsoft.com/windows/servercore:ltsc2019

#Make temp folders for the SQL Server and SQL Command Line Utilities media

RUN powershell -Command (mkdir C:\SQL2022)

#Copy the SQL Server media into the container

COPY \SQL2022 C:/SQL2022

#Install SQL Server

RUN C:/SQL2022/SETUP.exe /Q /ACTION=INSTALL /FEATURES=SQLENGINE /
INSTANCENAME=MSSQLSERVER \
/SECURITYMODE=SQL /SAPWD="TempPassw0rd" /SQLSVCACCOUNT="NT AUTHORITY\
System" \
/AGTSVCACCOUNT="NT AUTHORITY\System" /SQLSYSADMINACCOUNTS="BUILTIN\
Administrators" \
/IACCEPTSQLSERVERLICENSETERMS=1 /TCPENABLED=1 /UPDATEENABLED=False

#Set SQL Server to start automatically

RUN powershell -Command (Set-Service MSSQLSERVER -StartupType Automatic)

#Remove the installation media
```

```
RUN powershell -Command (Remove-Item -Path C:/SQL2022 -Recurse -Force)

#Create a mountpoint for data files

VOLUME C:/datafiles

#Switch shell to PowerShell

#SHELL ["powershell", "-Command", "$ErrorActionPreference = 'Stop';
$ProgressPreference = 'SilentlyContinue';"]

#Copy start.ps1 to container

COPY \start.ps1 /

WORKDIR /

CMD powershell -Command (.\start.ps1 -saPassword $env:saPassword -databases
$env:databases -agentStartupType $env:agentStartupType)
```

Our next step will be to create a new Start.ps1 file. This time, the file, which can be seen in Listing 4-34, is a lot more complex. The script accepts three parameters, which allow us to pass in a password for the sa account, an array of databases that should exist on the instance and the required startup type of the SQL Server Agent service.

The first command in the script is used to install the `sqlserver` PowerShell module, from the PowerShell Gallery. This allows us to use the `Invoke-SqlCmd` cmdlet. The script then runs a query against the SQL instance, authenticating using the temporary password of the sa account, and changes the password to the one passed in.

The next section of the script is the most complicated. This section checks to see if each database in the array of database names that was passed exists on the instance. If it doesn't, it attempts to attach the database from the mounted volume. If no database files exist, it will check to see if there is a backup file in the mounted volume and restore the database. Finally, if all else fails, a new database will be created.

Tip   This version of the script relies heavily on naming conventions of database and backup files. It also assumes that there will only ever be an `.mdf` and `.ldf` file. You can, of course, edit this script, however, to add support for `.ndf` files, or your own naming conventions or application requirements.

The next command in the script will alter the SQL Server Agent service to use the startup type that has been passed to the script. Finally, the script enters the same infinite loop as in the previous example. This stops the container from stopping, after the last instruction is passed.

Listing 4-34. Start.ps1

```
param(
[Parameter(Mandatory=$true)]
[string]$saPassword,

[Parameter(Mandatory=$false)]
[string]$databases,

[Parameter(Mandatory=$false)]
[String]$agentStartupType
)

#Install SQL Server PowerShell Provider

If(-not(Get-InstalledModule SQLServer -ErrorAction silentlycontinue)){
    Install-Module SQLServer -Confirm:$False -Force
}

#Update sa Password

$params = @{
    ServerInstance = "localhost"
    Username = "sa"
    Password = "TempPassw0rd"
    Query = "ALTER LOGIN [sa] WITH PASSWORD='{0}'; ALTER LOGIN sa ENABLE ;"
    -f $saPassword
}

Invoke-Sqlcmd @params

#Shred the database array

$databasesClean = $databases -split ","

#Create each database
```

```
ForEach ($database in $databasesClean) {
    $params = @{
        ServerInstance = "localhost"
        Username = "sa"
        Password = $saPassword
        Variable = "dbName='{0}'" -f $database
        Query = "SELECT COUNT(*) AS dbExists FROM sys.databases WHERE name
        = `$(dbName)"
    }

    $dbExists = Invoke-Sqlcmd @params

    if ($dbexists.dbExists -eq 0) {
        $mdf = "C:\datafiles\{0}.mdf" -f $database
        if (Test-Path $mdf) {
            $params = @{
                ServerInstance = "localhost"
                Username = "sa"
                Password = $saPassword
                Variable = "dbName='{0}'" -f $database
                Query = "DECLARE @SQL NVARCHAR(MAX) = 'CREATE DATABASE
                [' + `$(dbName) + '] ON ( FILENAME = N''C:\datafiles\' +
                `$(dbName) + '.mdf'' ),( FILENAME = N''C:\datafiles\' +
                `$(dbName) + '.ldf'' ) FOR ATTACH'; EXEC(@SQL)"
            }

            Invoke-Sqlcmd @params
        } else {
            $bak = "C:\datafiles\{0}.bak" -f $database
            if (Test-Path $bak) {
                $params = @{
                    ServerInstance = "localhost"
                    Username = "sa"
                    Password = $saPassword
                    Variable = "dbName='{0}'" -f $database
```

```
                Query = "DECLARE @SQL NVARCHAR(MAX) = 'RESTORE DATABASE
                [' + `$(dbName) + '] FROM  DISK = N''C:\datafiles\' +
                `$(dbName) + '.bak'';'; EXEC(@SQL)"
            }

            Invoke-Sqlcmd @params
        } else {
            $params = @{
                ServerInstance = "localhost"
                Username = "sa"
                Password = $saPassword
                Variable = "dbName='{0}'" -f $database
                Query = "DECLARE @SQL NVARCHAR(MAX) = 'CREATE DATABASE
                [' + `$(dbName) + ']' EXEC(@SQL)"
            }

            Invoke-Sqlcmd @params
        }
    }
  }
}

#Set Agent service startup type

Set-Service SQLSERVERAGENT -StartupType $agentStartupType

#Start infinite loop

$lastCheck = (Get-Date).AddSeconds(-2)

while ($true)
{
    $lastCheck = Get-Date
    Start-Sleep -Seconds 2
}
```

Tip   Environment variables do not support arrays. Therefore, we need to pass the list of databases as a comma-separated string. We then use Split in PowerShell to create the array.

We can now build the image using the command in Listing 4-35. Notice that I have incremented the major version number.

Listing 4-35. Build the Docker Image

```
docker build -t sql-2022:2.0 .
```

Finally, we can run the container, as demonstrated in Listing 4-36. Notice that we are using -e switches to create the environment variables in the container.

Listing 4-36. Run the Container

```
docker run -p 1433:1433 --name sql-2022 -e "saPassword=PermPassw0rd" -e
"databases=test,persisteddata" -e "agentStartupType=Automatic" -d --volume
c:\datafiles:c:\datafiles sql-2022:2.0
```

Tip   The possibilities for automation with containers are worthy of a book in its own right, and I would encourage you to experiment. For example, you could try wrapping the command that runs the container in a PowerShell script, where you pass the required name of the container. The script could then create a folder on the host, which includes the container name, making it unique. The container's mounted volume could then map to a unique folder name. You should also experiment with passing the sa password as a path to an encrypted file, as passing it in an environment variable is not secure for a production environment. You could also experiment with adding a gMSA to the container. This will allow SQL Server to interact with AD, despite domain join not being supported for containers.

Summary

SQL Server can now be installed not just on Windows but also on Linux and inside containers. This provides much more flexibility for database architects to host SQL Server on the platform that is most appropriate for their application's needs.

SQL Server is supported on Ubuntu, Red Hat, and SUSE Linux distributions. When planning the deployment of production systems, you should ensure that you are using a supported version, as well as a supported distribution of Linux.

SQL Server can be installed on both Windows and Linux containers, although Microsoft only provide support for SQL Server on Linux containers. Microsoft supply some basic Docker images, but you may need to build your own, custom Docker image for deploying SQL Server. This allows you to use your desired operating system and also configure the container appropriately for your requirements.

CHAPTER 5

Configuring the Instance

The installation and configuration of your SQL Server instance does not end when setup successfully completes. There are many other considerations that you should take into account, both inside the database engine and outside of it, using tools such as SQL Server Configuration Manager. In this chapter, we will discuss many of the most important instance-level configuration options, including processor and memory configuration, SQL Server's buffer pool extension, and hybrid buffer pools. We will also explore important configuration choices for system databases, how your instance can configure and how to configure SQL Server, to work with your firewall. We will also look at some useful trace flags and how to set them.

Tip A SQL Server instance is an installation of SQL Server. It is possible to have multiple instances of SQL Server on the same physical server, or VM. Each instance has its own isolated services, has its own set of system databases, and will be configured to listen on a different port.

Instance Configuration

At the instance level, there are countless settings and flags that can be configured. In the following sections, we will look at viewing and configuring these settings using tools such as sp_configure, sys.configurations, DBCC TRACEON, and ALTER SERVER.

Using sp_configure

You can change many of the settings that you can configure at the instance level using the system stored procedure sp_configure. You can use the sp_configure procedure to both view and change instance-level settings. This procedure will be used in many examples throughout this book, so it is important that you understand how it works. If a

135

procedure is the first statement in the batch, you can run it without the EXEC keyword, but you must use the EXEC keyword if there are any preceding statements. If the procedure is run with no parameters, then it will return a five-column result set. The meaning of these columns is detailed in Table 5-1.

Table 5-1. *Result Set Returned by sp_configure*

Column	Description
Name	The name of the instance-level setting.
Minimum	The minimum value that is acceptable for this setting.
Maximum	The maximum value that is accepted for this setting.
Config_value	The value that has been configured for this value. If this value differs from the value in the Run_value column, then the instance will need to be either restarted or reconfigured for this configuration to take effect.
Run_value	The value that is currently being used for this setting.

If you wish to use sp_configure to change the value of a setting, as opposed to just viewing it, then you must run the procedure with two parameters being passed in. The first of these parameters is called configname and is defined with a VARCHAR(35) data type. This parameter is used to pass the name of the setting that you wish to change. The second parameter is called configvalue and is defined as an integer. This parameter is used to pass the new value for the setting. After you have changed an instance-level setting using sp_configure, it will not immediately take effect. To activate the setting, you will need to either restart the Database Engine Service or reconfigure the instance.

There are two options for reconfiguring the instance. The first is a command called RECONFIGURE. The second is a command called RECONFIGURE WITH OVERRIDE. The RECONFIGURE command will change the running value of the setting as long as the newly configured value is regarded as "sensible" by SQL Server. For example, RECONFIGURE will not allow you to disable contained databases when they exist on the instance. If you use the RECONFIGURE WITH OVERRIDE command, however, this action would be allowed, even though your contained databases will no longer be accessible. Even with this command, however, SQL Server will still run checks to ensure that the value you have entered is between the Min and Max values for the setting. It will also not allow you to perform any operations that will cause serious errors. For example, it will not allow you to configure the Min Server Memory (MB) setting to be higher than the Max Server Memory (MB) setting, since this would cause a fatal error in the Database Engine.

The first time you run the sp_configure stored procedure with no parameters in SQL Server 2022, it will return 29 rows. These rows contain the basic configuration options for the instance. One of the options is called Show Advanced Options. If you turn on this option and then reconfigure the instance, as demonstrated in Listing 5-1, then an additional 52 advanced settings will be displayed when you run the procedure. If you try to change the value of one of the advanced options before turning on the Show Advanced Options setting, then the command will fail.

Listing 5-1. Showing Advanced Options

```
EXEC sp_configure 'show advanced options', 1
RECONFIGURE
```

As an alternative to viewing these settings with sp_configure, you can also retrieve the same information by querying sys.configurations. If you use sys.configurations to return the information, then two additional columns will be returned. One of these columns is called is_dynamic, and it designates if the option can be configured with the RECONFIGURE command (1) or if the instance needs to be restarted (0). The other column is called is_Advanced, and it indicates if the setting is configurable without Show Advanced Options being turned on.

Processor and Memory Configuration

When configuring your instance, one of your first considerations should be the configuration of processor and memory resources. There are two main considerations that you should give to the processor. One is processor affinity and the other is MAXDOP (maximum degree of parallelism).

Processor Affinity

By default, your instance will be able to use all of the processor cores within your server. (A physical processor, also known as a socket, or CPU, consists of multiple cores, which are individual processors.) If you use processor affinity, however, specific processor cores will be aligned with your instance and these will be the only cores that the instance has access to. There are two main reasons for limiting your instance in this way. The first is when you have multiple instances running on the same server. With this configuration, you may find that the instances are competing for the same processor resources and therefore blocking each other. Processor affinity is controlled via a setting called *affinity mask*.

Imagine you had a server with four physical processors, each of which had two cores. Assuming that hyper-threading is turned off for the purpose of this example, there would be a total of eight cores available to SQL Server. If you had four instances on the server, then to avoid the instances competing for resources, you could align cores 0 and 1 with instance 1, cores 2 and 3 with instance 2, cores 4 and 5 with instance 3, and cores 6 and 7 with instance 4. Of course, the disadvantage of this is CPU resources not being utilized, if an instance is idle.

If you have other services running on the server, such as SQL Server Integration Services (SSIS), you may wish to leave a core available for Windows and other applications, which cannot be used by any of the instances. In this case, you may have identified that instance 4 uses less processor resources than the other instances. It may be an instance dedicated to ETL (extract, transform, and load), for example, and be used primarily for hosting the SSIS catalog. In this case, you may align instance 4 with core 6 only. This would leave core 7 free for other purposes. This design is illustrated in Figure 5-1.

Note   SSIS is incorporated into the Database Engine. However, when SSIS packages run, they run in a separate DTSHost process and are, therefore, not aligned with the processor and memory configuration of the instance.

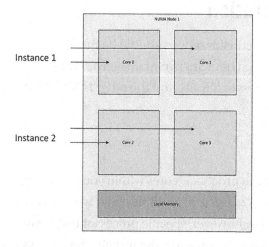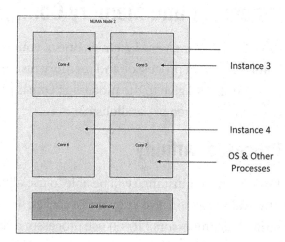

Figure 5-1. *Processor affinity diagram*

When using processor affinity, it is important for performance to align an instance with cores on the same NUMA (nonuniform memory access) node. This is because, if a processor needs to remotely access the memory of a different NUMA node, it needs to go via an interconnect, which is a lot slower than accessing the local NUMA node. In the example shown in Figure 5-1, if we had aligned instance 1 with cores 0 and 7, then we would have breached the NUMA boundary and performance would have been impaired.

Caution   Although it is not recommended for SQL Server, some virtual environments use a technique called *oversubscribed processors*. This means that more cores are allocated to guests than actually exist on the physical hosts. When this is the case, you should not use processor affinity because NUMA boundaries will not be respected.

The affinity mask reducing contention also holds true for clustered environments. Imagine you have a two-node cluster with an active/active configuration. Each node of the cluster is hosting a single instance. It may be important for your business that you can guarantee consistent performance in the event of a failover. In this case, assuming that each of your nodes has eight cores, then on node 1, you could configure instance 1 to use cores 0, 1, 2, and 3. On node 2, you could configure instance 2 to use cores 4, 5, 6, and 7. Now, in the event of failover, your instances will continue to use the same processor cores and not fight for resources.

The second reason for using processor affinity is to avoid the overhead associated with threads being moved between processors at the operating system level. When your instance is under heavy load, you may see a performance improvement by aligning SQL Server threads with specific cores. In this scenario, it would be possible to separate standard SQL Server tasks from SQL Server I/O–related tasks.

Imagine that you have a server with a single processor, which has two cores. Hyper-threading is turned off and you have a single instance installed. You may choose to align tasks associated with I/O affinity, such as Lazy Writer, with core 0, while aligning other SQL Server threads with core 1. To align I/O tasks with specific processors, you need to use an additional setting, called *Affinity I/O Mask*. When this setting is enabled, a hidden scheduler is created, which is used purely for Lazy Writer. Therefore, it is important that you do not align the affinity and affinity I/O masks with the same core. Otherwise, you will inadvertently create the contention that you are trying to avoid.

Caution   It is very rare that Affinity I/O Mask is required. To align workloads from multiple instances, Affinity Mask is sufficient. It is normally only appropriate for very large databases running on 32-bit systems. With 64-bit systems with larger amounts of RAM, I/O churn is less; hence, there is less context switching.

Both Affinity Mask and Affinity I/O Mask can be set through the GUI in SQL Server Management Studio by selecting the Processors tab in the Instance Properties dialog box, as shown in Figure 5-2.

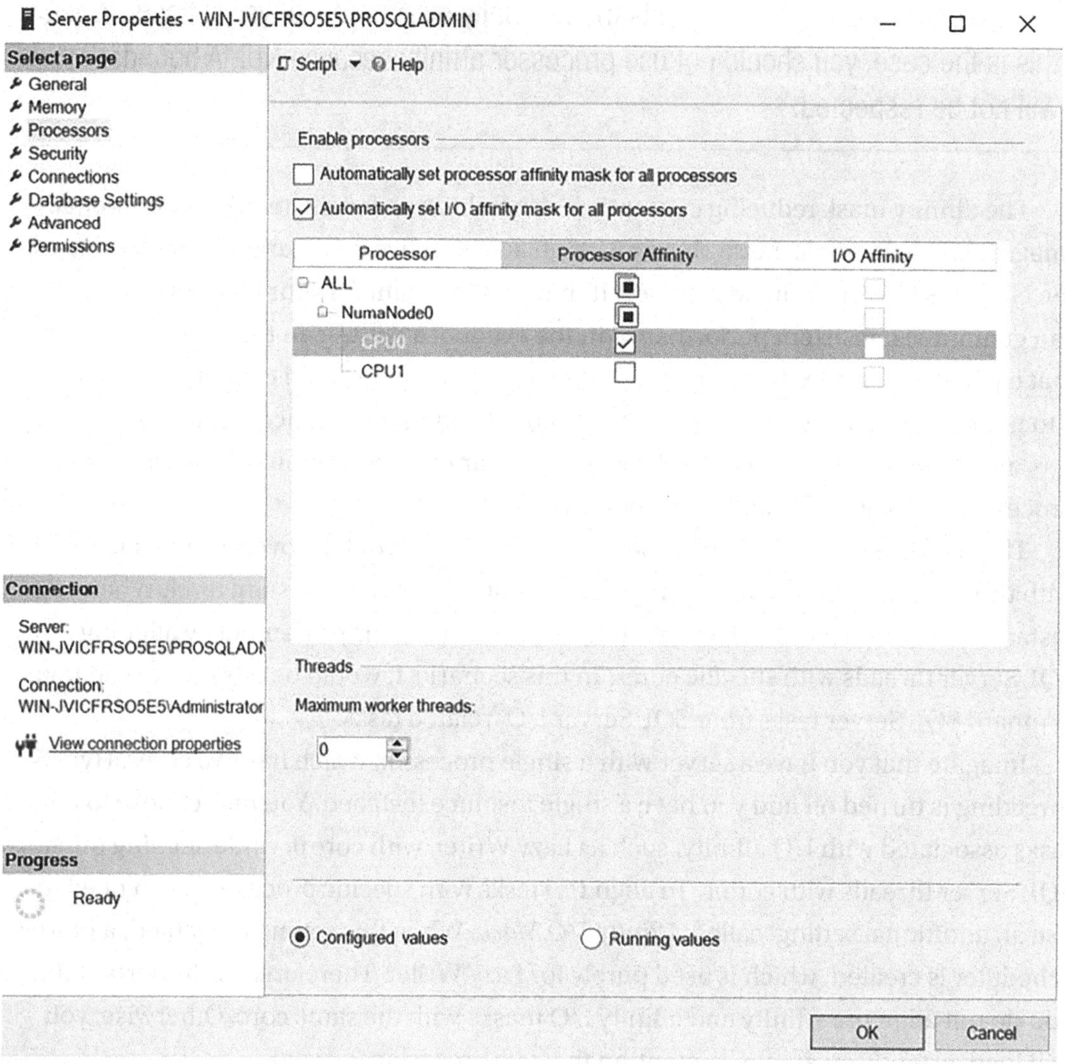

Figure 5-2. The Processors tab

Processor affinity works based on bit maps. Therefore, if you wish to use sp_configure to set processor affinity, then you first need to calculate the integer representation of the bit map value. This is made more complex because the INT data type is a 32-bit signed integer, meaning that some of the representations will be negative numbers. The value assigned to each processor is listed in Table 5-2.

Tip   Many free calculators are available on the Internet that will assist you in converting binary to signed integer.

Table 5-2. *Processor Affinity Bit Maps*

Processor Number	Bit Mask	Signed Integer Representation
0	0000 0000 0000 0000 0000 0000 0000 0001	1
1	0000 0000 0000 0000 0000 0000 0000 0010	2
2	0000 0000 0000 0000 0000 0000 0000 0100	4
3	0000 0000 0000 0000 0000 0000 0000 1000	8
4	0000 0000 0000 0000 0000 0000 0001 0000	16
5	0000 0000 0000 0000 0000 0000 0010 0000	32
6	0000 0000 0000 0000 0000 0000 0100 0000	64
7	0000 0000 0000 0000 0000 0000 1000 0000	128
8	0000 0000 0000 0000 0000 0001 0000 0000	256
9	0000 0000 0000 0000 0000 0010 0000 0000	512
10	0000 0000 0000 0000 0000 0100 0000 0000	1024
11	0000 0000 0000 0000 0000 1000 0000 0000	2028
12	0000 0000 0000 0000 0001 0000 0000 0000	4096
13	0000 0000 0000 0000 0010 0000 0000 0000	8192
14	0000 0000 0000 0000 0100 0000 0000 0000	16384
15	0000 0000 0000 0000 1000 0000 0000 0000	32768

(*continued*)

Table 5-2. (*continued*)

Processor Number	Bit Mask	Signed Integer Representation
16	0000 0000 0000 0001 0000 0000 0000 0000	65536
17	0000 0000 0000 0010 0000 0000 0000 0000	131072
18	0000 0000 0000 0100 0000 0000 0000 0000	262144
19	0000 0000 0000 1000 0000 0000 0000 0000	524288
20	0000 0000 0001 0000 0000 0000 0000 0000	1048576
21	0000 0000 0010 0000 0000 0000 0000 0000	2097152
22	0000 0000 0100 0000 0000 0000 0000 0000	4194304
23	0000 0000 1000 0000 0000 0000 0000 0000	8388608
24	0000 0001 0000 0000 0000 0000 0000 0000	16777216
25	0000 0010 0000 0000 0000 0000 0000 0000	33554432
26	0000 0100 0000 0000 0000 0000 0000 0000	67108864
27	0000 1000 0000 0000 0000 0000 0000 0000	134217728
28	0001 0000 0000 0000 0000 0000 0000 0000	268435456
29	0010 0000 0000 0000 0000 0000 0000 0000	536870912
30	0100 0000 0000 0000 0000 0000 0000 0000	1073741824
31	1000 0000 0000 0000 0000 0000 0000 0000	-2147483648

On a 32-core server, there are 2.631308369336935e+35 possible combinations for processor affinity, but a few examples are included in Table 5-3.

Table 5-3. *Examples of Affinity Masks*

Aligned Processors	Bit Mask	Signed Integer Representation
0 and 1	0000 0000 0000 0000 0000 0000 0000 0011	3
0, 1, 2, and 3	0000 0000 0000 0000 0000 0000 0000 1111	15
8 and 9	0000 0000 0000 0000 0000 0011 0000 0000	768
8, 9, 10, and 11	0000 0000 0000 0000 0000 1111 0000 0000	3840
30 and 31	1100 0000 0000 0000 0000 0000 0000 0000	-1073741824
28, 29, 30, and 31	1111 0000 0000 0000 0000 0000 0000 0000	-268435456

Because of the nature of the affinity mask and the integer data type having a maximum range of 2^{32}, if your server has between 33 and 64 processors, then you will also need to set the Affinity64 Mask and Affinity64 I/O Mask settings. These will provide the masks for the additional processors.

The settings discussed in this section can all be configured using sp_configure. The example in Listing 5-2 demonstrates aligning the instance with cores 0 to 3.

Listing 5-2. Setting Processor Affinity

```
EXEC sp_configure 'affinity mask', 15
RECONFIGURE
```

Even with the 64-bit masks, there is still a limitation of aligning the first 64 cores using this method, and SQL Server will support up to 256 logical processors. For this reason, newer versions of SQL Server have introduced an enhanced method of setting processor affinity. This is through a command called ALTER SERVER CONFIGURATION. Listing 5-3 demonstrated two ways that this command can be used. The first aligns the instance with specific processors in the way that we have seen up until now. In this example, the alignment is with CPUs 0, 1, 2, and 3. The second aligns the instance with all processors within two NUMA nodes, in this case, nodes 0 and 4. Just as when you make changes using sp_configure, changes made using ALTER SERVER CONFIGURATION will be reflected in sys.configurations.

Listing 5-3. ALTER SERVER CONFIGURATION

```
ALTER SERVER CONFIGURATION
    SET PROCESS AFFINITY CPU=0 TO 3

ALTER SERVER CONFIGURATION
    SET PROCESS AFFINITY NUMANODE=0, 4
```

MAXDOP

MAXDOP will set the maximum number of cores that will be made available to each individual execution of a query. The thought of this may initially sound counterintuitive. Surely you would want every query to be parallelized as much as possible? Well, this is not always the case.

Although some data warehousing queries may benefit from high levels of parallelization, many OLTP (online transaction processing) workloads may perform better with a lower degree of parallelization. This is because if a query executes over many parallel threads, and one thread takes much longer than the others to complete, then the other threads may sit waiting for the final thread to finish so that their streams can be synchronized. If this is occurring, you are likely to see a high number of waits with the wait type CXPACKET.

In many OLTP systems, high levels of parallelization being chosen by the Query Optimizer actually indicate issues such as missing or highly fragmented indexes or out-of-date statistics. Resolving these issues will improve performance far more than running queries with a high degree of parallelism.

For instances that support heavy data warehousing workloads, different MAXDOP configurations should be tested and set accordingly, with the understanding that MAXDOP can also be set at the query level, through the use of a Query Hint, if a handful of queries would benefit from a different setting to the majority of the instance's workload. In the vast majority of cases, however, the instance-level setting for MAXDOP should be configured using the following rules, for servers with a single NUMA node:

- Servers with less than eight logical CPUs should have MAXDOP set to be equal to the number of logical CPUs.

- Servers with more than eight logical CPUs should have MAXDOP set at 8.

For servers with multiple NUMA nodes, the MAXDOP for the instance should be configured using the following rules:

- Servers with less than 16 logical CPUs per NUMA node should have MAXDOP set to be equal to the number of logical CPUs per NUMA node.

- Servers with more than 16 logical CPUs per NUMA node should have MAXDOP set to 16.

The default value for MAXDOP is 0, which means that queries are only limited by the number of cores that are visible to the instance. You can configure MAXDOP via the GUI by configuring the Max Degree of Parallelism setting on the Advanced tab of the Server Properties. Figure 5-3 illustrates this setting being configured to 8.

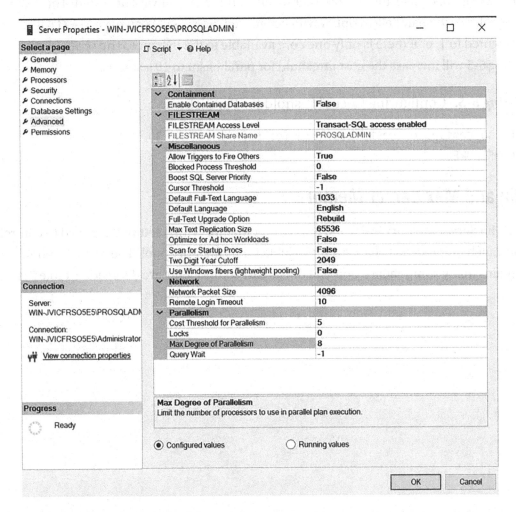

Figure 5-3. *The Advanced tab*

You can also configure MAXDOP using `sp_configure`. Listing 5-4 demonstrates using `sp_configure` to set MAXDOP to a value of 8.

Listing 5-4. Configuring MAXDOP with sp_configure

```
EXEC sys.sp_configure max degree of parallelism', 8
RECONFIGURE
```

An adjunct to lowering the MAXDOP setting is to increase the threshold at which the Query Optimizer will choose a parallel plan over a serial plan. The default setting for this is an estimated serial execution time of 5 seconds, but you can configure this to anything between 0 and 32767 seconds. A practical limit in many environments is around 30 seconds, but of course, this is workload specific and should always be tested. The cost threshold for the parallelism option will be ignored, however, if you have MAXDOP configured to 1, or if there is only one core available to the instance. The script in Listing 5-5 will increase the cost threshold for parallelism to 10 seconds.

Listing 5-5. Configuring Cost Threshold for Parallelism

```
EXEC sp_configure 'cost threshold for parallelism', 30
RECONFIGURE
```

Min and Max Server Memory

The Min Server Memory (MB) and Max Server Memory (MB) settings are used to control how much memory SQL Server has available for its memory pool. The memory pool contains many components. Some of the largest components are detailed in Table 5-4.

Table 5-4. *SQL Server Memory Pool*

Component	Description
Buffer cache	The buffer cache stores data and index pages before and after being read from or written to disk. Even if the pages your query requires are not in the cache, they will still be written to the buffer cache first and then retrieved from memory, as opposed to being written directly to disk.
Procedure cache	The procedure cache contains execution plans, not just for stored procedures, but also for ad hoc queries, prepared statements, and triggers. When SQL Server begins to optimize a query, it first checks this cache to see if a suitable plan already exists.
Log cache	The log cache stores log records before they are written to the transaction log.
Log pool	A hash table that allows HA/DR and data distribution technologies, such as AlwaysOn, Mirroring, and Replication, to quickly access required log records.
CLR	CLR refers to .NET code that is used inside the instance. In older versions of SQL Server, CLR sat outside of the main memory pool, as the memory pool only dealt with single, 8KB page allocations. From SQL Server 2012 onward, the memory pool now deals with both single and multipage allocations, so CLR has been brought in.

In many environments, it is likely that you will want to provide the same value, for both Min and Max Server Memory. This will avoid the overhead of SQL Server dynamically managing the amount of memory it has reserved.

If you have multiple instances, however, then dynamic memory management may be beneficial so that the instance with the heaviest workload at any given time can consume the most resources. You must give extra consideration if your instances are hosted on an active/active cluster. I have seen one example of a client turning on Lock

Pages In Memory and then configuring the min and max memory for the instances on each node as if they were stand-alone boxes. At the point of failover, the remaining node crashed, because there was not enough RAM to support the memory requirements of all instances on one box.

No matter how your environment is configured, you will always want to leave enough memory for the operating system. Assuming that you have one instance and no other applications, such as SSIS packages, running on the server, you would normally set both the min and max memory setting to be the lowest value from the following:

- RAM - 2GB

- (RAM / 8) * 7

If you have multiple instances, you would, of course, divide this number appropriately between the instances, depending on their requirements. If you have other applications running on the server, then you must also take their memory requirements into account and add those to the operating system requirements.

Min Server Memory (MB) and Max Server Memory (MB) can both be configured by using the Memory tab in the Server Properties dialog box, as shown in Figure 5-4.

Note   When adding more memory to a server, you should remember to change the min and max memory setting in the SQL Server instance.

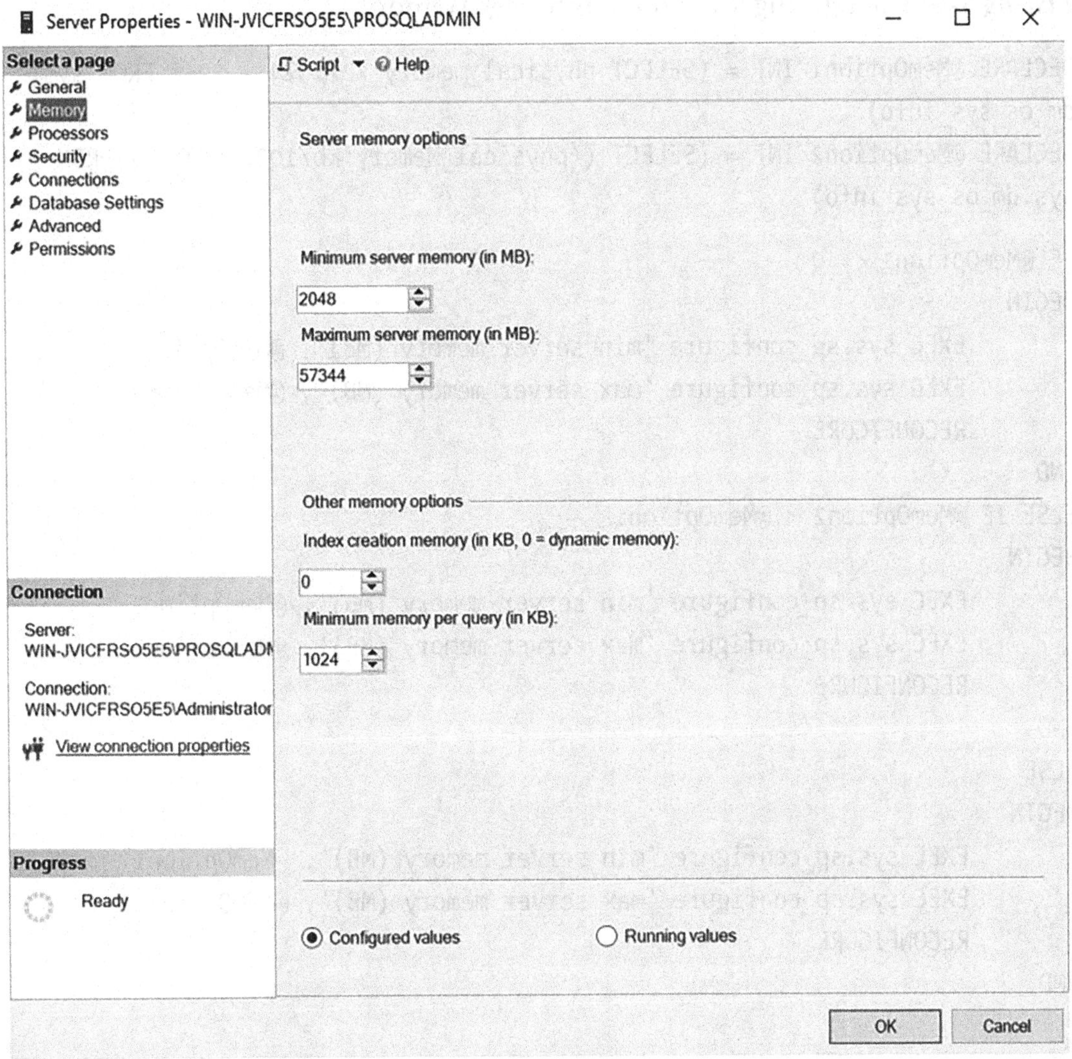

Figure 5-4. *The Memory tab*

You can also configure both the settings through T-SQL by using the sp_configure stored procedure. Listing 5-6 demonstrates this.

Listing 5-6. Configuring Min and Max Server Memory

```
DECLARE @MemOption1 INT = (SELECT physical_memory_kb/1024 - 2048 FROM sys.
dm_os_sys_info)
DECLARE @MemOption2 INT = (SELECT ((physical_Memory_kb/1024)/8) * 7 FROM
sys.dm_os_sys_info)

IF @MemOption1 <= 0
BEGIN
        EXEC sys.sp_configure 'min server memory (MB)', @MemOption2
        EXEC sys.sp_configure 'max server memory (MB)', @MemOption2
        RECONFIGURE
END
ELSE IF @MemOption2 < @MemOption1
BEGIN
        EXEC sys.sp_configure 'min server memory (MB)', @MemOption2
        EXEC sys.sp_configure 'max server memory (MB)', @MemOption2
        RECONFIGURE
END
ELSE
BEGIN
        EXEC sys.sp_configure 'min server memory (MB)', @MemOption1
        EXEC sys.sp_configure 'max server memory (MB)', @MemOption1
        RECONFIGURE
END
```

Trace Flags

Trace flags are switches within SQL Server that can be used to toggle functionality on and off. Within the instance, they can be set at the session level, or they can be applied to the instance globally, using a DBCC command called DBCC TRACEON. Not all trace flags can be set at the session level due to their nature. An example of this is trace flag 634. Setting this flag turns off the background thread responsible for periodically compressing rowgroups within columnstore indexes. Obviously, this would not apply to a specific session. The sample in Listing 5-7 uses DBCC TRACEON to set trace flag 634 globally. It also turns on 1211 for the current session only. Trace flag 1211 disables lock escalation based on memory pressure or number of locks. The script then uses DBCC TRACESTATUS to show the status of the flags before finally using DBCC TRACEOFF to toggle the behavior back to default. You can see that to specify the global scope, we use a second parameter of -1. The default is to set the flag at the session level.

Listing 5-7. Setting Trace Flags with DBCC TRACEON

```
DBCC TRACEON(634, -1)
DBCC TRACEON(1211)

DBCC TRACESTATUS

DBCC TRACEOFF(634, -1)
DBCC TRACEOFF(1211)
```

Caution   Trace flag 1211 is used here for the purpose of demonstrating DBCC TRACEON. However, it may cause an excessive number of locks and should be used with extreme caution. It may even cause SQL Server to throw errors due to lack of memory for allocating locks.

Figure 5-5 shows the results screen that is produced from running this script, assuming that no other trace flags have currently been toggled away from their default setting. There are no results to display from the DBCC TRACEON and DBCC TRACEOFF commands. The messages windows, however, will display execution completed messages or inform you of any errors.

	TraceFlag	Status	Global	Session
1	634	1	1	0
2	1211	1	0	1

⊘ Query executed successfully.

Figure 5-5. *DBCC TRACESTATUS results*

The limitation of using DBCC TRACEON, even with a global scope, is that the settings are transient and will not be persisted after the instance has been restarted. Therefore, if you wish to make permanent configuration changes to your instance, then you must use the -T startup parameter on the SQL Server service.

Startup parameters can be configured in SQL Server Configuration Manager. Expanding Service in the left-hand window will display a list of all SQL Server–related services on the server. Entering the properties for the Database Engine service and selecting the Startup Parameters tab will then allow you to add or remove startup parameters. Figure 5-6 illustrates setting trace flag 809. (Please refer to the "Hybrid Buffer Pool" section of this chapter to understand the effect of this Trace Flag.)

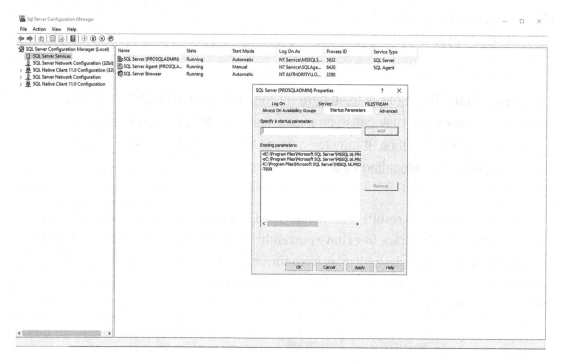

Figure 5-6. *Startup parameters*

If your instance is running on Windows Server Core, or if you want to script the configuration on a GUI-based server, then you could achieve the same results by running the PowerShell script in Listing 5-8. This script allows you to specify the instance name and trace flag to be configured in the top two variables. These could also be parameterized if you wish to create a reusable script. Similarly, the script could be added to the automatic installation script that we created in Chapter 3.

The PowerShell script works by determining the Registry path to the startup parameters and then by counting the number of arguments that already exist. Counting the arguments allows the next argument number in sequence to be determined. It then adds the new argument, specifying the required trace flag.

Listing 5-8. Configuring Trace Flags on Windows Server Core

```
# Define initial variables

$InstanceName = "PROSQLADMINCORE"
$TraceFlag = "809"

# Configure full service name to be inserted into Registry path

$Instance = "MSSQL16.$InstanceName"

#Create full registry path

$RegistryPath = "HKLM:\SOFTWARE\Microsoft\Microsoft SQL Server\
MSSQL16.$InstanceName\MSSQLServer\Parameters"

# Gather all properties from the Registry path

$Properties = Get-ItemProperty $RegistryPath

# Count the number of SQLArg properties that already exist so that the next
number in sequence can be determined

$Arguments = $Properties.psobject.properties | ?{$_.Name -like 'SQLArg*'} |
select Name, Value

# Create the name of the new argument based on the next argument number in
sequence

$NewArgument = "SQLArg"+($Arguments.Count)

# Construct the complete value of the argument

$FullTraceFlag = "-T$TraceFlag"

# Set the trace flag
Set-ItemProperty -Path $RegistryPath -Name $NewArgument -Value
$FullTraceFlag
```

Many trace flags can be specified as startup parameters and the vast majority of them are only helpful in very specific circumstances. There are a few that stand out, however, as having the potential for more widespread use. These trace flags are detailed in the following sections.

Note   Two often configured trace flags, in older versions of SQL Server, were T1117 and T1118, which respectively, caused all files with a filegroup to grow at the same rate and caused all extents (even for small tables) to be uniform. These features are now documented, database-level options, however. Therefore, T1117 and T1118 have no effect, and no longer need to be specified.

Trace Flag 3042

When you are performing backups using backup compression in SQL Server, a preallocation algorithm is used to allocate a defined percentage of the database size to the backup file. This gives you a performance advantage, over growing the size of the backup file, as required, on the fly. On the flip side, however, if you need to preserve disk space on your backup volume and use only the minimum amount of space required, then you can use trace flag 3042 to turn off this behavior and grow the file as required.

Trace Flag 3226

By default, every time you take a backup, a message will be recorded in the SQL Server log. If you take frequent log backups, however, then this can very quickly cause so much "noise" in the log that troubleshooting issues can become more difficult and time-consuming. If this is the case, then you can turn on trace flag 3226. This will cause successful backup messages to be suppressed in the log, resulting in a smaller, more manageable log. Another method of avoiding noise would be to create a script, which uses the sys.xp_readerrorlog system stored procedure to read the log. You can write the results to a table and filter them, for "interesting" events.

Trace Flag 3625

SQL Server enforces tight controls on the visibility of metadata. Users can only view metadata for objects they own, or where they have explicitly been granted permissions to view metadata. This method of protection is still fallible, however, and a skilled attacker could still gain information. One way in which they could achieve this is by manipulating the order of precedence in queries in order to produce error messages.

In order to mitigate this risk, you can set trace flag 3625. This trace flag will limit the amount of metadata visible in error messages by masking certain data with asterisks. The downside of this defensive tactic, however, is that error messages become less meaningful and harder to understand. This can make troubleshooting issues more difficult.

Ports and Firewalls

In modern enterprise topologies, it is likely that your SQL Server instance will need to communicate through at least two firewalls. One of these will be a hardware firewall and the other will be the Windows Firewall, also known as the local firewall. In order for your instance to communicate with other interfaces—whether those are applications or other instances on the network—while still maintaining the security provided by a firewall, ports will need to be opened so that SQL Server can communicate through those ports.

Process of Communication

In order to understand which ports will need to be opened to allow SQL Server traffic, you must first understand how clients communicate with SQL Server. Figure 5-7 illustrates the process flow for TCP/IP connections. This example assumes that the instance is listening on Port 1433 (the default port)—this will be discussed in more detail later in this chapter.

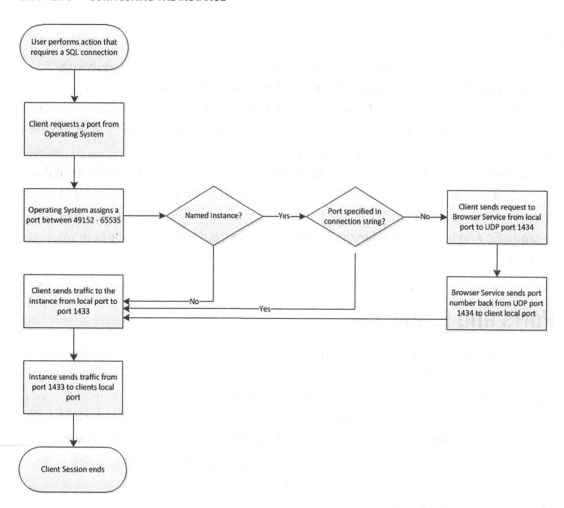

Figure 5-7. Communication process flow

If you wish clients to access the instance via named pipes, as opposed to TCP/IP, then SQL Server will communicate over port 445. This is the same port used by file and printer sharing.

Ports Required by SQL Server

If you install a default instance of SQL Server, then setup will automatically assign port 1433, which is the port registered for SQL Server in IANA (Internet Assigned Numbers Authority). Many DBAs choose to change this port number, however, for enhanced security. An attacker will know that you are likely to have instances running on port 1433 and will therefore know which port to attack. In smaller estates, unless you are confident of the security of your network, using nonstandard port numbers may be a good idea to add an extra layer of obfuscation. In larger enterprises, however, you will need to consider the impact on operational supportability. For example, if each instance has a different port number, you will need a method of recording and very quickly obtaining the port number for a given instance in case of failure of the browser service. This will be less of a concern in environments where multiple named instances are permitted on each server, since you will already have the inventory tooling for recording these port numbers.

Note   IANA, the Internet Assigned Numbers Authority, is responsible for coordinating the allocation of Internet protocol resources, such as IP addresses, domain names, protocol parameters, and port numbers of network services. Its website is www.internetassignednumbersauthority.org/.

If you install a named instance of SQL Server, then setup will configure the instance to use dynamic ports. When dynamic ports are configured, then every time the instance starts, it will request a port number from the operating system. The OS will then assign it a random available port from the dynamic range, which is from 49152 to 65535, assuming that you are running on Windows Server 2008 or above. In earlier versions of Windows, the dynamic port range was from 1024 to 5000, but Microsoft changed this in Windows Vista and Windows Server 2008 to comply with IANA.

If your instance is configured to use dynamic ports, then configuring firewalls can be challenging. At the Windows Firewall level, it is possible to configure a specific service to communicate on any port, but this can be hard to replicate at the hardware firewall level. Alternatively, you need to keep the full dynamic port range open bidirectionally. Therefore, I recommend that the instance is configured to use a specific port.

It is important to remember that SQL Server uses many other ports for various features. The full set of ports that may be required by the Database Engine is listed in Table 5-5. If you install features outside of the Database Engine, such as SSAS or SSRS, then additional ports will be required. There will also be additional requirements if you plan to use additional services with your instance, such as IPSec for encryption, MSDTC (Microsoft Distributed Transaction Coordinator) distributed transactions, or SCOM (System Center Operations Manager) for monitoring.

Table 5-5. *Ports Required by the Database Engine*

Feature	Port
Browser Service	UDP 1433.
Instance over TCP/IP	TCP 1433, dynamic or static configured.
Instance over named pipes	TCP 445.
DAC (dedicated administrator connection)	TCP 1434. If TCP 1434 is already in use, the port will be printed to the SQL Server log during instance startup.
Service Broker	TCP 4022 or as per configuration.
AlwaysOn Availability Groups	TCP 5022 or as per configuration.
Merge replication with Web sync	TCP 21, TCP 80, UDP 137, UDP 138, TCP 139, TCP 445.
T-SQL Debugger	TCP 135.

Configuring the Port That the Instance Will Listen On

As mentioned earlier in this chapter, if you have a named instance, then before configuring your firewall, it is likely that you will want to configure a static port for the instance. The port can be configured within the TCP/IP Properties dialog box of the TCP/IP protocol in SQL Server Configuration Manager. To navigate to this dialog box, drill down through SQL Server Network Configuration ➤ Protocols for *INSTANCENAME* (where *INSTANCENAME* is the name of your instance) in the left-hand pane of SQL Server Configuration Manager. Entering TCP/IP in the right-hand pane will display the dialog box.

On the Protocol tab, you will notice a setting named *Listen All*, which has a default value of Yes, as shown in Figure 5-8. The significance of this setting will become apparent shortly.

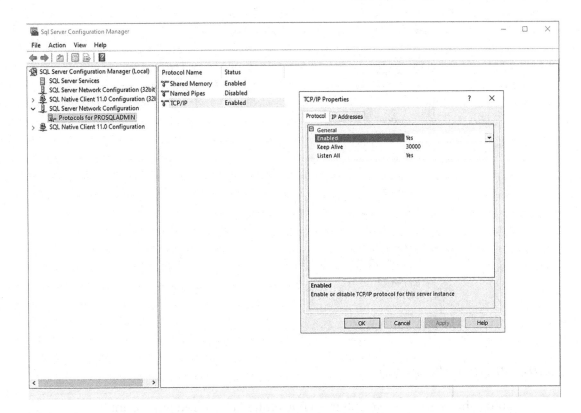

Figure 5-8. *The Protocol tab*

In the IP Addresses tab, you will notice that there are configuration details for multiple IP addresses. Because the Listen All setting is set to Yes, however, SQL Server will ignore all of these configurations. Instead, it will look solely at the settings specified for IP All at the very bottom of the dialog box. The TCP dynamic ports field will display the random port that has been assigned by the operating system and the TCP Port field will be blank, as illustrated in Figure 5-9. To assign a static port number, we need to flip this around. We will need to clear the TCP Dynamic Port field and populate the TCP Port field with 1433, which is our chosen port number. The SQL Server service will need to be restarted before this change can take effect.

Tip   Remember that the Default instance will take port 1433 by default. Therefore, if a Default instance already exists on the server, when you create the named instance, you must use a different port.

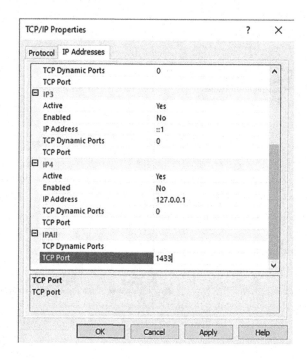

Figure 5-9. *IP Addresses tab*

We could achieve the same result from PowerShell by running the script in Listing 5-9. This script has two variables at the top where you should insert the name of your instance and the port number you want to assign. These could also be parameterized to create a reusable script. The script loads the relevant SMO Assembly. It then creates a new SMO object and connects to the TCP properties of the object to configure the port. The script must be run As Administrator.

Listing 5-9. Assigning a Static Port

```
# Initialize variables

$Instance = "PROSQLADMIN"
$Port = "1433"

# Load SMO Wmi.ManagedComputer assembly
[System.Reflection.Assembly]::LoadWithPartialName("Microsoft.SqlServer.
SqlWmiManagement") | out-null

# Create a new smo object
$m = New-Object ('Microsoft.SqlServer.Management.Smo.Wmi.ManagedComputer')
```

```
#Disable dynamic ports

$m.ServerInstances[$Instance].ServerProtocols['Tcp'].IPAddresses['IPAll'].
IPAddressProperties['TcpDynamicPorts'].Value = ""

# Set static port

$m.ServerInstances[$Instance].ServerProtocols['Tcp'].IPAddresses['IPAll'].
IPAddressProperties['TcpPort'].Value = "$Port"

# Reconfigure TCP

$m.ServerInstances[$Instance].ServerProtocols['Tcp'].Alter()
```

System Databases

SQL Server maintains five system databases, each of which is important to the efficient
running of your instance. The following sections describe each of these databases and
details any special considerations for configuring them.

mssqlsystemresource (Resource)

Although referred to as Resource, the full name of the Resource database is
mssqlsystemresource. It is the physical repository used to store the system objects that
appear within the sys schema of every database. It is read-only and should never be
modified, except under guidance from Microsoft. It is not visible within Management
Studio, and if you try to connect to it from a query window, it will fail, unless you are in
single-user mode. There are no considerations for configuring Resource.

MSDB

MSDB is used as a metadata repository for many SQL Server features, including Server
Agent, Backup/Restore, Database Mail, Log Shipping, Policies, and more. Although this
is obviously a critical and useful database, there are no specific configuration options to
consider. That being said, in a very large instance consisting of a very large number of
databases, all with frequent log backups, the database can grow very large. This means
that you will need to purge old data and sometimes consider indexing strategies. Historic

backup data can be purged using the sp_deletebackuphistory stored procedure or the History Cleanup Task in a Maintenance Plan. Automating routine maintenance tasks will be discussed in more detail in Chapter 24.

Master

Master is the system database that contains metadata for instance-level objects, such as Logins, Linked Servers, TCP endpoints, and master keys and certificates for implementing encryption. The biggest consideration for the Master database is the backup policy. Although it does not need to be backed up as frequently as user databases do, you should always ensure that you do have a current backup. At a minimum, the database should be backed up after creating or altering logins, linked servers, and system configurations; creating or altering keys and certificates; or after creating or dropping user databases. Many people select a weekly, full backup schedule for Master, but this will depend on your operational requirements, such as how often you create new users.

Note   Logins and users will be discussed in Chapter 10, backups will be discussed in Chapter 13, and keys and certificates will be discussed in Chapter 12.

Although technically possible, it is considered bad practice to store user objects in the Master database. I have seen clients implement this for stored procedures that need to be shared by all databases on the instance, but it adds complexity because they are fragmenting the storage of user objects and also increasing the frequency with which they must back up Master.

Tip   Because developers often do not set a default database, they end up creating stored procedures in the master database by mistake. You should check for this issue as part of your code deployment process.

Model

Model is used as a template for all new databases that are created on the instance. This means that spending some time configuring this database can save you time and reduce human error when you are creating user databases. For example, if you set the Recovery Model to be *Full* on the Model database, then all new user databases will automatically be configured in the same way. You still have the option to override this in your CREATE DATABASE statement. Additionally, if you need a specific object to exist in all databases, such as a maintenance-stored procedure or a database role, then creating this in Model will mean that the object will automatically be created inside every new database. Model is also used for creating TempDB every time the instance starts. This means that if you create objects in the Model database, they will automatically be added to TempDB when the instance restarts.

Tip   When you are configuring or adding new objects to Model, existing databases will not be updated. Changes will only apply to new databases that you create subsequently.

TempDB

TempDB is a workspace used by SQL Server when it needs to create temporary objects. This applies to temporary tables created by users, and less commonly known, it also applies to table variables. Table variables always cause an object to be created in TempDB, but data is only spooled to disk if it breaches size thresholds. There are also many internal reasons why SQL Server will require temporary objects to be created. Some of the key reasons are as follows:

- Sorting and spooling data
- Hashing data, such as for joins and aggregate grouping
- Online index operations
- Index operations where results are sorted in TempDB
- Triggers
- DBCC commands

- The OUTPUT clause of a DML (data manipulation language) statement

- Row versioning for snapshot isolation, read-committed snapshot isolation, queries over MARS, and so on

Because TempDB is responsible for so many tasks, in high-volume instances, it is likely to have a very high throughput. For this reason, it is the system database that you should spend the most time configuring in order to ensure the best performance for your data-tier applications.

The first thing you should consider is the size of TempDB. Ideally, TempDB will be subject to capacity planning for large or highly transactional instances. A full discussion of capacity planning is beyond the scope of this book, but ideally, this will involve using a test server to expand all of the user databases on the instance out, to the size that they are expected to grow to, discovered through their own capacity planning exercises. You would then run representative workloads through those databases and monitor the usage of TempDB. Additionally, you should also perform administrative tasks against the databases that you have expanded to their expected size. Specifically, this would include activities such as rebuilding indexes so that you can examine the usage profile of TempDB during these activities. There are a number of DMVs (dynamic management views) that can help you with this planning. Some of the most useful are described in Table 5-6.

Table 5-6. *DMVs for TempDB Capacity Planning*

DMV	Description
sys.dm_db_session_space_usage	Displays the number of pages allocated for each current session. This will include page counts for the following objects: • User and system tables • User and system indexes • Temporary tables • Temporary indexes • Table variables • Tables returned by functions • Internal objects for sorting and hashing operations • Internal objects for spools and large object operations

(continued)

Table 5-6. (*continued*)

DMV	Description
`sys.dm_db_task_space_usage`	Displays the number of pages allocated by tasks. This will include page counts from the same object types as `sys.dm_db_session_space_usage`.
`sys_dm_db_file_space_usage`	Displays full usage information for all files in the database, including page counts and extent counts. To return data for TempDB, you must query this DMV from the context of the TempDB database, since it can also return data from user databases.
`sys.dm_tran_version_store`	Returns a row for every record within the version store. You can view this data raw or aggregate it to get size totals.
`sys.dm_tran_active_snapshot_database_transactions`	Returns a row for every current transaction that may need to access the version store, due to isolation level, triggers, MARS (Multiple Active Results Sets), or online index operations.

Optimizing TempDB

In addition to the size of TempDB, you should also carefully consider the number of files that you will require. This is important because due to the nature of many objects being very rapidly created and dropped, if you have too few files, then you can suffer contention of the GAM and SGAM pages. If you have too many files, on the other hand, you may experience increased overhead. This is because SQL Server allocates pages to each file within the filegroup in turn in order to maintain proportional fill. With a large number of files, there will be an extra synchronization effort to determine if the allocation weighting for each file should be altered. TempDB files should be the same size.

> **Tip**   Some SQL Server experts suggest that temp tables should not be explicitly dropped and should be cleaned up by the garbage collector thread. Personally, while I see the benefits of this, I feel it needs to be traded off against other considerations, such as code quality, especially in large, complex stored procedures.

The current, general recommendation is that you should have one TempDB file for every core available to the instance, with a minimum of two files and a maximum of eight files. You should only add more than eight files if you specifically witness GAM/SGAM contention. This will manifest itself as PAGELATCH waits occurring against TempDB. You will find a discussion of how to add files and alter their size in Chapter 6.

Tip   PAGEIOLATCH waits indicate a different issue than PAGELATCH waits. If you see PAGEIOLATCH waits against TempDB, this indicates that the underlying storage is the bottleneck. Wait types will be discussed in more detail in Chapter 19.

SQL Server supports an optimization for TempDB, called Memory-Optimized TempDB Metadata. As its name suggests, this feature stores the system tables that are responsible for managing TempDB metadata, in nondurable memory-optimized tables.

Tip   Please see Chapter 7 for further details of memory-optimized tables.

This is an important new feature, which increases the scalability of SQL Server, by removing the contention bottleneck, on TempDB system pages. It does not come without a cost, however, and before implementing the feature, you must be aware that a single transaction cannot access memory-optimized tables across multiple databases. This may cause issues if you have scripts which perform activities such as custom monitoring.

For example, you may have a script which records the script in Listing 5-10. The first section of the script creates the Chapter5 database. The CaptureTempTableCount procedure inserts a count of temp tables into a memory-optimized table. Imagine that this procedure is configured to run once a minute with SQL Server Agent (see Chapter 24). You then use the TempTableCount table in your ongoing capacity planning endeavors.

Listing 5-10. Using Memory-Optimized Tables with TempDB

```
--Create the Chapter5 Database

CREATE DATABASE Chapter5
GO

USE Chapter5
GO
```

```
--Add a memory-optimized filegroup
ALTER DATABASE Chapter5 ADD FILEGROUP memopt
    CONTAINS MEMORY_OPTIMIZED_DATA;

ALTER DATABASE Chapter5 ADD FILE (
    name='memopt1', filename='c:\data\memopt1'
) TO FILEGROUP memopt ;

ALTER DATABASE Chapter5
    SET MEMORY_OPTIMIZED_ELEVATE_TO_SNAPSHOT = ON ;
GO

CREATE TABLE TempTableCount (
      ID              INT       IDENTITY(1,1) NOT NULL      PRIMARY KEY
NONCLUSTERED,
      TableCount    INT                       NOT NULL,
      DateTime      DateTime2                 NOT NULL
) WITH(MEMORY_OPTIMIZED=ON) ;
GO

CREATE PROCEDURE CaptureTempTableCount
AS
BEGIN
      BEGIN TRANSACTION
            INSERT INTO TempTableCount (TableCount, DateTime)
            SELECT COUNT(*) As TableCount, SYSDATETIME() AS DateTime
            FROM tempdb.sys.tables t
            WHERE type = 'U'
      COMMIT
END
GO
```

If you test this procedure, you will see that it works as expected. But now, let's turn on Memory-Optimized TempDB Metadata using the command in Listing 5-11.

Listing 5-11. Enable Memory-Optimized TempDB Metadata

```
ALTER SERVER CONFIGURATION SET MEMORY_OPTIMIZED TEMPDB_METADATA = ON ;
```

If you test the procedure again, you will notice that it now fails because it is attempting to access memory-optimized tables in multiple databases. To work around this issue, you would need to use a disk-based table rather than a memory-optimized table.

Buffer Pool Extension

As already mentioned, the buffer pool is an area of memory that SQL Server uses to cache pages before they are written to disk and after they have been read from disk. There are two distinct types of pages that exist in the buffer cache: clean pages and dirty pages. A *clean page* is a page to which no modifications have been made. Clean pages usually exist in the cache because they have been accessed by read operations, such as SELECT statements. Once in the cache, they can support all statements. For example, a DML statement can access the clean page, modify it, and then update its dirty page marker.

Dirty pages are pages that have been modified by statements such as INSERT, UPDATE, and DELETE, among others. These pages need to have their associated log record written to disk, and subsequently, the dirty pages themselves will be flushed to disk before they are regarded as clean. The process of writing the log record first is known as WAL (write-ahead logging), and it is how SQL Server ensures that no committed data can ever be lost, even in the event of a system failure.

Dirty pages are always kept in the cache until they are flushed to disk. Clean pages, on the other hand, are kept in cache for as long as possible, but are removed when space is required for new pages to be cached. SQL Server evicts pages based on a least-recently-used policy. This means that read-intensive workloads can rapidly start to suffer from memory pressure if the buffer cache is not correctly sized.

The issue here is that RAM is expensive compared to storage, and it may not be possible to keep throwing more and more memory at the problem. In order to address this, Microsoft introduced a technology in SQL Server 2014 called buffer pool extensions.

A buffer pool extension is designed to be used with very fast SSDs, which will normally be locally attached to the server, as opposed to being located on a SAN. In short, the storage needs to operate as fast as possible. The extension will then become a secondary cache for clean pages only. When clean pages are evicted from the cache, they will be moved to the buffer pool extension, where they can be retrieved faster than by going back to the main I/O subsystem.

This is a very useful feature, but it is not a magic bullet. First, it is important to remember that the buffer pool extension will never be able to provide the same performance improvement as a correctly sized buffer cache will without an extension. Second, the performance gain that you will experience from using a buffer pool extension is workload specific. For example, a read-intensive OLTP workload will probably benefit substantially from buffer pool extensions, whereas a write-intensive workload will see little benefit at all. This is because dirty pages cannot be flushed to the extension. Large data warehouses are also unlikely to benefit dramatically from buffer pool extensions. This is because the tables are likely to be so large that a full table scan, which is common with this workload scenario, is likely to consume the majority of both the cache and the extension. This means that it will wipe out other data from the extension and will be unlikely to benefit subsequent queries.

It is sensible to use a resilient SSD volume such as a RAID 10 stripe. This is because if the volume were to fail, with no resilience, your server would immediately see a drop in performance. In the event that the SSD drive that your extension is stored on fails, SQL Server will automatically disable the extension. It can be reenabled manually, or it will automatically attempt to reenable itself when the instance is restarted.

I also recommend that you size the extension between four and eight times the size of your Max Server Memory setting in order to obtain optimum performance. The maximum possible size of the extension is thirty-two times the size of the Max Server Memory setting.

Buffer pool extension can be enabled using the statement shown in Listing 5-12. This script assumes that the SSD drive that you wish to use is mapped as the S:\ volume. It also assumes that we have 32GB set as the Max Server Memory setting, so we will configure the extension to be 128GB, which is four times the size.

Listing 5-12. Enable Buffer Pool Extension

```
ALTER SERVER CONFIGURATION
SET BUFFER POOL EXTENSION ON
(FILENAME = 'S:\SSDCache.BPE', SIZE = 128 GB )
```

If required, the buffer pool extension can be disabled by using the command in Listing 5-13. Be warned, however, that removing a buffer pool extension is likely to result in a sudden drop in performance.

Listing 5-13. Disable Buffer Pool Extension

```
ALTER SERVER CONFIGURATION
SET BUFFER POOL EXTENSION OFF
```

Hybrid Buffer Pool

SQL Server supports the Hybrid Buffer Pool, offering support for PMEM (persistent memory). PMEM is also known as SCM (storage class memory). A PMEM device resides on the memory bus and is solid-state and byte-addressable. This makes it faster than flash disks and cheaper than DRAM. The data stored on a PMEM device persists, after the server has been powered off.

When formatting a PMEM device in Windows (PMEM devices are supported by Windows Server 2016 and higher) for use with a Hybrid Buffer Pool, you should enable DirectAccess and use an allocation unit size of 2MB on Windows Server 2019, or the largest available size, on other versions of Windows Server.

Once the drive has been created, SQL Server transaction logs can be stored on the device. SQL Server will then use memory-mapped I/O (also known as enlightenment) when reading clean pages from the Buffer Pool. This mitigates the need to copy the page into DRAM, before accessing it, therefore reducing I/O latency.

Enlightenment can only be used for clean pages. If a page becomes dirty, then it will be written to DRAM, before finally being flushed back to the PMEM device.

To enable PMEM support in SQL Server, running on a Windows operating system, simply enable Trace Flag 809 on the SQL Server service. For SQL Server running on Linux, Trace Flag 3979 must be enabled on the SQL Server service. (Please see the "Trace Flags" section of this chapter for information on how to enable a trace flag.)

Summary

You should consider how you should configure your processor and memory for the instance. With regard to the processor, these considerations should include affinity mask settings for multiple instances, or avoiding context switching during I/O operations. You should also consider the appropriate settings for MAXDOP in your environment.

With regard to memory, you should consider the most appropriate usage of Min and Max Server Memory and if it is appropriate to configure these to the same value. You should also consider if buffer pool extensions would help your system performance, and if so, you should use Max Server Memory as the base for calculating the correct size of this warm cache.

Trace flags toggle settings on and off, and adding them as startup parameters will ensure that your instance is always configured as you require it to be. Many trace flags are for very specific purposes, but some have more generic usage, such as 3226, which will suppress successful backup messages, to avoid noise in the logs masking issues.

For your SQL Server instance to be able to communicate with applications and other instances on the network, you should configure the instance port and local firewall appropriately. It is generally considered bad practice to use a dynamic port for SQL Server connections, so you should configure the instance to use a specific TCP port.

All five of the system databases are critical to the proper functioning of the instance. In terms of configuration, however, you should give most consideration to TempDB. TempDB is heavily used by many SQL Server features, and therefore it can quickly become a bottleneck in busy systems. You should ensure that you have the correct number of files and that they are sized correctly.

Uninstalling an instance or removing features from an instance can be done either from Control Panel or from the command line. You should be mindful of the fact that even after an instance is uninstalled, there will still be a residue left in the file system and also in the Registry.

PART II

Database Administration

CHAPTER 6

Database Configuration

Within a database, data is stored in one or more data files. These files are grouped into logical containers called filegroups. Every database also has at least one log file. Log files sit outside of filegroup containers and do not follow the same rules as data files. This chapter begins by discussing filegroup strategies that database administrators (DBAs) can adopt before it looks at how DBAs can maintain data and log files.

Data Storage

Before considering which filegroup strategies to adopt, it is important that you understand how SQL Server stores data. The diagram in Figure 6-1 illustrates the storage hierarchy within a database.

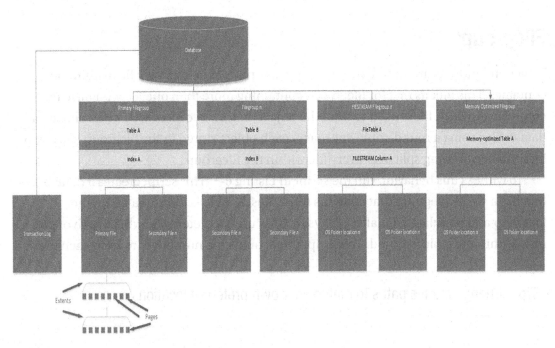

Figure 6-1. *How SQL Server stores data*

175

© Peter A. Carter 2023
P. A. Carter, *Pro SQL Server 2022 Administration*, https://doi.org/10.1007/978-1-4842-8864-1_6

A database always consists of at least one filegroup, which contains a minimum of one file. The first file in the database is known as the *primary file*. This file is given an .mdf file extension by default. You can, however, change this extension if you wish. This file can be used to store data, but it is also used to store metadata that provides database startup information and pointers to other files within the database. The filegroup that contains the primary file is called the *primary filegroup.*

If additional files are created within the database, they are known as *secondary files* and are given the .ndf extension by default. You can, however, change this extension if you wish. These files can be created in the primary filegroup and/or in secondary filegroups. Secondary files and filegroups are optional, but they can prove very useful to database administrators, as we will discuss later in this chapter.

Tip   It is a good idea to keep default file extensions. There are no real benefits in using different extensions and doing so adds extra complexity. For example, not only do you need to remember what extensions you used, but also, if your antivirus software uses file extensions for its exclusions list, you could suddenly see a nasty drop in performance.

Filegroups

Tables and indexes are stored on a filegroup, as opposed to a specific file within the container. This means that for filegroups containing more than one file, you have no control over which file is used to store the object. In fact, because SQL Server allocates data to files using a round-robin approach, each object stored in the filegroup has a very high chance of being split over every file within the filegroup.

To witness this behavior, run the script in Listing 6-1. This script creates a database that has a single filegroup that contains three files. A table is then created on the filegroup and populated. Finally, %%physloc%% is used to determine where each of the rows within the table is stored. The script then counts the number of rows in each file.

Tip   Change the file paths to match your own preferred locations.

Listing 6-1. SQL Server Round-Robin Allocation

```
USE Master
GO

--Create a database with three files in the primary filegroup.

CREATE DATABASE [Chapter6]
 CONTAINMENT = NONE
 ON  PRIMARY
( NAME = N'Chapter6', FILENAME = N'F:\MSSQL\MSSQL16.PROSQLADMIN\MSSQL\DATA\
Chapter6.mdf'),
( NAME = N'Chapter6_File2',
        FILENAME = N'F:\MSSQL\MSSQL16.PROSQLADMIN\MSSQL\DATA\Chapter6_
        File2.ndf'),
( NAME = N'Chapter6_File3',
        FILENAME = N'F:\MSSQL\MSSQL16.PROSQLADMIN\MSSQL\DATA\Chapter6_
        File3.ndf')
 LOG ON
( NAME = N'Chapter6_log',
        FILENAME = N'E:\MSSQL\MSSQL16.PROSQLADMIN\MSSQL\DATA\Chapter6_
        log.ldf');
GO
IF NOT EXISTS (SELECT name FROM sys.filegroups WHERE is_default=1 AND name
= N'PRIMARY')
        ALTER DATABASE [Chapter6] MODIFY FILEGROUP [PRIMARY] DEFAULT;
GO

USE Chapter6
GO

--Create a table in the new database. The table contains a wide, fixed-
length column
--to increase the number of allocations.
```

```sql
CREATE TABLE dbo.RoundRobinTable
(
        ID              INT         IDENTITY        PRIMARY KEY,
        DummyTxt        NCHAR(1000),
);
GO

--Create a Numbers table that will be used to assist the population of
the table.

DECLARE @Numbers TABLE
(
        Number      INT
)

--Populate the Numbers table.

;WITH CTE(Number)
AS
(
        SELECT 1 Number

        UNION ALL
        SELECT Number +1
        FROM CTE
        WHERE Number <= 99
)
INSERT INTO @Numbers
SELECT *
FROM CTE;

--Populate the example table with 100 rows of dummy text.

INSERT INTO dbo.RoundRobinTable
SELECT 'DummyText'
FROM @Numbers a
CROSS JOIN @Numbers b;
```

```
--Select all the data from the table, plus the details of the row's
physical location.
--Then group the row count.
--by file ID

SELECT b.file_id, COUNT(*) AS [RowCount]
FROM
(
        SELECT ID, DummyTxt, a.file_id
        FROM dbo.RoundRobinTable
        CROSS APPLY sys.fn_PhysLocCracker(%%physloc%%) a
) b
GROUP BY b.file_id;
```

The results displayed in Figure 6-2 show that the rows have been distributed evenly over the three files within the filegroup. If the files are different sizes, then the file with the most space receives more of the rows due to the proportional fill algorithm, which attempts to weigh the allocations to each file in order to evenly distribute data across each of the files.

Tip You may notice that there are no rows returned for File 2. This is because file_id 2 is always the transaction log file (or first transaction log file if you have more than one). file_id 1 is always the primary database file.

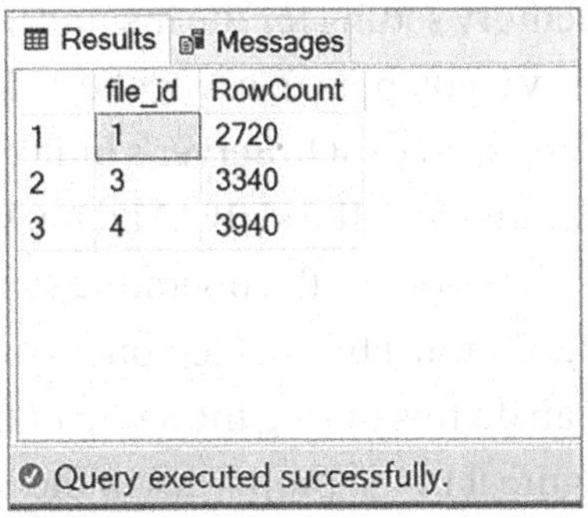

	file_id	RowCount
1	1	2720
2	3	3340
3	4	3940

Figure 6-2. *Evenly distributed rows*

Caution   The physloc functions are undocumented. Therefore, Microsoft will not provide support for their use.

Standard data and indexes are stored in a series of 8KB pages; these are made up of a 96-byte header that contains metadata about the page and 8096 bytes for storing the data itself. These 8KB pages are then organized into units of eight continuous pages, which together are called an extent. An *extent* is the smallest unit the SQL Server can read from disk.

FILESTREAM Filegroups

FILESTREAM is a technology that allows you to store binary data in an unstructured manner. Binary data is often stored in the operating system, as opposed to the database, and FILESTREAM gives you the ability to continue this while at the same time offering transactional consistency between this unstructured data and the structured metadata stored in the database. Using this technology will allow you to overcome SQL Server's 2GB maximum size limitation for a single object. You will also see a performance improvement for large binary objects over storing them in the database. If files are over 1MB in size, the read performance is likely to be faster with FILESTREAM.

You do need to bear in mind, however, that objects stored with FILESTREAM use Windows cache instead of the SQL Server buffer cache. This has the advantage that you do not have large files filling up your buffer cache causing other data to be flushed to either the buffer cache extension or to disk. On the flip side, it means that when you are configuring the Max Server Memory setting for the instance, you should remember that Windows requires extra memory if you plan to cache the objects because the binary cache in Windows is used, as opposed to SQL Server's buffer cache.

Separate filegroups are required for FILESTREAM data. Instead of containing files, these filegroups point to folder locations in the operating system. Each of these locations is called a *container*. FILESTREAM must be enabled on the instance in order to create a FILESTREAM filegroup. You can do this during the setup of the instance, as discussed in Chapter 2, or you can configure it in the properties of the instance in SQL Server Management Studio.

We can add a FILESTREAM filegroup to our Chapter6 database by using the Add Filegroup button on the Filegroups tab of the Database Properties dialog box and then adding a name for the filegroup in the Name field, as shown in Figure 6-3.

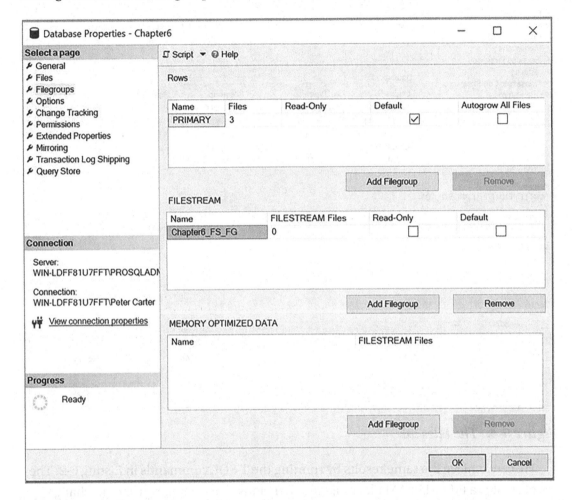

Figure 6-3. *The Filegroups tab*

We can then use the Files tab of the Database Properties dialog box to add the container. Here, we need to enter a name for the container and specify the file type as FILESTEAM data. We are then able to select our FILESTREAM filegroup from the Filegroup drop-down box, as illustrated in Figure 6-4.

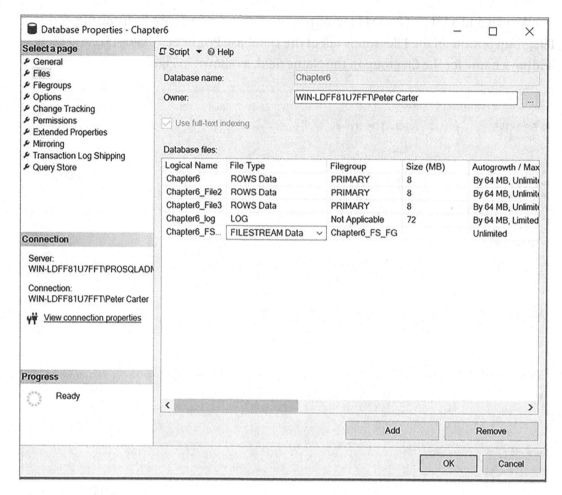

Figure 6-4. *The Files tab*

We can achieve the same results by running the T-SQL commands in Listing 6-2. The script creates a FILESTREAM filegroup and then adds a container. You should change the directories in the script to match your own configuration.

Listing 6-2. Adding a FILESTREAM Filegroup

```
ALTER DATABASE [Chapter6] ADD FILEGROUP [Chapter6_FS_FG] CONTAINS FILESTREAM;
GO

ALTER DATABASE [Chapter6] ADD FILE ( NAME = N'Chapter6_FA_File1', FILENAME
= N'F:\MSSQL\MSSQL16.PROSQLADMIN\MSSQL\DATA\Chapter6_FA_File1' ) TO
FILEGROUP [Chapter6_FS_FG];
GO
```

In order to explore the folder structure of a FILESTREAM container, we first need to create a table and populate it with data. The script in Listing 6-3 creates a table, which consists of a unique identifier—which is required for all tables that contain FILESTREAM data—a text description of the binary object, and a VARBINARY(MAX) column that we will use to store the illustration from Figure 6-1, earlier in this chapter. The file that we have used is unimportant, so to run the script yourself, change the name and location of the file being imported to a file on your system.

Listing 6-3. Creating a Table with FILESTREAM Data

```
USE Chapter6
GO

CREATE TABLE dbo.FilestreamExample
(
        ID                      UNIQUEIDENTIFIER ROWGUIDCOL NOT
                                NULL UNIQUE,
        PictureDescription      NVARCHAR(500),
        Picture                   VARBINARY(MAX) FILESTREAM
);
GO

INSERT INTO FilestreamExample
    SELECT NEWID(), 'Figure 6-1. Diagram showing the SQL Server storage
    hierarchy.', * FROM
    OPENROWSET(BULK N'c:\Figure_6-1.jpg', SINGLE_BLOB) AS import;
```

Note   We have used a UNIQUE constraint, as opposed to a primary key, since a GUID is not usually a good choice as a primary key. If the table must have a primary key, it may be more sensible to add an additional integer column with the IDENTITY property specified. We have used a GUID and set the ROWGUIDCOL property, since this is required by SQL Server to map to the FILESTREAM objects.

If we now open the location of the container in the file system, we can see that we have a folder, which has a GUID as its name. This represents the table that we created. Inside this folder is another folder that also has a GUID as its name. This folder represents the FILESTREAM column that we created. Inside this folder, we will find a file, which is the picture that we inserted into the column. This file's name is the log sequence number from when the file was created. It is theoretically possible to change the extension of this file to its original extension and then open it. This is certainly not recommended, however, because it may have undesirable effects within SQL Server. At the root level of the container, you will also find a file called filestream.hdr, which contains the metadata for the container and a folder called $FSLog. This folder contains a series of files that make up the FILESTREAM equivalent of the transaction log. This folder hierarchy is illustrated in Figure 6-5.

Tip   The SQL Server service account is automatically granted file system permissions on the FILESTREAM container. It is considered bad practice to grant any other users permissions to this folder structure. If you try to access the folder with a Windows Administrator account, you are given a permissions warning, stating that if you continue, you will be permanently granting yourself permissions to the folder.

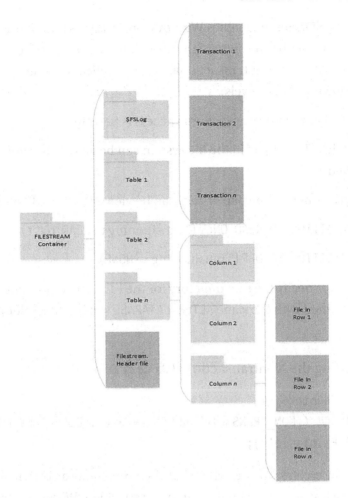

Figure 6-5.   *FILESTREAM folder hierarchy*

FileTable is a technology that builds on top of FILESTREAM and allows data to be stored in the file system. Therefore, to use it, you must enable FILESTREAM with streaming access. Unlike FILESTREAM, however, FileTable allows nontransactional access to the data. This means that you can move data so it is stored in the SQL Engine rather than in the operating system without needing to modify existing applications. You can also open and modify the files through Windows Explorer like any other files in the operating system.

To achieve this, SQL Server enables Windows applications to request a file handle without having a transaction. Because of this functionality, you need to specify, at the database level, what level of nontransactional access applications may request. You can configure the following access levels:

- NONE (Default—Only transactional access is permitted.)

- READ_ONLY (The object in the file system can be viewed but not modified.)

- FULL (The object in the file system can be viewed and modified.)

- IN_TRANSITION_TO_READ_ONLY (Transitioning to READ_ONLY)

- IN_TRANSITION_TO_OFF (Transitioning to NONE)

You also need to specify the root directory for the FileTable container. Both of these tasks can be performed with the same ALTER DATABASE statement, as demonstrated in Listing 6-4.

Listing 6-4. Setting the Nontransactional Access Level

```
ALTER DATABASE Chapter6
    SET FILESTREAM ( NON_TRANSACTED_ACCESS = FULL, DIRECTORY_NAME =
    N'Chapter6_FileTable' );
```

SQL Server now creates a share, which has the same name as your instance. Inside this share, you will find a folder with the name you specified. When you create a FileTable, you can again specify a directory name. This creates a subfolder with the name you specify. Because FileTables do not have a relational schema, and the metadata that is stored about the files is fixed, the syntax for created them includes only the name of the table, the directory, and the collation to use. The code in Listing 6-5 demonstrates how to create a FileTable called Chapter6_FileTable.

Listing 6-5. Creating a FileTable

```
USE Chapter6
GO

CREATE TABLE dbo.ch06_test AS FILETABLE
  WITH
```

```
(
  FILETABLE_DIRECTORY = 'Chapter6_FileTable',
  FILETABLE_COLLATE_FILENAME = database_default
);
GO
```

To load files into the table, you can simply copy or move them into the folder location, or developers can use the System.IO namespace within their applications. SQL Server will update the metadata columns of the FileTable accordingly. In our example, the file path to the container where the FileTable files can be found is \\127.0.0.1\ prosqladmin\Chapter6_FileTable\Chapter6_FileTable. Here, 127.0.0.1 is the loopback address of our server (the same effect as using localhost), prosqladmin is the share that was created based on our instance name, and Chapter6_FileTable\ Chapter6_Filetable FILESTREAM\FileTable is the container.

Memory-Optimized Filegroups

SQL Server supports a feature called *memory-optimized tables*. These tables are stored entirely in memory; however, the data is also written to files on disk. This is for durability. Transactions against in-memory tables have the same ACID (atomic, consistent, isolated, and durable) properties as traditional disk-based tables. We will discuss in-memory tables further in Chapter 7 and in-memory transactions in Chapter 18.

Because in-memory tables require a copy of the data to be stored on disk, in order to be durable, we have the memory-optimized filegroup. This type of filegroup is similar to a FILESTREAM filegroup but with some subtle differences. First, you can only create one memory-optimized filegroup per database. Second, you do not need to explicitly enable FILESTREAM unless you are planning to use both features.

In-memory data is persisted on disk through the use of two file types. One is a Data file and the other a Delta file. These two file types always operate in pairs and cover a specific range of transactions, so you should always have the same amount. The Data file is used to track inserts that are made to in-memory tables and the Delta file is used to track deletions. Update statements are tracked via a combination of the two files, because the update is tracked as a delete and an insert. The files are written sequentially and are table agnostic, meaning that each file may contain data for multiple tables.

We can add an in-memory optimized filegroup to our database in the Filegroups tab of the Database Properties dialog box by using the Add Filegroup button in the Memory Optimized Data area of the screen and by specifying a name for the filegroup. This is illustrated in Figure 6-6.

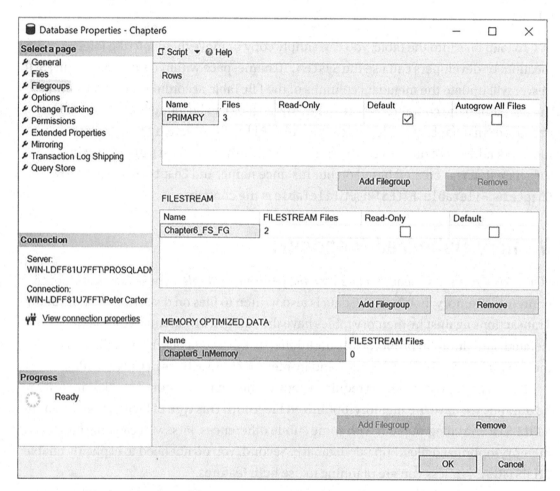

Figure 6-6. *Adding the in-memory filegroup*

We can then add the container to the filegroup by using the Add File button in the Files tab of the Database Properties Dialog box. Here we need to specify the logical name of our file and select the FILESTREAM file type. We will then be able to choose to add the file to our in-memory filegroup by using the drop-down box, as shown in Figure 6-7.

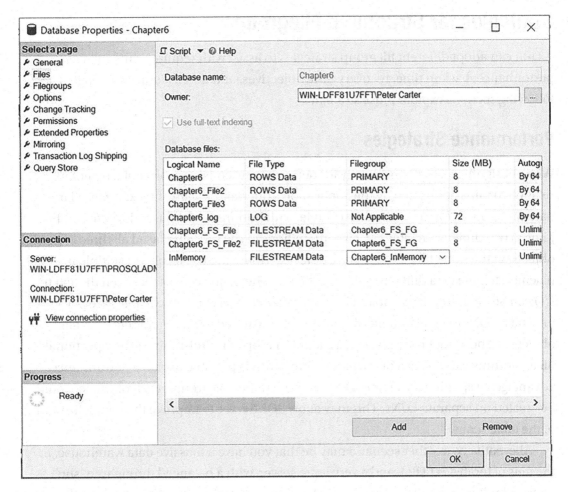

Figure 6-7. *Adding an in-memory container*

Alternatively, we can achieve the same results by using the T-SQL script in
Listing 6-6. Make sure to change the file location to match your directory structure.

Listing 6-6. Adding an In-memory Filegroup and Container

```
ALTER DATABASE [Chapter6] ADD FILEGROUP [Chapter6_InMemory] CONTAINS
MEMORY_OPTIMIZED_DATA;
GO

ALTER DATABASE [Chapter6] ADD FILE ( NAME = N'InMemory', FILENAME = N'F:\
MSSQL\MSSQL16.PROSQLADMIN\MSSQL\DATA\InMemory' ) TO FILEGROUP [Chapter6_
InMemory];
GO
```

Strategies for Structured Filegroups

A DBA can adopt different filegroup strategies to assist with requirements such as performance, backup time, recovery time objectives, and tiered storage offerings. The following sections explore those strategies.

Performance Strategies

When designing a filegroup strategy for performance, consider object placement in relation to joins performed by the application's queries. Imagine, for example, a large data warehouse. You have a wide fact table, with hundreds of thousands of rows, which joins to two dimension tables, each with millions of rows. If you placed all three of these objects on the same filegroup, then you can distribute the I/O by using multiple files, placing each file on a different spindle. The issue here, however, is that even though the I/O can be distributed, you do not have granular control over which tables are placed on which LUNs (logical unit numbers). As demonstrated earlier in this chapter, all objects will be stripped evenly, using a combination of round-robin and proportional fill algorithms, across each of the files. Therefore, it is possible to gain a performance advantage by splitting these tables onto three separate filegroups, each of which would be created on separate LUNs. This may allow SQL Server to improve the parallelization of the table scans.

Alternatively, another scenario may be that you have a massive data warehouse, in the tens of terabytes (TBs), and a very large server, with a balanced throughput, such as a server built using the Fast Track Data Warehouse Reference Architecture (details of which can be found on the MSDB library); in this case, you may get the best performance by creating filegroups over every single disk available. This gives the server the best performance in terms of I/O throughput and helps prevent the I/O subsystem from becoming the bottleneck.

Also consider the placement of tables that are subject to horizontal partitioning. Imagine a very large table where data is partitioned by month. If your application's workload means that several months of data are often being read at the same time, then you may see a performance improvement if you split each month out into separate filegroups, each of which uses a discrete set of spindles, in a similar way to the join example, mentioned earlier. There will be a full discussion on partitioning in Chapter 7.

> **Caution**   The downside to this approach is that placing partitions on separate filegroups prevents you from using partitioning functions, such as SWITCH.

If your database has a large amount of archive data, then you can harness read-only filegroups as a performance strategy. Here, you will place static data that is required for historical reporting on a read-only filegroup. Because the data is read-only, you do not need to worry about locks and concurrency issues (see Chapter 19) which can cause performance degradation. You also know that your indexes and statistics (see Chapter 8) will never be fragmented or need updating, respectively, again preventing performance degradation due to maintenance issues and ensuring that you always have a good query plan.

> **Caution**   The downside of this approach is that it can cause complexity for developers, who need to join the archive data back to "live" data, which needs to be on standard filegroups, as it is still subject to change.

Backup and Restore Strategies

SQL Server allows you to back up at the file and filegroup level as well as at the database level. You are subsequently able to perform what is known as a *piecemeal restore*. A piecemeal restore allows you to bring your database online in stages. This can be very useful for large databases that have a very low recovery time objective.

Imagine that you have a large database that contains a small amount of very critical data that the business cannot be without for more than a maximum of two hours. The database also contains a large amount of historic data that the business requires access to on a daily basis for the purpose of reporting, but it is not critical that it is restored within the two-hour window. In this scenario, it is good practice to have two secondary filegroups. The first contains the critical data and the second contains the historic data. In the event of a disaster, you can then restore the primary filegroup and the first secondary filegroup. At this point, you can bring the database online and the business will have access to this data. Subsequently, the filegroup containing the historic reporting data could be brought online.

Filegroups can also assist with backup strategies. Imagine a scenario where you have a large database that takes two hours to back up. Unfortunately, you have a long-running ETL process and only a one-hour window in which the database can be backed up nightly. If this is the case, then you can split the data between two filegroups. The first filegroup can be backed up on Monday, Wednesday, and Friday, and the second filegroup can be backed up on Tuesday, Thursday, and Saturday. Backups and restores are discussed full y in Chapter 12.

Storage-Tiering Strategies

Some organizations may decide that they want to implement storage tiering for large databases. If this is the case, then you will often need to implement this by using partitioning. For example, imagine that a table contains six years' worth of data. The data for the current year is accessed and updated many times a day. Data for the previous three years is accessed in monthly reports, but other than that is rarely touched. Data as far back as six years must be available instantly, if it is needed for regulatory reasons, but in practice, it is rarely accessed.

In the scenario just described, partitioning could be used with yearly partitions. The filegroup containing the current year's data could consist of files on locally attached RAID 10 LUNs for optimum performance. The partitions holding data for years 2 and 3 could be placed on the premium tier of the corporate SAN device. Partitions for data older than three years could be placed on near-line storage within the SAN, thus satisfying regulatory requirements in the most cost-effective manner.

Some organizations have also introduced automated storage tiering, such as AO (Adaptive Optimization). Although automated storage tiering technology works extremely well in some environments, its implementation for SQL Server can sometimes prove problematic. This is because it works in two phases. The first is an analysis phase, which decides which tier each block or file should reside on for the best trade-off between cost and expense. The second phase will actually move the data to the most appropriate tier.

The issue is that the window where data is being moved tends to reduce the performance of the SAN. Therefore, running analysis followed by moving the data frequently (i.e., hourly) can cause unacceptable performance degradation. On the flip side, however, running analysis less frequently (such as during business hours) and moving data overnight sometimes do not tally with SQL Server usage profiles. For example, imagine a reporting application that needs optimum performance, but where the weekly reports are generated on a Friday. Because the last analysis window before this peak period was Thursday, when not a lot was happening, the data is likely to reside on a slower, more cost-effective tier, meaning that performance will be impaired. When Saturday arrives, however, and the application is virtually idle again, the data will reside on the premium tier, because of the analysis window, during Friday's peak usage. For this reason, automated storage tiering often works best in environments where databases have set hours of operation, with little day-to-day variance in usage profiles.

Strategies for Memory-Optimized Filegroups

Just like structured filegroups, memory-optimized filegroups will use a round-robin approach to allocating data between containers. It is common practice to place these multiple containers on separate spindles in order to maximize I/O throughput. The issue is, however, that if you place one container on spindle A and one container on spindle B, then the round-robin approach will place all of the Data files on one volume and all of the Delta files on the other volume.

To avoid this issue, it is good practice to place two containers on each of the volumes that you wish to use for your memory-optimized filegroup. This will ensure that you get a balanced distribution of I/O, as illustrated in Figure 6-8. This is in line with Microsoft's recommended best practice.

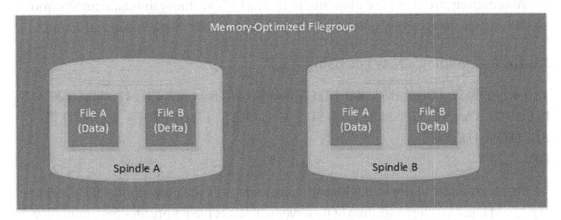

Figure 6-8. *Balanced I/O distribution for memory-optimized filegroups*

File and Filegroup Maintenance

During the life cycle of a data-tier application, at times you may need to perform maintenance activities on your database files and filegroups for reasons such as performance or capacity management. The following sections will describe how to add, expand, and shrink files.

Adding Files

You may need to add files to a filegroup for both capacity and performance reasons. If your database grows past your capacity estimates and the volume that hosts your data files cannot be resized, then you can add additional files to the filegroup, which is hosted on different LUNs.

You may also need to add additional files to the filegroup in order to increase the I/O throughput if the storage subsystem becomes a bottleneck for your application. We could add an additional file to our Chapter6 database by using the Files tab of the Database Properties dialog box. Here, we will use the Add button and then specify the logical name of the file, the filegroup that we want the file to reside in, the initial size of the file, the autogrowth settings, the maximum size of the file, and the physical path to where the file will be stored.

Alternatively, we could use the script in Listing 6-7 to achieve the same results. You should change the directory path in the script to match your own directory structure.

Listing 6-7. Adding a New File Using T-SQL

```
ALTER DATABASE [Chapter6] ADD FILE ( NAME = N'Chapter6_File4', FILENAME =
N'G:\DATA\Chapter6_File4.ndf' , SIZE = 5120KB , FILEGROWTH = 1024KB ) TO
FILEGROUP [PRIMARY];
GO
```

In this scenario, however, it is important to remember the proportional fill algorithm. If you add files to a filegroup, then SQL Server will target the empty files first, until they have the same amount of free space remaining as the original files. This means that if you create them with the same size as the original files, you may not receive the benefit that you are expecting. You can witness this behavior by running the script in Listing 6-8.

This script uses the same technique we used when we initially created and populated the RoundRobin table to generate an additional 10,000 rows and then identify how many rows are in each file.

Listing 6-8. Adding Additional Rows to the RoundRobin table

```
--Create a Numbers table that will be used to assist the population of
the table

DECLARE @Numbers TABLE
(
        Number          INT
)

--Populate the Numbers table

;WITH CTE(Number)
AS
(
        SELECT 1 Number
        UNION ALL
        SELECT Number +1
        FROM CTE
        WHERE Number <= 99
)
INSERT INTO @Numbers
SELECT *
FROM CTE;

--Populate the example table with 10000 rows of dummy text

INSERT INTO dbo.RoundRobinTable
SELECT 'DummyText'
FROM @Numbers a
CROSS JOIN @Numbers b;

--Select all the data from the table, plus the details of the rows'
physical location.
--Then group the row count
```

```
--by file ID
SELECT b.file_id, COUNT(*)
FROM
(
        SELECT ID, DummyTxt, a.file_id
        FROM dbo.RoundRobinTable
        CROSS APPLY sys.fn_PhysLocCracker(%%physloc%%) a
) b
GROUP BY b.file_id;
```

You can see from the results in Figure 6-9 that the proportional fill algorithm used the new file exclusively until it was full and then restarted the round-robin allocation between each file. After restarting the proportional fill algorithm, however, an autogrowth event has occurred on the first file in the filegroup. This means that the first file now has a lot more empty space than the other files and has received most of the remaining new rows.

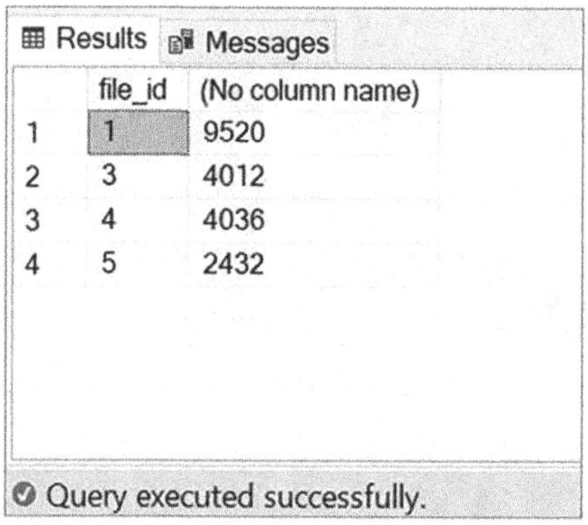

Results Messages

	file_id	(No column name)
1	1	9520
2	3	4012
3	4	4036
4	5	2432

Query executed successfully.

Figure 6-9. *Row allocations to new file*

The workaround for the new file being filled up first would be to either create smaller files or increase the size of the existing files. Either of these approaches would level out the amount of free space left in each file and make SQL Server distribute the writes evenly.

The other alternative is to use a database scoped configuration to force all files within the filegroup to grow every time an autogrowth event occurs. This will be discussed further in the "Database Scoped Configurations" section of this chapter.

We have discussed the implications for adding new files on the round-robin algorithm. It is also worth mentioning, however, that when you initially create your filegroup, you should create the files within that file group, with equal sizes, to take advantage of the algorithm.

Expanding Files

If you had added files using the GUI, rather than a script, then you may have noticed that the initial sizes, indicated next to each of our files, were 11MB, 6MB, and 7MB, respectively, as opposed to the 5MB that we configured for them earlier in this chapter. This is because a more accurate name for the Initial Size field would actually be Current Size. Because we have configured autogrowth for the files, as they have become full, SQL Server has automatically grown the files for us.

This is a very useful fail-safe feature, but ideally we should use it as just that—a fail-safe. Growing files uses resources and also causes locks to be taken out, blocking other processes. It is therefore advisable to presize the database files in line with capacity estimates, as opposed to starting with a small file and relying on autogrow.

For the same reason, when specifying a file's autogrowth settings, you should shy away from the default value of 1MB and specify a much larger value. If you don't, if your file becomes full and autogrowth kicks in, your files will grow in very tiny increments, which is likely to impair performance, even if you are using instant file initialization. The value that you should set your files to grow by will depend on your environment. You should take into account, for example, the amount of free space that is available on the volume and the number of other databases that share the volume. You can see how much space is left in a file by using the sys.dm_db_file_space_usage dynamic management view (DMV). This DMV will return a column named unallocated_extent_page_count, which will tell us how many free pages there are left to be allocated. We can use this to calculate the remaining free space in each file, as demonstrated in Listing 6-9.

Listing 6-9. Calculating Free Space in Each File

```
SELECT
    file_id
    ,unallocated_extent_page_count * 1.0 / 128 'Free Space (MB)'
FROM sys.dm_db_file_space_usage;
```

If we want to expand a file, we do not need to wait for autogrowth to kick in. We can expand the file manually by changing the value of the Initial Size field in the Files tab of the Database Properties dialog box, or by using the ALTER DATABASE command. The command in Listing 6-10 will resize the newest file in our Chapter6 database to be 20MB.

Listing 6-10. Expanding a File

```
ALTER DATABASE [Chapter6] MODIFY FILE ( NAME = N'Chapter6_File4', SIZE =
20480KB );
```

Shrinking Files

Just as you can expand database files, you can also shrink them. There are various methods for achieving this, including shrinking a single file, shrinking all files within a database including the log, or even setting an Auto Shrink option at the database level.

To shrink an individual file, you need to use the DBCC SHRINKFILE command. When you use this option, you can specify either the target size of the file or you can specify the EMPTYFILE option. The EMPTYFILE option will move all data within the file to other files within the same filegroup. This means that you can subsequently remove the file from the database.

If you specify a target size for the database, then you can choose to specify either TRUNCATEONLY or NOTRUNCATE. If you select the former, then SQL Server will start at the end of the file and reclaim space until it reaches the last allocated extent. If you choose the latter, then beginning at the end of the file, SQL Server will begin a process of moving allocated extents to the first free space at the start of the file.

To remove the unused space at the end of our expanded Chapter6_File4 file, we could use the Shrink File screen in SQL Server Management Studio, which can be found by right-clicking the database and drilling through Tasks ➤ Shrink ➤ Files. In the Shrink File screen, we can select the appropriate file from the File Name drop-down box and then ensure that the Release Unused Space radio button is selected. This option enforces TRUNCATEONLY.

We could also achieve the same result by running the command in Listing 6-11.

Listing 6-11. Shrinking a File with TRUNCATEONLY

```
USE [Chapter6]
GO

DBCC SHRINKFILE (N'Chapter6_File4' , 0, TRUNCATEONLY);
```

If we wanted to reclaim the unused space at the end of all files in the database, we could right-click the database and drill down through Tasks ➤ Shrink ➤ Database. We would then ensure that the Reorganize Files Before Releasing Unused Space option is not selected and click OK.

We could achieve the same result via T-SQL by running the command in Listing 6-12.

Listing 6-12. Shrinking a Database via T-SQL

```
USE [Chapter6]
GO

DBCC SHRINKDATABASE(N'Chapter6' );
```

There are very few occasions when it is acceptable to shrink a database, or even an individual file. There is a misconception that large, empty files take longer to back up, but this is a fallacy. In fact, I have had only one occasion in my career when I needed to shrink data files. This instance happened after we removed several hundred gigabytes of archive data from a database and were approaching our 2TB LUN limit, but this was an exceptional circumstance. Generally speaking, you should not look to shrink your database files, and you should certainly never, ever use the Auto Shrink option on a database.

In the event that you do have to shrink a database, be prepared for the process to be slow. It is a single-threaded operation and will consume resources while running. It can also cause contention issues. In SQL Server 2022, however, these contention issues can be mitigated with a new option: WAIT_AT_LOW_PRIORITY. This option will avoid queries that require a schema modify lock from being blocked during the wait phase of the shrink process. These queries will only become blocked during the execution phase. This means that if a shrink operation is unable to obtain a schema modify lock when it reaches the execution phase, it will wait for 1 minute and then time-out. If the operation times out, it will silently fail and need to be run again.

I recommend that you should never consider using the NOTRUNCATE option. As described earlier, this will cause extents to be moved around inside the file and will lead to massive fragmentation issues like those you can see using the script in Listing 6-13. This script first creates a clustered index on our RoundRobin table. It then uses the sys. dm_db_index_physical_stats DMV to examine the level of fragmentation at the leaf level of the clustered index. Subsequently, it shrinks the database and then reexamines the level of fragmentation of the leaf level of our clustered index.

Listing 6-13. Fragmentation Caused by Shrinking

```
USE Chapter6
GO

--Create a clustered index on RoundRobinTable
CREATE UNIQUE CLUSTERED INDEX CIX_RoundRobinTable ON dbo.
RoundRobinTable(ID);
GO

--Examine Fragmentation on new index
SELECT * FROM sys.dm_db_index_physical_stats(DB_ID('Chapter6'),OBJECT_
ID('dbo.RoundRobinTable'),1,NULL,'DETAILED')
WHERE index_level = 0;

--Shrink the database
DBCC SHRINKDATABASE(N'Chapter6', NOTRUNCATE);
GO

--Reexamine index fragmentation
SELECT * FROM sys.dm_db_index_physical_stats(DB_ID('Chapter6'),OBJECT_
ID('dbo.RoundRobinTable'),1,NULL,'DETAILED')
WHERE index_level = 0;
GO
```

As you can see from the results shown in Figure 6-10, the fragmentation of the leaf level of the index has increased from 0.08% to a massive 71.64%, which will severely impact queries run against the index. Indexes and fragmentation will be discussed in detail in Chapter 8.

Note   The fragmentation level may vary depending on the layout of extents within your file(s).

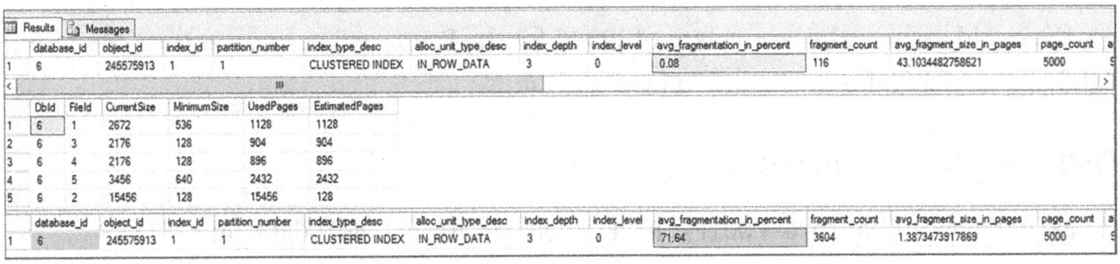

Figure 6-10. *Results of fragmentation*

Database Scoped Configurations

In older versions of SQL Server, Trace Flags could be configured on the SQL Server service (see Chapter 5), which changed the default behavior of how SQL Server stored data and performed autogrowth events. The first of these was T1117, which was used to make all files within a filegroup grow at the same time, which was helpful for distributing data evenly, especially in data warehousing scenarios. The other was T1118, which was used to force uniform extents to be used exclusively—essentially turning of mixed extents (where different pages within an extent can be allocated to different tables). T1118 was useful for optimizing TempDB, but could also prove useful in data warehousing scenarios.

In more recent versions of SQL Server, T1117 and T1118 have no effect, if they are turned on. They have been replaced by Database Scoped Configurations, which have two main benefits. Firstly, Database Scoped Configurations are configured at the database level instead of the instance level. This means that a single consolidated instance can easily support databases with different workload profiles. Secondly, Database Scoped Configurations are documented and supported by Microsoft. While T1117 and T1118 were well known and well used, they had no official support from Microsoft.

201

> **Note**   The equivalent behavior of T1117 and T1118 is assumed by default on the TempDB database. For user databases, however, the traditional default behavior is assumed.

We could assume the equivalent of T1117 for the Primary filegroup, in the Chapter6 database, by using the command in Listing 6-14.

Listing 6-14. Turn On Autogrow All Files

```
ALTER DATABASE Chapter6 MODIFY FILEGROUP [Primary] AUTOGROW_ALL_FILES
```

The command in Listing 6-15 will assume the equivalent behavior T1118 for the Chapter6 database.

Listing 6-15. Turn Off Mixed Page Allocations

```
ALTER DATABASE Chapter6 SET MIXED_PAGE_ALLOCATION OFF
```

SQL Server 2022 introduces new database scoped configurations, which allow the database engine to make performance enhancements to query plans based on previous executions of the same query.

The DOP_FEEDBACK configuration allows the database engine to alter the degree of parallelism for a query if it identifies inefficiencies in previous executions of the same query. This configuration can be toggled on and off using the ALTER DATABASE SCOPED CONFIGURATION command, as demonstrated in Listing 6-16.

Listing 6-16. Toggle DOP_FEEDBACK

```
ALTER DATABASE SCOPED CONFIGURATION SET DOP_FEEDBACK = ON ;
GO
ALTER DATABASE SCOPED CONFIGURATION SET DOP_FEEDBACK = OFF ;
GO
```

> **Tip**   It is worth noting that an additional database scoped configuration, MAXDOP, which sets the default maximum degree of parallelism, can be configured differently for Primary and Secondary databases within an Availability Group Database. For example, the command ALTER DATABASE SCOPED

CONFIGURATION SET MAXDOP = 2 will configure the Primary database, while the command ALTER DATABASE SCOPED CONFIGURATION FOR SECONDARY SET MAXDOP = 4 will configure the MAXDOP differently for the Secondary database. This allows you to tune readable secondary replicas for reporting workloads. Selecting an appropriate maximum degree of parallelism is discussed in Chapter 3 and Availability Groups are discussed in Chapter 15.

SQL Server 2022 also introduces the ability to adjust the amount of memory that is allocated to a query, based on the performance of previous query executions. There are two database scoped configurations that support this functionality. The MEMORY_ GRANT_FEEDBACK_PERCENTILE configuration introduces an algorithm that configures the memory grant, based on multiple past executions of a query. This helps optimize memory grants for queries that have memory requirements which swing dramatically.

The MEMORY_GRANT_FEEDBACK_PERSISTENCE configuration allows for memory grant information to be persisted for a query plan, even after the plan has been removed from the cache. Listing 6-17 shows how the two memory grant feedback configurations can be toggled on and off.

Listing 6-17. Toggle Memory Grant Feedback Configurations

```
--Turn on

ALTER DATABASE SCOPED CONFIGURATION SET MEMORY_GRANT_FEEDBACK_PERCENTILE_
GRANT = ON ;
GO
ALTER DATABASE SCOPED CONFIGURATION SET MEMORY_GRANT_FEEDBACK_
PERSISTENCE = ON ;
GO

--Turn off

ALTER DATABASE SCOPED CONFIGURATION SET MEMORY_GRANT_FEEDBACK_PERCENTILE_
GRANT =  OFF ;
GO
ALTER DATABASE SCOPED CONFIGURATION SET MEMORY_GRANT_FEEDBACK_
PERSISTENCE = OFF ;
GO
```

> **Caution**   At the time of writing, prior to General Availability of SQL Server 2022, Microsoft documentation refers to MEMORY_GRANT_FEEDBACK_PERCENTILE, while the feature is implemented as MEMORY_GRANT_FEEDBACK_PERCENTILE_GRANT. The description and examples in this chapter have been written using the command that currently implemented. However, it is unclear whether it is the documentation or the command will be updated. Therefore, if you find that the command does not work, it is likely that Microsoft have changed the name of the command to MEMORY_GRANT_FEEDBACK_PERCENTILE.

All database scoped configurations and their currently configured values, against both the Primary and Secondary database (where appropriate), can be retrieved by running the query in Listing 6-18.

Listing 6-18. View Database Scoped Configurations and Their Current Values

```
SELECT
      name
    , value
    , value_for_secondary
FROM sys.database_scoped_configurations
```

> **Tip**   The feedback mechanisms used for the *_FEEDBACK* configurations mentioned in this chapter rely on the functionality of Query Store. Therefore, Query Store must be enabled for the feedback mechanisms to work. Query Store is discussed in Chapter 22. Further database scoped configurations are discussed throughout this book.

Log Maintenance

The transaction log is a vital tool in SQL Server's armory; it provides recovery functionality but also supports many features, such as AlwaysOn Availability Groups, Transactional Replication, Change Data Capture, and many more.

Internally, the log file is split down into a series of VLFs (virtual log files). When the final VLF in the log file becomes full, SQL Server will attempt to wrap around to the first VLF at the beginning of the log. If this VLF has not been truncated and cannot be reused, then SQL Server will attempt to grow the log file. If it is not able to expand the file due to lack of disk space or max size settings, then a 9002 error will be thrown and the transaction will be rolled back. Figure 6-11 illustrates the structure of the log file and its circular usage.

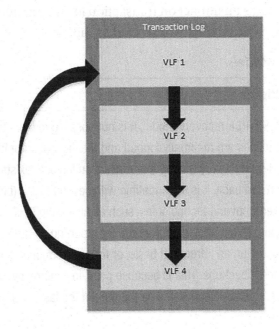

Figure 6-11. *Log file structure*

The amount of VLFs inside a log file is determined by the size of the log when it was initially created and also the size that it is expanded by each time it grows. If the log file is created at or grows in increments of less than 64MB, then 1 VLF will be added to the file. If it is created at or grows in increments between 64MB and 1GB, then 8 VLFs will be added to the file. If it is created at or grows by more than 1GB, then 16 VLFs will be added.

Tip   This is a change of behavior in SQL Server 2022. In previous versions, if the log grew in increments of less than 64MB, four new VLFs were created. This change reduces the amount of log fragmentation in log files that grow by small amounts.

The transaction log is a low-maintenance component of the SQL Server stack. There will be times, however, when maintenance scenarios occur; these are discussed in the following sections.

Recovery Model

The *recovery model* is a database-level property that controls how transactions are logged and, therefore, it has an impact on transaction log maintenance. The three recovery models within SQL Server are described in Table 6-1.

Table 6-1. *Recovery Models*

Recovery Model	Description
SIMPLE	In the SIMPLE recovery model, it is not possible to back up the transaction log. Transactions are minimally logged and the log will automatically be truncated. In SIMPLE recovery model, the transaction log only exists to allow transactions to be rolled back. It is incompatible with several HADR (high-availability and disaster recovery) technologies, such as AlwaysOn Availability Groups and Log Shipping. This model is appropriate for reporting databases where updates only occur on an infrequent basis, or for nonproduction databases that require infrequent backups. This is because point-in-time recovery is not possible. The recovery point objective will be the time of the last FULL or DIFFERENTIAL backup.
FULL	In the FULL recovery model, transaction log backups must be taken. The log will only be truncated during the log backup process. Transactions are fully logged and this means that point-in-time recovery is possible. It also means that you must have a complete chain of log file backups to restore a database to the most recent point.
BULK LOGGED	The BULK_LOGGED recovery model is meant to be used on a temporary basis when you are using the FULL recovery model but need to perform a large BULK INSERT operation. When you switch to this mode, BULK INSERT operations are minimally logged. You then switch back to FULL recovery model when the import is complete. In this recovery model, you can restore to the end of any backup, but not to a specific point in time between backups.

Note   Recovery models will be discussed further in Chapter 12.

Log File Count

Several times I have witnessed a misconception that having multiple log files can improve the performance of a database. This is a fallacy. The idea is driven by the belief that if you have multiple log files on separate drives, you can distribute I/O and relieve the log as a bottleneck.

The truth is that the transaction log is sequential, and even if you add multiple log files, SQL Server treats them as if they are a single file. This means that the second file will only be used after the first file becomes full. As a result, no performance benefit can be gained from this practice. In fact, the only possible reason that you would ever need more than one transaction log file is if you ran out of space on the LUN that was hosting the log, and for some reason, it cannot be moved elsewhere and the volume can't be expanded. In my professional career, although I have encountered multiple log files on several occasions, I have never encountered a valid reason for having them.

Shrinking the Log

Shrinking your log file should never be part of your standard maintenance routines. There is no benefit to adopting this policy. There are some occasions, however, when you may have to shrink a log file, and, thankfully, it does not come with the same hazards as shrinking a data file.

The usual reason for needing to shrink your log file is when an atypical activity occurs in your database, such as an initial data population or a one-time ETL load. If this is the case and your log file expands past the point where space thresholds on your volume are being breached, then reducing the size of the file is likely to be the best course of action, as opposed to expanding the volume that is hosting it. In this eventuality, however, you should carefully analyze the situation to ensure that it really is an atypical event. If it seems like it could occur again, then you should consider increasing capacity to deal with it.

Tip Before increasing capacity, it is worth investigating if smaller transactions or batches can be used.

To shrink a log file, you can use the Shrink File dialog box. Here, select Log in the File Type drop-down box. This causes the Filegroup drop-down box to be grayed out, and assuming you only have one log file, it will automatically be selected in the File Name drop-down. If you have multiple transaction log files, you will be able to select the appropriate file from the drop-down list. As with shrinking a data file, choosing the Release Unused Space option will cause TRUNCATEONLY to be used.

Alternatively, you can use the script in Listing 6-19 to achieve the same results. It is important to note, however, that shrinking the log file may not actually result in any space being reclaimed. This happens if the last VLF in the file cannot be reused. A full list of reasons why it may not be possible to reuse a VLF is included later in this chapter.

Listing 6-19. Shrinking a Log with TRUNCATEONLY

```
USE [Chapter6]
GO

DBCC SHRINKFILE (N'Chapter6_log' , 0, TRUNCATEONLY);
GO
```

Tip Because shrinking the transaction log always involves reclaiming space from the end of the log, until the first active VLF is reached, it is sensible to take a log backup and place the database in single-user mode before performing this activity.

Log Fragmentation

When the log is truncated because of a backup in the Full Recovery model or a Checkpoint operation in the Simple Recovery model, what actually happens is that any VLFs that can be reused are truncated. Reasons why a VLF may not be able to be reused include VLFs containing log records associated with active transactions or transactions that have not yet been sent to other databases in Replication or AlwaysOn topologies. In a similar fashion, if you shrink the log file, then VLFs will be removed from the end of the file until the first active VLF is reached.

There is no hard and fast rule for the optimum number of VLFs inside a log file, but I try to maintain approximately two VLFs per GB for large transaction logs, in the tens-of-gigabytes range. For smaller transaction logs, it is likely the ratio will be higher. If you have too many VLFs, then you may witness performance degradation of any activity that uses the transaction log. On the flip side, having too few VLFs can also pose a problem. In such a case where each VLF is GBs in size, when each VLF is truncated, it will take a substantial amount of time to clear, and you could witness a system slowdown while this takes place. Therefore, for large log files, it is recommended that you grow your transaction log in 8GB chunks to maintain the optimum number and size of VLFs.

To demonstrate this phenomenon, we will create a new database called Chapter6LogFragmentation, which has a single table on the primary filegroup, called Inserts, and then populate it with one million rows using the script in Listing 6-20. This will cause a large number of VLFs to be created, which will have a negative impact on performance.

Listing 6-20. Creating the Chapter6LogFragmentation Database

```
--Create Chapter6LogFragmentation database

CREATE DATABASE [Chapter6LogFragmentation]
 CONTAINMENT = NONE
 ON  PRIMARY
( NAME = N'Chapter6LogFragmentation', FILENAME = N'F:\MSSQL\MSSQL16.
PROSQLADMIN\MSSQL\DATA\Chapter6LogFragmentation.mdf' , SIZE = 5120KB ,
FILEGROWTH = 1024KB )
 LOG ON
( NAME = N'Chapter6LogFragmentation_log', FILENAME = N'E:\MSSQL\MSSQL16.
PROSQLADMIN\MSSQL\DATA\Chapter6LogFragmentation_log.ldf' , SIZE = 1024KB ,
FILEGROWTH = 10%);
GO

USE Chapter6LogFragmentation
GO

--Create Inserts table
```

```
CREATE TABLE dbo.Inserts
(ID                     INT                    IDENTITY,
DummyText          NVARCHAR(50)
);
```

--Create a Numbers table that will be used to assist the population of the table

```
DECLARE @Numbers TABLE
(
        Number      INT
)
```

--Populate the Numbers table

```
;WITH CTE(Number)
AS
(
        SELECT 1 Number

        UNION ALL
        SELECT Number +1
        FROM CTE
        WHERE Number <= 99
)
INSERT INTO @Numbers
SELECT *
FROM CTE;
```

--Populate the example table with 100 rows of dummy text

```
INSERT INTO dbo.Inserts
SELECT 'DummyText'
FROM @Numbers a
CROSS JOIN @Numbers b
CROSS JOIN @Numbers c;
```

You can review the size of your transaction log and see how many VLFs are in your log by running the script in Listing 6-21.

Listing 6-21. Size of Log and Number of VLFs

```
--Create a variable to store the results of DBCC LOGINFO

DECLARE @DBCCLogInfo TABLE
(
RecoveryUnitID          TINYINT
,FieldID                 TINYINT
,FileSize                 BIGINT
,StartOffset         BIGINT
,FseqNo               INT
,Status                  TINYINT
,Parity                  TINYINT
,CreateLSN          NUMERIC
);

--Populate the table variable with the results of DBCC LOGINFO

INSERT INTO @DBCCLogInfo
EXEC('DBCC LOGINFO');

--Display the size of the log file, combined with the number of VLFs and a
VLFs to GB ratio

SELECT
        name
        ,[Size in MBs]
        ,[Number of VLFs]
        ,[Number of VLFs] / ([Size in MBs] / 1024) 'VLFs per GB'
FROM
```

```
(
        SELECT
                name
                ,size * 1.0 / 128 'Size in MBs'
                ,(SELECT COUNT(*)
                        FROM @DBCCLogInfo) 'Number of VLFs'
        FROM sys.database_files
        WHERE type = 1
) a;
```

The results of running this script inside the Chapter6LogFragmentation database
are displayed in Figure 6-12. You can see that there are 61 VLFs, which is an excessive
amount given the log size is 345MB.

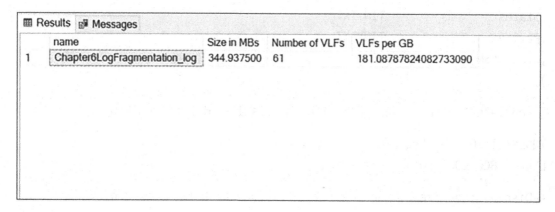

Figure 6-12. *VLFs per GB*

Caution   DBCC LOGINFO is undocumented, so it will not be supported by
Microsoft. For example, in SQL Server 2012, Microsoft added a column to the
output named RecoveryUnitID, but they have never made its description public.

The meaning of each column returned by DBCC LOGINFO is described in Table 6-2.

Table 6-2. *DBCC LOGINFO Columns*

Column	Description
FileID	The ID of the physical file. Assuming that you only have one file, this should always return the same value.
FileSize	The size of the VLF in bytes.
StartOffset	How many bytes there are from the beginning of the physical file until the start of the VLF.
FSeqNo	Defines the current usage order of the VLFs. The highest FSeqNo indicates the VLF that is currently being written to.
Status	A status of 2 means that the VLF is currently active. A status of 0 means that it is not and can therefore be reused.
Parity	Parity starts at 0. When a VLF is initially used, it is set to 64. Subsequently, it can be set to either 64 or 128. Each time a VLF is reused, this flag is switched to the opposite value.
CreateLSN	CreateLSN indicates the log sequence number that was used to create the VLF.

With an understanding of the columns, we can identify several interesting facts about the results shown earlier. First, because the first four VLFs have a CreateLSN value of 0, we know that these were the VLFs that were initially created when the log file itself was generated. The rest have been created by the log expanding, rather than cycling. We can also see that the final ten VLFs in the results have not yet been used, because they have a Parity of 0. The VLF with an FSeqNo of 83 is the VLF where records are currently being written, since it has the highest FSeqNo.

Most interestingly, for the purpose of this example, we can see that the first 51 VLFs are marked as active, meaning that they cannot be reused. This means that if we attempt to shrink our log file, only ten VLFs can be removed and the file would only shrink by the sum of their file sizes.

The reason that our log was growing and could not be cycled was because all the space was used during the course of a single transaction and, of course, our log has not been backed up. The query in Listing 6-22 will enable you to determine if there are any other reasons why you transaction log is growing. The query interrogates the sys. databases catalog view and returns the last reason that a VLF could not be reused.

Listing 6-22. sys.databases

```
SELECT log_reuse_wait_desc
FROM sys.databases
WHERE name = 'Chapter6LogFragmentation';
```

The log reuse waits that are still used in SQL Server 2022 and that are not for Microsoft's internal use only are described in Table 6-3. It is important to understand that the log reuse wait applies to the point when the log attempts to cycle and may still not be valid at the point you query sys.databases. For example, if there was an active transaction at the point that the last log cycle was attempted, it will be reflected in sys. databases, even though you may not currently have any active transactions at the point when you query sys.databases.

Table 6-3. *Log Reuse Waits*

Log_reuse_wait	Log_reuse_wait_description	Description
0	NOTHING	The log was able to cycle on its last attempt.
1	CHECKPOINT	Normally indicates that a CHECKPOINT has not occurred since the last time the log was truncated.
2	LOG_BACKUP	The log cannot be truncated until a log backup has been taken.
3	ACTIVE_BACKUP_OR_RESTORE	A backup or restore operation is currently in progress on the database.
4	ACTIVE_TRANSACTION	There is a long-running or deferred transaction. Deferred transactions will be discussed in Chapter 18.
5	DATABASE_MIRRORING	Either an asynchronous replica is still synchronizing or mirroring has been paused.
6	REPLICATION	There are transactions in the log that have not yet been received by the distributor.

(continued)

Table 6-3. (*continued*)

Log_reuse_wait	Log_reuse_wait_description	Description
7	DATABASE_SNAPSHOT_CREATION	A database snapshot is currently being created. Database snapshots will be discussed in Chapter 16.
8	LOG_SCAN	A log scan operation is in progress.
9	AVAILABILITY_REPLICA	Secondary replicas are not fully synchronized or the availability group has been paused.
13	OLDEST_PAGE	The oldest page of the database is older than the checkpoint LSN. This occurs when indirect checkpoints are being used.
16	XPT_CHECKPOINT	A memory-optimized CHECKPOINT is required before the log can be truncated.

In our scenario, in order to mark the VLFs as reusable, we need to back up our transaction log. Theoretically, we could also switch to the SIMPLE recovery model, but this would break our log chain. Before we do this, we need to take a full backup. This is because all backup sequences must begin with a full backup. (Backups and restores will be discussed in Chapter 12.) This will leave only the VLF with an FSeqNo of 83 as active and the others will be marked as reusable.

In order to improve log fragmentation, we need to shrink the log file and then expand it again, with a larger increment. So in our case, we would shrink the log as far as possible, which will be to VLF FSeqNo 83, because this is the last active VLF in the file. We then expand it back to 500MB. We can perform these tasks with the script in Listing 6-23.

Listing 6-23. Defragmenting the Transaction Log

```
USE Chapter6LogFragmentation
GO

DBCC SHRINKFILE ('Chapter6LogFragmentation _log' , 0, TRUNCATEONLY);
GO
```

```
ALTER DATABASE Chapter6LogFragmentation MODIFY FILE ( NAME =
'Chapter6LogFragmentation _log', SIZE = 512000KB );
GO
```

Finally, we run the query in Listing 6-21 again so that we can examine the differences. Figure 6-13 shows that despite growing the log by around 155GB, we have fewer VLFs than we started with.

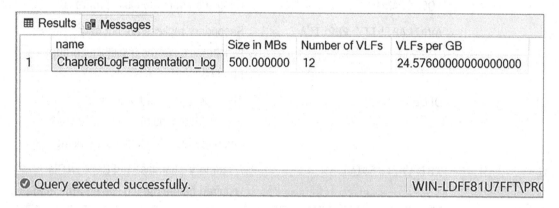

Figure 6-13. *Log fragmentation after shrinking and expanding*

Summary

Filegroups are logical containers for data files. Special filegroups also exist for FILESTREAM/FileTable data and for memory-optimized data. When tables and indexes are created, they are created on a filegroup as opposed to a file, and the data in the object is distributed evenly across the files within that filegroup.

You can adopt various strategies for filegroups to assist with performance, backup/restore activities, or even storage tiering. For performance, you can either choose to place frequently joined objects into separate filegroups or you can distribute all objects across all spindles on the server in order to maximize I/O throughput.

To support backups of very large databases when there is a limited maintenance window, you can split data across filegroups and you can back up those filegroups on alternate nights. To improve recovery times for critical data, you can isolate critical data in a separate filegroup and then restore it before other filegroups.

To support manual storage tiering, implement table partitioning so that each partition is stored on a separate filegroup. You can then place the files within each filegroup on an appropriate storage device.

Both FILESTREAM and memory-optimized filegroups point to folders in the operating system, as opposed to containing files. Each folder location is known as a container. For memory-optimized filegroups, consider having two containers for each disk array you use in order to evenly distribute I/O.

You can expand and shrink data files. Shrinking files, especially auto-shrink, however, is considered bad practice and can result in serious fragmentation issues, which lead to performance problems. When expanding files, you should use larger increments to reduce repeated overhead.

You can also expand and shrink log files, although it is rare that you need to shrink them. Expanding log files in small increments can lead to log fragmentation, which is where your log file contains a vast amount of VLFs. You can resolve log fragmentation by shrinking the log and then growing it again in larger increments.

## CHAPTER 7

Table Optimizations

During the life cycle of your data-tier applications, you may need to perform a number of maintenance tasks and performance optimizations against the tables that hold your application's data. These operations may include partitioning a table, compressing a table, or migrating data to a memory-optimized table. In this chapter, we will explore these three concepts in detail.

Table Partitioning

Partitioning is a performance optimization for large tables and indexes that splits the object horizontally into smaller units. When the tables or indexes are subsequently accessed, SQL Server can perform an optimization called *partition elimination*, which allows only the required partitions to be read, as opposed to the entire table. Additionally, each partition can be stored on a separate filegroup; this allows you to store different partitions on different storage tiers. For example, you can store older, less frequently accessed data on less expensive storage. Figure 7-1 illustrates how a large Orders table may be structured.

© Peter A. Carter 2023
P. A. Carter, *Pro SQL Server 2022 Administration*, https://doi.org/10.1007/978-1-4842-8864-1_7

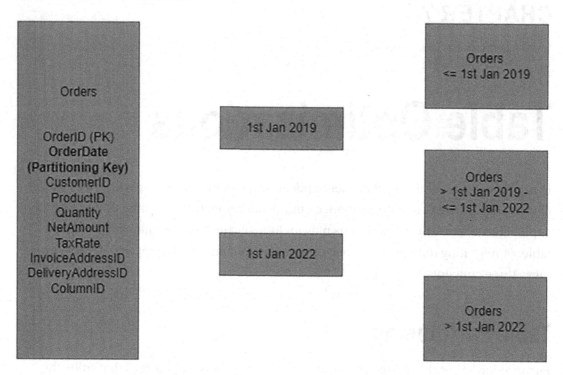

Figure 7-1. *Partitioning structure*

Partitioning Concepts

Before drilling into the technical implementation of partitioning, it helps if you understand the concepts, such as partitioning keys, partition functions, partition schemes, and partition alignment. These concepts are discussed in the following sections.

Partitioning Key

The *partitioning key* is used to determine in which partition each row of the table should be placed. If your table has a clustered index, then the partitioning key must be a subset of the clustered index key. All other UNIQUE indexes on the table, including the primary key (if this differs from the clustered index), also need to include the partitioning key. The partitioning key can consist of any data type, with the exception of TEXT, NTEXT, IMAGE, XML, TIMESTAMP, VARCHAR(MAX), NVARCHAR(MAX), and VARBINARY(MAX). It also cannot be a user-defined CLR Type column or a column with an alias data type. It can, however, be a computed column, as long as this column is persisted. Many scenarios will use a date or datetime column as the partitioning key. This allows you to implement sliding windows based on time. We discuss sliding windows later in this chapter. In Figure 7-1, the OrderDate column is being used as the partitioning key.

Because the column is used to distribute rows between partitions, you should use a column that will enable an even distribution of rows in order to gain the most benefit from the solution. The column you select should also be a column that queries will use as filter criteria. This will allow you to achieve partition elimination.

Partition Function

You use boundary points to set the upper and lower limits of each partition. In Figure 7-1, you can see that the boundary points are set as 1st Jan 2022 and 1st Jan 2019. These boundary points are configured in a database object called the *partition function*. When creating the partition function, you can specify if the range should be left or right. If you align the range to the left, then any values that are exactly equal to a boundary point value will be stored in the partition to the left of that boundary point. If you align the range with the right, then values exactly equal to the boundary point value will be placed in the partition to the right of that boundary point. The partition function also dictates the data type of the partitioning key.

Partition Scheme

Each partition can be stored on a separate filegroup. The *partition scheme* is an object that you create to specify which filegroup each partition will be stored on. As you can see from Figure 7-1, there is always one more partition than there is boundary point. When you create a partition scheme, however, it is possible to specify an "extra" filegroup. This will define the next filegroup that should be used if an additional boundary point is added. It is also possible to specify the ALL keyword, as opposed to specifying individual filegroups. This will force all partitions to be stored on the same filegroup.

Index Alignment

An index is considered aligned with the table if it is built on the same partition function as the table. It is also considered aligned if it is built on a different partition function, but the two functions are identical, in that they share the same data type, the same number of partitions, and the same boundary point values.

Because the leaf level of a clustered index consists of the actual data pages of the table, a clustered index is always aligned with the table. A nonclustered index, however, can be stored on a separate filegroup to the heap, or clustered index. This extends to partitioning, where either the base table or nonclustered indexes can be independently partitioned. If nonclustered indexes are stored on the same partition scheme or an identical partition scheme, then they are aligned. If this is not the case, then they are nonaligned.

Aligning indexes with the base table is good practice unless you have a specific reason not to. This is because aligning indexes can assist with partition elimination. Index alignment is also required for operations such as SWITCH, which will be discussed later in this chapter.

Partitioning Hierarchy

Objects involved in partitioning work in a one-to-many hierarchy, so multiple tables can share a partition scheme and multiple partition schemes can share a partition function, as illustrated in Figure 7-2.

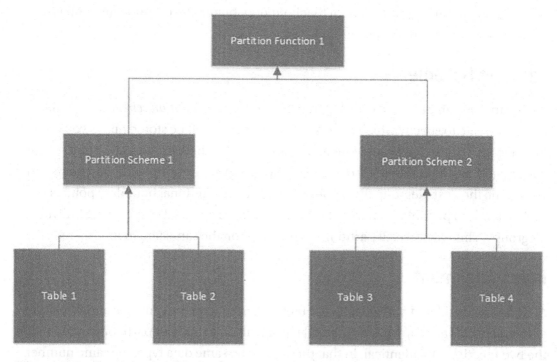

Figure 7-2. *Partitioning hierarchy*

> **Tip**   While Graph databases are beyond the scope of this book, it is worth mentioning that SQL Server supports partitioning graph database tables and indexes, which divides the data into units, which can be spread across multiple filegroups.

Implementing Partitioning

Implementing partitioning involves creating the partition function and partition scheme and then creating the table on the partition scheme. If the table already exists, then you will need to drop and re-create the table's clustered index. These tasks are discussed in the following sections.

Creating the Partitioning Objects

The first object that you will need to create is the partition function. This can be created using the CREATE PARTITION FUNCTION statement, as demonstrated in Listing 7-1. This script creates a database called Chapter7 and then creates a partition function called PartFunc. The function specifies a data type for partitioning keys of DATE and sets boundary points for 1st Jan 2022 and 1st Jan 2019. Table 7-1 details how dates will be distributed between partitions.

Table 7-1. *Distribution of Dates*

Date	Partition	Notes
6th June 2018	1	
1st Jan 2019	1	If we had used RANGE RIGHT, this value would be in partition 2.
11th October 2019	2	
1st Jan 2022	2	If we had used RANGE RIGHT, this value would be in partition 3.
9th May 2022	3	

Listing 7-1. Creating the Partition Function

```
USE Master
GO

--Create Database Chapter7 using default settings from Model

CREATE DATABASE Chapter7 ;
GO

USE Chapter7
GO

--Create Partition Function

CREATE PARTITION FUNCTION PartFunc(Date)
AS RANGE LEFT
FOR VALUES('2019-01-01', '2022-01-01') ;
```

The next object that we need to create is a partition scheme. This can be created using the CREATE PARTITION SCHEME statement, as demonstrated in Listing 7-2. This script creates a partition scheme called PartScheme against the PartFunc partition function and specifies that all partitions will be stored on the PRIMARY filegroup. Although storing all partitions on the same filegroup does not allow us to implement storage tiering, it does enable us to automate sliding windows.

Listing 7-2. Creating the Partition Scheme

```
CREATE PARTITION SCHEME PartScheme
AS PARTITION PartFunc
ALL TO ([PRIMARY]) ;
```

Creating a New Partitioned Table

Now that we have a partition function and partition scheme in place, all that remains is to create our partitioned table. The script in Listing 7-3 creates a table called Orders and partitions it based on the OrderDate column. Even though OrderNumber provides a natural primary key for our table, we need to include OrderDate in the key so that it can be used as our partitioning column. Obviously, the OrderDate column is not suitable for the primary key on its own, since it is not guaranteed to be unique.

Listing 7-3. Creating the Partition Table

```
CREATE TABLE dbo.Orders
        (
        OrderNumber int         NOT NULL,
        OrderDate date          NOT NULL,
        CustomerID int          NOT NULL,
        ProductID int           NOT NULL,
        Quantity int            NOT NULL,
        NetAmount money         NOT NULL,
        TaxAmount money         NOT NULL,
        InvoiceAddressID int    NOT NULL,
        DeliveryAddressID int   NOT NULL,
        DeliveryDate date       NULL
        ) ON PartScheme(OrderDate)  ;
GO

ALTER TABLE dbo.Orders ADD CONSTRAINT
        PK_Orders PRIMARY KEY CLUSTERED
        (
        OrderNumber,
        OrderDate
        ) WITH( STATISTICS_NORECOMPUTE = OFF, IGNORE_DUP_KEY = OFF,
                ALLOW_ROW_LOCKS = ON, ALLOW_PAGE_LOCKS = ON) ON
                PartScheme(OrderDate) ;

GO
```

The important thing to notice in this script is the ON clause. Normally, you would create a table "on" a filegroup, but in this case, we are creating the table "on" the partition scheme and passing in the name of the column that will be used as the partitioning key. The data type of the partitioning key must match the data type specified in the partition function.

Partitioning an Existing Table

Because the clustered index is always aligned with the base table, the process of moving a table to a partition scheme is as simple as dropping the clustered index and then recreating the clustered index on the partition scheme. The script in Listing 7-4 creates a table called ExistingOrders and populates it with data.

Listing 7-4. Creating a New Table and Populating It with Data

```
--Create the ExistingOrders table

CREATE TABLE dbo.ExistingOrders
    (
        OrderNumber int            IDENTITY        NOT NULL,
        OrderDate date          NOT NULL,
        CustomerID int          NOT NULL,
        ProductID int           NOT NULL,
        Quantity int            NOT NULL,
        NetAmount money      NOT NULL,
        TaxAmount money      NOT NULL,
        InvoiceAddressID int   NOT NULL,
        DeliveryAddressID int  NOT NULL,
        DeliveryDate date          NULL
    ) ON [PRIMARY] ;
GO

ALTER TABLE dbo.ExistingOrders ADD CONSTRAINT
    PK_ExistingOrders PRIMARY KEY CLUSTERED
    (
    OrderNumber,
    OrderDate
    ) WITH( STATISTICS_NORECOMPUTE = OFF, IGNORE_DUP_KEY = OFF,
            ALLOW_ROW_LOCKS = ON, ALLOW_PAGE_LOCKS = ON) ON
            [PRIMARY] ;

GO
```

```
--We will now populate the data with data so that we can view the storage
properties
--and then partition the table when the data already exists.

--Build a numbers table for the data population
DECLARE @Numbers TABLE
(
        Number          INT
)

;WITH CTE(Number)
AS
(
        SELECT 1 Number
        UNION ALL
        SELECT Number + 1
        FROM CTE
        WHERE Number < 20
)
INSERT INTO @Numbers
SELECT Number FROM CTE ;

--Populate ExistingOrders with data
INSERT INTO dbo.ExistingOrders
SELECT
        (SELECT CAST(DATEADD(dd,RAND(CHECKSUM(NEWID())))*b.Number*a.
        Number,'20220101') AS DATE)),
        (SELECT TOP 1 Number -10 FROM @Numbers ORDER BY NEWID()),
        (SELECT TOP 1 Number FROM @Numbers ORDER BY NEWID()),
        (SELECT TOP 1 Number FROM @Numbers ORDER BY NEWID()),
       500,
       100,
        (SELECT TOP 1 Number FROM @Numbers ORDER BY NEWID()),
        (SELECT TOP 1 Number FROM @Numbers ORDER BY NEWID()),
        (SELECT CAST(DATEADD(dd,(SELECT TOP 1 Number - 10
                            FROM @Numbers
```

```
                            ORDER BY NEWID(), a.Number,
                            b.Number),GETDATE()) as DATE))
FROM @Numbers a
CROSS JOIN @Numbers b ;
```

As shown in Figure 7-3, by looking at the Storage tab of the Table Properties dialog box, we can see that the table has been created on the PRIMARY filegroup and is not partitioned.

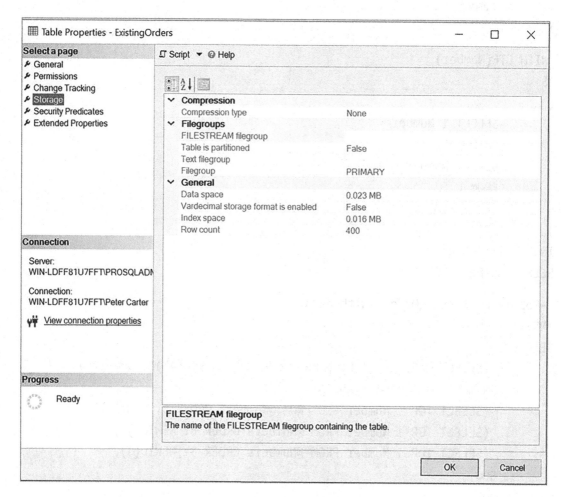

Figure 7-3. *Table properties nonpartitioned*

The script in Listing 7-5 now drops the clustered index of the ExistingOrders table and re-creates it on the PartScheme partition scheme. Again, the key line to note is the ON clause, which specifies PartScheme as the target partition function and passes in OrderDate as the partitioning key.

Listing 7-5. Moving the Existing Table onto the Partition Scheme

```
--Drop Clustered Index

ALTER TABLE dbo.ExistingOrders DROP CONSTRAINT PK_ExistingOrders ;
GO

--Re-created clustered index on PartScheme

ALTER TABLE dbo.ExistingOrders ADD  CONSTRAINT PK_ExistingOrders PRIMARY
KEY CLUSTERED
(
        OrderNumber ASC,
        OrderDate ASC
)WITH (PAD_INDEX = OFF, STATISTICS_NORECOMPUTE = OFF, SORT_IN_TEMPDB = OFF,
           IGNORE_DUP_KEY = OFF, ONLINE = OFF, ALLOW_ROW_LOCKS = ON,
           ALLOW_PAGE_LOCKS = ON) ON PartScheme(OrderDate) ;
GO
```

In Figure 7-4, you can see that if you look again at the Storage tab of the Table Properties dialog box, you find that the table is now partitioned against the PartScheme partition scheme.

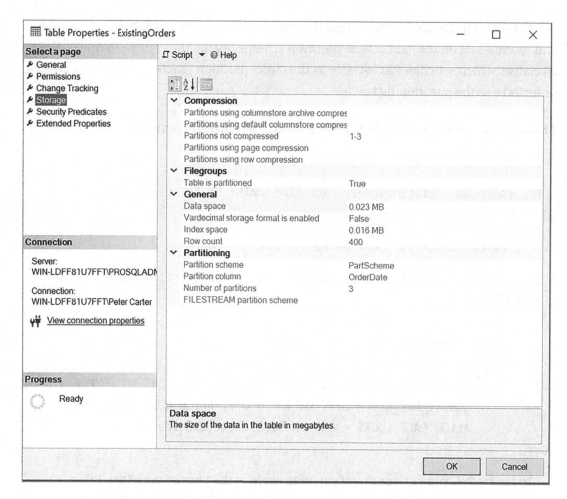

Figure 7-4. *Table properties partitioned*

Monitoring Partitioned Tables

You may wish to keep track of the number of rows in each partition of your table. Doing so allows you to ensure that your rows are being distributed evenly. If they are not, then you may wish to reassess your partitioning strategy to ensure you get the full benefit from the technology. You can view distribution by using the Disk Usage by Partition report in SSMS. If you require a programmatic solution, however, you can use the $PARTITION function as discussed in the following section.

$PARTITION Function

You can determine how many rows are in each partition of your table by using the
$PARTITION function. When you run this function against the partition function, it
accepts the column name of your partitioning key as a parameter, as demonstrated in
Listing 7-6.

Listing 7-6. Using the $PARTITION Function

```
SELECT
        COUNT(*) 'Number of Rows'
        ,$PARTITION.PartFunc(OrderDate) 'Partition'
FROM dbo.ExistingOrders
GROUP BY $PARTITION.PartFunc(OrderDate) ;
```

From the results in Figure 7-5, you can see that all of the rows in our table sit in the
same partition, which pretty much defies the point of partitioning and means that we
should reassess our strategy.

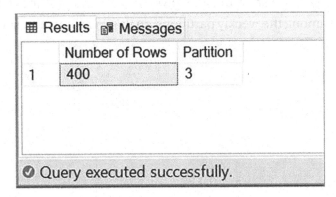

Figure 7-5. *The $PARTITION function run against a partitioned table*

We can also use the $PARTITION function to assess how a table would be partitioned
against a different partition function. This can help us plan to resolve the issue with our
ExistingOrders table. The script in Listing 7-7 creates a new partition function, called
PartFuncWeek, which creates weekly partitions for the month of March 2022. It then uses
the $PARTITION function to determine how the rows of our ExistingOrders table will
be split if we implemented this strategy. For the time being, we do not need to create a

partition scheme or repartition the table. Before running the script, change the boundary point values so they are based upon the date when you run the script. This is because the data in the table is generated using the GETDATE() function.

Listing 7-7. $PARTITION Function Against a New Partition Function

```
--Create new partition function
CREATE PARTITION FUNCTION PartFuncWeek(DATE)
AS RANGE LEFT
FOR VALUES ('2022-03-7','2022-03-14','2022-03-21','2022-03-28') ;

--Assess spread of rows
SELECT
        COUNT(*) 'Number of Rows'
        ,$PARTITION.PartFuncWeek(OrderDate) 'Partition'
FROM dbo.ExistingOrders
GROUP BY $PARTITION.PartFuncWeek(OrderDate) ;
```

The results in Figure 7-6 show that the rows of the ExistingOrders table are fairly evenly distributed among the weekly partitions, so this may provide a suitable strategy for our table.

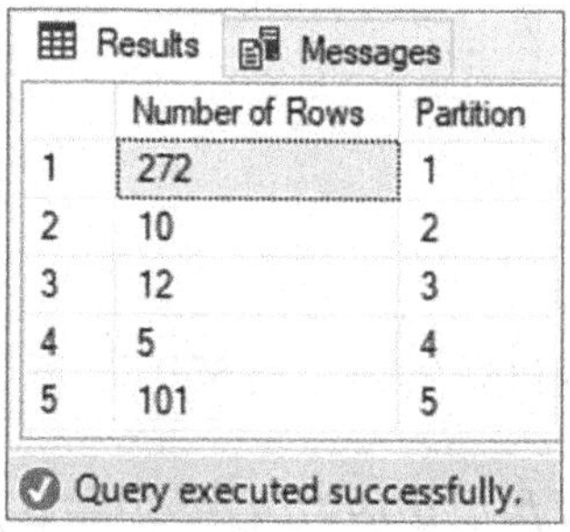

	Number of Rows	Partition
1	272	1
2	10	2
3	12	3
4	5	4
5	101	5

Query executed successfully.

Figure 7-6. *$PARTITION function against a new partition function*

Tip   Due to the randomization, your results may vary.

Sliding Windows

Our weekly partitioning strategy seems to work well, but what about when we reach December? As it currently stands, all new order placed after 28th November 2022 will all end up in the same partition, which will just grow and grow. To combat this issue, SQL Server provides us with the tools to create sliding windows. In our case, this means that each week, a new partition will be created for the following week and the earliest partition will be removed.

To achieve this, we can use the SPLIT, MERGE, and SWITCH operations. The SPLIT operation adds a new boundary point, thus creating a new partition. The MERGE operation removes a boundary point, thus merging two partitions together. The SWITCH operation moves a partition into an empty table or partition.

In our scenario, we create a staging table, called OldOrdersStaging. We use this table as a staging area to hold the data from our earliest partition. Once in the staging table, you can perform whatever operations or transformation may be required. For example, your developers may wish to create a script, to roll the data up, and to transfer it to a historical Orders table. Even though the OldOrdersStaging table is designed as a temporary object, it is important to note that you cannot use a temporary table. Instead, you must use a permanent table and *drop* it at the end. This is because temporary tables reside in TempDB, which means that they will be on a different filegroup, and SWITCH will not work. SWITCH is a metadata operation, and therefore, both partitions involved must reside on the same filegroup.

The script in Listing 7-8 implements a sliding window. First, it creates a staging table for the older orders. The indexes and constraints of this table must be the same as those of the partitioned table. The table must also reside on the same filegroup in order for the SWITCH operation to succeed. It then determines the highest and lowest boundary point values in the partitioned table, which it will use as parameters for the SPLIT and MERGE operations. It then uses the ALTER PARTITION FUNCTION command to remove the lowest boundary point value and add in the new boundary point. Finally, it reruns the $PARTITION function to display the new distribution of rows and interrogates the sys. partition_functions and sys.partition_range_values catalog views to display the new boundary point values for the PartFuncWeek partition function. The script assumes that the PartSchemeWeek partition scheme has been created and the ExistingOrders table has been moved to this partition scheme.

Listing 7-8. Implementing a Sliding Window

```
--Create the OldOrders table

CREATE TABLE dbo.OldOrdersStaging(
        [OrderNumber] [int] IDENTITY(1,1) NOT NULL,
         [OrderDate] [date] NOT NULL,
         [CustomerID] [int] NOT NULL,
         [ProductID] [int] NOT NULL,
         [Quantity] [int] NOT NULL,
         [NetAmount] [money] NOT NULL,
         [TaxAmount] [money] NOT NULL,
         [InvoiceAddressID] [int] NOT NULL,
         [DeliveryAddressID] [int] NOT NULL,
         [DeliveryDate] [date] NULL,
 CONSTRAINT PK_OldOrdersStaging PRIMARY KEY CLUSTERED
(
        OrderNumber ASC,
        OrderDate ASC
)WITH (PAD_INDEX = OFF, STATISTICS_NORECOMPUTE = OFF, IGNORE_DUP_KEY = OFF,
          ALLOW_ROW_LOCKS = ON, ALLOW_PAGE_LOCKS = ON)
) ;
GO

--Calculate the lowest boundary point value

DECLARE @LowestBoundaryPoint DATE = (
        SELECT TOP 1 CAST(value  AS DATE)
        FROM sys.partition_functions pf
        INNER JOIN sys.partition_range_values prv
                ON pf.function_id = prv.function_id
        WHERE pf.name = 'PartFuncWeek'
        ORDER BY value ASC) ;

--Calculate the newest boundary point value

DECLARE @HighestboundaryPoint DATE = (
SELECT TOP 1 CAST(value  AS DATE)
```

```
        FROM sys.partition_functions pf
        INNER JOIN sys.partition_range_values prv
                ON pf.function_id = prv.function_id
        WHERE pf.name = 'PartFuncWeek'
        ORDER BY value DESC) ;
```

--Add 7 days to the newest boundary point value to determine the new boundary point

```
DECLARE @NewSplitRange DATE = (
        SELECT DATEADD(dd,7,@HighestboundaryPoint)) ;
```

--Switch the oldest partition to the OldOrders table

```
ALTER TABLE ExistingOrders
        SWITCH PARTITION 1 TO OldOrdersStaging PARTITION 2 ;
```

--Remove the oldest partition

```
ALTER PARTITION FUNCTION PartFuncWeek()
        MERGE RANGE(@LowestBoundaryPoint) ;
```

--Create the new partition

```
ALTER PARTITION FUNCTION PartFuncWeek()
        SPLIT RANGE(@NewSplitRange) ;
GO
```

--Re-run $PARTITION to assess new spread of rows

```
SELECT
        COUNT(*) 'Number of Rows'
        ,$PARTITION.PartFuncWeek(OrderDate) 'Partition'
FROM dbo.ExistingOrders
GROUP BY $PARTITION.PartFuncWeek(OrderDate) ;

SELECT name, value FROM SYS.partition_functions PF
INNER JOIN SYS.partition_range_values PFR ON PF.function_id = PFR.
function_id
WHERE name = 'PARTFUNCWEEK' ;
```

The results displayed in Figure 7-7 show how the partitions have been realigned.

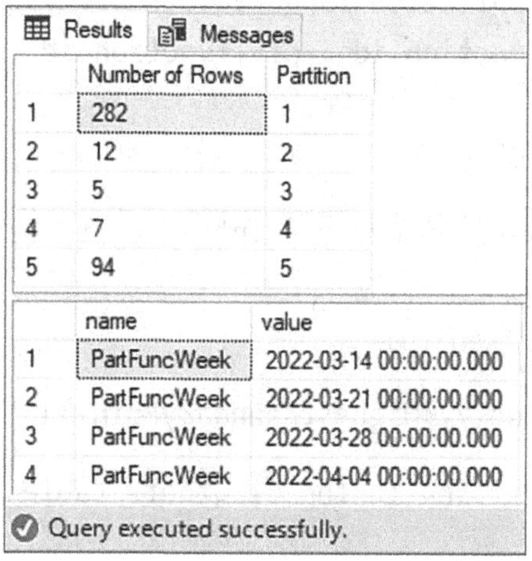
Results Messages

	Number of Rows	Partition
1	282	1
2	12	2
3	5	3
4	7	4
5	94	5

	name	value
1	PartFuncWeek	2022-03-14 00:00:00.000
2	PartFuncWeek	2022-03-21 00:00:00.000
3	PartFuncWeek	2022-03-28 00:00:00.000
4	PartFuncWeek	2022-04-04 00:00:00.000

Query executed successfully.

Figure 7-7. *New partition alignment*

When you are using the `SWITCH` function, there are several limitations. First, all nonclustered indexes of the table must be aligned with the base table. Also, the empty table or partition that you move the data into must have the same indexing structure. It must also reside on the same filegroup as the partition that you are switching out. This is because the `SWITCH` function does not actually move any data. It is a metadata operation that changes the pointers of the pages that make up the partition.

You can use `MERGE` and `SPLIT` with different filegroups, but there will be a performance impediment. Like `SWITCH`, `MERGE` and `SPLIT` can be performed as metadata operations if all partitions involved reside on the same filegroup. If they are on different filegroups, however, then physical data moves need to be performed by SQL Server, which can take substantially longer.

Partition Elimination

One of the key benefits of partitioning is that the Query Optimizer is able to access only the partitions required to satisfy the results of a query, instead of the entire table. For partition elimination to be successful, the partitioning key must be included as a filter in the `WHERE` clause. We can witness this functionality by running the query in Listing 7-9 against our `ExistingOrders` table and choosing the option to include the actual execution plan.

Listing 7-9. Query Using Partition Elimination

```
SELECT OrderNumber, OrderDate
FROM dbo.ExistingOrders
WHERE OrderDate BETWEEN '2022-03-02' AND '2022-03-06' ;
```

If we now view the execution plan and examine the properties of the Index Scan operator through Management Studio, we see that only one partition has been accessed, as shown in Figure 7-8.

| Actual Partition Count | 1 |
| Actual Partitions Accessed | 1 |

Figure 7-8. *Index Scan operator properties with partition elimination*

The partition elimination functionality can be a little fragile, however. For example, if you are manipulating the OrderDate column in any way, as opposed to just using it for evaluation, then partition elimination cannot occur. For example, if you cast the OrderDate column to the DATETIME2 data type, as demonstrated in Listing 7-10, then all partitions would need to be accessed. This issue can also impact partitioned indexes.

Listing 7-10. Query Not Using Partition Elimination

```
SELECT OrderNumber, OrderDate
FROM dbo.ExistingOrders
WHERE CAST(OrderDate AS DATETIME2) BETWEEN '2022-03-01' AND '2022-03-31' ;
```

Figure 7-9 illustrates the same properties of the Index Scan operator, viewed through Management Studio. Here you can see that all partitions have been accessed, as opposed to just one.

| Actual Partition Count | 3 |
| Actual Partitions Accessed | 1..3 |

Figure 7-9. *Index Scan properties, no partition elimination*

Table Compression

When you think of compression, it is natural to think of saving space at the expense of performance. However, this does not always hold true for SQL Server table compression. Compression in SQL Server can actually offer a performance benefit. This is because SQL Server is usually an I/O-bound application, as opposed to being CPU bound. This means that if SQL Server needs to read dramatically fewer pages from disk, then performance will increase, even if this is at the expense of CPU cycles. Of course, if your database is, in fact, CPU bound because you have very fast disks and only a single CPU core, for example, then compression could have a negative impact, because compression uses extra CPU, but this is atypical. In order to understand table compression, it helps to have insight into how SQL Server stores data within a page. Although a full discussion of page internals is beyond the scope of this book, Figure 7-10 gives you a high-level view of the default structure of an on-disk page and row.

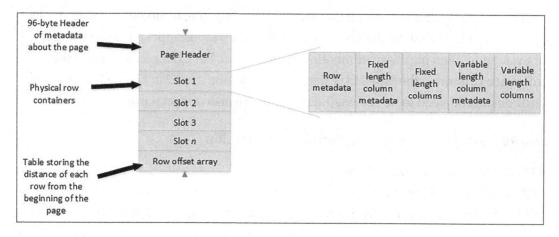

Figure 7-10. *Structure of a page*

Within the row, the row metadata contains details such as whether or not versioning information exists for the row and if the row has NULL values. The fixed-length column metadata records the length of the fixed-length portion of the page. The variable-length metadata includes a column offset array for the variable-length columns so that SQL Server can track where each column begins in relation to the beginning of the row.

Row Compression

On an uncompressed page, as just described, SQL Server stores fixed-length columns first, followed by variable-length columns. The only columns that can be variable length are columns with a variable-length data type, such as VARCHAR or VARBINARY. When row compression is implemented for a table, SQL Server uses the minimum amount of storage for other data types as well. For example, if you have an integer column that contains a NULL value in row 1, a value of 50 in row 2, and a value of 40,000 in row 3, then in row 1, the column does not use any space at all; it uses 1 byte in row 2, because it will store this value as a TINYINT; and it uses 4 bytes in row 3, because it will need to store this value as an INT. This is opposed to an uncompressed table using 4 bytes for every row, including row 1.

In addition, SQL Server also compresses Unicode columns so that characters that can be stored as a single byte only use a single byte, as opposed to 2 bytes, as they would in an uncompressed page. In order to achieve these optimizations, SQL Server has to use a different page format, which is outlined in Figure 7-11.

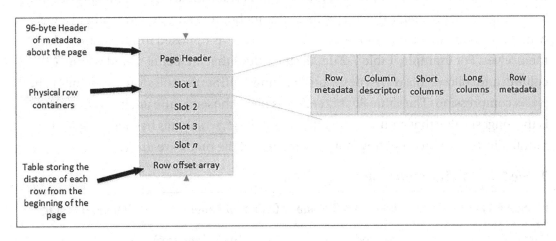

Figure 7-11. *Page structure with row compression*

Note   A short column is 8 bytes or less.

In Figure 7-11, the first area of row metadata contains details such as whether or not there is versioning information about the row and if any long data columns exist. The column descriptor contains the number of short columns and the length of each long column. The second area of metadata contains details such as versioning information and forwarding pointers for heaps.

Page Compression

When you implement page compression, row compression is implemented first. Page compression itself is actually comprised of two different forms of compression. The first is *prefix compression* and the second is *dictionary compression*. These compression types are outlined in the following sections.

Prefix Compression

Prefix compression works by establishing a common prefix for a column across rows within a page. Once the best prefix value has been established, SQL Server chooses the longest value that contains the full prefix as the anchor row and stores all other values within the column, as a differential of the anchor row, as opposed to storing the values themselves. For example, Table 7-2 details the values that are being stored within a column and follows this with a description of how SQL Server will store the values using prefix compression. The value Postfreeze has been chosen as the anchor value, since it is the longest value that contains the full prefix of Post, which has been identified. The number in <> is a marker of how many characters of the prefix are used.

Table 7-2. *Prefix Compression Differentials*

Column A Value	Column A Storage	Column B Value	Column B Storage
Postcode	<4>code	Teethings (Anchor)	—
Postfreeze (Anchor)	—	Teacher	<2>acher
Postpones	<4>pones	Teenager	<3>nager
Postilion	<4>ilion	Teeth	<5>
Imposters	<0>Imposters	Tent	<2>nt
Poacher	<2>acher	Rent	<0>Rent

Dictionary Compression

Dictionary compression is performed after all columns have been compressed using prefix compression. It looks across all columns within a page and finds values that match. The matching is performed using the binary representation of a value, which makes the process data-type agnostic. When it finds duplicate values, it adds them to a special dictionary at the top of the page, and in the row, it simply stores a pointer to the value's location in the dictionary. Table 7-3 expands on the previous table to give you an overview of this.

Table 7-3. *Dictionary Compression Pointers*

Column A Value	Column A Storage	Column B Value	Column B Storage
Postcode	<4>code	Teethings (Anchor)	—
Postfreeze (Anchor)	—	Teacher	[Pointer1]
Postpones	<4>pones	Teenager	<3>nager
Postilion	<4>ilion	Teeth	<5>
Imposters	<0>Imposters	Tent	<2>nt
Poacher	[Pointer1]	Rent	<0>Rent

Here, you can see that the value <2>acher, which appeared in both columns in the previous table, has been replaced with a pointer to the dictionary where the value is stored.

Page Compression Structure

In order to facilitate page compression, a special row is inserted in the page immediately after the page header, which contains the information regarding the anchor record and dictionary. This row is called the compression information record, and it is illustrated in Figure 7-12.

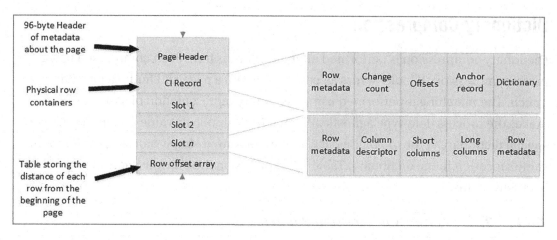

Figure 7-12. *Page structure with page compression*

The row metadata for the compression information record specifies if the record contains an anchor record and a dictionary. The change count records how many changes have been made to the page, which may affect the usefulness of the anchor and dictionary. When a table is rebuilt, SQL Server can use this information to determine if the page should be rebuilt. The offsets contain the start and end locations of the dictionary, from the beginning of the page. The anchor record contains each column's prefix value and the dictionary contains the duplicate values for which pointers have been created.

Columnstore Compression

Columnstore indexes are always compressed, automatically. This means that if you create a clustered columnstore index on your table, your table is also compressed, and this cannot be combined with row or page compression. There are two types of columnstore compression available to you: COLUMNSTORE and COLUMNSTORE_ARCHIVE.

You can think of COLUMNSTORE as the standard compression type for columnstore indexes and you should only use the COLUMNSTORE_ARCHIVE algorithm for data that is infrequently accessed. This is because this compression algorithm breaks the rules for SQL Server data compression as far as performance goes. If you implement this algorithm, expect a very high compression ratio, but prepare for it to be at the expense of query performance.

XML Compression

SQL Server 2022 introduces compression for XML data. The functionality reduces the amount of space used for XML data that is stored in overflow allocation units, at the expense of CPU cycles.

Tip   Columns, which have small data types, such as integers, are stored within the data page that contains the row. A row cannot span multiple data pages, however. Data types, such as VARCHAR( ) and XML, however, could cause a row to overflow the 8060 bytes available within the body of a page (8192 bytes—a 96-byte page header). SQL Server works around this by placing the data in separate allocation units, associated to the same table. These are called overflow allocation units.

XML compression can be implemented on tables that have XML columns and on XML indexes. When used with a table, it is important to note that it is a table-level setting. Therefore, you cannot have a mix of compression on and off for different XML columns within the same table.

The default for XML compression is Off and Primary XML indexes do not inherit the compression settings from table. Likewise, secondary XML indexes do not inherit their compression setting from Primary XML index. Therefore, if you want to use XML compression on a table and all its indexes, you should turn compression on in the table and in all indexes. Listing 7-11 demonstrates how to turn on XML compression for a table.

Tip   XML indexes are discussed in Chapter 8.

Listing 7-11. Turn On XML Compression

```
CREATE TABLE XMLData
(
    ID      INT     IDENTITY    PRIMARY KEY,
    XMLData         XML
)
WITH (XML_COMPRESSION = ON)
```

Implementing Compression

The planning and implementation of row and page compression is a straightforward process, and it is discussed in the following sections.

Selecting the Compression Level

As you probably realized from the earlier descriptions of row and page compression, page compression offers a higher compression ratio than row compression, which means better I/O performance. However, this is at the expense of CPU cycles, both when the table is being compressed and again when it is being accessed. Therefore, before you start compressing your tables, make sure you understand how much each of these compression types will reduce the size of your table so that you can assess how much I/O efficiency you can achieve.

You can accomplish this by using a system stored procedure called sp_estimate_data_compression_savings. This procedure estimates the amount of space that you could save by implementing compression. It accepts the parameters listed in Table 7-4.

Table 7-4. *sp_estimate_data_compression_savings Parameters*

Parameter	Comments
@schema_name	The name of the schema, which contains the table that you want to run the procedure against.
@object_name	The name of the table that you want to run the procedure against.
@index_ID	Pass in NULL for all indexes. For a heap, the index ID is always 0 and a clustered index always has an ID of 1.
@partition_number	Pass in NULL for all partitions.
@data_compression	Pass in ROW, PAGE, COLUMNSTORE, COLUMNSTORE_ARCHIVE, or NONE if you want to assess the impact of removing compression from a table that is already compressed.

The two executions of the sp_estimate_data_compression_savings stored procedure in Listing 7-12 assess the impact of row and page compression, respectively, on all partitions of our ExistingOrders table.

Listing 7-12. Sp_ estimate_data_compression_savings

```
EXEC sp_estimate_data_compression_savings @schema_name = 'dbo', @object_
name = 'ExistingOrders',
    @index_id = NULL, @partition_number = NULL, @data_compression ='ROW' ;

EXEC sp_estimate_data_compression_savings @schema_name = 'dbo', @object_
name = 'ExistingOrders',
    @index_id = NULL, @partition_number = NULL, @data_compression =
    'PAGE' ;
```

The results in Figure 7-13 show that for the two partitions that are currently in use, page compression will have no additional benefit over row compression. Therefore, it is pointless to add the extra CPU overhead associated with page compression. This is because row compression is always implemented on every row of every page in the table. Page compression, on the other hand, is assessed on a page-by-page basis, and only pages that will benefit from being compressed are rebuilt. Because of the random nature of the largely numeric data that we inserted into this table, SQL Server has determined that the pages of our table will not benefit from page compression.

	object_name	schema_name	index_id	partition_number	size_with_current_compression_setting(KB)	size_with_requested_compression_setting(KB)	sample_size_with_current_compression_setting(KB)	sample_size_with_requested_compress
1	ExistingOrders	dbo	1	1	0	0	0	0
2	ExistingOrders	dbo	1	2	0	0	0	0
3	ExistingOrders	dbo	1	3	40	32	48	40

	object_name	schema_name	index_id	partition_number	size_with_current_compression_setting(KB)	size_with_requested_compression_setting(KB)	sample_size_with_current_compression_setting(KB)	sample_size_with_requested_compress
1	ExistingOrders	dbo	1	1	0	0	0	0
2	ExistingOrders	dbo	1	2	0	0	0	0
3	ExistingOrders	dbo	1	3	40	8	48	16

Figure 7-13. *Results of sp_estimate_data_compression_savings*

Tip SQL Server supports Columnstore indexes in sp_estimate_data_compression_savings. The compression types COLUMNSTORE and COLUMNSTORE_ARCHIVE can now be used as both a source object and a compression type. Columnstore compression is discussed in the "Columnstore Compression" section of this chapter.

Compressing Tables and Partitions

We determined that row compression reduces the size of our table, but we can't gain any further benefits by implementing page compression. Therefore, we can compress our entire table using the command in Listing 7-13.

Listing 7-13. Implementing Row Compression on the Entire Table

```
ALTER TABLE ExistingOrders
    REBUILD WITH (DATA_COMPRESSION = ROW) ;
```

If we look more closely at the results, however, we can see that, in fact, only partition 1 benefits from row compression. Partition 2 remains the same size. Therefore, it is not worth the overhead to compress partition 2. Running the ALTER TABLE statement in Listing 7-14 will rebuild only partition 1. It will then remove compression from the entire table by rebuilding it with DATA_COMPRESSION = NONE.

Listing 7-14. Implementing Row Compression for Specific Partitions

```
--Compress partition 1 with ROW compression

ALTER TABLE ExistingOrders
    REBUILD PARTITION = 1 WITH (DATA_COMPRESSION = ROW) ;
GO

--Remove compression from the whole table

ALTER TABLE ExistingOrders
    REBUILD WITH (DATA_COMPRESSION = NONE) ;
```

Data Compression Wizard

The Data Compression Wizard can be reached via the context menu of a table by drilling down through Storage ➤ Manage Compression. It provides a graphical user interface (GUI) for managing compression. The main page of the wizard is illustrated in Figure 7-14. On this screen, you can utilize the Use same compression type for all partitions option to implement one type of compression uniformly across the table. Alternatively, you can specify different compression types for each individual partition. The Calculate button runs the sp_estimate_data_compression_savings stored procedure and displays the current and estimated results for each partition.

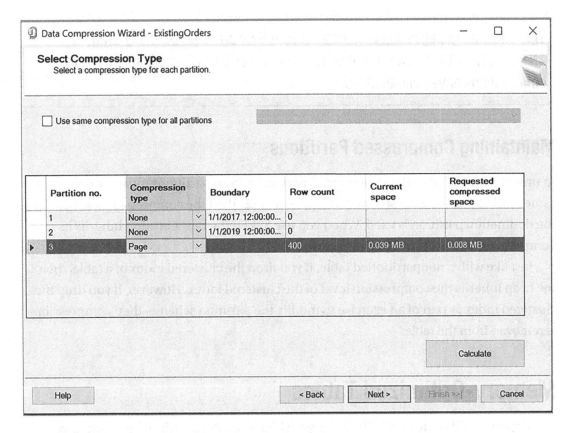

Figure 7-14. The Data Compression Wizard

On the final page of the wizard, you can choose to run the process immediately, script the action, or schedule it to run using SQL Server Agent.

Maintaining Compression on Heaps

When new pages are added to a heap (a table without a Clustered Index), they are not automatically compressed with page compression. This means that rebuilding a compressed table should be part of your standard maintenance routines when it does not have a clustered index. To rebuild the compression on a table, you should remove compression and then reimplement it.

Tip   New heap pages will be compressed if they are inserted using INSERT INTO...WITH (TABLOCK) or if they are inserted as part of a bulk insert where optimizations have been enabled.

Maintaining Compressed Partitions

In order to use the SWITCH operation with partitions, both partitions must have the same level of compression selected. If you use MERGE, then the compression level of the destination partition is used. When you use SPLIT, the new partition inherits its compression level from the original partition.

Just like with a nonpartitioned table, if you drop the clustered index of a table, then the heap inherits the compression level of the clustered index. However, if you drop the clustered index as part of an exercise to modify the partition scheme, then compression is removed from the table.

Memory-Optimized Tables

In-Memory OLTP is a feature of SQL Server, which can offer significant performance improvements by storing all of the table's data in memory. This, of course, can dramatically reduce I/O despite the fact that the tables are also saved to disk for durability. This is because the disk-based version of the tables is stored in an unstructured format, outside of the database engine, using a FILESTREAM-based technology. Also, memory-optimized checkpoints happen a lot more frequently. An automatic checkpoint is taken after the transaction log has grown by 512MB since the last time an automatic checkpoint occurred. This removes I/O spikes that are associated with checkpoint activity. I/O contention on transaction logs can also be reduced with memory-optimized tables since less data is logged. It is also worth mentioning that only table changes are logged, not index changes.

In addition to minimizing I/O, In-Memory OLTP can also reduce CPU overhead. This is because natively compiled stored procedures can be used to access the data, as opposed to traditional, interpreted code. Natively compiled stored procedures use significantly fewer instructions, meaning less CPU time. Memory-optimized tables do not help reduce network overhead, however, because the same amount of data still needs to be communicated to the client.

By their very nature, memory-optimized tables increase memory pressure as opposed to reducing it, because even if you never use the data, it still sits in memory, reducing the amount of space available in which traditional resources can be cached. This means that in-memory functionality is designed for OLTP workloads as opposed to data warehousing workloads. The expectation is that fact and dimension tables within a data warehouse are too large to reside in memory.

As well as lower resource usage, memory-optimized tables can also help reduce contention. When you access data in a memory-optimized table, SQL Server does not take out a latch. This means that both latch and spinlock contention are automatically removed. Blocking between read and write transactions can also be reduced because of a new optimistic concurrency method for implementing isolation levels. Transactions and isolation levels, including memory optimized, are discussed in Chapter 18.

Durability

When creating memory-optimized tables, you can specify either SCHEMA_AND_DATA or SCHEMA_ONLY as the durability setting. If you select SCHEMA_AND_DATA, then all of the table's data are persisted to disk and transactions are logged. If you select SCHEMA_ONLY, however, then data is not persisted, and transactions are not logged. This means that after the SQL Server service is restarted, the structure of the table will remain intact, but it will contain no data. This can be useful for transient processes, such as data staging during an ETL load.

Creating and Managing Memory-Optimized Tables

Tip   At first glance, it may be tempting to use memory-optimized tables throughout your database. They have many limitations, however, and, in fact, you should only use them on an exception basis. These limitations will be discussed later in this section.

Before you can create a memory-optimized table, a memory-optimized filegroup must already exist. Memory-optimized filegroups are discussed in Chapter 6.

You create memory-optimized tables using the CREATE TABLE T-SQL statement, as you would for a disk-based table. The difference is that you must specify a WITH clause, which specifies that the table will be memory optimized. The WITH clause is also used to indicate the level of durability that you require.

Memory-optimized tables must also include an index. We fully discuss indexes, including indexes for memory-optimized tables, in Chapter 8, but for now, you should know that memory-optimized tables support the following types of indexes:

- Nonclustered hash index

- Nonclustered index

Hash indexes are organized into buckets, and when you create them, you must specify a bucket count using the BUCKET_COUNT parameter. Ideally, your bucket count should be two times the number of distinct values within the index key. You will not always know how many distinct values you have; in such cases, you may wish to significantly increase the BUCKET_COUNT. The trade-off is that the more buckets you have, the more memory the index consumes. Once you have created the table, the index will be a fixed size and it is not possible to alter the table or its indexes.

The script in Listing 7-15 creates a memory-optimized table called OrdersMem with full durability and populates it with data. It creates a nonclustered hash index on the ID column with a bucket count of 2,000,000, since we will be inserting 1,000,000 rows. The script assumes that the memory-optimized filegroup has already been created.

Listing 7-15. Creating a Memory-Optimized Table

```
USE [Chapter7]
GO

CREATE TABLE dbo.OrdersMem(
        OrderNumber int IDENTITY(1,1) NOT NULL PRIMARY KEY
        NONCLUSTERED HASH
                                WITH (BUCKET_COUNT= 2000000),
        OrderDate date NOT NULL,
        CustomerID int NOT NULL,
        ProductID int NOT NULL,
        Quantity int NOT NULL,
        NetAmount money NOT NULL,
```

```
        TaxAmount money NOT NULL,
        InvoiceAddressID int NOT NULL,
        DeliveryAddressID int NOT NULL,
        DeliveryDate date NULL,
)WITH (MEMORY_OPTIMIZED = ON, DURABILITY = SCHEMA_AND_DATA) ;

DECLARE @Numbers TABLE
(
        Number          INT
)

;WITH CTE(Number)
AS
(
        SELECT 1 Number
        UNION ALL
        SELECT Number + 1
        FROM CTE
        WHERE Number < 100
)
INSERT INTO @Numbers
SELECT Number FROM CTE ;

--Populate ExistingOrders with data

INSERT INTO dbo.OrdersMem
SELECT
        (SELECT CAST(DATEADD(dd,(SELECT TOP 1 Number
                                FROM @Numbers
                                ORDER BY NEWID()),getdate())as DATE)),
        (SELECT TOP 1 Number -10 FROM @Numbers ORDER BY NEWID()),
        (SELECT TOP 1 Number FROM @Numbers ORDER BY NEWID()),
        (SELECT TOP 1 Number FROM @Numbers ORDER BY NEWID()),
        500,
        100,
        (SELECT TOP 1 Number FROM @Numbers ORDER BY NEWID()),
        (SELECT TOP 1 Number FROM @Numbers ORDER BY NEWID()),
```

```
                   (SELECT CAST(DATEADD(dd,(SELECT TOP 1 Number - 10
                                        FROM @Numbers
                                        ORDER BY NEWID()),getdate()) as DATE))
FROM @Numbers a
CROSS JOIN @Numbers b
CROSS JOIN @Numbers c ;
```

Performance Profile

While memory-optimized tables were in development, they were known as *Hekaton*, which is a play on words, meaning 100 times faster. So let's see how performance compares for different query types between in-memory and disk-based tables. The code in Listing 7-16 creates a new table, called OrdersDisc, and populates it with the data from OrdersMem so that you can run fair tests against the two tables.

Note   For this benchmarking, the tests are running on a VM, with 2×2 core vCPUs, 8GB RAM, and a hybrid SSHD (solid-state hybrid technology) SATA disk.

Listing 7-16. Creating a Disk-Based Table and Populating It with Data

```
USE [Chapter7]
GO

CREATE TABLE dbo.OrdersDisc(
        OrderNumber int NOT NULL,
        OrderDate date NOT NULL,
        CustomerID int NOT NULL,
        ProductID int NOT NULL,
        Quantity int NOT NULL,
        NetAmount money NOT NULL,
        TaxAmount money NOT NULL,
        InvoiceAddressID int NOT NULL,
        DeliveryAddressID int NOT NULL,
        DeliveryDate date NULL,
 CONSTRAINT [PK_OrdersDisc] PRIMARY KEY CLUSTERED
```

```
(
        [OrderNumber] ASC,
        [OrderDate] ASC
)
) ;
INSERT INTO dbo.OrdersDisc
        SELECT *
        FROM dbo.OrdersMem ;
```

First, we will run the most basic test—a SELECT * query from each table. The script in Listing 7-17 runs these queries after tearing down the plan cache and the buffer cache to ensure a fair test.

Listing 7-17. The SELECT * Benchmark

```
SET STATISTICS TIME ON

--Tear down the plan cache

DBCC FREEPROCCACHE

--Tear down the buffer cache

DBCC DROPCLEANBUFFERS

--Run the benchmarks

SELECT *
FROM dbo.OrdersMem ;

SELECT *
FROM dbo.OrdersDisc ;
```

Tip   Listing 7-17 uses DBCC FREEPROCCACHE to remove execution plans from the cache. It removes all plans from the plan cache. If you wanted to remove plans for a specific database, however, then you could do so by using ALTER DATABASE SCOPED CONFIGURATION CLEAR PROCEDURE_CACHE.

From the results in Figure 7-15, you can see that the memory-optimized table returned the results just under 4.5% faster.

Tip Naturally, the results you see may vary based on the system on which you run the scripts. For example, if you have SSDs, then the queries against the disk-based tables may be more comparable. Also, be aware that this test uses cold data (not in the buffer cache). If the data in the disk-based tables is warm (in the buffer cache), then you can expect the results to be comparable, or in some cases, the query against the disk-based table may even be slightly faster.

```
(1000000 row(s) affected)

SQL Server Execution Times:
   CPU time = 109 ms,  elapsed time = 7688 ms.

(1000000 row(s) affected)

SQL Server Execution Times:
   CPU time = 94 ms,  elapsed time = 8132 ms.
```

Figure 7-15. *SELECT * benchmark results*

In the next test, we see what happens if we add in an aggregation. The script in Listing 7-18 runs COUNT(*) queries against each of the tables.

Listing 7-18. The COUNT(*) Benchmark

```
SET STATISTICS TIME ON

--Tear down the plan cache

DBCC FREEPROCCACHE

--Tear down the buffer cache

DBCC DROPCLEANBUFFERS

--Run the benchmarks
```

```
SELECT COUNT(*)
FROM dbo.OrdersMem ;

SELECT COUNT(*)
FROM dbo.OrdersDisc ;
```

From the results in Figure 7-16, we can see that this time, the memory-optimized tabled performed considerably better than the disk-based table, offering us a 340% performance improvement over the disk-based table.

```
(1 row(s) affected)

 SQL Server Execution Times:
   CPU time = 172 ms,  elapsed time = 171 ms.

(1 row(s) affected)

 SQL Server Execution Times:
   CPU time = 63 ms,  elapsed time = 582 ms.
```

Figure 7-16. *COUNT(*) benchmark results*

It is also interesting to see how memory-optimized tables compare to disk-based tables when there is a filter on the OrderNumber column, since this column is covered by an index on both tables. The script in Listing 7-19 adds the data in the NetAmount column, but it also filters on the OrderNumber column so that only OrderNumbers over 950,000 are considered.

Listing 7-19. Primary Key Filter Benchmark

```
SET STATISTICS TIME ON

--Tear down the plan cache

DBCC FREEPROCCACHE

--Tear down the buffer cache

DBCC DROPCLEANBUFFERS

--Run the benchmarks

SELECT SUM(NetAmount)
FROM dbo.OrdersMem
```

```
WHERE OrderNumber > 950000 ;

SELECT SUM(NetAmount)
FROM dbo.OrdersDisc
WHERE OrderNumber > 950000 ;
```

In this instance, because the memory-optimized table was scanned but the clustered index on the disk-based table was able to perform an index seek, the disk-based table performed approximately ten times faster than the memory-optimized table. This is illustrated in Figure 7-17.

```
(1 row(s) affected)

 SQL Server Execution Times:
   CPU time = 203 ms,  elapsed time = 220 ms.
SQL Server parse and compile time:
   CPU time = 0 ms, elapsed time = 0 ms.

(1 row(s) affected)

 SQL Server Execution Times:
   CPU time = 0 ms,  elapsed time = 26 ms.
```

Figure 7-17. *SUM filtering on primary key benchmark results*

Note   We would have received a far superior performance for the final query on the memory-optimized table if we had implemented a nonclustered index as opposed to a nonclustered hash index, because a hash index requires an exact match as opposed to knowing a range, like a traditional index. Indexes are discussed further in Chapter 8.

Table Memory Optimization Advisor

The Table Memory Optimization Advisor is a wizard that can run against an existing disk-based table and it will walk you through the process of migration. The first page of the wizard checks your table for incompatible features, such as sparse columns and foreign key constraints against disk-based tables.

The following page provides you with a warning having to do with which features are not available for memory-optimized tables, such as distributed transactions and TRUNCATE TABLE statements.

The Migration Options page of the wizard allows you to specify the durability level of the table. Checking the box causes the table to be created with DURABILITY = SCHEMA_ ONLY. On this screen, you can also choose a new name for the disk-based table that you are migrating, since obviously, the new object cannot share the name of the existing object. Finally, you can use the check box to specify if you want the data from the existing table to be copied to the new table.

The Primary Key Migration page allows you to select the columns that you wish to use to form the primary key of the table as well as the index that you want to create on your table. If you choose a nonclustered hash index, you need to specify the bucket count, whereas if you choose a nonclustered index, you need to specify the columns and order.

The Summary screen of the wizard provides an overview of the activities that will be performed. Clicking the Migrate button causes the table to be migrated.

Caution   While the compatibility of memory-optimized tables with the SQL Server feature set has improved dramatically over the last few releases, there are still a number of features that memory-optimized tables do not support. A full list of nonsupported T-SQL constructs can be found at https://docs.microsoft. com/en-us/sql/relational-databases/in-memory-oltp/transact-sql-constructs-not-supported-by-in-memory-oltp?view=sql-server-ver16.

Natively Compiled Objects

In-Memory OLTP introduces native compilation, for both memory-optimized tables and for stored procedures, which can significantly improve performance. The following sections discuss these concepts.

Natively Compiled Tables

When you create a memory-optimized table, SQL Server compiles the table to a DLL (dynamic-link library) using native code and loads the DLL into memory. You can examine these DLLs by running the query in Listing 7-20. The script examines the dm_os_loaded_ modules DMV and then joins to sys.tables using the object_id of the table, which is embedded in the file name of the DLL. This allows the query to return the name of the table.

Listing 7-20. Viewing DLLs for Memory-Optimized Tables

```
SELECT
        m.name DLL
        ,t.name TableName
        ,description
FROM sys.dm_os_loaded_modules m
INNER JOIN sys.tables t
        ON t.object_id =
(SELECT SUBSTRING(m.name, LEN(m.name) + 2 - CHARINDEX('_',
REVERSE(m.name)),
len(m.name) - (LEN(m.name) + 2 - CHARINDEX('_', REVERSE(m.name)) + 3) ))
WHERE m.name like '%xtp_t_' + cast(db_id() as varchar(10)) + '%' ;
```

For security reasons, these files are recompiled based on database metadata every time the SQL Server service starts. This means that if the DLLs are tampered with, the changes made will not persist. Additionally, the files are linked to the SQL Server process to prevent them from being modified.

SQL Server automatically removes the DLLs when they are no longer needed. After a table has been dropped and a checkpoint has subsequently been issued, the DLLs are unloaded from memory and physically deleted from the file system, either when the instance is restarted or when the databases are taken offline, or dropped.

Natively Compiled Stored Procedures

In addition to natively compiled memory-optimized tables, SQL Server also supports natively compiled stored procedures. As mentioned earlier in this chapter, these procedures can reduce CPU overhead and offer a performance benefit over traditionally interpreted stored procedures because fewer CPU cycles are required during their execution.

The syntax for creating a natively compiled stored procedure is similar to the syntax for creating an interpreted stored procedure, but there are some subtle differences. First, the procedure must start with a BEGIN ATOMIC clause. The body of the procedure must include precisely one BEGIN ATOMIC clause. The transaction within this block will commit when the block ends. The block must terminate with an END statement. When you begin the atomic block, you *must* specify the isolation level and the language to use.

You will also notice that the WITH clause contains NATIVE_COMPILATION, SCHEMABINDING, and EXECUTE AS options. SCHEMABINDING must be specified for natively compiled procedures. This prevents the objects on which it depends from being altered. You must also specify the EXECUTE AS clause because the default value for EXECUTE AS is Caller, but this is not a supported option for native compilation. This has implications if you are looking to migrate your existing interpreted SQL to natively compiled procedures, and it means that you should reassess your security policy as a prerequisite to code migration. The option is fairly self-explanatory.

You can see an example of creating a natively compiled stored procedure in Listing 7-21. This procedure can be used to update the OrdersMem table.

Listing 7-21. Creating a Natively Compiled Stored Procedure

```
CREATE PROCEDURE UpdateOrdersMem
        WITH NATIVE_COMPILATION, SCHEMABINDING, EXECUTE AS OWNER
AS
BEGIN ATOMIC WITH (TRANSACTION ISOLATION LEVEL = SNAPSHOT, LANGUAGE =
'English')
        UPDATE dbo.OrdersMem
                SET DeliveryDate = DATEADD(dd,1,DeliveryDate)
        WHERE DeliveryDate < GETDATE()
END ;
```

When planning a code migration to natively compiled procedures, you should advise your development teams that there are many limitations, and they will not be able to use features including table variables, CTEs (common table expressions), subqueries, the OR operator in WHERE clauses, and UNION.

Like memory-optimized tables, DLLs are also created for natively compiled stored procedures. The modified script in Listing 7-22 displays a list of DLLs associated with natively compiled procedures.

Listing 7-22. Viewing DLLs for Natively Compiled Procedures

```
SELECT
        m.name DLL
        ,o.name ProcedureName
        ,description
FROM sys.dm_os_loaded_modules m
INNER JOIN sys.objects o
        ON o.object_id =
(SELECT SUBSTRING(m.name, LEN(m.name) + 2 - CHARINDEX('_',
REVERSE(m.name)),
len(m.name) - (LEN(m.name) + 2 - CHARINDEX('_', REVERSE(m.name)) + 3) ))
WHERE m.name like '%xtp_p_' + cast(db_id() as varchar(10)) + '%' ;
```

Summary

SQL Server offers many features for optimizing tables. Partitioning allows tables to be split down into smaller structures, which means that SQL Server can read fewer pages in order to locate the rows that it needs to return. This process is called partition elimination. Partitioning also allows you to perform storage tiering by storing older, less frequently accessed data on inexpensive storage.

SWITCH, SPLIT, and MERGE operations will help you implement sliding windows for your partitioned tables. SWITCH allows you to move data from its current partition to an empty partition or table as a metadata operation. SPLIT and MERGE allow you to insert and remove boundary points in a partition function.

Two compression options are available for row-based tables. These types of compression are designed as a performance enhancement, because they allow SQL Server to reduce the amount of I/O it needs to read all of the required rows from a table. Row compression works by storing numeric and Unicode values in the smallest space required, rather than the largest space required, for any acceptable value. Page compression implements row compression, and also prefix and dictionary compression. This provides a higher compression ratio, meaning even less I/O, but at the expense of CPU.

Columnstore indexes have two compression methods. COLUMNSTORE is the standard compression type. COLUMNSTORE_ARCHIVE should only be used for infrequently accessed data.

Memory-optimized tables are a feature of SQL Server, which enable massive performance gains by keeping an entire table resident in memory. This can significantly reduce I/O pressure. You can use such tables in conjunction with natively compiled stored procedures, which can also increase performance, by interacting directly with the natively compiled DLLs of the memory-optimized tables and by reducing the CPU cycles required, as compared to interpreted code.

CHAPTER 8

Indexes and Statistics

Recent versions of SQL Server support many different types of index that are used to enhance query performance. These include traditional clustered and nonclustered indexes, which are built on B-tree (balanced-tree) structures and enhance read performance on disk-based tables. There are also indexes that support complex data types, such as XML, JSON, and geospatial data types. These advanced data type indexes are beyond the scope of this book, but a full discussion can be found in the Apress title *SQL Server Advanced Data Types*, which can be found at www.apress.com/gp/book/9781484239001. DBAs can also create Columnstore indexes to support data warehouse–style queries, where analysis is performed on very large tables. SQL Server also supports in-memory indexes, which enhance the performance of tables that are stored using In-Memory OLTP. This chapter discusses many of the available index types inside the Database Engine.

SQL Server maintains statistics on index and table columns to enhance query performance by improving cardinality estimates. This allows the Query Optimizer to create an efficient query plan. This chapter also discusses how to use and maintain statistics.

Clustered Indexes

A *B-tree* is a data structure you can use to organize key values so a user can search for the data they are looking for much more quickly than if they had to read the entire table. It is a tree-based structure where each node is allowed more than two child nodes. The tree is balanced, meaning there will always be the same number of steps to retrieve any single row of data.

© Peter A. Carter 2023
P. A. Carter, *Pro SQL Server 2022 Administration*, https://doi.org/10.1007/978-1-4842-8864-1_8

A *clustered index* is a B-tree structure that causes the data pages of a table to be logically stored in the order of the clustered index key. The clustered index key can be a single column or a set of columns that enforce uniqueness of each row in the table. This key is often the table's primary key, and although this is the most typical usage, in some circumstances, you will want to use a different column. This is discussed in more detail later in this chapter.

Tables Without a Clustered Index

When a table exists without a clustered index, it is known as a *heap*. A heap consists of an IAM (index allocation map) page(s) and a series of data pages that are not linked together or stored in order. The only way SQL Server can determine the pages of the table is by reading the IAM page(s). When a table is stored as a heap, without an index, then every time the table is accessed, SQL Server must read every single page in the table, even if you only want to return one row. The diagram in Figure 8-1 illustrates how a heap is structured.

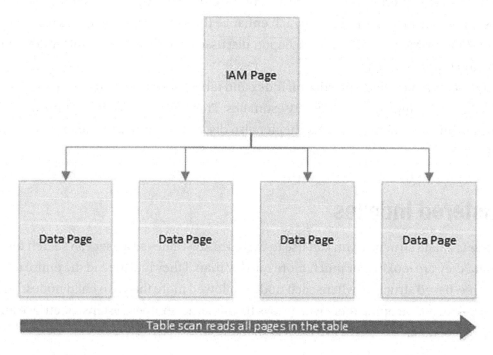

Figure 8-1. *Heap structure*

When data is stored on a heap, SQL Server needs to maintain a unique identifier for each row. It does this by creating a RID (row identifier). A RID has a format of `FileID: Page ID: Slot Number`, which is a physical location. Even if a table has nonclustered indexes, it is still stored as a heap, unless there is a clustered index. When nonclustered indexes are created on a heap, the RID is used as a pointer so that nonclustered indexes can link back to the correct row in the base table.

Tables with a Clustered Index

When you create a clustered index on a table, a B-tree structure is created. This B-tree is based on the values of the clustered key, and if the clustered index is not unique, it also includes a uniquifier. A *uniquifier* is a value used to identify rows if their key values are the same. This allows SQL Server to perform more efficient search operations by creating a tiered set of pointers to the data, as illustrated in Figure 8-2. The page at the top level of this hierarchy is called the *root node*. The bottom level of the structure is called the *leaf level*, and with a clustered index, the leaf level consists of the actual data pages of the table. B-tree structures can have one or more intermediate levels, depending on the size of the table.

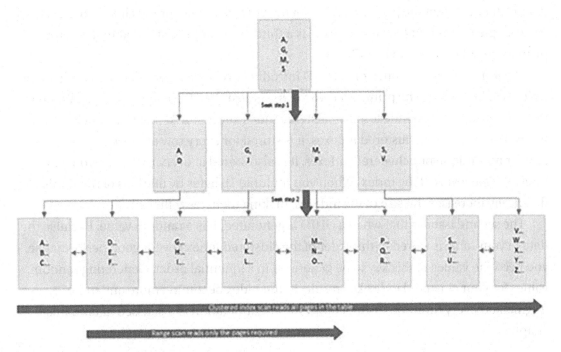

Figure 8-2. *Clustered index structure*

Figure 8-2 shows that although the leaf level is the data itself, the levels above contain pointers to the pages below them in the tree. This allows SQL Server to perform a seek operation, which is a very efficient method of returning a small number of rows. It works by navigating its way down the B-tree, using the pointers, to find the row(s) it requires. In this figure, we can see that if required, SQL Server can still scan all pages of the table in order to retrieve the required rows—this is known as a *clustered index scan.* Alternatively, SQL Server may decide to combine these two methods to perform a range scan. Here, SQL Server seeks the first value of the required range and then scans the leaf level until it encounters the first value that is not required. SQL Server can do this, because the table is ordered by the index key, which means that it can guarantee that no other matching values appear later in the table.

Clustering the Primary Key

The primary key of a table is often the natural choice for the clustered index, because many OLTP applications access 99% of data through the primary key. In fact, by default, unless you specify otherwise, or unless a clustered index already exists on the table, creating a primary key automatically generates a clustered index on that key. There are circumstances when the primary key is not the correct choice for the clustered index. An example of this that I have witnessed is a third-party application that requires the primary key of the table to be a GUID.

Creating a clustered index on a GUID introduces two major problems if the clustered index is to be built on the primary key. The first is size. A GUID is 16 bytes long. When a table has nonclustered indexes, the clustered index key is stored in every nonclustered index. For unique nonclustered indexes, it is stored for every row at the leaf level, and for nonunique nonclustered indexes, it is also stored at every row in the root and intermediate levels of the index. When you multiple 16 bytes by millions of rows, this drastically increases the size of the indexes, making them less efficient.

The second issue is that when a GUID is generated, it is a random value. Because the data in your table is stored in the order of the clustered index key for good performance, you need the values of this key to be generated in sequential order. Generating random values for your clustered index key results in the index becoming more and more fragmented every time you insert a new row. Fragmentation is discussed later in this chapter.

There is a workaround for the second issue, however. SQL Server has a function called NEWSEQUENTIALID(). This function always generates a GUID value that is higher than previous values generated on the server. Therefore, if you use this function in the default constraint of your primary key, you can enforce sequential inserts.

Caution   After the server has been restarted, NEWSEQUENTIALID() can start with a lower value. This may lead to fragmentation.

If the primary key must be a GUID or another wide column, such as a Social Security Number, or if it must be a set of columns that form a natural key, such as Customer ID, Order Date, and Product ID, then it is highly recommended that you create an additional column in your table. You can make this column an INT or BIGINT, depending on the number of rows you expect the table to have, and you can use either the IDENTITY property or a SEQUENCE in order to create a narrow, sequential key for your clustered index.

Tip   Remember a narrow clustered key is important because it will be included in all other indexes on the table.

Administering Clustered Indexes

You can create a clustered index by using the CREATE CLUSTERED INDEX statement, as shown in Listing 8-1. Other methods you can use to create a clustered index are using the ALTER TABLE statement with a PRIMARY KEY clause and using the INDEX clause in the CREATE TABLE statement, as long as you are using SQL Server 2014 or higher. This script creates a database called Chapter8 and then a table called CIDemo. Finally, it creates a clustered index on the ID column of this table.

Note   Remember to change the file locations to match your own configuration.

Listing 8-1. Creating a Clustered Index

```
--Create Chapter8 Database

CREATE DATABASE Chapter8
 ON  PRIMARY
( NAME = N'Chapter8', FILENAME =
    N'F:\Program Files\Microsoft SQL Server\MSSQL15.PROSQLADMIN\MSSQL\DATA\
    Chapter8.mdf'),
 FILEGROUP [MEM] CONTAINS MEMORY_OPTIMIZED_DATA  DEFAULT
( NAME = N'MEM', FILENAME = N'H:\DATA\CH08')
 LOG ON
( NAME = N'Chapter8_log', FILENAME =
    N'E:\Program Files\Microsoft SQL Server\MSSQL15.PROSQLADMIN\MSSQL\DATA\
    Chapter8_log.ldf') ;
GO

USE Chapter8
GO

--Create CIDemo table

CREATE TABLE dbo.CIDemo
(
        ID              INT                 IDENTITY,
        DummyText       VARCHAR(30)
) ;
GO

--Create clustered index

CREATE UNIQUE CLUSTERED INDEX CI_CIDemo ON dbo.CIDemo([ID]) ;
GO
```

When creating an index, you have a number of WITH options that you can specify. These options are outlined in Table 8-1.

Table 8-1. *Relational Index WITH Options*

Option	Description
MAXDOP	Specifies how many cores are used to build the index. Each core that is used builds its own portion of the index. The trade-off is that a higher MAXOP builds the index faster, but a lower MAXDOP means the index is built with less fragmentation.
FILLFACTOR	Specifies how much free space should be left in each page of the leaf level of the index. This can help reduce fragmentation caused by inserts at the expense of having a wider index, which requires more I/O to read. For a clustered index, with a nonchanging, ever-increasing key, always set this to 0, which means 100% full minus enough space for one row.
PAD_INDEX	Applies the fill factor percentage to the intermediate levels of the B-tree.
STATISTICS_ NORECOMPUTE	Turns on or off the automatic updating of distribution statistics. Statistics are discussed later in this chapter.
SORT_IN_TEMPDB	Specifies that the intermediate sort results of the index should be stored in TempDB. When you use this option, you can offload I/O to the spindles hosting TempDB, but this is at the expense of using more disk space. Cannot be ON if RESUMABLE is ON.
STATISTICS_ INCREMENTAL	Specifies if statistics should be created per partition. Limitations to this are discussed later in this chapter.
DROP_EXISTING	Used to drop and rebuild the existing index with the same name.
IGNORE_DUP_KEY	When you enable this option, an INSERT statement that tries to insert a duplicate key value into a unique index will not fail. Instead, a warning is generated and only the rows that break the unique constraint fail.
ONLINE	Can be set as ON or OFF, with a default of OFF. Specifies if the entire table and indexes should be locked for the duration of the index build or rebuild. If ON, then queries are still able to access the table during the operation. This is at the expense of the time it takes to build the index. For clustered indexes, this option is not available if the table contains LOB data.*

(continued)

Table 8-1. (*continued*)

Option	Description
OPTIMIZE_FOR_ SEQUENTIAL_KEY	Optimizes high concurrency inserts, where the index key is sequential. Introduced in SQL Server 2019, this feature is designed for indexes that suffer from last-page insert contention.
RESUMABLE	Can be set as ON or OFF, with a default of OFF. Specifies if the index creation or build can be paused and resumed, or can be resumed after a failure. Can only be set to ON if ONLINE is set to ON.
MAX_DURATION	Specifies, in minutes, the maximum duration that an index rebuild or rebuild will execute for, before pausing. Can only be specified if ONLINE is set to ON and RESUMABLE is set to ON.
ALLOW_ROW_LOCKS	Specifies that you can take row locks out when accessing the table. This does not means that they definitely will be taken.
ALLOW_PAGE_LOCKS	Specifies that you can take page locks out when accessing the table. This does not means that they definitely will be taken.
DATA_COMPRESSION	Allows you to specify ROW or PAGE, which denotes the type of compression that will be used for the index. Compression is discussed in Chapter 7. The default is NONE, which denotes that the index will not be compressed.
XML_COMPRESSION	Specifies if the index should use XML compression. XML Compression is discussed in Chapter 7.

*Spatial data is regarded as LOB data.

As mentioned earlier in this chapter, if you create a primary key on a table, then unless you specify the NONCLUSTERED keyword, or a clustered index already exists, a clustered index is created automatically to cover the column(s) of the primary key. Also, remember that at times you may wish to move the clustered index to a more suitable column if the primary key is wide or if it is not ever-increasing.

In order to achieve this, you need to drop the primary key constraint and then re-create it using the NONCLUSTERED keyword. This forces SQL Server to cover the primary key with a unique nonclustered index. Once this is complete, you are able to create the clustered index on the column of your choosing.

If you need to remove a clustered index that is not covering a primary key, you can do so by using the DROP INDEX statement, as demonstrated in Listing 8-2, which drops the clustered index that we created in the previous example.

Listing 8-2. Dropping the Index

```
DROP INDEX CI_CIDemo ON dbo.CIDemo ;
```

Nonclustered Indexes

A nonclustered index is based on a B-tree structure in the same way that a clustered index is. The difference is that the leaf level of a nonclustered index contains pointers to the data pages of the table, as opposed to being the data pages of the table, as illustrated in Figure 8-3. This means that a table can have multiple nonclustered indexes to support query performance.

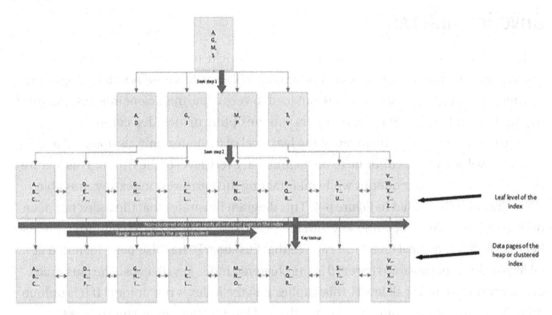

Figure 8-3. *Nonclustered index structure*

Just like a clustered index, a nonclustered index supports seek, scan, and range scan operations in order to find the required data. If the index key of the nonclustered index includes all columns that need to be accessed during a query, then you do not need for SQL Server to access the underlying table. This also holds true if the only columns

271

accessed are in the nonclustered index and the clustered index key. This is because the leaf level of a nonclustered index always contains the clustered index key. This is referred to as an index *covering the query*, which is discussed in the next section.

If the query needs to return columns that are not included in the nonclustered index or clustered index key, SQL Server needs to find the matching rows in the base table. This is done through a process called a *key lookup*. A key lookup operation accesses the rows required from the base table using either the clustered index key value or the RID if the table does not have a clustered index.

This can be efficient for a small number of rows, but it quickly becomes expensive if many rows are returned by the query. This means that if many rows will be returned, SQL Server may decide that it is less expensive to ignore the nonclustered index and use the clustered index or heap instead. This decision is known as *the tipping point* of the index. The tipping point varies from table to table, but it is generally between 0.5% and 2% of the table.

Covering Indexes

Although having all required columns within the nonclustered index means that you do not have to retrieve data from the underlying table, the trade-off is that having many columns within a nonclustered index can lead to very wide, inefficient indexes. In order to gain a better balance, SQL Server offers you the option of included columns.

Included columns are included at the leaf level of the index only, as opposed to the index key values, which continue to be included at every level of the B-tree. This feature can help you cover your queries while maintaining the narrowest index keys possible. This concept is illustrated in Figure 8-4. This diagram illustrates that the index has been built using `Balance` as the index key, but the `FirstName` and `LastName` columns have also been included at the leaf level. You can see that `CustomerID` has also been included at all levels; this is because `CustomerID` is the clustered index key. Because the clustered index key is included at all levels, this implies that the index is not unique. If it is unique, then the clustered key is only included at the leaf level of the B-tree. This means that unique, nonclustered indexes are always narrower than their nonunique equivalents. This index is perfect for a query that filters on `Balance` in the `WHERE` clause and returns the `FirstName` and `LastName` columns. It also covers queries that returned `CustomerID` in the results.

Tip   If both the clustered and nonclustered indexes are nonunique, each level of the nonclustered B-tree includes the clustering uniquifier, as well as the clustered key.

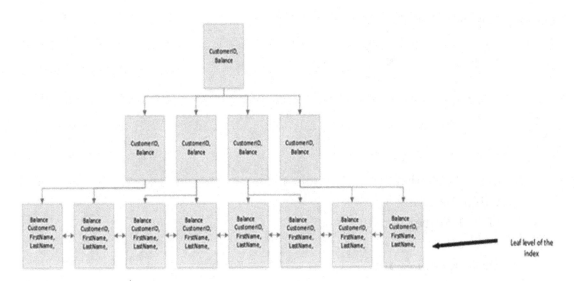

Figure 8-4. *Nonclustered index with included columns*

You can also use the index illustrated in Figure 8-4 to cover queries that filter on FirstName or LastName in the WHERE clause providing that other columns from the table are not returned. To process the query, however, SQL Server needs to perform an index scan, as opposed to an index seek or range scan, which is, of course, less efficient.

Administering Nonclustered Indexes

You can create nonclustered indexes using the CREATE NONCLUSTERED INDEX T-SQL statement. The script in Listing 8-3 creates a table called Customers and a table called Orders within the Chapter8 database. It then creates a foreign key constraint on the CustomerID column. Finally, a nonclustered index is created on the Balance column of the Customers table. Clustered indexes are created automatically on the primary key columns of each table.

Listing 8-3. Creating Tables and Then Adding a Nonclustered Index

```
USE Chapter8
GO

--Create and populate numbers table

DECLARE @Numbers TABLE
(
        Number          INT
)

;WITH CTE(Number)
AS
(
        SELECT 1 Number
        UNION ALL
        SELECT Number + 1
        FROM CTE
        WHERE Number < 100
)
INSERT INTO @Numbers
SELECT Number FROM CTE ;

--Create and populate name pieces

DECLARE @Names TABLE
(
        FirstName       VARCHAR(30),
        LastName        VARCHAR(30)
) ;

INSERT INTO @Names
VALUES('Peter', 'Carter'),
               ('Michael', 'Smith'),
               ('Danielle', 'Mead'),
               ('Reuben', 'Roberts'),
               ('Iris', 'Jones'),
```

```
                ('Sylvia', 'Davies'),
                ('Finola', 'Wright'),
                ('Edward', 'James'),
                ('Marie', 'Andrews'),
                ('Jennifer', 'Abraham') ;

--Create and populate Customers table

CREATE TABLE dbo.CustomersDisk
(
        CustomerID              INT                     NOT
NULL    IDENTITY    PRIMARY KEY,
        FirstName               VARCHAR(30)             NOT NULL,
        LastName                VARCHAR(30)             NOT NULL,
        BillingAddressID        INT                     NOT NULL,
        DeliveryAddressID       INT                     NOT NULL,
        CreditLimit             MONEY                   NOT NULL,
        Balance                 MONEY                   NOT NULL
) ;

SELECT * INTO #CustomersDisk
FROM
            (SELECT
                    (SELECT TOP 1 FirstName FROM @Names ORDER BY NEWID())
                    FirstName,
                    (SELECT TOP 1 LastName FROM @Names ORDER BY NEWID())
                    LastName,
                    (SELECT TOP 1 Number FROM @Numbers ORDER BY NEWID())
                    BillingAddressID,
                    (SELECT TOP 1 Number FROM @Numbers ORDER BY NEWID())
                    DeliveryAddressID,
                    (SELECT TOP 1
                        CAST(RAND() * Number AS INT) * 10000
                        FROM @Numbers
                        ORDER BY NEWID()) CreditLimit,
                    (SELECT TOP 1
                        CAST(RAND() * Number AS INT) * 9000
```

```
                        FROM @Numbers
                        ORDER BY NEWID()) Balance
        FROM @Numbers a
        CROSS JOIN @Numbers b
) a ;

INSERT INTO dbo.CustomersDisk
SELECT * FROM #CustomersDisk ;
GO

--Create Numbers table

DECLARE @Numbers TABLE
(
        Number          INT
)

;WITH CTE(Number)
AS
(
        SELECT 1 Number
        UNION ALL
        SELECT Number + 1
        FROM CTE
        WHERE Number < 100
)
INSERT INTO @Numbers
SELECT Number FROM CTE ;

--Create the Orders table

CREATE TABLE dbo.OrdersDisk
        (
        OrderNumber     INT     NOT NULL        IDENTITY
        PRIMARY KEY,
        OrderDate       DATE    NOT NULL,
        CustomerID      INT     NOT NULL,
        ProductID       INT     NOT NULL,
```

```
        Quantity        INT       NOT NULL,
        NetAmount       MONEY     NOT NULL,
        DeliveryDate    DATE        NULL
        ) ON [PRIMARY] ;

--Populate Orders with data

SELECT * INTO #OrdersDisk
FROM
        (SELECT
                (SELECT CAST(DATEADD(dd,(SELECT TOP 1 Number
                                        FROM @Numbers
                                        ORDER BY NEWID()),GETDATE())
                                        as DATE)) OrderDate,
                (SELECT TOP 1 CustomerID FROM CustomersDisk ORDER BY
                NEWID()) CustomerID,
                (SELECT TOP 1 Number FROM @Numbers ORDER BY NEWID())
                ProductID,
                (SELECT TOP 1 Number FROM @Numbers ORDER BY NEWID())
                Quantity,
                (SELECT TOP 1 CAST(RAND() * Number AS INT) +10 * 100
                        FROM @Numbers
                        ORDER BY NEWID()) NetAmount,
                (SELECT CAST(DATEADD(dd,(SELECT TOP 1 Number - 10
                                        FROM @Numbers
                                        ORDER BY NEWID()),GETDATE()) as
                                        DATE)) DeliveryDate

        FROM @Numbers a
        CROSS JOIN @Numbers b
        CROSS JOIN @Numbers c
) a ;

INSERT INTO OrdersDisk
SELECT * FROM #OrdersDisk ;
```

```
--Clean-up Temp Tables

DROP TABLE #CustomersDisk ;

DROP TABLE #OrdersDisk ;

--Add foreign key on CustomerID

ALTER TABLE dbo.OrdersDisk ADD CONSTRAINT
        FK_OrdersDisk_CustomersDisk FOREIGN KEY
        (
        CustomerID
        ) REFERENCES dbo.CustomersDisk
        (
        CustomerID
        ) ON UPDATE   NO ACTION
         ON DELETE   NO ACTION ;

--Create a nonclustered index on Balance

CREATE NONCLUSTERED INDEX NCI_Balance ON dbo.CustomersDisk(Balance) ;
```

We can change the definition of the NCI_Balance index to include the FirstName and LastName columns by using the CREATE NONCLUSTERED INDEX statement and specifying the DROP_EXISTING option as demonstrated in Listing 8-4.

Listing 8-4. Altering the Index to Include Columns

```
CREATE NONCLUSTERED INDEX NCI_Balance ON dbo.CustomersDisk(Balance)
    INCLUDE(LastName, FirstName)
    WITH(DROP_EXISTING = ON) ;
```

You can drop the index in the same way that we dropped the clustered index earlier in this chapter—using a DROP INDEX statement. In this case, the full statement would be DROP INDEX NCI_Balance ON dbo.CustomersDisk.

Filtered Indexes

A filtered index is an index built on a subset of the data stored within a table, as opposed to one that is built on all of the data in the table. Because the indexes are smaller, they can lead to improved query performance and reduced storage cost. They also have the potential to cause less overhead for DML operations, since they only need to be updated if the DML operation affects the data within the index. For example, if an index was filtered on `OrderDate >= '2019-01-01' AND OrderDate <= '2019-12-31'` and subsequently updated all rows in the table where the `OrderDate >= '2020-01-01'`, then the performance of the update would be the same as if the index did not exist.

Filtered indexes are constructed by using a `WHERE` clause on index creation. There are many things that you can do in the `WHERE` clause, such as filter on `NULL` or `NOT NULL` values; use equality and inequality operators, such as `=`, `>`, `<`, and `IN`; and use logical operators, such as `AND` and `OR`. There are also limitations, however. For example, you cannot use `BETWEEN`, `CASE`, or `NOT IN`. Also, you can only use simple predicates so, for example, using a date/time function is prohibited, so creating a rolling filter is not possible. You also cannot compare a column to other columns.

The statement in Listing 8-5 creates a filtered index on `DelieveryDate`, where the value is `NULL`. This allows you to make performance improvements on queries that are run to determine which orders are yet to have their delivery scheduled.

Listing 8-5. Creating Filtered Index

```
CREATE NONCLUSTERED INDEX NonDeliveredItems ON dbo.OrdersDisk(DeliveryDate)
        WHERE DeliveryDate IS NULL ;
```

Indexes for Specialized Application

In addition to traditional B-tree indexes, SQL Server also provides several types of special indexes to help query performance against memory-optimized tables and Columnstore indexes that help query performance in data warehouse scenarios. The following sections discuss these special indexes. Although beyond the scope of this book, SQL Server also offers special indexes for geospatial data, XML, and JSON.

Columnstore Indexes

As you have seen, traditional indexes store rows of data on data pages. This is known as a *rowstore*. SQL Server also supports *Columnstore* indexes. These indexes flip data around and use a page to store a column, as opposed to a set of rows. This is illustrated in Figure 8-5.

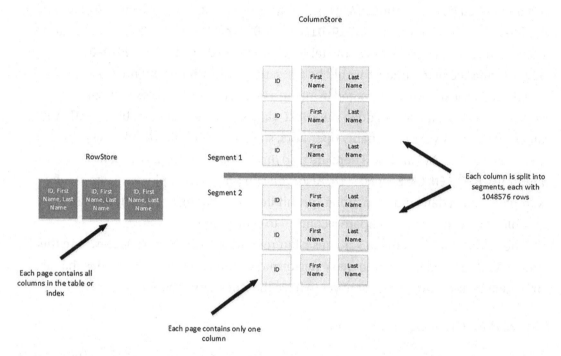

Figure 8-5. *Columnstore index structure*

A Columnstore index slices the rows of a table into chunks of between 102,400 and 1,048,576 rows each. Each slice is called a *rowgroup*. Data in each rowgroup is then split down into columns and compressed using VertiPaq technology. Each column within a rowgroup is called a *column segment*.

Columnstore indexes offer several benefits over traditional indexes, given appropriate usage scenarios. First, because they are highly compressed, they can improve I/O efficiency and reduce memory overhead. They can achieve such a high compression rate because data within a single column is often very similar between rows. Also, because a query is able to retrieve just the data pages of the column it requires, I/O can again be reduced. This is helped even further by the fact that each column segment contains a header with metadata about the data within the segment. This means that SQL Server can access just the segments it needs, as opposed to the whole column. A new query execution mechanism has also been introduced to support Columnstore indexes. It is called batch execution mode, and it allows data to be processed in chunks of 1000 rows, as opposed to on a row-by-row basis. This means that CPU usage is much more efficient. Columnstore indexes are not a magic bullet, however, and are designed to be optimal for data warehouse–style queries that perform read-only operations on very large tables. OLTP-style queries are not likely to see any benefit and, in some cases, may actually execute slower. SQL Server supports both clustered and nonclustered Columnstore indexes, and these are discussed in the following sections.

Clustered Columnstore Indexes

Clustered Columnstore indexes cause the entire table to be stored in a Columnstore format. There is no traditional rowstore storage for a table with a clustered Columnstore index; however, new rows that are inserted into the table may temporarily be placed into a rowstore table, called a *deltastore*. This is to prevent the Columnstore index from becoming fragmented and to enhance performance for DML operations. The diagram in Figure 8-6 illustrates this.

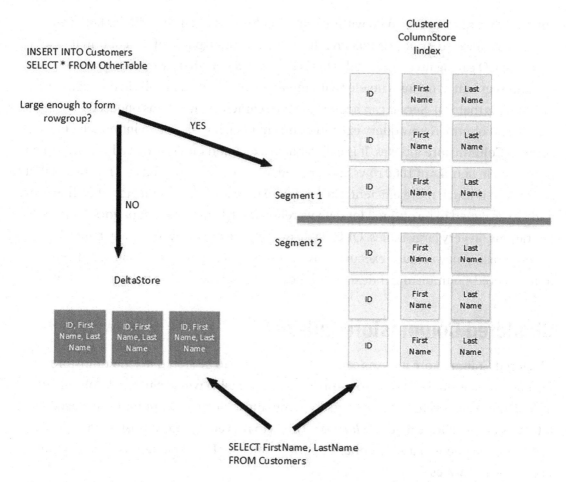

Figure 8-6. *Clustered columnstore index with deltastores*

The diagram shows that when data is inserted into a clustered Columnstore index, SQL Server assesses the number of rows. If the number of rows is high enough to achieve a good compression rate, SQL Server treats them as a rowgroup or rowgroups and immediately compresses them and adds them to the Columnstore index. If there are too few rows, however, SQL Server inserts them into the internal deltastore structure. When you run a query against the table, the database engine seamlessly joins the structures together and returns the results as one. Once there are enough rows, the deltastore is marked as closed and a background process called the *tuple* compresses the rows into a rowgroup in the Columnstore index.

There can be multiple deltastores for each clustered Columnstore index. This is because when SQL Server determines that an insert warrants using a deltastore, it attempts to access the existing deltastores. If all existing deltastores are locked, however, then a new one is created, instead of the query being forced to wait for a lock to be released.

When a row is deleted in a clustered Columnstore index, then the row is only logically removed. The data still physically stays in the rowgroup until the next time the index is reorganized or until the next time a background thread runs. The background thread was introduced in SQL Server 2019 and provides improved index quality, by compressing small deltastores and merging small rowgroups. SQL Server maintains a B-tree structure of pointers to deleted rows in order to easily identify them. If the row being deleted is located in a deltastore, as opposed to the index itself, then it is immediately deleted, both logically and physically. When you update a row in a clustered Columnstore index, then SQL Server marks the row as being logically deleted and inserts a new row into a deltastore, which contains the new values for the row.

You can create clustered Columnstore indexes using a `CREATE CLUSTERED COLUMNSTORE INDEX` statement. The script in Listing 8-6 copies the contents of the `OrdersDisk` table to a new table called `OrdersColumnstore` and then creates a clustered Columnstore index on the table. When you create the index, you do not need to specify a key column; this is because all of the columns are added to column segments within the Columnstore index. Your queries can then use the index to search on whichever column(s) it needs to satisfy the query. The clustered Columnstore index is the only index on the table. You are not able to create traditional nonclustered indexes or a nonclustered Columnstore index. Additionally, the table must not have primary key, foreign key, or unique constraints.

Listing 8-6. Creating a Clustered Columnstore Index

```
SELECT * INTO dbo.OrdersColumnstore
FROM dbo.OrdersDisk ;
GO

CREATE CLUSTERED COLUMNSTORE INDEX CCI_OrdersColumnstore ON dbo.
OrdersColumnstore ;
```

It is also possible to create nonclustered B-Tree indexes on a Clustered Columnstore index. It provides efficient seek operations against the underlying columnar data.

SQL Server 2022 introduces a performance optimization for clustered Columnstore indexes, called Ordered Clustered Columnstore Indexes. This allows improved performance by offering better elimination of segments, by ordering the data before it is compressed. The script in Listing 8-7 creates the same index as the script in Listing 8-6, except that it uses the ORDER clause to cause the data to be ordered by the OrderDate column.

Tip   If you have run the script in Listing 8-6, you will need to use a DROP INDEX statement to convert the OrdersDisk table back to a heap, before running the script in Listing 8-7.

Listing 8-7. Create an Ordered Clustered Columnstore Index

```
SELECT * INTO dbo.OrdersColumnstore
FROM dbo.OrdersDisk ;
GO

CREATE CLUSTERED COLUMNSTORE INDEX CCI_OrdersColumnstore ON dbo.
OrdersColumnstore ORDER (OrderDate) ;
```

Note   You cannot order clustered columnstore indexes on string columns.

Nonclustered Columnstore Indexes

A Nonclustered Columnstore index is essentially the same as a Clustered Columnstore Index. The difference is that a copy of the data is made from the columns that the index covers instead of the converting the data that is stored within the table to a columnar format, meaning that a table can have both B-Tree (clustered and nonclustered) indexes, as well as nonclustered Columnstore indexes. Obviously, this increases the storage space required for the data, but it provides the benefit of allowing you to target operational workloads at a clustered B-Tree while targeting analytical workloads against the nonclustered Columnstore. Given that a ten times compression ratio is typical within a Columnstore index, it will likely be worth the additional storage.

The statement in Listing 8-8 creates a nonclustered Columnstore index on the FirstName, LastName, Balance, and CustomerID columns of the CustomersDisk table.

Listing 8-8. Creating Nonclustered Columnstore Indexes

```
CREATE NONCLUSTERED COLUMNSTORE INDEX NCCI_FirstName_LastName_Balance_
CustomerID
    ON dbo.CustomersDisk(FirstName,LastName,Balance,CustomerID) ;
```

In-Memory Indexes

As we saw in *Chapter* 7, SQL Server provides two types of index for memory-optimized tables: nonclustered and nonclustered hash. Every memory-optimized table must have a minimum of one index. All in-memory indexes cover all columns in the table because they use a memory pointer to link to the data row.

Indexes on memory-optimized tables must be created in the CREATE TABLE statement. There is no CREATE INDEX statement for in-memory indexes. Indexes built on memory-optimized tables are always stored in memory only and are never persisted to disk, regardless of your table's durability setting. They are then re-created after the instance restarts, from the table's underlying data. You do not need to worry about fragmentation of in-memory indexes, since they never have a disk-based structure.

In-Memory Nonclustered Hash Indexes

A nonclustered hash index consists of an array of buckets. A hash function is run on each of the index keys, and then the hashed key values are placed into the buckets. The hashing algorithm used is deterministic, meaning that index keys with the same value always have the same hash value. This is important because repeated hash values are always placed in the same hash bucket. When many keys are in the same hash bucket, performance of the index can degrade, because the whole chain of duplicates needs to be scanned to find the correct key. Therefore, if you are building a hash index on a nonunique column with many repeated keys, you should create the index with a much larger number of buckets. This should be in the realm of 20 to 100 times the number of distinct key values, as opposed to 2 times the number of unique keys that is usually recommended for unique indexes. Alternatively, using a nonclustered index on a nonunique column may offer a better solution. The second consequence of the hash function being deterministic is that different versions of the same row are always stored in the same hash bucket.

Even in the case of a unique index where only a single, current row version exits, the distribution of hashed values into buckets is not even, and if there are an equal number of buckets to unique key values, then approximately one-third of the buckets is empty, one-third contains a single value, and one-third contains multiple values. When multiple values share a bucket, it is known as a *hash collision*, and a large number of hash collisions can lead to reduced performance. Hence, the recommendation for the number of buckets in a unique index is twice the number of unique values expected in the table.

Tip   When you have a unique nonclustered hash index, in some cases, many unique values may hash to the same bucket. If you experience this, then increasing the number of buckets helps, in the same way that a nonunique index does.

As an example, if your table has one million rows, and the indexed column is unique, the optimum number of buckets, known as the BUCKET_COUNT, is two million. If you know that you expect your table to grow to two million rows, however, then it may be prudent to create four million hash buckets. This number of buckets is low enough to not have an impact on memory. It also still allows for the expected increase in rows, without there being too few buckets, which would impair performance. An illustration of potential mappings between index values and hash buckets is illustrated in Figure 8-7.

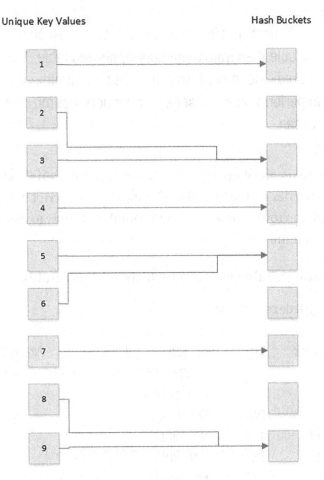

Figure 8-7. *Mappings to a nonclustered hash index*

Tip   The amount of memory used by a nonclustered hash index always remains static, since the number of buckets does not change.

Hash indexes are optimized for seek operations with the = predicate. For the seek operation, however, the full index key must be present in the predicate evaluation. If it is not, a full index scan is required. An index scan is also required if inequality predicates, such as < or >, are used. Also, because the index is not ordered, the index cannot return the data in the sort order of the index key.

Note   You may remember that in *Chapter 7*, we witnessed superior performance
from a disk-based table than from a memory-optimized table. This is explained
by us using the > predicate in our query; this meant that although the disk-based
index was able to perform an index seek, our memory-optimized hash index had to
perform an index scan.

Let's now create a memory-optimized version of our OrdersDisk table, which includes
a nonclustered hash index on the OrderID column, using the script in Listing 8-9. Initially,
this row has one million rows, but we expect the number to grow to two million, so we use
a BUCKET_COUNT of four million.

Listing 8-9. Creating a Table with a Nonclustered Hash Index

```
CREATE TABLE dbo.OrdersMemHash
(
        OrderNumber     INT     NOT NULL    IDENTITY    PRIMARY KEY
                                NONCLUSTERED HASH WITH(BUCKET_COUNT =
                                4000000),
        OrderDate       DATE    NOT NULL,
        CustomerID      INT     NOT NULL,
        ProductID       INT     NOT NULL,
        Quantity        INT     NOT NULL,
        NetAmount       MONEY   NOT NULL,
        DeliveryDate    DATE    NULL,
) WITH(MEMORY_OPTIMIZED = ON, DURABILITY = SCHEMA_AND_DATA) ;

INSERT INTO dbo.OrdersMemHash(OrderDate,CustomerID,ProductID,Quantity,
NetAmount,DeliveryDate)
SELECT OrderDate
        ,CustomerID
        ,ProductID
        ,Quantity
        ,NetAmount
        ,DeliveryDate
FROM dbo.OrdersDisk ;
```

If we now wish to add an additional index to the table, we need to drop and re-create it. We already have data in the table, however, so we first need to create a temp table and copy the data in so that we can drop and re-create the memory-optimized table. The script in Listing 8-10 adds a nonclustered index to the OrderDate column.

Listing 8-10. Adding an Index to a Memory-Optimized Table

```
--Create and populate temp table

SELECT * INTO #OrdersMemHash
FROM dbo.OrdersMemHash ;

--Drop existing table

DROP TABLE dbo.OrdersMemHash ;

--Re-create the table with the new index

CREATE TABLE dbo.OrdersMemHash
(
        OrderNumber    INT     NOT NULL    IDENTITY    PRIMARY KEY
                                   NONCLUSTERED HASH WITH(BUCKET_COUNT =
                                   4000000),
        OrderDate      DATE    NOT NULL           INDEX NCI_OrderDate
                                             NONCLUSTERED,
        CustomerID     INT     NOT NULL,
        ProductID      INT     NOT NULL,
        Quantity       INT     NOT NULL,
        NetAmount      MONEY   NOT NULL,
        DeliveryDate   DATE    NULL,
) WITH(MEMORY_OPTIMIZED = ON, DURABILITY = SCHEMA_AND_DATA) ;
GO

--Allow values to be inserted into the identity column

SET IDENTITY_INSERT OrdersMemHash ON ;
GO

--Repopulate the table
```

```
INSERT INTO
dbo.OrdersMemHash(OrderNumber,OrderDate,CustomerID,ProductID,Quantity,
NetAmount,DeliveryDate)
SELECT *
FROM #OrdersMemHash ;

--Stop further inserts to the identity column and clean up temp table

SET IDENTITY_INSERT OrdersMemHash OFF ;

DROP TABLE #OrdersMemHash ;
```

We can examine the distribution of the values in our hash index by interrogating the sys.dm_db_xtp_hash_index_stats DMV. The query in Listing 8-11 demonstrates using this DMV to view the number of hash collisions and calculate the percentage of empty buckets.

Listing 8-11. sys.dm_db_xtp_hash_index_stats

```
SELECT
  OBJECT_SCHEMA_NAME(HIS.OBJECT_ID) + '.' + OBJECT_NAME(HIS.OBJECT_ID)
  'Table Name',
  I.name as 'Index Name',
  HIS.total_bucket_count,
  HIS.empty_bucket_count,
  FLOOR((CAST(empty_bucket_count AS FLOAT)/total_bucket_count) * 100)
  'Empty Bucket Percentage',
  total_bucket_count - empty_bucket_count 'Used Bucket Count',
  HIS.avg_chain_length,
  HIS.max_chain_length
FROM sys.dm_db_xtp_hash_index_stats AS HIS
INNER JOIN sys.indexes AS I
        ON HIS.object_id = I.object_id
                AND HIS.index_id = I.index_id ;
```

From the results in Figure 8-8, we can see that for our hash index, 78% of the buckets are empty. The percentage is this high because we specified a large BUCKET_COUNT with table growth in mind. If the percentage was less than 33%, we would want to specify a higher number of buckets to avoid hash collisions. We can also see that we have an average chain length of 1, with a maximum chain length of 5. This is healthy. If the average chain count increases, then performance begins to tail off, since SQL Server has to scan multiple values to find the correct key. If the average chain length reaches 10 or higher, then the implication is that the key is nonunique and there are too many duplicate values in the key to make a hash index viable. At this point, we should either drop and re-create the table with a higher bucket count for the index or, ideally, look to implement a nonclustered index instead.

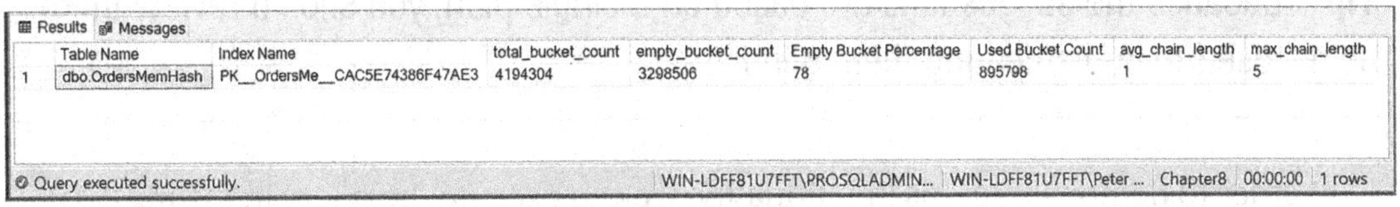

	Table Name	Index Name	total_bucket_count	empty_bucket_count	Empty Bucket Percentage	Used Bucket Count	avg_chain_length	max_chain_length
1	dbo.OrdersMemHash	PK__OrdersMe__CAC5E74386F47AE3	4194304	3298506	78	895798	1	5

Figure 8-8. *sys.dm_db_xtp_hash_index_stats results*

In-Memory Nonclustered Indexes

In-memory nonclustered indexes have a similar structure to a disk-based nonclustered index called a *bw-tree*. This structure uses a page-mapping table, as opposed to pointers, and is traversed using less than, as opposed to greater than, which is used when traversing disk-based indexes. The leaf level of the index is a singly linked list. Nonclustered indexes perform better than nonclustered hash indexes where a query uses inequality predicates, such as `BETWEEN`, >, or <. In-memory nonclustered indexes also perform better than a nonclustered hash index, where the = predicate is used, but not all of the columns in the key are used in the filter. Nonclustered indexes can also return the data in the sort order of the index key. Unlike disk-based indexes, however, these indexes cannot return the results in the reverse order of the index key.

Maintaining Indexes

Once indexes have been created, a DBA's work is not complete. Indexes need to be maintained on an ongoing basis. The following sections discuss considerations for index maintenance.

Missing Indexes

When you run queries, the Database Engine keeps track of any indexes that it would like to use when building a plan to aid your query performance. When you view an execution plan in SSMS, you are provided with advice on missing indexes, but the data is also available later through DMVs.

Tip   Because the suggestions are based on a single plan, you should review them as opposed to implementing them blindly.

In order to demonstrate this functionality, we can execute the query in Listing 8-12 and choose to include the actual execution plan.

Tip   You can see missing index information by viewing the estimated query plan.

Listing 8-12. Generating Missing Index Details

```
SELECT SUM(c.creditlimit) TotalExposure, SUM(o.netamount)
'TotalOrdersValue'
FROM dbo.CustomersDisk c
INNER JOIN dbo.OrdersDisk o
        ON c.CustomerID = o.CustomerID ;
```

Once we have run this query, we can examine the execution plan and see what it tells us. The execution plan for this query is shown in Figure 8-9.

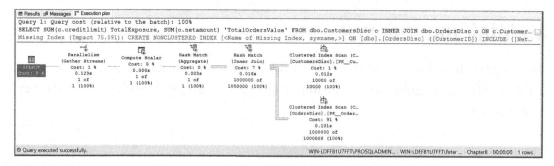

Figure 8-9. *Execution plan showing missing indexes*

At the top of the execution plan in Figure 8-9, you can see that SQL Server is recommending that we create an index on the `CustomerID` column of the `OrdersDisk` table and include the `NetAmount` column at the leaf level. We are also advised that this should provide a 75% performance improvement to the query.

As mentioned, SQL Server also makes this information available through DMVs. The `sys.dm_db_missing_index_details` DMV joins to the `sys.dm_db_missing_index_group_stats` through the intermediate DMV `sys.dm_db_missing_index_groups`, which avoids a many-to-many relationship. The script in Listing 8-13 demonstrates how we can use these DMVs to return details on missing indexes.

Listing 8-13. Missing Index DMVs

```
SELECT
        mid.statement TableName
        ,ISNULL(mid.equality_columns, '')
            + ','
            + ISNULL(mid.inequality_columns, '') IndexKeyColumns
        ,mid.included_columns
        ,migs.unique_compiles
        ,migs.user_seeks
        ,migs.user_scans
        ,migs.avg_total_user_cost
        ,migs.avg_user_impact
FROM sys.dm_db_missing_index_details mid
INNER JOIN sys.dm_db_missing_index_groups mig
        ON mid.index_handle = mig.index_handle
        INNER JOIN sys.dm_db_missing_index_group_stats migs
                ON mig.index_group_handle = migs.group_handle ;
```

The results of this query are shown in Figure 8-10. They show the following: the name of the table with the missing index; the column(s) that SQL Server recommends should form the index key; the columns that SQL Server recommends should be added as included columns at the leaf level of the B-tree; the number of times that queries that would have benefited from the index have been compiled; how many seeks would have been performed against the index, if it existed; the number of times that the index has been scanned if it existed; the average cost that would have been saved by using the index; and the average percentage cost that would have been saved by using the index. In our case, we can see that the query would have been 95% less expensive if the index existed when we ran our query.

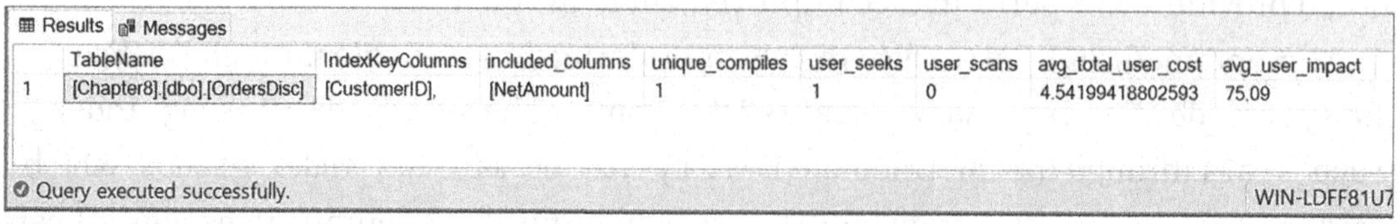

	TableName	IndexKeyColumns	included_columns	unique_compiles	user_seeks	user_scans	avg_total_user_cost	avg_user_impact
1	[Chapter8].[dbo].[OrdersDisc]	[CustomerID],	[NetAmount]	1	1	0	4.54199418802593	75.09

⊘ Query executed successfully.   WIN-LDFF81U7

Figure 8-10. Missing index results

Index Fragmentation

Disk-based indexes are subject to fragmentation. Two forms of fragmentation can occur in B-trees: internal fragmentation and external fragmentation. *Internal fragmentation* refers to pages having lots of free space. If pages have lots of free space, then SQL Server needs to read more pages than is necessary to return all of the required rows for a query. *External fragmentation* refers to the pages of the index becoming out of physical order. This can reduce performance, since the data cannot be read sequentially from disk.

For example, imagine that you have a table with one million rows of data and that all of these data rows fit into 5000 pages when the data pages are 100% full. This means that SQL Server needs to read just over 39MB of data in order to scan the entire table (8KB * 5000). If the pages of the table are only 50% full, however, this increases the number of pages in use to 10,000, which also increases the amount of data that needs to be read to 78MB. This is internal fragmentation.

Internal fragmentation can occur naturally when DELETE statements are issued and when DML statements occur, such as when a key value that is not ever-increasing is inserted. This is because SQL Server may respond to this situation by performing a *page split*. A page split creates a new page, moves half of the data from the existing page to the new page, and leaves the other half on the existing page, thus creating 50% free space on both pages. They can also occur artificially, however, through the misuse of the FILLFACTOR and PAD_INDEX settings.

FILLFACTOR controls how much free space is left on each leaf level page of an index when it is created or rebuilt. By default, the FILLFACTOR is set to 0, which means that it leaves enough space on the page for exactly one row. In some cases, however, when a high number of page splits is occurring due to DML operations, a DBA may be able to reduce fragmentation by altering the FILLFACTOR. Setting a FILLFACTOR of 80, for example, leaves 20% free space in the page, meaning that new rows can be added to the page without page splits occurring. Many DBAs change the FILLFACTOR when they are not required to, however, which automatically causes internal fragmentation as soon as the index is built. PAD_INDEX can be applied only when FILLFACTOR is used, and it applies the same percentage of free space to the intermediate levels of the B-tree.

External fragmentation is also caused by page splits and refers to the logical order of pages, as ordered by the index key, being out of sequence when compared to the physical order of pages on disk. External fragmentation makes it so SQL Server is less able to perform scan operations using a sequential read, because the head needs to move backward and forward over the disk to locate the pages within the file.

Note   This is not the same as fragmentation at the file system level where a data file can be split over multiple, unordered disk sectors.

Detecting Fragmentation

You can identify fragmentation of indexes by using the sys.dm_db_index_physical_stats DMF. This function accepts the parameters listed in Table 8-2.

Table 8-2. *sys.dm_db_index_physical_stats Parameters*

Parameter	Description
Database_ID	The ID of the database that you want to run the function against. If you do not know it, you can pass in DB_ID('MyDatabase') where MyDatabase is the name of your database.
Object_ID	The Object ID of the table that you want to run the function against. If you do not know it, pass in OBJECT_ID('MyTable') where MyTable is the name of your table. Pass in NULL to run the function against all tables in the database.
Index_ID	The index ID of the index you want to run the function against. This is always 1 for a clustered index. Pass in NULL to run the function against all indexes on the table.

(continued)

Table 8-2. (*continued*)

Parameter	Description
Partition_Number	The ID of the partition that you want to run the function against. Pass in NULL if you want to run the function against all partitions, or if the table is not partitioned.
Mode	Choose LIMITED, SAMPLED, or DETAILED. LIMITED only scans the non–leaf levels of an index. SAMPLED scans 1% of pages in the table, unless the table has 10,000 pages or less, in which case DETAILED mode is used. DETAILED mode scans 100% of the pages in the table. For very large tables, SAMPLED is often preferred due to the length of time it can take to return data in DETAILED mode.

Listing 8-14 demonstrates how we can use sys.dm_db_index_physical_stats to check the fragmentation levels of our OrdersDisk table.

Listing 8-14. sys.dm_db_index_physical_stats

```
USE Chapter8
GO

SELECT
i.name
,IPS.index_type_desc
,IPS.index_level
,IPS.avg_fragmentation_in_percent
,IPS.avg_page_space_used_in_percent
,i.fill_factor
,CASE
    WHEN i.fill_factor = 0
        THEN 100-IPS.avg_page_space_used_in_percent
    ELSE i.fill_factor-ips.avg_page_space_used_in_percent
END Internal_Frag_With_Fillfactor_Offset
,IPS.fragment_count
,IPS.avg_fragment_size_in_pages
```

```
FROM sys.dm_db_index_physical_stats(DB_ID('Chapter8'),OBJECT_ID('dbo.Orders
Disk'),NULL,NULL,'DETAILED') IPS
INNER JOIN sys.indexes i
        ON IPS.Object_id = i.object_id
                AND IPS.index_id = i.index_id ;
```

You can see, from the results of this query, that one row is returned for every level of each B-tree. If the table was partitioned, this would also be broken down by partition. The index_level column indicates which level of the B-tree is represented by the row. Level 0 implies the leaf level of the B-tree, whereas Level 1 is either the lowest intermediate level or the root level if no intermediate levels exist, and so on, with the highest number always reflecting the root node. The avg_fragmentation_in_percent column tells us how much external fragmentation is present. We want this value to be as close to zero as possible. The avg_page_space_used_in_percent tells us how much internal fragmentation is present, so we want this value to be as close to 100 as possible. The Internal_Frag_With_FillFactor_Offset column also tells us how much internal fragmentation is present, but this time, it applies an offset to allow for the fill factor that has been applied to the index. The fragment_count column indicates how many chunks of continuous pages exist for the index level, so we want this value to be as low as possible. The avg_fragment_size_in_pages column tells the average size of each fragment, so obviously this number should also be as high as possible.

Removing Fragmentation

You can remove fragmentation by either reorganizing or rebuilding an index. When you reorganize an index, SQL Server reorganizes the data within the leaf level of the index. It looks to see if there is free space on a page that it can use. If there is, then it moves rows from the next page onto this page. If there are empty pages at the end of this process, then they are removed. SQL Server only fills pages to the level of the FillFactor specified. Once this is complete, the data within the leaf level pages is shuffled so that their physical order is a closer match to their logical, key order. Reorganizing an index is always an ONLINE operation, meaning that the index can still be used by other processes while the operation is in progress. Where it is always an ONLINE operation, it will fail if the ALLOW_PAGE_LOCKS option is turned off. The process of reorganizing an index is suitable for removing internal fragmentation and low levels of external fragmentation of 30% or less. However, it makes no guarantees, even with this usage profile, that there will not be fragmentation left after the operation completes.

The script in Listing 8-15 creates an index called `NCI_CustomerID` on the `OrdersDisk` table and then demonstrates how we can reorganize it.

Listing 8-15. Reorganizing an Index

```
--Create the index that will be used in the examples, for the following
sections

CREATE NONCLUSTERED INDEX NCI_CustomerID ON dbo.OrdersDisk(CustomerID) ;
GO

--Reorganize the index

ALTER INDEX NCI_CustomerID ON dbo.OrdersDisk REORGANIZE ;
```

When you rebuild an index, the existing index is dropped and then completely rebuilt. This, by definition, removes internal and external fragmentation since the index is built from scratch. It is important to note, however, that you are still not guaranteed to be 100% fragmentation free after this operation. This is because SQL Server assigns different chunks of the index to each CPU core that is involved in the rebuild. Each CPU core should build its own section in the perfect sequence, but when the pieces are synchronized, there may be a small amount of fragmentation. You can minimize this issue by specifying `MAXDOP` = 1. Even when you set this option, you may still encounter fragmentation in some cases. For example, if `ALLOW_PAGES_LOCKS` is configured as `OFF`, then the workers share the allocation cache, which can cause fragmentation. Additionally, when you set `MAXDOP` = 1, it is at the expense of the time it takes to rebuild the index.

You can rebuild an index by performing either an `ONLINE` or `OFFLINE` operation. If you choose to rebuild the index as an `ONLINE` operation, then the original version of the index is still accessible while the operation takes place. The `ONLINE` operation comes at the expense of both time and resource utilization. You need to enable `ALLOW_PAGE_LOCKS` to make your `ONLINE` rebuild successful.

The script in Listing 8-16 demonstrates how we can rebuild the `NCI_Balance` index on the `OrdersDisk` table. Because we have not specified `ONLINE` = `ON`, it uses the default setting of `ONLINE` = `OFF`, and the index is locked for the entire operation. Because we specify `MAXDOP` = 1, the operation is slower, but has no fragmentation.

Listing 8-16. Rebuilding an Index

```
ALTER INDEX NCI_CustomerID ON dbo.OrdersDisk REBUILD WITH(MAXDOP = 1) ;
```

If you create a maintenance plan to rebuild or reorganize indexes, then all indexes within the specified database are rebuilt, regardless of whether they need to be—this can be time-consuming and eat resources. You can resolve this issue by using the sys. dm_db_index_physical_stats DMF to create an intelligent script that you can run from SQL Server Agent and use to reorganize or rebuild only those indexes that require it. This is discussed in more detail in *Chapter* 17.

Tip   There is a myth that using SSDs removes the issue of index fragmentation. This is not correct. Although SSDs reduce the performance impact of out-of-order pages, they do not remove it. They also have no impact on internal fragmentation.

Resumable Index Operations

SQL Server 2019 supports resumable online index creation and index rebuilds for both traditional (clustered and nonclustered) indexes and Columnstore indexes. Resumable index operations allow you to pause an online index operation (build or rebuild), in order to free up system resources and then restart it again, from where it left off, when resource utilization is no longer an issue. These operations also allow an online index operation to be restarted, after it has failed for common reasons, such as lack of disk space.

Some of the advantages that this functionality brings to a DBA are clear. For example, if a large index rebuild needs to fit inside a short maintenance window, then the rebuild can be paused at the end of a maintenance window and restarted at the beginning of the next, as opposed to having to abort the operation, to free up system resources. There are also other, hidden benefits, however. For example, resumable index operations do not consume large amount of log space, even when performed on large indexes. This is because all data required to restart the index operation is stored inside the database. A side note of this is that the index operation does not hold a long-running transaction while paused.

For the most part, there are very few drawbacks to using resumable index operations. The quality of defragmentation achieved is comparable to the quality of a standard online index operation, and there is no real difference in speed between resumable and standard online index operations (excluding the potential pause of course). As always, however, there is no such thing as a free lunch, and during a paused, resumable operation, there will be a degradation of write performance, to affected tables and indexes, due to two versions of the index needing to be updated. This degradation should not be more than 10%, in most cases. There should be no impact to read operations, during the pause, as they continue to use the original version of the index, until the operation has completed.

The command in Listing 8-17 demonstrated how to rebuild the NCI_CustomerID index, on the OrdersDisk table, as a resumable operation.

Listing 8-17. Resumable Index Rebuild

```
ALTER INDEX NCI_CustomerID ON dbo.OrdersDisk REBUILD WITH(MAXDOP = 1,
ONLINE=ON, RESUMABLE=ON) ;
```

The command in Listing 8-18 will pause the index rebuild, started in Listing 8-17.

Tip   The command in Listing 8-18 will only work if the execution of the command in Listing 8-16 has not yet completed.

Listing 8-18. Pause an Index Rebuild

```
ALTER INDEX NCI_CustomerID ON dbo.OrdersDisk PAUSE
```

After running this script, the index rebuild operation will pause, and the message displayed in Figure 8-11 will be displayed.

```
🗐 Messages
    Msg 1219, Level 16, State 1, Line 1
    Your session has been disconnected because of a high priority DDL operation.
    Msg 596, Level 21, State 1, Line 0
    Cannot continue the execution because the session is in the kill state.
    Msg 0, Level 20, State 0, Line 0
    A severe error occurred on the current command.  The results, if any, should be discarded.

100 %    ▼ ◀
```

Figure 8-11. *Message thrown, when index operation paused*

The script in Listing 8-19 will either resume or abort the index rebuild, based on the value assigned to the @Action variable.

Listing 8-19. Resume or Abort an Index Operation

```
DECLARE @Action NVARCHAR(6) = 'Resume'

IF (@Action = 'Resume')
BEGIN
      ALTER INDEX NCI_CustomerID ON dbo.OrdersDisk RESUME
END
ELSE
BEGIN
      ALTER INDEX NCI_CustomerID ON dbo.OrdersDisk ABORT
END
```

Instead of turning on ONLINE and RESUMABLE options for each, individual index operation, you can turn them on globally, at the database level, by using database scoped configurations. The ELEVATE_ONLINE configuration will change the default value of ONLINE to ON, for supported index operations, within the database. The configuration ELEVATE_RESUMABLE will default the value of RESUMABLE to ON.

Both ELEVATE_ONLINE and ELEVATE_RESUMABLE can be configured as OFF (the default behavior), WHEN_SUPPORTED, or FAIL_UNSUPPORTED. When set to WHEN_SUPPORTED, noncompatible operations, such as rebuilding XML indexes, will be performed offline and unresumable. If set to FAIL_UNSUPPORTED, however, such operations will fail, throwing an error.

The script in Listing 8-20 demonstrates how to set ELEVATE_ONLINE and ELEVATE_ RESUMABLE to WHEN_SUPPORTED, for the Chapter8 Database.

Listing 8-20. Default to ONLINE and RESUMABLE

```
USE Chapter8
GO

ALTER DATABASE SCOPED CONFIGURATION SET ELEVATE_ONLINE = WHEN_SUPPORTED ;
GO
ALTER DATABASE SCOPED CONFIGURATION SET ELEVATE_RESUMABLE = WHEN_
SUPPORTED ;
GO
```

Partitioned Indexes

As mentioned in *Chapter* 7, it is possible to partition indexes as well as tables. A clustered index always shares the same partition scheme as the underlying table, because the leaf level of the clustered index is made up of the actual data pages of the table. Nonclustered indexes, on the other hand, can either be aligned with the table or not. Indexes are aligned if they share the same partition scheme or if they are created on an identical partition scheme.

In most cases, it is good practice to align nonclustered indexes with the base table, but on occasion, you may wish to deviate from this strategy. For example, if the base table is not partitioned, you can still partition an index for performance. Also, if you index key is unique and does not contain the partitioning key, then it needs to be unaligned. There is also an opportunity to gain a performance boost from unaligned nonclustered indexes if the table is involved in collated joins with other tables on different columns.

You can create a partitioned index by using the ON clause to specify the partition scheme in the same way that you create a partitioned table. If the index already exists, you can rebuild it, specifying the partition scheme in the ON clause. The script in Listing 8-21 creates a partition function and a partition scheme. It then rebuilds the clustered index of the OrdersDisk table to move it to the new partition scheme. Finally, it creates a new nonclustered index, which is partition aligned with the table.

Tip   Before running the script, change the name of the primary key to match your own.

Listing 8-21. Rebuilding and Creating Partitioned Indexes

```
--Create partition function

CREATE PARTITION FUNCTION OrdersPartFunc(int)
AS RANGE LEFT
FOR VALUES(250000,500000,750000) ;
GO

--Create partition scheme

CREATE PARTITION SCHEME OrdersPartScheme
AS PARTITION OrdersPartFunc
ALL TO([PRIMARY]) ;
GO

--Partition OrdersDisk table

ALTER TABLE dbo.OrdersDisk DROP CONSTRAINT PK__OrdersDi__CAC5E7420B016A9F ;
GO

ALTER TABLE dbo.OrdersDisk
ADD PRIMARY KEY CLUSTERED(OrderNumber) ON OrdersPartScheme(OrderNumber) ;
GO

--Create partition aligned nonclustered index

CREATE NONCLUSTERED INDEX NCI_Part_CustID ON dbo.OrdersDisk(CustomerID,
OrderNumber)
    ON OrdersPartScheme(OrderNumber) ;
```

When you rebuild an index, you can also specify that only a certain partition is rebuilt. The example in Listing 8-22 rebuilds only Partition 1 of the NCI_Part_ CustID index.

Listing 2-22. Rebuilding a Specific Partition

```
ALTER INDEX NCI_Part_CustID ON dbo.OrdersDisk REBUILD PARTITION = 1 ;
```

Statistics

Cardinality refers to how many rows the query optimizer expects to be returned by a query and is a key part of how the optimizer choses the optimal plan for a given query. The primary method that the optimizer uses to estimate cardinality is statistics.

SQL Server maintains statistics regarding the distribution of data within a column or set of columns. These columns can either be within a table or a nonclustered index. When the statistics are built on a set of columns, then they also include correlation statistics between the distributions of values in those columns. The Query Optimizer can then use these statistics to build efficient query plans based on the number of rows that it expects a query to return (cardinality). A lack of statistics can lead to inefficient plans being generated. For example, the Query Optimizer may decide to perform an index scan when a seek operation would be more efficient.

You can allow SQL Server to manage statistics automatically. A databaselevel option called AUTO_CREATE_STATISTICS automatically generates single column statistics, where SQL Server believes better cardinality estimates will help query performance. There are limitations to this however. For example, filtered statistics or multicolumn statistics cannot be created automatically.

Tip   The only exception to this is when an index is created. When you create an index, statistics are always generated, even multicolumn statistics, to cover the index key. It also includes filtered statistics on filtered indexes. This is regardless of the AUTO_CREATE_STATS setting.

Auto Create Incremental Stats causes statistics on partitioned tables to be automatically created on a per-partition basis, as opposed to being generated for the whole table. This can reduce contention by stopping a scan of the full table from being required.

Statistics become out of date as DML operations are performed against a table. The database-level option, AUTO_UPDATE_STATISTICS, rebuilds statistics when they become outdated. The rules in Table 8-3 are used to determine if statistics are out of date.

Table 8-3. *Statistics Update Algorithms*

No of Rows in Table	Rule
0	Table has greater than 0 rows.
<= 500	500 or more values in the first column of the statistics object have changed.
> 500	500 + 20% or more values in the first column of the statistics object have changed.
Partitioned table with INCREMENTAL statistics	20% or more of values in the first column of the statistics object for a specific partition have changed.

The AUTO_UPDATE_STATISTICS process is very useful and it is normally a good idea to use it. An issue can arise, however, because the process is synchronous and blocking. Therefore, if a query is run, SQL Server checks to see if the statistics need to be updated. If they do, SQL Server updates them, but this blocks the query and any other queries that require the same statistics, until the operation completes. During times of high read/write load, such as an ETL process against very large tables, this can cause performance problems. The workaround for this is another database-level option, called AUTO_UPDATE_STATISTICS_ASYNC. Even when this option is turned on, it only takes effect if AUTO_UPDATE_STATISTICS is also turned on. When enabled, AUTO_UPDATE_STATS_ASYNC forces the update of the statistics object to run as an asynchronous background process. This means that the query that caused it to run and other queries are not blocked, providing that a schema stability lock is not required. The trade-off, however, is that these queries do not benefit from the updated statistics.

The options mentioned earlier can be configured on the Options page of the Database Properties dialog box. Alternatively, you can configure them using ALTER DATABASE commands, as demonstrated in Listing 8-23.

Listing 8-23. Toggling Automatic Statistics Options

```
--Turn on Auto_Create_Stats

ALTER DATABASE Chapter8 SET AUTO_CREATE_STATISTICS ON ;
GO

--Turn on Auto_Create_Incremental_Stats
```

```
ALTER DATABASE Chapter8 SET AUTO_CREATE_STATISTICS ON  (INCREMENTAL=ON) ;
GO
```

```
--Turn on Auto_Update_Stats_Async
```

```
ALTER DATABASE Chapter8 SET AUTO_UPDATE_STATISTICS ON WITH NO_WAIT ;
GO
```

```
--Turn on Auto_Update_Stats_Async
```

```
ALTER DATABASE Chapter8 SET AUTO_UPDATE_STATISTICS_ASYNC ON WITH NO_WAIT ;
GO
```

SQL Server 2022 introduces a new database scoped configuration (see Chapter 5 for further details about database scoped configurations), which avoids blocking other transactions that require a schema stability lock. The ASYNC_STATS_UPDATE_WAIT_AT_ LOW_PRIORITY option, which can be toggled on and off using the script in Listing 8-24, works by placing the lock request of a low priority queue. It will only have any effect if AUTO_UPDATE_STATISTICS is turned on for the database.

Listing 8-24. Toggle ASYNC_STATS_UPDATE_WAIT_AT_LOW_PRIORITY

```
--Turn On
```

```
ALTER DATABASE SCOPED CONFIGURATION SET ASYNC_STATS_UPDATE_WAIT_AT_LOW_
PRIORITY = ON
GO
```

```
--Turn Off
```

```
ALTER DATABASE SCOPED CONFIGURATION SET ASYNC_STATS_UPDATE_WAIT_AT_LOW_
PRIORITY = ON
GO
```

Filtered Statistics

Filtered statistics allow you to create statistics on a subset of data within a column through the use of a WHERE clause in the statistic creation. This allows the Query Optimizer to generate an even better plan, since the statistics only contain the distribution of values within the well-defined subset of data. For example, if we create filtered statistics on the NetAmount column of our OrdersDisk table filtered by OrderDate being greater than 1 Jan 2019, then the statistics will not include rows that contain old orders, allowing us to search for large, recent orders more efficiently.

Incremental Statistics

Incremental statistics can help reduce table scans caused by statistics updates on large partitioned tables. When enabled, statistics are created and updated on a per-partition basis, as opposed to globally, for the entire table. This can significantly reduce the amount of time you need to update statistics on large partitioned tables, since partitions where the statistics are not outdated are not touched, therefore reducing unnecessary overhead.

Incremental statistics are not supported in all scenarios, however. A warning is generated and the setting is ignored if the option is used with the following types of statistics:

- Statistics on views

- Statistics on XML columns

- Statistics on Geography or Geometry columns

- Statistics on filtered indexes

- Statistics for indexes that are not partition aligned

Additionally, you cannot use incremental statistics on read-only databases or on databases that are participating in an AlwaysOn Availability Group as a readable secondary replica.

Managing Statistics

In addition to being automatically created and updated by SQL Server, you can also create and update statistics manually using the CREATE STATISTICS statement. If you wish to create filtered statistics, add a WHERE clause at the end of the statement. The script in Listing 8-25 creates a multicolumn statistic on the FirstName and LastName columns of the CustomersDisk table. It then creates a filtered statistic on the NetAmount column of the OrdersDisk table, built only on rows where the OrderDate is greater than 1st Jan 2019.

Listing 8-25. Creating Statistics

```
USE Chapter8
GO

--Create multicolumn statistic on FirstName and LastName

CREATE STATISTICS Stat_FirstName_LastName ON dbo.CustomersDisk(FirstName,
LastName) ;
GO

--Create filtered statistic on NetAmount

CREATE STATISTICS Stat_NetAmount_Filter_OrderDate ON dbo.
OrdersDisk(NetAmount)
WHERE OrderDate > '2019-01-01' ;
GO
```

When creating statistics, you can use the options detailed in Table 8-4.

Table 8-4. *Creating Statistics Options*

Option	Description
FULLSCAN	Creates the statistic object on a sample of 100% of rows in the table. This option creates the most accurate statistics but takes the longest time to generate.
SAMPLE	Specifies the number of rows or percentage of rows you need to use to build the statistic object. The larger the sample, the more accurate the statistic, but the longer it takes to generate. Specifying 0 creates the statistic but does not populate it.
NORECOMPUTE	Excludes the statistic object from being automatically updated with AUTO_UPDATE_STATISTICS.
INCREMENTAL	Overrides the database-level setting for incremental statistics.

Individual statistics, or all statistics on an individual table, can be updated by using the UPDATE STATISTICS statement. The script in Listing 8-26 first updates the Stat_NetAmount_Filter_OrderDate statistics object that we created on the OrdersDisk table and then updates all statistics on the CustomersDisk table.

Listing 8-26. Updating Statistics

```
--Update a single statistics object

UPDATE STATISTICS dbo.OrdersDisk Stat_NetAmount_Filter_OrderDate ;
GO

--Update all statistics on a table

UPDATE STATISTICS dbo.CustomersDisk ;
GO
```

When using UPDATE STATISTICS, in addition to the options specified in Table 8-4 for creating statistics, which are all valid when updating statistics, the options detailed in Table 8-5 are also available.

Table 8-5. *Updating Statistics Options*

Option	Description
RESAMPLE	Uses the most recent sample rate to update the statistics.
ON PARTITIONS	Causes statistics to be generated for the partitions listed and then merges them together to create global statistics.
ALL | COLUMNS | INDEX	Specifies if statistics should be updated for just columns, just indexes, or both. The default is ALL.

You can also update statistics for an entire database by using the sp_updatestats system stored procedure. This procedure updates out-of-date statistics on disk-based tables and all statistics on memory-optimized tables regardless of whether they are out of date or not. Listing 8-27 demonstrates this system stored procedure's usage to update statistics in the Chapter8 database. Passing in the RESAMPLE parameter causes the most recent sample rate to be used. Omitting this parameter causes the default sample rate to be used.

Listing 8-27. Sp_updatestats

```
EXEC sp_updatestats 'RESAMPLE' ;
```

> **Note**   Updating statistics causes queries that use those statistics to be recompiled the next time they run. The only time this is not the case is if there is only one possible plan for the tables and indexes referenced. For example, `SELECT * FROM MyTable` always performs a clustered index scan, assuming that the table has a clustered index.

SQL Server 2019 introduces additional metadata information, to help diagnose issues that are caused by queries waiting for synchronous statistics updates to occur. Firstly, a new wait type has been added, called `WAIT_ON_SYNC_STATISTICS_REFRESH`. This wait type denotes the amount of time that queries have spent waiting on the completion of synchronous statistics updates. Secondly, a new command type, called `SELECT (STATMAN)`, has been added to the sys.dm_exec_requests DMV. This command type indicates that a `SELECT` statement is currently waiting for a synchronous statistics update to complete, before it can continue.

Managing Cardinality

Because cardinality estimation is critical to plan optimization, if the cardinality estimator makes the wrong assumptions, it can have serious implications for query performance. Therefore, major changes to the cardinality estimator are not often made. There was a major update in SQL Server 7. The next large update was in SQL Server 2014.

The update to the cardinality estimator in SQL Server 2014 had two main impacts on behavior. Firstly, the assumption that columns are independent was replaced with an assumption that there will be correlation between values in different columns.

The behavior for estimating if no data will be returned based on joining multiple tables has also changed. The original behavior was to estimate the selectivity in the predicates of each table before joining the histograms to estimate join selectivity. The new behavior is to estimate join selectivity from the base tables before estimating predicate selectivity. This is known as base containment.

The issue is that the new cardinality estimations may be suboptimal for your workloads. If this is the case, then you can force a query to use legacy cardinality estimations by using a plan hint. New in SQL Server 2022, you can also use a Query Store hint to force the behavior without changing the query. This will be discussed in Chapter 22.

There are also Database Scoped Configurations that allow you to change the behavior on a database level, however. You can use the commands in Listing 8-28 to toggle between legacy and standard cardinality estimations for all queries within the database.

Listing 8-28. Toggle Legacy Cardinality Estimations

```
--Turn Legacy Cardinality Estimations On
```

```
ALTER DATABASE SCOPED CONFIGURATION SET LEGACY_CARDINALITY_ESTIMATION = ON
GO
```

```
--Turn Legacy Cardinality Estimations Off
```

```
ALTER DATABASE SCOPED CONFIGURATION SET LEGACY_CARDINALITY_ESTIMATION = ON
GO
```

In SQL Server 2022, providing that Query Store is enabled, you can also use feedback to help the optimizer determine what cardinality assumptions should be used for a given query, based on previous optimizations of the same query. You can use the commands in Listing 8-29 to toggle this functionality on or off, within a database.

Tip   Query store is discussed in Chapter 22.

Listing 8-29. Toggle Cardinality Feedback

```
--Turn Cardinality Feedback On
```

```
ALTER DATABASE SCOPED CONFIGURATION SET CE_FEEDBACK = ON
GO
```

```
--Turn Cardinality Feedback Off
```

```
ALTER DATABASE SCOPED CONFIGURATION SET CE_FEEDBACK = ON
GO
```

Summary

A table that does not have a clustered index is called a heap and the data pages of the table are stored in no particular order. Clustered indexes build a B-tree structure, based on the clustered index key, and cause the data within the table to be ordered by that key. There can only ever be one clustered index on a table because the leaf level of the clustered index is the actual data pages of the table, and the pages can only be physically ordered in one way. The natural choice of key for a clustered index is the primary key of the table and, by default, SQL Server automatically creates a clustered index on the primary key. There are situations, however, when you may choose to use a different column as the clustered index key. This is usually when the primary key of the table is very wide, is updateable, or is not ever-increasing.

Nonclustered indexes are also B-tree structures built on other columns within a table. The difference is that the leaf level of a nonclustered index contains pointers to the data pages of the table, as opposed to the data pages themselves. Because a nonclustered index does not order the actual data pages of a table, you can create multiple nonclustered indexes. These can improve query performance when you create them on columns that are used in WHERE, JOIN, and GROUP BY clauses. You can also include other columns at the leaf level of the B-tree of a nonclustered index in order to cover a query. A query is covered by a nonclustered index, when you do not need to read the data from the underlying table. You can also filter a nonclustered index by adding a WHERE clause to the definition. This allows for improved query performance for queries that use a well-defined subset of data.

Columnstore indexes compress data and store each column in a distinct set of pages. This can significantly improve the performance of data warehouse–style queries, which perform analysis on large datasets, since only the required columns need to be accessed, as opposed to the entire row. Each column is also split into segments, with each segment containing a header with metadata about the data, in order to further improve performance by allowing SQL Server to only access the relevant segments, in order to satisfy a query. Nonclustered Columnstore indexes are similar to Clustered Columnstore indexes, except that they make a copy of the data. This provides large performance enhancements at the expense of space.

You can create two types of index on memory-optimized tables: nonclustered indexes and nonclustered hash indexes. Nonclustered hash indexes are very efficient for point lookups, but they can be much less efficient when you must perform a range scan. Nonclustered indexes perform better for operations such as inequality comparisons, and they are also able to return the data in the sort order of the index key.

Indexes need to be maintained over time. They become fragmented due to DML statements causing page splits and can be reorganized or rebuilt to reduce or remove fragmentation. When pages become out of sequence, this is known as external fragmentation, and when pages have lots of free space, this is known as internal fragmentation. SQL Server stores metadata regarding index fragmentation and can display this through a DMF called `sys.dm_db_index_physical_stats`. SQL Server also maintains information on indexes that it regards as missing. A missing index is an index that does not exist in the database but would improve query performance if it were created. DBAs can use this data to help them improve their indexing strategies.

SQL Server maintains statistics about the distribution of values within a column or set of columns to help improve the quality of query plans. Without good-quality statistics, SQL Server may make the wrong choice about which index or index operator to use in order to satisfy a query. For example, it may choose to perform an index scan when an index seek would have been more appropriate. You can update statistics manually or automatically, but either way causes queries to be recompiled. SQL Server also supports incremental statistics, which allow statistics to be created on a per-partition basis, as opposed to globally for an entire table.

As well as managing statistics, SQL Server 2022 also allows you a limited degree of management over the assumptions used for cardinality estimation. The `CE_FEEDBACK` and `LEGACY_CARDINALITY_ESTIMATIONS` Database Scoped Configurations can be used. Legacy cardinality estimation can also be set for a specific query, using a Plan Hint or a Query Store hint.

CHAPTER 9

Database Consistency

Databases involve lots of I/O. When you have a lot of I/O, you inherently run the risk of corruption. Your primary defense against database corruption is to take regular backups of your database and to periodically test that these backups can be restored. You need to look out for database corruption, however, and SQL Server provides tools you can use to check the consistency of your database, as well as to resolve consistency issues if backups are not available. This chapter will look at the options you have for both checking and fixing consistency issues.

Consistency Errors

Consistency errors can occur in user databases or system databases, leaving tables, databases, or even the entire instances in an inaccessible state. Consistency errors can occur for many reasons, including hardware failures and issues with the Database Engine. The following sections discuss the types of error that can occur, how to detect these errors, and what to do if your system databases become corrupt.

Understand Consistency Errors

Different database consistency errors can occur; these cause a query to fail or a session to be disconnected and a message to be written to the SQL Server error log. The most common errors are detailed in the following sections.

605 Error

A 605 error can point to one of two issues, depending on the error severity. If the severity is level 12, then it indicates a dirty read. A *dirty read* is a transactional anomaly that occurs when you are using the Read Uncommitted isolation level or the NOLOCK query hint. It occurs when a transaction reads a row that never existed in the database, due

315

© Peter A. Carter 2023
P. A. Carter, *Pro SQL Server 2022 Administration*, https://doi.org/10.1007/978-1-4842-8864-1_9

to another transaction being rolled back. Transactional anomalies will be discussed in more detail in Chapter 18. To resolve this issue, either rerun the query until it succeeds or rewrite the query to avoid the use of the Read Uncommitted isolation level or the NOLOCK query hint.

The 605 error may indicate a more serious issue, however, and often it indicates a hardware failure. If the severity level is 21, then the page may be damaged, or the incorrect page may be being served up from the operating system. If this is the case, then you need to either restore from a backup or use DBCC CHECKDB to fix the issue. (DBCC CHECKDB is discussed later in this chapter.) Additionally, you should also have the Windows administrators and storage team check for possible hardware or disk-level issues.

823 Error

An 823 error occurs when SQL Server attempts to perform an I/O operation and the Windows API that it uses to perform this action returns an error to the Database Engine. An 823 error is almost always associated with a hardware or driver issue.

If an 823 error occurs, then you should use DBCC CHECKDB to check the consistency of the rest of the database and any other databases that reside on the same volume. You should liaise with your storage team to resolve the issue with the storage. Your Windows administrator should also check the Windows event log for correlated error messages. Finally, you should either restore the database from a backup or use DBCC CHECKDB to "fix" the issue.

824 Error

If the call to the Windows API succeeds but there are logical consistency issues with the data returned, then an 824 error is generated. Just like an 823 error, an 824 error usually means that there is an issue with the storage subsystem. If an 824 error is generated, then you should follow the same course of action as you do when an 823 error is generated.

5180 Error

A 5180 error occurs when a file ID is discovered that is not valid. File IDs are stored in page pointers, as well as in system pages at the beginning of each file. This error is usually caused by a corrupt pointer within a page, but it can potentially also indicate an issue with the Database Engine. If you experience this error, you should restore from a backup or run DBCC CHECKDB to fix the error.

7105 Error

A 7105 error occurs when a row within a table references an LOB (Large Object Block) structure that does not exist. This can happen because of a dirty read in the same manner as a 605 severity 12 error, or it can happen as the result of a corrupt page. The corruption can either be in the data page that points to the LOB structure or in a page of the LOB structure itself.

If you encounter a 7105 error, then you should run DBCC CHECKDB to check for errors. If you don't find any, then the error is likely the result of a dirty read. If you find errors, however, then either restore the database from a backup or use DBCC CHECKDB to fix the issue.

Detecting Consistency Errors

SQL Server provides mechanisms for verifying the integrity of pages as they are read from and written to disk. It also provides a log of corrupt pages that helps you identify the type of error that has occurred, how many times it has occurred, and the current status of the page that has become corrupt. These features are discussed in the following sections.

Page Verify Option

A database-level option called Page Verify determines how SQL Server checks for page corruption that the I/O subsystem causes when it is reading and writing pages to disk. It can be configured as CHECKSUM, which is the default option, TORN_PAGE_DETECTION, or NONE.

The recommended setting for Page Verify is CHECKSUM. When this option is selected, every time a page is written, a CHECKSUM value is created against the entire page and saved in the page header. A CHECKSUM value is a hash sum, which is deterministic and unique based on the value that the hashing function is run against. This value is then recalculated when a page is read into the buffer cache and compared to the original value.

When TORN_PAGE_DETECTION is specified, whenever a page is written to disk, the first 2 bytes of every 512-byte sector of the page are written to the page's header. When the page is subsequently read into memory, these values are checked to ensure that they are the same. The flaw here is obvious; it is perfectly possible for a page to be corrupt, and for this corruption not to be noticed, because it is not within the bytes that are checked.

TORN_PAGE_DETECTION is a deprecated feature of SQL Server, which means that it will not be available in future versions. You should avoid using it. If Page Verify is set to NONE, then SQL Server performs no page verification whatsoever. This is not good practice.

If all of your databases have been created in a SQL Server 2022 instance, then they are all configured to use CHECKSUM by default. If you have migrated your databases from a previous version of SQL Server, however, then they may be configured to use TORN_PAGE_ DETECTION. You can check the Page Verify setting of your databases by using the script in Listing 9-1.

Listing 9-1. Checking the Page Verify Option

```
--Create the Chapter9 database

CREATE DATABASE Chapter9 ;
GO

--View page verify option, for all databases on the instance

SELECT
        name
        ,page_verify_option_desc
FROM sys.databases ;
```

If you find that a database is using TORN_PAGE_DETECTION, or worse was set to NONE, then you can resolve the issue by altering the setting in the Options page of the Database Properties dialog box, as shown in Figure 9-1.

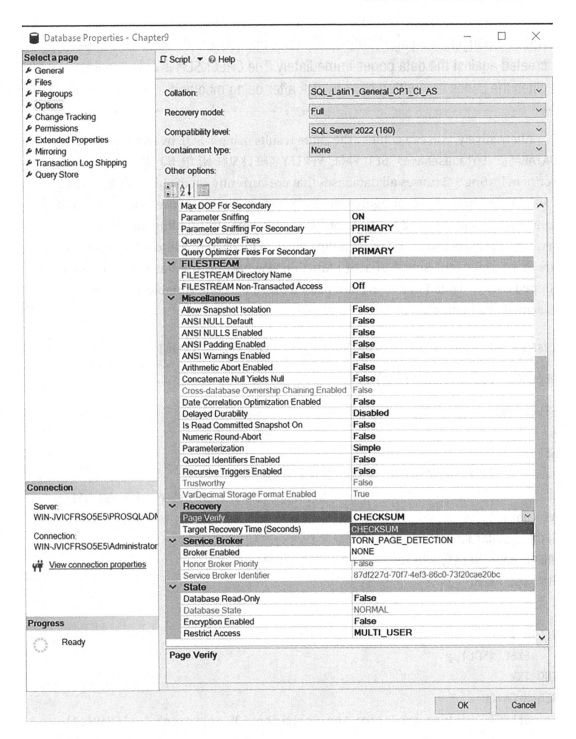

Figure 9-1. *The Options page*

Note   Changing the Page Verify option does not cause the CHECKSUM to be created against the data pages immediately. The CHECKSUM is only generated when the pages are written back to disk after being modified.

Alternatively, you can achieve the same results using T-SQL by using an ALTER DATABASE <DatabaseName> SET PAGE_VERIFY CHECKSUM WITH NO_WAIT statement. The script in Listing 9-2 causes all databases that are currently set to either NONE or TORN_ PAGE_DETECTION to be reconfigured to use CHECKSUM. The script uses the XQuery data() function to avoid the need for a cursor. The script works by building the statement required for every row in the table. It flips the data for each row into XML, but the tags are then striped out using the Data() function, leaving only the statement. It is then flipped back to a relational string and passed into a Unicode variable, which is then executed as dynamic SQL.

Listing 9-2.   Reconfiguring All Databases to Use CHECKSUM

```
DECLARE @SQL NVARCHAR(MAX)

SELECT @SQL =
(
SELECT
        'ALTER DATABASE ' + QUOTENAME(Name) +
                            ' SET PAGE_VERIFY CHECKSUM WITH NO_WAIT; '
AS [data()]
FROM sys.databases
WHERE page_verify_option_desc <> 'CHECKSUM'
FOR XML PATH('')
) ;

BEGIN TRY
    EXEC(@SQL) ;
END TRY
BEGIN CATCH
    SELECT 'Failure executing the following SQL statement ' + CHAR(13)
    +CHAR(10) + @SQL ;
END CATCH
```

Tip   You can use this technique any time you require a script to perform an operation against multiple databases. The code is far more efficient than using a cursor and promotes good practice by allowing DBAs to lead by example. You are always telling your developers not to use the cursor, right?

Suspect Pages

If SQL Server discovers a page with a bad checksum or a torn page, then it records the pages in the MSDB database in a table called dbo.suspect_pages. It also records any pages that encounter an 823 or 824 error in this table. The table consists of six columns, as described in Table 9-1.

Table 9-1. *suspect_pages Columns*

Column	Description
Database_id	The ID of the database that contains the suspect page
File_id	The ID of the file that contains the suspect page
Page_id	The ID of the page that is suspect
Event_Type	The nature of the event that caused the suspect pages to be updated
Error_count	An incremental counter that records the number of times that the event has occurred
Last_updated_date	The last time the row was updated

The possible values for the event_type column are explained in Table 9-2.

Table 9-2. *Event Types*

Event_type	Description
1	823 or 824 error
2	Bad checksum
3	Torn page
4	Restored
5	Repaired
7	Deallocated by DBCC CHECKDB

After recording the suspect page in the suspect_pages table, SQL Server updates the row after you have fixed the issue by either restoring the page from a backup or by using DBCC CHECKDB. It also increments the error count every time an error with the same event_type is encountered. You should monitor this table for new and updated entries and you should also periodically delete rows from this table, which have an event_type of 4 or 5, to stop the table from becoming full.

Note   Page restores will be discussed in Chapter 12.

The script in Listing 9-3 creates a table in the Chapter9, called CorruptTable, which is then populated with data. It then causes one of the table's pages to become corrupt.

Listing 9-3. Corrupting a Page

```
USE Chapter9
GO

--Create the table that we will corrupt

CREATE TABLE dbo.CorruptTable
(
ID    INT    NOT NULL    PRIMARY KEY CLUSTERED    IDENTITY,
SampleText NVARCHAR(50)
) ;
```

```
--Populate the table

DECLARE @Numbers TABLE
(ID        INT)

;WITH CTE(Num)
AS
(
SELECT 1 Num
UNION ALL
SELECT Num + 1
FROM CTE
WHERE Num <= 100
)
INSERT INTO @Numbers
SELECT Num
FROM CTE ;

INSERT INTO dbo.CorruptTable
SELECT 'SampleText'
FROM @Numbers a
CROSS JOIN @Numbers b ;

--DBCC WRITEPAGE will be used to corrupt a page in the table. This
requires the
--database to be placed in single user mode.
--THIS IS VERY DANGEROUS - DO NOT EVER USE THIS IN A PRODUCTION ENVIRONMENT

ALTER DATABASE Chapter9 SET  SINGLE_USER WITH NO_WAIT ;
GO

DECLARE @SQL NVARCHAR(MAX) ;

SELECT @SQL = 'DBCC WRITEPAGE(' +
(
        SELECT CAST(DB_ID('Chapter9') AS NVARCHAR)
) +
', 1, ' +
```

```
(
        SELECT TOP 1 CAST(page_id AS NVARCHAR)
        FROM dbo.CorruptTable
        CROSS APPLY sys.fn_PhysLocCracker(%%physloc%%)
) +
', 2000, 1, 0x61, 1)' ;

EXEC(@SQL) ;

ALTER DATABASE Chapter9 SET  MULTI_USER WITH NO_WAIT ;
GO

SELECT *
FROM dbo.CorruptTable ;
```

The results in Figure 9-2 show that the final query in the script, which tried to read the data from the table, failed because one of the pages is corrupt, and therefore, there is a bad checksum.

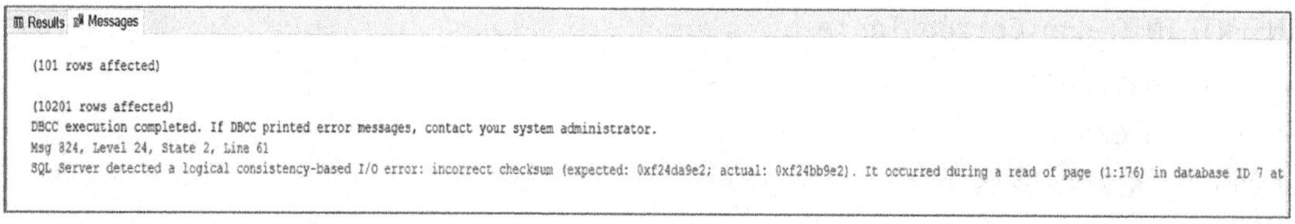

Figure 9-2. *Bad checksum error*

Caution   DBCC WRITEPAGE is used here for educational purposes only. It is undocumented and also extremely dangerous. It should *never* be used on a production system and should only be used on any database with extreme caution.

324

You can use the query in Listing 9-4 to generate a friendly output from the msdb. dbo.suspect_pages table. This query uses the DB_NAME() function to find the name of the database, joins to the sys.master_files system table to find the name of the file involved, and uses a CASE statement to translate the event_type into an event type description.

Listing 9-4. Querying suspect_pages

```
SELECT
    DB_NAME(sp.database_id) [Database]
    ,mf.name
    ,sp.page_id
    ,CASE sp.event_type
        WHEN 1 THEN '823 or 824 or Torn Page'
        WHEN 2 THEN 'Bad Checksum'
        WHEN 3 THEN 'Torn Page'
        WHEN 4 THEN 'Restored'
        WHEN 5 THEN 'Repaired (DBCC)'
        WHEN 7 THEN 'Deallocated (DBCC)'
    END AS [Event]
    ,sp.error_count
    ,sp.last_update_date
FROM msdb.dbo.suspect_pages sp
INNER JOIN sys.master_files mf
        ON sp.database_id = mf.database_id
                AND sp.file_id = mf.file_id ;
```

After corrupting a page of our CorruptTable table, running this query will produce the results in Figure 9-3. Obviously, the page_id is likely to be different if you were to run the scripts on your own system, since the Database Engine is likely to have allocated different pages to the table that you created.

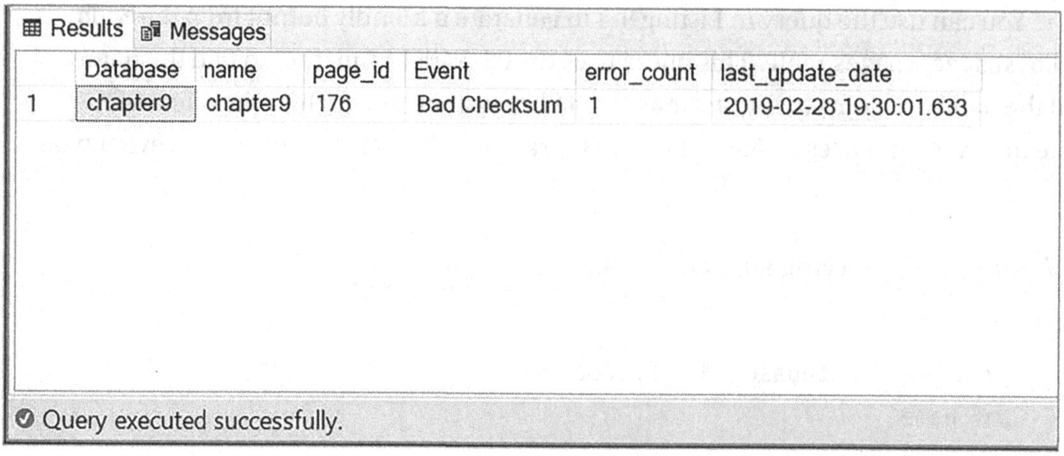

	Database	name	page_id	Event	error_count	last_update_date
1	chapter9	chapter9	176	Bad Checksum	1	2019-02-28 19:30:01.633

Query executed successfully.

Figure 9-3. *Results of querying suspect_pages*

Note   We will fix the error later in this chapter, but that involves losing data that was stored on the page. If a backup is available, then a page restore is a better option than a repair in this scenario.

Consistency Issues for Memory-Optimized Tables

Corruption usually occurs during a physical I/O operation, so you can be forgiven for thinking that memory-optimized tables are immune to corruption, but this is a fallacy. As you may remember from Chapter 7, although memory-optimized tables reside in memory, a copy of the tables—and depending on your durability settings, a copy of your data—is kept in physical files. This is to ensure that the tables and data are still available after a restart of the instance. These files can be subject to corruption. It is also possible for data to become corrupt in memory, due to issues such as a faulty RAM chip.

Unfortunately, the repair options of DBCC CHECKDB are not supported against memory tables. However, when you take a backup of a database that contains a memory-optimized filegroup, a checksum validation is performed against the files within this filegroup. It is therefore imperative that you not only take regular backups, but that you also check that they can be restored successfully, on a regular basis. This is because your only option, in the event of a corrupted memory-optimized table, is to restore from the last known good backup.

System Database Corruption

If system databases become corrupt, your instance can be left in an inaccessible state. The following sections discuss how to respond to corruption in the Master database and the Resource database.

Corruption of the Master Database

If the Master database becomes corrupted, it is possible that your instance will be unable to start. If this is the case, then you need to rebuild the system databases and then restore the latest copies from backups. Chapter 12 discusses strategies for database backups in more detail, but this highlights why backing up your system databases is important. In the event that you need to rebuild your system databases, you will lose all instance-level information, such as Logins, SQL Server Agent jobs, Linked Servers, and so on, if you are not able to restore from a backup. Even knowledge of the user databases within the instance will be lost and you will need to reattach the databases.

In order to rebuild the system databases, you need to run setup. When you are rebuilding system databases using setup, the parameters described in Table 9-3 are available.

Table 9-3. *System Database Rebuild Parameters*

Parameter	Description
/ACTION	Specifies Rebuilddatabase for the action parameter.
/INSTANCENAME	Specifies the instance name of the instance that contains the corrupt system database.
/Q	This parameter stands for quiet. Use this to run setup without any user interaction.
/SQLCOLLATION	This is an optional parameter that you can use to specify a collation for the instance. If you omit it, the collation of the Windows OS is used.
/SAPWD	If your instance uses mixed-mode authentication, then use this parameter to specify the password for the SA account.
/SQLSYSADMINACCOUNTS	Use this parameter to specify which accounts should be made sysadmins of the instance.

The PowerShell command in Listing 9-5 rebuilds the system databases of the PROSQLADMIN instance.

Listing 9-5. Rebuilding System Databases

```
.\setup.exe /ACTION=rebuilddatabase /INSTANCENAME=PROSQLADMIN /SQLSYSADMINA
CCOUNTS=SQLAdministrator
```

As mentioned, when this action is complete, ideally we restore the latest copy of the Master database from a backup. Since we do not have one, we need to reattach our Chapter9 database in order to continue. Additionally, the detail of the corrupt page within the suspect_pages table will also be lost. Attempting to read the CorruptTable table in the Chapter9 database causes this data to be repopulated, however. The script in Listing 9-6 reattaches the Chapter9 database. You should change the file paths to match you own configuration before you run the script.

Listing 9-6. Reattaching a Database

```
CREATE DATABASE Chapter9 ON
( FILENAME = N'F:\MSSQL\DATA\Chapter9.mdf' ),
( FILENAME = N'F:\MSSQL\DATA\Chapter9_log.ldf' )
 FOR ATTACH ;
```

Corruption of the Resource Database or Binaries

It is possible for the instance itself to become corrupt. This can include corrupt Registry keys or the Resource database becoming corrupt. If this happens, then find the repair utility that ships with the SQL Server installation media. To invoke this tool, select Repair from the Maintenance tab of the SQL Server Installation Center.

After the wizard has run the appropriate rule checks, you are presented with the Select Instance page, as illustrated in Figure 9-4.

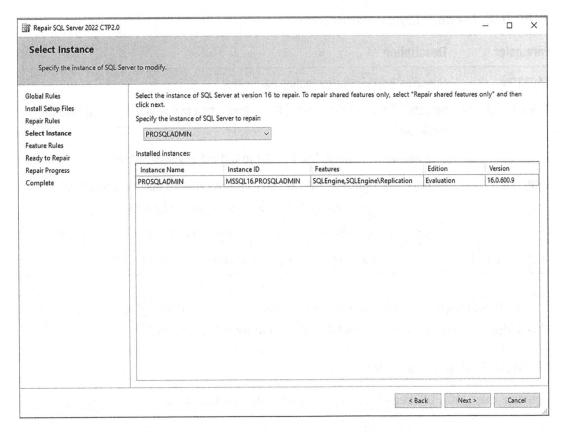

Figure 9-4. *The Select Instance page*

After you select the instance that needs to be repaired, the following page of the wizard runs an additional rules check to ensure that the required features can be repaired. Finally, on the Ready To Repair page, you see a summary of the actions that are to be performed. After choosing to repair, you see the repair progress report. Once the repair completes, a Summary page displays, which provides you with the status of each operation that was performed and also a link to a log file that you may wish to review if you need to perform troubleshooting.

As an alternative to using SQL Server Installation Center, you can achieve the same rebuild from the command line. This is useful if your instance is running on Windows Server Core. When you are repairing an instance from the command line, the parameters available to you are those listed in Table 9-4. Because the Master database is not being rebuilt when you are repairing an instance, you do not need to specify a collation or Administrator details.

Table 9-4. *Instance Repair Parameters*

Parameter	Description
/ACTION	Specifies Repair for the action parameter.
/INSTANCENAME	Specifies the instance name of the instance that contains the corrupt system database.
/Q	This parameter is Quiet. Use this to run without any user interaction.
/ENU	An optional parameter that you can use on a localized operating system to specify that the English version of SQL Server should be used.
/FEATURES	An optional parameter you can use to specify a list of components to repair.
/HIDECONSOLE	An optional parameter that causes the console to be suppressed.

The PowerShell command in Listing 9-7 also rebuilds the PPROSQLADMIN instance. This script also works for instances hosted on Windows Server Core.

Listing 9-7. Repairing an Instance

```
.\setup.exe /ACTION=repair /INSTANCENAME=PROSQLADMIN /q
```

DBCC CHECKDB

DBCC CHECKDB is a utility that can be used to both discover corruption and also fix the errors. When you run DBCC CHECKDB, by default it creates a database snapshot and runs the consistency checks against this snapshot. This provides a transactionally consistent point from which the checks can occur while at the same time reducing contention in the database. It can check multiple objects in parallel to improve performance, but this depends on the number of cores that are available and the MAXDOP setting of the instance.

Checking for Errors

When you run DBCC CHECKDB for the purpose of discovering corruption only, then you can specify the arguments, detailed in Table 9-5.

Table 9-5. *DBCC CHECKDB Arguments*

Argument	Description
NOINDEX	Specifies that that integrity checks should be performed on heap and clustered index structures but not on nonclustered indexes.
EXTENDED_ LOGICAL_CHECKS	Forces the logical consistency of XML indexes, indexed views, and spatial indexes to be performed.
NO_INFOMSGS	Prevents informational messages from being returned in the results. This can reduce noise when you are searching for an issue, since only errors and warnings with a severity level greater than 10 are returned.
TABLOCK	DBCC CHECKDB creates a database snapshot and runs its consistency checks against this structure to avoid taking out locks in the database, which cause contention. Specifying this option changes that behavior so that instead of creating a snapshot, SQL Server takes out a temporary exclusive lock on the database, followed by exclusive locks on the structures that it is checking. In the event of high write load, this can reduce the time it takes to run DBCC CHECKDB, but at the expense of contention with other processes that may be running. It also causes the system table metadata validation and service broker validation to be skipped.
ESTIMATEONLY	When this argument is specified, no checks are performed. The only thing that happens is that the space required in TempDB to perform the checks is calculated based on the other arguments specified.
PHYSICAL_ONLY	When this argument is used, DBCC CHECKDB is limited to performing allocation consistency checks on the database, consistency checks on system catalogs, and validation on each page of every table within the database. This option cannot be used in conjunction with DATA_PURITY.
DATA_PURITY	Specifies that column integrity checks are carried out, such as ensuring that values are within their data type boundaries. For use with databases that have been upgraded from SQL Server 2000 or below only. For any newer databases, or SQL Server 2000 databases that have already been scanned with DATA_PURITY, the checks happen by default.
ALL_ERRORMSGS	For backward compatibility only. Has no effect on SQL 2022 databases.

DBCC CHECKDB is a very intensive process that can consume many CPU and I/O resources. Therefore, it is advisable to run it during a maintenance window to avoid performance issues for applications. The Database Engine automatically decides how many CPU cores to assign the DBCC CHECKDB based on the Instance level setting for MAXDOP and the amount of throughput to the sever when the process begins. If you expect load to increase during the window when DBCC CHECKDB will be running, however, then you can throttle the process to a single core by turning on Trace Flag 2528. This flag should be used with caution, however, because it causes DBC CHECKDB to take much longer to complete. If a snapshot is not generated, either because you have specified TABLOCK or because there was not enough space on disk to generate a snapshot, then it also causes each table to be locked for a much longer period.

The sample in Listing 9-8 does not perform any checks but calculates the amount of space required in TempDB in order for DBCC CHECKDB to run successfully against the Chapter9 database.

Listing 9-8. Checking TempDB Space Required for DBCC CHECKDB

```
USE Chapter9
GO

DBCC CHECKDB WITH ESTIMATEONLY ;
```

Because our Chapter9 database is tiny, we only require less than half a megabyte of space in TempDB. This is reflected in the results, shown in Figure 9-5.

```
Messages
 DBCC results for 'chapter9'.
 Estimated TEMPDB space (in KB) needed for CHECKDB on database chapter9 = 2293.
 DBCC execution completed. If DBCC printed error messages, contact your system administrator.



100 %    ▼
✓ Query executed successfully.                                              WIN-LDFF81U7FFT\PRC
```

Figure 9-5. *TempDB space required for DBC CHECKDB results*

The script in Listing 9-9 uses DBCC CHECKDB to perform consistency checks across the entire Chapter9 database.

Listing 9-9. Running DBCC CHECKDB

```
USE Chapter9
GO

DBCC CHECKDB ;
```

Figure 9-6 displays a fragment of the results of running this command. As you can see, the issue with the corrupt page in the CorruptTable table has been identified.

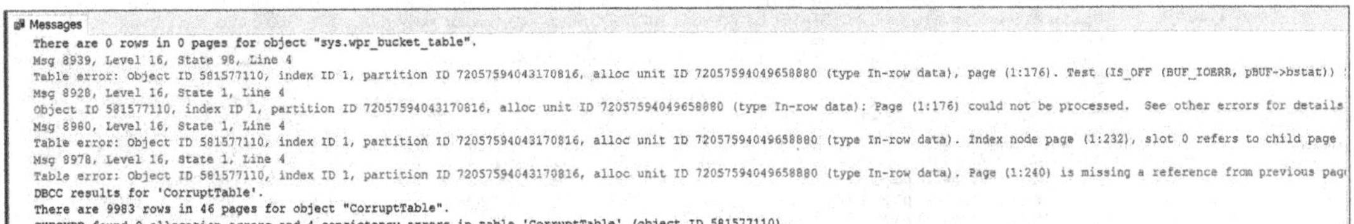

Figure 9-6. DBCC CHECKDB identifies corrupt page

In real life, unless you are troubleshooting a specific error, you are unlikely to be running DBCC CHECKDB manually. It is normally scheduled to run with SQL Server Agent or a maintenance plan. So how do you know when it encounters an error? Simply, the SQL Server Agent job step fails. Figure 9-7 shows the error message being displayed in the history of the failed job. The output from DBCC CHECKDB is also written to the SQL Server Error log. This is regardless of whether or not it was invoked manually or through a SQL Server Agent job.

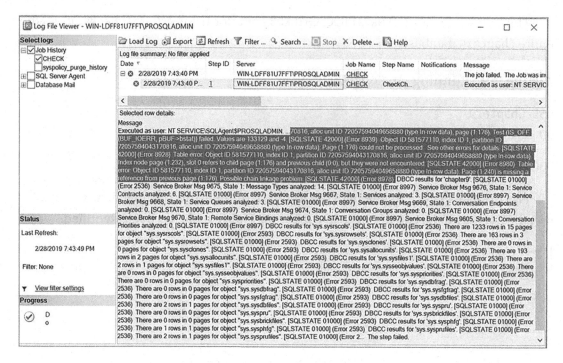

Figure 9-7. *Errors in job history*

Because `DBCC CHECKDB` finding errors causes the job to fail, you can set up a notification so that a DBA receives an alert. Assuming that Database Mail is configured on the sever, you can create a new operator that receives e-mails by selecting New Operator from the context menu of the Operators folder under the SQL Server Agent folder in SQL Server Management Studio, as illustrated in Figure 9-8.

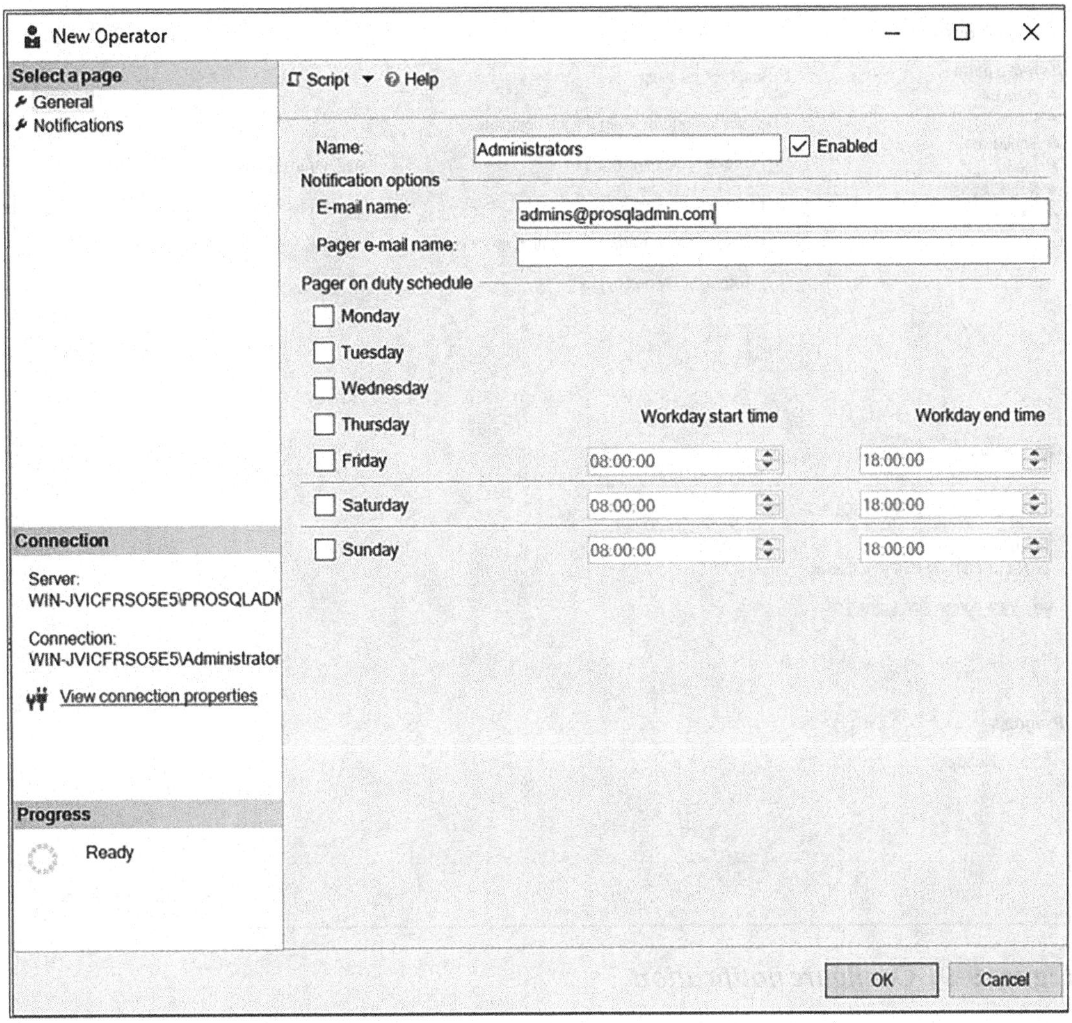

Figure 9-8. *Create a new operator*

Once you have created the operator, you are able to specify that operator in the Notifications tab of the Job Properties page of the SQL Server Agent job. This is illustrated in Figure 9-9.

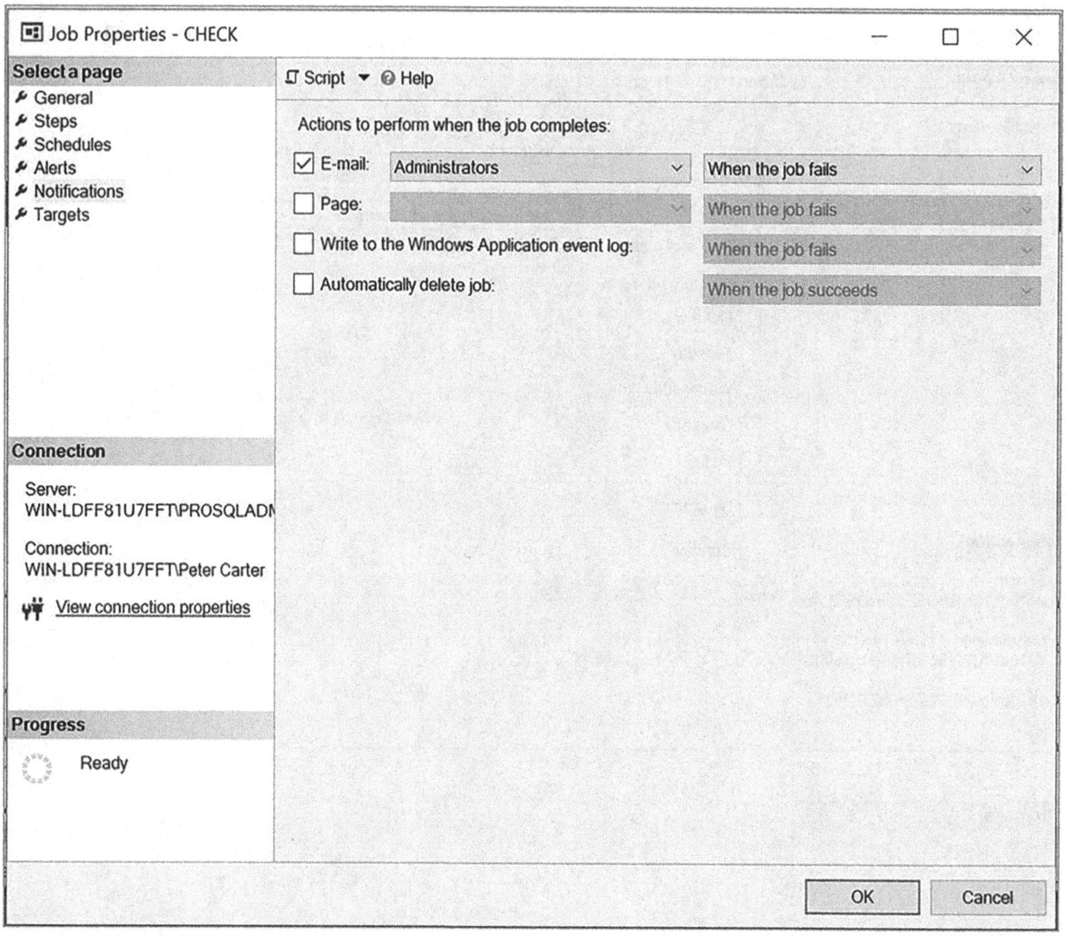

Figure 9-9. *Configure notification*

SQL Server Agent jobs are discussed fully in Chapter 24.

Fixing Errors

When we use DBCC CHECKDB to repair a corruption in the database, we need to specify an additional argument that determines the repair level to use. The options available are REPAIR_REBUILD or REPAIR_ALLOW_DATA_LOSS. REPAIR_REBUILD is, of course, the preferred option, and it can be used to resolve issues that will not cause data loss, such as bad page pointers, or corruption inside a nonclustered index. REPAIR_ALLOW_DATA_LOSS attempts to fix all errors it encounters, but as its name suggests, this may involve data being lost.

Caution   You should only use this option to restore the data if no backup is available.

Before specifying a repair option for DBCC CHECKDB, always run it without a repair option first. This is because when you do so, it will tell you the minimum repair option that you can use to resolve the errors. If we look again at the output of the run against the Chapter9 database, then we can see that the end of the output advises the most appropriate repair option to use. This is illustrated in Figure 9-10.

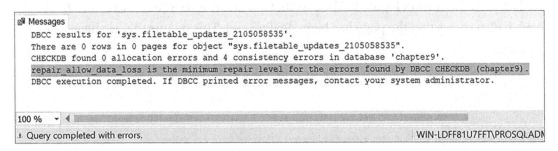

Figure 9-10. *Suggested repair option*

In our case, we are informed that we need to use the REPAIR_ALOW_DATA_LOSS option. If we try to use the REPAIR_REBUILD option, we receive the following message, from DBCC CHECKDB:

```
CHECKDB found 0 allocation errors and 4 consistency errors in database
'chapter9'.repair_allow_data_loss is the minimum repair level for the
errors found by DBCC CHECKDB (chapter9, repair_rebuild)
```

Since we do not have a backup of the Chapter9 database, this is our only chance of fixing the corruption. In order to use the repair options, we also have to put our database in SINGLE_USER mode. The script in Listing 9-10 places the Chapter9 database in SINGLE_USER mode, runs the repair, and then alters the database again to allow multiple connections.

Listing 9-10. Repairing Corruption with DBCC CHECKDB

```
ALTER DATABASE Chapter9 SET SINGLE_USER ;
GO

DBCC CHECKDB (Chapter9, REPAIR_ALLOW_DATA_LOSS) ;
GO

ALTER DATABASE Chapter9 SET MULTI_USER ;
GO
```

The partial results in Figure 9-11 show that the errors in `CorruptTable` have been fixed. It also shows that the page has been deallocated. This means that we have lost all data on the page.

Figure 9-11. *Results of repairing corruption with DBCC CHECKDB*

If we query the `msdb.dbo.suspect_pages` table again using the same query as demonstrated in Listing 9-4, we see that the `Event` column has been updated to state that the page has been deallocated. We can also see that the `error_count` column has been incremented every time we accessed the page, through either `SELECT` statements or `DBCC CHECKDB`. These results are displayed in Figure 9-12.

Results | Messages

	Database	name	page_id	Event	error_count	last_update_date
1	chapter9	chapter9	176	Deallocated (DBCC)	9	2019-02-28 20:00:37.560

Query executed successfully.

Figure 9-12. *Suspect_pages table, following repair*

Emergency Mode

If your database files are damaged to the extent that your database is inaccessible and unrecoverable, even by using the `REPAIR_ALLOW_DATA_LOSS` option, and you do not have usable backups, then your last resort is to run `DBCC CHECKDB` in emergency mode using the `REPAIR_ALLOW_DATA_LOSS` option. Remember, emergency mode is a last resort option for repairing your databases, and if you cannot access them through this mode, you will not be able to access them via any other means. When you perform this action with the database in emergency mode, `DBCC CHECKDB` treats pages that are inaccessible due to corruption as if they do not have errors in an attempt to recover data.

This operation can also back up databases that are inaccessible due to log corruption. This is because it attempts to force the transaction log to recover, even if it encounters errors. If this fails, it rebuilds the transaction log. Of course, this may lead to transaction inconsistencies, but as mentioned, this is an option of last resort.

As an example, we will delete the transaction log file for the `Chapter9` database in the operating system. You can find the operating system location of the transaction log file by running the query in Listing 9-11.

Listing 9-11. Finding the Transaction Log Path

```
SELECT physical_name
FROM sys.master_files
WHERE database_id = DB_ID('Chapter9')
    AND type_desc = 'Log' ;
```

Because data and log files are locked by the SQL Server process, we first need to stop the instance. After starting the instance again, we can see that our Chapter9 database has been marked as Recovery Pending, as shown in Figure 9-13.

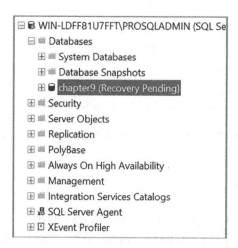

Figure 9-13. *Database in Recovery Pending*

Since we have no backup available for the Chapter9 database, the only option that we have is to use DBCC CHECKDB in emergency mode. The script in Listing 9-12 puts the Chapter9 database in emergency mode and then uses DBCC CHECKDB with the REPAIR_ALLOW_DATA_LOSS option to fix the error.

Listing 9-12. DBCC CHECKDB in Emergency Mode

```
ALTER DATABASE Chapter9 SET EMERGENCY ;
GO

ALTER DATABASE Chapter9 SET SINGLE_USER ;
GO

DBCC CHECKDB ('Chapter9', REPAIR_ALLOW_DATA_LOSS) ;
GO

ALTER DATABASE Chapter9 SET MULTI_USER ;
GO
```

The partial results, displayed in Figure 9-14, show that SQL Server was able to bring the database online by rebuilding the transaction log. However, it also shows that this means that transactional consistency has been lost and the restore chain has been broken. Because we have lost transactional consistency, we should now run DBCC CHECKCONSTRAINTS to find errors in foreign key constraints, and CHECK constraints. DBCC CHECKCONSTRAINTS is covered later in this chapter.

```
Messages
File activation failure. The physical file name "C:\Program Files\Microsoft SQL Server\MSSQL15.PROSQLADMIN\MSSQL\DATA\chapter9_log.ldf" may be incorrect.
The log cannot be rebuilt because there were open transactions/users when the database was shutdown, no checkpoint occurred to the database, or the database was read-only. This error
Warning: The log for database 'chapter9' has been rebuilt. Transactional consistency has been lost. The RESTORE chain was broken, and the server no longer has context on the previous
DBCC results for 'chapter9'.
Service Broker Msg 9675, State 1: Message Types analyzed: 14.
Service Broker Msg 9676, State 1: Service Contracts analyzed: 6.
Service Broker Msg 9667, State 1: Services analyzed: 3.
Service Broker Msg 9668, State 1: Service Queues analyzed: 3.
Service Broker Msg 9669, State 1: Conversation Endpoints analyzed: 0.
Service Broker Msg 9674, State 1: Conversation Groups analyzed: 0.
Service Broker Msg 9670, State 1: Remote Service Bindings analyzed: 0.
Service Broker Msg 9605, State 1: Conversation Priorities analyzed: 0.
DBCC results for 'sys.sysrscols'.
```

Figure 9-14. Results of DBCC CHECKDB in emergency mode

Note If running DBCC CHECKDB in emergency mode fails, then there is no other way that the database can be repaired.

Other DBCC Commands for Corruption

A number of other DBCC commands perform a subset of the work carried out by DBCC CHECKDB. These are discussed in the following sections.

DBCC CHECKCATALOG

In SQL Server, the system catalog is a collection of metadata that describes the database and data held within it. When DBCC CHECKCATALOG is run, it performs consistency checks on this catalog. This command is run as part of DBCC CHECKDB but can also run as a command in its own right. When run in its own right, it accepts the same arguments as DBCC CHECKDB, with the exception of PHYSICAL_ONLY and DATA_PURITY, which are not available for this command.

DBCC CHECKALLOC

DBCC CHECKALLOC performs consistency checks against the disk allocation structures within a database. It is run as part of DBCC CHECKDB but can also be run as a command in its own right. When run in its own right, it accepts many of the same arguments as DBCC CHECKDB, with the exception of PHYSICAL_ONLY, DATA_PURITY, and REPAIR_REBUILD, which are not available for this command. The output is by table, index, and partition.

DBCC CHECKTABLE

DBCC CHECKTABLE is run against every table and indexed view in a database, as part of DBCC CHECKDB. However, it can also be run as a separate command in its own right against a specific table and the indexes of that table. It performs consistency checks against that specific table, and if any indexed views reference the table, it also performs cross table consistency checks. It accepts the same arguments as DBCC CHECKDB, but with it, you also need to specify the name or ID of the table that you want to check.

Caution   I have witnessed people split their tables into two buckets and replace DBCC CHECKDB with a run DBCC CHECKTABLE against half of their tables on alternate nights. This not only leaves gaps in what is being checked, but a new database snapshot is generated for every table that is checked, as opposed to one snapshot being generated for all checks to be performed. This can lead to longer run times, per table.

DBCC CHECKFILEGROUP

DBCC CHECKFILEGROUP performs consistency checks on the system catalog, the allocation structures, tables, and indexed views within a specified filegroup. There are some limitations to this, however, when a table has indexes that are stored on a different filegroup. In this scenario, the indexes are not checked for consistency. This still applies if it is the indexes that are stored on the filegroup that you are checking, but the corresponding base table is on a different filegroup.

If you have a partitioned table, which is stored on multiple filegroups, DBCC CHECKFILEGROUP only checks the consistency of the partition(s) that are stored on the filegroup being checked. The arguments for DBCC CHECKFILEGROUP are the same as those for DBCC CHECKDB, with the exception of DATA_PURITY, which is not valid and you cannot specify any repair options. You also need to specify the filegroup name or ID.

DBCC CHECKIDENT

DBCC CHECKIDENT scans all rows within a specified table to find the highest value in the IDENTITY column. It then checks to ensure that the next IDENTITY value, which is stored in a table's metadata, is higher than the highest value in the IDENTITY column of the table. DBCC CHECKIDENT accepts the arguments detailed in Table 9-6.

Table 9-6. *DBCC CHECKIDENT Arguments*

Argument	Description
Table Name	The name of the table to be checked.
NORESEEED	Returns the maximum value of the IDENTITY column and the current IDENITY value, but will not reseed the column, even if required.
RESEED	Reseeds the current IDENITY value to that of the maximum IDENTITY value in the table.
New Reseed Value	Used with RESEED, specifies a seed for the IDENITY value. This should be used with caution, since setting the IDENTITY value to lower than the maximum value in the table can cause errors to be generated, if there is a primary key or unique constraint on the IDENTITY column.
WITH NO_INFOMSGS	Causes informational messages to be suppressed.

We could check the IDENTITY value against the maximum IDENTITY value in our CorruptTable table by using the command in Listing 9-13.

Listing 9-13. DBCC CHECKIDENT

```
DBCC CHECKIDENT('CorruptTable',NORESEED) ;
```

The results, displayed in Figure 9-15, show that both the maximum value in the IDENITY column and the current IDENTITY value are both 10201, meaning that there is not currently an issue with the IDENTTY value in our table.

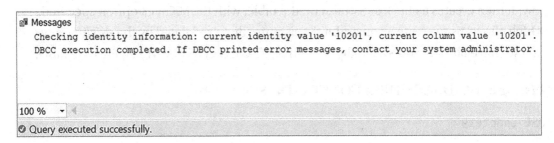

Figure 9-15. *DBCC CHECKIDENT results*

DBCC CHECKCONSTRAINTS

DBCC CHECKCONSTRAINTS can check the integrity of a specific foreign key or check constraint within a table, check all constraints on a single table, or check all constraints on all tables of a database. DBCC CHECKCONSTRAINTS accepts the arguments detailed in Table 9-7.

Table 9-7. *DBCC CHECKCONSTRAINTS Arguments*

Argument	Description
Table or Constraint	Specifies either the name or ID of the constraint you wish to check, or specifies the name or ID of a table to check all enabled constraints on that table. Omitting this argument causes all enabled constraints on all tables within the database to be checked.
ALL_CONSTRAINTS	If DBCC CHECKCONSTRAINTS is being run against an entire table or entire database, then this option forces disabled constraints to be checked as well as enabled ones.
ALL_ERRORMSGS	By default, if DBCC CHECKCONSTRAINTS finds rows that violate a constraint, it returns the first 200 of these rows. Specifying ALL_ERRORMSGS causes all rows violating the constraint to be returned, even if this number exceeds 200.
NO_INFOMSGS	Causes informational messages to be suppressed.

The script in Listing 9-14 creates a table called BadConstraint and inserts a single row. It then creates a check constraint on the table, with the NOCHECK option specified, which allows us to create a constraint that is immediately violated by the existing row that we have already added. Finally, we run DBCC CHECKCONSTRAINTS against the table.

Listing 9-14. DBCC CHECKCONSTRAINTS

```
USE Chapter9
GO

--Create the BadConstraint table

CREATE TABLE dbo.BadConstraint
(
```

```
ID          INT PRIMARY KEY
) ;

--Insert a negative value into the BadConstraint table

INSERT INTO dbo.BadConstraint
VALUES(-1) ;

--Create a CHECK constraint, which enforces positive values in the
ID column

ALTER TABLE dbo.BadConstraint WITH NOCHECK ADD CONSTRAINT chkBadConstraint
CHECK (ID > 0) ;
GO

--Run DBCC CHECKCONSTRAINTS against the table

DBCC CHECKCONSTRAINTS('dbo.BadConstraint') ;
```

The results of running this script are shown in Figure 9-16. You can see that DBCC CHECKCONSTRAINTS has returned the details of the row that breaches the constraint.

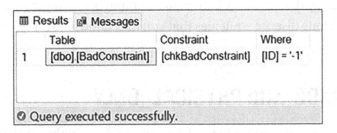

Figure 9-16. *DBCC CHECKCONSTRAINTS results*

Tip   After running DBCC CHECKDB, or other DBCC commands to repair corruption, it is good practice to run DBCC CHECKCONSTRAINTS. This is because the repair options of the DBCC commands do not take constraint integrity into account.

Even if DBCC CHECKCONSTRAINTS does not find any bad data, it still does not mark the constraint as trusted. You must do this manually. The script in Listing 9-15 first runs a query to see if the constraint is trusted and then manually marks it as trusted.

Listing 9-15. Marking a Constraint as Trusted

```
SELECT
    is_not_trusted
FROM sys.check_constraints
WHERE name = 'chkBadConstraint' ;

ALTER TABLE dbo.BadConstraint WITH CHECK CHECK CONSTRAINT
chkDadConstraint ;
```

Consistency Checks on VLDBs

If you have VLDBs (very large databases), then it may be difficult to find a maintenance window long enough to run DBCC CHECKDB, and running it while users or ETL processes are connected is likely to cause performance issues. You may also encounter a similar issue if you have a large estate of smaller databases that are using a common infrastructure, such as a SAN or a private cloud. Ensuring that your databases are consistent, however, should be a priority near the top of your agenda, so you should try and find a strategy that achieves both your maintenance and performance goals. The following sections discuss strategies that you may choose to adopt to achieve this balance.

DBCC CHECKDB with PHYSICAL_ONLY

One strategy that you can adopt is to run DBCC CHECKDB regularly, ideally nightly, using the PHYSICAL_ONLY option, and then run a complete check on a periodic, but less-frequent basis, ideally weekly. When you run DBCC CHECKDB with the PHYSICAL_ONLY option, consistency checks are carried out of system catalogs and allocation structures and each page of every table is scanned and validated. The net result of this is that corruption caused by I/O errors is trapped, but other issues, such as logical consistency errors, are identified. This is why it is important to still run a full scan weekly.

Backing Up WITH CHECKSUM and DBCC CHECKALLOC

If you are in a position where all of your databases have a full backup every night and all are configured with a PAGE_VERIFY option of CHECKSUM, then an alternative approach to the one mentioned in the previous section is to add the WITH CHECKSUM option to your full backups, followed by a DBCC CHECKALLOC, to replace the DBCC CHECKDB with the PHYSICAL_ONLY option specified on a nightly basis. The DBCC CHECKALLOC command, which is actually a subset of the DBCC CHECKDB command, validates the allocation structures within the database. When the full backups are taken WITH CHECKSUM, then this fulfills the requirement to scan and verify each page of every table for I/O errors. Just like running DBCC CHECKDB, with the PHYSICAL_ONLY option specified, this identifies any corruption caused by I/O operations and identifies any bad checksums. Any page errors that occurred in memory, however, are not identified. This means that like the PHYSICAL_ONLY strategy, you still require a full run of DBCC CHECKDB once a week to trap logical consistency errors or corruptions that occurred in memory. This option is very useful if you have an environment with common infrastructure and you are performing full nightly backups of all databases, since you will reduce the overall amount of I/O on a nightly basis. This is at the expense of the duration of your backup window, however, and it increases the resources used during this time.

Splitting the Workload

Another strategy for VLDBs may be to split the load of DBCC CHECKDB over multiple nights. For example, if your VLDB has multiple filegroups, then you could run DBCC CHECKFILEGROUP against half of the filegroups on Monday, Wednesday, and Friday, and against the other half of the filegroups on Tuesday, Thursday, and Saturday. You could reserve Sunday for a full run of DBCC CHECKDB. A full run of DBCC CHECKDB is still advised on a weekly basis, since DBCC CHECKFILEGROUP does not perform checks, such as validating Service Broker objects.

If your issue is common infrastructure, as opposed to VLDBs, then you can adapt the concept just described so that you run DBCC CHECKDB on a subset of databases on alternate nights. This can be a little complex, since the approach here, in order to avoid swamping the SAN, is to segregate the databases intelligently, and based on size, as opposed to a random 50/50 split. This will often involve centralizing the maintenance routines, on a central server, known as a Central Management Server (CMS). A CMS is a SQL Server instance, which sits in the middle of your SQL Server estate, and provides centralized monitoring and maintenance. Often, for intelligent maintenance, such as I am describing here, the CMS will control maintenance routines by scheduling PowerShell scripts, which will interact with metadata, stored on the CMS, to decide which maintenance jobs to run.

Offloading to a Secondary Server

The final strategy for reducing the load on production systems caused by DBCC CHECKDB is to offload the work to a secondary server. If you decide to take this approach, it involves taking a full backup of the VLDB and then restoring it on a secondary server before you run DBCC CHECKDB on the secondary server. This approach has several disadvantages, however. First, and most obviously, it means that you have the expense of procuring and maintaining a secondary server, just for the purpose of running consistency checks. This makes it the most expensive of the options discussed (unless of course, you reuse an existing server, such as a UAT server). Also, if you find corruption, you will not know if the corruption was generated on the production system and copied over in the backup or if the corruption was actually generated on the secondary server. This means that if errors are found, you still have to run DBCC CHECKDB on the production server.

Summary

Many types of corruption can occur in SQL Server. These include pages that have been damaged at the file system level, logical consistency errors, and corrupt pages that have a bad checksum. Pages can also be damaged in memory, which would not be identified through a checksum.

Three-page verification options can be selected for a database. The NONE option leaves you totally exposed to issues and is regarded as bad practice. The TORN_PAGE_ DETECTION option is deprecated and should not be used, since it only checks the first 2 bytes in every 512-byte sector. The final option is CHECKSUM. This is the default option and should always be selected.

Pages that are damaged are stored in a table called dbo.suspect_pages in the MSDB database. Here, the error count is increased every time the error is encountered and the event type of the page is updated to indicate that it has been repaired or restored as appropriate.

If a system database, especially Master, becomes corrupt, you may be unable to start your instance. If this is the case, then you can rectify the issue by running setup with the ACTION parameter set to Rebuilddatabases. Alternatively, if the instance itself has become corrupt, then you can run setup with the ACTION parameter set to repair. This resolves issues such as corrupt Registry keys or corruption to the Resource database.

DBCC CHECKDB is a command that you should run on a regular basis to check for corruption. If you find corruption, then you can also use this command to fix the issue. There are two repair modes that are available, depending on the nature of the corruption: REPAIR_REBUILD or REPAIR_ALLOW_DATA_LOSS. You should only use the REPAIR_ALLOW_DATA_LOSS option as a last resort in the event that no backup is available from which to restore the database or corrupt pages. This is because the REPAIR_ALLOW_DATA_LOSS option is liable to deallocate the corrupt pages, causing all data on these pages to be lost.

Other DBCC commands can be used to perform a subset of DBCC CHECKDB functionality. These include DBCC CHECKTABLE, which can validate the integrity of a specific table, and DBCC CONSTRAINTS, which you can use to verify the integrity of foreign keys and check constraints, especially after you run DBCC CHECKDB with a repair option.

For VLDBs or estates that share infrastructure, running DBCC CHECKDB can be an issue because of performance impact and resource utilization. You can mitigate this by adopting a strategy that offers a trade-off between maintenance and performance goals. These strategies include splitting the workload, offloading the workload to a secondary server, or running only subsets of the checking functionality on a nightly basis and then performing a full check on a weekly basis.

PART III

Security, Resilience, and Scaling Workloads

## CHAPTER 10

SQL Server Security Model

SQL Server 2022 offers a complex security model with overlapping layers of security that help database administrators (DBAs) counter the risks and threats in a manageable way. It is important for DBAs to understand the SQL Server security model so that they can implement the technologies in the way that best fits the needs of their organization and applications. This chapter discusses the SQL Server security hierarchy before demonstrating how to implement security at the instance, database, and object levels.

Tip SQL Server 2022 introduces new security features which integrate SQL Server with Defender and Purview that can be leveraged in Hybrid Cloud scenarios. These features will be discussed in Chapter 21.

Security Hierarchy

The security hierarchy for SQL Server begins at the Windows domain level and cascades down through the local server, the SQL Server instance, the databases, and right on down to the object level. The model is based on the concept of principals, securables, and permissions. *Principals* are entities to which permissions are granted, denied, or revoked. Revoking a permission means deleting an existing grant or deny assignment. Groups and roles are principals that contain zero or more security principals and simplify the management of security by allowing you to assign permissions to similar principals as a single unit.

© Peter A. Carter 2023
P. A. Carter, *Pro SQL Server 2022 Administration*, https://doi.org/10.1007/978-1-4842-8864-1_10

Securables are objects that can have permissions granted on them—for example, an endpoint at the instance level, or a table within a database. Therefore, you grant a permission on a securable to a principal. Figure 10-1 provides an overview of each level of the security hierarchy and how principals are layered.

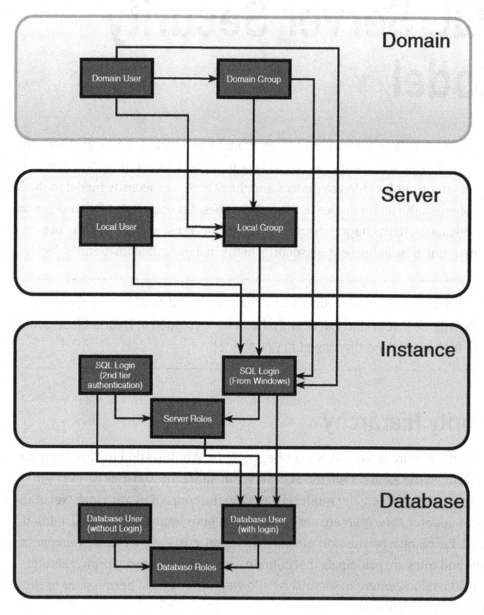

Figure 10-1. *Security principal hierarchy*

The diagram shows that a login, created within the SQL Server instance, can be mapped to a local Windows user or group or to a domain user or group. In SQL Server 2022, domain Users and Groups can also include Azure Active Directory Users and Groups. This will be discussed later in this chapter. Usually, in an Enterprise environment, this is a domain user or group. (A *group* is a collection of users that are granted permissions as a unit.) This eases the administration of security. Imagine that a new person joins the sales team. When added to the domain group called SalesTeam— which already has all of the required permissions to file system locations, SQL Server databases, and so on—they immediately inherit all required permissions to perform their role.

The diagram also illustrates how local server accounts or domain accounts and groups can be mapped to a user at the database level (a database user without login). This is part of the functionality of contained databases. This technology was introduced as far back as SQL Server 2012, to support high availability with AlwaysOn Availability Groups. Contained database authentication is discussed later in this chapter.

You can then add the Windows login, which you create at the SQL Server instance level or at a second-tier SQL Server login (if you are using mixed-mode authentication), to fix server roles and user-defined server roles at the instance level. Doing this allows you to grant the user common sets of permissions to instance-level objects, such as linked servers and endpoints. You can also map logins to database users.

Database users sit at the database level of the hierarchy. You can grant them permissions directly on schemas and objects within the database, or you can add them to database roles. Database roles are similar to server roles, except they are granted a common set of permissions on objects that sit inside the database, such as schemas, tables, views, stored procedures, and so on.

Tip   Generally, the preferred method is to add users to groups and assign the groups to database roles, as opposed to assigning permissions directly to users. This simplifies security management.

Before moving any further, we will now create the Chapter10 database, which will be used by examples in this chapter. This can be achieved by running the script in Listing 10-1.

Listing 10-1. Create the Chapter10 Database

```
--Create Chapter10 database

CREATE DATABASE Chapter10 ;
GO

USE Chapter10
GO

--Create SensitiveData table

CREATE TABLE dbo.SensitiveData
(
ID     INT    PRIMARY KEY    IDENTITY,
SensitiveText         NVARCHAR(100)
) ;

--Populate SensitiveData table

DECLARE @Numbers TABLE
(
ID          INT
)

;WITH CTE(Num)
AS
(
SELECT 1 AS Num
UNION ALL
SELECT Num + 1
FROM CTE
WHERE Num < 100
)

INSERT INTO @Numbers
SELECT Num
FROM CTE ;
```

```
INSERT INTO dbo.SensitiveData
SELECT 'SampleData'
FROM @Numbers ;
```

Implementing Instance-Level Security

Unless you are using contained databases (discussed later in this chapter), all users must be authenticated at the instance level. You can use two authentication modes with SQL Server: Windows authentication and mixed-mode authentication. When you select Windows authentication, a login at the instance level is created and mapped to a Windows user or group, which exists either at the domain level or at the local server level.

For example, let's say you have two users, Pete and Danielle. Both users have domain accounts, PROSQLADMIN\Pete and PROSQLADMIN\Danielle. Both users are also part of a Windows group called PROSQLADMIN\SQLUsers. Creating two logins, one mapped to Pete's account and one mapped to Danielle's account, is functionally equivalent to creating one login, mapped to the SQLUsers group, as long as you grant the exact same set of permissions. Creating two separate logins provides more granular control over the permissions, however.

When you create a login mapped to a Windows user or group, SQL Server records the SID (security identifier) of this principal and stores it in the Master database. It then uses this SID to identify users who are attempting to connect, from the context that they have used, to log in to the server or domain.

In addition to creating a login mapped to a Windows user or group, you can also map a login to a certificate or an asymmetric key. Doing so does not allow a user to authenticate to the instance by using a certificate, but it does allow for code signing so that permissions to procedures can be abstracted, rather than granted directly to a login. This helps when you are using dynamic SQL, which breaks the ownership chain; in this scenario, when you run the procedure, SQL Server combines the permissions from the user who called the procedure and the user who maps to the certificate. Ownership chains are discussed later in this chapter.

If you select mixed-mode authentication for your instance, however, then in addition to using Windows authentication, as described earlier, users can also connect by using second-tier authentication. When you use second-tier authentication, you create a SQL login, which has a username and password. This username and password is stored in the Master database with its own SID. When the user attempts to authenticate to the instance, they supply the username and password, and this is validated against the credentials stored.

When you are using mixed-mode authentication, there will be a special user, called the SA. This is the System Administrator account, and it has administrative rights to the entire instance. This can be a security vulnerability, because anybody looking to hack into a SQL Server instance will first try to crack the password for the SA account. Because of this, it is imperative that you use a very strong password for this account.

An additional security tip is to rename the SA account. This means that a potential hacker will not know the name of the administrative account, which makes it a lot harder to break into the instance. You can rename the SA account by using the command in Listing 10-2.

Listing 10-2. Renaming the SA Account

```
ALTER LOGIN sa WITH NAME = PROSQLADMINSA ;
```

By its very nature, Windows authentication is more secure than second-tier authentication. Therefore, it is good practice to configure your instance to use Windows authentication only, unless you have a specific need to use second-tier authentication. You can set the authentication mode in SQL Server Management Studio within the Security tab of the Server Properties dialog box. You will need to restart the SQL Server service for the change to take effect.

Server Roles

SQL Server provides a set of server roles, out of the box, that allow you to assign instance-level permissions to logins that map to common requirements. These are called *fixed server roles*, and you cannot change the permissions that are assigned to them; you can only add and remove logins. Table 10-1 describes each of these fixed server roles.

Table 10-1. *Fixed Server Roles*

Role	Description
sysadmin	The sysadmin role gives administrative permissions to the entire instance. A member of the sysadmin role can perform any action within the instance of the SQL Server relational engine.
bulkadmin	In conjunction with the INSERT permission on the target table within a database, the bulkadmin role allows a user to import data from a file using the BULK INSERT statement. This role is normally given to service accounts that run ETL processes.
dbcreator	The dbcreator role allows its members to create new databases within the instance. Once a user creates a database, he is automatically the owner of that database and is able to perform any action inside it.
diskadmin	The diskadmin role gives its members the permissions to manage backup devices within SQL Server.
processadmin	Members of the processadmin role are able to stop the instance from T-SQL or SSMS. They are also able to kill running processes.
public	All SQL Server logins are added to the public role. Although you can assign permissions to the public role, this does not fit with the principle of least privilege. This role is normally only used for internal SQL Server operations, such as authentication to TempDB.

(continued)

Table 10-1. (*continued*)

Role	Description
securityadmin	Members of the securityadmin role are able to manage logins at the instance level. For example, members may add a login to a server role (except sysadmin) or assign permissions to an instance-level resource, such as an endpoint. However, they cannot assign permissions within a database to database users.
serveradmin	Serveradmin combines the diskadmin and processadmin roles. As well as being able to start or stop the instance, however, members of this role can also shut down the instance using the SHUTDOWN T-SQL command. The subtle difference here is that the SHUTDOWN command gives you the option of not running a CHECKPOINT in each database if you use it with the NOWAIT option. Additionally, members of this role can alter endpoints and view all instance metadata.
setupadmin	Members of the setupadmin role are able to create and manage linked servers.
##MS_DatabaseConnector##	Members can connect to any database on the instance, without the requirement to have a database user mapped in each database.
##MS_DatabaseManager##	Gives members the permissions to create database and also to drop any database on the instance. If a member of this role creates a database, they will be made the owner of that database, by default.

(continued)

Table 10-1. (*continued*)

Role	Description
##MS_PerformanceDefinitionReader##	Members are able to view all instance-level catalog views which are performance related. Members will also be able to view any database-level catalog views, which are security related, within databases that they are allowed to access.
##MS_SecurityDefinitionReader##	Members can view all instance-level catalog views which are security related. Members will also be able to view any database-level catalog views which are security related, within databases that they are allowed to access.
##MS_DefinitionReader##	Members are able to see the definitions of objects, generate scripts, and view metadata for any objects at the instance level, or within databases that they can access.
##MS_LoginManager##	Members can create and drop and logins within the instance.
##MS_ServerPerformanceStateReader##	Members are granted permissions to view any performance-related DMVs (dynamic management views) and DMFs (dynamic management functions) at the instance level and are also granted the VIEW DATABASE PERFORMANCE STATE permission within any databases that they can access.
##MS_ServerSecurityStateReader##	Members are granted permissions to view any security-related DMVs (dynamic management views) and DMFs (dynamic management functions) at the instance level and are also granted the VIEW DATABASE SECURITY STATE permission within any databases that they can access.

(*continued*)

Table 10-1. (*continued*)

Role	Description
##MS_ServerStateReader##	Members can read all DMVs and DMFs at the instance level and in databases where they have a user mapped.
##MS_ServerStateManager##	Members can read all DMVs and DMFs at the instance level and in databases where they have a user mapped. Additionally, members are granted the ALTER SERVER STATE permission, which allows for operations such as clearing down the cache and viewing performance counters.

Note   The roles encapsulated in ## were newly introduced in SQL Server 2022. Microsoft have defined the ## encapsulation to easily identify them as fixed server roles, as opposed to user-defined server roles (see the following texts). While roles which are not encapsulated in ## are not formally deprecated, Microsoft regard them as provided for backward compatibility.

You can create your own server roles, which group users who need a common set of permissions that are tailored to your environment. For example, if you have a highly available environment that relies on availability groups, then you may wish to create a server role called AOAG and grant this group the following permissions:

Alter any availability group

Alter any endpoint

Create availability group

Create endpoint

You can then add the junior DBAs, who are not authorized to have full sysadmin permissions, but who you want to manage the high availability of the instance, to this role. You can create this server role by selecting New Server Role from the context menu of Security ➤ Server Roles in SSMS. The General tab of the New Server Role dialog box is illustrated in Figure 10-2.

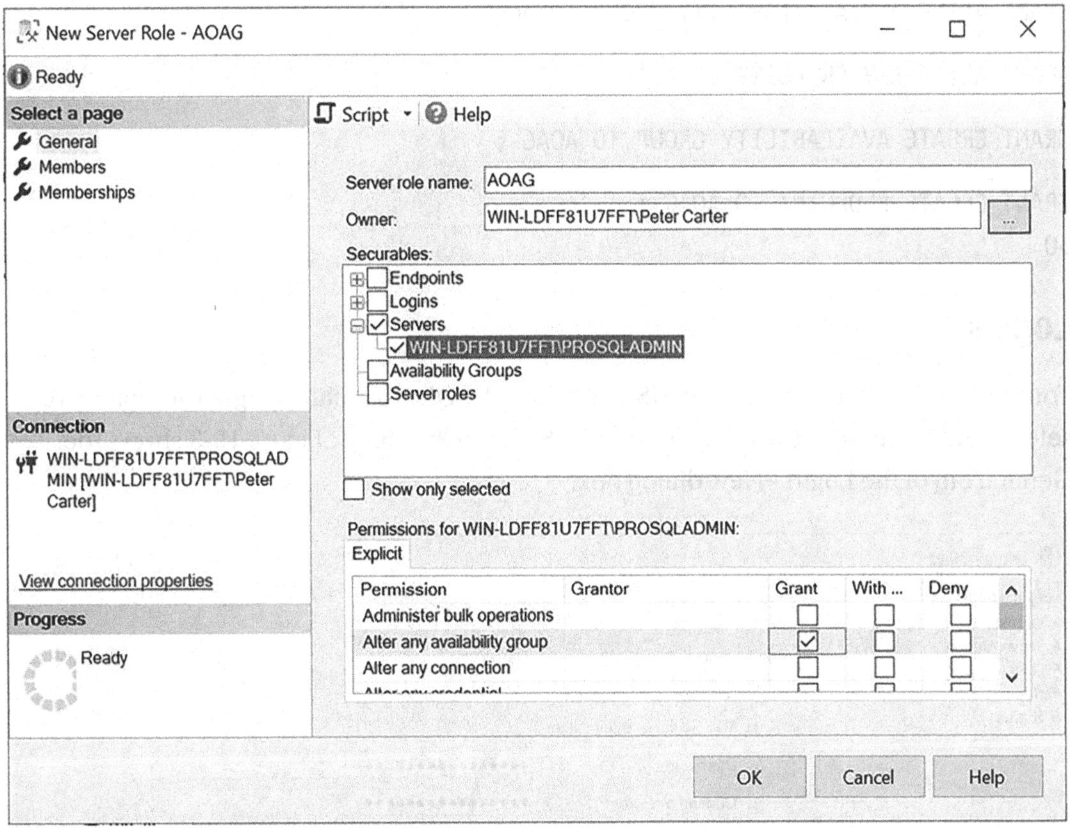

Figure 10-2. *The General tab*

You can see that we have assigned the name of the role as AOAG, we have specified an owner for the role, and we have selected the permissions required under the instance that we are configuring. On the Members tab of the dialog box, we can search for preexisting logins that we will add to the role, and in the Membership tab, we can optionally choose to nest the role inside another server role.

Alternatively, you can create the group through T-SQL. The script in Listing 10-3 also creates this group. We add logins to the role later in this chapter.

Listing 10-3. Creating a Server Role and Assigning Permissions

```
USE Master
GO

CREATE SERVER ROLE AOAG AUTHORIZATION [WIN-KIAGK4GN1MJ\Administrator] ;
GO
```

```
GRANT ALTER ANY AVAILABILITY GROUP TO AOAG ;

GRANT ALTER ANY ENDPOINT TO AOAG ;

GRANT CREATE AVAILABILITY GROUP TO AOAG ;

GRANT CREATE ENDPOINT TO AOAG ;
GO
```

Logins

You can create a login through SSMS or through T-SQL. To create a login through SSMS, select New Login from the context menu of Security ➤ Logins. Figure 10-3 shows the General tab of the Login - New dialog box.

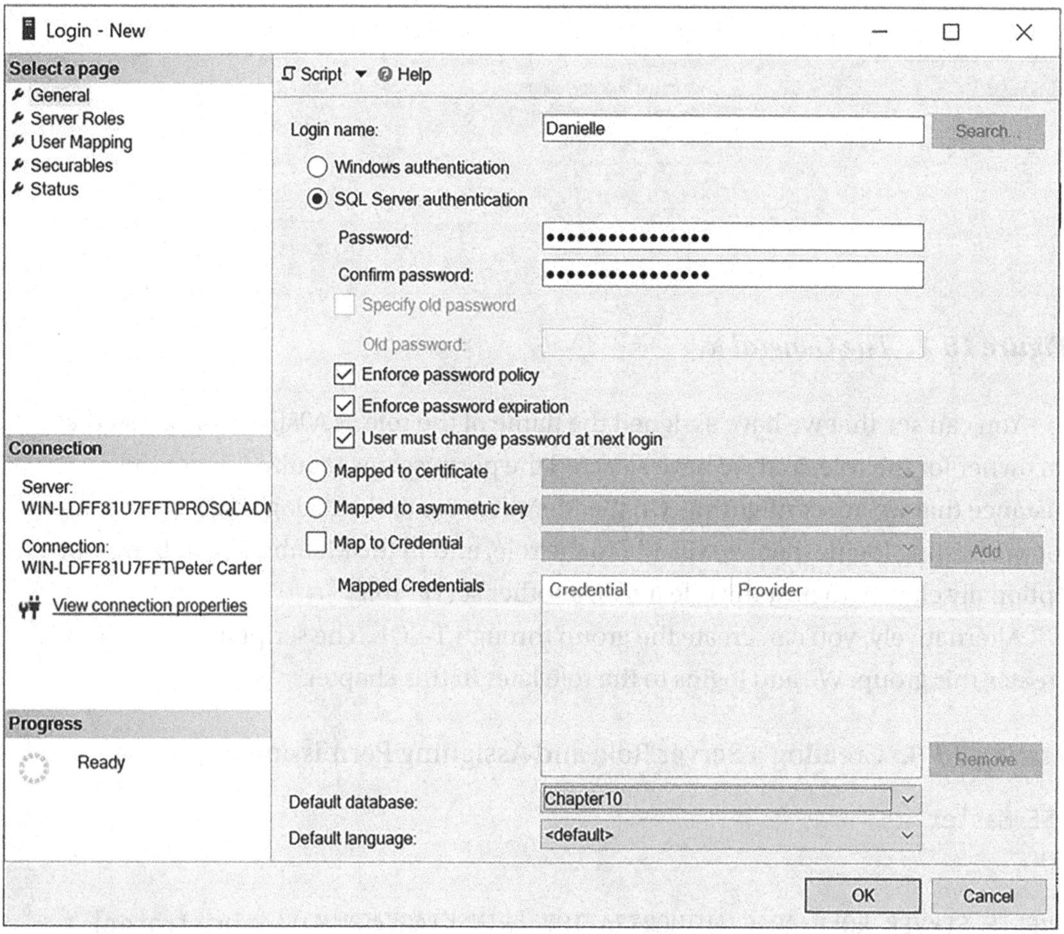

Figure 10-3. *The General tab*

You can see that we have named the login Danielle, and we have specified SQL Server authentication as opposed to Windows authentication. This means that we have also had to specify a password and then confirm it. You may also note that three boxes are checked: enforce password policy, enforce password expiration, and user must change password at next login. These three options are cumulative, meaning that you cannot select Enforce password expiration without also having enforce password policy selected. You also cannot select user must change password at next login without also selecting the Enforce password expiration option.

When you select the enforce password policy option, SQL Server checks the password policies for Windows users at the domain level and applies them to SQL Server logins as well. So, for example, if you have a domain policy that enforces that network user's passwords are eight characters or longer, then the same applies to the SQL Server login. If you do not select this option, then no password policies are enforced against the login's password. In a similar vein, if you select the option to enforce password expiration, the expiration period is taken from the domain policies.

We have also set the login's default database to be Chapter10. This does not assign the user any permissions to the Chapter10 database, but it specifies that this database will be the login's landing zone, when the user authenticate to the instance. It also means that if the user does not have permissions to the Chapter10 database, or if the Chapter 10 database is dropped or becomes inaccessible, the user will not be able to log in to the instance.

On the Server Roles tab, you can add the login to server roles. In our case, we have chosen not to add the login to any additional server roles. Adding logins to server roles is discussed in the next section of this chapter.

On the User Mapping tab, we can map the login to users at the database level. On this screen, you should create a database user within the Chapter10 database. The name of the database user in each database has defaulted to the same name as the login. This is not mandatory, and you can change the names of the database users; however, it is good practice to keep the names consistent. Failure to do so only leads to confusion and increases the time you must spend managing your security principals. We have not added the users to any database roles at this point. Database roles are discussed later in this chapter.

On the Securables tab, we can search for specific instance-level objects on which to grant the login permissions. In the Status tab, we can grant or deny the login permissions to log in to the instance and enable or disable the login. Also, if the login has become locked out because an incorrect password has been entered too many times, we can unlock the user. The number of failed password attempts is based on the Group Policy settings for the Server, but the CHECK_POLICY option must be used on the login.

The same user can be created through T-SQL by running the script in Listing 10-4. You can see that in order to achieve the same results, multiple commands are required. The first creates the login and the others create database users that map to the login.

Listing 10-4. Creating a SQL Server Login

```
USE Master
GO

CREATE LOGIN Danielle
    WITH PASSWORD=N'Pa$$word' MUST_CHANGE, DEFAULT_DATABASE=Chapter10,
    CHECK_EXPIRATION=ON, CHECK_POLICY=ON ;
GO

USE Chapter10
GO

CREATE USER Danielle FOR LOGIN Danielle ;
GO
```

We can also use either the New Login dialog box or T-SQL to create Windows logins. If using the GUI, we can select the Windows login as opposed to the SQL Server login option and then search for the user or group that we want the login to map to. Listing 10-5 demonstrates how to create a Windows login using T-SQL. It maps the login to a domain user called Pete, with the same configuration as Danielle.

Listing 10-5. Creating a Windows Login

```
CREATE LOGIN [PROSQLADMIN\pete] FROM WINDOWS WITH DEFAULT_
DATABASE=Chapter10 ;
GO

USE Chapter10
GO

CREATE USER [PROSQLADMIN\pete] FOR LOGIN [PROSQLADMIN\pete] ;
```

Starting with SQL Server 2022, logins can also be created from Azure AD Security Principals, namely, Azure AD Users, Azure AD Groups, and Azure AD Applications. To integrate with Azure AD, the instance will need to be registered with Azure Arc, which is discussed in Chapter 21. You will also need to register an Azure AD Application and assign a certificate. Once their prerequisites are met, you will be able to create a Login for an Azure AD User, using the command in Listing 10-6.

Tip   At the time of writing, Azure AD integration is only available for on-premises servers. It does not work with SQL Server on Azure VMs.

Listing 10.6.   Create a Login for an Azure AD User

```
CREATE LOGIN [pete@prosqladmin.com] FROM EXTERNAL PROVIDER
```

Granting Permissions

When assigning permissions to logins, you can use following actions:

> GRANT
>
> DENY
>
> REVOKE

GRANT gives principal permissions on a securable. You can use the WITH option with GRANT to also provide a principal with the ability to assign the same permission to other principals. DENY specifically denies login permissions on a securable; DENY overrules GRANT. Therefore, if a login is a member of a server role or roles that give the login permissions to alter an endpoint, but the principal was explicitly denied permissions to alter the same endpoint, then the principal is not able to manage the endpoint. REVOKE removes a permission association to a securable. This includes DENY associations as well as GRANT associations. If a login has been assigned permissions through a server role, however, then revoking the permissions to that securable, against the login itself, has no effect. In order to have an effect, you would need to use DENY, remove the permissions from the role, or change the permissions assigned to the role.

The command in Listing 10-7 grants Danielle permission to alter any login, but then it specifically denies her the permissions to alter the service account.

Listing 10-7. Granting and Denying Permissions

```
GRANT ALTER ANY LOGIN TO Danielle ;
GO

DENY ALTER ON LOGIN::[NT Service\MSSQL$PROSQLADMIN] TO Danielle ;
```

Note the difference in syntax between assigning permissions on a class of object, in this case, logins, and assigning permissions on a specific object. For an object type, the ANY [Object Type] syntax is used, but for a specific object, we use [Object Class]::[Securable].

We can add or remove logins from a server role by using the ALTER SERVER ROLE statement. Listing 10-8 demonstrates how to add Danielle to the ##MS_DatabaseManager## role and then remove her again.

Listing 10-8. Adding and Removing Server Roles

```
--Add Danielle to the sysadmin Role

ALTER SERVER ROLE ##MS_DatabaseManager## ADD MEMBER Danielle ;
GO

--Remove Danielle from the sysadmin role

ALTER SERVER ROLE ##MS_DatabaseManager## DROP MEMBER Danielle ;
GO
```

Implementing Database-Level Security

We have seen how security at the instance level is managed using logins and server roles. Security at the level of the individual database has a similar model, consisting of database users and database roles. The following sections describe this functionality.

Database Roles

Just as there are server roles at the instance level that help manage permissions, there are also database roles at the database level that can group principals together to assign common permissions. There are built-in database roles, but it is also possible to define your own, ones that meet the requirements of your specific data-tier application.

The built-in database roles that are available in SQL Server 2022 are described in Table 10-2.

Table 10-2. *Database Roles*

Database Role	Description
db_accessadmin	Members of this role can add and remove database users from the database.
db_backupoperator	The db_backupoperator role gives users the permissions they need to back up the database, natively. It may not work for third-party backup tools, such as CommVault or Backup Exec, since these tools often require sysadmin rights.
db_datareader	Members of the db_datareader role can run SELECT statements against any table in the database. It is possible to override this for specific tables by explicitly denying a user permissions to those tables. DENY overrides the GRANT.
db_datawriter	Members of the db_datawriter role can perform DML (data manipulation language) statements against any table in the database. It is possible to override this for specific tables by specifically denying a user permissions against a table. The DENY will override the GRANT.
db_denydatareader	The db_denydatareader role denies the SELECT permission against every table in the database.
db_denydatawriter	The db_denydatawriter role denies its members the permissions to perform DML statements against every table in the database.
db_ddladmin	Members of this role are given the ability to run CREATE, ALTER, and DROP statements against any object in the database. This role is rarely used, but I have seen a couple of examples or poorly written applications that create database objects on the fly. If you are responsible for administering an application such as this, then the ddl_admin role may be useful.
db_owner	Members of the db_owner role can perform any action within the database that has not been specifically denied.
db_securityadmin	Members of this role can grant, deny, and revoke a user's permissions to securables. They can also add or remove role memberships, with the exception of the db_owner role.

You can create your own database roles in SQL Server Management Studio by drilling down through Databases ➤ Your Database ➤ Security and then selected New Database Role from the context menu of database roles in Object Explorer. This displays the General tab of the Database Role - New dialog box. Here, you should specify db_ ReadOnlyUsers as the name of our role and state that the role will be owned by dbo. dbo is system user that members of the sysadmin server role map to. We have then used the Add button to add Danielle to the role.

On the Securables tab, we can search for objects that we want to grant permissions on, and then we can select the appropriate permissions for the objects. Figure 10-4 illustrates the results of searching for objects that are part of the dbo schema. We have then selected that the role should have SELECT permissions against the SensitiveData table, but that DELETE, INSERT, and UPDATE permissions should be specifically denied.

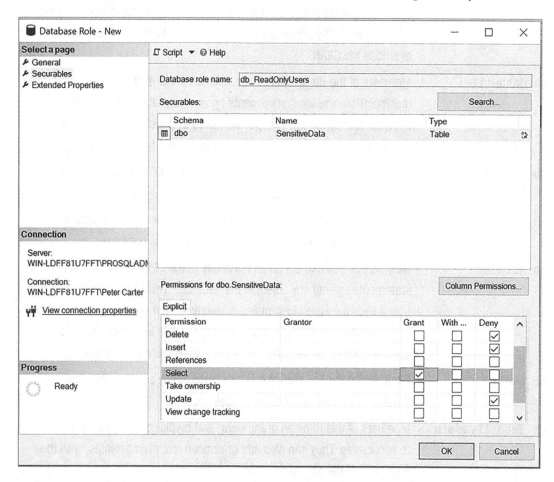

Figure 10-4. *The Securables tab*

Because there is currently only one table in our Chapter10 database, this role is functionally equivalent to adding Danielle to the db_datareader and db_denydatawriter built-in database roles. The big difference is that when we create new tables in our database, the permissions assigned to our db_ReadOnlyUsers role continue to apply only to the SensitiveData table. This is in contrast to the db_datareader and db_denydatawriter roles, which assign the same permission set to any new tables that are created.

An alternative way to create the db_ReadOnlyUsers role is to use the T-SQL script in Listing 10-9. You can see that we have had to use several commands to set up the role. The first command creates the role and uses the authorization clause to specify the owner. The second command adds Danielle as a member of the role, and the subsequent commands use GRANT and DENY keywords to assign the appropriate *permissions on* the securable *to* the principal.

Listing 10-9. Creating a Database Role

```
--Set Up the Role

CREATE ROLE db_ReadOnlyUsers AUTHORIZATION dbo ;
GO

ALTER ROLE db_ReadOnlyUsers ADD MEMBER Danielle ;

GRANT SELECT ON dbo.SensitiveData TO db_ReadOnlyUsers ;

DENY DELETE ON dbo.SensitiveData TO db_ReadOnlyUsers ;

DENY INSERT ON dbo.SensitiveData TO db_ReadOnlyUsers ;

DENY UPDATE ON dbo.SensitiveData TO db_ReadOnlyUsers ;
GO
```

Tip   Although DENY assignments can be helpful in some scenarios—for example, if you want to assign securable permissions to all but one table—in a well-structured security hierarchy, use them with caution. DENY assignments can increase the complexity of managing security, and you can enforce the principle of least privilege by exclusively using GRANT assignments in the majority of cases.

Schemas

Schemas provide a logical namespace for database objects while at the same time abstracting an object from its owner. Every object within a database must be owned by a database user. In much older versions of SQL Server, this ownership was direct. In other words, a user named Bob could have owned ten individual tables. From SQL Server 2005 onward, however, this model has changed so that Bob now owns a schema, and the ten tables are part of that schema.

This abstraction simplifies changing the ownership of database objects; in this example, to change the owner of the ten tables from Bob to Colin, you need to change the ownership in one single place (the schema) as opposed to changing it on all ten tables.

Well-defined schemas can also help simplify the management of permissions, because you can assign principal permissions on a schema, as opposed to the individual objects within that schema. For example, if you had five sales related tables—OrdersHeaders, OrderDetails, StockList, PriceList, and Customers—putting all five tables within a single schema named Sales allows you to apply the SELECT, UPDATE, and INSERT permissions *on* the Sales schema *to* the SalesUsers database role. Assigning permissions to an entire schema does not just affect tables, however. For example, granting SELECT on a schema also gives SELECT permissions to all views within the schema. Granting the EXECUTE permission on a schema grants EXECUTE on all procedures and functions within the schema.

For this reason, well-designed schemas group tables by business rules, as opposed to technical joins. Consider the entity relationship diagram in Figure 10-5.

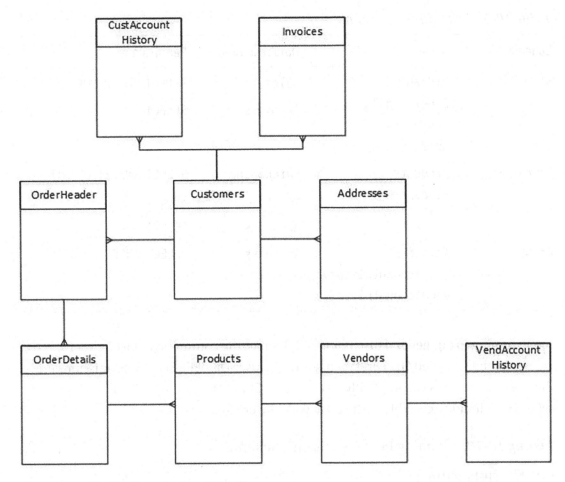

Figure 10-5. *Entity relationship diagram*

A good schema design for this example would involve three schemas, which are split by business responsibility—Sales, Procurement, and Accounts. Table 10-3 demonstrates how these tables can be split and permissions can then be assigned to the tables via database roles.

Table 10-3. *Schema Permissions*

Schema	Table	Database Role	Permissions
Sales	OrderHeader OrderDetails Customers Addresses	Sales Accounts	SELECT, INSERT, UPDATE SELECT
Procurement	Products Vendors	Purchasing Sales Accounts	SELECT, INSERT, UPDATE SELECT SELECT
Accounts	Invoices CustAccountHistory VendAccountHistory	Accounts	SELECT, INSERT, UPDATE

Returning to our general discussion of schemas, the command in Listing 10-10 creates a schema called CH10 and then grants the user Danielle SELECT permissions on the dbo schema. This will implicitly give her SELECT permissions on all tables within this schema, including new tables, which are yet to be created.

Listing 10-10. Granting Permissions on a Schema

```
CREATE SCHEMA CH10 ;
GO

GRANT SELECT ON SCHEMA::CH10 TO Danielle ;
```

To change a table's schema post creation, use the ALTER SCHEMA TRANSFER command, as demonstrated in Listing 10-11. This script creates a table without specifying a schema. This means that it is automatically placed in the dbo schema. It is then moved to the CH10 schema.

Listing 10-11. Transferring an Object Between Schemas

```
CREATE TABLE TransferTest
(
        ID int
) ;
GO

ALTER SCHEMA CH10 TRANSFER dbo.TransferTest ;
GO
```

Creating and Managing Contained Users

We have already seen how to create a database user, which maps to a login at the instance level. It is also possible to create a database user, which does not map to a server principal, however. This is to support a technology called *contained databases*.

Contained databases allow you to reduce a database's dependency on the instance by isolating aspects such as security. This makes the database easier to move between instances and helps support technologies such as AlwaysOn Availability Groups, which are discussed in Chapter 14.

Currently, SQL Server supports the database containment levels of NONE, which is the default, and PARTIAL. PARTIAL indicates that the database supports contained database users and that metadata is stored inside the database using the same collation. However, the database can still interact with noncontained features, such as users mapped to logins at the instance level. There is currently no option for FULL containment, since there is no way to stop the database from interacting with objects outside its boundaries.

In order to use contained databases, you must enable them at both the instance and the database level. You can enable them at both levels by using the Server Properties and Database Properties dialog boxes in SQL Server Management Studio. Alternatively, you can enable them at the instance level by using sp_configure and at the database level by using the ALTER DATABASE statement. The script in Listing 10-12 demonstrates how to enable contained databases for the instance and the Chapter10 database using T-SQL. To use the ALTER DATABASE command, you need to disconnect users from the database.

Listing 10-12. Enabling Contained Databases

```
--Enable contained databases at the instance level

EXEC sp_configure 'show advanced options', 1 ;
GO

RECONFIGURE ;
GO

EXEC sp_configure 'contained database authentication', '1' ;
GO

RECONFIGURE WITH OVERRIDE ;
GO

--Set Chapter10 database to use partial containment

USE Master
GO

ALTER DATABASE [Chapter10] SET CONTAINMENT = PARTIAL WITH NO_WAIT ;
GO
```

Once you have enabled contained databases, you can create database users that are not associated with a login at the instance level. You can create a user from a Windows user or group by using the syntax demonstrated in Listing 10-13. This script creates a database user that maps to the Chapter10Users domain group. It specifies that dbo is the default schema.

Listing 10-13. Creating a Database User from a Windows Login

```
USE Chapter10
GO

CREATE USER [PROSQLADMIN\Chapter10Uusers] WITH DEFAULT_SCHEMA=dbo ;
GO
```

Alternatively, to create a database user who is not mapped to a login at the instance level but who still relies on second-tier authentication, you can use the syntax in Listing 10-14. This script creates a user in the Chapter10 database called ContainedUser.

Listing 10-14. Creating a Database User with Second-Tier Authentication

```
USE Chapter10
GO

CREATE USER ContainedUser WITH PASSWORD=N'Pa$$w0rd', DEFAULT_SCHEMA=dbo ;
GO
```

When you use contained database users, you need to take a number of additional security considerations into account. First, some applications may require that a user have permissions to multiple databases. If the user is mapped to a Windows user or group, then this is straightforward because the SID that is being authenticated is that of the Windows object. If the database user is using second-tier authentication, however, then it is possible to duplicate the SID of the user from the first database. For example, we can create a user called ContainedUser in the Chapter10 database that will use second-tier authentication. We can then duplicate this user in the Chapter10Twain database by specifying the SID, as demonstrated in Listing 10-15. Before duplicating the user, the script first creates the Chapter10Twain database and configures it to be contained.

Listing 10-15. Creating a Duplicate User

```
USE Master
GO

CREATE DATABASE Chapter10Twain ;
GO

ALTER DATABASE Chapter10Twain SET CONTAINMENT = PARTIAL WITH NO_WAIT ;
GO

USE Chapter10Twain
GO

CREATE USER ContainedUser WITH PASSWORD = 'Pa$$w0rd',
    SID = 0x0105000000000009030000009134B23303A7184590E152AE6A1197DF ;
```

We can determine the SID by querying the sys.database_principals catalog view from the Chapter10 database, as demonstrated in Listing 10-16.

Listing 10-16. Finding the User's SID

```
SELECT sid
FROM sys.database_principals
WHERE name = 'ContainedUser' ;
```

Once we have duplicated the user in the second database, we also need to turn on the TRUSTWORTHY property of the first database in order to allow cross-database queries to take place. We can turn on TRUSTWORTHY in the Chapter10 database by using the command in Listing 10-17.

Listing 10-17. Turning on TRUSTWORTHY

```
ALTER DATABASE Chapter10 SET TRUSTWORTHY ON ;
```

Even if we do not create a duplicate user, it is still possible for a contained user to access other databases via the Guest account of another database if the Guest account is enabled. This is a technical requirement so that the contained user can access TempDB.

DBAs should also be careful when they attach a contained database to an instance to ensure that they are not inadvertently granting permissions to users who are not meant to have access. This can happen when you are moving a database from a preproduction environment to a production instance and UAT (user acceptance testing) or development users were not removed from the database before the attach.

SQL Server 2022 supports Azure AD Authentication. Both Logins and contained database users can be created from Azure AD user. The script in Listing 10-18 demonstrates how to create a contained database user from an Azure AD security principal. In this case, it is created for an Azure AD user, but it is also possible to create contained database users from an Azure AD group or Azure AD application, using the same syntax.

Listing 10-18. Create Contained Database User from Azure AD Security Principal

```
CREATE USER [pete@prosqladmin.com] FROM EXTERNAL PROVIDER
```

Tip   To be able to integrate with Azure AD, Azure Arc will need to be configured. You will also need to register an Azure AD application, as well as creating and assigning a certificate. Integration with Azure Arc will be discussed in Chapter 21.

Implementing Object-Level Security

There are two variations of syntax for granting a database user permissions to an object. The first uses the OBJECT phrase, whereas the second does not. For example, the two commands in Listing 10-19 are functionally equivalent.

Listing 10-19. Assigning Permissions

```
USE Chapter10
GO

--Grant with OBJECT notation

GRANT SELECT ON OBJECT::dbo.SensitiveData TO [PROSQLADMIN\Chapter10Users] ;
GO

--Grant without OBJECT notation

GRANT SELECT ON dbo.SensitiveData TO [PROSQLADMIN\Chapter10Users] ;
GO
```

Many permissions can be granted and not all permissions are relevant to each object. For example, the SELECT permission can be granted on a table or a view, but not to a stored procedure. The EXECUTE permission, on the other hand, can be granted on a stored procedure, but not to a table or view.

When granting permissions on a table, it is possible to grant permissions to specific columns, as opposed to the table itself. The script in Listing 10-20 gives the user ContainedUser SELECT permissions on the SensitiveData table in the Chapter10 database. Instead of being able to read the entire table, however, permissions are only granted on the SensitiveText column.

Listing 10-20. Granting Column-Level Permissions

```
GRANT SELECT ON dbo.SensitiveData ([SensitiveText]) TO ContainedUser ;
```

Summary

SQL Server offers a complex security framework for managing permissions that contains multiple, overlapping layers. At the instance level, you can create logins from Windows users or groups, or you can create them as second-tier logins, with passwords stored inside the database engine. Second-tier authentication requires that you enable mixed-mode authentication at the instance level.

Server roles allow logins to be grouped together so that you can assign them common permissions. This eases the administrative overhead of managing security. SQL Server provides built-in server roles for common scenarios, or you can create your own server roles that meet the needs of your data-tier applications.

At the database level, logins can map to database users. If you are using contained databases, then it is also possible to create database users that map directly to a Windows security principal or have their own second-tier authentication credentials. This can help isolate the database from the instance by removing the dependency on an instance-level login. This can help you make the database more portable, but at the expense of additional security considerations.

Fine-grain permissions can become difficult to manage, especially when you need to secure data at the column level. SQL Server offers ownership chaining, which can reduce this complexity. With ownership chaining, it is possible to assign permissions on a view, as opposed to on the underlying tables. It is even possible to use ownership chasing across multiple databases—which, of course, is not without its own complexities. For ownership chaining to succeed, all of the objects in the chain must share the same owner. Otherwise, the ownership chain is broken and permissions on the underlying objects are evaluated.

CHAPTER 11

Auditing and Ledger

Passive security refers to the practice of logging user activity in order to avoid the threat of nonrepudiation. This is important because if an attack is launched by a privileged user, it allows for appropriate disciplinary or even legal action to be taken. SQL Server provides SQL Server Audit to assist with implementing passive security. SQL Server 2022 also introduces Ledger, which uses blockchain technology to make data tamper-evident, which allows for streamlined auditing processes. In this chapter, we will discuss the new ledger functionality, how to implement it and how to use it to discover who has changed data. We will also explore the concepts involved in auditing before demonstrating how to implement SQL Server Audit, including the creation of custom audit event.

Ledger

Any DBA who has been involved in a regulatory audit will know how troublesome and laborious proving the authenticity of your data can be. SQL Server 2022 addresses this issue by introducing a blockchain technology, which can not only provide a change history for your data, but also prove that your data has not been tampered with and avoid nonrepudiation in the event that tampering has occurred—even by accounts with administrative access. Because ledger functionality is built on blockchain technology, it can also be used to fulfill use cases such as secure supply chain processes between companies.

SQL Server 2022 introduces two types of ledger table, to provide this functionality: append-only ledger tables and updateable ledger tables. These table types, along with ledger databases, digest management, and ledger management will be discussed in the following sections.

© Peter A. Carter 2023
P. A. Carter, *Pro SQL Server 2022 Administration*, https://doi.org/10.1007/978-1-4842-8864-1_11

Append-Only Ledger Tables

Append-only ledger tables do not allow any UPDATE or DELETE statements to be issued
against them. Therefore, they are perfect for tables that store data such as transactional
information against a credit account, for example.

While the table will probably be created by a developer, it is important for a DBA
involved with audit requirements to understand the process. Therefore, Listing 11-1
first creates the Chapter11 database and then creates an append-only table, within the
database, called dbo.AccountTransactions. The script uses the new GENERATE ALWAYS
AS syntax in the column definitions to create two system columns, which will hold the
transaction ID of the transaction that inserted the row and the sequence number, within
the transaction of that insert. If you omit these column definitions, for an append-only
ledger table, then SQL Server will automatically create them, using the names ledger_
start_transaction_id and ledger_start_sequence_number, respectively. The script
also uses the WITH clause to specify that the table will be an append-only ledger table.
Lastly, the script inserts some data into the table.

Listing 11-1. Create an Append-Only Ledger Table

```
CREATE DATABASE Chapter11
GO

USE Chapter11
GO

CREATE TABLE dbo.AccountTransactions (
    AccountTransactionID INT                NOT NULL    IDENTITY
    PRIMARY KEY,
    CustomerID              INT             NOT NULL,
    TxDescription           NVARCHAR(256)   NOT NULL,
    TxAmount                DECIMAL(6,2)    NOT NULL,
    NewBalance              DECIMAL(6,2)    NOT NULL,
    account_tx_transaction_id    BIGINT GENERATED ALWAYS AS transaction_id
    START HIDDEN NOT NULL,
    account_tx_sequence_number   BIGINT GENERATED ALWAYS AS sequence_number
    START HIDDEN NOT NULL,
) WITH(LEDGER = ON (APPEND_ONLY = ON)) ;
```

```
INSERT INTO dbo.AccountTransactions (CustomerID, TxDescription, TxAmount,
NewBalance)
VALUES (5, 'Card Payment', 5.00, 995.00),
       (5, 'Card Payment', 250.00, 745.00),
       (5, 'Repayment', 255.00, 1000.00),
       (5, 'Card Payment', 20.00, 980.00) ;
```

So let's see what happens if we try to tamper with the data in this table and update a row. This is demonstrated in Listing 11-2.

Listing 11-2. Attempt to Modify Data in Table

```
UPDATE dbo.AccountTransactions
SET TxAmount = 5000.00
WHERE TxDescription = 'Repayment' ;
```

The result of running this query is displayed in Figure 11-1.

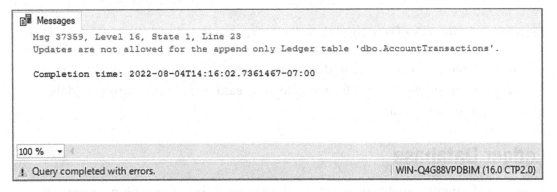

Figure 11-1. *Result of trying to modify data in append-only table*

If we wanted to check who had inserted a row into the table, or when a row was inserted, then we could make use of the system-populated columns that we created in the table and join them to a catalog view called sys.database_ledger_transactions, which records information about all DML (data manipulation language) statements which have been run against all ledger tables. The script in Listing 11-3 demonstrates how to return the time that each row was inserted and the account that inserted them.

Listing 11-3. Discover Who Inserted Data

```
SELECT
        dlt.commit_time
      , dlt.principal_name
      , atx.*
      , atx.account_tx_sequence_number
FROM dbo.AccountTransactions atx
INNER JOIN sys.database_ledger_transactions dlt
      ON atx.account_tx_transaction_id = dlt.transaction_id
```

The results of this query are shown in Figure 11-2. You can see that it is a simple task to identify who inserted each row and when, giving a forensic capability.

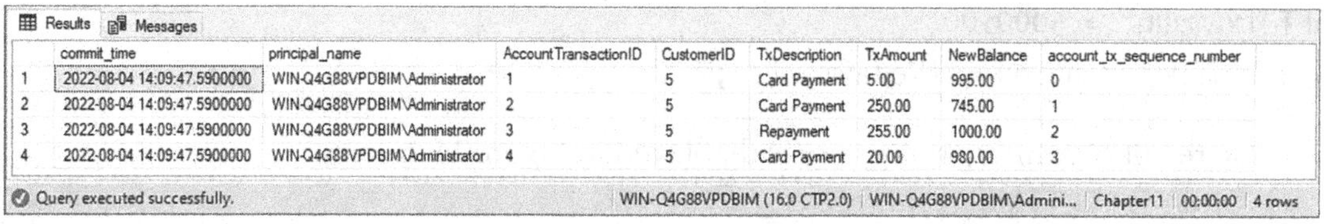

	commit_time	principal_name	Account TransactionID	CustomerID	TxDescription	TxAmount	NewBalance	account_tx_sequence_number
1	2022-08-04 14:09:47.5900000	WIN-Q4G88VPDBIM\Administrator	1	5	Card Payment	5.00	995.00	0
2	2022-08-04 14:09:47.5900000	WIN-Q4G88VPDBIM\Administrator	2	5	Card Payment	250.00	745.00	1
3	2022-08-04 14:09:47.5900000	WIN-Q4G88VPDBIM\Administrator	3	5	Repayment	255.00	1000.00	2
4	2022-08-04 14:09:47.5900000	WIN-Q4G88VPDBIM\Administrator	4	5	Card Payment	20.00	980.00	3

Query executed successfully.   WIN-Q4G88VPDBIM (16.0 CTP2.0) | WIN-Q4G88VPDBIM\Admini... | Chapter11 | 00:00:00 | 4 rows

Figure 11-2. *Results of row insertion discovery*

Once a table has been configured as append-only, it cannot be turned off. This prevents a highly privileged user from turning the feature off, inserting rows and then turning the feature back on.

Ledger Database

As previously mentioned, it will usually be the responsibility of a developer to create tables and there is a risk of human error, where a developer may forget to configure a table as a ledger table. This risk can be mitigated for databases where all tables should be ledger tables, with the use of a ledger database.

When a ledger database is used, all tables within the database will automatically become ledger tables, even if LEDGER = ON is not specified when creating the table. The default behavior is for tables to be created as updateable ledger tables, but developers can use the WITH(LEDGER = ON (APPEND_ONLY = ON)) syntax and specify the table should be an append-only table. Developers can also specify the LEDGER = ON syntax explicitly to control the names of ledger columns, the ledger view, or the history table. If you attempt to create a table in a ledger database with the LEDGER = OFF syntax, the table creation will fail.

The script in Listing 11-4 creates a ledger database called Chapter11Ledger. It then creates two tables. The GoodsIn table is automatically created as an updateable ledger table, while the AccountTransactions table is created as an append-only table.

Listing 11-4. Create a Ledger Database

```
CREATE DATABASE Chapter11Ledger WITH LEDGER = ON ;
GO

USE Chapter11Ledger
GO

CREATE TABLE dbo.GoodsIn (
    ID              INT             NOT NULL   IDENTITY   PRIMARY KEY,
    StockID         INT             NOT NULL,
    QtyOrdered      INT             NOT NULL,
    QtyReceived     INT             NOT NULL,
    ReceivedBy      NVARCHAR(128)   NOT NULL,
    ReceivedDate    DATETIME2       NOT NULL,
    Damaged         BIT             NOT NULL
) ; --Will automatically be created as an updateable ledger table

CREATE TABLE dbo.AccountTransactions (
    AccountTransactionID  INT            NOT NULL   IDENTITY   PRIMARY KEY,
    CustomerID            INT            NOT NULL,
    TxDescription         NVARCHAR(256)  NOT NULL,
    TxAmount              DECIMAL(6,2)   NOT NULL,
    NewBalance            DECIMAL(6,2)   NOT NULL
) WITH(LEDGER = ON (APPEND_ONLY = ON)) ; --Will be created as an append-
only ledger table
```

Figure 11-3 shows how Ledger tables are displayed within SQL Server Management Studio's Object Explorer. You will notice that SSMS v19 adds folders for dropped ledger columns and dropped ledger tables. You will also notice that the updatable ledger table provides a drill-through to the history table.

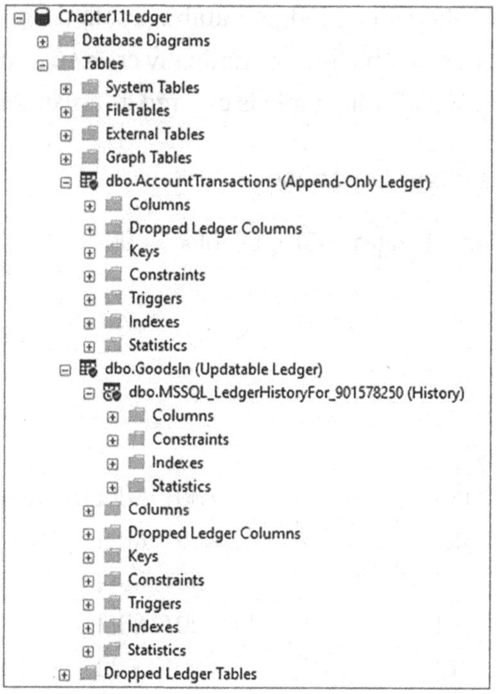

Figure 11-3. Ledger tables in SSMS

Ledger status of databases and tables can also be viewed through the sys.databases and sys.tables catalog views. The script in Listing 11-5 demonstrates how to return the ledger status at the database level, for the Chapter11 and Chapter11Ledger databases. It then demonstrates how to return the ledger table status for each table across the two databases.

Listing 11-5. Return Ledger Status Information

```
SELECT
        name
      , is_ledger_on
FROM sys.databases
WHERE name LIKE 'Chapter11%'

SELECT
        'Chapter11' AS DatabaseName
      , name
      , ledger_type_desc
```

```
        , ledger_view_id
        , is_dropped_ledger_table
FROM Chapter11.sys.tables
UNION ALL
SELECT
        'Chapter11Ledger'
        , name
        , ledger_type_desc
        , ledger_view_id
        , is_dropped_ledger_table
FROM Chapter11Ledger.sys.tables
```

Database Ledger and Digest Management

Ledger works using blockchain technology to incrementally capture the state of a database over time. When DML statements are executed against ledger tables, the query engine extends the execution plan to record the transaction ID, ordinal sequence number of the operation within the transaction for the INSERT and/or DELETE operations. The new version of the row is then serialized and a hash of the serialized content is appended, at the transaction level, to a Merkle Tree. A separate Merkle Tree is created for each table updated within the transaction, and as well as the row versions, metadata is also stored about the updated columns (such as datatype, ordinal column position, etc.) and the transaction (such as transaction ID, timestamp, etc.).

Tip   A deep discussion of Merkle Trees is beyond the scope of this book, but further detail can be found at `https://en.wikipedia.org/wiki/Merkle_tree`.

These Merkle Trees are added to a tamper-evident data structure called a block. A block is a hashed representation of all hashed transactions that have occurred since the block was opened. The most recent block is known as the database digest.

A block closes when any one of the following conditions are met:

- A database digest is automatically generated.

- A database digest is manually generated.

- The block contains 100,000 transactions.

When a block is closed, the following operations are performed on the closed block:

- All transactions of both the `sys.database_ledger_transactions` catalog view (which was discussed in the previous section) and the in-memory queue of transactions that have not yet been flushed to the catalog view.

- The Merkle Tree of the transactions within the block and the hash of content is calculated.

- The block is persisted to the `sys.database_ledger_blocks` catalog view.

It is very important to note that the trustworthiness of the database depends on the trustworthiness of the digests. Therefore, generated digests should always be stored on trusted WORM (write once read many) storage devices.

To assist with this, SQL Server 2022 provides integration with Azure Confidential Ledger and Azure Blob Storage with immutability. Automatic digest generation can only be configured if this Azure integration is used. When digests are generated automatically with Azure integration, the digest will be generated every 30 seconds, providing that there has been at least one transaction impacting ledger tables within that time. To configure this, you will need to create a `CREDENTIAL` that uses the URL of the Blob storage as its name, the shared access signature as the identity, and the shared access signature key as the secret.

Caution   You should develop a (ideally automated) process for rotating the shared access signature key simultaneously in both Azure and SQL Server.

The command in Listing 11-6 demonstrates how to manually generate a digest for the `Chapter11Ledger` database and then view the persisted block in `sys.database_ledger_blocks`.

Listing 11-6. Generate a Digest and View Persisted Block

```
--Manually generate a digest

EXEC sys.sp_generate_database_ledger_digest

--View the persisted digest
```

```
SELECT *
FROM sys.database_ledger_blocks
```

Listing 11-7 shows the JSON document that was generated. It includes the hash of the block, as well as metadata about the block.

Listing 11-7. Generated JSON

```
{
  "database_name":"Chapter11Ledger",
  "block_id":0,
  "hash":"0x5D529C2464D66909F2F20ED418D48D8542B049347C897705930E32
  BA46278825",
  "last_transaction_commit_time":"2022-08-07T11:19:42.7500000",
  "digest_time":"2022-08-07T19:45:56.5364972"
}
```

The script in Listing 11-8 compares two digests to verify the Chapter11Ledger database and ensure that the data has not been tampered with.

Tip   You will notice that the first activity of the script is to turn on Snapshot isolation. This is a requirement for database verification. Transaction isolation levels are discussed in Chapter 19.

Listing 11-8. Verify a Database

```
ALTER DATABASE Chapter11Ledger SET ALLOW_SNAPSHOT_ISOLATION ON
GO

EXECUTE sp_verify_database_ledger N'
[
    {
      "database_name":"Chapter11Ledger",
      "block_id":0,
```

"hash":"0x5D529C2464D66909F2F20ED418D48D8542B049347C897705930E32
      BA46278825",
      "last_transaction_commit_time":"2022-08-07T11:19:42.7500000",
      "digest_time":"2022-08-07T19:45:56.5364972"
    },
    {
      "database_name":"Chapter11Ledger",
        "block_id":0,
        "hash":"0x5D529C2464D66909F2F20ED418D48D8542B049347C897705930E32
        BA46278825",
        "last_transaction_commit_time":"2022-08-07T11:19:42.7500000",
        "digest_time":"2022-08-07T19:56:44.7114967"
    }
]';

Figure 11-4 illustrates a successful database verification.

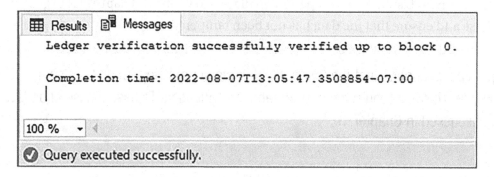

Figure 11-4. *Successful database verification*

Figure 11-5 illustrates a failed database verification, which implies the data has been tampered with.

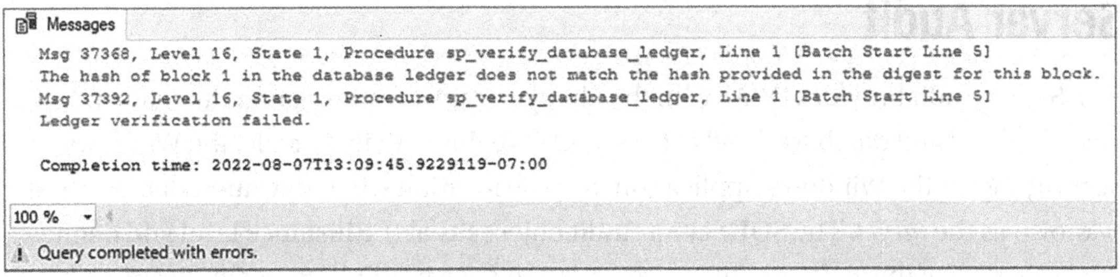

Figure 11-5. *Failed database verification*

If you are using automatic digest generation and storage, then you can ingest the locations from the sys.database_ledger_digest_locations catalog view. When converted to a JSON document using the FOR JSON clause, the locations in this catalog view can be passed to the sys.sp_verify_database_ledger_from_digest_storage stored procedure, to verify a database. This is demonstrated in Listing 11-9.

Listing 11-9. Verify a Database from Automatically Generated Digests

```
DECLARE @digest_locations NVARCHAR(MAX)

SET @digest_locations = (
      SELECT *
      FROM sys.database_ledger_digest_locations
      FOR JSON AUTO, INCLUDE_NULL_VALUES
);

EXEC sys.sp_verify_database_ledger_from_digest_storage @digest_locations ;
```

Caution   It is very important that you schedule database verification to happen on a regular basis. Doing so will alert you promptly to an attack. Details of using Server Agent to automate maintenance can be found in Chapter 23.

Server Audit

SQL Server Audit provides DBAs with the ability to capture granular audits against instance-level and database-level activity and save this activity to a file, the Windows Security log, or the Windows Application log. The location where the audit data is saved is known as the *target*. The SQL Server Audit object sits at the instance level and defines the properties of the audit and the target. You can have multiple server audits in each instance. This is useful if you have to audit many events in a busy environment, since you can distribute the I/O by using a file as the target and placing each target file on a separate volume.

Choosing the correct target is important from a security perspective. If you choose the Windows Application log as a target, then any Windows user who is authenticated to the server is able to access it. The Security log is a lot more secure than the Application log but can also be more complex to configure for SQL Server Audit. The service account that is running the SQL Server service requires the Generate Security Audits user rights assignment within the server's local security policy. Application-generated auditing also needs to be enabled for success and failure within the audit policy. The other consideration for the target is size. If you decide to use the Application log or Security log, then it is important that you consider, and potentially increase, the size of these logs before you begin using them for your audit. Also, work with your Windows administration team to decide on how the log will be cycled when full and if you will be archiving the log by backing it up to tape.

The SQL Server Audit can then be associated with one or more server audit specifications and database audit specifications. These specifications define the activity that will be audited at the instance level and the database level, respectively. It is helpful to have multiple server or database audit specifications if you are auditing many actions, because you can categorize them to make management easier while still associating them with the same server audit. Each database within the instance needs its own database audit specification if you plan to audit activity in multiple databases.

Creating a Server Audit

When you create a server audit, you can use the options detailed in Table 11-1.

Table 11-1. *Server Audit Options*

Option	Description
FILEPATH	Only applies if you choose a file target. Specifies the file path, where the audit logs will be generated.
MAXSIZE	Only applies if you choose a file target. Specifies the largest size that the audit file can grow to. The minimum size you can specify for this is 2MB.
MAX_ ROLLOVER_ FILES	Only applies if you choose a file target. When the audit file becomes full, you can either cycle that file or generate a new file. The MAX_ROLLOVER_FILES setting controls how many new files can be generated before they begin to cycle. The default value is UNLIMITED, but specifying a number caps the number of files to this limit. If you set it to 0, then there will only ever be one file, and it will cycle every time it becomes full. Any value above 0 indicates the number of rollover files that will be permitted. So, for example, if you specify 5, then there will be a maximum of six files in total.
MAX_FILES	Only applies if you choose a file target. As an alternative to MAX_ROLLOVER_FILES, the MAX_FILES setting specifies a limit for the number of audit files that can be generated, but when this number is reached, the logs will not cycle. Instead, the audit fails and events that cause an audit action to occur are handled based on the setting for ON_FAILURE.
RESERVE_ DISK_SPACE	Only applies if you choose a file target. Preallocate space on the volume equal to the value set in MAXSIZE, as opposed to allowing the audit log to grow as required.
QUEUE_ DELAY	Specify if audit events are written synchronously or asynchronously. If set to 0, events are written to the log synchronously. Otherwise, specify the duration in milliseconds that can elapse before events are forced to write. The default value is 1000 (1 second), which is also the minimum value.
ON_FAILURE	Specify what should happen if events that cause an audit action fail to be audited to the log. Acceptable values are CONTINUE, SHUTDOWN, or FAIL_OPERATION. When CONTINUE is specified, the operation is allowed to continue. This can lead to unaudited activity occurring. FAIL_OPERATION causes auditable events to fail, but allows other actions to continue. SHUTDOWN forces the instance to stop if auditable events cannot be written to the log.

(continued)

Table 11-1. (*continued*)

Option	Description
AUDIT_ GUID	Because server and database audit specifications link to the server audit through a GUID, there are occasions when an audit specification can become orphaned. These include when you attach a database to an instance, or when you implement technologies such as database mirroring. This option allows you to specify a specific GUID for the server audit, as opposed to having SQL Server generate a new one.

It is also possible to create a filter on the server audit. This can be useful when your audit specification captures activity against an entire class of object, but you are only interested in auditing a subset. For example, you may configure a server audit specification to log any member changes to server roles; however, you are only actually interested in members of the sysadmin server role being modified. In this scenario, you can filter on the sysadmin role.

You can create a server audit through the GUI in SQL Server Management Studio by drilling through Security in Object Explorer and choosing New Audit from the Audits node. Figure 11-6 illustrates the Create Audit dialog box.

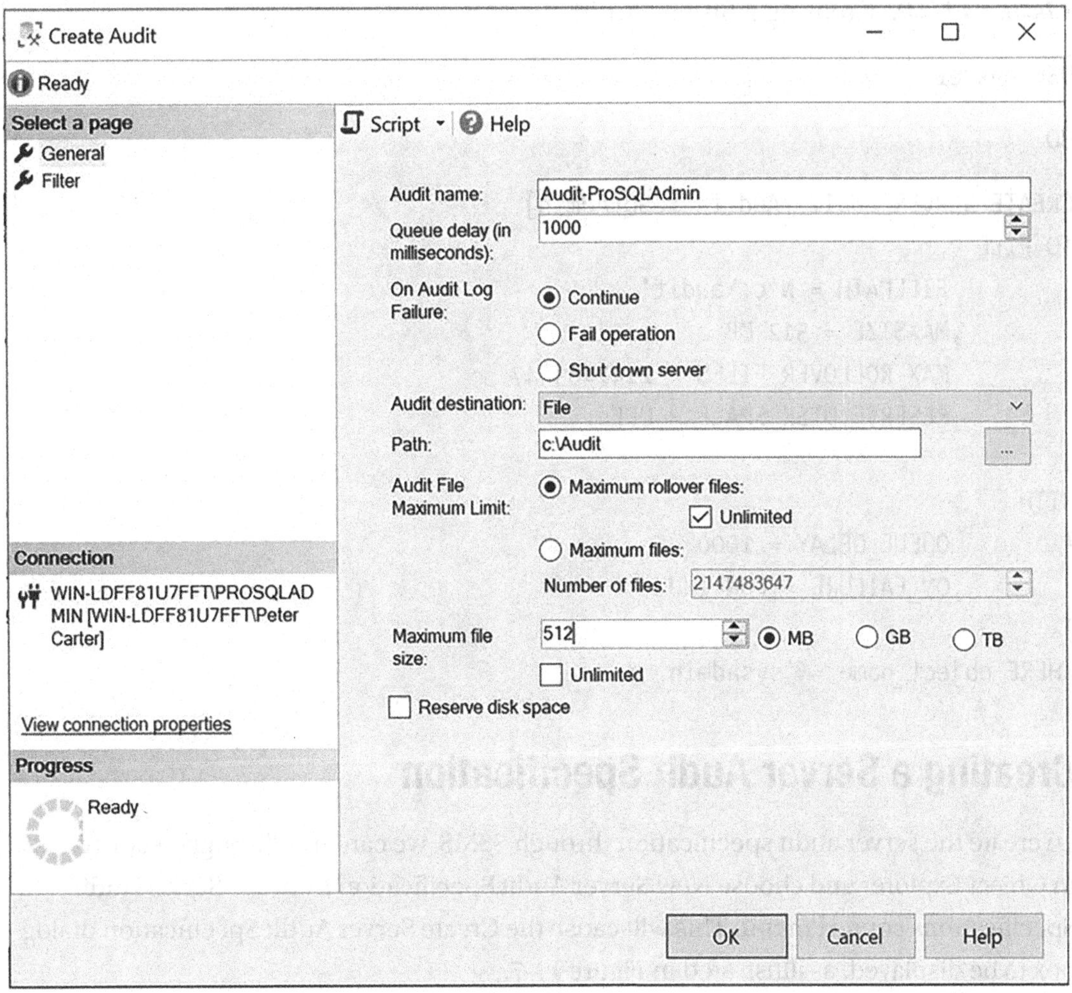

Figure 11-6. *The General tab*

You can see that we have decided to save our audit to a flat file, as opposed to a Windows log. Therefore, we need to specify the file-related parameters. We set our file to roll over and enforce the maximum size for any one file to be 512MB. We leave the default value of 1 second (1000 milliseconds) as a maximum duration before audit entries are forced to be written to the log and name the audit Audit-ProSQLAdmin.

On the Filter tab of the Create Audit dialog box, you should specify that we wish to filter on the object_name and only audit changes to the sysadmin role.

Alternatively, we can use T-SQL to perform the same action. The script in Listing 11-10 creates the same server audit.

Listing 11-10. Creating a Server Audit

```
USE Master

GO

CREATE SERVER AUDIT [Audit-ProSQLAdmin]
TO FILE
(        FILEPATH = N'c:\audit'
        ,MAXSIZE = 512 MB
        ,MAX_ROLLOVER_FILES = 2147483647
        ,RESERVE_DISK_SPACE = OFF
)
WITH
(        QUEUE_DELAY = 1000
        ,ON_FAILURE = CONTINUE
)
WHERE object_name = 'sysadmin' ;
```

Creating a Server Audit Specification

To create the server audit specification through SSMS, we can drill through Security
in Object Explorer and choose New Server Audit Specification from the Server Audit
Specifications context menu. This will cause the Create Server Audit Specification dialog
box to be displayed, as illustrated in Figure 11-7.

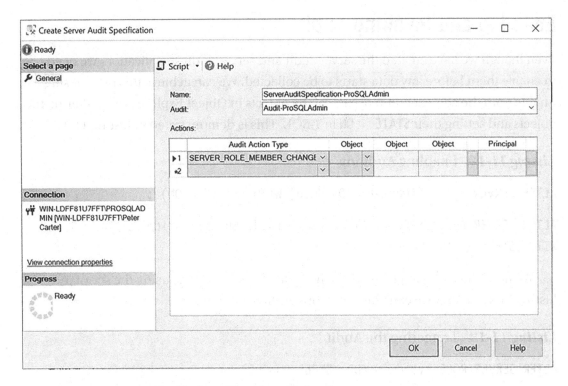

Figure 11-7. *Server Audit Specification dialog box*

You can see that we have selected the SERVER_ROLE_MEMBER_CHANGE_GROUP as the audit action type. This audits any additions or removals of the membership of server roles. Combined with the filter that we have put on the Server Audit object, however, the new result is that only changes to the sysadmin server role will be logged. We also selected the Audit-ProSQLAdmin audit from the Audit drop-down box to tie the objects together.

Alternatively, we can create the same server audit specification through T-SQL by running the command in Listing 11-11. In this command, we are using the FOR SERVER AUDIT clause to link the server audit specification to the Audit-ProSQLAdmin server audit, and the ADD clause to specify the audit action type to capture.

Listing 11-11. Creating the Server Audit Specification

```
CREATE SERVER AUDIT SPECIFICATION [ServerAuditSpecification-ProSQLAdmin]
FOR SERVER AUDIT [Audit-ProSQLAdmin]
ADD (SERVER_ROLE_MEMBER_CHANGE_GROUP) ;
```

Enabling and Invoking Audits

Even though we have created the server audit and server audit specification, we need
to enable them before any data starts to be collected. We can achieve this by choosing
Enable from the context menu of each of the objects in Object Explorer, or by altering the
objects and setting their STATE = ON in T-SQL. This is demonstrated in Listing 11-12.

Listing 11-12. Enabling Auditing

```
ALTER SERVER AUDIT [Audit-ProSQLAdmin] WITH (STATE = ON) ;

ALTER SERVER AUDIT SPECIFICATION [ServerAuditSpecification-ProSQLAdmin]
WITH (STATE = ON) ;
```

We now add the Danielle login to the sysadmin server roles using the script in
Listing 11-13 so that we can check that our audit is working.

Listing 11-13. Triggering the Audit

```
ALTER SERVER ROLE sysadmin ADD MEMBER Danielle ;
```

We expect that our server audit specification's definition has captured both actions,
but that the WHERE clause has filtered out the first action we applied to the server audit.
If we view the audit log by selecting View Audit Log from the context menu of the Audit-
ProSQLAdmin server audit in Object Explorer, as illustrated in Figure 11-8, we can see that
this is working as expected and review the audit entry that has been captured.

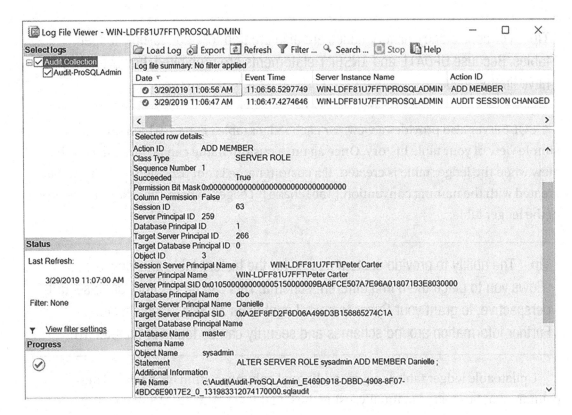

Figure 11-8. *Audit Log File Viewer*

We can see that a granular level of information has been captured. Most notably, this information includes the full statement that caused the audit to fire, the database and object involved, the target login, and the login that ran the statement.

Updateable Ledger Tables

Just like append-only ledger tables, updateable ledger tables also provide nonrepudiation and table history. The difference is that they allow INSERT and UPDATE statements to be made against the table. To make the table versions available, they use a history table, which records every DML statement that was made against the table. A custom name can be provided for this history table, on creation of the updateable ledger table. If a custom name is not provided, then it defaults to the format MSSQL_ LedgerHistoryFor_[Object_ID], where Object_ID is the object ID of the updateable ledger table.

> **Tip**   For consistency, history tables are also created for append-only ledger tables. Because UPDATE and INSERT statements are prohibited, however, they have limited value.

SQL Server also provides a view, for each ledger table created, which provides a simple view of your table history. Once again, a custom name can be provided for the view when the ledger table is created. If a custom name is not provided, then it will be created with the naming convention [TableName]_Ledger, where TableName is the name of the ledger table.

> **Tip**   The ability to provide custom names for the history table and view also allows you to place them in a different schema. This can be helpful from a security perspective, to grant your Cyber team or Legal team access to table history. Further information around schemas and security can be found in Chapter 10.

Updateable ledger tables require additional columns within each table. These columns can be created manually, using the GENERATE ALWAYS AS syntax discussed in the previous section, or if the column definitions are omitted, they will be created automatically, using the column names detailed in Table 11-2.

Table 11-2. *Columns Required for Updatable Ledger Tables*

Column	Data Type	Description
ledger_start_transaction_id	BIGINT	The transaction ID of the transaction that inserted the row
ledger_end_transaction_id	BIGINT	The transaction ID of the transaction that deleted the row
ledger_start_sequence_number	BIGINT	The operation sequence number, within the transaction, that created a row version
ledger_end_sequence_number	BIGINT	The operation sequence number, within the transaction, that deleted a row version

The script in Listing 11-14 creates an updateable ledger table within the Chapter11 database and inserts some initial data, before making modifications to the data. In this example, we specify custom names for the ledger view and history table, but we omit the ledger columns. This means that they will be created automatically, with default names. You will notice that the table also specifies SYSTEM_VERSIONING = ON. This is a requirement and must always be set, when creating an updateable ledger table.

Note   Different activities are simulated as being run by different users, using the EXECUTE AS clause. This creates an interesting repudiation point that we will discuss a little later.

Tip   To run the script in Listing 11-14, you will need Logins and Users called Andrew and GoodsInApplication. These users will need permissions to perform INSERT, UPDATE, and DELETE operations against the ledger tables. Please see Chapter 10 for information on how to create Logins and Users. Alternatively, you could change the EXECUTE AS clauses to use any other Logins which exist and have the appropriate permissions to the ledger tables.

Listing 11-14. Create an Updateable Ledger Table

```
USE Chapter11
GO

--Create Updateable Ledger Table

CREATE TABLE dbo.GoodsIn (
    ID              INT             NOT NULL    IDENTITY    PRIMARY KEY,
    StockID         INT             NOT NULL,
    QtyOrdered      INT             NOT NULL,
    QtyReceived     INT             NOT NULL,
    ReceivedBy      NVARCHAR(128)   NOT NULL,
    ReceivedDate    DATETIME2       NOT NULL,
    Damaged         BIT             NOT NULL
```

```
) WITH (
    SYSTEM_VERSIONING = ON ( --Updateable ledger tables must always have
    system_versioning turned on
        HISTORY_TABLE = dbo.GoodsIn_Ledger_History --Specify custom
        name for history table
    ),
    LEDGER = ON (
        LEDGER_VIEW = dbo.GoodsIn_Ledger_View --Specify custom name for
        ledger view
    )
) ;
GO

EXECUTE AS LOGIN = 'GoodsInApplication' --Simulate activity by application

--Insert Initial Data

INSERT INTO dbo.GoodsIn (StockID, QtyOrdered, QtyReceived, ReceivedBy,
ReceivedDate, Damaged)
VALUES(17, 25, 25, 'Pete', '20220807 10:59', 0),
    (6, 20, 19, 'Brian', '20220810 15:01', 0),
    (17, 20, 20, 'Steve', '20220810 16:56', 1),
    (36, 10, 10, 'Steve', '20220815 18:11', 0),
    (36, 10, 10, 'Steve', '20220815 18:12', 1),
    (1, 85, 85, 'Andrew', '20220820 10:27', 0) ;

--Duplicate row deleted by application

DELETE FROM dbo.GoodsIn WHERE ID = 4 ;

REVERT --Stop impersonating GoodsInApplication

EXECUTE AS LOGIN = 'Andrew' --Simulate activity by user

--Row updated by Andrew, from outside the application (RED FLAG)
```

```
UPDATE dbo.GoodsIn
SET QtyReceived = 70
WHERE ID = 6 ;

REVERT --Stop impersonating Andrew

EXECUTE AS LOGIN = 'GoodsInApplication' --Simulate activity by application

--Rows updated by application

UPDATE dbo.GoodsIn
SET Damaged = 1
WHERE ID = 1 ;

INSERT INTO dbo.GoodsIn (StockID, QtyOrdered, QtyReceived, ReceivedBy,
ReceivedDate, Damaged)
VALUES (17, 25, 25, 'Pete', '20220822 08:59', 0)

REVERT --Stop impersonating GoodsInApplication
```

To avoid searching for the view and history table that are associated with the GoodsIn updateable ledger table, we can use the query in Listing 11-15 to return the object names.

Listing 11-15. Discover Ledger View and History Table Names

```
SELECT
        t.name AS Updateable_Ledger_Table
      , h.name AS History_Table
      , v.name AS Ledger_View
FROM sys.tables AS t
INNER JOIN sys.tables AS h
      ON h.object_id = t.history_table_id
JOIN sys.views v
      ON v.object_id = t.ledger_view_id
WHERE t.name = 'GoodsIn' ;
```

Tip   This query could be expanded to meet your needs. For example, if you decide to store history tables in a different schema, you could join to `sys.schemas` to include the schema name.

The script in Listing 11-16 expands out the script, using dynamic SQL, to return the contents of the updateable ledger table, the history table, and the ledger view.

Listing 11-16. View Updateable Ledger Table, Ledger View, and History Table

```
DECLARE @SQL NVARCHAR(MAX)

SET @SQL = (
SELECT
        'SELECT * FROM ' + t.name --Updateable Ledger Table
    + ' SELECT * FROM ' + h.name --History Table
    + ' SELECT * FROM ' + v.name + ' ORDER BY ledger_transaction_id,
ledger_sequence_number ' --Ledger View
FROM sys.tables AS t
INNER JOIN sys.tables AS h
    ON h.object_id = t.history_table_id
JOIN sys.views v
    ON v.object_id = t.ledger_view_id
WHERE t.name = 'GoodsIn' )

EXEC(@SQL)
```

The results of this query are displayed in Figure 11-9.

Results | Messages

	ID	StockID	QtyOrdered	QtyReceived	ReceivedBy	ReceivedDate	Damaged
1	1	17	25	25	Pete	2022-08-07 10:59:00.0000000	1
2	2	6	20	19	Brian	2022-08-10 15:01:00.0000000	0
3	3	17	20	20	Steve	2022-08-10 16:56:00.0000000	1
4	5	36	10	10	Steve	2022-08-15 18:12:00.0000000	1
5	6	1	85	70	Andrew	2022-08-20 10:27:00.0000000	0
6	7	17	25	25	Pete	2022-08-22 08:59:00.0000000	0

	ID	StockID	QtyOrdered	QtyReceived	ReceivedBy	ReceivedDate	Damaged	ledger_start_transaction_id	ledger_end_transaction_id	ledger_start_sequence_number	ledger_end_sequence_number
1	4	36	10	10	Steve	2022-08-15 18:11:00.0000000	0	1066	1069	3	0
2	6	1	85	85	Andrew	2022-08-20 10:27:00.0000000	0	1066	1072	5	1
3	1	17	25	25	Pete	2022-08-07 10:59:00.0000000	0	1066	1073	0	1

	ID	StockID	QtyOrdered	QtyReceived	ReceivedBy	ReceivedDate	Damaged	ledger_transaction_id	ledger_sequence_number	ledger_operation_type	ledger_operation_type_desc
1	1	17	25	25	Pete	2022-08-07 10:59:00.0000000	0	1066	0	1	INSERT
2	2	6	20	19	Brian	2022-08-10 15:01:00.0000000	0	1066	1	1	INSERT
3	3	17	20	20	Steve	2022-08-10 16:56:00.0000000	1	1066	2	1	INSERT
4	4	36	10	10	Steve	2022-08-15 18:11:00.0000000	0	1066	3	1	INSERT
5	5	36	10	10	Steve	2022-08-15 18:12:00.0000000	1	1066	4	1	INSERT
6	6	1	85	85	Andrew	2022-08-20 10:27:00.0000000	0	1066	5	1	INSERT
7	4	36	10	10	Steve	2022-08-15 18:11:00.0000000	0	1069	0	2	DELETE
8	6	1	85	70	Andrew	2022-08-20 10:27:00.0000000	0	1072	0	1	INSERT
9	6	1	85	85	Andrew	2022-08-20 10:27:00.0000000	0	1072	1	2	DELETE
10	1	17	25	25	Pete	2022-08-07 10:59:00.0000000	1	1073	0	1	INSERT
11	1	17	25	25	Pete	2022-08-07 10:59:00.0000000	0	1073	1	2	DELETE
12	7	17	25	25	Pete	2022-08-22 08:59:00.0000000	0	1074	0	1	INSERT

Query executed successfully.   WIN-Q4G88\

Figure 11-9. *Results of viewing ledger table objects*

You can see from the results that the history table contains one row for each transaction or batch that has modified the table. In our example, we did not use explicit transactions. Therefore, the demarcation is by batch. Because of our use of the EXECUTE AS clause, the updates are divided into three batches and, hence, three transactions.

The ledger view provides a view of the data within the table as it has changed over time. There is no UPDATE operation recorded. Instead, for updates, two rows appear in the view: one for the insert of the new version of the row and another for the deletion of the old row version. For example, there are two rows with the Transaction ID 1073 containing rows for the "before" and "after" versions of the row that was updated by Andrew.

As is the case with append-only ledger tables, you can also view the principal who ran the updates against an updateable ledger table and the time that the transaction was committed. This is demonstrated in Listing 11-17.

Listing 11-17. Discover Who Modified the Table

```
SELECT
        lv.ID
      , lv.StockID
      , lv.QtyOrdered
      , lv.QtyReceived
      , lv.ReceivedBy
```

```
        , lv.ReceivedDate
        , lv.Damaged
        , lv.ledger_operation_type_desc
        , dlt.commit_time
        , dlt.principal_name
FROM dbo.GoodsIn_Ledger_View lv
INNER JOIN sys.database_ledger_transactions dlt
        ON dlt.transaction_id = lv.ledger_transaction_id
```

You may remember that earlier in this section, I mentioned an interesting repudiation consideration around the use of impersonation. The results of the preceding query, shown in Figure 11-10, demonstrate that this is actually not a concern. Despite the use of EXECUTE AS to impersonate different users, for all updates, the principal with which we are logged into SQL Server has been recorded as the principal that modified the data.

	ID	StockID	QtyOrdered	QtyReceived	ReceivedBy	ReceivedDate	Damaged	ledger_operation_type_desc	commit_time	principal_name
1	2	6	20	19	Brian	2022-08-10 15:01:00.0000000	0	INSERT	2022-08-07 06:11:24.7566667	WIN-Q4G88VPDBIM\Administrator
2	3	17	20	20	Steve	2022-08-10 16:56:00.0000000	1	INSERT	2022-08-07 06:11:24.7566667	WIN-Q4G88VPDBIM\Administrator
3	5	36	10	10	Steve	2022-08-15 18:12:00.0000000	1	INSERT	2022-08-07 06:11:24.7566667	WIN-Q4G88VPDBIM\Administrator
4	4	36	10	10	Steve	2022-08-15 18:11:00.0000000	0	INSERT	2022-08-07 06:11:24.7566667	WIN-Q4G88VPDBIM\Administrator
5	6	1	85	85	Andrew	2022-08-20 10:27:00.0000000	0	INSERT	2022-08-07 06:11:24.7566667	WIN-Q4G88VPDBIM\Administrator
6	1	17	25	25	Pete	2022-08-07 10:59:00.0000000	0	INSERT	2022-08-07 06:11:24.7566667	WIN-Q4G88VPDBIM\Administrator
7	4	36	10	10	Steve	2022-08-15 18:11:00.0000000	0	DELETE	2022-08-07 06:11:24.7600000	WIN-Q4G88VPDBIM\Administrator
8	6	1	85	70	Andrew	2022-08-20 10:27:00.0000000	0	INSERT	2022-08-07 06:11:24.7666667	WIN-Q4G88VPDBIM\Administrator
9	6	1	85	85	Andrew	2022-08-20 10:27:00.0000000	0	DELETE	2022-08-07 06:11:24.7666667	WIN-Q4G88VPDBIM\Administrator
10	1	17	25	25	Pete	2022-08-07 10:59:00.0000000	1	INSERT	2022-08-07 06:11:24.7700000	WIN-Q4G88VPDBIM\Administrator
11	1	17	25	25	Pete	2022-08-07 10:59:00.0000000	0	DELETE	2022-08-07 06:11:24.7700000	WIN-Q4G88VPDBIM\Administrator
12	7	17	25	25	Pete	2022-08-22 08:59:00.0000000	0	INSERT	2022-08-07 06:11:24.7700000	WIN-Q4G88VPDBIM\Administrator

Query executed successfully.

Figure 11-10. *Results of viewing who modified data*

Just like append-only ledger tables, once a table has been configured as an updateable ledger table, that feature cannot be turned off. This prevents privileged users from turning the feature off, updating data, and then reenabling the feature. Another interesting consideration for updatable ledger tables is what happens if the whole table is deleted? For example, what if a privileged user copies the data out of the GoodsIn table, drops the table, and then reinserts the modified data? The simple answer is that DROP does not drop a ledger table, it simply renames it, along with its associated objects. For example, let's use the script in Listing 11-18 to drop the GoodsIn table before rerunning the query that discovers ledger object names.

Listing 11-18. Dropping Ledger Objects

```
USE Chapter11
GO

DROP TABLE dbo.GoodsIn
GO

SELECT
        t.name AS Updateable_Ledger_Table
      , h.name AS History_Table
      , v.name AS Ledger_View
FROM sys.tables AS t
INNER JOIN sys.tables AS h
      ON h.object_id = t.history_table_id
JOIN sys.views v
      ON v.object_id = t.ledger_view_id ;
```

The results, shown in Figure 11-11, show that instead of being deleted, the objects have simply been renamed and can still be queried.

Figure 11-11. *Viewing dropped ledger objects*

Caution   This does not stop an entire database from being dropped and modified data being copied back in.

Database Audit Specifications

A database audit specification is similar to a server audit specification but specifies audit requirements at the database level, as opposed to at the instance level. In order to demonstrate this functionality, we map the Danielle login to a user in this database and assign SELECT permissions to the SensitiveData table. We also create a new server audit, called Audit-Chapter11, which we use as the audit to which our database audit specification attaches. These actions are performed in Listing 11-19. Before executing the script, change the file path to match your own configuration.

Listing 11-19. Creating the Chapter11Audit Database

```
USE Master
GO

--Create Chapter11Audit Database

CREATE DATABASE Chapter11Audit
GO

USE Chapter11Audit
GO

CREATE TABLE dbo.SensitiveData (
    ID      INT      PRIMARY KEY      NOT NULL,
    Data    NVARCHAR(256) NOT NULL
) ;

--Create Server Audit

USE master
GO

CREATE SERVER AUDIT [Audit-Chapter11Audit]
TO FILE
(        FILEPATH = N'C:\Audit'
        ,MAXSIZE = 512 MB
        ,MAX_ROLLOVER_FILES = 2147483647
        ,RESERVE_DISK_SPACE = OFF
)
WITH
(        QUEUE_DELAY = 1000
        ,ON_FAILURE = CONTINUE
) ;

USE Chapter11Audit
```

```
GO

--Create database user from Danielle Login

CREATE USER Danielle FOR LOGIN Danielle WITH DEFAULT_SCHEMA=dbo ;
GO

GRANT SELECT ON dbo.SensitiveData TO Danielle ;
```

We now look to create a database audit specification that captures any INSERT statements made against the SensitiveData table by any user but also captures SELECT statements run specifically by Danielle.

We can create the database audit specification in SQL Server Management Studio by drilling through the Chapter11Audit database ➤ Security and selecting New Database Audit Specification from the context menu of Database Audit Specifications. This invokes the Create Database Audit Specification dialog box, as illustrated in Figure 11-12.

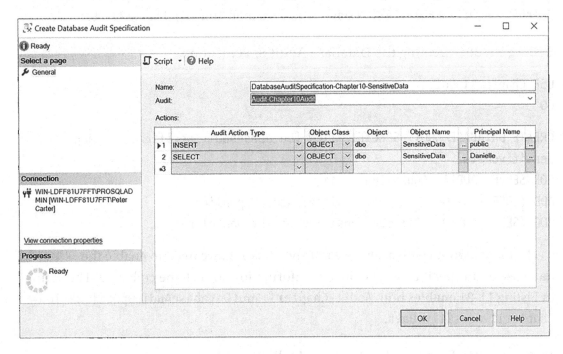

Figure 11-12. *Database Audit Specification dialog box*

You can see that we named the database audit specification DatabaseAuditSpecification-Chapter11-SensitiveData and linked it to the Audit-Chapter11 server audit using the drop-down list. In the lower half of the screen, we specified two audit action types, INSERT and SELECT. Because we specified an object class of OBJECT, as opposed to the other available options of DATABASE or SCHEMA, we also need to specify the object name of the table that we want to audit. Because we only want Danielle's SELECT activity to be audited, we add this user to the Principal field for the SELECT action type, but we add the Public role as the principal for the INSERT action type. This is because all database users will be members of the Public role, and hence, all INSERT activity will be captured, regardless of the user.

Tip   You can display a complete list of audit class types by running the query SELECT * FROM sys.dm_audit_class_type_map. You can find a complete list of auditable actions by running the query SELECT * FROM sys.dm_audit_ actions.

We can create the same database audit specification in T-SQL by using the CREATE DATABASE AUDIT SPECIFICATION statement, as demonstrated in Listing 11-20.

Listing 11-20. Creating the Database Audit Specification

```
USE Chapter11Audit
GO

CREATE DATABASE AUDIT SPECIFICATION [DatabaseAuditSpecification-Chapter11-
SensitiveData]
FOR SERVER AUDIT [Audit-Chapter11]
ADD (INSERT ON OBJECT::dbo.SensitiveData BY public),
ADD (SELECT ON OBJECT::dbo.SensitiveData BY Danielle) ;
```

Just as we would with a server audit specification, we need to enable the database audit specification before any information starts to be collected. The script in Listing 11-21 enables both Audit-Chapter11 and DatabaseAuditSpecification-Chapter11-SensitiveData.

Listing 11-21. Enabling the Database Audit Specification

```
USE Chapter11Audit
GO
```

```
ALTER DATABASE AUDIT SPECIFICATION [DatabaseAuditSpecification-Chapter11-
SensitiveData]
WITH (STATE = ON) ;
GO

USE Master
GO

ALTER SERVER AUDIT [Audit-Chapter11] WITH (STATE = ON) ;
```

To test security, SQL Server allows you to impersonate a user. To do this, you must be a sysadmin or be granted the impersonate permissions on the user in question. The script in Listing 11-22 impersonates the user Danielle in order to check that the auditing is successful. It does this by using the EXECUTE AS USER command. The REVERT command switches the security context back to the user who ran the script.

Listing 11-22. Testing Security with Impersonation

```
USE Chapter11Audit
GO

GRANT INSERT, UPDATE ON dbo.sensitiveData TO Danielle ;
GO

INSERT INTO dbo.SensitiveData (SensitiveText)
VALUES ('testing') ;
GO

UPDATE dbo.SensitiveData
SET SensitiveText = 'Boo'
WHERE ID = 2 ;
GO

EXECUTE AS USER ='Danielle'
GO

INSERT dbo.SensitiveData (SensitiveText)
VALUES ('testing again') ;
GO

UPDATE dbo.SensitiveData
```

```
SET SensitiveText = 'Boo'
WHERE ID = 1 ;
GO

REVERT
```

Auditing the Audit

With the auditing that we have implemented up to this point, there is a security hole. If an administrator with the permissions to manage server audit has ill intent, then it is possible for them to change the audit specification before performing a malicious action and then finally reconfiguring the audit to its original state in order to remove reputability.

Server audit allows you to protect against this threat, however, by giving you the ability to audit the audit itself. If you add the AUDIT_CHANGE_GROUP to your server audit specification or database audit specification, then any changes to the specification are captured.

Using the Audit-Chapter11 server audit and the DatabaseAuditSpecification-Chapter11 database audit specification as an example, we are auditing any INSERT statements, by any user, to the SensitiveData table. To avoid a privileged user with ill intent inserting data into this table without traceability, we can use the script in Listing 11-23 to add the AUDIT_CHANGE_GROUP. Note that we have to disable the database audit specification before we make the change and then reenable it.

Listing 11-23. Adding AUDIT_CHANGE_GROUP

```
USE Chapter11Audit
GO

ALTER DATABASE AUDIT SPECIFICATION [DatabaseAuditSpecification-Chapter11-
SensitiveData]
WITH (STATE=OFF) ;
GO

ALTER DATABASE AUDIT SPECIFICATION [DatabaseAuditSpecification-Chapter11-
SensitiveData]
ADD (AUDIT_CHANGE_GROUP) ;
GO
```

```
ALTER DATABASE AUDIT SPECIFICATION [DatabaseAuditSpecification-Chapter11-
SensitiveData]
WITH(STATE = ON) ;
GO
```

After executing this command, any changes we make to the auditing are captured. If you view the audit log, you can see that the Administrator login has been audited, removing the INSERT audit on the SensitiveData table.

Summary

SQL Server 2022 introduces Ledger, which uses blockchain technology to prove the trustworthiness of your data. This can fulfill use cases such as satisfying audit requirements and creating supply chain management processes between companies.

There are two types of ledger table available: append-only ledger tables and updateable ledger tables. Append-only tables only permit INSERT statements and do not permit UPDATE OR DELETE statements. Nonreputability is ensured by logging the time and security principal which made each insert.

Updateable ledger tables allow INSERT, UPDATE, and DELETE statements. They use a history table to store each row version, and again, nonreputability is ensured by logging the time and security principal of each transaction.

The latest block is known as a database digest. Digests can be generated automatically, if you integrate with Azure or can be generated manually. However, once your digests are generated, you should ensure that they are used to regularly verify the trustworthiness of your database.

Server audit allows a fine-grain audit of activity at both the instance and database levels. It also includes the ability to audit the audit itself, thus removing the threat of a privileged user bypassing the audit with malicious intent. You can save audits to a file in the operating system and control permissions through NTFS. Alternatively, you can save audits to the Windows Security log or Windows Application log.

## CHAPTER 12

Encryption

Encryption is a process of obfuscating data with an algorithm that uses keys and certificates so that if security is bypassed and data is accessed or stolen by unauthorized users, then it will be useless, unless the keys that were used to encrypt it are also obtained. This adds an additional layer of security over and above access control, but it does not replace the need for an access control implementation. Encrypting data also has the potential to considerably degrade performance, so you should use it on the basis of need, as opposed to implementing it on all data as a matter of routine.

In this chapter, we discuss the SQL Server encryption hierarchy before demonstrating how to implement transparent data encryption (TDE) as well as cell-level encryption. We also discuss Always Encrypted, and secure enclaves.

Encryption Hierarchy

SQL Server offers the ability to encrypt data through a hierarchy of keys and certificates. Each layer within the hierarchy encrypts the layer below it.

Encryption Concepts

Before we discuss the hierarchy in detail, it is important to understand the concepts that relate to encryption. The following sections provide an overview of the main artifacts that are involved in encryption.

Symmetric Keys

A *symmetric key* is an algorithm that you can use to encrypt data. It is the weakest form of encryption because it uses the same algorithm for both encrypting and decrypting the data. It is also the encryption method that has the least performance overhead. You can encrypt a symmetric key with a password or with another key or certificate.

415

© Peter A. Carter 2023
P. A. Carter, *Pro SQL Server 2022 Administration*, https://doi.org/10.1007/978-1-4842-8864-1_12

Asymmetric Keys

In contrast to a symmetric key, which uses the same algorithm to both encrypt and decrypt data, an *asymmetric key* uses a pair of keys or algorithms. You can use one for encryption only and the other for decryption only. The key that is used to encrypt the data is called the *private key* and the key that is used to decrypt the data is known as the *public key*.

Certificates

A certificate is issued by a trusted source, known as a *certificate authority (CA)*. It uses an asymmetric key and provides a digitally signed statement, which binds the public key to a principal or device, which holds the corresponding private key.

Windows Data Protection API

The Windows Data Protection API (DPAPI) is a cryptographic application programming interface (API) that ships with the Windows operating system. It allows keys to be encrypted by using user or domain secret information. DPAPI is used to encrypt the Service Master Key, which is the top level of the SQL Server encryption hierarchy.

SQL Server Encryption Concepts

SQL Server's cryptography functionality relies on a hierarchy of keys and certificates, with the root level being the Service Master Key. The following sections describe the use of master keys, as well as SQL Server's encryption hierarchy.

Master Keys

The root level of the SQL Server encryption hierarchy is the Service Master Key. The Service Master Key is created automatically when the instance is built, and it is used to encrypt database master keys, credentials, and linked servers' passwords using the DPAPI. The Service Master Key is stored in the Master database and there is always precisely one per instance. The Service Master Key is a symmetric key that is generated using the AES 256 algorithm. This is in contrast to older versions of SQL Server, which use the Triple DES algorithm.

If you ever need to regenerate the Service Master Key, it involves decrypting and then reencrypting every key and certificate that sits below it in the hierarchy. This is a very resource-intensive process and should only be attempted during a maintenance window.

You can regenerate the Service Master Key using the command in Listing 12-1. You should be aware, however, that if the process fails to decrypt and reencrypt any key that is below it in the hierarchy, then the whole regeneration process fails. You can change this behavior by using the FORCE keyword. The FORCE keyword forces the process to continue, after errors. Be warned that this will leave any data that cannot be decrypted and reencrypted unusable. You will have no way to regain access to this data.

Listing 12-1. Regenerating the Service Master Key

```
ALTER SERVICE MASTER KEY REGENERATE
```

Because the Service Master Key is so vital, you must take a backup of it after it has been created or regenerated and store it in a secure, off-site location for the purpose of disaster recovery. You can also restore the backup of this key if you are migrating an instance to a different server to avoid issues with the encryption hierarchy. The script in Listing 12-2 demonstrates how to back up and restore the Service Master Key. If the master key you restore is identical, then SQL Server lets you know and data does not need to be reencrypted.

Listing 12-2. Backing Up and Restoring the Service Master Key

```
BACKUP SERVICE MASTER KEY
    TO FILE = 'c:\keys\service_master_key'
    ENCRYPTION BY PASSWORD = 'Pa$$w0rd'

RESTORE SERVICE MASTER KEY
    FROM FILE = 'c:\keys\service_master_key'
    DECRYPTION BY PASSWORD = 'Pa$$w0rd'
```

Tip service_master_key is the name of the key file as opposed to a folder. By convention, it does not have an extension.

As when you are regenerating a Service Master Key, when you restore it, you can also use the FORCE keyword with the same consequences.

A Database Master Key is a symmetric key, encrypted using the AES 256 algorithm that is used to encrypt the private keys and certificates that are stored within a database. It is encrypted using a password, but a copy is created that is encrypted using the Service Master Key. This allows the Database Master Key to be opened automatically when it is needed. If this copy does not exist, then you need to open it manually. This means that the key needs to be explicitly opened in order for you to use a key that has been encrypted by it. A copy of the Database Master Key is stored within the database and another copy is stored within the Master database. You can create a Database Master Key using the command in Listing 12-3.

Listing 12-3. Creating a Database Master Key

```
CREATE DATABASE Chapter12MasterKeyExample ;
GO

USE Chapter12MasterKeyExample
GO

CREATE MASTER KEY ENCRYPTION BY PASSWORD = 'Pa$$wOrd'
```

As with the Service Master Key, Database Master Keys should be backed up and stored in a secure off-site location. You can back up and restore a Database Master Key by using the commands in Listing 12-4.

Listing 12-4. Backing Up and Restoring a Database Master Key

```
BACKUP MASTER KEY
    TO FILE = 'c:\keys\Chapter12_master_key'
    ENCRYPTION BY PASSWORD = 'Pa$$wOrd';

RESTORE MASTER KEY
    FROM FILE = 'c:\keys\Chapter12_master_key'
    DECRYPTION BY PASSWORD = 'Pa$$wOrd' --The password in the backup file
    ENCRYPTION BY PASSWORD = 'Pa$$wOrd'; --The password it will be
    encrypted within the database
```

As with the Service Master Key, if the restore is unable to decrypt and reencrypt any of the keys below it in the hierarchy, the restore fails. You are able to use the FORCE keyword to force the restore to succeed, but when you do so, you permanently lose access to the data encrypted using the key(s) that could not be decrypted and reencrypted.

SQL Server 2022 introduces support for backing up the Database Master key to Azure Blob storage. To use this option, you will need to create a SQL Server Credential that uses the URL of the Blob storage as its name, the shared access signature as the identity, and the shared access signature key as the secret. Credentials are discussed in Chapter 10 and creating credentials for Azure is demonstrated in Chapter 21.

Once you have a Credential in place, you can simply replace the TO FILE clause of the BACKUP MASTER KEY and RESTORE MASTER KEY statements with TO URL and FROM URL clauses, where the URL is the same as the URL used by the Credential.

Hierarchy

The SQL Server encryption hierarchy is illustrated in Figure 12-1.

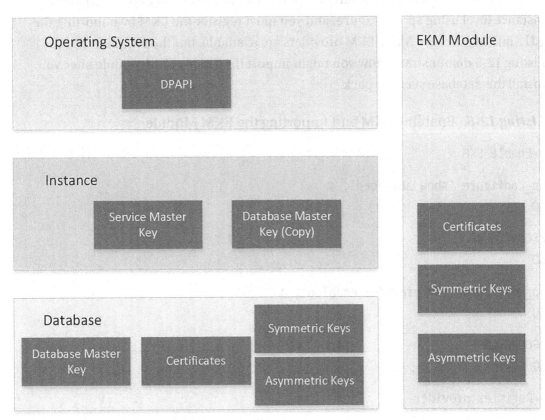

Figure 12-1. *Encryption hierarchy*

The diagram shows that the Service Master Key and a copy of the Database Master Key are stored at the instance level, with the Database Master Key also being stored within the database. The certificates, symmetric keys, and asymmetric keys that are encrypted using the Database Master Key are also stored within the database.

To the right of the diagram, you see a section called the EKM Module. An Extensible Key Management (EKM) module allows you to generate and manage keys and certificates used to secure SQL Server data in third-party hardware security modules, which interface with SQL Server using the Microsoft Cryptographic API (MSCAPI). This is more secure because the key is not being stored with the data, but it also means that you can benefit from advanced features that may be offered by the third-party vendor, such as key rotation and secure key disposal.

Before you can use a third-party EKM module, you need to enable EKM at the instance level using sp_configure, and you must register the EKM by importing the .dll into SQL Server. Many EKM providers are available, but the sample script in Listing 12-5 demonstrates how you might import the Thales EKM module after you install the database security pack.

Listing 12-5. Enabling EKM and Importing the EKM Module

```
--Enable EKM

sp_configure 'show advanced', 1
GO

RECONFIGURE
GO

sp_configure 'EKM provider enabled', 1
GO

RECONFIGURE
GO

--Register provider

CREATE CRYPTOGRAPHIC PROVIDER nCipher_Provider FROM FILE =
 'C:\Program Files\nCipher\nfast\bin\ncsqlekm64.dll'
```

Note   A full discussion of EKM is beyond the scope of this book, but you can obtain further information from your cryptographic provider.

Transparent Data Encryption

When implementing a security strategy for your sensitive data, one important aspect to consider is the risk of data being stolen. Imagine a situation in which a privileged user with malicious intent uses detach/attach to move a database to a new instance in order to gain access to data they are not authorized to view. Alternatively, if a malicious user gains access to the database backups, they can restore the backups to a new server in order to gain access to the data.

Transparent data encryption (TDE) protects against these scenarios by encrypting the data pages and log file of a database and by storing the key, known as a Database Encryption Key, in the boot record of the database. Once you enable TDE on a database, pages are encrypted before they are written to disk and they are decrypted when they are read into memory.

TDE also provides several advantages over cell-level encryption, which will be discussed later in this chapter. First, it does not cause bloat. A database encrypted with TDE is the same size as it was before it was encrypted. Also, although there is a performance overhead, this is significantly less than the performance overhead associated with cell-level encryption. Another significant advantage is that the encryption is transparent to applications, meaning that developers do not need to modify their code to access the data.

When planning the implementation of TDE, be mindful of how it interacts with other technologies. For example, you are able to encrypt a database that uses In-Memory OLTP, but the data within the In-Memory filegroup is not encrypted because the data resides in memory, and TDE only encrypts data at rest, meaning when it is on disk. Even though the memory-optimized data is not encrypted, log records associated with in-memory transactions are encrypted.

It is also possible to encrypt databases that use FILESTREAM, but again, data within a FILESTREAM filegroup is not encrypted. If you use full-text indexes (FTE), then new full-text indexes are encrypted. Existing full-text indexes are only encrypted after they are imported during an upgrade. It is regarded as bad practice to use full-text indexing with TDE, however. This is because data is written to disk in plain text during the full-text indexing scan operation, which leaves a window of opportunity for attackers to access sensitive data.

High availability and disaster recovery technologies such as database mirroring, AlwaysOn Availability Groups, and log shipping are supported with databases that have TDE enabled. Data on the replica database is also encrypted, and the data within the log is encrypted, meaning that it cannot be intercepted as it is being sent between the servers. Replication is also supported with TDE, but the data in the subscriber is not automatically encrypted. You must enable TDE manually on subscribers and the distributor.

Caution   Even if you enable TDE at the subscriber, data is still stored in plain text while it is in intermediate files. This, arguably, poses a greater risk than using FTE (full-text indexes), so you should closely consider the risk/benefit scenario.

It is also important to note that enabling TDE for any database within an instance causes TDE to be enabled on TempDB. The reason for this is that TempDB is used to store user data for intermediate results sets, during sort operations, spool operations, and so on. TempDB also stores user data when you are using Temp Tables, or row versioning operations occur. This can have the undesirable effect of decreasing the performance of other user databases that have not had TDE enabled.

It is also important to note, from the viewpoint of the performance of database maintenance, that TDE is incompatible with instant file initialization. Instant file initialization speeds up operations that create or expand files, as the files do not need to be zeroed out. If your instance is configured to use instant file initialization, then it no longer works for the files associated with any databases that you encrypt. It is a hard technical requirement that files are zeroed out when TDE is enabled.

Implementing TDE

To implement transparent data encryption, you must first create a Database Master Key. Once this key is in place, you can create a certificate. You must use the Database Master Key to encrypt the certificate. If you attempt to encrypt the certificate using a password only, then it will be rejected when you attempt to use it to encrypt the Database

Encryption Key. The Database Encryption Key is the next object that you need to create, and as implied earlier, you encrypt this using the certificate. Finally, you can alter the database to turn encryption on.

Note   It is possible to encrypt the Database Encryption Key using an asymmetric key as opposed to a server certificate, but only if the asymmetric key is protected using an EKM module.

When you enable TDE for a database, a background process moves through each page in every data file and encrypts it. This does not stop the database from being accessible, but it does take out locks, which stop maintenance operations from taking place. While the encryption scan is in progress, the following operations cannot be performed:

- Dropping a file
- Dropping a filegroup
- Dropping the database
- Detaching the database
- Taking the database offline
- Setting the database as read_only

Luckily, a feature in recent versions of SQL Server gives DBAs more control over this process, with the ability to pause and restart the encryption scan, using an ALTER DATABASE statement, with either SET ENCRYPTION SUSPEND or SET ENCRYPTION RESTART options specified.

It is also important to note that the operation to enable TDE will fail if any of the filegroups within a database are marked as read_only. This is because all pages within all files need to be encrypted when TDE is enabled, and this involves changing the data within the pages to obfuscate them.

The script in Listing 12-6 creates a database called Chapter12Encrypted and then creates a table that is populated with data. Finally, it creates a Database Master Key and a server certificate.

Listing 12-6. Creating the Chapter12Encrypted Database

```
--Create the Database

CREATE DATABASE Chapter12Encrypted ;
GO

USE Chapter12Encrypted
GO

--Create the table

CREATE TABLE dbo.SensitiveData
(
ID              INT                     PRIMARY KEY         IDENTITY,
FirstName       NVARCHAR(30),
LastName        NVARCHAR(30),
CreditCardNumber        VARBINARY(8000)
) ;
GO

--Populate the table

DECLARE @Numbers TABLE
(
        Number          INT
)

;WITH CTE(Number)
AS
(
        SELECT 1 Number
        UNION ALL
        SELECT Number + 1
        FROM CTE
        WHERE Number < 100
)
INSERT INTO @Numbers
SELECT Number FROM CTE ;
```

```
DECLARE @Names TABLE
(
        FirstName           VARCHAR(30),
        LastName            VARCHAR(30)
) ;

INSERT INTO @Names
VALUES('Peter', 'Carter'),
                ('Michael', 'Smith'),
                ('Danielle', 'Mead'),
                ('Reuben', 'Roberts'),
                ('Iris', 'Jones'),
                ('Sylvia', 'Davies'),
                ('Finola', 'Wright'),
                ('Edward', 'James'),
                ('Marie', 'Andrews'),
                ('Jennifer', 'Abraham'),
                ('Margaret', 'Jones') ;

INSERT INTO dbo.SensitiveData(Firstname, LastName, CreditCardNumber)
SELECT  FirstName, LastName, CreditCardNumber FROM
        (SELECT
                (SELECT TOP 1 FirstName FROM @Names ORDER BY NEWID())
                FirstName
                ,(SELECT TOP 1 LastName FROM @Names ORDER BY NEWID())
                LastName
                ,(SELECT CONVERT(VARBINARY(8000)
                ,(SELECT TOP 1 CAST(Number * 100 AS CHAR(4))
                  FROM @Numbers
                  WHERE Number BETWEEN 10 AND 99 ORDER BY NEWID()) + '-' +
                        (SELECT TOP 1 CAST(Number * 100 AS CHAR(4))
                          FROM @Numbers
                          WHERE Number BETWEEN 10 AND 99 ORDER BY
                          NEWID()) + '-' +
                        (SELECT TOP 1 CAST(Number * 100 AS CHAR(4))
                          FROM @Numbers
```

```
                            WHERE Number BETWEEN 10 AND 99 ORDER BY
                            NEWID()) + '-' +
                        (SELECT TOP 1 CAST(Number * 100 AS CHAR(4))
                            FROM @Numbers
                            WHERE Number BETWEEN 10 AND 99 ORDER BY
                            NEWID())))) CreditCardNumber
FROM @Numbers a
CROSS JOIN @Numbers b
CROSS JOIN @Numbers c
) d ;

USE Master
GO

--Create the Database Master Key

CREATE MASTER KEY ENCRYPTION BY PASSWORD = 'Pa$$w0rd';
GO

--Create the Server Certificate

CREATE CERTIFICATE TDECert WITH SUBJECT = 'Certificate For TDE';
GO
```

Now that we have created our database, along with the Database Master Key and certificate, we can now encrypt our database. To do this through SQL Server Management Studio, we can select Manage Database Encryption, from under Tasks, in the context menu of our database. This invokes the Manage Database Encryption wizard illustrated in Figure 12-2.

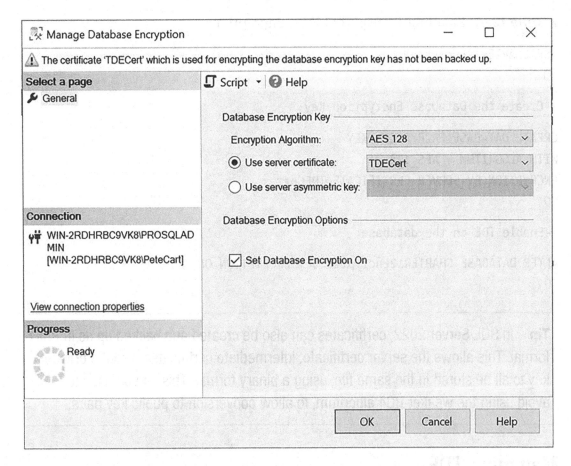

Figure 12-2. *Manage Database Encryption wizard*

You can see that we have selected our server certificate from the drop-down box and have chosen to enable database encryption. In the Encryption Algorithm drop-down box, we have selected AES 128, which is the default option.

Note   Choosing an algorithm is essentially a trade-off between security and performance. Longer keys consume more CPU resources but are more difficult to crack.

Transparent data encryption can also be configured through T-SQL. We can achieve the same results via T-SQL by executing the script in Listing 12-7.

Listing 12-7. Enabling Transparent Data Encryption

```
USE CHAPTER12Encrypted
GO

--Create the Database Encryption Key

CREATE DATABASE ENCRYPTION KEY
WITH ALGORITHM = AES_128
ENCRYPTION BY SERVER CERTIFICATE TDECert ;
GO

--Enable TDE on the database

ALTER DATABASE CHAPTER12Encrypted SET ENCRYPTION ON ;
GO
```

Tip   In SQL Server 2022, certificates can also be created and backed up as in PFX format. This allows the server certificate, intermediate certificates, and the private key to all be stored in the same file, using a binary format. This can be used to avoid using the weaker RC4 algorithm, to allow conversion to public key pairs.

Managing TDE

When configuring TDE, we are given a warning that the certificate used to encrypt the Database Encryption Key has not been backed up. Backing up this certificate is critical and you should do so before you configure TDE or immediately afterward. If the certificate becomes unavailable, you have no way to recover the data within your database. You can back up the certificate by using the script in Listing 12-8.

Listing 12-8. Backing Up the Certificate

```
USE Master
GO

BACKUP CERTIFICATE TDECert
TO FILE = 'C:\certificates\TDECert'
WITH PRIVATE KEY (file='C:\certificates\TDECertKey',
ENCRYPTION BY PASSWORD='Pa$$w0rd')
```

Migrating an Encrypted Database

By the very nature of TDE, if we attempt to move our Chapter12Encrypted database
to a new instance, the operation fails, unless we take our cryptographic artifacts into
account. Figure 12-3 illustrates the message we receive if we take a backup of the
Chapter12Encrypted database and try to restore it on a new instance. You can find a full
discussion of backups and restores in Chapter 13.

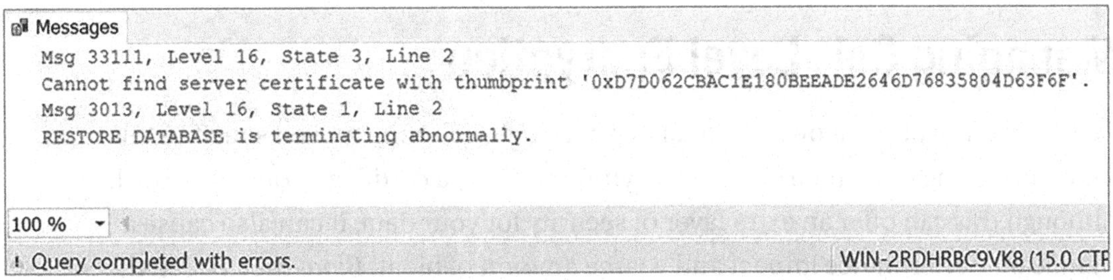

```
Messages
    Msg 33111, Level 16, State 3, Line 2
    Cannot find server certificate with thumbprint '0xD7D062CBAC1E180BEEADE2646D76835804D63F6F'.
    Msg 3013, Level 16, State 1, Line 2
    RESTORE DATABASE is terminating abnormally.
```

100 %

Query completed with errors.   WIN-2RDHRBC9VK8 (15.0 CTF

Figure 12-3. *An attempt to restore an encrypted database on a new instance*

We would receive the same error if we detached the database and attempted to
attach it to the new instance. Instead, we must first create a Database Master Key with
the same password and then restore the server certificate and private key to the new
instance. We can restore the server certificate that we created earlier using the script in
Listing 12-9.

Listing 12-9. Restoring the Server Certificate

```
CREATE MASTER KEY ENCRYPTION BY PASSWORD = 'Pa$$w0rd' ;
GO

CREATE CERTIFICATE TDECert
FROM FILE = 'C:\Certificates\TDECert'
WITH PRIVATE KEY
(
    FILE = 'C:\Certificates\TDECertKey',
    DECRYPTION BY PASSWORD = 'Pa$$w0rd'
) ;
```

TIP   Make sure that the SQL Server service account has permissions to the certificate and key files in the operating system. Otherwise, you will receive an error stating that the certificate is not valid, does not exist, or that you do not have permissions to it. This means that you should check the restore immediately and periodically repeat the test.

Managing Cell-Level Encryption

Cell-level encryption allows you to encrypt a single column, or even specific cells from a column, using a symmetric key, an asymmetric key, a certificate, or a password. Although this can offer an extra layer of security for your data, it can also cause a significant performance impact and a large amount of bloat. *Bloat* means that the size of the data is much larger after the data has been encrypted than it was before. Additionally, implementing cell-level encryption is a manual process that requires you to make code changes to applications. Therefore, encrypting data should not be your default position, and you should only do it when you have a regulatory requirement or clear business justification.

Although it is common practice to encrypt data using a symmetric key, it is also possible to encrypt data using an asymmetric key, a certificate, or even a passphrase. If you encrypt data using a passphrase, then the TRIPLE DES algorithm is used to encrypt the data. Table 12-1 lists the cryptographic functions that you can use to encrypt or decrypt data using these methods.

Table 12-1. *Cryptographic Functions*

Encryption Method	Encryption Function	Decryption Function
Asymmetric key	ENCRYPTBYASYMKEY()	DECRYPTBYASYMKEY()
Certificate	ENCRYPTBYCERT()	DECRYPTBYCERT()
Passphrase	ENCRYPTBYPASSPHRASE()	DECRYPTBYPASSPHRASE()

When we created the SensitiveData table in our database, you may have noticed that we used the VARBINARY(8000) data type for the CreditCardNumber column when the obvious choice would have been a CHAR(19). This is because encrypted data must be stored as one of the binary data types. We have set the length to 8000 bytes, because this is the maximum length of the data that is returned from the function used to encrypt it.

The script in Listing 12-10 will create a duplicate of the Chapter12Encrypted database. The script then creates a Database Master Key for this database and a certificate. After that, it creates a symmetric key that will be encrypted using the certificate. Finally, it opens the symmetric key and uses it to encrypt the CreditCardNumber column in our SensitiveData table.

Listing 12-10. Encrypting a Column of Data

```
--Create the duplicate Database

CREATE DATABASE Chapter12CellEncrypted ;
GO

USE Chapter12CellEncrypted
GO

--Create the table

CREATE TABLE dbo.SensitiveData
(
ID                 INT                  PRIMARY KEY        IDENTITY,
FirstName          NVARCHAR(30),
LastName           NVARCHAR(30),
CreditCardNumber          VARBINARY(8000)
)
GO

--Populate the table

SET identity_insert dbo.SensitiveData ON

INSERT INTO dbo.SensitiveData(id, firstname, lastname, CreditCardNumber)
```

```
SELECT id
        ,firstname
        ,lastname
        ,CreditCardNumber
FROM   Chapter12Encrypted.dbo.SensitiveData

SET identity_insert dbo.SensitiveData OFF

--Create Database Master Key

CREATE MASTER KEY ENCRYPTION BY PASSWORD = 'Pa$$w0rd';
GO

--Create Certificate

CREATE CERTIFICATE CreditCardCert
    WITH SUBJECT = 'Credit Card Numbers';
GO

--Create Symmetric Key

CREATE SYMMETRIC KEY CreditCardKey
    WITH ALGORITHM = AES_128
    ENCRYPTION BY CERTIFICATE CreditCardCert;
GO

--Backup Symmetric Key

BACKUP SYMMETRIC KEY CreditCardKey
    TO FILE = 'c:\keys\CreditCardKey.key'
    ENCRYPTION BY PASSWORD = 'Pa$$w0rd';

--Open Symmetric Key

OPEN SYMMETRIC KEY CreditCardKey
    DECRYPTION BY CERTIFICATE CreditCardCert;

--Encrypt the CreditCardNumber column
```

```
UPDATE dbo.SensitiveData
SET CreditCardNumber = ENCRYPTBYKEY(KEY_GUID('CreditCardKey'),
CreditCardNumber);
GO

CLOSE SYMMETRIC KEY CreditCardKey --Close the key so it cannot be used
again, unless reopened
```

You will notice that we back up the symmetric key before using it. This is a new feature of SQL Server 2022. In previous versions, only Service Master Keys, Database Master Keys, and Certificates could be backed up. The feature allows for the backup of symmetric keys to either file (as demonstrated) or to Azure Blob storage. To back up to Azure Blob storage, use a Credential to authenticate and replace the TO FILE clause with a TO URL clause, as discussed for Database Master Keys, earlier in this chapter. Keys can then be restored using a RESTORE SYMMETRIC KEY statement. Once again, this statement accepts FROM FILE or FROM URL clauses.

The UPDATE statement that we used to encrypt the data uses a function called ENCRYPTBYKEY() to encrypt the data. Table 12-2 describes the parameters the ENCRYPTBYKEY() function accepts. If we wish only to encrypt a subset of cells, we can add a WHERE clause to the UPDATE statement.

Table 12-2. *EncryptByKey() Parameters*

Parameter	Description
Key_GUID	The GUID of the symmetric key that is used to encrypt the data
ClearText	The binary representation of the data that you wish to encrypt
Add_authenticator	A BIT parameter that indicates if an authenticator column should be added
Authenticator	A parameter that specifies the column that should be used as an authenticator

Also notice that before we use the key to encrypt the data, we issue a statement to open the key. The key must always be opened before it is used for either encrypting or decrypting data. To do this, the user must have permissions to open the key.

When you encrypt a column of data using the method shown in Listing 12-10, you still have a security risk caused by the deterministic nature of the algorithm used for encryption, which means when you encrypt the same value, you get the same hash. Imagine a scenario in which a user has access to the SensitiveData table but is not authorized to view the credit card numbers. If that user is also a customer with a record in that table, they could update their own credit card number with the same hashed value as that of another customer in the table. They have then successfully stolen another customer's credit card number, without having to decrypt the data in the CreditCardNumber column. This is known as a *whole-value substitution attack.*

To protect against this scenario, you can add an authenticator column, which is also known as a *salt value.* This can be any column but is usually the primary key column of the table. When the data is encrypted, the authenticator column is encrypted along with the data. At the point of decryption, the authenticator value is then checked, and if it does not match, then the decryption fails.

Caution   It is very important that the values in the authenticator column are never updated. If they are, you may lose access to your sensitive data.

The script in Listing 12-11 shows how we can use an authenticator column to encrypt the CreditCardNumber column using the primary key of the table as an Authenticator column. Here, we use the HASHBYTES() function to create a hash value of the Authenticator column, and then we use the hash representation to encrypt the data. If you have already encrypted the column, the values are updated to include the salt.

Tip   This script is included as an example, but you should avoid running it at this point so you are able to follow later code examples.

Listing 12-11. Encrypting a Column Using an Authenticator

```
OPEN SYMMETRIC KEY CreditCardKey
    DECRYPTION BY CERTIFICATE CreditCardCert;

--Encrypt the CreditCardNumber column
```

```
UPDATE SensitiveData
SET CreditCardNumber = ENCRYPTBYKEY(Key_GUID('CreditCardKey')
                     ,CreditCardNumber
                     ,1
                     ,HASHBYTES('SHA1', CONVERT(VARBINARY(8000), ID)));
GO

CLOSE SYMMETRIC KEY CreditCardKey ;
```

At the end of the script, we close the key. If we do not close it explicitly, then it remains open for the rest of the session. This can be useful if we are going to perform multiple activities using the same key, but it is good practice to explicitly close it immediately following its final usage within a session.

Even though it is possible to encrypt data using symmetric keys, asymmetric keys, or certificates for performance reasons, you will usually choose to use a symmetric key and then encrypt that key using either an asymmetric key or a certificate.

Accessing Encrypted Data

In order to read the data in the column encrypted using ENCRYPTBYKEY(), we need to decrypt it using the DECRYPTBYKEY() function. Table 12-3 describes the parameters for this function.

Table 12-3. *DecryptByKey Parameters*

Parameter	Description
Cyphertext	The encrypted data that you want to decrypt
AddAuthenticator	A BIT value specifying if an authenticator column is required
Authenticator	The column to be used as an authenticator

The script in Listing 12-12 demonstrates how to read the encrypted data in the CreditCardNumber column using the DECRYPTBYKEY() function after it has been encrypted without an authenticator.

Listing 12-12. Reading an Encrypted Column

```
--Open Key

OPEN SYMMETRIC KEY CreditCardKey
    DECRYPTION BY CERTIFICATE CreditCardCert;

--Read the Data using DECRYPTBYKEY()

SELECT
        FirstName
        ,LastName
        ,CreditCardNumber AS [Credit Card Number Encrypted]
        ,CONVERT(VARCHAR(30), DECRYPTBYKEY(CreditCardNumber)) AS [Credit
        Card Number Decrypted]
        ,CONVERT(VARCHAR(30), CreditCardNumber)
                                    AS [Credit Card Number Converted
                                    Without Decryption]
FROM dbo.SensitiveData ;

--Close the Key

CLOSE SYMMETRIC KEY CreditCardKey ;
```

The sample of the results from the final query in this script is shown in Figure 12-4.
You can see that querying the encrypted column directly returns the encrypted binary
value. Querying the encrypted column with a straight conversion to the VARCHAR
data type succeeds, but no data is returned. Querying the encrypted column using
the DECRYPTBYKEY() function, however, returns the correct result when the value is
converted to the VARCAH data type.

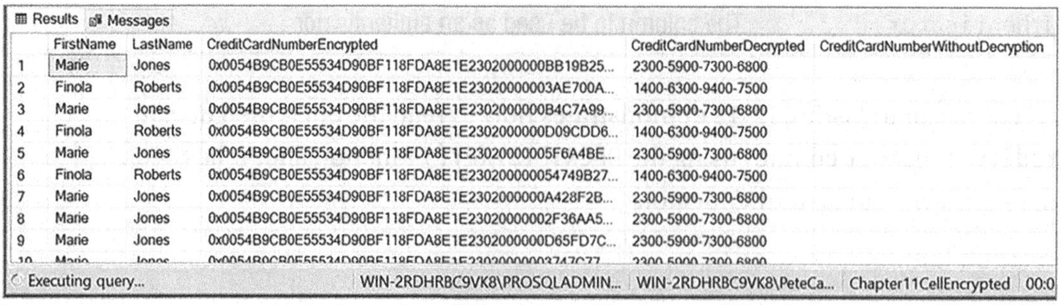

	FirstName	LastName	CreditCardNumberEncrypted	CreditCardNumberDecrypted	CreditCardNumberWithoutDecryption
1	Marie	Jones	0x0054B9CB0E55534D90BF118FDA8E1E2302000000BB19B25...	2300-5900-7300-6800	
2	Finola	Roberts	0x0054B9CB0E55534D90BF118FDA8E1E23020000003AE700A...	1400-6300-9400-7500	
3	Marie	Jones	0x0054B9CB0E55534D90BF118FDA8E1E2302000000B4C7A99...	2300-5900-7300-6800	
4	Finola	Roberts	0x0054B9CB0E55534D90BF118FDA8E1E2302000000D09CDD6...	1400-6300-9400-7500	
5	Marie	Jones	0x0054B9CB0E55534D90BF118FDA8E1E23020000005F6A4BE...	2300-5900-7300-6800	
6	Finola	Roberts	0x0054B9CB0E55534D90BF118FDA8E1E230200000054749B27...	1400-6300-9400-7500	
7	Marie	Jones	0x0054B9CB0E55534D90BF118FDA8E1E2302000000A428F2B...	2300-5900-7300-6800	
8	Marie	Jones	0x0054B9CB0E55534D90BF118FDA8E1E23020000002F36AA5...	2300-5900-7300-6800	
9	Marie	Jones	0x0054B9CB0E55534D90BF118FDA8E1E2302000000D65FD7C...	2300-5900-7300-6800	
10	Marie	Jones	0x0054B9CB0E55534D90BF118FDA8E1E23020000003747C77...	2300-5900-7300-6800	

Executing query...   WIN-2RDHRBC9VK8\PROSQLADMIN...   WIN-2RDHRBC9VK8\PeteCa...   Chapter11CellEncrypted   00:0

Figure 12-4. *Results of DECRYPTBYKEY()*

Always Encrypted

Always Encrypted is a technology which protects data against privileged users, such as members of the sysadmin role. Because DBAs cannot view the encrypted data, Always Encrypted provides true segregation of duties. This can help with compliance issues for sensitive data when your platform support is outsourced to a third-party vendor. This is especially true if you have a regulatory requirement not to make your data available outside of your country's jurisdiction and the third-party vendor is using offshore teams.

Always Encrypted uses two separate types of key: a column encryption key and a column master key. The column encryption key is used to encrypt the data within a column and the column master key is used to encrypt the column encryption keys.

Tip   The column master key is a key or a certificate, located within an external store.

Having the second layer of key means that SQL Server needs only to store an encrypted value of the column encryption key, instead of storing it in plain text. The column master key is not stored in the database engine at all. Instead, it is stored in an external key store. The key store used could be an HSM (hardware security module), Windows Certificate Store, or an EKM provider, such as Azure Key Vault or Thales. SQL Server then stores the location of the column master key, within the database metadata.

Instead of SQL Server being responsible for the encryption and decryption of data, this responsibility is handled by the client driver. Of course, this means that the application must be using a supported driver, and the following link contains details of working with supported drivers: `https://msdn.microsoft.com/en-gb/library/mt147923.aspx`.

When an application issues a request, which will require data to either be encrypted or decrypted, the client driver liaises with the database engine to determine the location of the column master key. The database engine also provides the encrypted column encryption key and the algorithm used to encrypt it.

The client driver can now contact the external key store and retrieve the column master key, which it uses to decrypt the column encryption key. The plaintext version of the column encryption key can then be used to encrypt or decrypt the data, as required.

The entire process is transparent to the application, meaning that changes are not required to the application's code in order to use Always Encrypted. The only change that may be required is to use a later supported driver.

Note   The client driver will cache the plaintext version of column encryption keys as an optimization, which attempts to avoid repeated round trips to the external key store.

Always Encrypted has some significant limitations, including an inability to perform nonequality comparisons (even equality comparisons are only available with deterministic encryption). SQL Server 2019 introduced Secure Enclaves to address some of these issues. With secure enclaves, operators such as <, >, and even LIKE are supported, providing that randomized encryption is used. Secure Enclaves also support in-place encryption.

Secure Enclaves work, by using a protected area of memory, inside the SQL Server process, as a trusted execution environment. Within this memory region, data is decrypted and computations are performed. It is not possible for the rest of the SQL Server process, or any other process on the server, to access the secure memory, meaning that the decrypted data cannot be leaked, even when using debugging tools.

If SQL Server determines that a secure enclave is required to satisfy a query, then the client driver uses a secure channel, to send the encryption keys to the secure enclave. The client driver then submits the query, and encrypted query parameters, for execution. Because the data (even the encrypted parameters) are only ever decrypted inside the enclave, the data, parameters, and encryption keys are never exposed, in plain text.

Because the decrypted data and keys are available inside of the enclave, the client driver needs to verify that the enclave is genuine. To do this, it requires an external arbiter, known as an attestation service, such as the Windows Server Host Guardian Service. Before sending any data to the enclave, the client driver will contact the attestation service to determine the enclave's validity.

When using Always Encrypted, there are many limitations. For example, advanced data types are not supported. A full list of limitations can be found at docs.microsoft. com/en-us/sql/relational-databases/security/encryption/always-encrypted-database-engine?view=sql-server-2022#feature-details.

Implementing Always Encrypted

In this section, we will encrypt data, within a database called Chapter12AlwaysEncrypted, using Always Encrypted with Secure Enclaves. We will use VBS (virtualization-based security) enclaves. In production environments, you should ensure that your enclaves use TPM (Trusted Platform Module) attestation, for enhanced security. TPM is hardware-based attestation and is beyond the scope of this chapter. Further details can be found at https://docs.microsoft.com/en-us/windows-server/identity/ad-ds/manage/component-updates/tpm-key-attestation.

In this section, we will configure a second server, as the attestation service, and register our SQL Server with it, so that it may arbitrate, when client wishes to use the enclave.

The first step is to use the PowerShell script in Listing 12-13 to configure a second server as the attestation service. This server must be running Windows Server 2019 or higher. The process requires the server to perform several reboots. Therefore, the script uses comments to mark the sections. After running each section of the script, the subsequent section should not be run, until the reboot is complete. Remember that you cannot use the same server, which hosts your SQL Server instance. It is also worthy of note that the server acting as the attestation service may not be domain joined, at the point it is configured. This is because a new domain is created, for the host guardian.

Tip   The PowerShell terminal should be run as Administrator, for the script to execute successfully.

Listing 12-13. Configure the Attestation Server

```
#Part 1 - Install the Host Guardian Service role

Install-WindowsFeature -Name HostGuardianServiceRole -Include
ManagementTools -Restart

#Part 2 - Install the Host Guardian Service & configure its domain

$DSRepairModePassword = ConvertTo-SecureString -AsPlainText
'MyVerySecurePa$$w0rd' -Force
```

```
Install-HgsServer -HgsDomainName 'HostGuardian.local' -SafeMode
AdministratorPassword $DSRepairModePassword -Restart
```

```
#After the reboot, log in using the admin account, which will now be
elevated to Domain Admin of the HostGuardian.local domain
```

```
#Part 3 - Configure Host Key Attestatio
```

```
Initialize-HgsAttestation -HgsServiceName 'hgs' -TrustHostKey
```

We now need to register the server hosting the SQL Server instance as a guarded host. We can prepare for this, using the script in Listing 12-14. Once again, the script uses comments to split it into sections. This is because restarts are required during the process. Again, the PowerShell terminal should be run as Administrator.

Listing 12-14. Prepare to Register the Host As a Guarded Host

```
#Part 1 - Enable the HostGuardian feature
```

```
Enable-WindowsOptionalFeature -Online -FeatureName HostGuardian -All
```

```
#Part 2 - Remove VBS requirement. Only required if you are using a VM
```

```
Set-ItemProperty -Path HKLM:\SYSTEM\CurrentControlSet\Control\
DeviceGuard -Name RequirePlatformSecurityFeatures -Value 0
shutdown /r
```

```
#Part 3 - Generate a host key pair and export public key to a file
```

```
#Generate the host key pair
Set-HgsClientHostKey
```

```
#Create a folder to store the keys
New-Item -Path c:\ -Name Keys -ItemType directory
```

```
#Export the public key to a file
Get-HgsClientHostKey -Path ("c:\Keys\{0}key.cer" -f $env:computername)
```

At this point, you should manually copy the certificate file that is generated in the c:\ keys folder to the attestation server. Assuming that you copy the certificate to a folder called c:\keys, the script in Listing 12-15 will import the key into the attestation service.

Note   Be sure to change the server and key names to match your own.

Listing 12-15. Import Client Key into Attestation Service

```
Add-HgsAttestationHostKey -Name WIN-2RDHRBC9VK8 -Path c:\keys\
WIN-2RDHRBC9VK8key.cer
```

The final step in the registration process is to configure the client, which can be achieved using the script in Listing 12-16. Be sure to change the IP address of the attestation service to match your own before running the script.

Listing 12-16. Configure the Client

```
$params = @{
    AttestationServerUrl   = 'http://10.0.0.3/Attestation'
    KeyProtectionServerUrl = 'http://10.0.0.3/KeyProtection'
}
Set-HgsClientConfiguration @params
```

Now that our server is registered as a guarded host, we can create the certificate and keys that will be used by Always Encrypted. This can be done using the script in Listing 12-17.

Listing 12-17. Create the Always Encrypted Cryptographic Objects

```
# Create a certificate, to encrypt the column master key. It will be stored
in the Windows Certificate Store, under Current User
$params = @{
    Subject           = "AlwaysEncryptedCert"
    CertStoreLocation = 'Cert:\CurrentUser\My'
    KeyExportPolicy   = 'Exportable'
    Type              = 'DocumentEncryptionCert'
    KeyUsage          = 'DataEncipherment'
    KeySpec           = 'KeyExchange'
}
$certificate = New-SelfSignedCertificate @params
```

```
# Import the SqlServer module.
Import-Module "SqlServer"

# Connect to the Chapter12AlwaysEncrypted database
$serverName = "{0}\prosqladmin" -f $env:COMPUTERNAME
$databaseName = "Chapter12AlwaysEncrypted"
$connectionString = "Data Source = {0}; Initial Catalog = {1}; Integrated
Security = true" -f @(
    $serverName
    $databaseName
)
$database = Get-SqlDatabase -ConnectionString $connectionString

# Create a settings object, specifying -AllowEnclaveComputations to make
the key Enclave Enabled
$params = @{
    CertificateStoreLocation = 'CurrentUser'
    Thumbprint = $certificate.Thumbprint
    AllowEnclaveComputations = $true
}
$cmkSettings = New-SqlCertificateStoreColumnMasterKeySettings @params

# Create the Column Master Key.
$cmkName = 'ColumnMasterKey'

$params = @{
    Name = $cmkName
    InputObject = $database
    ColumnMasterKeySettings = $cmkSettings
}
New-SqlColumnMasterKey @params

# Create a Column Encryption Key, encrypted with the Column Master Key
$params = @{
    Name = 'ColumnEncryptionKey'
    InputObject = $database
    ColumnMasterKey = $cmkName
}
New-SqlColumnEncryptionKey @params
```

When creating the Column Master Key, we specified a Key Store parameter. Table 12-4 details the key stores that are supported for Always Encrypted. If we wish to use Secure Enclaves, however, we must not choose the CNG store.

Table 12-4. *Key Store Values*

Key Store Type	Description
Windows Certificate Store - Current User	The key or certificate is stored in the area of the Windows Certificate Store that is reserved for the profile of the user that created the certificate. This option may be appropriate if you use the database engine's service account interactively, to create the certificate.
Windows Certificate Store - Local Machine	The key or certificate is stored in the area of the Windows Certificate Store that is reserved for the local machine.
Azure Key Vault	The key or certificate is stored in the Azure Key Vault EKM service.
Key Storage Provider (CNG)	The key or certificate is stored in an EKM store that supports Cryptography API: Next Generation.

The next step is to enable secure enclaves within the SQL Server instance. Unlike most instance configurations, the instance must be restarted for the change to take effect. The script in Listing 12-18 will change the configuration.

Listing 12-18. Enable Secure Enclaves

```
EXEC sys.sp_configure 'column encryption enclave type', 1;
RECONFIGURE ;
```

We now want to encrypt the CreditCardNumber, ExpMonth, and ExpYear columns of the dbo.CreditCards table, which is loosely based on the Sales.CreditCard table of the AdventureWorks database.

When encrypting the data, we have a choice of two methods: deterministic or randomized. This is an important decision to understand, as it may have an impact on performance, security, and the features that are available with secure enclaves.

Deterministic encryption will always produce the same encrypted value, for the same plaintext value. This means that if deterministic encryption is used, operations including equality joins, grouping, and indexing are possible on an encrypted column, proving a BIN2 collation is used for the column. This leaves the possibility of attacks against the encryption, however.

If you use randomized encryption, then different encrypted values can be generated for the same plaintext values. This means that while encryption loopholes are plugged, for standard Always Encrypted implementations, equality joins, grouping, and indexing are not supported against the encrypted data.

When implementing Always Encrypted with secure enclaves, however, more functionality is available when using randomized encryption than it is when using deterministic encryption. Table 12-5 details the compatibility of deterministic and randomized encryption, with and without secure enclaves.

Table 12-5. *Encryption Types and Feature Compatibility*

Encryption Type	In-Place Encryption	Equality Comparisons	Rich Computations	LIKE
Deterministic Without Enclaves	No	Yes	No	No
Deterministic With Enclaves	Yes	Yes	No	No
Randomized Without Enclaves	No	No	No	No
Randomized With Enclaves	Yes	Yes (Inside Enclave)	Yes	Yes

We will use randomized encryption so that we can fully benefit from secure enclave functionality. The script in Listing 12-19 will create the `Chapter12AlwaysEncrypted` database, before creating the `dbo.CreditCards` table, which is loosely based on the `Sales.CreditCards` table from the `AdventureWorks` database.

Listing 12-19. Create the CreditCards Table, with Encrypted Columns

```
CREATE TABLE dbo.CreditCards
(
CardID     INT      IDENTITY     NOT NULL,
CardType   NVARCHAR(20)  NOT NULL,
CardNumber NVARCHAR(20)  COLLATE Latin1_General_BIN2 ENCRYPTED WITH (
        COLUMN_ENCRYPTION_KEY = [ColumnEncryptionKey],
```

```
        ENCRYPTION_TYPE = Randomized,
        ALGORITHM = 'AEAD_AES_256_CBC_HMAC_SHA_256') NOT NULL,
ExpMonth   INT ENCRYPTED WITH (
        COLUMN_ENCRYPTION_KEY = [ColumnEncryptionKey],
        ENCRYPTION_TYPE = Randomized,
        ALGORITHM = 'AEAD_AES_256_CBC_HMAC_SHA_256') NOT NULL,
ExpYear    INT ENCRYPTED WITH (
        COLUMN_ENCRYPTION_KEY = [ColumnEncryptionKey],
        ENCRYPTION_TYPE = Randomized,
        ALGORITHM = 'AEAD_AES_256_CBC_HMAC_SHA_256') NOT NULL,
CustomerID INT NOT NULL
) ;
```

Caution   If encrypting existing data, only ever perform the operation during a maintenance window, as DML statements against the table, while encryption is in progress could potentially result in data loss.

We will now use PowerShell to demonstrate how a client may insert data into encrypted columns. Note that the connection string includes the Column Encryption Setting. The technique is demonstrated in Listing 12-20.

Listing 12-20. Insert Data into Encrypted Columns

```
#Create a SqlConnection object, specifying Column Encryption Setting
= enabled
$sqlConn = New-Object System.Data.SqlClient.SqlConnection
$sqlConn.ConnectionString = "Server=localhost\prosqladmin;Integrated
Security=true; Initial Catalog=Chapter12AlwaysEncrypted; Column Encryption
Setting=enabled;"

#Open the connection
$sqlConn.Open()

#Create a SqlCommand object, and add the query and parameters
$sqlcmd = New-Object System.Data.SqlClient.SqlCommand
$sqlcmd.Connection = $sqlConn
```

```
$sqlcmd.CommandText = "INSERT INTO dbo.CreditCards (CardType, CardNumber,
ExpMonth, ExpYear, CustomerID) VALUES (@CardType, @CardNumber, @ExpMonth,
@ExpYear, @CustomerID)"
$sqlcmd.Parameters.Add((New-Object Data.SqlClient.SqlParameter
("@CardType",[Data.SQLDBType]::nVarChar,20)))
$sqlcmd.Parameters["@CardType"].Value = "SuperiorCard"
$sqlcmd.Parameters.Add((New-Object Data.SqlClient.SqlParameter
("@CardNumber",[Data.SQLDBType]::nVarChar,20)))
$sqlcmd.Parameters["@CardNumber"].Value = "33332664695310"
$sqlcmd.Parameters.Add((New-Object Data.SqlClient.SqlParameter
("@ExpMonth",[Data.SQLDBType]::Int)))
$sqlcmd.Parameters["@ExpMonth"].Value = "12"
$sqlcmd.Parameters.Add((New-Object Data.SqlClient.SqlParameter
("@ExpYear",[Data.SQLDBType]::Int)))
$sqlcmd.Parameters["@ExpYear"].Value = "22"
$sqlcmd.Parameters.Add((New-Object Data.SqlClient.SqlParameter
("@CustomerID",[Data.SQLDBType]::Int)))
$sqlcmd.Parameters["@CustomerID"].Value = "1"

#Insert the data
$sqlcmd.ExecuteNonQuery();

#Close the connection
$sqlConn.Close()
```

Administering Keys

As you would expect, metadata about keys is exposed through system tables and dynamic management views. Details regarding Column Master Keys can be found in the sys.column_master_keys table. The columns returned by this table are detailed in Table 12-6.

Table 12-6. *sys.column_master_keys Columns*

Column	Description
Name	The name of the column master key.
Column_master_key_id	The internal identifier of the column master key.
Create_date	The date and time that the key was created.
Modify_date	The date and time that the key was last modified.
Key_store_provider_name	The type of key store provider, where the key is stored.
Key_path	The path to the key, within the key store.
Allow_enclave_computations	Specifies if the key is enclave enabled.
Signature	A digital signature, combining `key_path` and `allow_enclave_ computations`. This stops malicious administrators from changing the key's enclave enabled setting.

The details of Column Encryption Keys can be found in the `sys.column_ encryption_keys` system table. This table returns the columns detailed in Table 12-7.

Table 12-7. *Columns Returned by sys.column_encryption_keys*

Name	Description
Name	The name of the column encryption key
Column_encryption_key_id	The internal ID of the column encryption key
Create_date	The date and time that the key was created
Modify_date	The date and time that the key was last modified

An additional system table, called `sys.column_encryption_key_vales`, provides a join between the `sys.column_master_keys` and `sys.column_encryption_keys` system tables while at the same time providing the encrypted value of the column encryption key, when encrypted by the column master key. Table 12-8 details the columns returned by this system table.

Table 12-8. *sys.column_encryption_key_values Columns*

Name	Description
Column_encryption_key_id	The internal ID of the column encryption key
Column_master_key_id	The internal ID of the column master key
Encrypted_value	The encrypted value of the column encryption key
Encrypted_algorithm_name	The algorithm used to encrypt the column encryption key

Therefore, we could use the query in Listing 12-21 to find all columns in a database that have been encrypted with enclave enabled keys.

Tip   Remove the WHERE clause to return all columns that are secure with Always Encrypted, and determine which columns do and do not support secure enclaves.

Listing 12-21. Return Details of Columns That Use Secure Enclaves

```
SELECT
        c.name AS ColumnName
      , OBJECT_NAME(c.object_id) AS TableName
      , cek.name AS ColumnEncryptionKey
      , cmk.name AS ColumnMasterKey
      , CASE
            WHEN cmk.allow_enclave_computations = 1
                    THEN 'Yes'
            ELSE 'No'
        END AS SecureEnclaves
FROM sys.columns c
INNER JOIN sys.column_encryption_keys cek
    ON c.column_encryption_key_id = cek.column_encryption_key_id
```

```
INNER JOIN sys.column_encryption_key_values cekv
    ON cekv.column_encryption_key_id = cek.column_encryption_key_id
INNER JOIN sys.column_master_keys cmk
    ON cmk.column_master_key_id = cekv.column_master_key_id
WHERE allow_enclave_computations = 1
```

It is not possible for an Administrator to toggle a key between enclave enabled and not enclave enabled. This is a conscious design decision by Microsoft to protect against malicious Administrators. It is possible to rotate keys, however, and when rotating keys, you can rotate out a key that is not enclave enabled, and replace it with one that is (or vice versa).

Tip The following demonstration assumes that an additional column master key exists within the Chapter12AlwaysEncrypted database.

The simplest way to rotate a key is by using SQL Server Management Studio. Drill through Databases ➤ Chapter12AlwaysEncrypted ➤ Security ➤ Always Encrypted Keys ➤ Column Master Keys and then select Rotate from the context menu of the key which you wish to rotate out. This will cause the Column Master Key Rotation dialog box to be displayed, as illustrated in Figure 12-5. Here, you can select the new key, which should be used to encrypt the underlying column encryption keys.

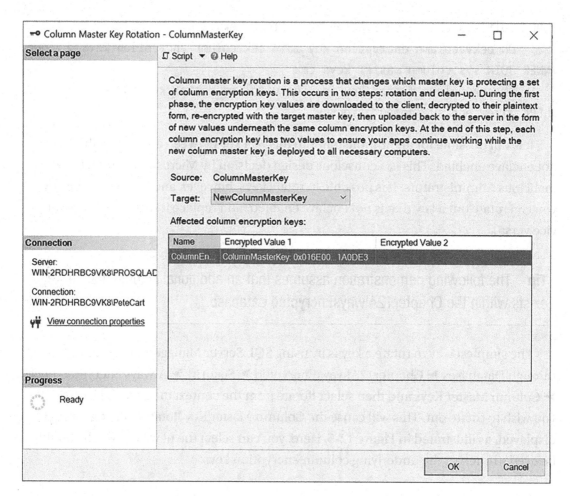

Figure 12-5.   Column Master Key Rotation dialog box

Now that the encryption keys have been reencrypted using the new keys, the old key values need to be cleaned up. This can be achieved by selecting Cleanup from the context menu of the old column master key, causing the Column Master Key Cleanup dialog box to be invoked. This is illustrated in Figure 12-6.

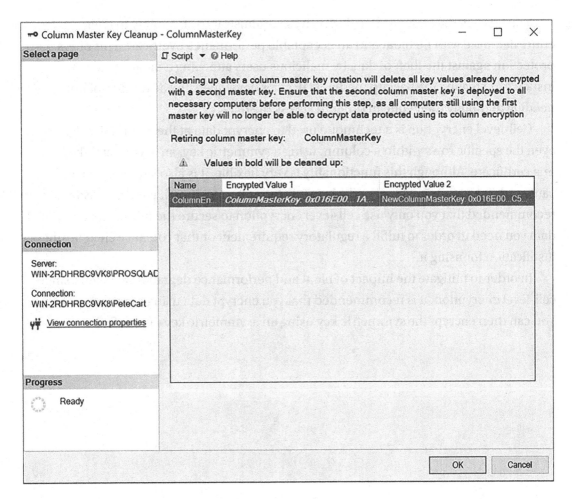

Figure 12-6. Column Master Key Cleanup dialog box

Summary

The SQL Server encryption hierarchy begins with the Service Master Key, which is encrypted using the Data Protection API (DPAPI) in the Windows operating system. You can then use this key to encrypt the Database Master Key. In turn, you can use this key to encrypt keys and certificates stored within the database. SQL Server also supports third-party Extensible Key Management (EKM) providers to allow for advanced key management of keys used to secure data.

Transparent data encryption (TDE) gives administrators the ability to encrypt an entire database with no bloat and an acceptable performance overhead. This offers protection against the theft of data by malicious users attaching a database to a new instance or stealing the backup media. TDE gives developers the advantage of not needing to modify their code in order to access the data.

Cell-level encryption is a technique used to encrypt data at the column level, or even the specific rows within a column, using a symmetric key, an asymmetric key, or a certificate. Although this functionality is very flexible, it is also very manual and causes a large amount of bloat and a large performance overhead. For this reason, I recommended that you only use cell-level encryption to secure the minimum amount of data you need in order to fulfill a regulatory requirement or that you have clear business justification for using it.

In order to mitigate the impact of bloat and performance degradation when using cell-level encryption, it is recommended that you encrypt data using a symmetric key. You can then encrypt the symmetric key using an asymmetric key or certificate.

## CHAPTER 13

Backups and Restores

Backing up a database is one of the most important tasks that a DBA can perform. Therefore, after discussing the principles of backups, we look at some of the backup strategies that you can implement for SQL Server databases. We then discuss how to perform the backup of a database before we finally look in-depth at restoring it, including restoring to a point in time, restoring individual files and pages, and performing piecemeal restores.

Backup Fundamentals

Depending on the recovery model you are using, you can take three types of backup within SQL Server: full, differential, and log. We discuss the recovery models in addition to each of the backup types in the following sections.

Recovery Models

As discussed in Chapter 6, you can configure a database in one of three recovery models: SIMPLE, FULL, and BULK LOGGED. These models are discussed in the following sections.

SIMPLE Recovery Model

When configured in SIMPLE recovery model, the transaction log (or to be more specific, VLFs [virtual log files] within the transaction log that contain transactions that are no longer required) is truncated after each checkpoint operation. This means that usually you do not have to administer the transaction log. However, it also means that you can't take transaction log backups.

© Peter A. Carter 2023
P. A. Carter, *Pro SQL Server 2022 Administration*, https://doi.org/10.1007/978-1-4842-8864-1_13

The `SIMPLE` recovery model can increase performance, for some operations, because transactions are minimally logged. Operations that can benefit from minimal logging are as follows:

- Bulk imports

- `SELECT INTO`

- `UPDATE` statements against large data types that use the `.WRITE` clause

- `WRITETEXT`

- `UPDATETEXT`

- Index creation

- Index rebuilds

The main disadvantage of the `SIMPLE` recovery model is that it is not possible to recover to a specific point in time; you can only restore to the end of a full backup. This disadvantage is amplified by the fact that full backups can have a performance impact, so you are unlikely to be able to take them as frequently as you would take a transaction log backup without causing an impact to users. Another disadvantage is that the `SIMPLE` recovery model is incompatible with some SQL Server HA/DR features, namely:

- AlwaysOn Availability Groups

- Database mirroring

- Log shipping

Therefore, in production environments (it is common for nonproduction environments), the most appropriate way to use the `SIMPLE` recovery model is for large data warehouse–style applications where you have a nightly ETL load, followed by read-only reporting for the rest of the day. This is because this model provides the benefit of minimally logged transactions, while at the same time, it does not have an impact on recovery, since you can take a full backup after the nightly ETL run.

FULL Recovery Model

When a database is configured in `FULL` recovery model, the log truncation does not occur after a `CHECKPOINT` operation. Instead, it occurs after a transaction log backup, as long as a `CHECKPOINT` operation has occurred since the previous transaction log backup. This means that you must schedule transaction log backups to run on a frequent basis. Failing to do so not only leaves your database at risk of being unrecoverable in the event of a failure, but it also means that your transaction log continues to grow until it runs out of space and a 9002 error is thrown.

When a database is in FULL recovery model, many factors can cause the VLFs within a transaction log not to be truncated. This is known as *delayed truncation.* You can find the last reason for delayed truncation to occur in the log_reuse_wait_desc column of sys.databases; a full list of reasons for delayed truncation appears in Chapter 6.

The main advantage of the FULL recovery model is that point-in-time recovery is possible, which means that you can restore your database to a point in the middle of a transaction log backup, as opposed to only being able to restore it to the end of a backup. Point-in-time recovery is discussed in detail later in this chapter. Additionally, FULL recovery model is compatible with all SQL Server functionality. It is usually the best choice of recovery model for production databases.

Tip   If you switch from SIMPLE recovery model to FULL recovery model, you are not actually in FULL recovery model until after you take a transaction log backup. Therefore, make sure to back up your transaction log immediately.

BULK LOGGED Recovery Model

The BULK LOGGED recovery model is designed to be used on a short-term basis while a bulk import operation takes place. The idea is that your normal model of operations is to use FULL recovery model, and then temporarily switch to the BULK LOGGED recovery model just before a bulk import takes place; you then switch back to FULL recovery model when the import completes. This may give you a performance benefit and also stop the transaction log from filling up, since bulk import operations are minimally logged.

Immediately before you switch to the BULK LOGGED recovery model, and immediately after you switch back to FULL recovery model, it is good practice to take a transaction log backup. This is because you cannot use any transaction log backups that contain minimally logged transactions for point-in-time recovery. For the same reason, it is also good practice to safe-state your application before you switch to the BULK LOGGED recovery model. You normally achieve this by disabling any logins, except for the login that performs the bulk import and logins that are administrators, to ensure that no other data modifications take place. You should also ensure that the data you are importing is recoverable by a means other than a restore. Following these rules mitigates the risk of data loss in the event of a disaster.

Although the minimally logged inserts keep the transaction log small and reduce the amount of I/O to the log, during the bulk import, the transaction log backup is more expensive than it is in FULL recovery model in terms of I/O. This is because when you back up a transaction log that contains minimally logged transactions, SQL Server also backs up any data extents, which contain pages that have been altered using minimally logged transactions. SQL Server keeps track of these pages by using bitmap pages, called ML (minimally logged) pages. ML pages occur once in every 64,000 extents and use a flag to indicate if each extent in the corresponding block of extents contains minimally logged pages.

Caution   BULK LOGGED recovery model may not be faster than FULL recovery model for bulk imports unless you have a very fast I/O subsystem. This is because the BULK LOGGED recovery model forces data pages updated with minimally logged pages to flush to disk as soon as the operation completes instead of waiting for a checkpoint operation.

Changing the Recovery Model

Before we show you how to change the recovery model of a database, let's first create the Chapter13 database, which we use for demonstrations in this chapter. You can create this database using the script in Listing 13-1.

Listing 13-1. Creating the Chapter13 Database

```
CREATE DATABASE Chapter13
 ON  PRIMARY
( NAME = 'Chapter13', FILENAME = 'C:\MSSQL\DATA\Chapter13.mdf'),
 FILEGROUP FileGroupA
( NAME = 'Chapter13FileA', FILENAME = 'C:\MSSQL\DATA\Chapter13FileA.ndf' ),
 FILEGROUP FileGroupB
```

```
( NAME = 'Chapter13FileB', FILENAME = 'C:\MSSQL\DATA\Chapter13FileB.ndf' )
 LOG ON
( NAME = 'Chapter13_log', FILENAME = 'C:\MSSQL\DATA\Chapter13_log.ldf' ) ;
GO

ALTER DATABASE [Chapter13] SET RECOVERY FULL ;
GO

USE Chapter13
GO

CREATE TABLE dbo.Contacts
(
ContactID        INT         NOT NULL        IDENTITY        PRIMARY KEY,
FirstName        NVARCHAR(30),
LastName         NVARCHAR(30),
AddressID        INT
) ON FileGroupA ;

CREATE TABLE dbo.Addresses
(
AddressID        INT         NOT NULL        IDENTITY        PRIMARY KEY,
AddressLine1        NVARCHAR(50),
AddressLine2        NVARCHAR(50),
AddressLine3        NVARCHAR(50),
PostCode        NCHAR(8)
) ON FileGroupB ;
```

You can change the recovery model of a database from SQL Server Management Studio (SSMS) by selecting Properties from the context menu of the database and navigating to the Options page, as illustrated in Figure 13-1. You can then select the appropriate recovery model from the Recovery Model drop-down list.

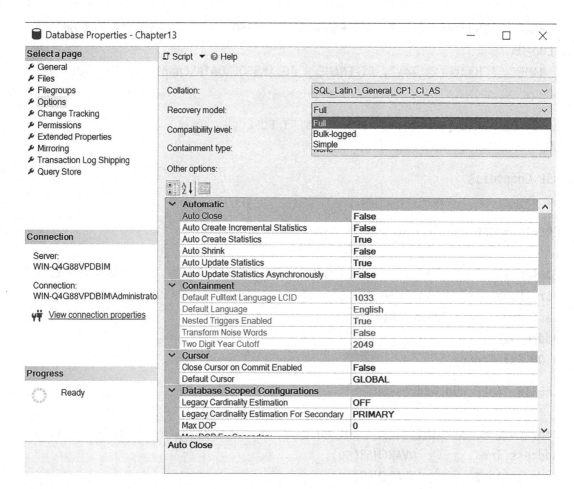

Figure 13-1. *The Options tab*

We can also use the script in Listing 13-2 to switch our Chapter13 database from the FULL recovery model to the SIMPLE recovery model and then back again.

Listing 13-2. Switching Recovery Models

```
ALTER DATABASE Chapter13 SET RECOVERY SIMPLE ;
GO

ALTER DATABASE Chapter13 SET RECOVERY FULL ;
GO
```

Tip   After changing the recovery model, refresh the database in Object Explorer to ensure that the correct recovery model displays.

Backup Types

You can take three types of backup in SQL Server: full, differential, and log. We discuss these backup types in the following sections.

Full Backup

You can take a full backup in any recovery model. When you issue a backup command, SQL Server first issues a CHECKPOINT, which causes any dirty pages to be written to disk. It then backs up every page within the database (this is known as the *data read phase*) before it finally backs up enough of the transaction log (this is known as the *log read phase*) to be able to guarantee transactional consistency. This ensures that you are able to restore your database to the most recent point, including any transactions that are committed during the data read phase of the backup.

Differential Backup

A differential backup backs up every page in the database that has been modified since the last full backup. SQL Server keeps track of these pages by using bitmap pages called DIFF pages, which occur once in every 64,000 extents. These pages use flags to indicate if each extent in their corresponding block of extents contains pages that have been updated since the last full backup.

The cumulative nature of differential backups means that your restore chain only ever needs to include one differential backup—the latest one. Only ever needing to restore one differential backup is very useful if there is a significant time lapse between full backups, but log backups are taken very frequently, because restoring the last differential can drastically decrease the number of transaction log backups you need to restore.

Log Backup

A transaction log backup can only be taken in the FULL or BULK LOGGED recovery models. When a transaction log backup is issued in the FULL recovery model, it backs up all transaction log records since the last backup. When it is performed in the BULK LOGGED recovery model, it also backs up any pages that include minimally logged transactions. When the backup is complete, SQL Server truncates VLFs within the transaction log until the first active VLF is reached.

Transaction log backups are especially important on databases that support OLTP (online transaction processing), since they allow a point-in-time recovery to the point immediately before the disaster occurred. They are also the least resource-intensive type of backup, meaning that you can perform them more frequently than you can perform a full or differential backup without having a significant impact on database performance.

Backup Media

Databases can be backed up to disk, or URL. The terminology surrounding backup media consists of backup devices, logical backup devices, media sets, media families, and backup sets. The structure of a media set is depicted in Figure 13-2, and the concepts are discussed in the following sections.

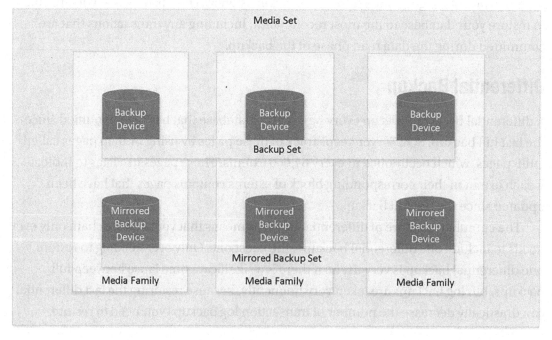

Figure 13-2. *Backup media diagram*

Backup Device

A *backup device* is a physical file on disk, or cloud storage. Previous versions of SQL Server only supported Windows Azure Blob storage as a URL target, but SQL Server 2022 also supports S3 storage in AWS. When the device is a disk, the disk can reside locally on the server or on a share. A media set can contain a maximum of 64 backup devices, and data can be striped across the backup devices and can also be mirrored. In Figure 13-2, there are six backup devices, split into three mirrored pairs. This means that the backup set is striped across three of the devices and then mirrored to the other three.

Striping the backup can be useful for a large database, because doing so allows you to place each device on a different drive array to increase throughput. It can also pose administrative challenges, however; if one of the disks in the devices in the stripe becomes unavailable, you are unable to restore your backup. You can mitigate this by using a mirror. When you use a mirror, the contents of each device are duplicated to an additional device for redundancy. If one backup device in a media set is mirrored, then all devices within the media set must be mirrored. Each backup device or mirrored set of backup devices is known as a *media family*. Each device can have up to four mirrors.

Each backup device within a media set must be all disk or all URL. If they are mirrored, then the mirror devices must have similar properties; otherwise, an error is thrown. For this reason, Microsoft recommends using the same make and model of device for mirrors.

It is also possible to create logical backup devices, which abstract a physical backup device. Using logical devices can simplify administration, especially if you are planning to use many backup devices in the same physical location. A *logical backup device* is an instance-level object and can be created in SSMS by choosing New Backup Device from the context menu of Server Objects ➤ Backup Devices; this causes the Backup Device dialog box to be displayed, where you can specify a logical device name and a physical path.

Alternatively, you can create the same logical backup device via T-SQL using the `sp_addumpdevice` system stored procedure. The command in Listing 13-3 uses the `sp_addumpdevice` procedure to create the `Chapter13Backup` logical backup device. In this example, we use the `@devtype` parameter to pass in the type of the device, in our case, disk. We then pass the abstracted name of the device into the `@logicalname` parameter and the physical file into the `@physicalname` parameter.

Listing 13-3. Creating a Logical Backup Device

```
EXEC sp_addumpdevice  @devtype = 'disk',
                      @logicalname = 'Chapter13Backup',
                      @physicalname = 'C:\MSSQL\Backup\
                                        Chapter13Backup.bak' ;
GO
```

Media Sets

A media set contains the backup devices to which the backup is written. Each media family within a media set is assigned a sequential number based upon their position in the media set. This is called the *family sequence number*. Additionally, each physical device is allocated a *physical sequence number* to identify its physical position within the media set.

When a media set is created, the backup devices are formatted, and a media header is written to each device. This media header remains until the devices are formatted and contains details, such as the name of the media set, the GUID of the media set, the GUIDs and sequence numbers of the media families, the number of mirrors in the set, and the date/time that the header was written.

Backup Sets

Each time a backup is taken to the media set, it is known as a *backup set*. New backup sets can be appended to the media, or you can overwrite the existing backup sets. If the media set contains only one media family, then that media family contains the entire backup set. Otherwise, the backup set is distributed across the media families. Each backup set within the media set is given a sequential number; this allows you to select which backup set to restore.

Backup Strategies

A DBA can implement numerous backup strategies for a database, but always base your strategy on the RTO (recovery time objective) and RPO (recovery point objective) requirements of your application(s). For example, if an application has an RPO of 60 minutes, you are not able to achieve this goal if you only back up the database once every 24 hours.

Tip   Please see Chapter 14 for a full discussion around RPO and RTO.

Full Backup Only

Backup strategies where you only take full backups are the least flexible. If databases are infrequently updated and there is a regular backup window that is long enough to take a full backup, then this may be an appropriate strategy. Also, a full backup-only strategy is often used for the Master and MSDB system databases.

It may also be appropriate for user databases, which are used for reporting only, and are not updated by users. In this scenario, it may be that the only updates to the database are made via an ETL load. If this is the case, then your backup only needs to be as frequent as this load. You should, however, consider adding a dependency between the ETL load and the full backup, such as putting them in the same SQL Server Agent job. This is because if your backup takes place halfway through an ETL load, it may render the backup useless when you come to restore. At least, not without unpicking the transactions performed in the ETL load that were included in the backup before finally rerunning the ETL load.

Using a full backup-only strategy also limits your flexibility for restores. If you only take full backups, then your only restore option is to restore the database from the point of the last full backup. This can pose two issues. The first is that if you take nightly backups at midnight every night and your database becomes corrupt at 23:00, then you lose 23 hours of data modifications.

The second issue occurs if a user accidently truncates a table at 23:00. The earliest restore point for the database is midnight the previous night. In this scenario, once again, your RPO for the incident is 23 hours, meaning 23 hours of data modifications are lost.

Full and Transaction Log Backups

If your database is in FULL recovery model, then you are able to take transaction log backups, as well as the full backups. This means that you can take much more frequent backups, since the transaction log backup is quicker than the full backup and uses fewer resources. This is appropriate for databases that are updated throughout the day, and it also offers more flexible restores, since you are able to restore to a point in time just before a disaster occurred.

If you are taking transaction log backups, then you schedule your log backups to be in line with your RPO. For example, if you have an RPO of one hour, then you can schedule your log backups to occur every 60 minutes, because this means that you can never lose more than one hour of data. (This is true as long as you have a complete log chain, none of your backups are corrupt, and the share or folder where the backups are stored is accessible when you need it.)

When you use this strategy, you should also consider your RTO. Imagine that you have an RPO of 30 minutes, so you are taking transaction log backups every half hour, but you are only taking a full backup once per week, at 01:00 on a Saturday. If your database becomes corrupt on Friday night at 23:00, you need to restore 330 backups. This is perfectly feasible from a technical view point, but if you have an RTO of one hour, then you may not be able to restore the database within the allotted time.

Full, Differential, and Transaction Log Backups

To overcome the issue just described, you may choose to add differential backups to your strategy. Because a differential backup is cumulative, as opposed to incremental in the way that log backups are, if you took a differential backup on a nightly basis at 01:00, then you only need to restore 43 backups to recover your database to the point just before the failure. This restore sequence consists of the full backup, the differential backup taken on the Friday morning at 01:00, and then the transaction logs, in sequence, between 01:30 and 23:00.

Filegroup Backups

For very large databases, it may not be possible to find a maintenance window that is large enough to take a full backup of the entire database. In this scenario, you may be able to split your data across filegroups and back up half of the filegroups on alternate nights. When you come to a restore scenario, you are able to restore only the filegroup that contains the corrupt data, providing that you have a complete log chain from the time the filegroup was backed up to the end of the log.

Tip Although it is possible to back up individual files as well as a whole filegroup, I find this less helpful, because tables are spread across all files within a filegroup. Therefore, if a table is corrupted, you need to restore all files within the filegroup, or if you only have a handful of corrupt pages, then you can restore just these pages.

Partial Backup

A partial backup involves backing up all read/write filegroups, but not backing up any read-only filegroups. This can be very helpful if you have a large amount of archive data in the database. The BACKUP DATABASE command in T-SQL also supports the READ_WRITE_FILEGROUP option. This means that you can easily perform a partial backup of a database without having to list out the read/write filegroups, which of course can leave you prone to human error if you have many filegroups.

Backing Up a Database

A database can be backed up through SSMS or via T-SQL. We examine these techniques in the following sections. Usually, regular backups are scheduled to run with SQL Server Agent or are incorporated into a maintenance plan. These topics are discussed in Chapter 22.

Backing Up in SQL Server Management Studio

You can back up a database through SSMS by selecting Tasks ➤ Backup from the context menu of the database; this causes the General page of the Back Up Database dialog box to display, as shown in Figure 13-3.

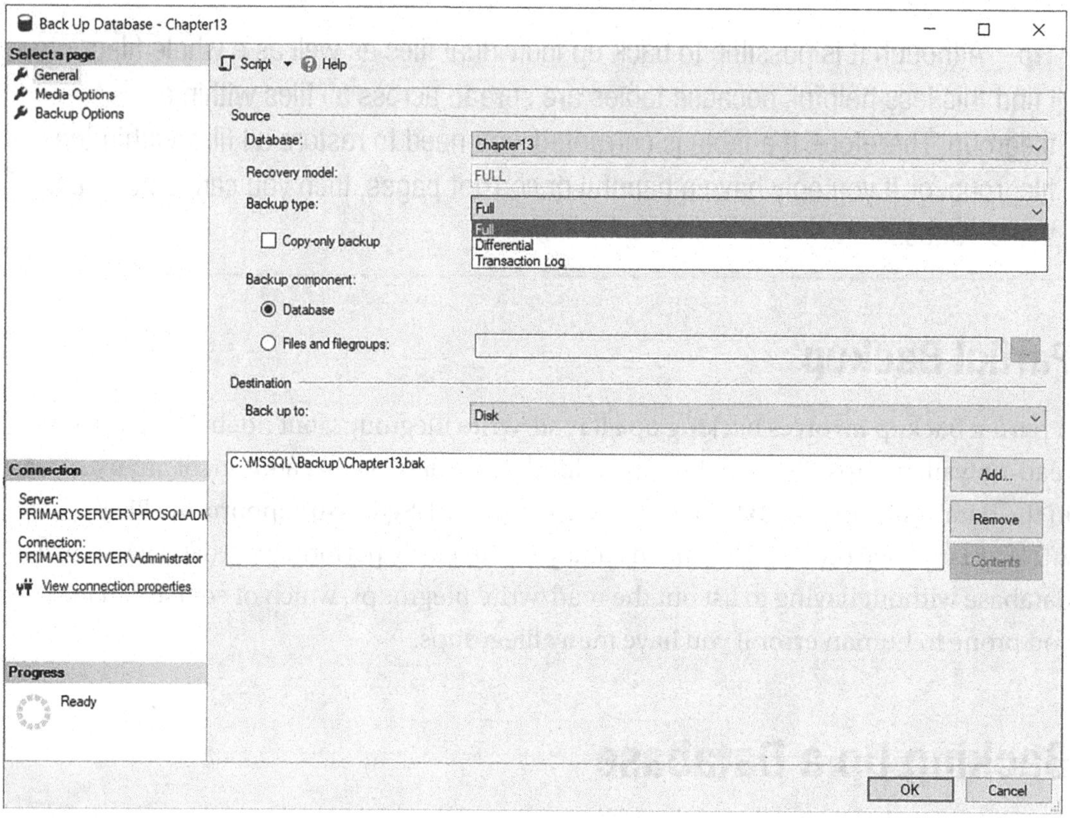

Figure 13-3. *The General page*

In the Database drop-down list, select the database that you wish to back up, and in the Backup type drop-down, choose to perform either a Full, a Differential, or a Transaction Log backup. The Copy-only backup check box allows you to perform a backup that does not affect the restore sequence. Therefore, if you take a copy-only full backup, it does not affect the differential base. Under the covers, this means that the DIFF pages are not reset. Taking a copy-only log backup does not affect the log archive point, and therefore the log is not truncated. Taking a copy-only log backup can be helpful in some online restore scenarios. It is not possible to take a copy-only differential backup.

If you have selected a full or differential backup in the Backup Component section, choose if you want to back up the entire database or specific files and filegroups. Selecting the Files and filegroups radio button causes the Select File and Filegroups dialog box to display, as illustrated in Figure 13-4. Here, you can select individual files or entire filegroups to back up.

Figure 13-4. *The Select Files and Filegroups dialog box*

In the Back up to section of the screen, you can select either Disk or URL from the drop-down list before you use the Add and Remove buttons to specify the backup devices that form the definition of the media set. You can specify a maximum of 64 backup devices. The backup device may contain multiple backups (backup sets), and when you click the Contents button, the details of each backup set contained within the backup device will be displayed.

On the Media Options page, you can specify if you want to use an existing media set or create a new one. If you choose to use an existing media set, then specify if you want to overwrite the content of the media set or append a new backup set to the media set. If you choose to create a new media set, then you can specify the name, and optionally, a description for the media set. If you use an existing media set, you can verify the date and time that the media set and backup set expire. These checks may cause the backup set to be appended to the existing backup device, instead of overwriting the backup sets.

Under the Reliability section, specify if the backup should be verified after completion. This is usually a good idea, especially if you are backing up to a URL, since backups across the network are prone to corruption. Choosing the Perform Checksum Before Writing to Media option causes the page checksum of each page of the database to be verified before it is written to the backup device. This causes the backup operation to use additional resources, but if you are not running DBCC CHECKDB as frequently as you take backups, then this option may give you an early warning of any database corruption. (Please see Chapter 9 for more details.) The Continue On Error option causes the backup to continue, even if a bad checksum is discovered during verification of the pages.

On the Backup Options page, you are able to set the expiration date of the backup set as well as select if you want the backup set to be compressed or encrypted. For compression, you can choose to use the instance default setting, or you can override this setting by specifically choosing to compress, or not compress, the backup.

If you choose to encrypt the backup, then you need to select a preexisting certificate. (You can find details of how to create a certificate in Chapter 11.) You then need to select the algorithm that you wish to use to encrypt the backup. Available algorithms in SQL Server 2022 are AES 128, AES 192, AES 256, or 3DES (Triple_DES_3Key). You should usually select an AES algorithm, because support for 3DES will be removed in a future version of SQL Server.

Backing Up via T-SQL

When you back up a database or log via T-SQL, you can specify many arguments. These can be broken down into the following categories:

- Backup options (described in Table 13-1).

- WITH options (described in Table 13-2).

- Backup set options (described in Table 13-3).

- Media set options (described in Table 13-4).

- Error management options (described in Table 13-5).

- Tape options have been deprecated for many versions and should not be used. Therefore, details of tape options are omitted from this chapter.

- Log-specific options (described in Table 13-6).

- Miscellaneous options (described in Table 13-7).

Table 13-1. *Backup Options*

Argument	Description
DATABASE/LOG	Specify DATABASE to perform a full or differential backup. Specify LOG to perform a transaction log backup.
database_name	The name of the database to perform the backup operation against. Can also be a variable containing the name of the database.
file_or_filegroup	A comma-separated list of files or filegroups to back up, in the format FILE = logical file name or FILEGROUP = Logical filegroup name.
READ_WRITE_ FILEGROUPS	Performs a partial backup by backing up all read/write filegroups. Optionally, use comma-separated FILEGROUP = syntax after this clause to add read-only filegroups.
TO	A comma-separated list of backup devices to stripe the backup set over, with the syntax DISK = physical device, or URL = physical device.
MIRROR TO	A comma-separated list of backup devices to which to mirror the backup set. If the MIRROR TO clause is used, the number of backup devices specified must equal the number of backup devices specified in the TO clause.

Table 13-2. *WITH Options*

Argument	Description
CREDENTIAL	Use when backing up to a Windows Azure Blob.
DIFFERENTIAL	Specifies that a differential backup should be taken. If this option is omitted, then a full backup is taken.
ENCRYPTION	Specifies the algorithm to use for the encryption of the backup. If the backup is not to be encrypted, then NO_ENCRYPTION can be specified, which is the default option. Backup encryption is only available in Enterprise, Business Intelligence, and Standard editions of SQL Server.
encryptor_name	The name of the encryptor in the format SERVER CERTIFICATE = encryptor name or SERVER ASYMMETRIC KEY = encryptor name.
BACKUP_OPTION	If backing up to S3 storage, then region can be specified by passing JSON, using the following format: '{"s3": {"region":"eu-west-1"}}'

Table 13-3. *Backup Set Options*

Argument	Description
COPY_ONLY	Specifies that a copy_only backup of the database or log should be taken. This option is ignored if you perform a differential backup.
COMPRESSION/NO COMPRESSION	By default, SQL Server decides if the backup should be compressed based on the instance-level setting. (These can be viewed in sys.configurations.) You can override this setting, however, by specifying COMPRESSION or NO COMPRESSION, as appropriate. Backup compression is only available in Enterprise, Business Intelligence, and Standard editions of SQL Server. In SQL Server 2022, if COMPRESSION is used, then ALGORITHM can also be specified, in braces. The default is MS_XPRESS, but this can be changed to work with third-party accelerator technologies.
NAME	Specifies a name for the backup set.
DESCRIPTION	Adds a description to the backup set.
EXPIRYDATE/ RETAINEDDAYS	Use EXPIRYDATE = datetime to specify a precise date and time that the backup set expires. After this date, the backup set can be overwritten. Specify RETAINDAYS = int to specify a number of days before the backup set expires.

Table 13-4. *Media Set Options*

Argument	Description
INIT/NOINIT	INIT attempts to overwrite the existing backup sets in the media set but leaves the media header intact. It first checks the name and expiry date of the backup set, unless SKIP is specified. NOINIT appends the backup set to the media set, which is the default behavior.
SKIP/NOSKIP	SKIP causes the INIT checks of backup set name and expiration date to be skipped. NOSKIP enforces them, which is the default behavior.
FORMAT/NOFORMAT	FORMAT causes the media header to be overwritten, leaving any backup sets within the media set unusable. This essentially creates a new media set. The backup set names and expiry dates are not checked. NOFORMAT preserves the existing media header, which is the default behavior.

(continued)

Table 13-4. (*continued*)

Argument	Description
MEDIANAME	Specifies the name of the media set.
MEDIADESCRIPTION	Adds a description of the media set.
BLOCKSIZE	Specifies the block size in bytes that will be used for the backup. The BLOCKSIZE defaults to 512 for disk and URL.

Table 13-5. *Error Management Options*

Argument	Description
CHECKSUM/NO_CHECKSUM	Specifies if the page checksum of each page should be validated before the page is written to the media set.
CONTINUE_AFTER_ERROR/ STOP_ON_ERROR	STOP_ON_ERROR is the default behavior and causes the backup to fail if a bad checksum is discovered when verifying the page checksum. CONTINUE_AFTER_ERROR allows the backup to continue if a bad checksum is discovered.

Table 13-6. *Log-Specific Options*

Argument	Description
NORECOVERY/STANDBY	NORECOVERY causes the database to be left in a restoring state when the backup completes, making it inaccessible to users. STANDBY leaves the database in a read-only state when the backup completes. STANDBY requires that you specify the path and file name of the transaction undo file, so it should be used with the format STANDBY = transaction_ undo_file. If neither option is specified, then the database remains online when the backup completes.
NO_TRUNCATE	Specifies that the log backup should be attempted, even if the database is not in a healthy state. It also does not attempt to truncate an inactive portion of the log. Taking a tail-log backup involves backing up the log with NORECOVERY and NO_TRUNCATE specified.

Table 13-7. *Miscellaneous Options*

Argument	Description
BUFFERCOUNT	The total number of I/O buffers used for the backup operation.
MAXTRANSFERSIZE	The largest possible unit of transfer between SQL Server and the backup media, specified in bytes.
STATS	Specifies how often progress messages should be displayed. The default is to display a progress message in 10% increments.

To perform the full database backup of the Chapter13 database, which we demonstrate through the GUI, we can use the command in Listing 13-4. Before running this script, modify the path of the backup device to meet your system's configuration.

Listing 13-4. Performing a Full Backup

```
BACKUP DATABASE Chapter13
        TO  DISK = 'C:\MSSQL\Backup\Chapter13.bak'
        WITH  RETAINDAYS = 90
        , FORMAT
        , INIT
        , MEDIANAME = 'Chapter13'
        , NAME = 'Chapter13-Full Database Backup'
        , COMPRESSION ;
GO
```

If we want to perform a differential backup of the Chapter13 database and append the backup to the same media set, we can add the WITH DIFFERENTIAL option to our statement, as demonstrated in Listing 13-5. Before running this script, modify the path of the backup device to meet your system's configuration.

Listing 13-5. Performing a Differential Backup

```
BACKUP DATABASE Chapter13
        TO  DISK = 'C:\MSSQL\Backup\Chapter13.bak'
        WITH  DIFFERENTIAL
        , RETAINDAYS = 90
        , NOINIT
```

```
, MEDIANAME = 'Chapter13'
, NAME = 'Chapter13-Diff Database Backup'
, COMPRESSION ;
GO
```

If we want to back up the transaction log of the Chapter13 database, again appending the backup set to the same media set, we can use the command in Listing 13-6. Before running this script, modify the path of the backup device to meet your system's configuration.

Listing 13-6. Performing a Transaction Log Backup

```
BACKUP LOG Chapter13
      TO  DISK = 'C:\MSSQL\Backup\Chapter13.bak'
      WITH  RETAINDAYS = 90
      , NOINIT
      , MEDIANAME = 'Chapter13'
      , NAME = 'Chapter13-Log Backup'
      , COMPRESSION ;
GO
```

Tip   In enterprise scenarios, you may wish to store full, differential, and log backups in different folders, to assist administrators, when looking for files to recover.

If we are implementing a filegroup backup strategy and want to back up only FileGroupA, we can use the command in Listing 13-7. We create a new media set for this backup set. Before running this script, modify the path of the backup device to meet your system's configuration.

Listing 13-7. Performing a Filegroup Backup

```
BACKUP DATABASE Chapter13 FILEGROUP = 'FileGroupA'
      TO  DISK = 'C:\MSSQL\Backup\Chapter13FGA.bak'
      WITH  RETAINDAYS = 90
      , FORMAT
```

```
     , INIT
     , MEDIANAME = 'Chapter13FG'
     , NAME = 'Chapter13-Full Database Backup-FilegroupA'
     , COMPRESSION ;
GO
```

To repeat the full backup of the Chapter13 but stripe the backup set across two backup devices, we can use the command in Listing 13-8. This helps increase the throughput of the backup. Before running this script, you should modify the paths of the backup devices to meet your system's configuration.

Listing 13-8. Using Multiple Backup Devices

```
BACKUP DATABASE Chapter13
       TO  DISK = 'H:\MSSQL\Backup\Chapter13Stripe1.bak',
           DISK = 'G:\MSSQL\Backup\Chapter13Stripe2.bak'
       WITH  RETAINDAYS = 90
       , FORMAT
       , INIT
       , MEDIANAME = 'Chapter13Stripe'
       , NAME = 'Chapter13-Full Database Backup-Stripe'
       , COMPRESSION ;
GO
```

For increased redundancy, we can create a mirrored media set by using the command in Listing 13-9. Before running this script, modify the paths of the backup devices to meet your system's configuration.

Listing 13-9. Using a Mirrored Media Set

```
BACKUP DATABASE Chapter13
         TO  DISK = 'H:\MSSQL\Backup\Chapter13Stripe1.bak',
             DISK = 'G:\MSSQL\Backup\Chapter13Stripe2.bak'
         MIRROR TO DISK = 'J:\MSSQL\Backup\Chapter13Mirror1.bak',
```

```
                    DISK = 'K:\MSSQL\Backup\Chapter13Mirror2.bak'
        WITH  RETAINDAYS = 90
        , FORMAT
        , INIT
        , MEDIANAME = 'Chapter13Mirror'
        , NAME = 'Chapter13-Full Database Backup-Mirror'
        , COMPRESSION ;
GO
```

Restoring a Database

You can restore a database either through SSMS or via T-SQL. We explore both of these options in the following sections.

Restoring in SQL Server Management Studio

To begin a restore in SSMS, select Restore Database from the context menu of Databases in Object Explorer. This causes the General page of the Restore Database dialog box to display, as illustrated in Figure 13-5. Selecting the database to be restored from the drop-down list causes the rest of the tab to be automatically populated.

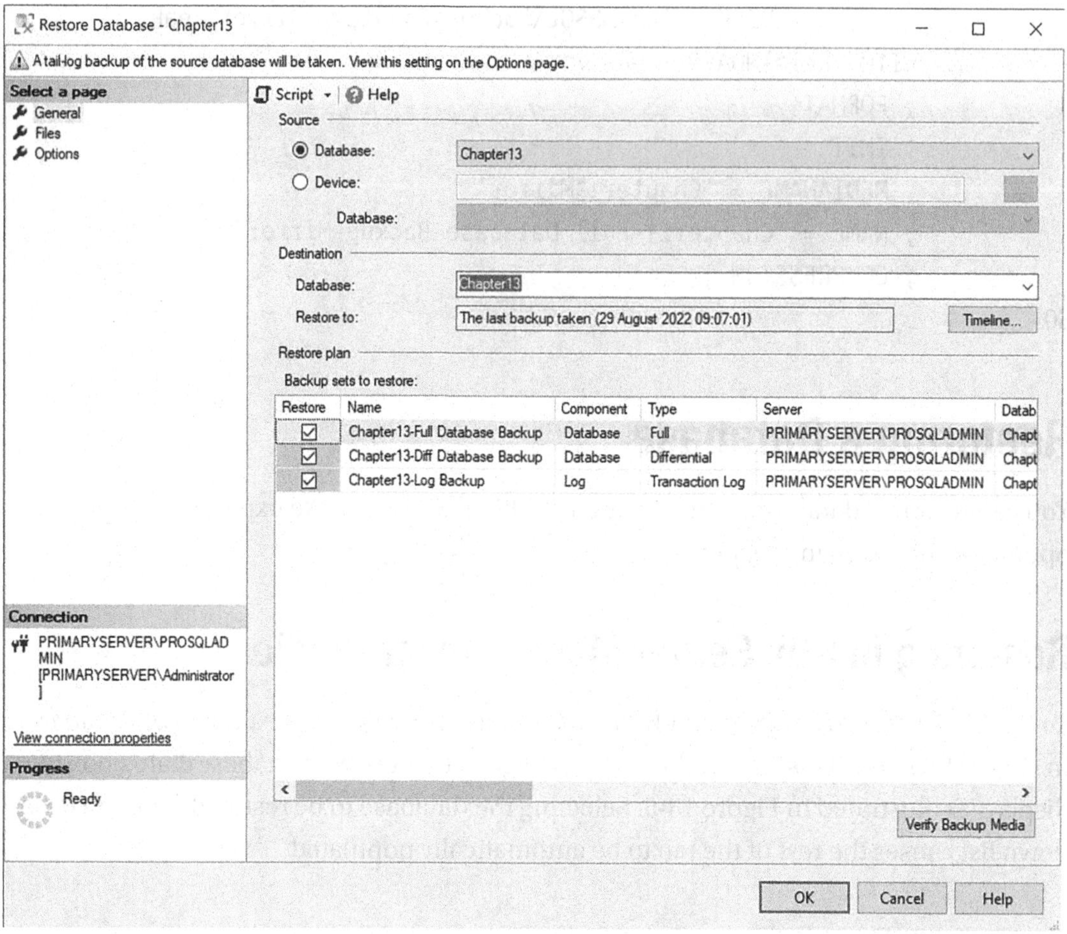

Figure 13-5. *The General page*

You can see that the contents of the Chapter13 media set are displayed in the Backup sets to restore pane of the page. In this case, we can see the contents of the Chapter13 media set. The Restore check boxes allow you to select the backup sets that you wish to restore.

The Timeline button provides a graphical illustration of when each backup set was created, as illustrated in Figure 13-6. This allows you to easily see how much data loss exposure you have, depending on the backup sets that you choose to restore. In the Timeline window, you can also specify if you want to recover to the end of the log, or if you wish to restore to a specific date/time.

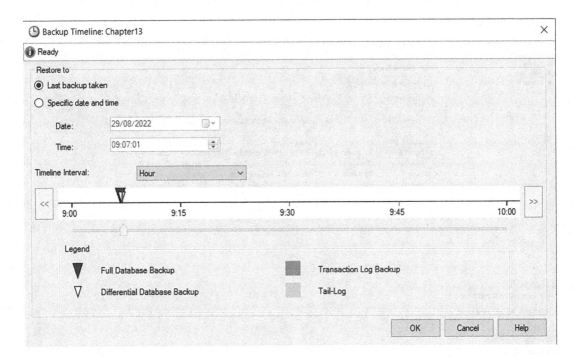

Figure 13-6. *The Backup Timeline page*

Clicking the Verify Backup Media button on the General page causes a RESTORE WITH VERIFYONLY operation to be carried out. This operation verifies the backup media without attempting to restore it. In order to do this, it performs the following checks:

- The backup set is complete.

- All backup devices are readable.

- The CHECKSUM is valid (only applies if WITH CHECKSUM was specified during the backup operation).

- Page headers are verified.

- There is enough space on the target restore volume for the backups to be restored.

On the Files page, illustrated in Figure 13-7, you can select a different location to which to restore each file. The default behavior is to restore the files to the current location. You can use the ellipses, next to each file, to specify a different location for each individual file, or you can use the Relocate all files to folder option to specify a single folder for all data files and a single folder for all log files.

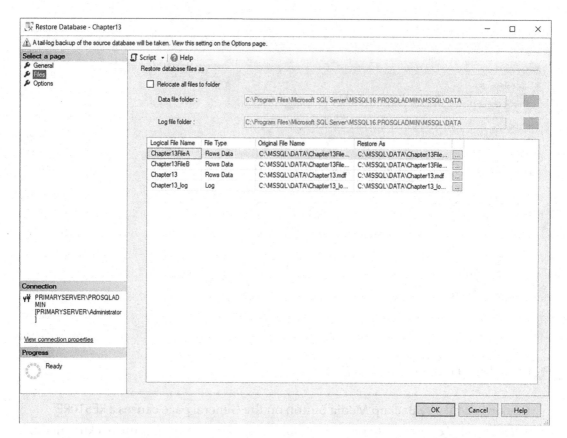

Figure 13-7. *The File page*

On the Options page, shown in Figure 13-8, you are able to specify the restore options that you plan to use. In the Restore Options section of the page, you can specify that you want to overwrite an existing database, preserve the replication settings within the database (which you should use if you are configuring log shipping to work with replication), and restore the database with restricted access. This last option makes the database accessible only to administrators and members of the db_owner and db_creator roles after the restore completes. This can be helpful if you want to verify the data, or perform any data repairs, before you make the database accessible to users.

In the Restore Options section, you can also specify the recovery state of the database. Restoring the database with RECOVERY brings the database online when the restore completes. NORECOVERY leaves the database in a restoring state, which means that further backups can be applied. STANDBY brings the database online but leaves it in a read-only state. This option can be helpful if you are failing over to a secondary server. If you choose this option, you are also able to specify the location of the Transaction Undo file.

Tip   If you specify WITH PARTIAL during the restore of the first backup file, you are able to apply additional backups, even if you restore WITH RECOVERY. There is no GUI support for piecemeal restores, however. Performing piecemeal restores via T-SQL is discussed later in this chapter.

In the Tail-Log Backup section of the screen, you can choose to attempt a tail-log backup before the restore operation begins, and if you choose to do so, you can choose to leave the database in a restoring state. A tail-log backup may be possible even if the database is damaged. Leaving the source database in a restoring state essentially safe-states it to mitigate the risk of data loss. If you choose to take a tail-log backup, you can also specify the file path for the backup device to use. You can also specify if you want to close existing connections to the destination database before the restore begins and if you want to be prompted before restoring each individual backup set.

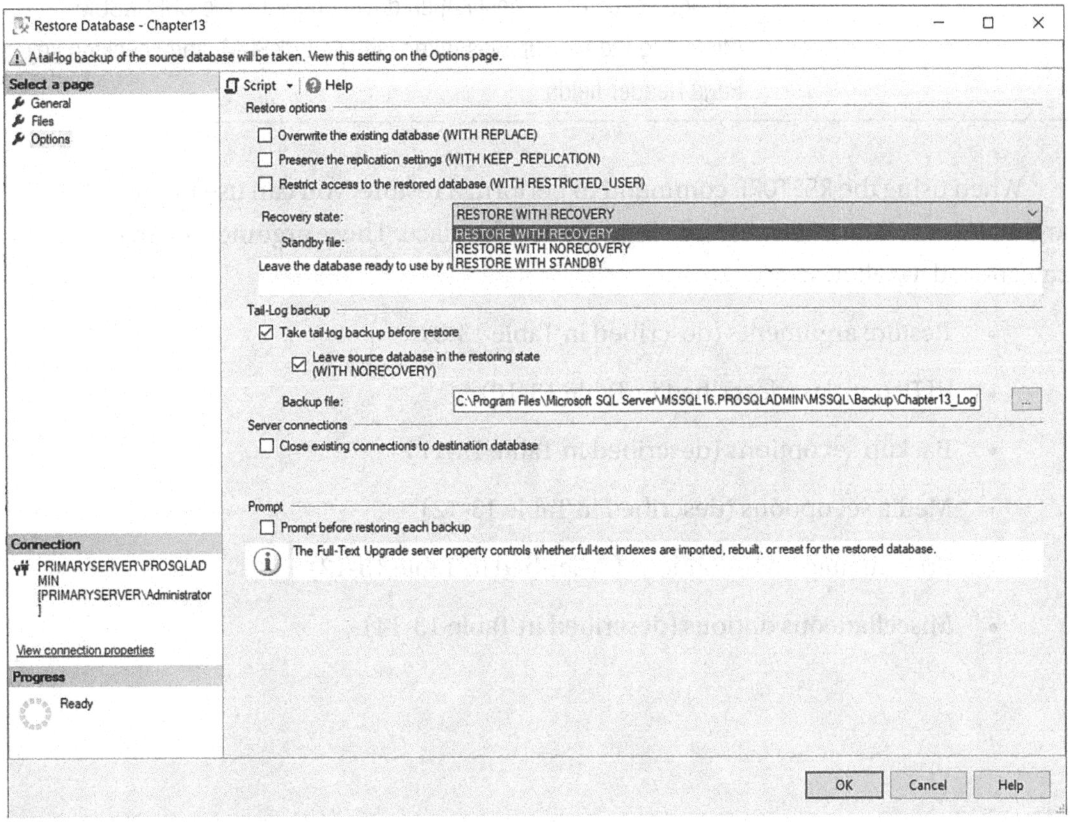

Figure 13-8. *The Options page*

Restoring via T-SQL

When using the RESTORE command in T-SQL, in addition to restoring a database, the options detailed in Table 13-8 are available.

Table 13-8. *Restore Options*

Restore Option	Description
RESTORE FILELISTONLY	Returns a list of all files in the backup device.
RESTORE HEADERONLY	Returns the backup headers for all backup sets within a backup device.
RESTORE LABELONLY	Returns information regarding the media set and media family to which the backup device belongs.
RESTORE VERIFYONLY	Checks that all backup devices exist and are readable. Also performs other high-level verification checks, such as ensuring there is enough space of the destination drive, checking the CHECKSUM (providing the backup was taken with CHECKSUM) and checking key Page Header fields.

When using the RESTORE command to perform a restore, you can use many arguments to allow many restore scenarios to take place. These arguments can be categorized as follows:

- Restore arguments (described in Table 13-9)

- WITH options (described in Table 13-10)

- Backup set options (described in Table 13-11)

- Media set options (described in Table 13-12)

- Error management options (described in Table 13-13)

- Miscellaneous options (described in Table 13-14)

Table 13-9. *Restore Arguments*

Argument	Description
DATABASE/LOG	Specify DATABASE to which to restore all or some of the files that constitute the database. Specify LOG to restore a transaction log backup.
database_name	Specifies the name of the target database that will be restored.
file_or_filegroup_or_pages	Specifies a comma-separated list of the files, filegroups, or pages to be restored. If restoring pages, use the format PAGE = FileID:PageID. In simple recovery model, files and filegroups can only be specified if they are read-only or if you are performing a partial restore using WITH PARTIAL.
READ_WRITE_FILEGROUPS	Restores all read/write filegroups but no read-only filegroups.
FROM	A comma-separated list of backup devices that contains the backup set to restore or the name of the database snapshot from which you wish to restore. Database snapshots are discussed in Chapter 16.

Table 13-10. *WITH Options*

Argument	Description
PARTIAL	Indicates that this is the first restore in a piecemeal restore, which is discussed later in this chapter.
RECOVERY/NORECOVERY/STANDBY	Specifies the state that the database should be left in when the restore operation completes. RECOVERY indicates that the database will be brought online. NORECOVERY indicates that the database will remain in a restoring state so that subsequent restores can be applied. STANDBY indicates that the database will be brought online in read-only mode.

(continued)

Table 13-10. (*continued*)

Argument	Description
MOVE	Used to specify the file system location that the files should be restored to if this is different from the original location.
CREDENTIAL	Used when performing a restore from a Windows Azure Blob.
REPLACE	If a database already exists on the instance with the target database name that you have specified in the restore statement, or if the files already exist in the operating system with the same name or location, then REPLACE indicates that the database or files should be overwritten.
RESTART	Indicates that if the restore operation is interrupted, it should be restarted from that point.
RESTRICTED_USER	Indicates that only administrators and members of the db_owner and db_creator roles should have access to the database after the restore operation completes.

Table 13-11. *Backup Set Options*

Argument	Description
FILE	Indicates the sequential number of the backup set, within the media set, to be used.
PASSWORD	If you are restoring a backup that was taken in SQL Server 2008 or earlier where a password was specified during the backup operation, then you need to use this argument to be able to restore the backup.

Table 13-12. *Media Set Options*

Argument	Description
MEDIANAME	If you use this argument, then the MEDIANAME must match the name of the media set allocated during the creation of the media set.
MEDIAPASSWORD	If you are restoring from a media set created using SQL Server 2008 or earlier and a password was specified for the media set, then you must use this argument during the restore operation.
BLOCKSIZE	Specifies the block size to use for the restore operation, in bytes, to override the default value of 512 for disk or URL.

Table 13-13. *Error Management Options*

Argument	Description
CHECKSUM/NOCHECKSUM	If CHECKSUM was specified during the backup operation, then specifying CHECKSUM during the restore operation will verify page integrity during the restore operation. Specifying NOCKECKSUM disables this verification.
CONTINUE_AFTER_ERROR/STOP_ON_ERROR	STOP_ON_ERROR causes the restore operation to terminate if any damaged pages are discovered. CONTINUE_AFTER_ERROR causes the restore operation to continue, even if damaged pages are discovered.

Table 13-14. *Miscellaneous Options*

Argument	Description
BUFFERCOUNT	The total number of I/O buffers used for the restore operation.
MAXTRANSFERSIZE	The largest possible unit of transfer between SQL Server and the backup media, specified in bytes.
STATS	Specifies how often progress messages should be displayed. The default is to display a progress message in 5% increments.
FILESTREAM (DIRECTORY_NAME)	Specifies the name of the folder to which FILESTREAM data should be restored.
KEEP_REPLICATION	Preserves the replication settings. Use this option when configuring log shipping with replication.
KEEP_CDC	Preserves the Change Data Capture (CDC) settings of a database when it is being restored. Only relevant if CDC was enabled at the time of the backup operation.
ENABLE_BROKER/ ERROR_BROKER_ CONVERSATIONS/ NEW_BROKER	ENABLE_BROKER specifies that service broker message delivery will be enabled after the restore operation completes so that messages can immediately be sent. ERROR_BROKER_CONVERSATIONS specifies that all conversations will be terminated with an error message before message delivery is enabled. NEW_BROKER specifies that conversations will be removed without throwing an error and the database will be assigned a new Service Broker identifier. Only relevant if Service Broker was enabled when the backup was created.
STOPAT/STOPATMARK/ STOPBEFOREMARK	Used for point-in-time recovery and only supported in FULL recovery model. STOPAT specifies a datetime value, which will determine the time of the last transaction to restore. STOPATMARK specifies either an LSN (log sequence number) to restore to, or the name of a marked transaction, which will be the final transaction that is restored. STOPBEFOREMARK restores up to the transaction prior to the LSN or marked transaction specified.

To perform the same restore operation that we performed through SSMS, we use the command in Listing 13-10. Before running the script, change the path of the backup devices to match your own configuration.

Listing 13-10. Restoring a Database

```
USE master
GO

--Back Up the tail of the log

BACKUP LOG Chapter13
TO  DISK = N'H:\MSSQL\Backup\Chapter13_LogBackup_2022-02-16_12-17-49.bak'
        WITH NOFORMAT,
                NAME = N'Chapter13_LogBackup_2022-02-16_12-17-49',
                NORECOVERY ,
                STATS = 5 ;

--Restore the full backup

RESTORE DATABASE Chapter13
FROM  DISK = N'H:\MSSQL\Backup\Chapter13.bak'
        WITH  FILE = 1,
                NORECOVERY,
                STATS = 5 ;

--Restore the differential

RESTORE DATABASE Chapter13
FROM  DISK = N'H:\MSSQL\Backup\Chapter13.bak'
        WITH  FILE = 2,
            NORECOVERY,
            STATS = 5 ;

--Restore the transaction log

RESTORE LOG Chapter13
FROM  DISK = N'H:\MSSQL\Backup\Chapter13.bak'
        WITH  FILE = 3,
                STATS = 5 ;

GO
```

Restoring to a Point in Time

In order to demonstrate restoring a database to a point in time, we first take a series of backups, manipulating data between each one. The script in Listing 13-11 first creates a base full backup of the Chapter13 database. It then inserts some rows into the Addresses table before it takes a transaction log backup. It then inserts some further rows into the Addresses table before truncating the table, and then finally, it takes another transaction log backup.

Listing 13-11. Preparing the Chapter13 Database

```
USE Chapter13
GO

BACKUP DATABASE Chapter13
        TO  DISK = 'H:\MSSQL\Backup\Chapter13PointinTime.bak'
        WITH  RETAINDAYS = 90
        , FORMAT
        , INIT, SKIP
        , MEDIANAME = 'Chapter13Point-in-time'
        , NAME = 'Chapter13-Full Database Backup'
        , COMPRESSION ;

INSERT INTO dbo.Addresses
VALUES('1 Carter Drive', 'Hedge End', 'Southampton', 'SO32 6GH')
        ,('10 Apress Way', NULL, 'London', 'WC10 2FG') ;

BACKUP LOG Chapter13
        TO  DISK = 'H:\MSSQL\Backup\Chapter13PointinTime.bak'
        WITH  RETAINDAYS = 90
        , NOINIT
        , MEDIANAME = 'Chapter13Point-in-time'
        , NAME = 'Chapter13-Log Backup'
        , COMPRESSION ;

INSERT INTO dbo.Addresses
VALUES('12 SQL Street', 'Botley', 'Southampton', 'SO32 8RT')
        ,('19 Springer Way', NULL, 'London', 'EC1 5GG') ;
```

```
TRUNCATE TABLE dbo.Addresses ;

BACKUP LOG Chapter13
        TO   DISK = 'H:\MSSQL\Backup\Chapter13PointinTime.bak'
        WITH  RETAINDAYS = 90
        , NOINIT
        , MEDIANAME = 'Chapter13Point-in-time'
        , NAME = 'Chapter13-Log Backup'
        , COMPRESSION ;
GO
```

Imagine that after the series of events that occurred in this script, we discover that the Addresses table was truncated in error and we need to restore to the point immediately before this truncation occurred. To do this, we either need to know the exact time of the truncation and need to restore to the date/time immediately before, or to be more accurate, we need to discover the LSN of the transaction where the truncation occurred and restore up to this transaction. In this demonstration, we choose the latter option.

We can use a system function called sys.fn_dump_dblog() to display the contents of the final log backup that includes the second insert statement and the table truncation. The procedure accepts a massive 68 parameters, and none of them can be omitted!

The first and second parameters allow you to specify a beginning and end LSN with which to filter the results. These parameters can both be set to NULL to return all entries in the backup. The third parameter specifies if the backup set is disk or tape, whereas the fourth parameter specifies the sequential ID of the backup set within the device. The next 64 parameters accept the names of the backup devices within the media set. If the media set contains less than 64 devices, then you should use the value DEFAULT for any parameters that are not required.

The script in Listing 13-12 uses the undocumented fn_dump_dblog() system function to identify the starting LSN of the autocommit transaction in which the truncation occurred. The issue with this function is that it does not return the LSN in the same format required by the RESTORE command. Therefore, the calculated column, ConvertedLSN, converts each of the three sections of the LSN from binary to decimal, pads them out with zeros as required, and finally concatenates them back together to produce an LSN that can be passed into the RESTORE operation.

Listing 13-12. Finding the LSN of the Truncation

```
SELECT
        CAST(
            CAST(
                CONVERT(VARBINARY, '0x'
                        + RIGHT(REPLICATE('0', 8)
                        + SUBSTRING([Current LSN], 1, 8), 8), 1
                ) AS INT
            ) AS VARCHAR(11)
        ) +
        RIGHT(REPLICATE('0', 10) +
        CAST(
            CAST(
                CONVERT(VARBINARY, '0x'
                        + RIGHT(REPLICATE('0', 8)
                        + SUBSTRING([Current LSN], 10, 8), 8), 1
                ) AS INT
            ) AS VARCHAR(10)), 10) +
        RIGHT(REPLICATE('0',5) +
        CAST(
            CAST(CONVERT(VARBINARY, '0x'
                        + RIGHT(REPLICATE('0', 8)
                        + SUBSTRING([Current LSN], 19, 4), 8), 1
                ) AS INT
            ) AS VARCHAR
        ), 5) AS ConvertedLSN
        ,*
FROM
    sys.fn_dump_dblog (
        NULL, NULL, N'DISK', 3, N'H:\MSSQL\Backup\Chapter13PointinTime.bak'
        DEFAULT, DEFAULT, DEFAULT, DEFAULT, DEFAULT, DEFAULT, DEFAULT,
        DEFAULT, DEFAULT, DEFAULT, DEFAULT, DEFAULT, DEFAULT, DEFAULT,
        DEFAULT, DEFAULT, DEFAULT, DEFAULT, DEFAULT, DEFAULT, DEFAULT,
        DEFAULT, DEFAULT, DEFAULT, DEFAULT, DEFAULT, DEFAULT, DEFAULT,
        DEFAULT, DEFAULT, DEFAULT, DEFAULT, DEFAULT, DEFAULT, DEFAULT,
```

```
        DEFAULT, DEFAULT, DEFAULT, DEFAULT, DEFAULT, DEFAULT, DEFAULT,
        DEFAULT, DEFAULT, DEFAULT, DEFAULT, DEFAULT, DEFAULT, DEFAULT,
        DEFAULT, DEFAULT, DEFAULT, DEFAULT, DEFAULT, DEFAULT, DEFAULT,
        DEFAULT, DEFAULT, DEFAULT, DEFAULT, DEFAULT, DEFAULT, DEFAULT)
WHERE [Transaction Name] = 'TRUNCATE TABLE' ;
```

Now that we have discovered the LSN of the transaction that truncated the
Addresses table, we can restore the Chapter13 database to this point. The script in
Listing 13-13 restores the full and first transaction log backups in their entirety. It then
restores the final transaction log but uses the STOPBEFOREMARK argument to specify the
first LSN that should not be restored. Before running the script, change the locations of
the backup devices, as per your own configuration. You should also replace the LSN with
the LSN that you generated using sys.fn_dump_dblog().

Listing 13-13. Restoring to a Point in Time

```
USE master
GO

RESTORE DATABASE Chapter13
        FROM  DISK = N'H:\MSSQL\Backup\Chapter13PointinTime.bak'
        WITH  FILE = 1
        ,  NORECOVERY
        ,  STATS = 5
        , REPLACE ;

RESTORE LOG Chapter13
        FROM  DISK = N'H:\MSSQL\Backup\Chapter13PointinTime.bak'
        WITH  FILE = 2
        ,  NORECOVERY
        ,  STATS = 5
        , REPLACE ;

RESTORE LOG Chapter13
        FROM  DISK = N'H:\MSSQL\Backup\Chapter13PointinTime.bak'
        WITH  FILE = 3
        ,  STATS = 5
```

```
, STOPBEFOREMARK = 'lsn:35000000036000001'
, RECOVERY
, REPLACE ;
```

Restoring Files and Pages

The ability to restore a filegroup, a file, or even a page gives you great control and flexibility in disaster recovery scenarios. The following sections demonstrate how to perform a file restore and a page restore.

Restoring a File

You may come across situations in which only some files or filegroups within the database are corrupt. If this is the case, then it is possible to restore just the corrupt file, assuming you have the complete log chain available, between the point when you took the file or filegroup backup and the end of the log. In order to demonstrate this functionality, we first insert some rows into the Contacts table of the Chapter13 database before we back up the primary filegroup and FileGroupA. We then insert some rows into the Addresses table, which resides on FileGroupB before we take a transaction log backup. These tasks are performed by the script in Listing 13-14.

Listing 13-14. Preparing the Database

```
INSERT INTO dbo.Contacts
VALUES('Peter', 'Carter', 1),
       ('Danielle', 'Carter', 1) ;

BACKUP DATABASE Chapter13 FILEGROUP = N'PRIMARY',  FILEGROUP =
N'FileGroupA'
       TO  DISK = N'H:\MSSQL\Backup\Chapter13FileRestore.bak'
       WITH FORMAT
       , NAME = N'Chapter13-Filegroup Backup'
       , STATS = 10 ;

INSERT INTO dbo.Addresses
VALUES('SQL House', 'Server Buildings', NULL, 'SQ42 4BY'),
       ('Carter Mansions', 'Admin Road', 'London', 'E3 3GJ') ;
```

```
BACKUP LOG Chapter13
        TO  DISK = N'H:\MSSQL\Backup\Chapter13FileRestore.bak'
        WITH NOFORMAT
        , NOINIT
        ,  NAME = N'Chapter13-Log Backup'
        , NOSKIP
        , STATS = 10 ;
```

If we imagine that Chapter13FileA has become corrupt, we are able to restore
this file, even though we do not have a corresponding backup for Chapter13FileB,
and recover to the latest point in time by using the script in Listing 13-15. This script
performs a file restore on the file Chapter13FileA before taking a tail-log backup of the
transaction log and then finally applying all transaction logs in sequence. Before running
this script, change the location of the backup devices to reflect your own configuration.

Caution   If we had not taken the tail-log backup, then we would no longer have
been able to access the Contacts table (in FileGroupB), unless we had also
been able to restore the Chapter13FileB file.

Listing 13-15. Restoring a File

```
USE master
GO

RESTORE DATABASE Chapter13 FILE = N'Chapter13FileA'
        FROM  DISK = N'H:\MSSQL\Backup\Chapter13FileRestore.bak'
        WITH  FILE = 1
        , NORECOVERY
        , STATS = 10
        , REPLACE ;
GO

BACKUP LOG Chapter13
        TO  DISK = N'H:\MSSQL\Backup\Chapter13_LogBackup_2022-02-17_12-26-09.bak'
        WITH NOFORMAT
        , NOINIT
```

```
        ,   NAME = N'Chapter13_LogBackup_2022-02-17_12-26-09'
        , NOSKIP
        , NORECOVERY
            ,   STATS = 5 ;

RESTORE LOG Chapter13
        FROM   DISK = N'H:\MSSQL\Backup\Chapter13FileRestore.bak'
        WITH   FILE = 2
        , STATS = 10
        , NORECOVERY ;

RESTORE LOG Chapter13
        FROM   DISK = N'H:\MSSQL\Backup\Chapter13_LogBackup_2022-02-17_
        12-26-09.bak'
        WITH FILE = 1
        , STATS = 10
        , RECOVERY ;
GO
```

Restoring a Page

If a page becomes corrupt, then it is possible to restore this page instead of restoring the complete file or even the database. This can significantly reduce downtime in a minor DR scenario. In order to demonstrate this functionality, we take a full backup of the Chapter13 database and then use the undocumented DBCC WRITEPAGE to cause a corruption in one of the pages of our Contacts table. These steps are performed in Listing 13-16.

Caution   DBCC WRITEPAGE is used here for educational purposes only. It is undocumented, but also extremely dangerous. It should not ever be used on a production system and should only ever be used on any database with extreme caution.

Listing 13-16. Preparing the Database

```
--Back up the database

BACKUP DATABASE Chapter13
        TO  DISK = N'H:\MSSQL\Backup\Chapter13PageRestore.bak'
        WITH FORMAT
        , NAME = N'Chapter13-Full Backup'
        , STATS = 10 ;

--Corrupt a page in the Contacts table

ALTER DATABASE Chapter13 SET SINGLE_USER WITH NO_WAIT ;
GO

DECLARE @SQL NVARCHAR(MAX)

SELECT @SQL = 'DBCC WRITEPAGE(' +
(
        SELECT CAST(DB_ID('Chapter13') AS NVARCHAR)
) +
', ' +
(
        SELECT TOP 1 CAST(file_id AS NVARCHAR)
        FROM dbo.Contacts
        CROSS APPLY sys.fn_PhysLocCracker(%%physloc%%)
) +
 ', ' +
(
        SELECT TOP 1 CAST(page_id AS NVARCHAR)
        FROM dbo.Contacts
        CROSS APPLY sys.fn_PhysLocCracker(%%physloc%%)
) +
', 2000, 1, 0x61, 1)' ;
```

```
EXEC(@SQL) ;
```

```
ALTER DATABASE Chapter13 SET MULTI_USER ;
GO
```

If we attempt to access the Contacts table after running the script, we receive the error message warning us of a logical consistency-based I/O error, and the statement fails. The error message also provides details of the page that is corrupt, which we can use in our RESTORE statement. To resolve this, we can run the script in Listing 13-17. The script restores the corrupt page before taking a tail-log backup, and then finally it applies the tail of the log. Before running the script, modify the location of the backup devices to reflect your configuration. You should also update the PageID to reflect the page that is corrupt in your version of the Chapter13 database. Specify the page to be restored in the format FileID:PageID.

Tip   The details of the corrupt page can also be found in MSDB.dbo. suspect_pages.

Listing 13-17. Restoring a Page

```
USE Master
GO
```

```
RESTORE DATABASE Chapter13 PAGE='3:8'
        FROM  DISK = N'H:\MSSQL\Backup\Chapter13PageRestore.bak'
        WITH  FILE = 1
        , NORECOVERY
        ,   STATS = 5 ;
```

```
BACKUP LOG Chapter13
        TO  DISK = N'H:\MSSQL\Backup\Chapter13_LogBackup_2022-02-17_
        16-47-46.bak'
        WITH NOFORMAT, NOINIT
        , NAME = N'Chapter13_LogBackup_2022-02-17_16-32-46'
        , NOSKIP
        , STATS = 5 ;
```

```
RESTORE LOG Chapter13
        FROM  DISK = N'H:\MSSQL\Backup\Chapter13_LogBackup_2022-02-17_
        16-47-46.bak'
        WITH  STATS = 5
                , RECOVERY ;
GO
```

Piecemeal Restores

A piecemeal restore involves bringing the filegroups of a database online one by one. This can offer a big benefit for a large database, since you can make some data accessible while other data is still being restored. In order to demonstrate this technique, we first take filegroup backups of all filegroups in the Chapter13 database and follow this with a transaction log backup. The script in Listing 13-18 performs this task. Before running the script, modify the locations of the backup devices to reflect your own configurations.

Listing 13-18. Filegroup Backup

```
BACKUP DATABASE Chapter13
        FILEGROUP = N'PRIMARY',  FILEGROUP = N'FileGroupA',
        FILEGROUP = N'FileGroupB'
        TO  DISK = N'H:\MSSQL\Backup\Chapter13Piecemeal.bak'
        WITH FORMAT
        , NAME = N'Chapter13-Fiegroup Backup'
        , STATS = 10 ;

BACKUP LOG Chapter13
        TO  DISK = N'H:\MSSQL\Backup\Chapter13Piecemeal.bak'
        WITH NOFORMAT, NOINIT
        ,  NAME = N'Chapter13-Full Database Backup'
        ,  STATS = 10 ;
```

The script in Listing 13-19 now brings the filegroups online, one by one, starting with the primary filegroup, followed by FileGroupA, and finally, FileGroupB. Before beginning the restore, we back up the tail of the log. This backup is restored

WITH RECOVERY after each filegroup is restored. This brings the restored databases back online. It is possible to restore further backups because we specify the PARTIAL option on the first restore operation.

Listing 13-19. Piecemeal Restore

```
USE master
GO

BACKUP LOG Chapter13
        TO  DISK = N'H:\MSSQL\Backup\Chapter13_LogBackup_2022-02-17_
        27-29-46.bak'
        WITH NOFORMAT, NOINIT
        , NAME = N'Chapter13_LogBackup_2022-02-17_17-29-46'
        , NOSKIP
        , NORECOVERY
        , NO_TRUNCATE
        , STATS = 5 ;

RESTORE DATABASE Chapter13
        FILEGROUP = N'PRIMARY'
        FROM  DISK = N'H:\MSSQL\Backup\Chapter13Piecemeal.bak'
        WITH  FILE = 1
        , NORECOVERY
        , PARTIAL
        , STATS = 10 ;

RESTORE LOG Chapter13
        FROM  DISK = N'H:\MSSQL\Backup\Chapter13Piecemeal.bak'
        WITH  FILE = 2
        , NORECOVERY
        , STATS = 10 ;

RESTORE LOG Chapter13
        FROM  DISK = N'H:\MSSQL\Backup\Chapter13_LogBackup_2022-02-17_
        27-29-46.bak'
        WITH  FILE = 1
        , STATS = 10
        , RECOVERY ;
```

```
----------------The PRIMARY Filegroup is now online--------------------

RESTORE DATABASE Chapter13
        FILEGROUP = N'FileGroupA'
        FROM  DISK = N'H:\MSSQL\Backup\Chapter13Piecemeal.bak'
        WITH  FILE = 1
        , NORECOVERY
        , STATS = 10 ;

RESTORE LOG Chapter13
        FROM  DISK = N'H:\MSSQL\Backup\Chapter13Piecemeal.bak'
        WITH  FILE = 2
        , NORECOVERY
        , STATS = 10 ;

RESTORE LOG Chapter13
        FROM  DISK = N'H:\MSSQL\Backup\Chapter13_
LogBackup_2022-02-17_27-29-46.bak'
        WITH  FILE = 1
        , STATS = 10
        , RECOVERY ;

----------------The FilegroupA Filegroup is now online--------------------

RESTORE DATABASE Chapter13
        FILEGROUP = N'FileGroupB'
        FROM  DISK = N'H:\MSSQL\Backup\Chapter13Piecemeal.bak'
        WITH  FILE = 1
        , NORECOVERY
        , STATS = 10 ;

RESTORE LOG Chapter13
        FROM  DISK = N'H:\MSSQL\Backup\Chapter13Piecemeal.bak'
        WITH  FILE = 2
        , NORECOVERY
        , STATS = 10 ;

RESTORE LOG Chapter13
```

```
FROM  DISK = N'H:\MSSQL\Backup\Chapter13_LogBackup_2022-02-17_
27-29-46.bak'
WITH  FILE = 1
, STATS = 10
, RECOVERY ;
```

-----------------The database is now fully online--------------------

Accelerated Database Recovery

When an instance starts, after an unplanned event, where you have not been able to place the instance in a safe-state first, then depending on the workloads, it can take a long time for databases to come back online. This happens, specifically, when there are long-running transactions. This is due to the mechanism SQL Server uses to recover the database. The recovery happens in three phases.

The first phase is called the analysis phase. Here, SQL Server scans the transaction log from the last checkpoint, or the oldest transaction that modified a page, which is still dirty, and determines the state of each transaction at the point where the SQL Server service stopped.

The second phase is the redo phase. Here, SQL Server scans the log, starting at the oldest uncommitted transaction, and performs redoes all operations from committed transactions, up to the point where SQL Server stopped.

The final phase is called the redo phase. This phase starts at the end of the transaction log and runs backward, to the last uncommitted transaction, rolling back any transactions that were not committed before the instance stopped.

SQL Server 2019 introduced a new recovery process, called Accelerated Database Recovery (ADR), which has been improved in SQL Server 2022. This process introduces a persisted version store (PVS) into a user database, which has the side effect of increasing storage requirements for the database, but reducing storage requirements for TempDB, as PVS replaces the version store in TempDB.

An asynchronous process, known as logical revert, is then able to perform an instant rollback for transactions that are stored in PVS, because the versions are marked as aborted and can simply be ignored.

ADR also introduces a secondary log stream, in memory, which is used to log transactions for operations which cannot use the PVS version store, such as DDL operations. This secondary log stream is called the SLOG. It serializes records to disk during checkpoint operations and is truncated as transactions commit.

Additionally, an asynchronous Cleaner process has been implemented, which periodically cleans up page versions, which are no longer required.

When ADR is enabled for a database, recovery still consists of three phases, but those phases are optimized for the new mechanisms.

In the analysis phase, SQL Server scans the transaction log from the last checkpoint, or the oldest transaction that modified a page, which is still dirty, and determines the state of each transaction at the point where the SQL Server service stopped. It also gathers nonversioned operations from the SLOG.

The redo phase is broken into two parts. In the first part, transactions are recommitted from the SLOG. In the second part, operations from the transaction log are redone. The design of ADR, however, means that this redo phase can commence from the last checkpoint, or the transaction of the last dirty page, instead of starting from the last uncommitted transaction.

The undo phase is incredibly fast. This is because the logical revert process can quickly determine which versions in PVS are aborted and undo any nonversioned transactions from the SLOG.

ADR also brings benefits to databases that participate in use cases such as ETL loads, where large operations or bulk inserts occur, causing long-running transactions. Traditionally, this can cause transaction logs to grow very large (see Chapter 6 for a discussion on log maintenance). ADR allows for aggressive log truncation, on log backup and checkpoints, because the log no longer needs to be processed from the last uncommitted transaction.

ADR can be enabled for a database using the ALTER DATABASE command. The command in Listing 13-20 enables ADR for the Chapter13 database.

Listing 13-20. Enable ADR

```
ALTER DATABASE Chapter13 SET ACCELERATED_DATABASE_RECOVERY = ON
```

In this example, we have not specified a filegroup that PVS should be stored on. Therefore, it will be stored on the default filegroup, which is PRIMARY by default. I recommend, however, that you store the PVS on an isolated filegroup that case be placed on the fastest possible storage.

Once ADR has been enabled, you will need to disable it, to change the PVS filegroup, however. The script in Listing 13-21 first removes ADR. It then configures a filegroup for PVS, before reconfiguring ADR to use the new filegroup.

Listing 13-21. Configure PVS on a Different Filegroup

```
--Disable ADR

ALTER DATABASE Chapter13 SET ACCELERATED_DATABASE_RECOVERY = OFF
GO

--Cleanup the existing PVS

EXEC sys.sp_persistent_version_cleanup Chapter13
GO

--Add PVS Filegroup

ALTER DATABASE Chapter13 ADD FILEGROUP PVS_FG
GO

--Add file to PVS Filegroup

ALTER DATABASE Chapter13 ADD FILE (
        NAME = 'PVS'
      , FILENAME = N'C:\MSSQL\DATA\PVS.ndf'
)
TO FILEGROUP PVS_FG
GO

--Enable ADR using new Filegroup for PVS

ALTER DATABASE Chapter13 SET ACCELERATED_DATABASE_RECOVERY = ON
(PERSISTENT_VERSION_STORE_FILEGROUP = PVS_FG);
GO
```

An enhancement in SQL Server 2022 is the ability to specify the number of threads, per database, that will be used for the cleanup process. In SQL Server 2019, there was a single thread for the whole instance. The number of threads is configurable, and increasing them can yield performance improvements when you have multiple large databases on the instance. The script in Listing 13-22 firstly turns on trace flag 3515, which enables multiple threads per database. It then uses sp_configure to specify the number of threads that the cleanup process can use.

Listing 13-22. Enable Multithreaded Cleanup

```
DBCC TRACEON(3515, -1)
GO

EXEC sp_configure 'Show advanced options', 1
RECONFIGURE

EXEC sp_configure 'ADR Cleaner Thread Count', '4'
RECONFIGURE WITH OVERRIDE;

EXEC sp_configure 'Show advanced options', 0
RECONFIGURE
```

Summary

A SQL Server database can operate in three recovery models. The SIMPLE recovery model automatically truncates the transaction log after CHECKPOINT operations occur. This means that log backups cannot be taken and, therefore, point-in-time restores are not available. In FULL recovery model, the transaction log is only truncated after a log backup operation. This means that you must take transaction log backups for both disaster recovery and log space. The BULK LOGGED recovery model is meant to be used only while a bulk insert operation is happening. In this case, you switch to this model if you normally use the FULL recovery model.

SQL Server supports three types of backup. A full backup copies all database pages to the backup device. A differential backup copies all database pages that have been modified since the last full backup to the backup device. A transaction log backup copies the contents of the transaction log to the backup device.

A DBA can adopt many backup strategies to provide the best possible RTO and RPO in the event of a disaster that requires a database to be restored. These include taking full backups only, which is applicable to SIMPLE recovery model; scheduling full backups along with transaction log backups; or scheduling full, differential, and transaction log backups. Scheduling differential backups can help improve the RTO of a database if frequent log backups are taken. DBAs may also elect to implement a filegroup backup strategy; this allows them to stage their backups into more manageable windows or perform a partial backup, which involves backing up only read/write filegroups.

Ad hoc backups can be taken via T-SQL or SQL Server Management Studio (SSMS). In production environments, you invariably want to schedule the backups to run periodically, and we discuss how to automate this action in Chapter 22.

You can also perform restores either through SSMS or with T-SQL. However, you can only perform complex restore scenarios, such as piecemeal restores, via T-SQL. SQL Server also provides you with the ability to restore a single page or file. You can restore a corrupt page as an online operation, and doing so usually provides a better alternative to fixing small-scale corruption than either restoring a whole database or using DBCC CHECKDB with the ALLOW_DATA_LOSS option. More details on DBCC CHECKDB can be found in Chapter 9.

Tip   Many other restore scenarios are beyond the scope of this book, because a full description of every possible scenario would be worthy of a volume in its own right. I encourage you to explore various restore scenarios in a sandpit environment before you need to use them for real! It is also advisable to have a run book, with decision tree, so that you are not under pressure to figure things out in a real disaster scenario.

Accelerated Database Recovery provides a new database recovery mechanism that can benefit databases that have long-running transactions, by reducing the time it takes to recover the database when the instance starts.

When using ADR, it is advisable to locate the PVS (persisted version store) on a dedicated filegroup, which contains files that reside on the fastest possible storage.

In addition to reducing recovery time, ADR can also help save disk space for databases that are the targets of ETL loads, or other long-running transactions. This is because the transaction log can be truncated more aggressively during backup and checkpoint operations, as the log no longer needs to be processed from the first uncommitted transaction.

Tip   In Azure, SQL Server Managed Instances and Azure SQL Database have ADR turned on by default and the feature cannot be disabled.

## CHAPTER 14

High Availability and Disaster Recovery Concepts

In today's 24×7 environments that are running mission-critical applications, businesses rely heavily on the availability of their data. Although servers and their software are generally reliable, there is always the risk of a hardware failure or a software bug, each of which could bring a server down. To mitigate these risks, business-critical applications often rely on redundant hardware to provide fault tolerance. If the primary system fails, then the application can automatically fail over to the redundant system. This is the underlying principle of high availability (HA).

Even with the implementation of HA technologies, there is always a small risk of an event that causes the application to become unavailable. This could be due to a major incident, such as the loss of a data center, due to a natural disaster, or due to an act of terrorism. It could also be caused by data corruption or human error, resulting in the application's data becoming lost or damaged beyond repair.

In these situations, some applications may rely on restoring the latest backup to recover as much data as possible. However, more critical applications may require a redundant server to hold a synchronized copy of the data in a secondary location. This is the underpinning concept of disaster recovery (DR). This chapter discusses the concepts behind HA and DR before providing an overview of the technologies that are available to implement these concepts.

© Peter A. Carter 2023
P. A. Carter, *Pro SQL Server 2022 Administration*, https://doi.org/10.1007/978-1-4842-8864-1_14

Availability Concepts

In order to analyze the HA and DR requirements of an application and implement the most appropriate solution, you need to understand various concepts. We discuss these concepts in the following sections.

Level of Availability

The amount of time that a solution is available to end users is known as the *level of availability*, or *uptime*. To provide a true picture of uptime, a company should measure the availability of a solution from a user's desktop. In other words, even if your SQL Server has been running uninterrupted for over a month, users may still experience outages to their solution caused by other factors. These factors can include network outages or an application server failure.

In some instances, however, you have no choice but to measure the level of availability at the SQL Server level. This may be because you lack holistic monitoring tools within the Enterprise. Most often, however, the requirement to measure the level of availability at the instance level is political, as opposed to technical. In the IT industry, it has become a trend to outsource the management of data centers to third-party providers. In such cases, the provider responsible for managing the SQL servers may not necessarily be the provider responsible for the network or application servers. In this scenario, you need to monitor uptime at the SQL Server level to accurately judge the performance of the service provider.

The level of availability is measured as a percentage of the time that the application or server is available. Companies often strive to achieve 99%, 99.9%, 99.99%, or 99.999% availability. As a result, the level of availability is often referred to in 9s. For example, five 9s of availability means 99.999% uptime and three 9s means 99.9% uptime.

Table 14-1 details the amount of acceptable downtime per week, per month, and per year for each level of availability.

All values are rounded down to the nearest second.

Table 14-1. *Levels of Availability*

Level of Availability	Downtime per Week	Downtime per Month	Downtime per Year
99%	1 hour, 40 minutes, 48 seconds	7 hours, 18 minutes, 17 seconds	3 days, 15 hours, 39 minutes, 28 seconds
99.9%	10 minutes, 4 seconds	43 minutes, 49 seconds	8 hours, 45 minutes, 56 seconds
99.99%	1 minute	4 minutes, 23 seconds	52 minutes, 35 seconds
99.999%	6 seconds	26 seconds	5 minutes, 15 seconds

To calculate other levels of availability, you can use the script in Listing 14-1. Before running this script, replace the value of @Uptime to represent the level of uptime that you wish to calculate. You should also replace the value of @UptimeInterval to reflect uptime per week, month, or year.

Listing 14-1. Calculating the Level of Availability

```
DECLARE @Uptime        DECIMAL(5,3) ;

--Specify the uptime level to calculate

SET @Uptime = 99.9 ;

DECLARE @UptimeInterval VARCHAR(5) ;

--Specify WEEK, MONTH, or YEAR

SET @UptimeInterval = 'YEAR' ;

DECLARE @SecondsPerInterval FLOAT ;

--Calculate seconds per interval

SET @SecondsPerInterval =
(
```

```
SELECT CASE
        WHEN @UptimeInterval = 'YEAR'
                THEN 60*60*24*365.243
        WHEN @UptimeInterval = 'MONTH'
                THEN 60*60*24*30.437
        WHEN @UptimeInterval = 'WEEK'
                THEN 60*60*24*7
        END
) ;

DECLARE @UptimeSeconds DECIMAL(12,4) ;

--Calculate uptime

SET @UptimeSeconds = @SecondsPerInterval * (100-@Uptime) / 100 ;

--Format results
SELECT
    CONVERT(VARCHAR(12), FLOOR(@UptimeSeconds /60/60/24))   + ' Day(s), '
  + CONVERT(VARCHAR(12), FLOOR(@UptimeSeconds /60/60 % 24)) + ' Hour(s), '
  + CONVERT(VARCHAR(12),  FLOOR(@UptimeSeconds /60 % 60))   + ' Minute(s), '
  + CONVERT(VARCHAR(12),  FLOOR(@UptimeSeconds % 60))       + ' Second(s).' ;
```

Service-Level Agreements and Service-Level Objectives

When a third-party provider is responsible for managing servers, the contract usually includes service-level agreements (SLAs). These SLAs define many parameters, including how much downtime is acceptable, the maximum length of time a server can be down in the event of failure, and how much data loss is acceptable if failure occurs. Normally, there are financial penalties for the provider if these SLAs are not met.

In the event that servers are managed in-house, DBAs still have the concept of customers. These are usually the end users of the application, with the primary contact being the business owner. An application's business owner is the stakeholder within the business who commissioned the application and who is responsible for signing off on funding enhancements, among other things.

In an in-house scenario, it is still possible to define SLAs, and in such a case, the IT Infrastructure or Platform departments may be liable for charge-back to the business teams if these SLAs are not being met. However, in internal scenarios, it is much more common for IT departments to negotiate service-level objectives (SLOs) with the business teams, as opposed to SLAs. SLOs are very similar in nature to SLAs, but their use implies that the business do not impose financial penalties on the IT department in the event that they are not met.

Proactive Maintenance

It is important to remember that downtime is not only caused by failure, but also by proactive maintenance. For example, if you need to patch the operating system, or SQL Server itself, with the latest service pack, then you must have some downtime during installation.

Depending on the upgrade you are applying, the downtime in such a scenario could be substantial—several hours for a stand-alone server. In this situation, high availability is essential for many business-critical applications—not to protect against unplanned downtime, but to avoid prolonged outages during planned maintenance.

Recovery Point Objective and Recovery Time Objective

The recovery point objective (RPO) of an application indicates how much data loss is acceptable in the event of a failure. For a data warehouse that supports a reporting application, for example, this may be an extended period, such as 24 hours, given that it may only be updated once per day by an ETL process and all other activity is read-only reporting. For highly transactional systems, however, such as an OLTP database supporting trading platforms or web applications, the RPO will be zero. An RPO of zero means that no data loss is acceptable.

Applications may have different RPOs for high availability and for disaster recovery. For example, for reasons of cost or application performance, an RPO of zero may be required for a failover within the site. If the same application fails over to a DR data center, however, five or ten minutes of data loss may be acceptable. This is because of technology differences used to implement intra-site availability and inter-site recovery.

The recovery time objective (RTO) for an application specifies the maximum amount of time an application can be down before recovery is complete and users can reconnect. When calculating the achievable RTO for an application, you need to consider many aspects. For example, it may take less than a minute for a cluster to fail over from one node to another and for the SQL Server service to come back up; however, it may take far longer for the databases to recover. The time it takes for databases to recover depends on many factors, including the size of the databases, the quantity of databases within an instance, and how many transactions were in-flight when the failover occurred. This is because all noncommitted transactions need to be rolled back.

Just like RPO, it is common for there to be different RTOs depending on whether you have an intra-site or inter-site failover. Again, this is primarily due to differences in technologies, but it also factors in the amount of time you need to bring up the entire estate in the DR data center if the primary data center is lost.

The RPO and RTO of an application may also vary in the event of data corruption. Depending on the nature of the corruption and the HA/DR technologies that have been implemented, data corruption may result in you needing to restore a database from a backup.

If you must restore a database, the worst-case scenario is that the achievable point of recovery may be the time of the last backup. This means that you must factor a hard business requirement for a specific RPO into your backup strategy. (Backups are discussed fully in Chapter 13.) If only part of the database is corrupt, however, you may be able to salvage some data from the live database and restore only the corrupt data from the restored database.

Data corruption is also likely to have an impact on the RTO. One of the biggest influencing factors is if backups are stored locally on the server, or if you need to retrieve them from tape (or in cloud, potentially from offline archive storage, which is more cost effective than standard storage). Retrieving backup files from tape, archive storage, or even from off-site locations is likely to add significant time to the recovery process.

Another influencing factor is what caused the corruption. If it is caused by a faulty I/O subsystem, then you may need to factor in time for the Windows administrators to run the check disk command (CHKDSK) against the volume and potentially more time for disks to be replaced. If the corruption is caused by a user accidently truncating a table or deleting a data file, however, then this is not of concern.

Cost of Downtime

If you ask any business owners how much downtime is acceptable for their applications and how much data loss is acceptable, the answers invariably come back as zero and zero, respectively. Of course, it is never possible to guarantee zero downtime, and once you begin to explain the costs associated with the different levels of availability, it starts to get easier to negotiate a mutually acceptable level of service.

The key factor in deciding how many 9s you should try to achieve is the cost of downtime. Two categories of cost are associated with downtime: tangible costs and intangible costs. Tangible costs are usually fairly straightforward to calculate. Let's use a sales application as an example. In this case, the most obvious tangible cost is lost revenue because the sales staff cannot take orders. Intangible costs are more difficult to quantify but can be far more expensive. For example, if a customer is unable to place an order with your company, they may place their order with a rival company and never return. Other intangible costs can include loss of staff morale, which leads to higher staff turnover, or even loss of company reputation. Because intangible costs, by their very nature, can only be estimated, the industry rule of thumb is to multiply the tangible costs by three and use this figure to represent your intangible costs.

Once you have an hourly figure for the total cost of downtime for your application, you can scale this figure out, across the predicted life cycle of your application, and compare the costs of implementing different availability levels. For example, imagine that you calculate that your total cost of downtime is $2,000/hour and the predicted life cycle of your application is three years. Table 14-2 illustrates the cost of downtime for your application, comparing the costs that you have calculated for implementing each level of availability, after you have factored in hardware, licenses, power, cabling, additional storage, and additional supporting equipment, such as new racks, administrative costs, and so on. This is known as the total cost of ownership (TCO) of a solution.

Table 14-2. *Cost of Downtime*

Level of Availability	Cost of Downtime (Three Years)	Cost of Availability Solution
99%	$525,600	$108,000
99.9%	$52,560	$224,000
99.99%	$5,256	$462,000
99.999%	$526	$910,000

In this table, you can see that implementing five 9s of availability saves $525,474 over a two-9s solution, but the cost of implementing the solution is an additional $802,000, meaning that it is not economical to implement. Four 9s of availability saves $520,334 over a two-9s solution and only costs an additional $354,000 to implement. Therefore, for this particular application, a three-9s solution is the most appropriate level of service to design for.

Classification of Standby Servers

There are three classes of standby solution. You can implement each using different technologies, although you can use some technologies to implement multiple classes of standby server. Table 14-3 outlines the different classes of standby that you can implement.

Table 14-3. *Standby Classifications*

Class	Description	Example Technologies
Hot	A synchronized solution where failover can occur automatically or manually. Often used for high availability.	Clustering, AlwaysOn Availability Groups (Synchronous)
Warm	A synchronized solution where failover can only occur manually. Often used for disaster recovery.	Log Shipping, AlwaysOn Availability Groups (Asynchronous)
Cold	An unsynchronized solution where failover can only occur manually. This is only suitable for read-only data, which is never modified.	—

Note   Cold standby does not show an example technology because no synchronization is required and, thus, no technology implementation is required. For example, in a cloud scenario, you may have a VMWare SDDC in an AWS availability zone. If an availability zone is lost, automation spins up an SDDC in a different availability zone and restores VM snapshots from an S3 bucket.

High Availability and Recovery Technologies

SQL Server provides a full suite of technologies for implementing high availability and disaster recovery. The following sections provide an overview of these technologies and discuss their most appropriate uses.

AlwaysOn Failover Clustering

A Windows cluster is a technology for providing high availability in which a group of up to 64 servers works together to provide redundancy. An AlwaysOn Failover Clustered Instance (FCI) is an instance of SQL Server that spans the servers within this group. If one of the servers within this group fails, another server takes ownership of the instance. Its most appropriate usage is for high availability scenarios where the databases are large or have high write profiles. This is because clustering relies on shared storage, meaning the data is only written to disk once. With SQL Server–level HA technologies, write operations occur on the primary database, and then again on all secondary databases, before the commit on the primary completes. This can cause performance issues. Even though it is possible to stretch a cluster across multiple sites, this involves SAN replication, which means that a cluster is normally configured within a single site.

Each server within a cluster is called a *node*. Therefore, if a cluster consists of three servers, it is known as a three-node cluster. Each node within a cluster has the SQL Server binaries installed, but the SQL Server service is only started on one of the nodes, which is known as the *active node*. Each node within the cluster also shares the same storage for the SQL Server data and log files. The storage, however, is only attached to the active node.

Tip   In geographically dispersed clusters (geoclusters), each server is attached to different storage. The volumes are updated by SAN replication or Windows Storage Replica (a Windows Server technology, introduced in Windows Server 2016, which performs storage replication). The cluster regards the two volumes as a single, shared volume, which can only be attached to one node at a time.

If the active node fails, then the SQL Server service is stopped and the storage is detached. The storage is then reattached to one of the other nodes in the cluster, and the SQL Server service is started on this node, which is now the active node. The instance is also assigned its own network name and IP address, which are also bound to the active node. This means that applications can connect seamlessly to the instance, regardless of which node has ownership.

The diagram in Figure 14-1 illustrates a two-node cluster. It shows that although the databases are stored on a shared storage array, each node still has a dedicated system volume. This volume contains the SQL Server binaries. It also illustrates how the shared storage, IP address, and network name are rebound to the passive node in the event of failover.

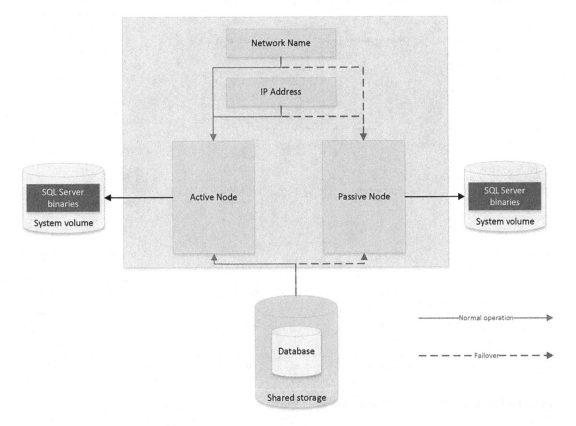

Figure 14-1. *Two-node cluster*

Active/Active Configuration

Although the diagram in Figure 14-1 illustrates an active/passive configuration, it is also possible to have an active/active configuration. Although it is not possible for more than one node at a time to own a single instance, therefore it is not possible to implement load balancing. It is, however, possible to install multiple instances on a cluster, and a different node may own each instance. In this scenario, each node has its own unique network name and IP address. Each instance's shared storage also consists of a unique set of volumes.

Therefore, in an active/active configuration, during normal operations, Node1 may host Instance1 and Node2 may host Instance2. If Node1 fails, both instances are then hosted by Node2, and vice versa. The diagram in Figure 14-2 illustrates a two-node active/active cluster.

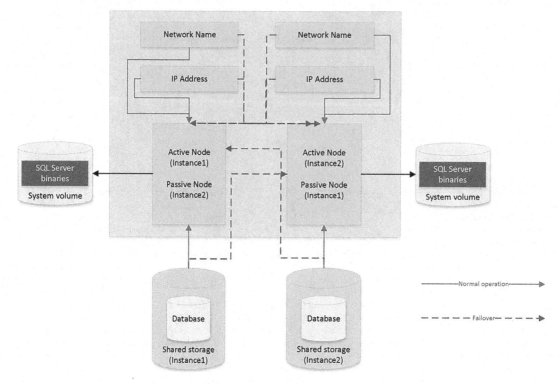

Figure 14-2. *Active/active cluster*

Caution   In an active/active cluster, it is important to consider resources in the event of failover. For example, if each node has 128GB of RAM and the instance hosted on each node is using 96GB of RAM and locking pages in memory, then when one node fails over to the other node, this node fails as well, because it does not have enough memory to allocate to both instances. Make sure you plan both memory and processor requirements as if the two nodes are a single server. For this reason, active/active clusters are not generally recommended for SQL Server.

Three-Plus Node Configurations

As previously mentioned, it is possible to have up to 64 nodes in a cluster. When you have three or more nodes, it is unlikely that you will want to have a single active node and two redundant nodes, due to the associated costs. Instead, you can choose to implement an N+1 or N+M configuration.

In an N+1 configuration, you have multiple active nodes and a single passive node. If a failure occurs on any of the active nodes, they fail over to the passive node. The diagram in Figure 14-3 depicts a three-node N+1 cluster.

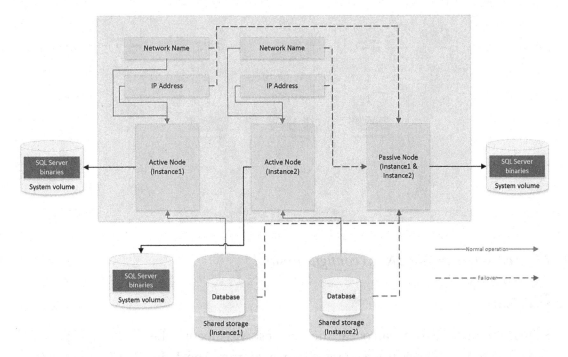

Figure 14-3. *Three-node N+1 configuration*

In an N+1 configuration, in a multifailure scenario, multiple nodes may fail over to the passive node. For this reason, you must be very careful when you plan resources to ensure that the passive node is able to support multiple instances. However, you can mitigate this issue by using an N+M configuration.

Whereas an N+1 configuration has multiple active nodes and a single passive node, an N+M cluster has multiple active nodes and multiple passive nodes, although there are usually fewer passive nodes than there are active nodes. The diagram in Figure 14-4 shows a five-node N+M configuration. The diagram shows that Instance3 is configured to always fail over to one of the passive nodes, whereas Instance1 and Instance2 are configured to always fail over to the other passive node. This gives you the flexibility to control resources on the passive nodes, but you can also configure the cluster to allow any of the active nodes to fail over to either of the passive nodes, if this is a more appropriate design for your environment.

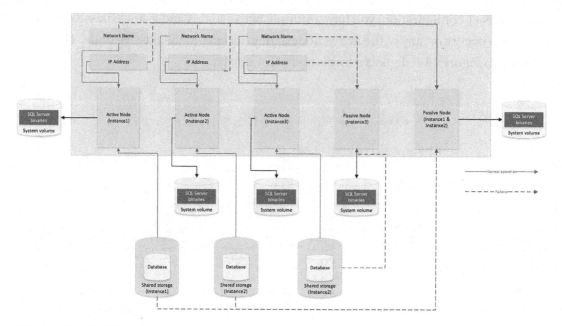

Figure 14-4. *Five-node N+M configuration*

Quorum

So that automatic failover can occur, the cluster service needs to know if a node goes down. In order to achieve this, you must form a quorum. The definition of a quorum is *"The minimum number of members required in order for business to be carried out."* In terms of high availability, this means that each node within a cluster, and optionally a witness device (which may be a cluster disk or a file share that is external to the cluster), receives a vote. If more than half of the voting members are unable to communicate with a node, then the cluster service knows that it has gone down and any cluster-aware applications on the server fail over to another node. The reason that more than half of the voting members need to be unable to communicate with the node is to avoid a situation known as a *split brain*.

To explain a split-brain scenario, imagine that you have three nodes in Data Center 1 and three nodes in Data Center 2. Now imagine that you lose network connectivity between the two data centers, yet all six nodes remain online. The three nodes in Data Center 1 believe that all of the nodes in Data Center 2 are unavailable. Conversely, the nodes in Data Center 2 believe that the nodes in Data Center 1 are unavailable. This leaves both sides (known as partitions) of the cluster thinking that they should take control. This can have unpredictable and undesirable consequences for any application that successfully connects to one or the other partition. *The Quorum = (Voting Members / 2) + 1* formula protects against this scenario.

Tip If your cluster loses quorum, then you can force one partition online, by starting the cluster service using the /fq switch. The partition that you force online is considered the *authoritative partition*. This means that other partitions can automatically rejoin the cluster when connectivity is reestablished.

Various quorum models are available and the most appropriate model depends on your environment. Table 14-4 lists the models that you can utilize and details the most appropriate way to use them.

Table 14-4. *Quorum Models*

Quorum Model	Appropriate Usage
Node Majority	When you have an odd number of nodes in the cluster
Node + Disk Witness Majority	When you have an even number of nodes in the cluster
Node + File Share Witness Majority	When you have nodes split across multiple sites or when you have an even number of nodes and are required to avoid shared disks*

Reasons for needing to avoid shared disks due to virtualization are discussed later in this chapter.

Although the default option is one node, one vote, it is possible to manually remove a nodes vote by changing the NodeWeight property to zero. This is useful if you have a *multi-subnet cluster* (a cluster in which the nodes are split across multiple sites). In this scenario, it is recommended that you use a file-share witness in a third site. This helps you avoid a cluster outage as a result of network failure between data centers. If you have an odd number of nodes in the quorum, however, then adding a file-share witness leaves you with an even number of votes, which is dangerous. Removing the vote from one of the nodes in the secondary data center eliminates this issue.

Caution   A file-share witness does not store a full copy of the quorum database. This means that a two-node cluster with a file-share witness is vulnerable to a scenario known as *partition in time*. In this scenario, if one node fails while you are in the process of patching or altering the cluster service on the second node, then there is no up-to-date copy of the quorum database. This leaves you in a position in which you need to destroy and rebuild the cluster.

Modern versions of Windows Server also support the concepts of Dynamic Quorum and Tie Breaker for 50% Node Split. When Dynamic Quorum is enabled, the cluster service automatically decides whether or not to give the quorum witness a vote, depending on the number of nodes in the cluster. If you have an even number of nodes, then it is assigned a vote. If you have an odd number of nodes, it is not assigned a vote. Tie Breaker for 50% Node Split expands on this concept. If you have an even number of nodes and a witness and the witness fails, then the cluster service automatically removes a vote from one random node within the cluster. This maintains an odd number of votes in the quorum and reduces the risk of a cluster going offline, due to a witness failure.

Tip   If your cluster is running in Windows Server 2016 or higher, with Datacenter Edition, then Storage Spaces Direct is supported. This allows high availability to be realized, using locally attached physical storage, with a software-defined storage layer on top. A full conversation around Storage Spaces Direct is beyond the scope of this book, but further details can be found at docs.microsoft.com/en-us/ windows-server/storage/storage-spaces/storage-spaces-direct-overview.

AlwaysOn Availability Groups

AlwaysOn Availability Groups (AOAG) replaces database mirroring and is essentially a merger of database mirroring and clustering technologies. SQL Server is installed as a stand-alone instance (as opposed to an AlwaysOn Failover Clustered Instance) on each node of a cluster. A cluster-aware application, called an Availability Group Listener, is then installed on the cluster; it is used to direct traffic to the correct node. Instead of relying on shared disks, however, AOAG compresses the log stream and sends it to the other nodes, in a similar fashion to database mirroring.

AOAG is the most appropriate technology for high availability in scenarios where you have small databases with low write profiles. This is because when used synchronously, it requires that the data is committed on all synchronous replicas before it is committed on the primary database. You can have up to eight replicas, including three synchronous replicas. AOAG may also be the most appropriate technology for implementing high availability in a virtualized environment. This is because the shared disk required by clustering may not be compatible with some features of the virtual estate. As an example, VMware does not support the use of vMotion, which is used to manually move virtual machines (VMs) between physical servers, and the Distributed Resource Scheduler (DRS), which is used to automatically move VMs between physical servers, based on resource utilization, when the VMs use shared disks, presented over Fiber Channel.

Tip   The limitations surrounding shared disks with VMware features can be worked around by presenting the storage directly to the guest OS over an iSCSI connection at the expense of performance degradation.

AOAG is the most appropriate technology for DR when you have a proactive failover requirement but when you do not need to implement a load delay. AOAG may also be suitable for disaster recovery in scenarios where you wish to utilize your DR server for offloading reporting. This allows the redundant servers to be utilized. When used for disaster recovery, AOAG works in an asynchronous mode. This means that it is possible to lose data in the event of a failover. The RPO is nondeterministic and is based on the time of the last uncommitted transaction.

Availability Groups allow you to configure one or more replicas as readable. The only limitation is that readable replicas and automatic failover cannot be configured on the same secondaries. The norm, however, would be to configure readable secondary replicas in asynchronous commit mode so that they do not impair performance.

To further simplify this, the Availability Group Replica checks for the read-only or read-intent properties in an application's connection string and points the application to the appropriate node. This means that you can easily scale reporting and database maintenance routines horizontally with very little development effort and with the applications being able to use a single connection string.

Because AOAG allows you to combine synchronous replicas (with or without automatic failover), asynchronous replicas, and replicas for read-only access, it allows you to satisfy high availability, disaster recovery, and reporting scale-out requirements using a single technology. If you're sole requirement is read scaling, as opposed to HA or DR, then it is actually possible to configure Availability Groups with no cluster. In this case, there is no cluster service, and hence no automatic redirection. Replicas within the Availability Group use certificate when communicating with each other. This is also true if you configure Availability Groups without AD, in a workgroup, or cross-domain.

When you are using AOAG, failover does not occur at the database level, nor at the instance level. Instead, failover occurs at the level of the availability group. The availability group is a concept that allows you to group related databases together so that they can fail over as an atomic unit. This is particularly useful in consolidated environments, because it allows you to group together the databases that map to a single application. You can then fail over this application to another replica for the purposes of DR testing, among other reasons, without having an impact on the other data-tier applications that are hosted on the instance.

No hard limits are imposed for the number of availability groups you can configure on an instance, nor are there any hard limits for the number of databases on an instance that can take part in AOAG. Microsoft, however, has tested up to, and officially recommends, a maximum of 100 databases and 10 availability groups per instance. The main limiting factor in scaling the number of databases is that AOAG uses a database mirroring endpoint and there can only be one per instance. This means that the log stream for all data modifications is sent over the same endpoint.

Figure 14-5 depicts how you can map data-tier applications to availability groups for independent failover. In this example, a single instance hosts two data-tier applications. Each application has been added to a separate availability group. The first availability group has failed over to Node2. Therefore, the availability group listeners point traffic for Application1 to Node2 and traffic for Application2 to Node1. Because each availability group has its own network name and IP address, and because these resources fail over with the AOAG, the application is able to seamlessly reconnect to the databases after failover.

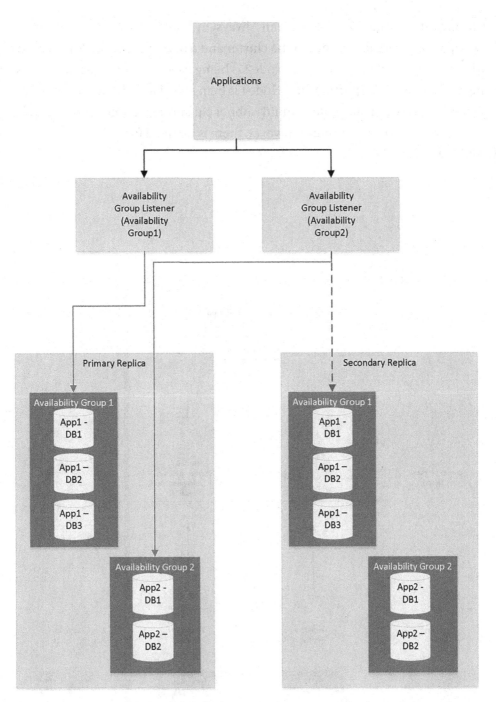

Figure 14-5. *Availability groups failover*

The diagram in Figure 14-6 depicts an AlwaysOn Availability Group topology. In this example, there are four nodes in the cluster and a disk witness. Node1 is hosting the primary replicas of the databases, Node2 is being used for automatic failover, Node3 is being used to offload reporting, and Node4 is being used for DR. Because the cluster is stretched across two data centers, multi-subnet clustering has been implemented. Because there is no shared storage, however, there is no need for SAN replication between the sites.

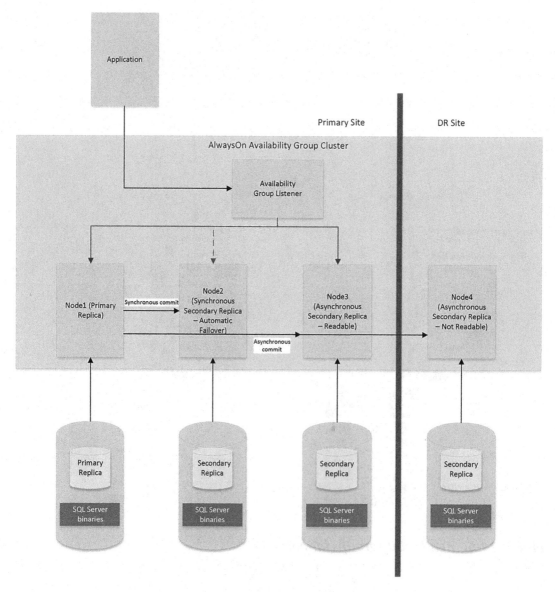

Figure 14-6. *AlwaysOn Availability Group topology*

Note   AlwaysOn Availability Groups are discussed in more detail in Chapter 15.

Automatic Page Repair

If a page becomes corrupt in a database configured as a replica in an AlwaysOn Availability Group topology, then SQL Server attempts to fix the corruption by obtaining a copy of the pages from one of the secondary replicas. This means that a logical corruption can be resolved without you needing to perform a restore or for you to run DBCC CHECKDB with a repair option. However, automatic page repair does not work for the following page types:

- File Header page

- Database Boot page

- Allocation pages

    - GAM (Global Allocation Map)

    - SGAM (Shared Global Allocation Map)

    - PFS (Page Free Space)

If the primary replica fails to read a page because it is corrupt, it first logs the page in the MSDB.dbo.suspect_pages table. It then checks that at least one replica is in the SYNCHRONIZED state and that transactions are still being sent to the replica. If these conditions are met, then the primary sends a broadcast to all replicas, specifying the PageID and LSN (log sequence number) at the end of the flushed log. The page is then marked as restore pending, meaning that any attempts to access it will fail, with error code 829.

After receiving the broadcast, the secondary replicas wait, until they have redone transactions up to the LSN specified in the broadcast message. At this point, they try to access the page. If they cannot access it, they return an error. If they *can* access the page, they send the page back to the primary replica. The primary replica accepts the page from the first secondary to respond.

The primary replica will then replace the corrupt copy of the page with the version that it received from the secondary replica. When this process completes, it updates the page in the MSDB.dbo.suspect_pages table to reflect that it has been repaired by setting the event_type column to a value of 5 (Repaired).

If the secondary replica fails to read a page while redoing the log because it is corrupt, it places the secondary into the SUSPENDED state. It then logs the page in the MSDB.dbo.suspect_pages table and requests a copy of the page from the primary replica. The primary replica attempts to access the page. If it is inaccessible, then it returns an error and the secondary replica remains in the SUSPENDED state.

If it can access the page, then it sends it to the secondary replica that requested it. The secondary replica replaces the corrupt page with the version that it obtained from the primary replica. It then updates the MSDB.dbo.suspect_pages table with an event_id of 5. Finally, it attempts to resume the AOAG session.

Note   It is possible to manually resume the session, but if you do, the corrupt page is hit again during the synchronization. Make sure you repair or restore the page on the primary replica first.

Log Shipping

Log shipping is a technology that you can use to implement disaster recovery. It works by backing up the transaction log on the principal server, copying it to the secondary server, and then restoring it. It is most appropriate to use log shipping in DR scenarios in which you require a load delay, because this is not possible with AOAG. As an example of where a load delay may be useful, consider a scenario in which a user accidently deletes all of the data from a table. If there is a delay before the database on the DR server is updated, then it is possible to recover the data for this table, from the DR server, and then repopulate the production server. This means that you do not need to restore a backup to recover the data. Log shipping is not appropriate for high availability, since there is no automatic failover functionality. The diagram in Figure 14-7 illustrates a log shipping topology.

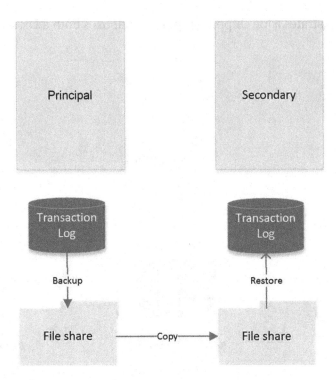

Figure 14-7. *Log Shipping topology*

Recovery Modes

In a log shipping topology, there is always exactly one principal server, which is the production server. It is possible to have multiple secondary servers, however, and these servers can be a mix of DR servers and servers used to offload reporting.

When you restore a transaction log, you can specify three recovery modes: Recovery, NoRecovery, and Standby. The Recovery mode brings the database online, which is not supported with Log Shipping. The NoRecovery mode keeps the database offline so that more backups can be restored. This is the normal configuration for log shipping and is the appropriate choice for DR scenarios.

The Standby option brings the database online, but in a read-only state so that you can restore further backups. This functionality works by maintaining a TUF (Transaction Undo File). The TUF file records any uncommitted transactions in the transaction log. This means that you can roll back these uncommitted transactions in the transaction log, which allows the database to be more accessible (although it is read-only). The next time a restore needs to be applied, you can reapply the uncommitted transaction in the TUF file to the log before the redo phase of the next log restore begins.

Figure 14-8 illustrates a log shipping topology that uses both a DR server and a reporting server.

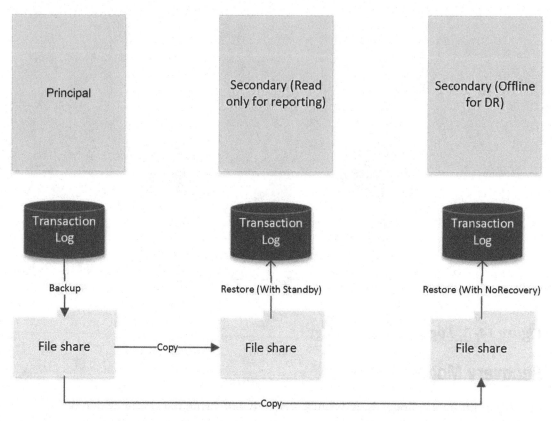

Figure 14-8. *Log shipping with DR and reporting servers*

Remote Monitor Server

Optionally, you can configure a monitor server in your log shipping topology. This helps you centralize monitoring and alerting. When you implement a monitor server, the history and status of all backup, copy, and restore operations are stored on the monitor server. A monitor server also allows you to have a single alert job, which is configured to monitor the backup, copy, and restore operations on all servers, as opposed to it needing separate alerts on each server in the topology.

> **Caution**   If you wish to use a monitor server, it is important to configure it when you set up log shipping. After log shipping has been configured, the only way to add a monitor server is to tear down and reconfigure log shipping.

Failover

Unlike other high availability and disaster recovery technologies, an amount of administrative effort is associated with failing over log shipping. To fail over log shipping, you must back up the tail end of the transaction log, and copy it, along with any other uncopied backup files, to the secondary server.

You now need to apply the remaining transaction log backups to the secondary server in sequence, finishing with the tail-log backup. You apply the final restore using the WITH RECOVERY option to bring the database back online in a consistent state. If you are not planning to fail back, you can reconfigure log shipping with the secondary server as the new primary server.

> **Note**   Log shipping is discussed in further detail in Chapter 16. Backups and restores are discussed in further detail in Chapter 13.

Combining Technologies

To meet your business objectives and nonfunctional requirements (NFRs), you need to combine multiple high availability and disaster recovery technologies together to create a reliable, scalable platform. A classic example of this is the requirement to combine an AlwaysOn Failover Cluster with AlwaysOn Availability Groups.

The reason you may need to combine these technologies is that when you use AlwaysOn Availability Groups in synchronous mode, which you must do for automatic failover, it can cause a performance impediment. As discussed earlier in this chapter, the performance issue is caused by the transaction being committed on the secondary server before being committed on the primary server. Clustering does not suffer from this issue, however, because it relies on a shared disk resource, and therefore the transaction is only committed once.

Therefore, it is common practice to first use a cluster to achieve high availability and then use AlwaysOn Availability Groups to perform DR and/or offload reporting. The diagram in Figure 14-9 illustrates a HA/DR topology that combines clustering and AOAG to achieve high availability and disaster recovery, respectively.

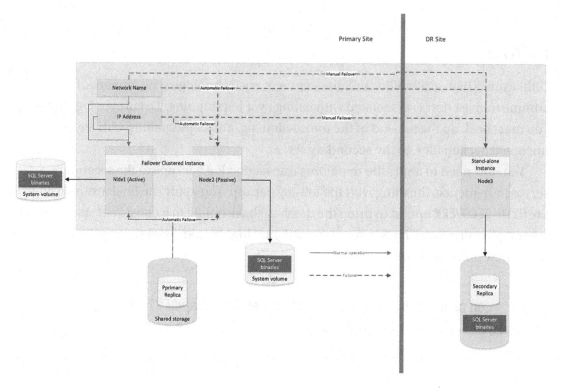

Figure 14-9. *Clustering and AlwaysOn Availability Groups combined*

The diagram in Figure 14-9 shows that the primary replica of the database is hosted on a two-node active/passive cluster. If the active node fails, the rules of clustering apply, and the shared storage, network name, and IP address are reattached to the passive node, which then becomes the active node. If both nodes are inaccessible, however, the availability group listener points the traffic to the third node of the cluster, which is situated in the DR site and is synchronized using log stream replication. Of course, when asynchronous mode is used, the database must be failed over manually by a DBA.

Another common scenario is the combination of a cluster and log shipping to achieve high availability and disaster recovery, respectively. This combination works in much the same way as clustering combined with AlwaysOn Availability Groups and is illustrated in Figure 14-10.

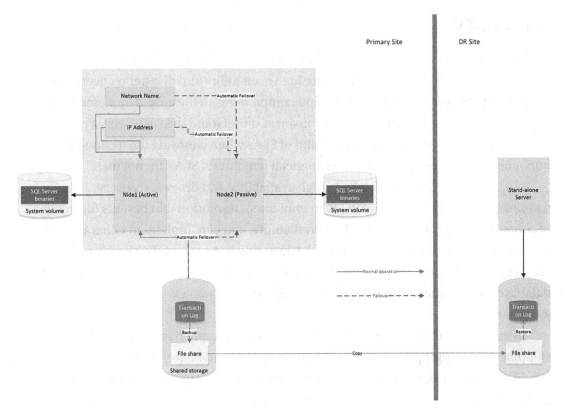

Figure 14-10. *Clustering combined with log shipping*

The diagram shows that a two-node active/passive cluster has been configured in the primary data center. The transaction log(s) of the database(s) hosted on this instance are then shipped to a stand-alone server in the DR data center. Because the cluster uses shared storage, you should also use shared storage for the backup volume and add the backup volume as a resource in the role. This means that when the instance fails over to the other node, the backup share also fails over, and log shipping continues to synchronize, uninterrupted.

Caution   If failover occurs while the log shipping backup or copy jobs are in progress, then log shipping may become unsynchronized and require manual intervention. This means that after a failover, you should check the health of your log shipping jobs.

Summary

Understanding the concepts of availability is key to making the correct implementation choices for your applications that require high availability and disaster recovery. You should calculate the cost of downtime and compare this to the cost of implementing choices of HA/DR solutions to help the business understand the cost/benefit profile of each option. You should also be mindful of SLAs when choosing the technology implementation, since there could be financial penalties if SLAs are not met.

SQL Server provides a full suite of high availability and disaster recovery technologies, giving you the flexibility to implement a solution that best fits the needs of your data-tier applications. For high availability, you can implement either clustering or AlwaysOn Availability Groups (AOAG). Clustering uses a shared disk resource and failover occurs at the instance level. AOAG, on the other hand, synchronizes data at the database level by maintaining a redundant copy of the database with a synchronous log stream.

To implement disaster recovery, you can choose to implement AOAG or log shipping. Log shipping works by backing up, copying, and restoring the transaction logs of the databases, whereas AOAG synchronizes the data using an asynchronous log stream.

It is also possible to combine multiple HA and DR technologies together in order to implement the most appropriate availability strategy. Common examples of this are combining clustering for high availability with AOAG or log shipping to provide DR.

## CHAPTER 15

Implementing AlwaysOn Availability Groups

AlwaysOn Availability Groups provide a flexible option for achieving high availability, recovering from disasters, and scaling out read-only workloads. The technology synchronizes data at the database level, but health monitoring and quorum are provided by a Windows cluster.

There are different variations of AlwaysOn Availability Groups. The traditional flavor sits on a Windows Failover Cluster, but if SQL Server is installed on Linux, then Pacemaker can be used. Since SQL Server 2017, AlwaysOn Availability Groups can also be configured with no cluster at all. This is acceptable for offloading reporting but is not a valid HA or DR configuration. When using SQL Server 2019 with Windows Server 2019, Availability Groups can even be configured for containerized SQL, with Kubernetes.

This chapter focuses on configuring Availability Groups on a Windows Failover Cluster, for the purpose of providing both high availability (HA) and disaster recovery (DR). We also discuss Availability Groups on Linux and Distributed Availability Groups. We discuss using availability groups to scale out read-only workloads in Chapter 17.

Note   For the demonstrations in this chapter, we use a domain that contains a domain controller and a three-node cluster. The cluster has no shared storage for data and there is no AlwaysOn Failover Clustered Instance. Each node has a stand-alone instance of SQL Server installed on it named `ClusterNode1\PrimaryReplica`, `ClusterNode2\SyncHA`, and `ClusterNode3\AsyncDR`, respectively. CLUSTERNODE1 and CLUSTERNODE2 are in Site1 and CLUSTERNODE3 resides in Site2, meaning that the cluster is stretched across

---

© Peter A. Carter 2023
P. A. Carter, *Pro SQL Server 2022 Administration*, https://doi.org/10.1007/978-1-4842-8864-1_15

subnets. Full details of how to build a Failover Cluster or a Failover Clustered Instance are beyond the scope of this book, but full details can be found in the Apress title *AlwaysOn Revealed*, which can be found at `www.apress.com/gb/ book/9781484223963`.

Implementing AlwaysOn Availability Groups

Before implementing AlwaysOn Availability Groups, we first create three databases, which we will use during the demonstrations in this chapter. Two of the databases relate to the fictional application, App1, and the third database relates to the fictional application, App2. Each contains a single table, which we populate with data. Each database is configured with Recovery mode set to FULL. This is a hard requirement for a database to use AlwaysOn Availability Groups because data is synchronized via a log stream. The script in Listing 15-1 creates these databases.

Listing 15-1. Creating Databases

```
CREATE DATABASE Chapter15App1Customers ;
GO

ALTER DATABASE Chapter15App1Customers SET RECOVERY FULL ;
GO

USE Chapter15App1Customers
GO

CREATE TABLE App1Customers
(
ID                 INT              PRIMARY KEY      IDENTITY,
FirstName          NVARCHAR(30),
LastName           NVARCHAR(30),
CreditCardNumber   VARBINARY(8000)
) ;
GO
```

```
--Populate the table

DECLARE @Numbers TABLE
(
        Number          INT
)

;WITH CTE(Number)
AS
(
        SELECT 1 Number
        UNION ALL
        SELECT Number + 1
        FROM CTE
        WHERE Number < 100
)
INSERT INTO @Numbers
SELECT Number FROM CTE

DECLARE @Names TABLE
(
        FirstName          VARCHAR(30),
        LastName           VARCHAR(30)
) ;

INSERT INTO @Names
VALUES('Peter', 'Carter'),
                ('Michael', 'Smith'),
                ('Danielle', 'Mead'),
                ('Reuben', 'Roberts'),
                ('Iris', 'Jones'),
                ('Sylvia', 'Davies'),
                ('Finola', 'Wright'),
                ('Edward', 'James'),
                ('Marie', 'Andrews'),
                ('Jennifer', 'Abraham'),
                ('Margaret', 'Jones')
```

```sql
INSERT INTO App1Customers(Firstname, LastName, CreditCardNumber)
SELECT   FirstName, LastName, CreditCardNumber FROM
         (SELECT
                 (SELECT TOP 1 FirstName FROM @Names ORDER BY NEWID())
                 FirstName
                 ,(SELECT TOP 1 LastName FROM @Names ORDER BY NEWID())
                 LastName
                 ,(SELECT CONVERT(VARBINARY(8000)
                 ,(SELECT TOP 1 CAST(Number * 100 AS CHAR(4))
                   FROM @Numbers
                   WHERE Number BETWEEN 10 AND 99 ORDER BY NEWID()) + '-' +
                         (SELECT TOP 1 CAST(Number * 100 AS CHAR(4))
                          FROM @Numbers
                          WHERE Number BETWEEN 10 AND 99 ORDER BY
                          NEWID()) + '-' +
                         (SELECT TOP 1 CAST(Number * 100 AS CHAR(4))
                          FROM @Numbers
                          WHERE Number BETWEEN 10 AND 99 ORDER BY
                          NEWID()) + '-' +
                         (SELECT TOP 1 CAST(Number * 100 AS CHAR(4))
                          FROM @Numbers
                          WHERE Number BETWEEN 10 AND 99 ORDER BY NEWID()))))
                         CreditCardNumber
FROM @Numbers a
CROSS JOIN @Numbers b
CROSS JOIN @Numbers c
) d ;

CREATE DATABASE Chapter15App1Sales ;
GO

ALTER DATABASE Chapter15App1Sales SET RECOVERY FULL ;
GO

USE Chapter15App1Sales
GO
```

```
CREATE TABLE [dbo].[Orders](
        [OrderNumber] [int] IDENTITY(1,1) NOT NULL PRIMARY KEY CLUSTERED,
        [OrderDate] [date]  NOT NULL,
        [CustomerID] [int]  NOT NULL,
        [ProductID] [int]   NOT NULL,
        [Quantity] [int]    NOT NULL,
        [NetAmount] [money] NOT NULL,
        [TaxAmount] [money] NOT NULL,
        [InvoiceAddressID] [int] NOT NULL,
        [DeliveryAddressID] [int] NOT NULL,
        [DeliveryDate] [date] NULL,
) ;

DECLARE @Numbers TABLE
(
        Number          INT
)

;WITH CTE(Number)
AS
(
        SELECT 1 Number
        UNION ALL
        SELECT Number + 1
        FROM CTE
        WHERE Number < 100
)
INSERT INTO @Numbers
SELECT Number FROM CTE

--Populate ExistingOrders with data

INSERT INTO Orders
SELECT
        (SELECT CAST(DATEADD(dd,(SELECT TOP 1 Number
                            FROM @Numbers
                            ORDER BY NEWID()),getdate())as DATE)),
```

```
            (SELECT TOP 1 Number -10 FROM @Numbers ORDER BY NEWID()),
            (SELECT TOP 1 Number FROM @Numbers ORDER BY NEWID()),
            (SELECT TOP 1 Number FROM @Numbers ORDER BY NEWID()),
        500,
        100,
            (SELECT TOP 1 Number FROM @Numbers ORDER BY NEWID()),
            (SELECT TOP 1 Number FROM @Numbers ORDER BY NEWID()),
            (SELECT CAST(DATEADD(dd,(SELECT TOP 1 Number - 10
             FROM @Numbers
             ORDER BY NEWID()),getdate() as DATE))
FROM @Numbers a
CROSS JOIN @Numbers b
CROSS JOIN @Numbers c ;

CREATE DATABASE Chapter15App2Customers ;
GO

ALTER DATABASE Chapter15App2Customers SET RECOVERY FULL ;
GO

USE Chapter15App2Customers
GO

CREATE TABLE App2Customers
(
ID                 INT                PRIMARY KEY        IDENTITY,
FirstName          NVARCHAR(30),
LastName           NVARCHAR(30),
CreditCardNumber   VARBINARY(8000)
) ;
GO

--Populate the table

DECLARE @Numbers TABLE
(
        Number        INT
) ;
```

```
;WITH CTE(Number)
AS
(
        SELECT 1 Number
        UNION ALL
        SELECT Number + 1
        FROM CTE
        WHERE Number < 100
)
INSERT INTO @Numbers
SELECT Number FROM CTE ;

DECLARE @Names TABLE
(
        FirstName          VARCHAR(30),
        LastName           VARCHAR(30)
) ;

INSERT INTO @Names
VALUES('Peter', 'Carter'),
                ('Michael', 'Smith'),
                ('Danielle', 'Mead'),
                ('Reuben', 'Roberts'),
                ('Iris', 'Jones'),
                ('Sylvia', 'Davies'),
                ('Finola', 'Wright'),
                ('Edward', 'James'),
                ('Marie', 'Andrews'),
                ('Jennifer', 'Abraham'),
                ('Margaret', 'Jones')

INSERT INTO App2Customers(Firstname, LastName, CreditCardNumber)
SELECT  FirstName, LastName, CreditCardNumber FROM
        (SELECT
                (SELECT TOP 1 FirstName FROM @Names ORDER BY NEWID())
                FirstName
```

```
        ,(SELECT TOP 1 LastName FROM @Names ORDER BY NEWID())
        LastName
        ,(SELECT CONVERT(VARBINARY(8000)
        ,(SELECT TOP 1 CAST(Number * 100 AS CHAR(4))
          FROM @Numbers
          WHERE Number BETWEEN 10 AND 99 ORDER BY NEWID()) + '-' +
              (SELECT TOP 1 CAST(Number * 100 AS CHAR(4))
               FROM @Numbers
               WHERE Number BETWEEN 10 AND 99 ORDER BY
               NEWID()) + '-' +
              (SELECT TOP 1 CAST(Number * 100 AS CHAR(4))
               FROM @Numbers
               WHERE Number BETWEEN 10 AND 99 ORDER BY
               NEWID()) + '-' +
              (SELECT TOP 1 CAST(Number * 100 AS CHAR(4))
               FROM @Numbers
               WHERE Number BETWEEN 10 AND 99 ORDER BY NEWID())))
        CreditCardNumber
FROM @Numbers a
CROSS JOIN @Numbers b
CROSS JOIN @Numbers c
) d ;
```

Configuring SQL Server

The first step in configuring AlwaysOn Availability Groups is enabling this feature
on the SQL Server service. To enable the feature from the GUI, we open SQL Server
Configuration Manager, drill through SQL Server Services and select Properties from the
context menu of the SQL Server service. When we do this, the service properties display
and we navigate to the AlwaysOn High Availability tab, shown in Figure 15-1.

On this tab, we check the Enable AlwaysOn Availability Groups box and ensure that
the cluster name displayed in the Windows Failover Cluster Name box is correct. We
then need to restart the SQL Server service. Because AlwaysOn Availability Groups use
stand-alone instances, which are installed locally on each cluster node, as opposed to a
failover clustered instance, which spans multiple nodes, we need to repeat these steps
for each stand-alone instance hosted on the cluster.

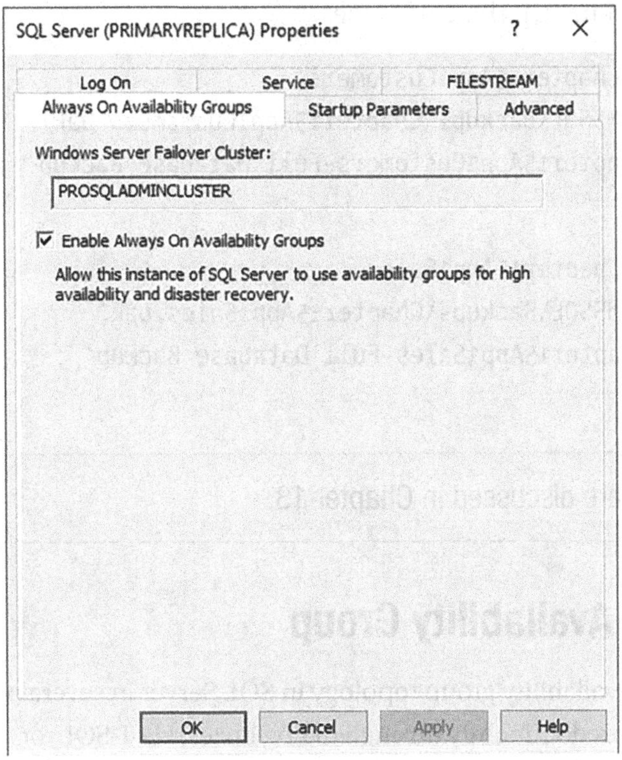

Figure 15-1. *The AlwaysOn High Avaiability tab*

We can also use PowerShell to enable AlwaysOn Availability Groups. To do this, we use the PowerShell command in Listing 15-2. The script assumes that CLUSTERNODE1 is the name of the server and that PRIMARYREPLICA is the name of the SQL Server instance.

Listing 15-2. Enabling AlwaysOn Availability Groups

```
Enable-SqlAlwaysOn -Path SQLSERVER:\SQL\CLUSTERNODE1\PRIMARYREPLICA
```

The next step is to take a full backup of all databases that will be part of the availability group. We will not be able to add them to an Availability Group until this has been done. We create separate availability groups for App1 and App2, respectively, so to create an availability group for App1, we need to back up the Chapter15App1Customers and Chapter15App1Sales databases. We do this by running the script in Listing 15-3.

Listing 15-3. Backing Up the Databases

```
BACKUP DATABASE Chapter15App1Customers
TO  DISK = N'C:\MSSQL\Backups\Chapter15App1Customers.bak'
WITH NAME = N'Chapter15App1Customers-Full Database Backup' ;
GO

BACKUP DATABASE Chapter15App1Sales
TO  DISK = N'C:\MSSQL\Backups\Chapter15App1Sales.bak'
WITH NAME = N'Chapter15App1Sales-Full Database Backup' ;
GO
```

Note   Backups are discussed in Chapter 13.

Creating the Availability Group

You can create an availability group topology in SQL Server in several ways. It can be created manually, predominantly through dialog boxes, via T-SQL, or through a wizard. In this chapter, we will explore the wizard and the dialog boxes.

Using the New Availability Group Wizard

When the backups complete successfully, we invoke the New Availability Group wizard by drilling through AlwaysOn High Availability in Object Explorer and selecting the New Availability Group wizard from the context menu of the Availability Groups folder. The Introduction page of the wizard is displayed, giving us an overview of the steps that we need to undertake.

On the Specify Name page (see Figure 15-2), we are prompted to enter a name for our availability group. We will also select Windows Server Failover Cluster as the Cluster Type. Other options for cluster type are external, which supports Pacemaker on Linux and None, which is used for Clusterless Availability Groups. The Database Level Health Detection option will cause the Availability Group to fail over, should any database within the group go offline. The Per Database DTC Support option will specify if cross-database transactions are supported, using MSDTC (Microsoft Distributed Transaction Coordinator). The option to make the Availability Group contained makes synchronizing instance-level objects easier. Contained availability groups are discussed later in this chapter.

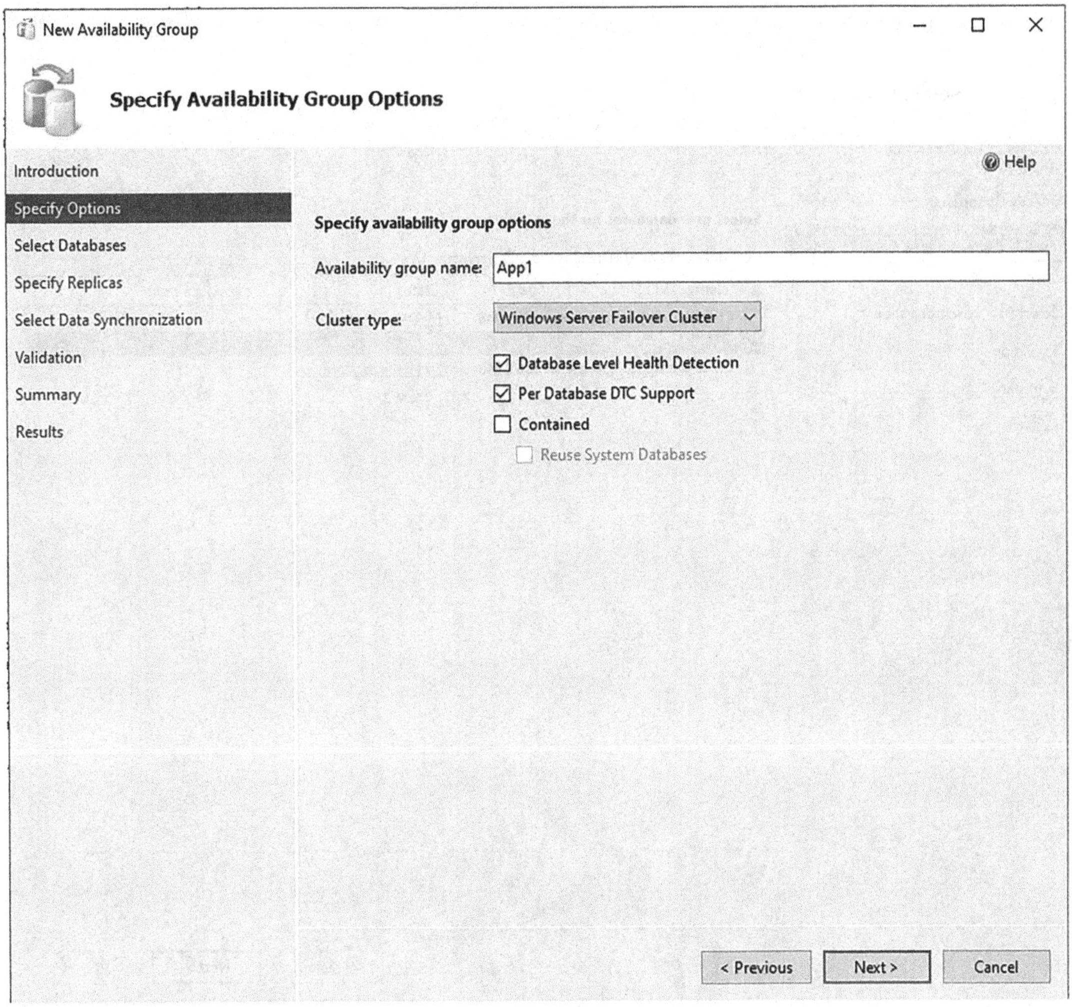

Figure 15-2. *The Specify Name page*

On the Select Databases page, we are prompted to select the database(s) that we wish to participate in the availability group, as illustrated in Figure 15-3. On this screen, notice that we cannot select the Chapter15App2Customers database, because we have not yet taken a full backup of the database.

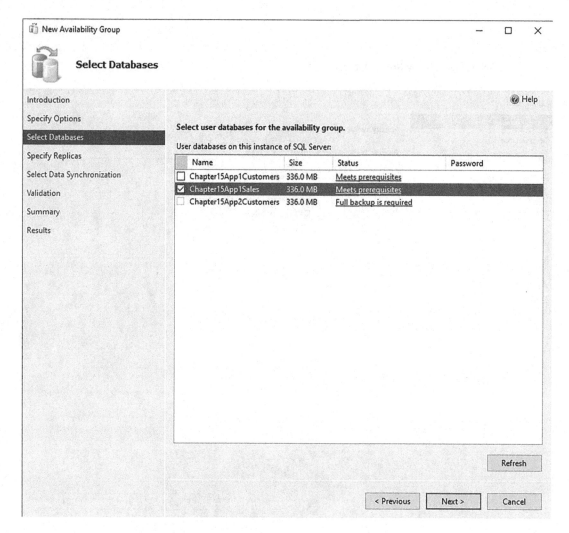

Figure 15-3. *The Select Databases page*

The Specify Replicas page consists of four tabs. We use the first tab, Replicas, to add the secondary replicas to the topology. Checking the Synchronous Commit option causes data to be committed on the secondary replica before it is committed on the primary replica. (This is also referred to as *hardening the log* on the secondary before the primary.) This means that, in the event of a failover, data loss is not possible, meaning that we can meet an SLA (service-level agreement) with an RPO (recovery point objective) of 0 (zero). It also means that there will be a performance degradation, however. If we choose Asynchronous Commit, then the replica operates in Asynchronous Commit mode. This means that data is committed on the primary replica before being committed on the secondary replica. This stops us from suffering performance degradation, but it also means that, in the event of failover, the RPO is nondeterministic. Performance considerations for synchronous replicas are discussed later in this chapter.

When we check the Automatic Failover option, the Synchronous Commit option is also selected automatically if we have not already selected it. This is because automatic failover is only possible in Synchronous Commit mode. We can set the Readable Secondary drop-down to No, Yes, or Read-intent. When we set it to No, the database is not accessible on replicas that are in a secondary role. When we set it to Read-intent, the Availability Group Listener can redirect read-only workloads to this secondary replica, but only if the application has specified `Application Intent=Read-only` in the connection string. Setting it to Yes enables the listener to redirect read-only traffic, regardless of whether the `Application Intent` parameter is present in the application's connection string. Although we can change the value of Readable Secondary through the GUI while at the same time configuring a replica for automatic failover without error, this is simply a quirk of the wizard. In fact, the replica is not accessible, since active secondaries are not supported when configured for automatic failover. The Replicas tab is illustrated in Figure 15-4. To meet our requirement of achieving HA and DR, we have configured the secondary server within the same site as a synchronous replica and configured the server in a different site as asynchronous. This means that the latency between data centers will not compound the performance degradation, which is associated with synchronous commits.

Note   Using secondary replicas for read-only workloads is discussed in more depth in Chapter 17.

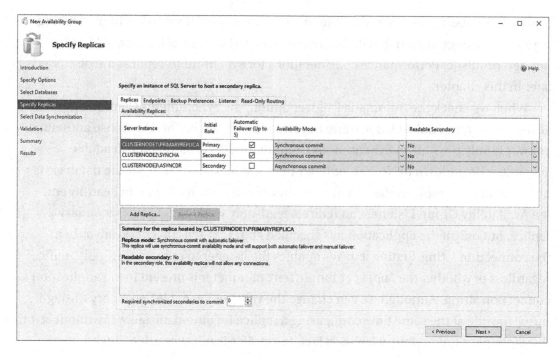

Figure 15-4. *The Replicas tab*

On the Endpoints tab of the Specify Replicas page, illustrated in Figure 15-5, we specify the port number for each endpoint. The default port is 5022, but we can specify a different port if we need to. On this tab, we also specify if data should be encrypted when it is sent between the endpoints. It is usually a good idea to check this option, and if we do, then AES (Advanced Encryption Standard) is used as the encryption algorithm.

Optionally, you can also change the name of the endpoint that is created. Because only one database mirroring endpoint is allowed per instance, however, and because the default name is fairly descriptive, there is not always a reason to change it. Some DBAs choose to rename it to include the name of the instance, since this can simplify the management of multiple servers. This is a good idea if your enterprise has many availability group clusters.

The service account each instance uses is displayed for informational purposes. It simplifies security administration if you ensure that the same service account is used by both instances. If you fail to do this, you will need to grant each instance permissions to each service account. This means that instead of reducing the security footprint of each service account by using it for one instance only, you simply push the footprint up to the SQL Server level instead of the operating system level.

The endpoint URL specifies the URL of the endpoint that availability groups will use to communicate. The format of the URL is `[Transport Protocol]://[Path]:[Port]`. The transport protocol for a database mirroring endpoint is always TCP (Transmission Control Protocol). The path can either be the fully qualified domain name (FQDN) of the server, the server name on its own, or an IP address, which is unique across the network. I recommend using the FQDN of the server, because this is always guaranteed to work. It is also the default value populated. The port should match the port number that you specify for the endpoint.

Note   Availability groups communicate with a database mirroring endpoint. Although database mirroring is deprecated, the endpoints are not.

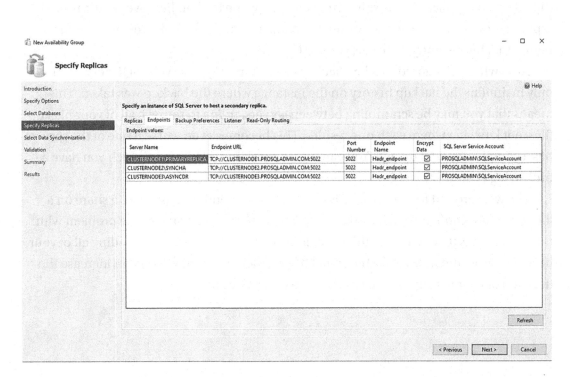

Figure 15-5. *The Endpoints tab*

On the Backup Preferences tab (see Figure 15-6), we can specify the replica on which automated backups will be taken. One of the big advantages of AlwaysOn Availability Groups is that when you use them, you can scale out maintenance tasks, such as backups, to secondary servers. Therefore, automated backups can seamlessly be directed to active secondaries. The possible options are Prefer Secondary, Secondary Only, Primary, or Any Replica. It is also possible to set priorities for each replica. When determining which replica to run the backup job against, SQL Server evaluates the backup priorities of each node and is more likely to choose the replica with the highest priority.

Although the advantages of reducing I/O on the primary replica are obvious, I, somewhat controversially, recommend against scaling automated backups to secondary replicas in many cases. This is especially the case when RTO (recovery time objective) is a priority for the application because of operational supportability issues. Imagine a scenario in which backups are being taken against a secondary replica and a user calls to say that they have accidently deleted all data from a critical table. You now need to restore a copy of the database and repopulate the table. The backup files, however, sit on the secondary replica. As a result, you need to copy the backup files over to the primary replica before you can begin to restore the database (or perform the restore over the network). This instantly increases your RTO.

Also, when configured to allow backups against multiple servers, SQL Server still only maintains the backup history on the instance where the backup was taken. This means that you may be scrambling between servers, trying to retrieve all of your backup files, not knowing where each one resides. This becomes even worse if one of the servers has a complete system outage. You can find yourself in a scenario in which you have a broken log chain.

The workaround for most of the issues that I just mentioned is to use a share on a file server and configure each instance to back up to the same share. The problem with this, however, is that by setting things up in this manner, you are now sending all of your backups across the network rather than backing them up locally. This can increase the duration of your backups as well as increase network traffic.

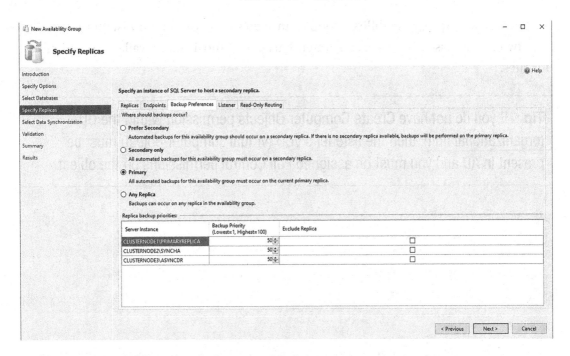

Figure 15-6. *The Backup Preferences tab*

On the Listener tab, shown in Figure 15-7, we choose if we want to create an availability group listener or if we want to defer this task until later. If we choose to create the listener, then we need to specify the listener's name, the port that it should listen on, and the IP address(es) that it should use. We specify one address for each subnet, in multi-subnet clusters. The details provided here are used to create the client access point resource in the availability group's cluster role. You may notice that we have specified port 1433 for the listener, although our instance is also running on port 1433. This is a valid configuration, because the listener is configured on a different IP address than the SQL Server instance. It is also not mandatory to use the same port number, but it can be beneficial, if you are implementing AlwaysOn Availability Groups on an existing instance because applications that specify the port number to connect may need fewer application changes. Remember that the server name will still be different, however, because applications will be connecting to the virtual name of the listener, as opposed to the name of the physical server\instance. In our example, applications connect to `APP1LISTEN\PRIMARYREPLICA` instead of `CLUSTERNODE1\PRIMARYREPLICA`. Although connections via `CLUSTERNODE1` are still permitted, they do not benefit from high availability or scale-out reporting.

Because our App1 Availability Group spans two subnets, then our Listener must have two IP addresses, one in each subnet. This makes the listener available in either of our sites.

Tip   If you do not have Create Computer Objects permission within the OU (organizational unit), then the listener's VCO (virtual computer object) must be present in AD and you must be assigned Full Control permissions on the object.

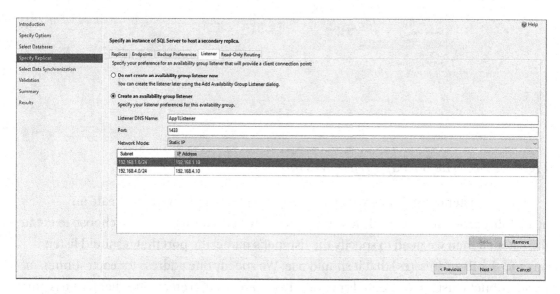

Figure 15-7. *The Listener tab*

On the Select Initial Data Synchronization screen, shown in Figure 15-8, we choose how the initial data synchronization of the replicas is performed. If you choose Full, then each database that participates in the availability group is subject to a full backup, followed by a log backup. The backup files are backed up to a share, which you specify, before they are restored to the secondary servers. The share path can be specified using either Windows or Linux formats, depending on your requirements. After the restore is complete, data synchronization, via log stream, commences.

If you have already backed up your databases and restored them onto the secondaries, then you can select the Join Only option. This starts the data synchronization, via log stream, on the databases within the availability group. Selecting Skip initial data synchronization allows you to back up and restore the databases yourself after you complete the setup.

If you select the Automatic seeding option, then an empty database is initially created on each Replica. The data is then seeding using VDI over the log stream transport. This option is slower than initializing with a backup but avoid transferring large backup files between shares.

> **Tip**   If your availability group will contain many databases, then it may be best to perform the backup/restore yourself. This is because the inbuilt utility will perform the actions sequentially, and therefore, it may take a long time to complete.

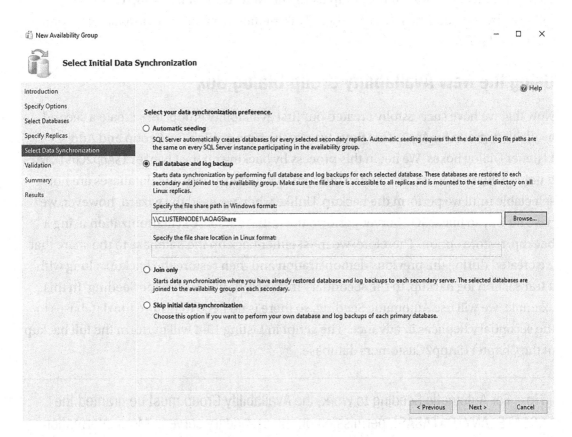

Figure 15-8. *The Select Data Synchronization page*

On the Validation page, rules that may cause the setup to fail are checked. If any of the results come back as Failed, then you need to resolve them before you attempt to continue.

Once validation tests are complete and we move to the Summary page, we are presented with a list of the tasks that are to be carried out during the setup.

As setup progresses, the results of each configuration task display on the Results page. If any errors occur on this page, be sure to investigate them, but this does not necessarily mean that the entire availability group needs to be reconfigured. For example, if the creation of the availability group listener fails because the VCO had not been presented in AD, then you can re-create the listener without needing to re-create the entire availability group.

As an alternative to using the New Availability Group wizard, you can perform the configuration of the availability group using the New Availability Group dialog box, followed by the Add Listener dialog box. This method of creating an availability group is examined later in this chapter.

Using the New Availability Group Dialog Box

Now that we have successfully created our first availability group, let's create a second availability group for App2. This time, we use the New Availability Group and Add Listener Dialog boxes. We begin this process by backing up the Chapter15App2Customers database. Just like when we created the App1 availability group, the databases are not selectable until we perform the backup. Unlike when we used the wizard, however, we have no way to make SQL Server perform the initial database synchronization using a backup/restore option. Therefore, we must either back up the database to the share that we created during the previous demonstration and then restore the backup, along with a transaction log backup, to the secondary instance, or use Automatic Seeding. In this example, we will use Automatic Seeding, so there is no need to restore the databases to the secondary Replicas in advance. The script in Listing 15-4 will perform the full backup of the Chapter15App2Customers database.

Tip   For Automatic Seeding to work, the Availability Group must be granted the CREATE ANY DATABASE permission on the secondary servers. More information about granting permissions can be found in Chapter 10.

Listing 15-4. Backing Up and Restoring the Database

```
--Back Up Database

BACKUP DATABASE [Chapter15App2Customers] TO  DISK = N'\\CLUSTERNODE1\
AOAGShare\Chapter15App2Customers.bak' WITH  COPY_ONLY, FORMAT, INIT,
REWIND, COMPRESSION,  STATS = 5 ;
GO
```

Tip   COPY_ONLY takes a full backup, but does not break the backup chain. Please see Chapter 13 for further details on backups.

If we had not already created an availability group, then our next job would be to create a TCP endpoint so the instances could communicate. We would then need to create a login for the service account on each instance and grant it the connect permissions on the endpoints. Because we can only ever have one database mirroring endpoint per instance, however, we are not required to create a new one, and obviously we have no reason to grant the service account additional privileges. Therefore, we continue by creating the availability group. To do this, we drill through AlwaysOn High Availability in Object Explorer and select New Availability Group from the context menu of availability groups.

This causes the General tab of the New Availability Group dialog box to display, as illustrated in Figure 15-9. On this screen, we type the name of the availability group in the first field. Then we click the Add button under the Availability Databases window before we type the name of the database that we wish to add to the group. We then need to click the Add button under the Availability Replicas window before we type the server\instance name of the secondary replica in the new row. For our use case, there is no need to specify the Per database DTC support or Database level health detection settings, as there is only a single database within the Availability Group. We have set Required synchronized secondaries to commit to 1, however. This setting guarantees that the specified number of secondary replicas writes the transaction data to log before the primary replica commits each transaction. In our scenario, where we only have a single synchronous secondary, that in the event of a failure on the Primary Replica, failover will happen automatically, but the Secondary Replica will not allow user transactions to be written to the database, until the original Primary Replica comes back online. This absolutely guarantees that there can be no data loss in any circumstances.

If we had left this setting as 0 (as we did in the first example in this chapter), then in the event that the Primary Replica failed and users wrote transactions to the Secondary Replica, before this Replica also failed, then data loss could occur, as the only other Replica uses asynchronous commit mode. The default setting is 0 and the maximum setting is the number of synchronous replicas—1. In SQL Server 2022, it is now possible to configure required synchronous replicas for Distributed Availability Groups. Distributed Availability Groups are discussed later in this chapter.

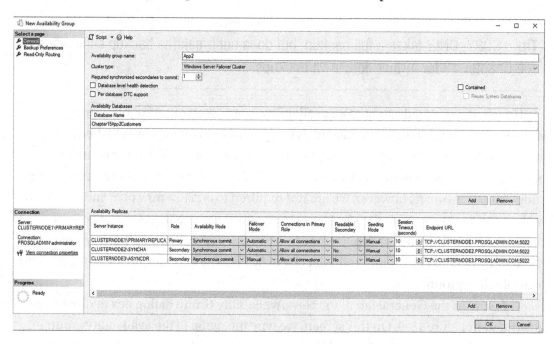

Figure 15-9. *The New Availability Group dialog box*

Now we can begin to set the replica properties. We discussed the Role, Availability Mode, Failover Mode, Readable Secondary, and Endpoint URL properties when we created the App1 availability group. The Connection In Primary Role property defines what connections can be made to the replica if the replica is in the primary role. You can configure this as either Allow All Connections or Allow Read/Write Connections. When Read/Write is specified, applications using the Application Intent = Read only parameter in their connection string will not be able to connect to the replica.

The Session Timeout property sets how long the replicas can go without receiving a ping from one another before they enter the DISCONNECTED state and the session ends. Although it is possible to set this value to as low as 5 seconds, it is usually a good idea to keep the setting at 60 seconds; otherwise, you run the risk of a false positive response, resulting in unnecessary failover. If a replica times out, it needs to be resynchronized, since transactions on the primary will no longer wait for the secondary, even if the secondary is running in Synchronous Commit mode.

On the Backup Preferences tab of the dialog box, we define the preferred replica to use for automated backup jobs, as shown in Figure 15-10. Just like when using the wizard, we can specify Primary, or we can choose between enforcing and preferring backups to occur on a secondary replica. We can also configure a weight, between 0 and 100 for each replica, and use the Exclude Replica check box to avoid backups being taken on a specific node.

Tip   Excluding Replicas from backups can help if you are using Software Assurance, and although your licensing allows you to keep a secondary replica synchronized for the purpose of either HA or DR, it does not allow you to perform other tasks (such as backups) on this secondary server.

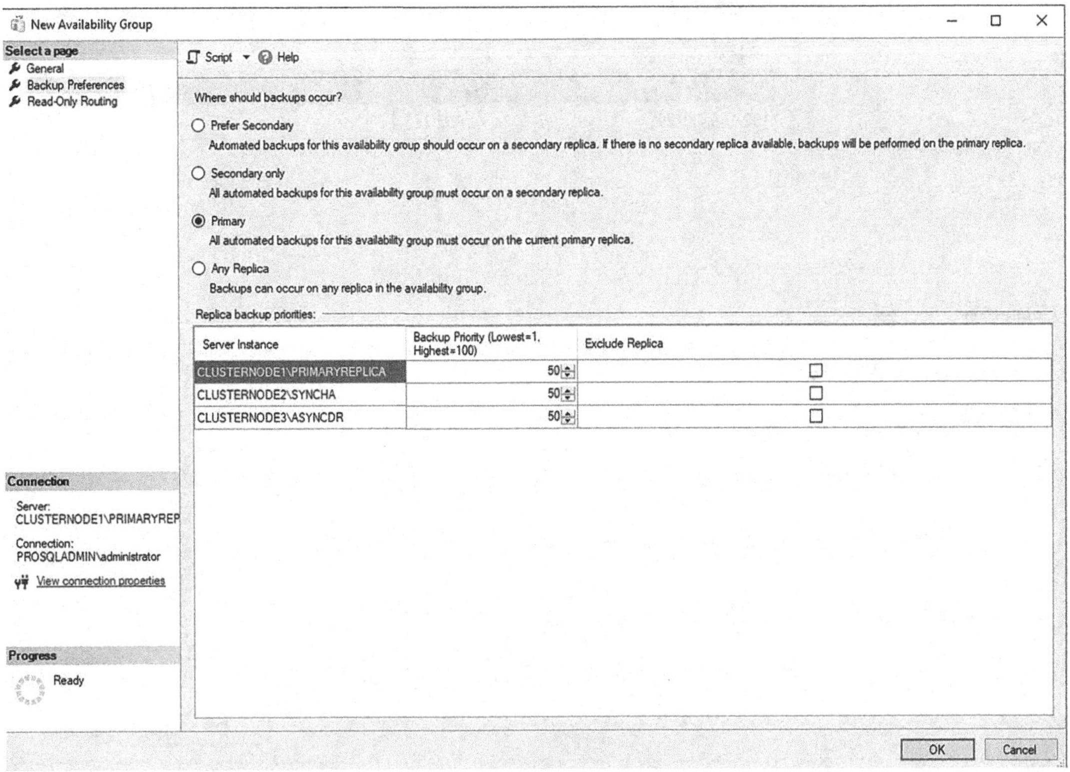

Figure 15-10. *The Backup Preferences tab*

Once we have created the availability group, we need to create the availability group listener. To do this, we select New Listener from the context menu of the App2 availability group, which should now be visible in Object Explorer. This invokes the New Availability Group Listener dialog box, which can be seen in Figure 15-11.

In this dialog box, we start by entering the virtual name for the listener. We then define the port that it will listen on and the IP address that will be assigned to it.

Tip   We are able to use the same port for both of the listeners, as well as the SQL Server instance, because all three use different IP addresses.

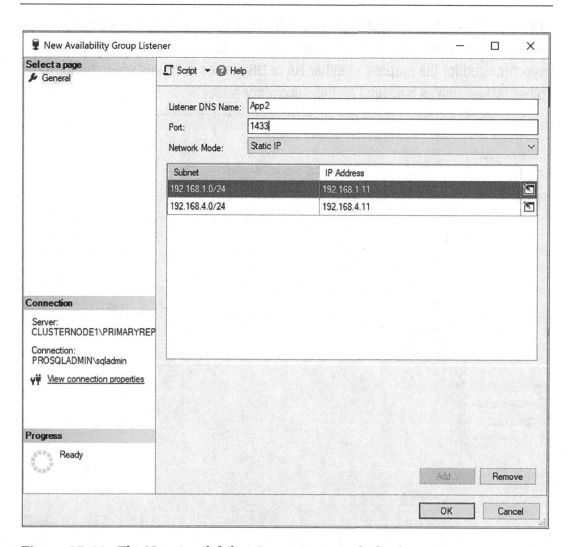

Figure 15-11. *The New Availability Group Listener dialog box*

Availability Groups On Linux

As well as working on a Windows Cluster, Availability Groups can also be configured on SQL Server instances running on Linux. In this section, we will discuss how to configure availability groups for high availability on Linux. In our specific scenario, we have two servers, namely, ubuntu-primary and ubuntu-secondary, which will form our server topology.

Tip   For further information on installing SQL Server on Linux, please see Chapter 4.

Just as you do in a Windows environment, the first step in configuring Availability Groups on Linux is to enable the feature, at the service level. The script in Listing 15-5 demonstrates how to enable Availability Groups and then restart the service. This script needs to be executed on each server that will host a Replica.

Tip   As discussed in Chapter 4, sudo is the equivalent of Run As Administrator in Windows. You will be prompted to enter the root password when using sudo.

Listing 15-5. Enable AlwaysOn Availability Groups

```
sudo /opt/mssql/bin/mssql-conf set hadr.hadrenabled  1
sudo systemctl restart mssql-server
```

Because Linux servers cannot authenticate with each other, using AD authentication, the next step is to create certificates, which can be used for authentication. You can create the certificates by connecting to the primary server and running the script in Listing 15-6. The script creates a certificate in the SQL Server instance and then backs it up to the operating system, so that we can copy it to the secondary server. Remember, that you can connect to a SQL Server instance, running on Linux, by using sqlcmd or by connecting from SSMS, installed on a Windows-based machine.

Tip   Further details of certificates can be found in Chapter 12.

Listing 15-6. Creating a Certificate

```
CREATE MASTER KEY ENCRYPTION BY PASSWORD = 'Pa$$w0rd';
GO

CREATE CERTIFICATE aoag_certificate WITH SUBJECT = 'AvailabilityGroups';
GO

BACKUP CERTIFICATE aoag_certificate
    TO FILE = '/var/opt/mssql/data/aoag_certificate.cer'
    WITH PRIVATE KEY (
        FILE = '/var/opt/mssql/data/aoag_certificate.pvk',
        ENCRYPTION BY PASSWORD = 'Pa$$w0rd'
    );
GO
```

We now need to copy the keys to the secondary server. To do this, we first need to grant the user permissions to the /var/opt/mssql/ data folder. We can do this with the command in Listing 15-7, which needs to be run on both servers.

Listing 15-7. Grant Permissions

```
sudo chmod -R 777 /var/opt/mssql/data
```

The command in Listing 15-8, if run on the primary server, will copy the public and private key of the certificate to the secondary server. For this command to work, SSH should be installed and configured on each server. A full discussion of SSH is beyond the scope of this book, but a guide can be found at https://linuxconfig.org/enable-ssh-on-ubuntu-20-04-focal-fossa-linux.

Tip   You should change the user and server names to match your own configuration.

Listing 15-8. Copy the Keys

```
scp aoag_certificate.* pete@ubuntu-secondary:/var/opt/mssql/data
```

We now need to create the certificate on the secondary server by importing the certificate and key from the file system. This can be achieved using the script in Listing 15-9.

Listing 15-9. Create the Certificate on the Secondary Server

```
CREATE MASTER KEY ENCRYPTION BY PASSWORD = 'Pa$$w0rd' ;
GO

CREATE CERTIFICATE aoag_certificate
    FROM FILE = '/var/opt/mssql/data/aoag_certificate.cer'
    WITH PRIVATE KEY (
            FILE = '/var/opt/mssql/data/aoag_certificate.pvk',
            DECRYPTION BY PASSWORD = 'Pa$$w0rd'
    ) ;
GO
```

Now that our certificates are in place, we need to create the endpoints that will be used for connections. The script in Listing 15-10 will create an endpoint called AOAG_Endpoint, which listens on port 5022 and uses our certificate for authentication. This script should be run on both instances.

Listing 15-10. Create the Endpoints

```
CREATE ENDPOINT AOAG_Endpoint
STATE = STARTED
AS TCP (LISTENER_PORT = 5022)
FOR DATABASE_MIRRORING (
    ROLE = ALL,
    AUTHENTICATION = CERTIFICATE aoag_certificate,
      ENCRYPTION = REQUIRED ALGORITHM AES
);
```

Next, we can create the Availability Group on the Primary Replica. This can be achieved using the command in Listing 15-11. We will not discuss the full syntax of the CREATE AVAILABILITY GROUP command here, which can be found at docs.microsoft. com/en-us/sql/t-sql/statements/create-availability-group-transact-sql?view=sql-server-2019, but there are a couple specific points of interest that I would like to point out. Firstly, you will notice that CLUSTER_TYPE is set to EXTERNAL. This is the only valid option when the underlying cluster is Pacemaker, on Linux. You will also notice that the FAILOVER_MODE is set to manual. This is the only valid option when the CLUSTER_TYPE is set to EXTERNAL. It means that failover should never be performed via T-SQL. Failover should only ever be managed by the external cluster manager.

Listing 15-11. Create the Availability Group

```
CREATE AVAILABILITY GROUP Linux_AOAG
    WITH (CLUSTER_TYPE = EXTERNAL)
   FOR REPLICA ON 'ubuntu-primary' WITH (
              ENDPOINT_URL = N'tcp://ubuntu-primary:5022',
              AVAILABILITY_MODE = SYNCHRONOUS_COMMIT,
              FAILOVER_MODE = EXTERNAL,
              SEEDING_MODE = AUTOMATIC
     ),
     'ubuntu-secondary' WITH (
              ENDPOINT_URL = N'tcp://ubuntu-secondary:5022',
              AVAILABILITY_MODE = SYNCHRONOUS_COMMIT,
              FAILOVER_MODE = EXTERNAL,
              SEEDING_MODE = AUTOMATIC
     ) ;
GO
```

We will now use the command in Listing 15-12 to grant the Availability Group permissions to create databases.

Listing 15-12. Grant Permissions

```
ALTER AVAILABILITY GROUP Linux_AOAG GRANT CREATE ANY DATABASE ;
GO
```

We can now join our secondary replica to the Availability Group and ensure that it has the appropriate permissions by running the script in Listing 15-13 while connected to the secondary instance.

Tip For the following script to succeed, the Linux user running the Pacemaker service should be granted VIEW SERVER STATE on the replica and ALTER, CONTROL, and VIEW DEFINITION on the Availability Group.

Listing 15-13. Join the Secondary Replica

```
ALTER AVAILABILITY GROUP Linux_AOAG JOIN WITH (CLUSTER_TYPE = EXTERNAL) ;
GO

ALTER AVAILABILITY GROUP Linux_AOAG GRANT CREATE ANY DATABASE ;
GO
```

Databases can now be added to the Availability Group. The script in Listing 15-14 will create a database called LinuxDB and populate it with data. It will then take the required backup, before adding it to the Linux_AOAG Availability Group.

Listing 15-14. Adding a Database

```
CREATE DATABASE LinuxDB ;
GO

ALTER DATABASE LinuxDB SET RECOVERY FULL ;
GO

USE LinuxDB
GO

CREATE TABLE [dbo].[Orders](
        [OrderNumber] [int] IDENTITY(1,1) NOT NULL PRIMARY KEY CLUSTERED,
        [OrderDate] [date]  NOT NULL,
        [CustomerID] [int]  NOT NULL,
        [ProductID] [int]  NOT NULL,
        [Quantity] [int]   NOT NULL,
        [NetAmount] [money] NOT NULL,
        [TaxAmount] [money] NOT NULL,
        [InvoiceAddressID] [int] NOT NULL,
```

```
        [DeliveryAddressID] [int] NOT NULL,
        [DeliveryDate] [date] NULL,
) ;

DECLARE @Numbers TABLE
(
        Number          INT
)

;WITH CTE(Number)
AS
(
        SELECT 1 Number
        UNION ALL
        SELECT Number + 1
        FROM CTE
        WHERE Number < 100
)
INSERT INTO @Numbers
SELECT Number FROM CTE

--Populate ExistingOrders with data

INSERT INTO Orders
SELECT
        (SELECT CAST(DATEADD(dd,(SELECT TOP 1 Number
                            FROM @Numbers
                            ORDER BY NEWID()),getdate())as DATE)),
        (SELECT TOP 1 Number -10 FROM @Numbers ORDER BY NEWID()),
        (SELECT TOP 1 Number FROM @Numbers ORDER BY NEWID()),
        (SELECT TOP 1 Number FROM @Numbers ORDER BY NEWID()),
        500,
        100,
        (SELECT TOP 1 Number FROM @Numbers ORDER BY NEWID()),
        (SELECT TOP 1 Number FROM @Numbers ORDER BY NEWID()),
        (SELECT CAST(DATEADD(dd,(SELECT TOP 1 Number - 10
```

```
        FROM @Numbers
        ORDER BY NEWID()),getdate() as DATE))
FROM @Numbers a
CROSS JOIN @Numbers b
CROSS JOIN @Numbers c ;

--Backup Database

BACKUP DATABASE LinuxDB
    TO DISK = N'/var/opt/mssql/data/LinuxDB.bak';
GO

--Add database to Availability Group

USE master
GO

ALTER AVAILABILITY GROUP Linux_AOAG ADD DATABASE LinuxDB
GO
```

Connecting to the primary instance, with SSMS, should now show that the Availability Group is configured and contains your database, as illustrated in Figure 15-12.

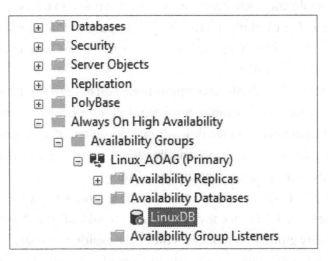

Figure 15-12. *Configured Availability Group on Linux server*

Finally, we will create a Listener for the Availability Group using the command in Listing 15-15.

Listing 15-15. Create an Availability Group Listener

```
ALTER AVAILABILITY GROUP Linux_AOAG
ADD LISTENER N'LinuxListener' (
WITH IP
(
    ('192.168.1.62', N'255.255.255.0')
)
, PORT=5022) ;
GO
```

Contained Availability Group

One of the challenges of using Availability Groups is that instance-level objects that the databases rely on, such as Logins and SQL Agent Jobs, are not replicated between nodes. This means that DBAs need to manually synchronize instance-level objects for data-tier applications to be operational after failover.

While I have seen some DBAs take the word "manually" in the literal context, this of course is not advisable and there are various methods that can be used to keep instance-level objects in sync. For example, I have used Maintenance Plans and have also used configuration management tooling, including PowerShell DSC and Puppet, to ensure that objects always exist on all nodes.

The aforementioned methods have operational considerations, however. DBAs need to update their automation as instance-level requirements evolve. They also need to monitor the automation to minimize downtime in the event of a failover. Additionally, the configuration management option usually requires a DBA with a degree of platform engineering skill to develop and maintain the solution.

SQL Server 2022 introduces contained availability groups to address this issue. This feature creates an additional copy of the master and msdb databases for each contained availability group and replicates them, alongside the availability databases. Because master and msdb contain the instance-level objects, these objects are replicated between nodes.

It is important to understand, however, that you are not replicating the system databases themselves. Instead, you are replicating copies of those system databases that exist solely for the purpose of supporting the contained availability group. When the availability group is first created, only administrators are added as logins to the new system databases. Other logins, as well as other instance-level objects, need to be configured. The replicated instance-level objects are only visible when connected to the availability group listener. Therefore, contained availability groups will only work as intended if an availability group listener exists, and if you force connections to be via that availability group listener.

This design has some interesting side effects. Firstly, when connected to an availability group listener, the replicated system databases will appear to be called `master` and `msdb` and have the database IDs of 1 and 2, respectively. If you connect to the instance, however, these databases will have names appended with the name of the availability group which they support and will have different database IDs to the instance's system databases. For example, if your availability group is called App3, the replicated system databases will be called `master_App3` and `msdb_App3`.

Tip   While contained availability groups dramatically simplify the process of simplifying instance-level objects, they can cause some complexities to scripts that perform other automated tasks. For example, imagine you have a maintenance script which either excludes databases with database IDs > 4 or excludes system databases by name. This script would need to be updated to use a wildcard on name to exclude `master_%`.

Let's see how this works in practice. The script in Listing 15-16 creates the `Chapter15App3Sales` database and then backs it up. We will use this database to create a contained availability group called App3.

Listing 15-16.   Create the Chapter15App3Sales Database

```
CREATE DATABASE Chapter15App3Sales ;
GO

ALTER DATABASE Chapter15App3Sales SET RECOVERY FULL ;
GO
```

```
USE Chapter15App3Sales
GO

CREATE TABLE [dbo].[Orders](
        [OrderNumber] [int] IDENTITY(1,1) NOT NULL PRIMARY KEY CLUSTERED,
        [OrderDate] [date]  NOT NULL,
        [CustomerID] [int]  NOT NULL,
        [ProductID] [int]   NOT NULL,
        [Quantity] [int]    NOT NULL,
        [NetAmount] [money] NOT NULL,
        [TaxAmount] [money] NOT NULL,
        [InvoiceAddressID] [int] NOT NULL,
        [DeliveryAddressID] [int] NOT NULL,
        [DeliveryDate] [date] NULL,
) ;

DECLARE @Numbers TABLE
(
        Number          INT
)

;WITH CTE(Number)
AS
(
        SELECT 1 Number
        UNION ALL
        SELECT Number + 1
        FROM CTE
        WHERE Number < 100
)
INSERT INTO @Numbers
SELECT Number FROM CTE

--Populate ExistingOrders with data
```

```
INSERT INTO Orders
SELECT
        (SELECT CAST(DATEADD(dd,(SELECT TOP 1 Number
                            FROM @Numbers
                            ORDER BY NEWID()),getdate())as DATE)),
        (SELECT TOP 1 Number -10 FROM @Numbers ORDER BY NEWID()),
        (SELECT TOP 1 Number FROM @Numbers ORDER BY NEWID()),
        (SELECT TOP 1 Number FROM @Numbers ORDER BY NEWID()),
      500,
      100,
        (SELECT TOP 1 Number FROM @Numbers ORDER BY NEWID()),
        (SELECT TOP 1 Number FROM @Numbers ORDER BY NEWID()),
        (SELECT CAST(DATEADD(dd,(SELECT TOP 1 Number - 10
         FROM @Numbers
         ORDER BY NEWID()),getdate()) as DATE))
FROM @Numbers a
CROSS JOIN @Numbers b
CROSS JOIN @Numbers c ;

GO


BACKUP DATABASE Chapter15App3Sales
TO  DISK = N'C:\MSSQL\Backups\Chapter15App3Sales.bak'
WITH NAME = N'Chapter15App3Sales-Full Database Backup' ;
GO
```

Figure 15-13 illustrates the Options page of the New Availability Group wizard. You will notice that we have checked the option to make the availability group contained. The Reuse System Databases option is not applicable in our scenario. This option can be used if you need to drop and re-create an existing contained availability group, allowing you to reuse the replicated system databases from the original availability group, so you can avoid having to reconfigure all the instance-level objects that need to be replicated.

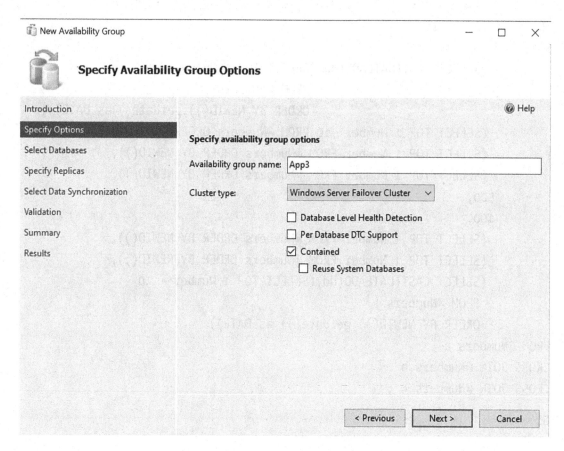

Figure 15-13. *Options page (contained availability group)*

Tip   For brevity, we will not walk through the rest of the wizard here, but details of how to use it can be found earlier in this chapter.

The images in Figure 15-14 and Figure 15-15 show the difference between how databases are viewed when connected to `CLUSTERNODE1\PRIMARYREPLICA` and `App3Listener`, respectively.

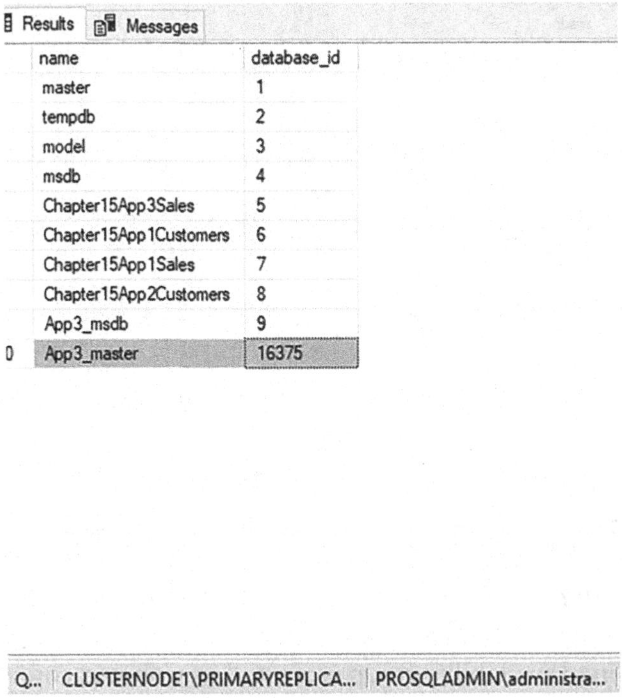
Results
Messages
name
database_id
master
1
tempdb
2
model
3
msdb
4
Chapter15App3Sales
5
Chapter15App1Customers
6
Chapter15App1Sales
7
Chapter15App2Customers
8
App3_msdb
9
App3_master
16375
Q...
CLUSTERNODE1\PRIMARYREPLICA...
PROSQLADMIN\administra...

***Figure 15-14.** Databases viewed through instance*

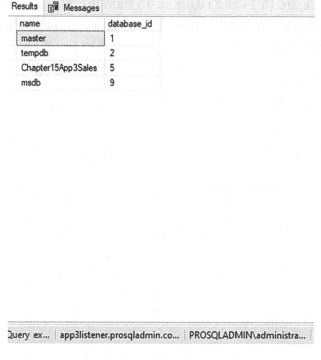

Figure 15-15. Databases viewed through contained availability group listener

Once the contained availability group is created, you should connect to the availability group listener to create the instance-level objects that should be replicated between nodes.

Distributed Availability Groups

Distributed Availability Groups (DAGs) are an extension of Availability Groups, which allow for data to be synchronized between two separate Availability Groups. This is an exciting technology, with many different use cases. For example, it allows data synchronization between Windows- and Linux-based Availability Groups, it allows the number of readable secondary replicas to be extended beyond 8 (which is the limit for a standard Availability Group), and it allows cross-site replication, without the complexity of a stretch cluster. DAGs can also help server migrations by providing data synchronization when an in-place upgrade is not possible and a side-by-side migration is required.

While each side of the DAG can be a Windows Failover Cluster, this is not a requirement, as the focus is very much on maintaining the databases, and no cluster configuration occurs.

In this section, we will illustrate the technology by configuring DAGs for our App1 Availability Group, between our PROSQLADMINCLUSTER cluster and the Linux_AOAG Availability Group hosted on two Linux servers, participating in a Pacemaker cluster.

The first step is to create the Distributed Availability Group on the Linux cluster. This can be achieved by using the script in Listing 15-17. Note the WITH (DISTRIBUTED) syntax, followed by the specifications of each Availability Group.

Note   Before starting, you should remove existing databases from the App1 Availability Group; otherwise, it will not be able to join the Distributed Availability Group, as the secondary Availability Group must be empty.

Listing 15-17. Create the Distributed Availability Group

```
CREATE AVAILABILITY GROUP DistributedAG
   WITH (DISTRIBUTED)
   AVAILABILITY GROUP ON
      'App1' WITH
      (
         LISTENER_URL = 'tcp://App1Listener.prosqladmin.com:1433',
         AVAILABILITY_MODE = ASYNCHRONOUS_COMMIT,
         FAILOVER_MODE = MANUAL,
         SEEDING_MODE = AUTOMATIC
      ),
      'Linux_AOAG' WITH
      (
         LISTENER_URL = 'tcp://LinuxListener:5022',
         AVAILABILITY_MODE = ASYNCHRONOUS_COMMIT,
         FAILOVER_MODE = MANUAL,
         SEEDING_MODE = AUTOMATIC
      );
GO
```

We can now run the command in Listing 15-18, against the
PROSQLADMINCLUSTER cluster, to join it to the Distributed Availability Group.

Listing 15-18. Join the Second Availability Group

```
ALTER AVAILABILITY GROUP DistributedAG
    JOIN
    AVAILABILITY GROUP ON
        'App1' WITH
        (
            LISTENER_URL = 'tcp://App1Listener.prosqladmin.com:1433',
            AVAILABILITY_MODE = ASYNCHRONOUS_COMMIT,
            FAILOVER_MODE = MANUAL,
            SEEDING_MODE = AUTOMATIC
        ),
        'Linux_AOAG' WITH
        (
            LISTENER_URL = 'tcp://LinuxListener:5022',
            AVAILABILITY_MODE = ASYNCHRONOUS_COMMIT,
            FAILOVER_MODE = MANUAL,
            SEEDING_MODE = AUTOMATIC
        ) ;
GO
```

Tip   Databases will need to be manually joined to secondary replicas within the
secondary Availability Group.

Managing AlwaysOn Availability Groups

Once the initial setup of your availability group is complete, you still need to perform administrative tasks. These include failing over the availability group, monitoring, and on rare occasions, adding additional listeners. These topics are discussed in the following sections.

Failover

If a replica is in Synchronous Commit mode and is configured for automatic failover, then the availability group automatically moves to a redundant replica in the event of an error condition being met on the primary replica. There are occasions, however, when you will want to manually fail over an availability group. This could be because of DR testing, proactive maintenance, or because you need to bring up an asynchronous replica following a failure of the primary replica or the primary data center.

Synchronous Failover

If you wish to fail over a replica that is in Synchronous Commit mode, launch the Failover Availability Group wizard by selecting Failover from the context menu of your availability group in Object Explorer. After moving past the Introduction page, you find the Select New Primary Replica page (see Figure 15-16). On this page, check the box of the replica to which you want to fail over. Before doing so, however, review the Failover Readiness column to ensure that the replicas are synchronized, and that no data loss will occur.

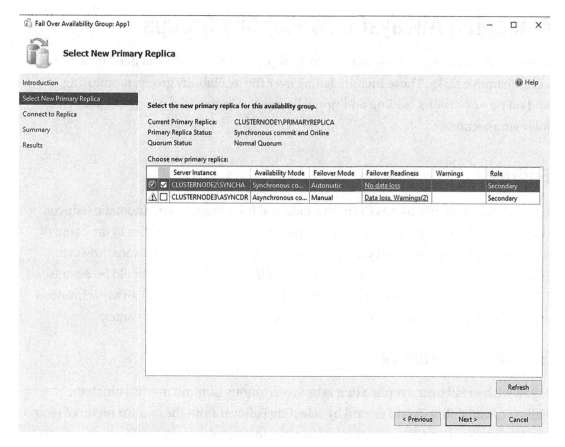

Figure 15-16. *The Select New Primary Replica page*

On the Connect to Replica page, illustrated in Figure 15-17, use the Connect button to establish a connection to the new primary replica.

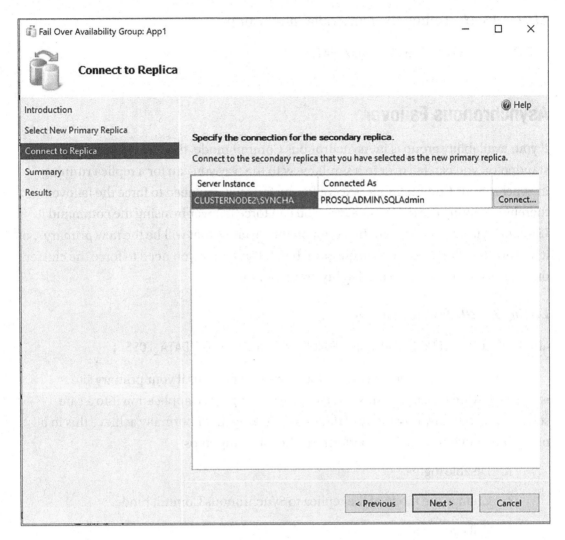

Figure 15-17. The Connect to Replica page

On the Summary page, you are given details of the task to be performed, followed by a progress indicator on the Results page. Once the failover completes, check that all tasks were successful, and investigate any errors or warnings that you receive.

We can also use T-SQL to fail over the availability group. The command in Listing 15-19 achieves the same results. Make sure to run this script from the replica that will be the new primary replica. If you run it from the current primary replica, use SQLCMD mode and connect to the new primary within the script.

Listing 15-19. Failing Over an Availability Group

```
ALTER AVAILABILITY GROUP App2 FAILOVER ;
GO
```

Asynchronous Failover

If your availability group is in Asynchronous Commit mode, then from a technical standpoint, you can fail over in a similar way to the way you can for a replica running in Synchronous Commit mode, except for the fact that you need to force the failover, thereby accepting the risk of data loss. You can force failover by using the command in Listing 15-20. You should run this script on the instance that will be the new primary. For it to work, the cluster must have quorum. If it doesn't, then you need to force the cluster online before you force the availability group online.

Listing 15-20. Forcing Failover

```
ALTER AVAILABILITY GROUP App2 FORCE_FAILOVER_ALLOW_DATA_LOSS ;
```

From a process perspective, you should only ever do this if your primary site is completely unavailable. If this is not the case, first put the application into a safe state. This avoids any possibility of data loss. The way that I normally achieve this in a production environment is by performing the following steps:

1. Disable logins.

2. Change the mode of the replica to Synchronous Commit mode.

3. Fail over.

4. Change the replica back to Asynchronous Commit mode.

5. Enable the logins.

You can perform these steps with the script in Listing 15-21. When run from the DR instance, this script places the databases in App2 into a safe state before failing over, and then it reconfigures the application to work under normal operations.

Listing 15-21. Safe-Stating an Application and Failing Over

```
--DISABLE LOGINS

DECLARE @AOAGDBs TABLE
(
DBName NVARCHAR(128)
) ;

INSERT INTO @AOAGDBs
SELECT database_name
FROM sys.availability_groups AG
INNER JOIN sys.availability_databases_cluster ADC
        ON AG.group_id = ADC.group_id
WHERE AG.name = 'App2' ;

DECLARE @Mappings TABLE
(
        LoginName NVARCHAR(128),
    DBname NVARCHAR(128),
    Username NVARCHAR(128),
    AliasName NVARCHAR(128)
) ;

INSERT INTO @Mappings
EXEC sp_msloginmappings ;

DECLARE @SQL NVARCHAR(MAX)

SELECT DISTINCT @SQL =
(
        SELECT 'ALTER LOGIN [' + LoginName + '] DISABLE; ' AS [data()]
        FROM @Mappings M
        INNER JOIN @AOAGDBs A
                ON M.DBname = A.DBName
        WHERE LoginName <> SUSER_NAME()
        FOR XML PATH ('')
)
```

```
EXEC(@SQL)
GO

--SWITCH TO SYNCHRONOUS COMMIT MODE

ALTER AVAILABILITY GROUP App2
MODIFY REPLICA ON N'CLUSTERNODE3\ASYNCDR' WITH (AVAILABILITY_MODE =
SYNCHRONOUS_COMMIT) ;
GO

--FAIL OVER

ALTER AVAILABILITY GROUP App2 FAILOVER
GO

--SWITCH BACK TO ASYNCHRONOUS COMMIT MODE

ALTER AVAILABILITY GROUP App2
MODIFY REPLICA ON N'CLUSTERNODE3\ASYNCDR' WITH (AVAILABILITY_MODE =
ASYNCHRONOUS_COMMIT) ;
GO

--ENABLE LOGINS

DECLARE @AOAGDBs TABLE
(
DBName NVARCHAR(128)
) ;

INSERT INTO @AOAGDBs
SELECT database_name
FROM sys.availability_groups AG
INNER JOIN sys.availability_databases_cluster ADC
        ON AG.group_id = ADC.group_id
WHERE AG.name = 'App2' ;

DECLARE @Mappings TABLE
(
        LoginName NVARCHAR(128),
```

```
    DBname NVARCHAR(128),
    Username NVARCHAR(128),
    AliasName NVARCHAR(128)
) ;

INSERT INTO @Mappings
EXEC sp_msloginmappings

DECLARE @SQL NVARCHAR(MAX)

SELECT DISTINCT @SQL =
(
        SELECT 'ALTER LOGIN [' + LoginName + '] ENABLE; ' AS [data()]
        FROM @Mappings M
        INNER JOIN @AOAGDBs A
                ON M.DBname = A.DBName
        WHERE LoginName <> SUSER_NAME()
        FOR XML PATH ('')
) ;

EXEC(@SQL)
```

Caution   If your instance has already disabled Logins, you will need to factor this into your logic, to avoid them being reenabled.

Synchronizing Uncontained Objects

Regardless of the method you use to fail over, assuming that all of the databases within the availability group are not contained, and assuming that you have not implemented contained availability groups, then you will need to ensure that instance-level objects are synchronized. The most straightforward way to keep your instance-level objects synchronized is by implementing an SSIS package, which is scheduled to run on a periodic basis.

Whether you choose to schedule a SSIS package to execute or you choose a different approach, such as a SQL Server Agent job that scripts and re-creates the objects on the secondary servers, these are the objects that you should consider synchronizing:

- Logins

- Credentials

- SQL Server Agent jobs

- Custom error messages

- Linked servers

- Server-level event notifications

- Stored procedures in Master

- Server-level triggers

- Encryption keys and certificates

Monitoring

Once you have implemented availability groups, you need to monitor them and respond to any errors or warnings that could affect the availability of your data. If you have many availability groups implemented throughout the enterprise, then the only way to monitor them effectively and holistically is by using an enterprise monitoring tool, such as SOC (System Operations Center). If you only have a small number of availability groups, however, or if you are troubleshooting a specific issue, then SQL Server provides the AlwaysOn Dashboard and the AlwaysOn Health Trace. The following sections examine these two features.

AlwaysOn Dashboard

The AlwaysOn Dashboard is an interactive report that allows you to view the health of your AlwaysOn environment and drill through, or roll up elements within the topology. You can invoke the report from the context menu of the Availability Groups folder in Object Explorer, or from the context menu of the availability group itself. Figure 15-18 shows the report that is generated from the context menu of the App2 availability group. You can see that currently, synchronization of both replicas is in a healthy state.

The three possible synchronization states that a database can be in are
SYNCHRONIZED, SYNCRONIZING, and NOT SYNCHRONIZING. A synchronous replica should
be in the SYNCHRONIZED state, and any other state is unhealthy. An asynchronous
replica, however, will never be in the SYNCHRONIZED state, and a state of SYNCHRONIZING
is considered healthy. Regardless of the mode, NOT SYNCHRONIZING indicates that the
replica is not connected.

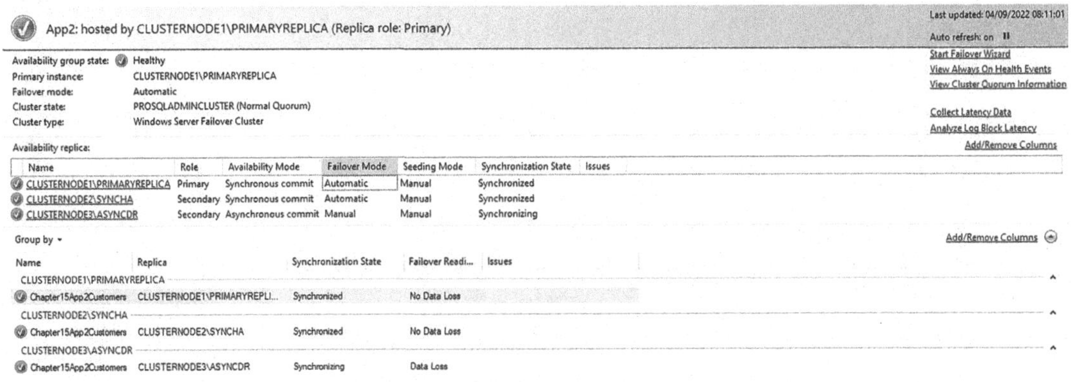

Figure 15-18. *The availability group dashboard*

Note   In addition to the synchronization states, a replica also has one of the
following operational states: PENDING_FAILOVER, PENDING, ONLINE, OFFLINE,
FAILED, FAILED_NO_QUORUM, and NULL (when the replica is disconnected).
The operational state of a replica can be viewed using the sys.dm_hadr_
availability_replica_states DMV.

At the top right of the report, there are links to the failover wizard, which we
discussed earlier in this chapter; the AlwaysOn Health events, which we discussed in the
next section; and also, a link to view cluster quorum information. The Cluster Quorum
Information screen, which is invoked by this link, is displayed in Figure 15-19. You can
also drill through each replica in the Availability Replicas window to see replica-specific
details.

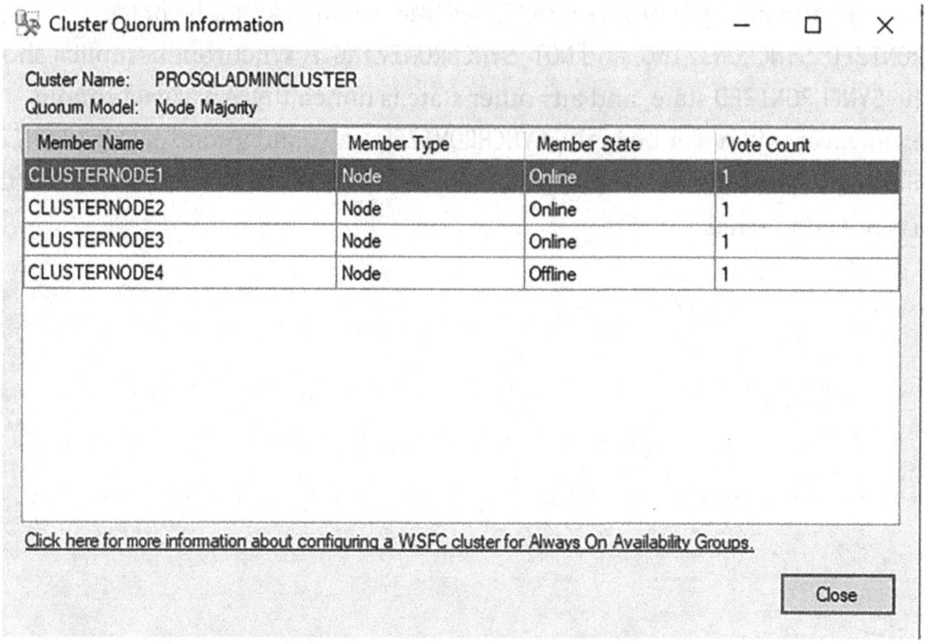

Figure 15-19. *The Cluster Quorum Information screen*

AlwaysOn Health Trace

The AlwaysOn Health Trace is an Extended Events session, which is created when you create you first availability group. It can be located in SQL Server Management Studio, under Extended Events ➤ Sessions, and via its context menu, you can view live data that is being captured, or you can enter the session's properties to change the configuration of the events that are captured.

Drilling through the session exposes the session's package, and from the context menu of the package, you can view previously captured events. Figure 15-20 shows that the latest event captured was Database 5 (which, in our case, is Chapter15App2Customers) and was waiting for the log to be hardened on the synchronous replica. Extended Events is discussed in detail in Chapter 20.

Displaying 587 Events	
name	timestamp
alwayson_ddl_executed	2019-05-30 12:38:00.6337606
alwayson_ddl_executed	2019-05-30 12:38:00.9334599
alwayson_ddl_executed	2019-05-30 12:43:36.8755627
alwayson_ddl_executed	2019-05-30 12:43:37.2157175
alwayson_ddl_executed	2019-05-30 12:47:51.3797680
alwayson_ddl_executed	2019-05-30 12:47:51.4761597
alwayson_ddl_executed	2019-05-30 12:47:51.7889510
alwayson_ddl_executed	2019-05-30 12:47:51.8915198
alwayson_ddl_executed	2019-05-30 12:47:52.1317534
alwayson_ddl_executed	2019-05-30 12:47:52.5519430
▶ hadr_db_partner_set_sync_state	2019-05-30 12:47:53.9656714

Event:hadr_db_partner_set_sync_state (2019-05-30 12:47:53.9656714)

Details

Field	Value
ag_database_id	9B556EA3-7F5E-4052-946A-4E8385A26412
commit_policy	WaitForHarden
commit_policy_target	WaitForHarden
database_id	5
group_id	E54CEF93-68A0-4D98-80D8-05E4BBAB0A3B
replica_id	87FE64A4-BFC7-416C-9810-DE21A12EF7D6
sync_log_block	154618823128
sync_state	LOG

Figure 15-20. *The target data*

Other Administrative Considerations

When databases are made highly available with AlwaysOn Availability Groups, several limitations are imposed. One of the most restrictive of these is that databases cannot be placed in single_user mode or be made read only. This can have an impact when you need to safe-state your application for maintenance. This is why, in the "Failover" section of this chapter, we disabled the logins that have users mapped to the databases. If you must place your database in single-user mode, then you must first remove it from the availability group.

A database can be removed from an availability group by running the command in Listing 15-22. This command removes the `Chapter15App2Customers` database from the availability group.

Listing 15-22. Removing a Database from an Availability Group

```
ALTER DATABASE Chapter15App2Customers SET HADR OFF ;
```

There may also be occasions in which you want a database to remain in an availability group, but you wish to suspend data movement to other replicas. This is usually because the availability group is in Synchronous Commit mode and you have a period of high utilization, where you need a performance improvement. You can suspend the data movement to a database by using the command in Listing 15-23, which suspends data movement for the `Chapter15App1Sales` database and then resumes it.

Caution   If you suspend data movement, the transaction log on the primary replica continues to grow, which leads to issues with disk space, and you are not able to truncate it until data movement resumes and the databases are synchronized.

Listing 15-23. Suspending Data Movement

```
ALTER DATABASE Chapter15App2Customers SET HADR SUSPEND ;
GO

ALTER DATABASE Chapter15App2Customers SET HADR RESUME ;
GO
```

Another important consideration is the placement of database and log files. These files must be in the same location on each replica. This means that if you use named instances, it is a hard technical requirement that you change the default file locations for data and logs, because the default location includes the name of the instance. This is assuming, of course, that you do not use the same instance name on each node, which would defy many of the benefits of having a named instance.

Summary

AlwaysOn Availability Groups can be implemented with up to eight secondary replicas, combining both Synchronous and Asynchronous Commit modes. When implementing high availability with availability groups, you always use Synchronous Commit mode, because Asynchronous Commit mode does not support automatic failover. When implementing Synchronous Commit mode, however, you must be aware of the associated performance penalty caused by committing the transaction on the secondary replica before it is committed on the primary replica. For disaster recovery, you will normally choose to implement Asynchronous Commit mode.

The availability group can be created via the New Availability Group wizard, through dialog boxes, through T-SQL, or even through PowerShell. If you create an availability group using dialog boxes, then some aspects, such as the endpoint and associated permissions, must be scripted using T-SQL or PowerShell.

If you implement disaster recovery with availability groups, then you need to configure a multi-subnet cluster. This does not mean that you must have SAN replication between the sites, however, since availability groups do not rely on shared storage. What you do need to do is add additional IP addresses for the administrative cluster access point and also for the Availability Group Listener. You also need to pay attention to the properties of the cluster that support client reconnection to ensure that clients do not experience a high number of time-outs.

Failover to a synchronous replica in the event of a failure of the primary replica is automatic. There are instances, however, in which you will also need to fail over manually. This could be because of a disaster that requires failover to the DR site, or it could be for proactive maintenance. Although it is possible to fail over to an asynchronous replica with the possibility of data loss, it is good practice to place the databases in a safe state first. Because you cannot place a database in read-only or single_user mode, if it is participating in an availability group, safe-stating usually consists of disabling the logins and then switching to Synchronous Commit mode before failover.

To monitor availability groups throughout the enterprise, you need to use a monitoring tool, such as System Operations Center. If you need to monitor a small number of availability groups or troubleshoot a specific issue, however, use one of the tools included with SQL Server, such as a dashboard for monitoring the health of the topology and an extended events session, called the AlwaysOn Health Trace.

You should also consider other maintenance tasks. These include where to place database and log files, as they must have the same location on each replica, and removing a database from an availability group so that you can place it in `single_user` mode, for example. Changing to `single_user` mode may be due to a requirement to run `DBCC CHECKDB` in a repair mode and suspend data movement. Suspending data movement allows you to remove the performance overhead during a period of high utilization, but be warned, it also causes the transaction log on the primary replica to grow, without an option to truncate it, until data movement has resumed and the databases are once again synchronized.

Tip   There is a saying that you do not have backups until you have tested restoring them. The same applies to failover. You should always test your failover plans before you need them in a real disaster scenario.

CHAPTER 16

Implementing Log Shipping

As discussed in Chapter 14, log shipping is a technology you can use to implement disaster recovery and the scale out of read-only reporting. It works by taking the transaction log backups of a database, copying them to one or more secondary servers, and then restoring them, in order to keep the secondary server(s) synchronized. This chapter demonstrates how to implement log shipping for disaster recovery (DR). You also discover how to monitor and fail over log shipping.

Note For the purpose of the demonstrations in this chapter, we use a domain, consisting of a domain controller and four stand-alone servers, each with an instance of SQL Server installed. The server/instance names are PRIMARYSERVER\PROSQLADMIN, DRSERVER\PROSQLDR, REPORTSERVER\ PROSQLREPORTS, and MONITORSERVER\PROSQLMONITOR, respectively.

Implementing Log Shipping for DR

Before we begin to implement log shipping for disaster recovery, we first create a database that we will use for the demonstrations in this chapter. The script in Listing 16-1 creates a database called Chapter16 with its recovery model set to FULL. We create one table within the database and populate it with data.

© Peter A. Carter 2023
P. A. Carter, *Pro SQL Server 2022 Administration*, https://doi.org/10.1007/978-1-4842-8864-1_16

Listing 16-1. Creating the Database to Be Log Shipped

```
--Create the database

CREATE DATABASE Chapter16;
GO

ALTER DATABASE Chapter16 SET RECOVERY FULL;
GO

USE Chapter16
GO

--Create and populate numbers table

DECLARE @Numbers TABLE
(
        Number          INT
)

;WITH CTE(Number)
AS
(
        SELECT 1 Number
        UNION ALL
        SELECT Number + 1
        FROM CTE
        WHERE Number < 100
)
INSERT INTO @Numbers
SELECT Number FROM CTE;

--Create and populate name pieces

DECLARE @Names TABLE
(
        FirstName          VARCHAR(30),
        LastName           VARCHAR(30)
);
```

```
INSERT INTO @Names
VALUES('Peter', 'Carter'),
                ('Michael', 'Smith'),
                ('Danielle', 'Mead'),
                ('Reuben', 'Roberts'),
                ('Iris', 'Jones'),
                ('Sylvia', 'Davies'),
                ('Finola', 'Wright'),
                ('Edward', 'James'),
                ('Marie', 'Andrews'),
                ('Jennifer', 'Abraham') ;

--Create and populate Customers table

CREATE TABLE dbo.Customers
(
        CustomerID              INT             NOT
NULL    IDENTITY     PRIMARY KEY,
        FirstName               VARCHAR(30)     NOT NULL,
        LastName                VARCHAR(30)     NOT NULL,
        BillingAddressID        INT             NOT NULL,
        DeliveryAddressID       INT             NOT NULL,
        CreditLimit             MONEY           NOT NULL,
        Balance                 MONEY           NOT NULL
);
SELECT * INTO #Customers
FROM
        (SELECT
                (SELECT TOP 1 FirstName FROM @Names ORDER BY NEWID())
                FirstName,
                (SELECT TOP 1 LastName FROM @Names ORDER BY NEWID())
                LastName,
                (SELECT TOP 1 Number FROM @Numbers ORDER BY NEWID())
                BillingAddressID,
                (SELECT TOP 1 Number FROM @Numbers ORDER BY NEWID())
                DeliveryAddressID,
```

```
                (SELECT TOP 1 CAST(RAND() * Number AS INT) * 10000
                    FROM @Numbers
                    ORDER BY NEWID()) CreditLimit,
                (SELECT TOP 1 CAST(RAND() * Number AS INT) * 9000
                    FROM @Numbers
                    ORDER BY NEWID()) Balance
        FROM @Numbers a
        CROSS JOIN @Numbers b
) a;

INSERT INTO dbo.Customers
SELECT * FROM #Customers;
GO
```

For the purpose of this demonstration, we would like to configure disaster recovery for the Chapter16 database so that we have an RPO (recovery point objective) of ten minutes. We will also implement a ten-minute load delay on the DR server. This means that if an application team notifies us immediately of an incident that has led to data loss—for example, a user accidently deletes rows from a table—then we are able to rectify the issue by using the data on the DR server before the log that contains the erroneous transaction is restored.

GUI Configuration

We can configure log shipping for our Chapter16 database through SQL Server Management Studio (SSMS). To do this, we select Properties from the context menu of the database and navigate to the Transaction Log Shipping page, which is displayed in Figure 16-1. The first task on this page is to check the Enable this as the primary database in a log shipping configuration check box.

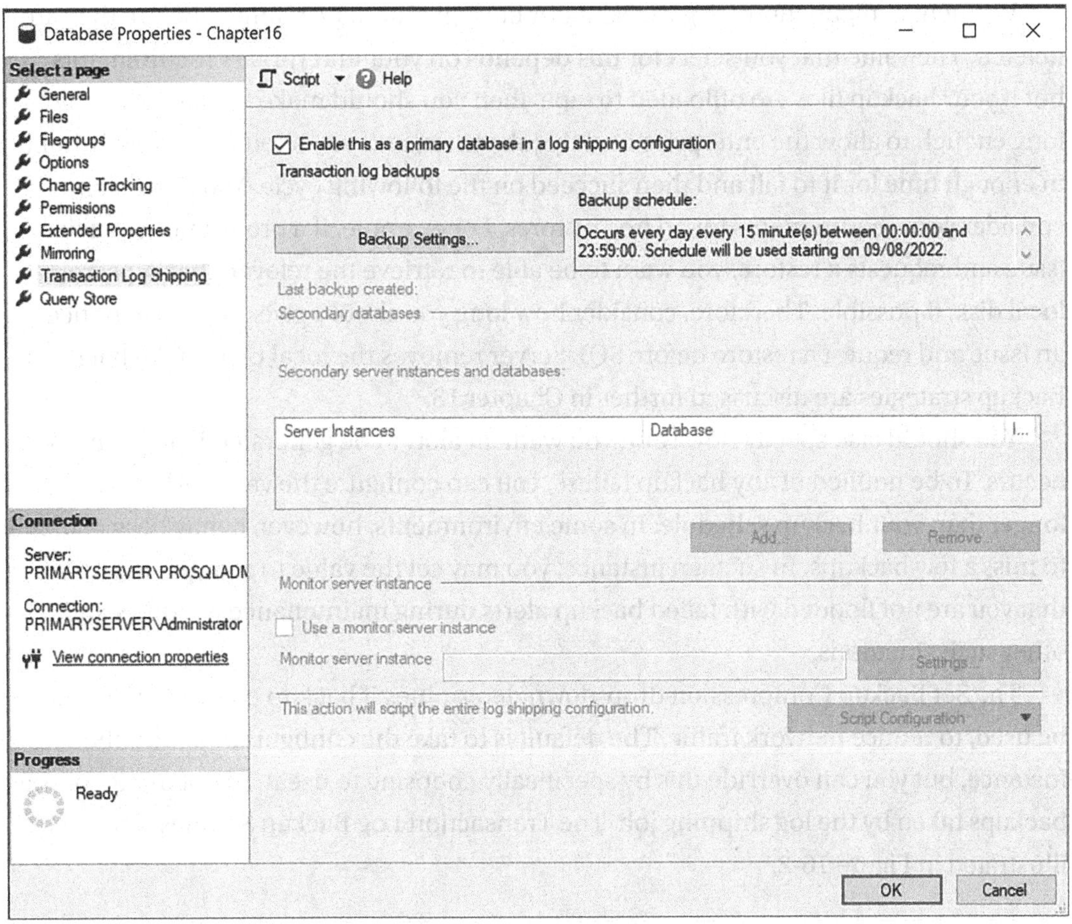

Figure 16-1. *The Transaction Log Shipping page*

We can now use the Backup Settings button to display the Transaction Log Backup Settings screen. On this screen, we enter the UNC (Universal Naming Convention) to the share that will be used for storing the log backups that log shipping takes. Because this share is actually configured on our primary server, we also enter the local path in the field below. The account that will be used to run the backup job needs to be granted read and change permissions on this share. By default, this will be the SQL Server service account, but for more granular security, it is possible to configure log shipping jobs to run under a proxy account, which reduces the security footprint of the implementation. Proxy accounts are discussed in Chapter 23.

We then configure how long we want our backup files to be retained before they are deleted. The value that you select for this depends on your enterprise's requirements, but if your backup files are offloaded to tape, then you should make the files available long enough to allow the enterprise backup job to run, and you should potentially build in enough time for it to fail and then succeed on the following cycle. You should also consider your requirements for ad hoc restores. For example, if a project notices a data issue and requests a restore, you want to be able to retrieve the relevant backups from local disk, if possible. Therefore, consider how long you should give projects to notice an issue and request a restore before SQL Server removes the local copy of the backups. Backup strategies are discussed further in Chapter 13.

You should also specify how soon you want an alert to be generated if no log backup occurs. To be notified of any backup failure, you can configure the value to be a minute longer than your backup schedule. In some environments, however, it may be acceptable to miss a few backups. In such an instance, you may set the value to a larger interval so that you are not flooded with failed backup alerts during maintenance windows and other such situations.

The Set Backup Compression drop-down determines if backup compression should be used, to reduce network traffic. The default is to take the configuration from the instance, but you can override this by specifically choosing to use it, or not use it, for the backups taken by the log shipping job. The Transaction Log Backup Settings screen is illustrated in Figure 16-2.

Tip   Your decision of whether or not you should use compression depends on the resource constraints of the server. If you are experiencing network bandwidth constraints, you will likely want to implement compression. If your server is CPU bound, however, then you may not be able to spare the extra cycles that compression uses.

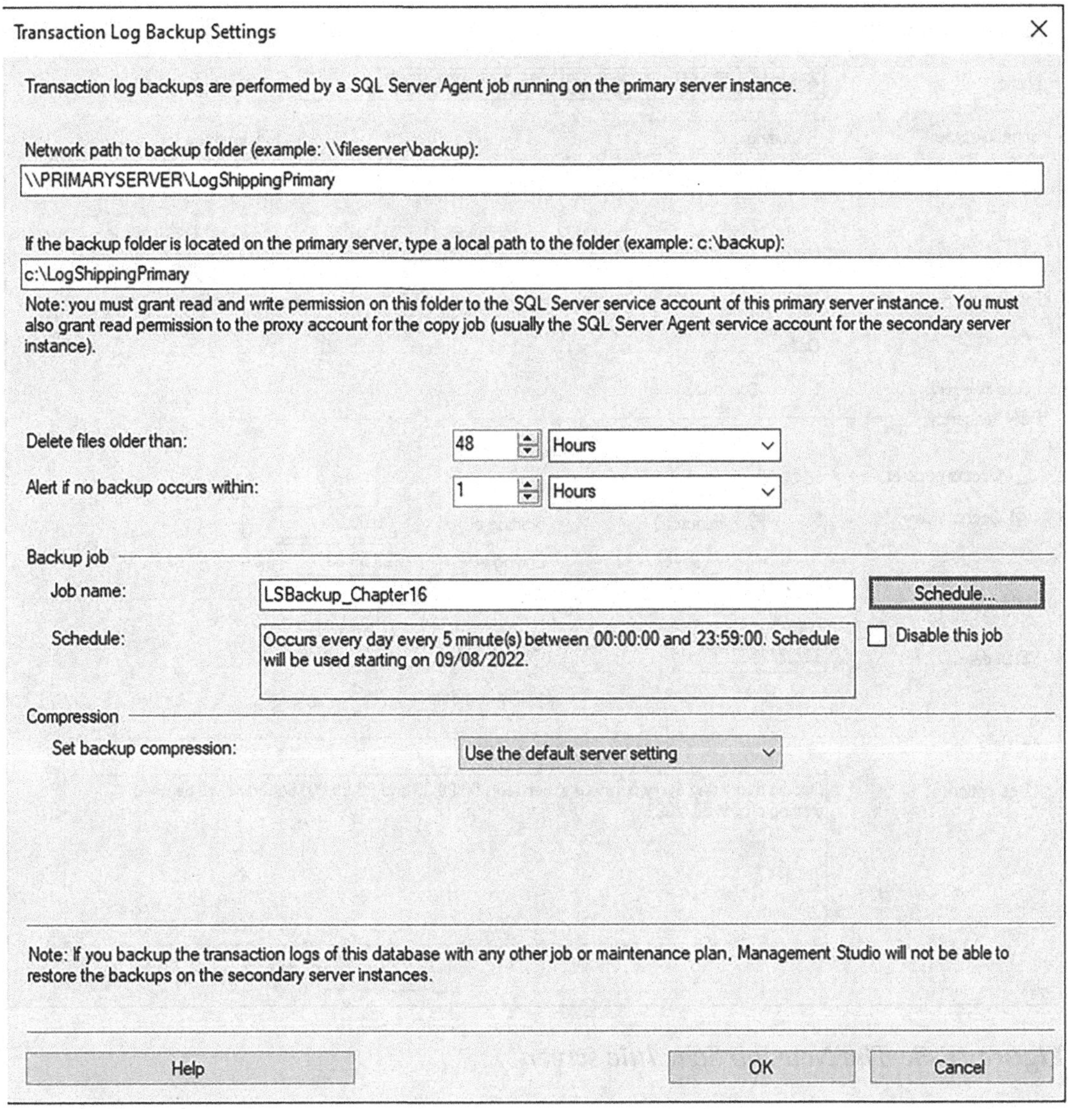

Figure 16-2. The Transaction Log Backup Settings screen

Clicking the Schedule button causes the New Job Schedule screen to be invoked. This screen, which is illustrated in Figure 16-3, is the standard SQL Server Agent screen used for creating job schedules, except that it has been prepopulated with the default name of the log shipping backup job. Because we are trying to achieve an RPO of ten minutes, we configure the backup job to run every five minutes. This is because we also need to allow time for the copy job to run. In a DR planning, we cannot assume that the primary server will be available for retrieving our log backup.

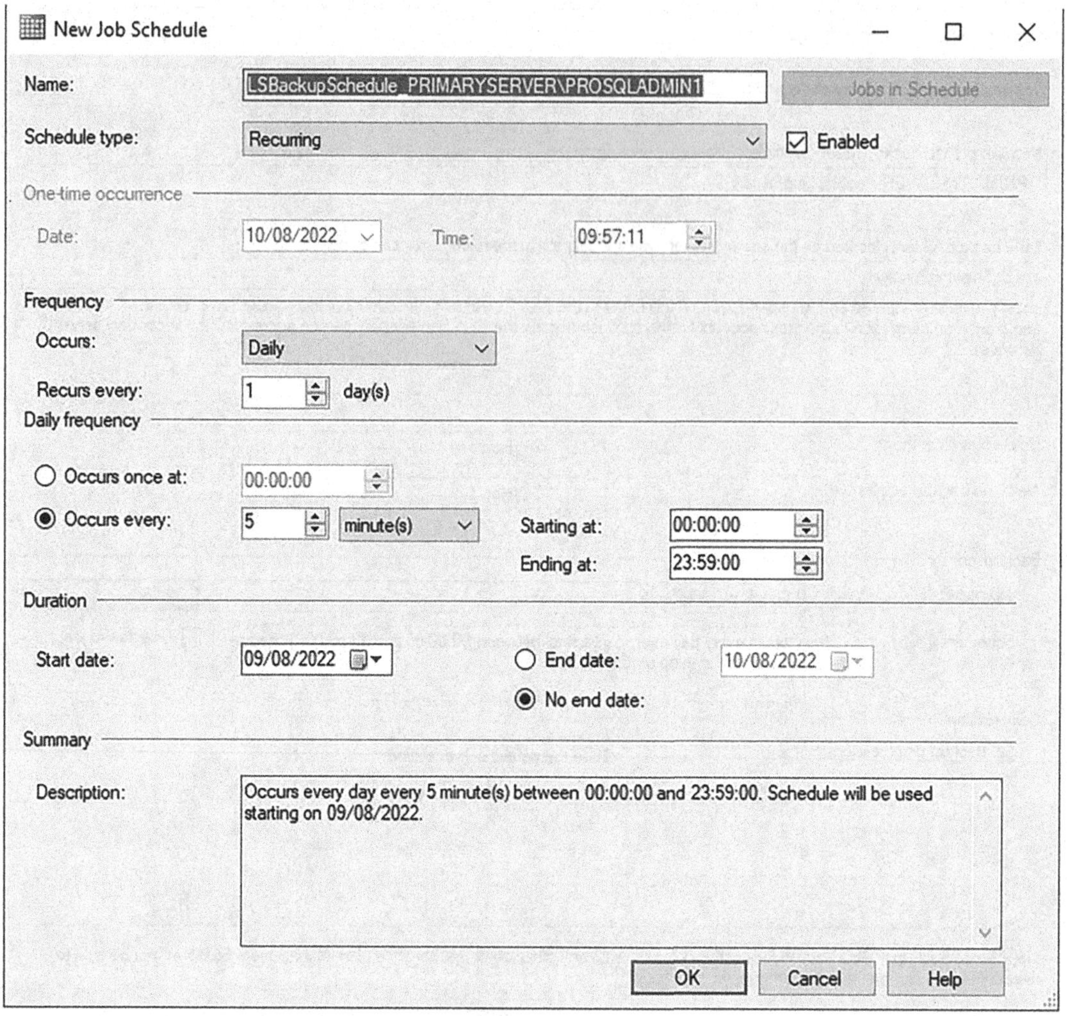

Figure 16-3. *The New Job Schedule screen*

After returning to the Transaction Log Shipping page, we can use the Add button to configure the secondary server(s) for our Log Shipping topology. Using this button causes the Secondary Database Settings page to display. This page consists of three tabs. The first of these is the Initialize Secondary Database tab, which is displayed in Figure 16-4.

On this tab, we configure how we want to initialize our secondary database. We can preinitialize our databases by taking a full backup of the database and then manually restoring them to the secondary server using the NORECOVERY option. In this kind of instance, we would select the No, the secondary database is initialized option.

If we already have a full backup available, then we can place it in a file share that the SQL Server service account has read and modify permissions on, and then use the Yes, restore an existing backup of the primary database into the secondary database option and specify the location of the backup file.

In our case, however, we do not have an existing full backup of the Chapter16 database, so we select the option to Yes, generate a full backup of the primary database and restore it into the secondary database. This causes the Restore Options window to display; it is here where we enter the locations that we want the data and transaction log files to be created on the secondary server, as illustrated in Figure 16-4.

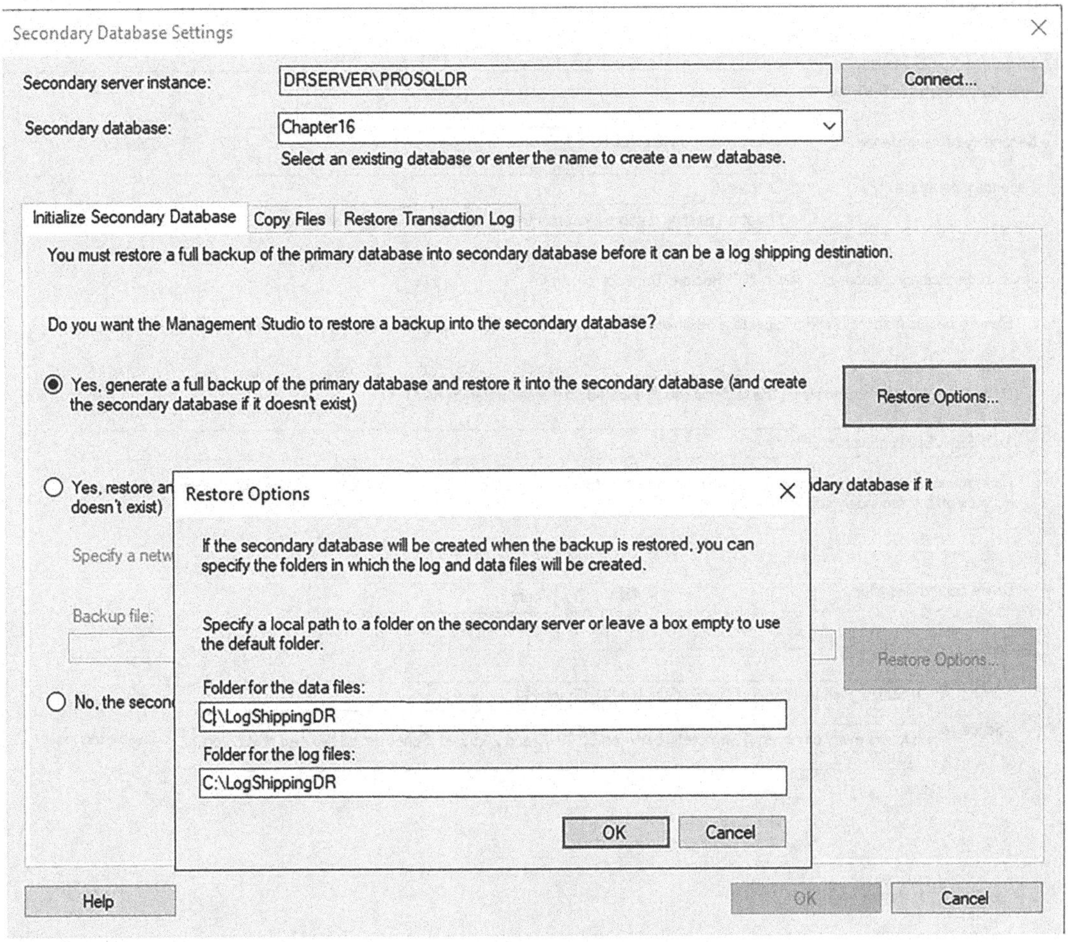

Figure 16-4. *The Initialize Secondary Database tab*

On the Copy Files tab, illustrated in Figure 16-5, we configure the job that is responsible for copying the transaction log files from the primary server to the secondary server(s). First, we specify the share on the secondary server to which we will copy the transaction logs. The account that runs the copy job must be configured with read and modify permissions on the share. Just like the backup job, this job defaults to running under the context of the SQL Server service account, but you can also configure it to run under a proxy account.

We also use this tab to configure how long the backup files should be retained on the secondary server before they are deleted. I usually recommend keeping this value in line with the value that you specify for retaining the backups on the primary server for consistency.

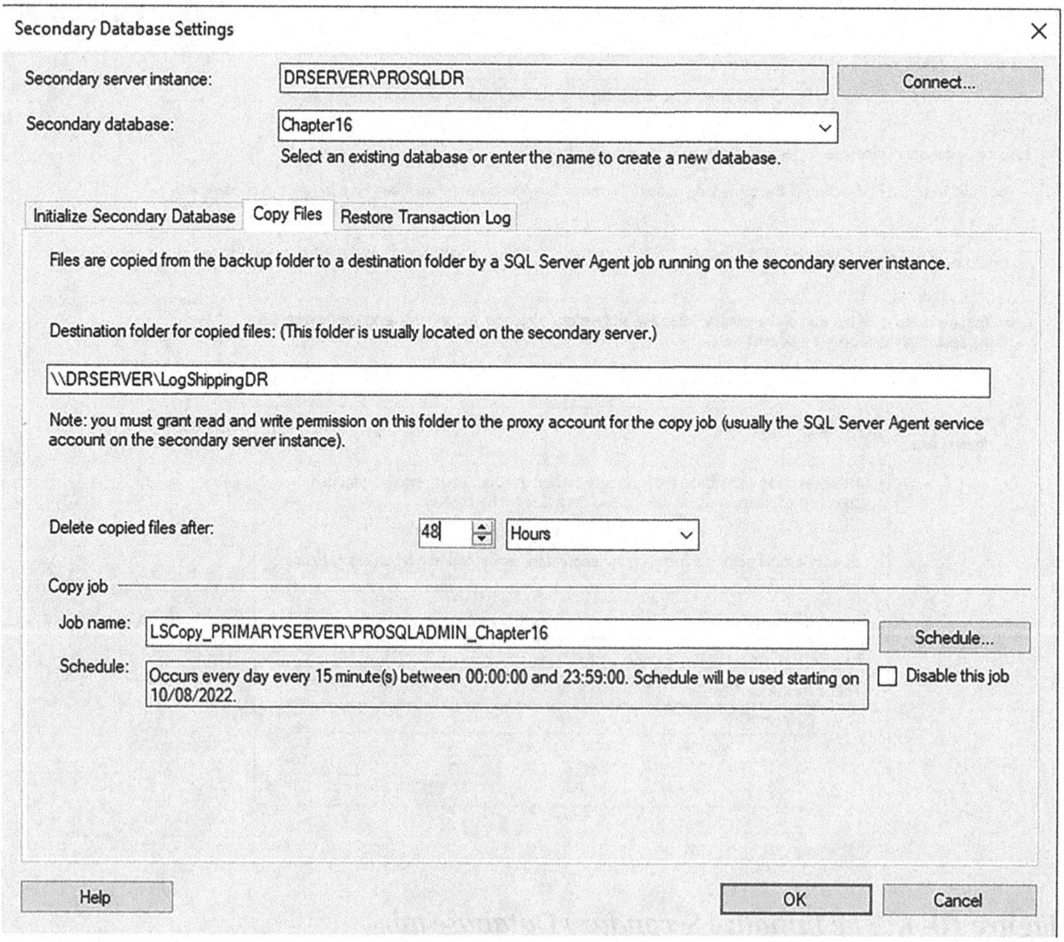

Figure 16-5. *The Copy Files tab*

The Job name field is automatically populated with the default name for a log shipping copy job, and using the Schedule button, you can invoke the New Job Schedule screen, where you can configure the schedule for the copy job. As illustrated in Figure 16-6, we have configured this job to run every five minutes, which is in line with our RPO requirement of ten minutes. It takes five minutes before the log is backed up, and then another five minutes before it is moved to the secondary sever. Once the file has been moved to the secondary server, we can be confident that, except in the most extreme circumstances, we will be able to retrieve the backup from either the primary or the secondary server, thus achieving our ten-minute RPO.

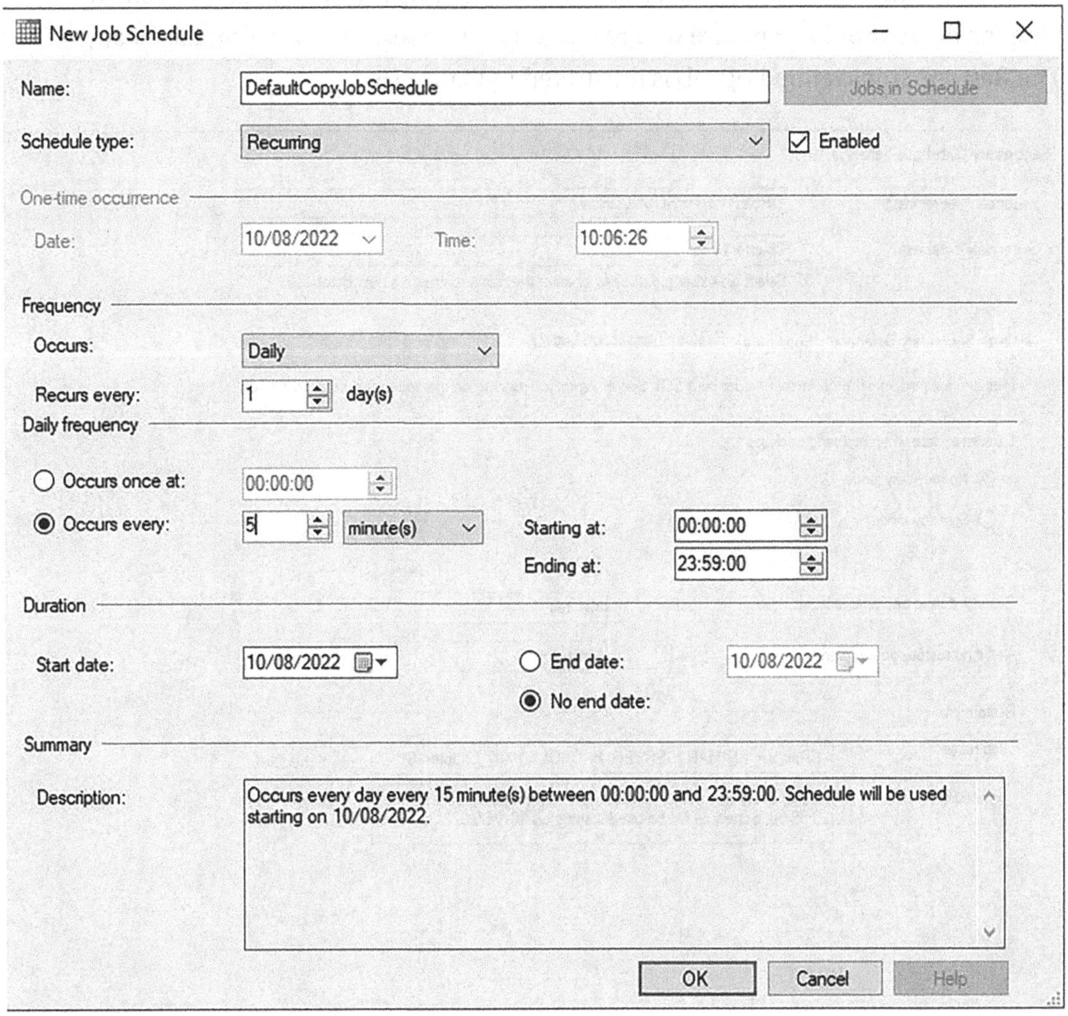

Figure 16-6. *The New Job Schedule screen*

On the Restore Transaction Log tab, we configure the job that is responsible for restoring the backups on the secondary server. The most important option on this screen is what database state we choose when restoring. Selecting the No recovery mode option is the applicable choice for a DR server. This is because if you choose Standby mode, uncommitted transactions are saved to a Transaction Undo File, which means the database can be brought online in read-only mode (as discussed in Chapter 14). However, this action increases the recovery time, because these transactions then need to be reapplied before the redo phase of the next restore.

On this tab, we also use the Delay restoring backups for at least option to apply the load delay, which gives users a chance to report data issues. We can also specify how long the delay should be before we are alerted that no restore operation has occurred. The Restore Transaction Log tab is illustrated in Figure 16-7.

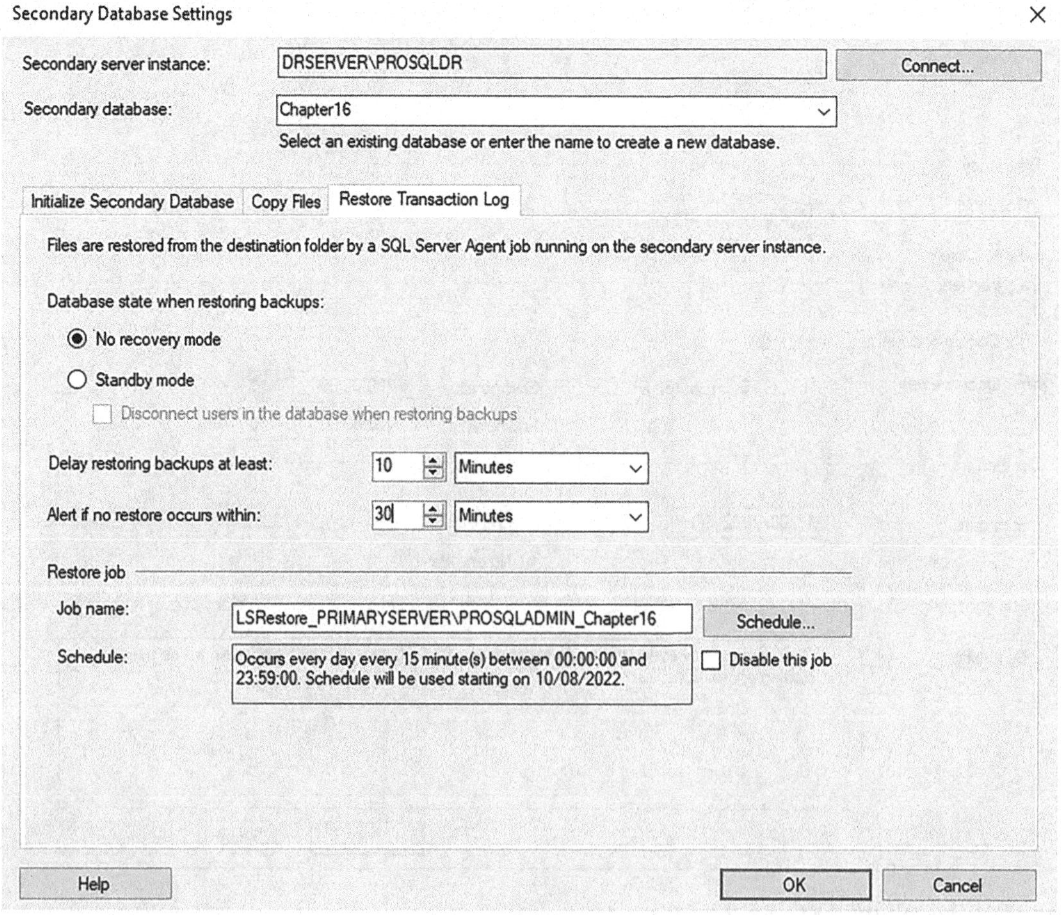

Figure 16-7. *The Restore Transaction Log tab*

The Schedule button invokes the New Job Schedule screen, displayed in Figure 16-8. On this screen, we can configure the job schedule for the restore of our transaction logs. Although doing so is not mandatory, for consistency, I usually recommend configuring this value so it is the same as the backup and copy jobs.

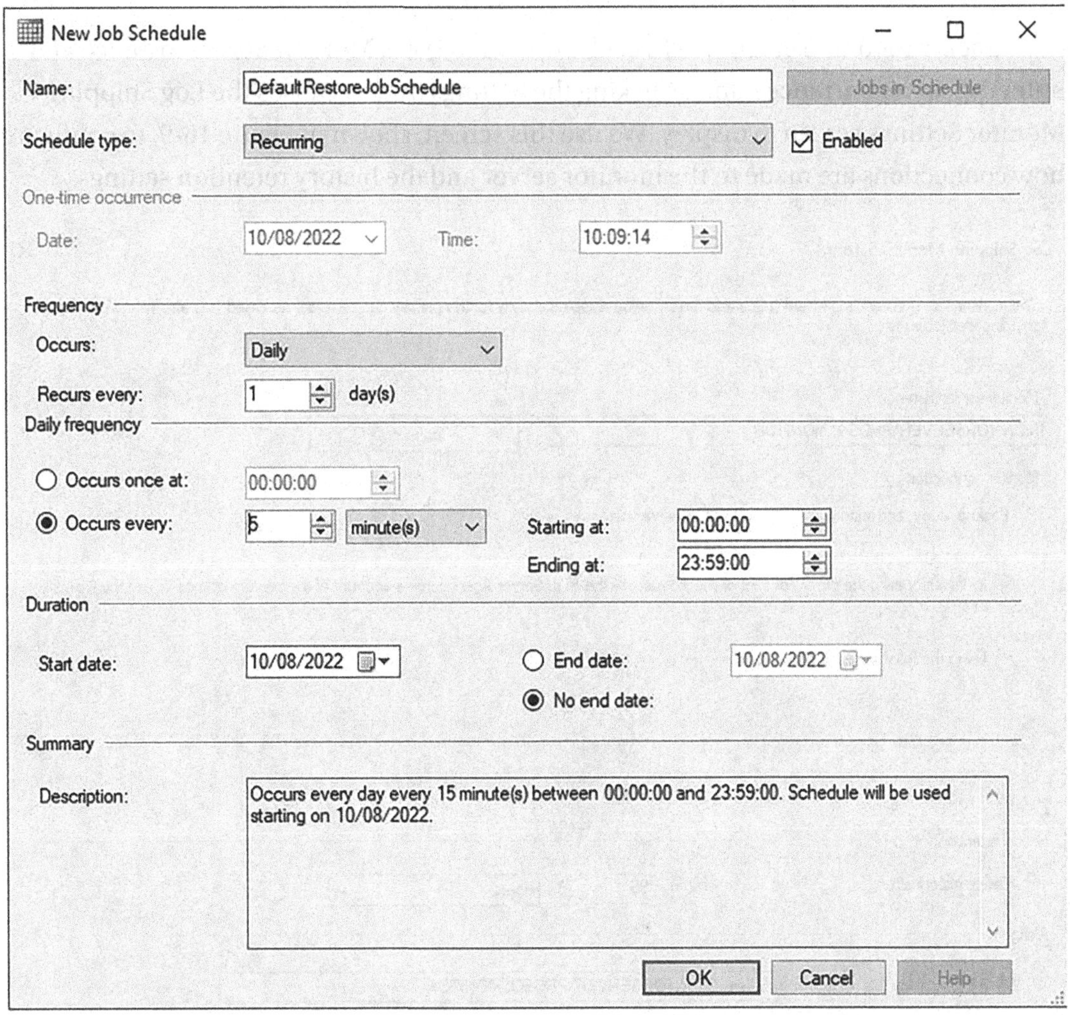

Figure 16-8. *New Job Schedule screen*

Once back on the Transaction Log Shipping page, we need to decide if we want to implement a monitor server. This option allows us to configure an instance, which acts as a centralized point for monitoring our Log Shipping topology. This is an important decision to make at this point, because after configuration is complete, there is no official way to add a monitor server to the topology without tearing down and reconfigured log shipping.

> **Tip**   It is technically possible to force in a monitor server at a later time, but the process involves manually updating log shipping metadata tables in MSDB. Therefore, it is not recommended, or supported.

To add a monitor server, we check the option to Use a Monitor Server Instance and enter the server/instance name. Clicking the Settings button causes the Log Shipping Monitor Settings screen to display. We use this screen, shown in Figure 16-9, to configure how connections are made to the monitor server and the history retention settings.

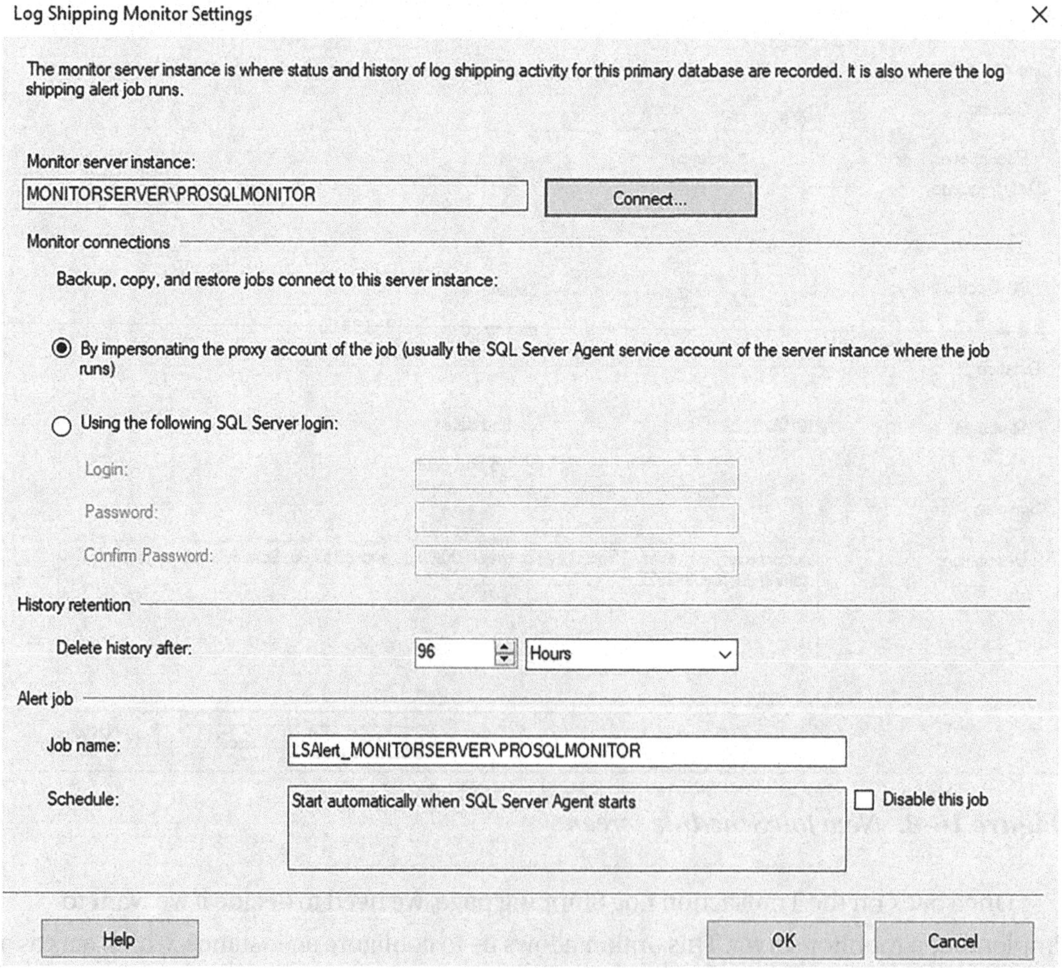

Figure 16-9.   *The Log Shipping Monitor Settings screen*

Now that our Log Shipping topology is fully configured, we can choose to script the configuration, which can be helpful for the purposes of documentation and change control. We can then complete the configuration. The progress of the configuration displays in the Save Log Shipping Configuration window (see Figure 16-10). Once configuration is complete, we should check this window for any errors that may have occurred during configuration and resolve them as needed. The most common cause of issues with log shipping configuration tends to be permissions related, so we need to ensure that the SQL Server service account (or proxy account) has the correct permissions on the file shares and instances before we continue.

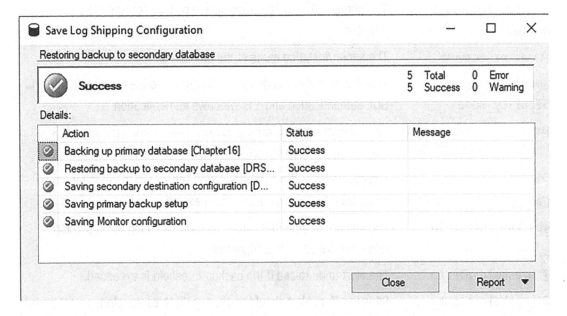

Figure 16-10. *The Save Log Shipping Configuration page*

T-SQL Configuration

To configure log shipping through T-SQL, we need to run a number of system stored procedures. The first of these procedures is sp_add_log_shipping_primary_database, which we use to configure the backup job and monitor the primary database. The parameters used by this procedure are described in Table 16-1.

Table 16-1. *sp_add_log_shipping_primary_database Parameters*

Parameter	Description
@database	The name of the database for which you are configuring log shipping.
@backup_directory	The local path to the backup folder.
@backup_share	The network path to the backup folder.
@backup_job_name	The name to use for the job that backs up the log.
@backup_retention_period	The duration that log backups should be kept for, specified in minutes.
@monitor_server	The server/instance name of the monitor server.
@monitor_server_Security_mode	The authentication mode to use to connect to the monitor server. 0 is SQL authentication and 1 is Windows authentication.
@monitor_server_login	The account used to connect to the monitor server (only use if SQL authentication is specified).
@monitor_server_password	The password of the account used to connect to the monitor server (only use if SQL authentication is specified).
@backup_threshold	The amount of time that can elapse, without a log backup being taken, before an alert is triggered.
@threshold_alert	The alert to be raised if the backup threshold is exceeded.
@threshold_alert_enabled	Specifies if an alert should be fired. 0 disables the alert; 1 enables it.
@history_retention_period	The duration for which the log backup job history will be retained, specified in minutes.
@backup_job_id	An OUTPUT parameter that specifies the GUID of the backup job that is created by the procedure.
@primary_id	An OUTPUT parameter that specifies the ID of the primary database.
@backup_compression	Specifies if backup compression should be used. 0 means disabled, 1 means enabled, and 2 means use the instance's default configuration.

Listing 16-2 demonstrates how we can use the sp_add_log_shipping_primary_ database procedure to configure Chapter16 for log shipping. This script uses the @backup_job_id output parameter to pass the job's GUID into the sp_update_job stored procedure. It also uses the sp_add_schedule and sp_attach_schedule system stored procedures to create the job schedule and attach it to the job. Because configuring log shipping involves connecting to multiple instances, we have added a connection to the primary instance. This means that we should run the script in SQLCMD mode.

Note sp_update_job, sp_add_schedule, and sp_attach_schedule are system stored procedures used to manipulate SQL Server Agent objects. A full discussion of SQL Server Agent can be found in Chapter 23.

Listing 16-2. Sp_add_log_shipping_primary_database

```
--Note that this script should be run in sqlcmd mode
:connect primaryserver\prosqladmin

DECLARE @LS_BackupJobId        UNIQUEIDENTIFIER
DECLARE @LS_BackUpScheduleID   INT

--Configure Chapter16 database as the Primary for Log Shipping

EXEC master.dbo.sp_add_log_shipping_primary_database
            @database = N'Chapter16'
            ,@backup_directory = N'c:\logshippingprimary'
            ,@backup_share = N'\\primaryserver\logshippingprimary'
            ,@backup_job_name = N'LSBackup_Chapter16'
            ,@backup_retention_period = 2880
            ,@backup_compression = 2
            ,@monitor_server = N'monitorserver.prosqladmin.com\
            prosqlmonitor'
            ,@monitor_server_security_mode = 1
            ,@backup_threshold = 60
```

```
                ,@threshold_alert_enabled = 1
                ,@history_retention_period = 5760
                ,@backup_job_id = @LS_BackupJobId OUTPUT ;

--Create a job schedule for the backup job

EXEC msdb.dbo.sp_add_schedule
                @schedule_name =N'LSBackupSchedule_primaryserver\
                prosqladmin1'
                ,@enabled = 1
                ,@freq_type = 4
                ,@freq_interval = 1
                ,@freq_subday_type = 4
                ,@freq_subday_interval = 5
                ,@freq_recurrence_factor = 0
                ,@active_start_date = 20220517
                ,@active_end_date = 99991231
                ,@active_start_time = 0
                ,@active_end_time = 235900
                ,@schedule_id = @LS_BackUpScheduleID OUTPUT ;

--Attach the job schedule to the job

EXEC msdb.dbo.sp_attach_schedule
                @job_id = @LS_BackupJobId
                ,@schedule_id = @LS_BackUpScheduleID  ;

--Enable the backup job
EXEC msdb.dbo.sp_update_job
                @job_id = @LS_BackupJobId
                ,@enabled = 1 ;
```

We use the `sp_add_log_shipping_primary_secondary` system stored procedure to update the metadata on the primary server in order to add a record for each secondary server in the Log Shipping topology. The parameters that it accepts are described in Table 16-2.

Table 16-2. *sp_add_log_shipping_primary_secondary Parameters*

Parameter	Description
@primary_database	The name of the primary database
@secondary_server	The server/instance of the secondary server
@secondary_database	The name of the database on the secondary server

Listing 16-3 demonstrates how we can use the `sp_add_log_shipping_primary_secondary` procedure to add a record of our DRSERVER\PROSQLDR instance to our primary server. Again, we specifically connect to the primary server, meaning that the script should run in SQLCMS mode.

Listing 16-3. Sp_add_log_shipping_primary_secondary

```
:connect primaryserver\prosqladmin

EXEC master.dbo.sp_add_log_shipping_primary_secondary
            @primary_database = N'Chapter16'
            ,@secondary_server = N'drserver\prosqldr'
            ,@secondary_database = N'Chapter16'
```

We now need to configure our DR server. The first task in this process is to run the `sp_add_log_shipping_secondary_primary` system stored procedure. This procedure creates the SQL Server Agent jobs that copy the transaction logs to the secondary server and restore them. It also configures monitoring. The parameters accepted by this stored procedure are detailed in Table 16-3.

Table 16-3. *sp_add_log_shipping_secondary_primary Parameters*

Parameter	Description
@primary_server	The server/instance name of the primary server.
@primary_database	The name of the primary database.
@backup_source_directory	The folder that the log backups are copied from.
@backup_destination_directory	The folder that the log backups are copied to.
@copy_job_name	The name that is given to the SQL Server Agent job used to copy the transaction logs.
@restore_job_name	The name that is given to the SQL Server Agent job used to restore the transaction logs.
@file_retention_period	The duration for which log backup history should be retained, specified in minutes.
@monitor_server	The server/instance name of the monitor server.
@monitor_server_security_mode	The authentication mode to be used to connect to the monitor server. 0 is SQL authentication and 1 is Windows authentication.
@monitor_server_login	The account used to connect to the monitor server (only use if SQL authentication is specified).
@monitor_server_password	The password of the account used to connect to the monitor server (only use if SQL authentication is specified).
@copy_job_id	OUTPUT parameter that specifies the GUID of the job that has been created to copy the transaction logs.
@restore_job_id	OUTPUT parameter that specifies the GUID of the job that has been created to restore the transaction logs.
@secondary_id	An OUTPUT parameter that specifies the ID of secondary database.

Listing 16-4 demonstrates how we can use the sp_add_log_shipping_secondary_ primary stored procedure to configure our DRSERVER\PROSQLDR instance as a secondary server in our Log Shipping topology. The script connects explicitly to the DR instance, so we should run it in SQL command mode. Just as when we set up the primary server, we use output parameters to pass to the SQL Server Agent stored procedures, to create the job schedules and enable the jobs.

Listing 16-4. Sp_add_log_shipping_secondary_primary

```
--Note This script should be run in sqlcmd mode
:connect drserver\prosqldr

DECLARE @LS_Secondary__CopyJobId        AS uniqueidentifier
DECLARE @LS_Secondary__RestoreJobId      AS uniqueidentifier
DECLARE @LS_SecondaryCopyJobScheduleID   AS int
DECLARE @LS_SecondaryRestoreJobScheduleID  AS int

--Configure the secondary server

EXEC master.dbo.sp_add_log_shipping_secondary_primary
            @primary_server = N'primaryserver\prosqladmin'
            @primary_database = N'Chapter16'
            ,@backup_source_directory = N'\\primaryserver\
            logshippingprimary'
            ,@backup_destination_directory = N'\\drserver\
            logshippingdr'
            ,@copy_job_name = N'LSCopy_primaryserver\prosqladmin_
            Chapter16'
            ,@restore_job_name = N'LSRestore_primaryserver\prosqladmin_
            Chapter16'
            ,@file_retention_period = 2880
            ,@monitor_server = N'monitorserver.prosqladmin.com\
            prosqlmonitor'
            ,@monitor_server_security_mode = 1
            ,@copy_job_id = @LS_Secondary__CopyJobId OUTPUT
            ,@restore_job_id = @LS_Secondary__RestoreJobId OUTPUT ;

--Create the schedule for the copy job

EXEC msdb.dbo.sp_add_schedule
            @schedule_name =N'DefaultCopyJobSchedule'
            ,@enabled = 1
```

```
                    ,@freq_type = 4
                    ,@freq_interval = 1
                    ,@freq_subday_type = 4
                    ,@freq_subday_interval = 15
                    ,@freq_recurrence_factor = 0
                    ,@active_start_date = 20220517
                    ,@active_end_date = 99991231
                    ,@active_start_time = 0
                    ,@active_end_time = 235900
                    ,@schedule_id = @LS_SecondaryCopyJobScheduleID OUTPUT ;

--Attach the schedule to the copy job

EXEC msdb.dbo.sp_attach_schedule
                    @job_id = @LS_Secondary__CopyJobId
                    ,@schedule_id = @LS_SecondaryCopyJobScheduleID  ;

--Create the job schedule for the restore job

EXEC msdb.dbo.sp_add_schedule
                    @schedule_name =N'DefaultRestoreJobSchedule'
                    ,@enabled = 1
                    ,@freq_type = 4
                    ,@freq_interval = 1
                    ,@freq_subday_type = 4
                    ,@freq_subday_interval = 15
                    ,@freq_recurrence_factor = 0
                    ,@active_start_date = 20220517
                    ,@active_end_date = 99991231
                    ,@active_start_time = 0
                    ,@active_end_time = 235900
                    ,@schedule_id = @LS_SecondaryRestoreJobScheduleID OUTPUT ;

--Attach the schedule to the restore job

EXEC msdb.dbo.sp_attach_schedule
                    @job_id = @LS_Secondary__RestoreJobId
                    ,@schedule_id = @LS_SecondaryRestoreJobScheduleID  ;
```

```
--Enable the jobs

EXEC msdb.dbo.sp_update_job
                @job_id = @LS_Secondary__CopyJobId
                ,@enabled = 1 ;

EXEC msdb.dbo.sp_update_job
                @job_id = @LS_Secondary__RestoreJobId
                ,@enabled = 1 ;
```

Our next step is to configure the secondary database. We can perform this task by using the sp_add_log_shipping_secondary_database stored procedure. The parameters accepted by this procedure are detailed in Table 16-4.

Table 16-4. *sp_add_log_shipping_secondary_database Parameters*

Parameter	Description
@secondary_database	The name of the secondary database.
@primary_server	The server/instance of the primary server.
@primary_database	The name of the primary database.
@restore_delay	Specifies the load delay, in minutes.
@restore_all	When set to 1, the restore job restores all available log backups. When set to 0, the restore job only applies a single log backup.
@restore_mode	Specifies the backup mode for the restore job to use. 1 means STANDBY and 0 means NORECOVERY.
@disconnect_users	Determines if users should be disconnected from the database while transaction log backups are being applied. 1 means that they are and 0 means that they are not. Only applies when restoring logs in STANDBY mode.
@block_size	Specifies the block size for the backup device, in bytes.
@buffer_count	Specifies the total number of memory buffers that can be used by a restore operation.
@max_transfer_size	Specifies the maximum size of the request that can be sent to the backup device, in bytes.

(*continued*)

Table 16-4. (*continued*)

Parameter	Description
@restore_threshold	The amount of time that can elapse, without a restore being applied, before an alert is generated; specified in minutes.
@threshold_alert	The alert to be raised if the restore threshold is exceeded.
@threshold_alert_enabled	Specifies if the alert is enabled. 1 means that it is enabled and 0 means that it is disabled.
@history_retention_period	The retention period of the restore history, specified in minutes.
@Ignoreremotemonitor	An undocumented parameter that partially controls how the internal log shipping database journal is updated.

Listing 16-5 demonstrates how we can use the sp_add_log_shipping_secondary_ database to configure our secondary database for log shipping. Since we are explicitly connecting to the DRSERVER\PROSQLDR instance, the script should run in SQLCMD mode.

Listing 16-5. Sp_add_log_shipping_secondary_database

```
:connect drserver\prosqldr

EXEC master.dbo.sp_add_log_shipping_secondary_database
              @secondary_database = N'Chapter16'
              ,@primary_server = N'primaryserver\prosqladmin'
              ,@primary_database = N'Chapter16'
              ,@restore_delay = 10
              ,@restore_mode = 0
              ,@disconnect_users     = 0
              ,@restore_threshold = 30
              ,@threshold_alert_enabled = 1
              ,@history_retention_period = 5760
              ,@ignoreremotemonitor = 1
```

The final task is to synchronize the monitor server and the DR server. We do this by using the (surprisingly) undocumented stored procedure sp_ processlogshippingmonitorsecondary. The parameters accepted by this procedure are detailed in Table 16-5.

Table 16-5. *sp_processlogshippingmonitorsecondary*

Parameter	Description
@mode	The recovery mode to use for the database. 0 indicates NORECOVERY and 1 indicates STANDBY.
@secondary_server	The server/instance of the secondary server.
@secondary_database	The name of the secondary database.
@secondary_id	The ID of the secondary server.
@primary_server	The server/instance of the primary server.
@monitor_server	The server/instance of the monitor server.
@monitor_server_security_mode	The authentication mode used to connect to the monitor server.
@primary_database	The name of the primary database.
@restore_threshold	The amount of time that can elapse without a restore being applied before an alert is triggered; specified in minutes.
@threshold_alert	The alert that fires if the alert restore threshold is exceeded.
@threshold_alert_enabled	Specifies if the alert is enabled or disabled.
@last_coppied_file	The file name of the last log backup to be copied to the secondary server.
@last_coppied_date	The date and time of the last time a log was copied to the secondary server.
@last_coppied_date_utc	The date and time of the last time a log was copied to the secondary server, converted to UTC (Coordinated Universal Time).
@last_restored_file	The file name of the last transaction log backup to be restored on the secondary server.
@last_restored_date	The date and time of the last time a log was restored on the secondary server.

(continued)

611

Table 16-5. *(continued)*

Parameter	Description
@last_restored_date_utc	The date and time of the last time a log was restored on the secondary server, converted to UTC.
@last_restored_latency	The elapsed time between the last log backup on the primary and its corresponding restore operation completing on the secondary.
@history_rentention_period	The duration that the history is retained, specified in minutes.

The script in Listing 16-6 demonstrates how to use the sp_ processlogshippingmonitorsecondary stored procedure to synchronize the information between our DR server and our monitor server. We should run the script against the monitor server, and since we are connecting explicitly to the MONITORSERVER\ PROSQLMONITOR instance, we should run the script in SQLCMD mode.

Listing 16-6. Sp_ processlogshippingmonitorsecondary

```
:connect monitorserver\prosqlmonitor

EXEC msdb.dbo.sp_processlogshippingmonitorsecondary
                @mode = 1
                ,@secondary_server = N'drserver\prosqldr'
                ,@secondary_database = N'Chapter16'
                ,@secondary_id = N''
                ,@primary_server = N'primaryserver\prosqladmin'
                ,@primary_database = N'Chapter16'
                ,@restore_threshold = 30
                ,@threshold_alert = 14420
                ,@threshold_alert_enabled = 1
                ,@history_retention_period        = 5760
                ,@monitor_server = N'monitorserver.prosqladmin.com\
                prosqlmonitor'
                ,@monitor_server_security_mode = 1
```

Log Shipping Maintenance

After you configure log shipping, you still have ongoing maintenance tasks to perform, such as failing over to the secondary server, if you need to, and switching the primary and secondary roles. These topics are discussed in the following sections. We also discuss how to use the monitor server to monitor the log shipping environment.

Failing Over Log Shipping

If your primary server has an issue, or your primary site fails, you need to fail over to your secondary server. To do this, first back up the tail end of the log. We discuss this process fully in Chapter 13, but the process essentially involves backing up the transaction log without truncating it and with NORECOVERY. This stops users from being able to connect to the database, therefore avoiding any further data loss. Obviously, this is only possible if the primary database is accessible. You can perform this action for the Chapter16 database by using the script in Listing 16-7.

Listing 16-7. Backing Up the Tail End of the Log

```
BACKUP LOG Chapter16
TO  DISK = N'c:\logshippingprimary\Chapter16_tail.trn'
WITH  NO_TRUNCATE , NAME = N'Chapter16-Full Database Backup', NORECOVERY
GO
```

The next step is to manually copy the tail end of the log and any other logs that have not yet been copied to the secondary server. Once this is complete, you need to manually restore the outstanding transaction log backups to the secondary server, in sequence. You need to apply the backups with NORECOVERY until the final backup is reached. This final backup is applied with RECOVERY. This causes any uncommitted transactions to be rolled back and the database to be brought online. Listing 16-8 demonstrates applying the final two transaction logs to the secondary database.

Listing 16-8. Applying Transaction Logs

```
--Restore the first transaction log

RESTORE LOG Chapter16
FROM  DISK = N'C:\LogShippingDR\Chapter16.trn'
WITH  FILE = 1,  NORECOVERY,  STATS = 10 ;
GO

--Restore the tail end of the log

RESTORE LOG Chapter16
FROM  DISK = N'C:\LogShippingDR\Chapter16_tail.trn'
WITH  FILE = 1,  RECOVERY, STATS = 10 ;
GO
```

Switching Roles

After you have failed over log shipping to the secondary server, you may want to swap the server roles so that the secondary that you failed over to becomes the new primary server and the original primary server becomes the secondary. In order to achieve this, first you need to disable the backup job on the primary server and the copy and restore jobs on the secondary server. If you are not planning to fail back the service, then it's a good idea to do this as soon as possible. We can perform this task for our Log Shipping topology by using the script in Listing 16-9. Because we are connecting to multiple servers, we need to run this script in SQLCMD mode.

Listing 16-9. Disabling Log Shipping Jobs

```
:connect primaryserver\prosqladmin

USE [msdb]
GO

--Disable backup job

EXEC msdb.dbo.sp_update_job @job_name = 'LSBackup_Chapter16',
              @enabled=0 ;
GO

:connect drserver\prosqldr
```

```
USE [msdb]
GO

--Disable copy job

EXEC msdb.dbo.sp_update_job @job_name='LSCopy_primaryserver\prosqladmin_
Chapter16',
                @enabled=0 ;
GO

--Disable restore job

EXEC msdb.dbo.sp_update_job @job_name='LSRestore_primaryserver\prosqladmin_
Chapter16',
                @enabled=0 ;
GO
```

The next step is to reconfigure log shipping on the new primary server. When you do this, configure the following:

- Ensure that you use the same backup share that you used for the original primary server.

- Ensure that when you add the secondary database, you specify the database that was originally the primary database.

- Specify the synchronization No, the secondary database is initialized option.

The script in Listing 16-10 performs this action for our new secondary server. Since we are connecting to multiple servers, we should run the script in SQLCMD mode.

Listing 16-10. Reconfiguring Log Shipping

```
:connect drserver\prosqldr

DECLARE @LS_BackupJobId      AS uniqueidentifier
DECLARE @SP_Add_RetCode      As int
DECLARE @LS_BackUpScheduleID AS int
```

```
EXEC @SP_Add_RetCode = master.dbo.sp_add_log_shipping_primary_database
                @database = N'Chapter16'
                ,@backup_directory = N'\\primaryserver\logshippingprimary'
                ,@backup_share = N'\\primaryserver\logshippingprimary'
                ,@backup_job_name = N'LSBackup_Chapter16'
                ,@backup_retention_period = 2880
                ,@backup_compression = 2
                ,@backup_threshold = 60
                ,@threshold_alert_enabled = 1
                ,@history_retention_period = 5760
                ,@backup_job_id = @LS_BackupJobId OUTPUT
                ,@overwrite = 1

EXEC msdb.dbo.sp_add_schedule
                @schedule_name =N'LSBackupSchedule_DRSERVER\PROSQLDR1'
                ,@enabled = 1
                ,@freq_type = 4
                ,@freq_interval = 1
                ,@freq_subday_type = 4
                ,@freq_subday_interval = 5
                ,@freq_recurrence_factor = 0
                ,@active_start_date = 20220517
                ,@active_end_date = 99991231
                ,@active_start_time = 0
                ,@active_end_time = 235900
                ,@schedule_id = @LS_BackUpScheduleID OUTPUT

EXEC msdb.dbo.sp_attach_schedule
                @job_id = @LS_BackupJobId
                ,@schedule_id = @LS_BackUpScheduleID

EXEC msdb.dbo.sp_update_job
                @job_id = @LS_BackupJobId
                ,@enabled = 1
```

```
EXEC master.dbo.sp_add_log_shipping_primary_secondary
              @primary_database = N'Chapter16'
              ,@secondary_server = N'primaryserver\prosqladmin'
              ,@secondary_database = N'Chapter16'
              ,@overwrite = 1

:connect primaryserver\prosqladmin

DECLARE @LS_Secondary__CopyJobId          AS uniqueidentifier
DECLARE @LS_Secondary__RestoreJobId        AS uniqueidentifier
DECLARE @LS_Add_RetCode          As int
DECLARE @LS_SecondaryCopyJobScheduleID          AS int
DECLARE @LS_SecondaryRestoreJobScheduleID          AS int

EXEC @LS_Add_RetCode = master.dbo.sp_add_log_shipping_secondary_primary
              @primary_server = N'DRSERVER\PROSQLDR'
              ,@primary_database = N'Chapter16'
              ,@backup_source_directory = N'\\primaryserver\
              logshippingprimary'
              ,@backup_destination_directory = N'\\primaryserver\
              logshippingprimary'
              ,@copy_job_name = N'LSCopy_DRSERVER\PROSQLDR_Chapter16'
              ,@restore_job_name = N'LSRestore_DRSERVER\PROSQLDR_
              Chapter16'
              ,@file_retention_period = 2880
              ,@overwrite = 1
              ,@copy_job_id = @LS_Secondary__CopyJobId OUTPUT
              ,@restore_job_id = @LS_Secondary__RestoreJobId OUTPUT

EXEC msdb.dbo.sp_add_schedule
              @schedule_name =N'DefaultCopyJobSchedule'
              ,@enabled = 1
              ,@freq_type = 4
              ,@freq_interval = 1
              ,@freq_subday_type = 4
              ,@freq_subday_interval = 5
              ,@freq_recurrence_factor = 0
              ,@active_start_date = 20220517
```

```
            ,@active_end_date = 99991231
            ,@active_start_time = 0
            ,@active_end_time = 235900
            ,@schedule_id = @LS_SecondaryCopyJobScheduleID OUTPUT

EXEC msdb.dbo.sp_attach_schedule
            @job_id = @LS_Secondary__CopyJobId
            ,@schedule_id = @LS_SecondaryCopyJobScheduleID

EXEC msdb.dbo.sp_add_schedule
            @schedule_name =N'DefaultRestoreJobSchedule'
            ,@enabled = 1
            ,@freq_type = 4
            ,@freq_interval = 1
            ,@freq_subday_type = 4
            ,@freq_subday_interval = 5
            ,@freq_recurrence_factor = 0
            ,@active_start_date = 20220517
            ,@active_end_date = 99991231
            ,@active_start_time = 0
            ,@active_end_time = 235900
            ,@schedule_id = @LS_SecondaryRestoreJobScheduleID OUTPUT

EXEC msdb.dbo.sp_attach_schedule
            @job_id = @LS_Secondary__RestoreJobId
            ,@schedule_id = @LS_SecondaryRestoreJobScheduleID

EXEC master.dbo.sp_add_log_shipping_secondary_database
            @secondary_database = N'Chapter16'
            ,@primary_server = N'DRSERVER\PROSQLDR'
            ,@primary_database = N'Chapter16'
            ,@restore_delay = 10
            ,@restore_mode = 0
            ,@disconnect_users        = 0
            ,@restore_threshold = 30
            ,@threshold_alert_enabled = 1
            ,@history_retention_period = 5760
            ,@overwrite = 1
```

```
EXEC msdb.dbo.sp_update_job
                @job_id = @LS_Secondary__CopyJobId
                ,@enabled = 1

EXEC msdb.dbo.sp_update_job
                @job_id = @LS_Secondary__RestoreJobId
                ,@enabled = 1
```

The final step is to reconfigure monitoring so it correctly monitors our new configuration. We can achieve this for our log shipping environment by using the script in Listing 16-11. This script connects to both the primary and secondary servers, so we should run it in SQLCMD mode.

Listing 16-11. Reconfiguring Monitoring

```
:connect drserver\prosqldr

USE msdb
GO

EXEC master.dbo.sp_change_log_shipping_secondary_database
        @secondary_database = N'database_name',
        @threshold_alert_enabled = 0 ;
GO

:connect primaryserver\prosqladmin

USE msdb
GO

EXEC master.dbo.sp_change_log_shipping_primary_database
        @database=N'database_name',
        @threshold_alert_enabled = 0 ;
GO
```

Because we have now created the backup, copy, and restore jobs on both servers, switching the roles after subsequent failovers is much more straightforward. From now on, after we have failed over, we can switch roles by simply disabling the backup job on the original primary server and the copy and restore jobs on the secondary server, and then enabling the backup job on the new primary server and the copy and restore jobs on the new secondary server.

Monitoring

The most important aspect of monitoring your Log Shipping topology is ensuring that the backups are occurring on the primary and being restored on the secondary. For this reason, when we configure log shipping in this chapter, we tweak the acceptable thresholds for backups and restores, and Server Agent Alerts are created on the monitor server. Before these alerts are useful, however, we need to configure them with an operator to notify.

On the monitor server, we have configured two alerts. The first is called Log Shipping Primary Server Alert, and when you view the General tab of this alert's properties, you see that it is configured to respond to Error 14420, as shown in Figure 16-11. Error 14420 indicates that a backup has not been taken of the primary database within the defined threshold.

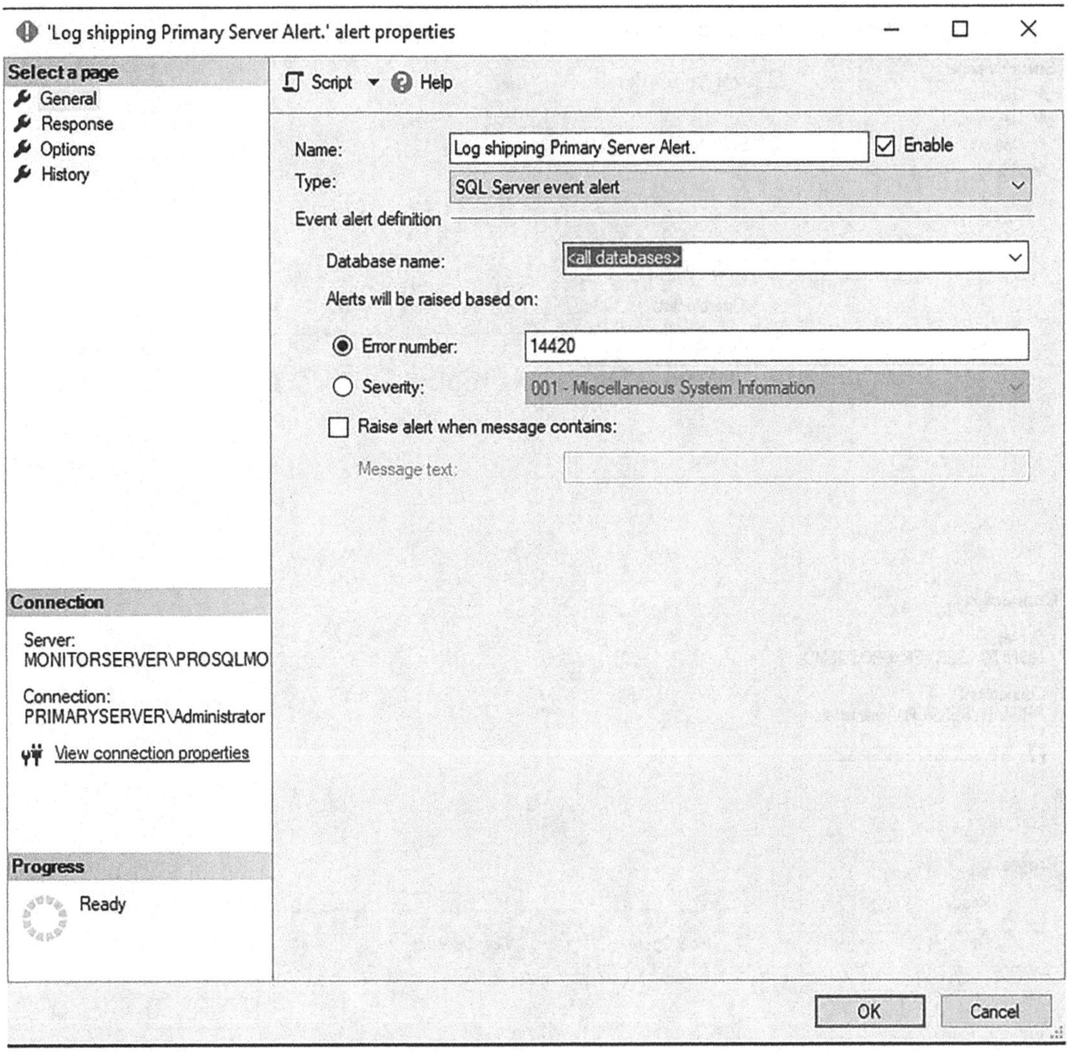

Figure 16-11. *The General tab*

On the Response tab, displayed in Figure 16-12, we need to configure an operator to receive the alerts. You can either use the New Operator button to configure a new operator, or as in our case, simply select the appropriate notification channel for the appropriate operator(s) in the list. You can also select to run a SQL Server Agent job, which attempts to remediate the condition.

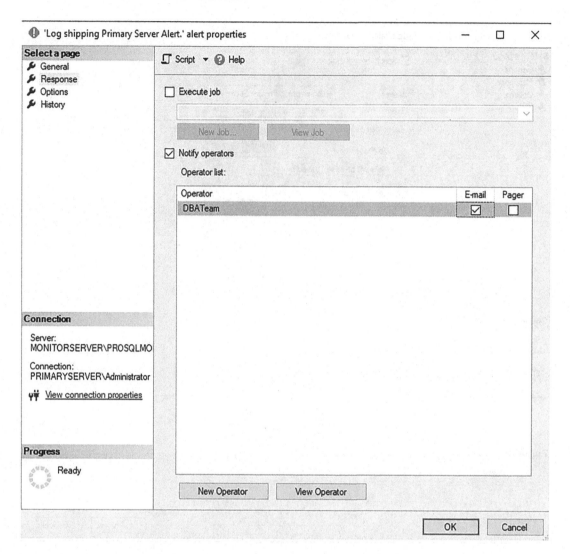

Figure 16-12. *The Response tab*

You should configure the Log Shipping Secondary Server Alert in the same way you configured the Log Shipping Primary Server Alert. The secondary server alert works in the same way, except that it is monitoring for Error 14421 instead of 14420. Error 14421 indicates that a transaction log has not been restored to the secondary server within the threshold period.

The log shipping report can be run from SQL Server Management Studio, and when you run it on the monitor server, it displays the status of the primary server and each secondary server. When run on the primary server, it shows the status of each database based on the backup jobs and includes a line for each secondary. When run on the DR server, it shows the status of each database based on the restore jobs. You can access the report by invoking the context menu of the instance and drilling through Reports ➤ Standard Reports, before selecting the Transaction Log Shipping Status report.

Figure 16-13 illustrates the report when run against the primary server. In our case, the replication is in good health, but if there were threshold breaches, then the rows would be highlighted in red. We could have obtained the same information by using the sp_help_log_shipping_monitor stored procedure.

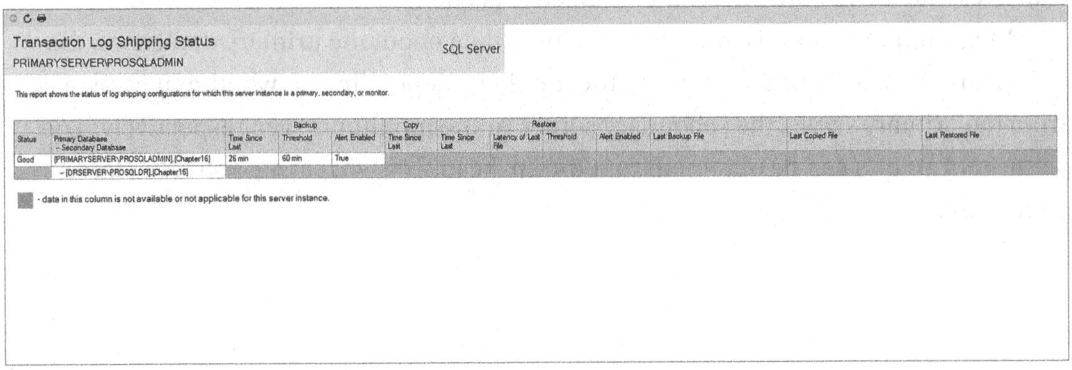

Figure 16-13. *The Log Shipping report*

Summary

Log shipping is a technology that you can use to implement DR for databases. It synchronizes data by backing up the transaction log of the primary database, copying it to a secondary server, and then restoring it. If the log is restored with STANDBY, then uncommitted transactions are stored in a Transaction Undo File and you can reapply them before subsequent backups. This means that you can bring the database online in read-only mode for reporting. If the logs are restored with NORECOVERY, however, then the servers are ready for a DR invocation, but the databases are in an offline state.

Failing over a database to a secondary server involves backing up the tail end of the transaction log and then applying any outstanding log backups to the secondary database, before finally bringing the database online by issuing the final restore with RECOVERY. If you wish to switch the server roles, then you need to disable the current log shipping jobs, reconfigure log shipping so that the secondary server is now the primary, and then reconfigure monitoring. After subsequent failovers, however, switching the roles becomes easier, because you are able to simply disable and enable the appropriate SQL Server Agent jobs used by log shipping.

To monitor the health of your Log Shipping topology, you should configure the log shipping alerts and add an operator who will be notified if the alert fires. The alert for the primary server is monitoring for Error 14420, which means that the backup threshold has been exceeded. The alert for the secondary server(s) monitors for Error 14421, which indicates that the restore threshold has been exceeded.

A log shipping report is available; it returns data about the primary databases, the secondary databases, or all servers in the topology, depending on whether it is invoked from the primary server, the secondary server, or the monitor server, respectively. The same information can be obtained from the `sp_help_log_shipping_monitor` stored procedure.

CHAPTER 17

Scaling Workloads

SQL Server provides multiple technologies that allow DBAs to horizontally scale
their workloads between multiple databases to avoid lock contention or to scale
them horizontally between servers to spread resource utilization. These technologies
include database snapshots, replication, and AlwaysOn Availability Groups. This
chapter discusses the considerations for these technologies and demonstrates how to
implement them.

Database Snapshots

A *database snapshot* is a point-in-time view of a database that never changes after it is
generated. It works using copy-on-write technology; this means that if a page is modified
in the source database, the original version of the page is copied to an NTFS sparse file,
which is used by the database snapshot. A *sparse file* is a file that starts off empty, with
no disk space allocated. As pages are updated in the source database and these pages
are copied to the sparse file, it grows to accommodate them. This process is illustrated in
Figure 17-1.

© Peter A. Carter 2023
P. A. Carter, *Pro SQL Server 2022 Administration*, https://doi.org/10.1007/978-1-4842-8864-1_17

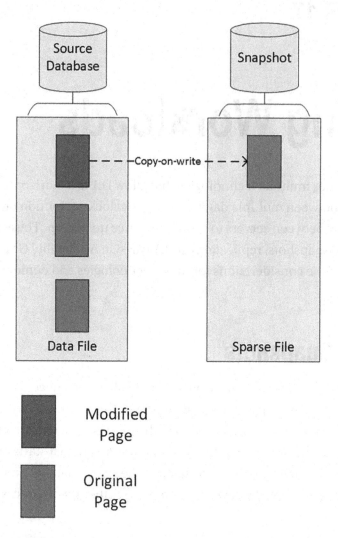

Figure 17-1. *Database snapshots*

If a user runs a query against the database snapshot, SQL Server checks to see if the required pages exist in the database snapshot. Any pages that do exist are returned from the database snapshot, whereas any other pages are retrieved from the source database, as illustrated in Figure 17-2. In this example, to satisfy the query, SQL Server needs to return Page 1:100 and Page 1:101. Page 1:100 has been modified in the source database since the snapshot was taken. Therefore, the original version of the page has been copied to the sparse file and SQL Server retrieves it from there. Page 1:101, on the other hand, has not been modified in the source database since the snapshot was created. Therefore, it does not exist in the sparse file, and SQL Server retrieves it from the source database.

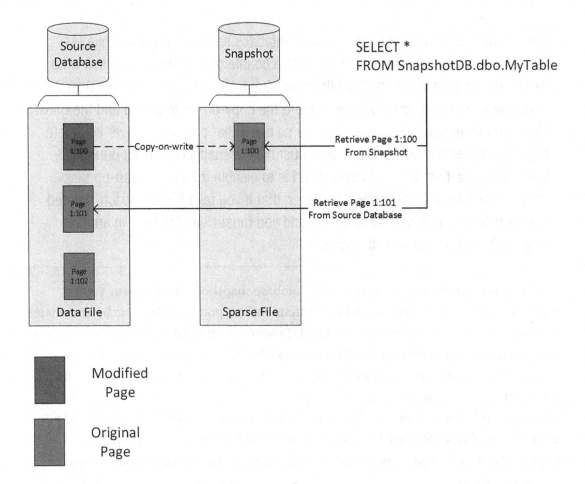

Figure 17-2. *Querying a database snapshot*

If your data-tier application is suffering from contention caused by locking, then you can scale out reporting to a database snapshot. It is important to note, however, that because a database snapshot must reside on the same instance as the source database, it does not help overcome resource utilization issues. In fact, the opposite is true. Because any modified pages must be copied to the sparse file, the I/O overhead increases. The memory footprint also increases, since pages are duplicated in the buffer cache for each database.

Tip   It may not be appropriate to have a database snapshot present while I/O-intensive tasks are carried out. I have seen a couple of scenarios—one involving index rebuilds on a VLDB and the other involving a snapshot on the Subscriber database in a Replication topology—where the copy-on-write thread and the ghost clean-up thread have blocked each other so badly that processes never complete. If you encounter this scenario and you must have a snapshot present during I/O-intensive tasks, then the only workaround is to disable the ghost clean-up task using Trace Flag 661. Be warned, however, that if you take this approach, deleted rows are never automatically removed, and you must clean them up in another way, such as by rebuilding all indexes.

In addition to the resource overhead of database snapshots, another issue you encounter when you use them to reduce contention for reporting is that data becomes stale as pages in the source database are modified. To overcome this, you can create a metadata-driven script to periodically refresh the snapshot. This is demonstrated in Chapter 18.

The issue of data becoming stale can also be an advantage, however, because it gives you two benefits: first, it means that you can use snapshots for historic reporting purposes, and second, it means that you can use database snapshots to recover data after user error has occurred. Be warned, however, that these snapshots provide no resilience against I/O errors or database failures, and you cannot use them to replace database backups.

Implementing Database Snapshots

Before demonstrating how to create a database snapshot, we first create the Chapter17 database, which we use for demonstrations throughout this chapter. The script in Listing 17-1 creates this database and populates it with data.

Listing 17-1. Creating the Chapter17 Database

```
CREATE DATABASE Chapter17 ;
GO

USE Chapter17
GO
```

```
CREATE TABLE Customers
(
ID                    INT              PRIMARY KEY        IDENTITY,
FirstName             NVARCHAR(30),
LastName              NVARCHAR(30),
CreditCardNumber      VARBINARY(8000)
) ;
GO

--Populate the table

DECLARE @Numbers TABLE
(
         Number          INT
)

;WITH CTE(Number)
AS
(
         SELECT 1 Number
         UNION ALL
         SELECT Number + 1
         FROM CTE
         WHERE Number < 100
)
INSERT INTO @Numbers
SELECT Number FROM CTE ;

DECLARE @Names TABLE
(
         FirstName       VARCHAR(30),
         LastName        VARCHAR(30)
) ;

INSERT INTO @Names
VALUES('Peter', 'Carter'),
                ('Michael', 'Smith'),
                ('Danielle', 'Mead'),
```

```
                ('Reuben', 'Roberts'),
                ('Iris', 'Jones'),
                ('Sylvia', 'Davies'),
                ('Finola', 'Wright'),
                ('Edward', 'James'),
                ('Marie', 'Andrews'),
                ('Jennifer', 'Abraham'),
                ('Margaret', 'Jones') ;

INSERT INTO Customers(Firstname, LastName, CreditCardNumber)
SELECT  FirstName, LastName, CreditCardNumber FROM
        (SELECT
                (SELECT TOP 1 FirstName FROM @Names ORDER BY NEWID())
                FirstName
                ,(SELECT TOP 1 LastName FROM @Names ORDER BY NEWID())
                LastName
                ,(SELECT CONVERT(VARBINARY(8000)
                ,(SELECT TOP 1 CAST(Number * 100 AS CHAR(4))
                  FROM @Numbers
                  WHERE Number BETWEEN 10 AND 99
                  ORDER BY NEWID()) + '-' +
                        (SELECT TOP 1 CAST(Number * 100 AS CHAR(4))
                         FROM @Numbers
                         WHERE Number BETWEEN 10 AND 99
                         ORDER BY NEWID()) + '-' +
                        (SELECT TOP 1 CAST(Number * 100 AS CHAR(4))
                         FROM @Numbers
                         WHERE Number BETWEEN 10 AND 99
                         ORDER BY NEWID()) + '-' +
                        (SELECT TOP 1 CAST(Number * 100 AS CHAR(4))
                         FROM @Numbers
                         WHERE Number BETWEEN 10 AND 99
                         ORDER BY NEWID()))) CreditCardNumber
FROM @Numbers a
CROSS JOIN @Numbers b
) d ;
```

To create a database snapshot on the Chapter17 database, we use the CREATE DATABASE syntax, adding the AS SNAPSHOT OF clause, as demonstrated in Listing 17-2. The number of files must match the number of files of the source database, and the snapshot must be created with a unique name. The .ss file extension is standard, but not mandatory. I have known some DBAs to use an .ndf extension if they cannot gain an antivirus exception for an additional file extension. I recommend using the .ss extension if possible, however, because this clearly identifies the file as being associated with a snapshot.

Listing 17-2. Creating a Database Snapshot

```
CREATE DATABASE Chapter17_ss_0630
ON PRIMARY
( NAME = N'Chapter17', FILENAME = N'F:\MSSQL\DATA\Chapter17_ss_0630.ss' )
AS SNAPSHOT OF Chapter17 ;
```

The fact that each database snapshot must have a unique name can cause an issue for connecting applications if you plan to use multiple snapshots; this is because the applications do not know the name of the database to which they should connect. You can resolve this issue by programmatically pointing applications to the latest database snapshot. You can find an example of how to do this in Listing 17-3. This script creates and runs a procedure that returns all data from the Contacts table. It first dynamically checks the name of the most recent snapshot that is based on the Chapter17 database, which means that the data will always be returned from the most recent snapshot.

Listing 17-3. Directing Clients to LatestSnapshot

```
USE Chapter17
GO

CREATE PROCEDURE dbo.usp_Dynamic_Snapshot_Query
AS
BEGIN
        DECLARE @LatestSnapshot NVARCHAR(128)
        DECLARE @SQL NVARCHAR(MAX)

        SET @LatestSnapshot = (
            SELECT TOP 1 name from sys.databases
```

```
            WHERE source_database_id = DB_ID('Chapter17')
            ORDER BY create_date DESC ) ;

        SET @SQL = 'SELECT * FROM ' + @LatestSnapshot + '.dbo.Customers' ;

        EXEC(@SQL) ;
END

EXEC dbo.usp_Dynamic_Snapshot_Query ;
```

Recovering Data from a Snapshot

If user error leads to data loss, then a database snapshot can allow a DBA to recover data without needing to restore a database from a backup, which can reduce the RTO for resolving the issue. Imagine that a user accidently truncates the Contacts table in the Chapter17 database; we can recover this data by reinserting it from the snapshot, as demonstrated in Listing 17-4.

Listing 17-4. Recovering Lost Data

```
--Truncate the table

TRUNCATE TABLE Chapter17.dbo.Customers ;

--Allow Identity values to be reinserted

SET IDENTITY_INSERT Chapter17.dbo.Customers ON ;

--Insert the data

INSERT INTO Chapter17.dbo.Customers(ID, FirstName, LastName,
CreditCardNumber)
SELECT *
        FROM Chapter17_ss_0630.dbo.Customers ;

--Turn off IDENTITY_INSERT

SET IDENTITY_INSERT Chapter17.dbo.Customers OFF ;
```

If a large portion of the source database has been damaged by user error, then instead of fixing each data issue individually, it may be quicker to recover the entire database from the snapshot. You can do this using the RESTORE command with the FROM DATABASE_SNAPSHOT syntax, as demonstrated in Listing 17-5.

Note   If more than one snapshot of the database that you wish to recover exists, then you must drop all the snapshots but the one you are going to restore from before you run this script.

Listing 17-5. Recovering from a Database Snapshot

```
USE Master
GO

RESTORE DATABASE Chapter17
        FROM DATABASE_SNAPSHOT = 'Chapter17_ss_0630' ;
```

Replication

SQL Server provides a suite of replication technologies, which you can use to disperse data between instances. You can use replication for many purposes, including offloading reporting, integrating data from multiple sites, supporting data warehousing, and exchanging data with mobile users.

Replication Concepts

Replication draws its terminology from the publishing industry. The components of a Replication topology are described in Table 17-1.

Table 17-1. *Replication Components*

Component	Description
Publisher	The publisher is the instance that makes data available to other locations. This is essentially the primary server.
Subscriber	The subscriber is the instance that receives data from the publisher. This is essentially the secondary server. A Replication topology can have multiple subscribers.
Distributor	The distributor is the instance that stores the metadata for the replication technology and may also take the workload of processing. This instance may be the same instance as the publisher.
Article	An article is a database object that is replicated, such as a table or a view. The article can be filtered to reduce the amount of data that needs to be replicated.
Publication	A publication is a collection of articles from a database that is replicated as a single unit.
Subscription	A subscription is a request from a subscriber to receive publications. It defines which publications are received by the subscriber. There are two types of subscription: push and pull. In a pull subscription model, the distribution or merge agent that is responsible for moving the data runs on each subscriber. In a push model, the distribution or merge agent runs on the distributor.
Replication Agents	Replication agents are applications that sit outside of SQL Server that are used to perform various tasks. The agents that are used depend on the type of replication that you implement.

Figure 17-3 illustrates how the replication components fit together within a Replication topology. In this example, two subscribers each receiving the same publication and the distributor have been separated from the publisher. This is known as a *remote distributor*. If the publisher and distributor shared an instance, then it is known as a *local distributor*.

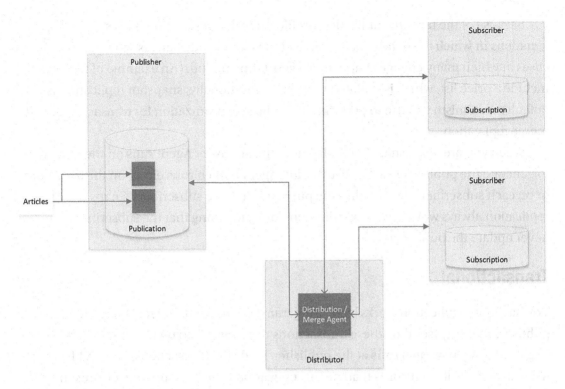

Figure 17-3. *Replication component overview*

Types of Replication

SQL Server offers three broad types of replication: snapshot, transactional, and merge. These replication technologies are introduced in the following sections.

Snapshot

Snapshot replication works by taking a complete copy of all articles at the point when synchronizations occurs; therefore, it does not need to track data changes between synchronizations. If you have defined a filter on the article, then only the filtered data is copied. This means that snapshot replication has no overhead, except when synchronization is occurring. When synchronization does occur, however, the resource overhead can be very high if there is a large amount of data to replicate.

The Snapshot Agent creates a system view and system stored procedure for each article in the publication. It uses these objects to generate the contents of the articles. It also creates schema files, which it applies to the subscription database before it uses BCP (Bulk Copy Program) to bulk copy the data.

Because of the resource utilization profile, snapshot replication is most suited to situations in which the dataset being replicated is small and changes infrequently, or in cases in which many changes happen in a short time period. (An example of this may include a price list, which is updated monthly.) Additionally, snapshot replication is the default mechanism you use to perform the initial synchronization for transactional and merge replication.

When you are using snapshot replication, the Snapshot Agent runs on the publisher to generate the publication. The Distribution Agent (which runs either on the distributor or on each subscriber) then applies the publication to the subscribers. Snapshot replication always works in a single direction only, meaning that the subscribers can never update the publisher.

Transactional

Transactional replication works by reading transactions from the transaction log on the publisher and then sending these transactions to be reapplied on the subscribers. The Log Reader Agent, which runs at the publisher, reads the transactions, and a VLF is not truncated until all log records marked for replication have been processed. This means that if there is a long period between synchronizations and many data modifications occur, there is a risk that your transaction log will grow or even run out of space. After the transactions have been read from the log, the Distribution Agent applies the transactions to the subscribers. This agent runs at the distributor in a push subscription model or at each of the subscribers in a pull subscription model. Synchronization is scheduled by SQL Server Agent jobs, which are configured to run the replication agents, and you can configure synchronization, so it happens continuously or periodically, depending on your requirements. The initial data synchronization is performed using the Snapshot Agent by default.

Transactional replication is normally used in server-to-server scenarios where there is a high volume of data modifications at the publisher and there is a reliable network connection between the publisher and subscriber. A global data warehouse is an example of this, having subsets of data replicated to regional data warehouses.

Standard transactional replication always works in a single direction only, which means that it is not possible for the subscribers to update the publisher. SQL Server also offers peer-to-peer transactional replication, however. In a Peer-to-Peer topology, each server acts as a publisher and a subscriber to the other servers in the topology. This means that changes you make on any server are replicated to all other servers in the topology.

Because all servers can accept updates, it is possible for conflicts to occur. For this reason, peer-to-peer replication is most suitable when each peer accepts updates on a different partition of data. If a conflict does occur, you can configure SQL Server to apply the transaction with the highest OriginatorID (a unique integer that is assigned to each node in the topology), or you can choose to resolve the conflict manually, which is the recommended approach.

Tip   If you are unable to partition the updateable data between nodes, and conflicts are likely, you may find merge replication to be a better choice of technology.

Merge

Merge replication allows you to update both the publisher and the subscribers. This is a good choice for client/server scenarios, such as mobile salespersons who can enter orders on their laptops and then have them sync with the main sales database. It can also be useful in some server/server scenarios—for example, regional data warehouses that are updated via ETL processes and then rolled up into a global data warehouse.

Merge replication works by maintaining a rowguid on every table that is an article within the publication. If the table does not have a uniqueidentifier column with the ROWGUID property set, then merge replication adds one. When a data modification is made to a table, a trigger fires, which maintains a series of change-tracking tables. When the Merge Agent runs, it applies only the latest version of the row. This means that resource utilization is high for tracking changes that occur, but the trade-off is that merge replication has the lowest overhead for actually synchronizing the changes.

Because the subscribers, as well as the publisher, can be updated, there is a risk that conflicts between rows will occur. You manage these using conflict resolvers. Merge replication offers 12 conflict resolvers out of the box, including earliest wins, latest wins, and subscriber always wins. You can also program your own COM-based conflict resolvers or choose to resolve conflicts manually.

Because you can use merge replication in client/server scenarios, it offers you a technology called web synchronization for updating subscribers. When you use web synchronization, after extracting the changes, the Merge Agent makes an HTTPS request to IIS and sends the data changes to the subscribers in the form of an XML message. Replication Listener and Merge Replication Reconciler, which are processes running on the subscriber, process the data changes, after sending any data modifications made at the subscriber back to the publisher.

Implementing Transactional Replication

The most appropriate type of replication for scaling workloads is standard transactional replication. We discuss how to implement this technology in the following sections.

Note   For the demonstrations in this section, we use two instances: PRIMARYSERVER\PROSQLADMIN and SECONDARYSERVER\PROSQLADMIN2ND.

Implementing the Distributor

Before configuring transactional replication for the Chapter17 database, we will configure our instance as a Distributor. This can be achieved with the Configure Distribution Wizard, which can be invoked by selecting Configure Distribution from the context menu of Replication. The first page in the wizard is the Distributor page, illustrated in Figure 17-4. On this page, we can choose to use the current instance as the distributor or specify a different instance.

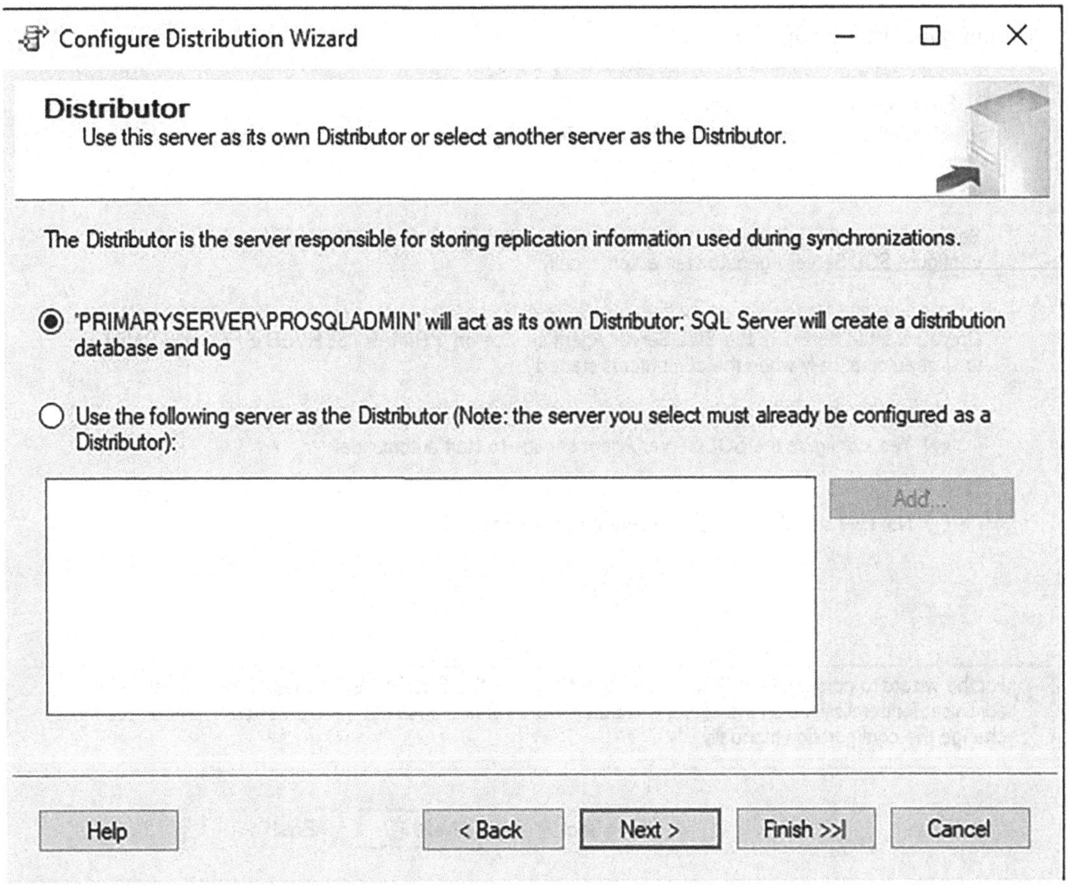

Figure 17-4. *The Distributor page*

Because our instance is not currently configured for SQL Server Agent service
to start automatically, we now see the SQL Server Agent Start page, which warns us
of this situation. This is because replication agents rely on SQL Server Agent to be
scheduled and run. We choose the option for SQL Server Agent to be configured to start
automatically, as shown in Figure 17-5.

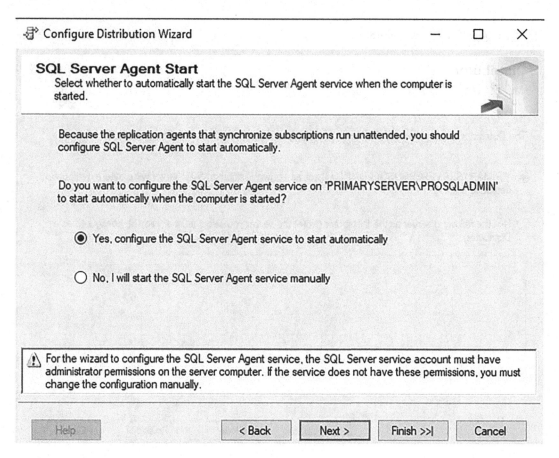

Figure 17-5. *The SQL Server Agent Start page*

On the Snapshot Folder page of the wizard, we select the location the Snapshot Agent will use to store the initial data for synchronization. This can be a local folder or a network share, but if you specify a local folder, then pull subscriptions are not supported, since the subscribers are unable to access it. In our case, we use a network share. The Snapshot Folder page is illustrated in Figure 17-6.

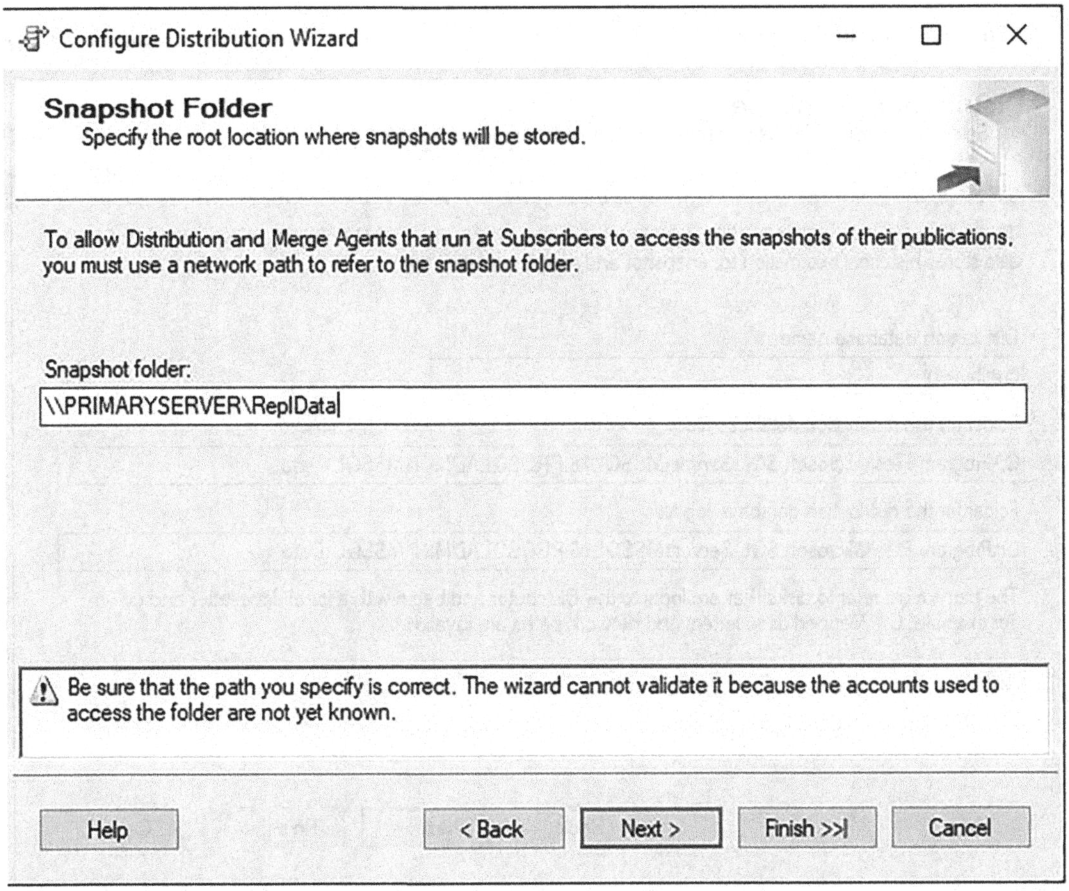

Figure 17-6. Snapshot Folder page

Next, on the Distribution Database page of the wizard, we must specify a name for the distribution database, and supply to folder locations, where the data and log files should be stored. This is represented in Figure 17-7.

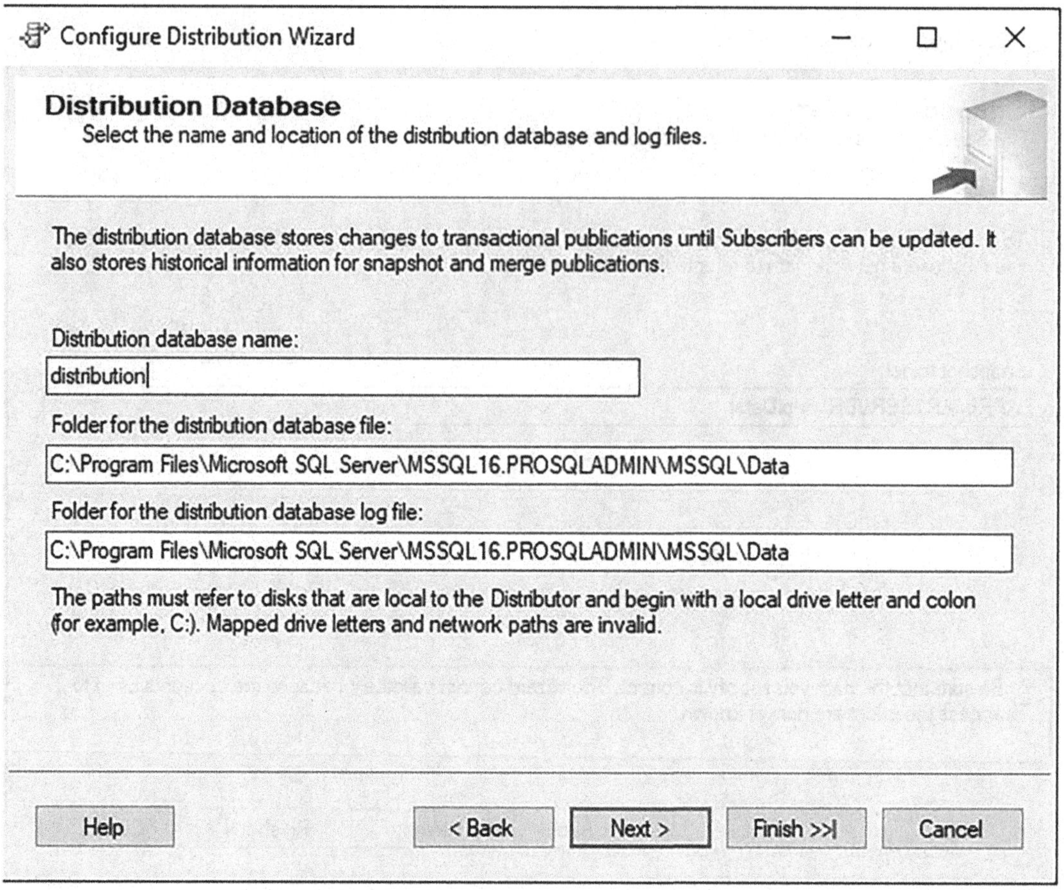

Figure 17-7. Distribution Database page

On the Publishers page of the wizard, shown in Figure 17-8, we specify the instances that will be used as Publishers, for the Distributor. The current instance will be added automatically but can be deselected. The Add button, in the bottom right of the page can be used to add additional SQL Server instances, or Oracle databases.

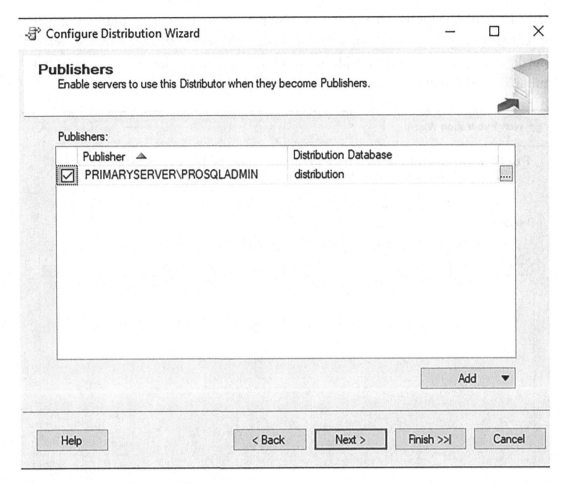

Figure 17-8. *Publishers Page*

Finally, we can choose to either configure the distributor, script the configuration, or both. In this case, we will configure the Distributor straight away.

Implementing the Publication

Now that the Distributor is configured, we will set up a Publication, for the Chapter17 database. To begin configuring transaction replication, we select New Publication from the context menu of Replication ➤ Local Publications in Object Explorer. This causes the New Publication Wizard to be invoked. After passing through the welcome screen, we see the Publication Database page, shown in Figure 17-9. Here, we select the database that contains the objects that we wish to use as articles in our publication. All articles within a publication must reside in the same database, so we can only select one database on this screen. To replicate articles from multiple databases, we must have multiple publications.

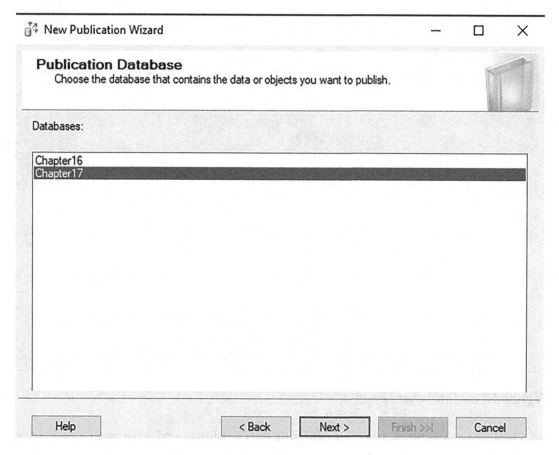

Figure 17-9. *The Publication Database page*

On the Publication Type page, shown in Figure 17-10, we select the type of replication we wish to use for the publication—in our case, transactional.

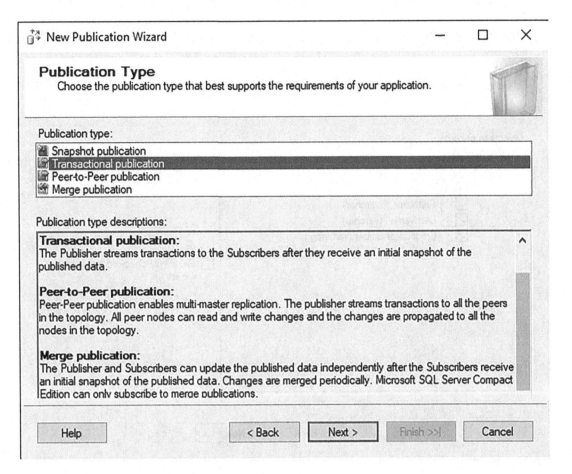

Figure 17-10. *The Publication Type page*

On the Articles page of the wizard, illustrated in Figure 17-11, we select the objects that we wish to include in our publication. All tables that you wish to publish must have a primary key, or you are not able to select them. Within a table, you can also select individual columns to replicate, if you need to.

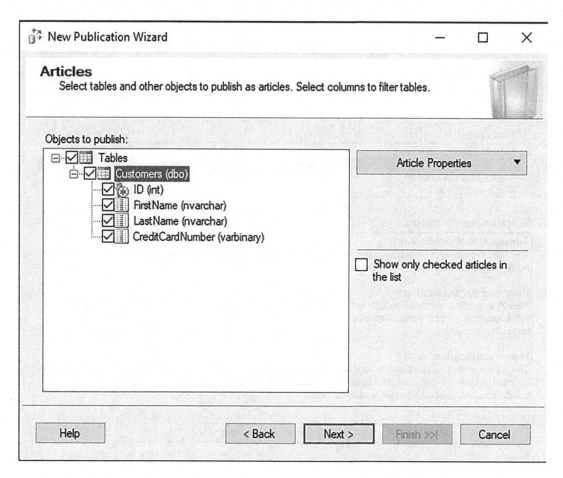

Figure 17-11. *The Articles page*

The Article Properties button allows us to alter the properties, either for the selected article or for all articles within the Article Properties dialog box, which is shown in Figure 17-12. You should usually leave most properties as the default unless you have a specific reason to change them. However, you should pay particular attention to some properties.

You use the Action If Name Is in Use property to determine the behavior if a table with the same name already exists in the subscriber database. The possible options are as follows:

- Keep the existing object unchanged.

- Drop the existing object and create a new one.

- Delete data. If the article has a row filter, delete only the data that matches the filter.

- Truncate all data in the existing object.

The Copy Permissions property demines if object-level permissions are copied to the subscriber. This is important, since you may or may not want to configure the permissions the same as they are for the publisher depending on how you are using the environment.

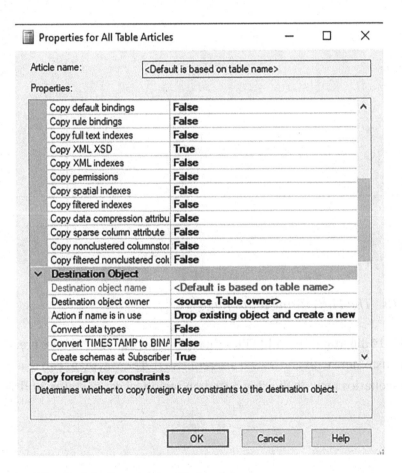

Figure 17-12. *The Article Properties dialog box*

On the Filter Table Rows page of the wizard, shown in Figure 17-13, we can use the Add, Edit, and Delete buttons to manage filters. Filters essentially add a WHERE clause to the article so that you can limit the number of rows that are replicated. You'll find this is especially useful for partitioning the data across multiple subscribers.

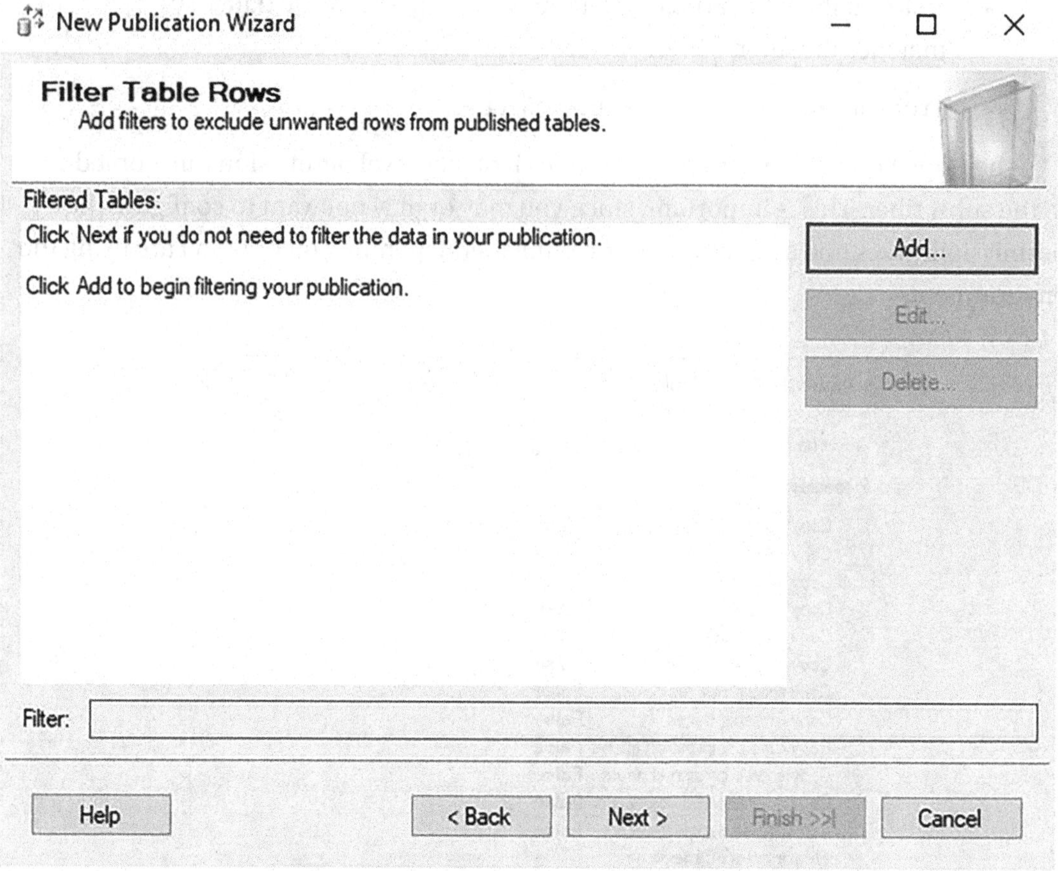

Figure 17-13. *The Filter Table Rows page*

Figure 17-14 illustrates the Add Filter dialog box. In our case, we are creating a filter so that only customers with an ID>500 are replicated. The ways you can use this in production scenarios include filtering based on region, account status, and so on.

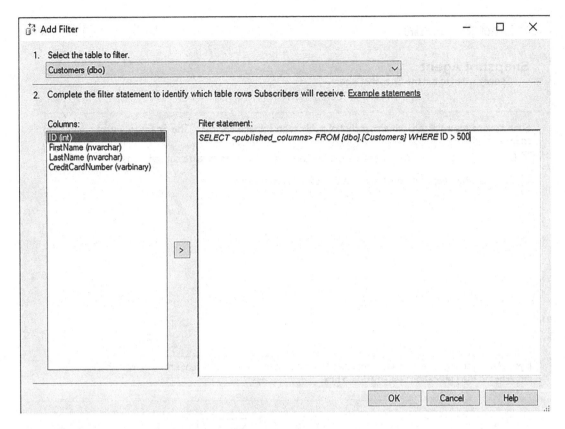

Figure 17-14. *The Add Filter dialog box*

On the Snapshot Agent page, illustrated in Figure 17-15, you can configure the initial snapshot to be created immediately, as we have done here, or you can schedule the Snapshot Agent to run at a specific time.

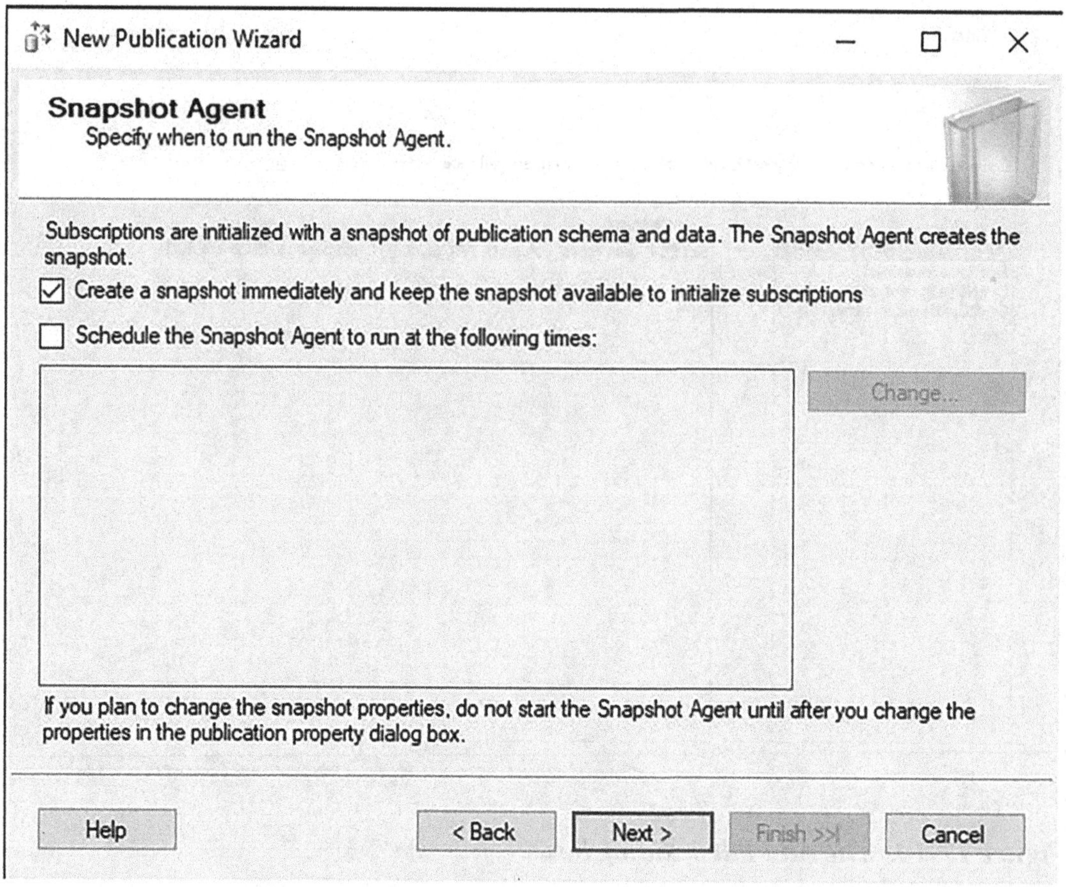

Figure 17-15. *The Snapshot Agent page*

On the Agent Security page, illustrated in Figure 17-16, you are invited to configure
the accounts that are used for running each of the replication agents. At a minimum, the
account that runs the Snapshot Agent should have the following permissions:

- Be a member of the db_owner database role in the distribution
  database

- Have read, write, and modify permissions on the share that contains
  the snapshot

At a minimum, the account that runs the Log Reader Agent must have the following
permissions:

- Be a member of the db_owner database role in the distribution
  database

When you create the subscription, choose the sync_type. This configuration choice affects the Log Reader account's required permissions in the following ways:

- Automatic: No additional permissions required

- Anything else: sysadmin on the distributor

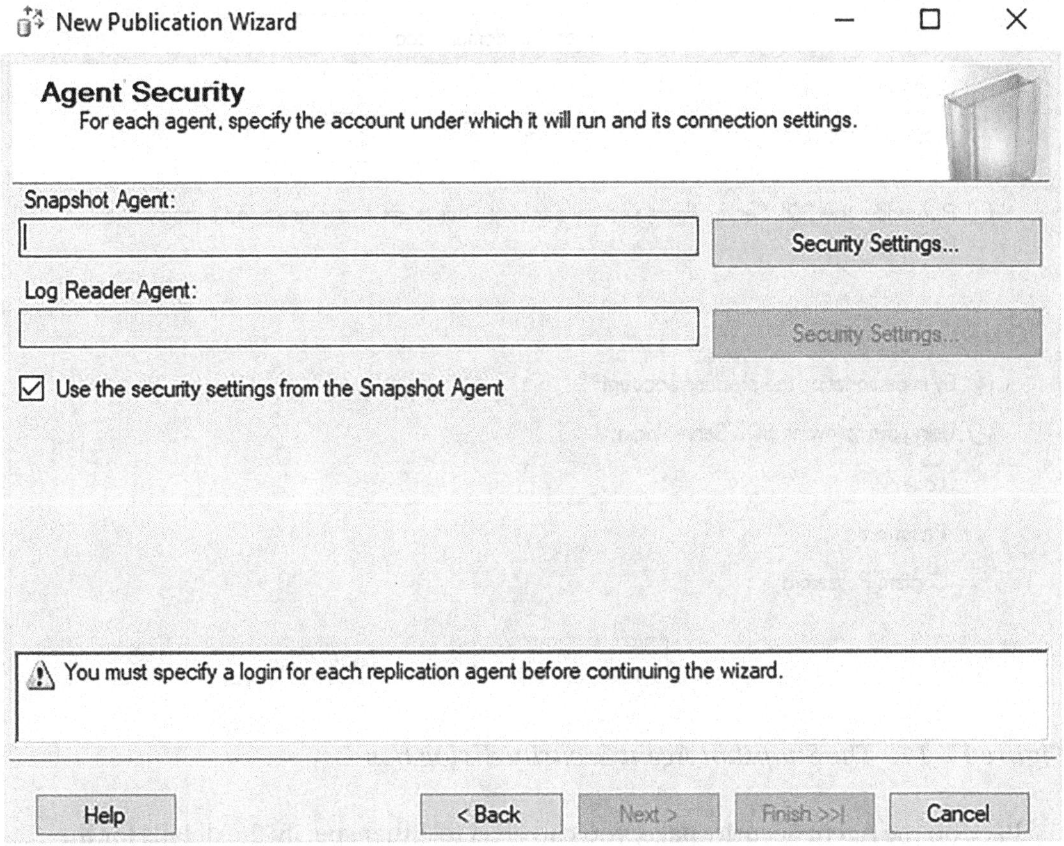

Figure 17-16. *The Agent Security page*

Clicking the Security Settings button for the Snapshot Agent causes the Snapshot Agent Security dialog box to display, as shown in Figure 17-17. In this dialog box, you can choose to run the Snapshot Agent under the context of the Server Agent service account, or you can specify a different Windows account to use. To follow the principle of least privilege, you should use a separate account. It is also possible to specify a different account from which to make connections to the publisher instance. In our case though, we specify that the same account should make all the connections.

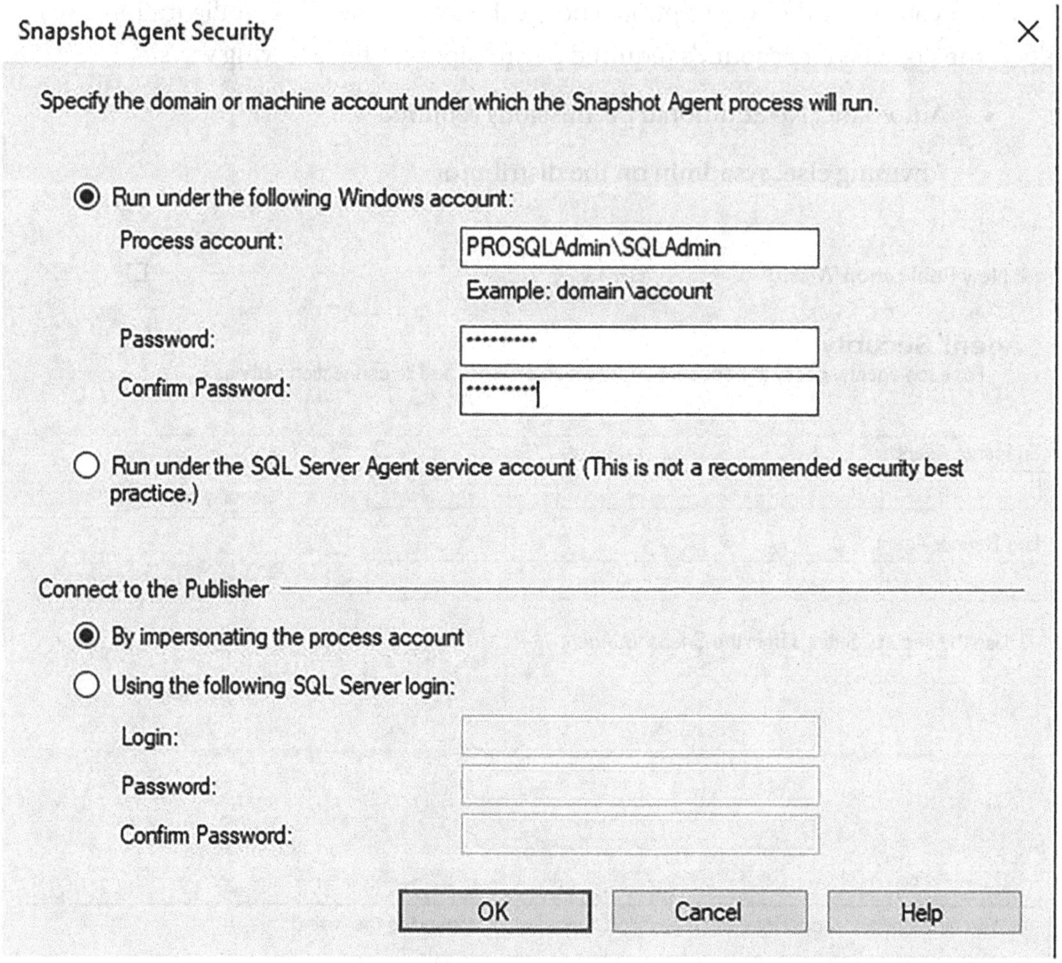

Figure 17-17. *The Snapshot Agent Security dialog box*

Back on the Agent Security page, you can elect to either specify the details for the account that will run the Log Reader Agent, or you can clone the information you have already entered for the account that will run the Snapshot Agent.

On the Wizard Actions page, you can elect to either generate the publication, as we have done, script the generation of the publication, or both. We will create the Publication immediately. Finally, on the Completion page, specify a name for the Publication. We will call ours **Chapter17**.

Implementing the Subscriber

Now that the PROSQLADMIN instance is configured as a distributor and publisher and our publication has been created, we need to configure our PROSQLADMIN2 instance as a subscriber. We can perform this task from either the publisher or from the subscriber. From the subscriber, we perform this task by connecting to the PROSQLADMIN2 instance and then by drilling through replication and selecting New Subscription from the context menu of Local Subscriptions. This causes the New Subscription Wizard to be invoked. After passing through the Welcome page of this wizard, you are presented with the Publication page, as illustrated in Figure 17-18. On this page, you use the Publisher drop-down box to connect to the instance that is configured as the publisher, and then you select the appropriate publication from the Databases and publications area of the screen.

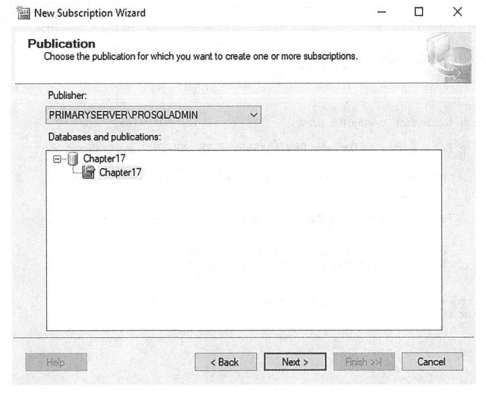

Figure 17-18. *The Publication page*

On the Distribution Agent Location page, you choose if you want to use push subscriptions or pull subscriptions. The appropriate choice here depends on your topology. If you have many subscribers, then you may choose to implement a remote distributor. If this is the case, then it is likely that you will use push subscriptions so that the server configured as the distributor has the impact of agents running. If you have many subscribers and you are using a local distributor, however, then it is likely that you will use pull subscriptions so that you can spread the cost of the agents between the subscribers. In our case, we have a local distributor, but we also only have a single subscriber, so from a performance perspective, it is an obvious choice of which server is most equipped to deal with the workload. We also must consider security when we place the distribution agent, however; we discuss this later in this section. For this demonstration, we use push subscriptions. The Distribution Agent Location page is illustrated in Figure 17-19.

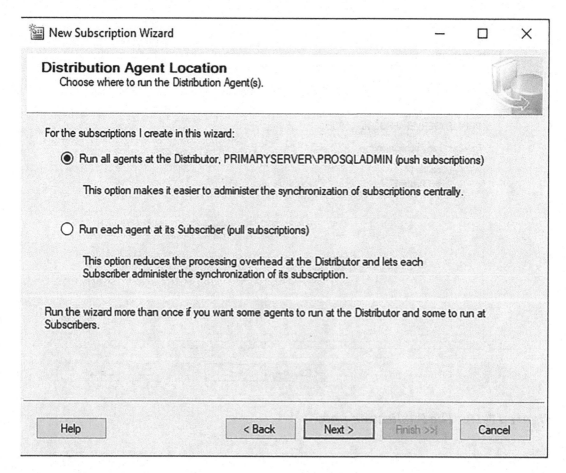

Figure 17-19. *The Distribution Agent Location page*

On the Subscribers page, we can select the name of our subscription database from the drop-down list. Because our subscription database doesn't already exist, however, we select New Database, as shown in Figure 17-20, which causes the New Database dialog box to be invoked.

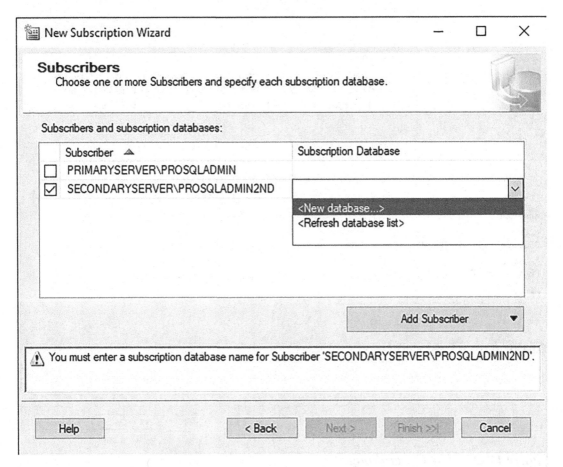

Figure 17-20. *The Subscribers page*

On the General page of the New Database dialog box, shown in Figure 17-21, you need to enter appropriate settings for the subscription database based upon its planned usage. If you need to, you can configure many of the database properties on the Options page.

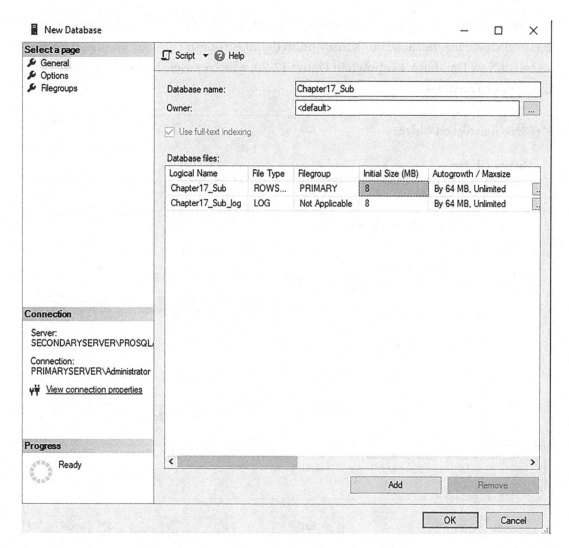

Figure 17-21. *The General page*

On the Distribution Agent Security page, illustrated in Figure 17-22, click the ellipses to invoke the Distribution Agent Security dialog box.

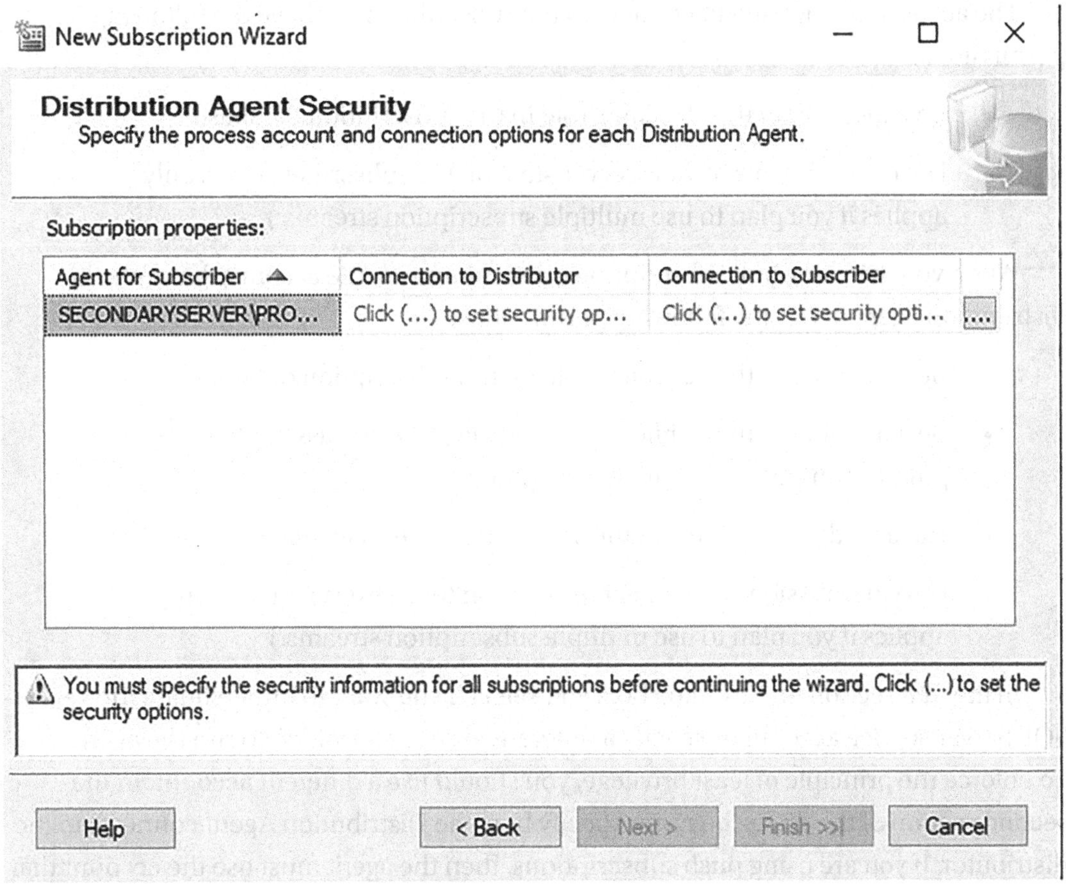

Figure 17-22. *The Distribution Agent Security page*

In the Distribution Agent Security dialog box, illustrated in Figure 17-23, specify the details of the account that runs the Distribution Agent. When you are using push subscription, at a minimum, the account that runs the Distribution Agent should have the following permissions:

- Be a member of the db_owner role on the Distribution database

- Be a member of the publication access list (We discuss configuring publication access later in this chapter.)

- Have read permissions on the share where the snapshot is located

The account that is used to connect to the subscriber must have the following permissions:

- Be a member of the db_owner role in the subscription database

- Have permissions to view server state on the subscribers (This only applies if you plan to use multiple subscription streams.)

When you are using pull subscriptions, at a minimum, the account that runs the distribution agent needs the following permissions:

- Be a member of the db_owner role on the subscription database

- Be a member of the publication access list (We discuss configuring publication access later in this chapter.)

- Have read permissions on the share where the snapshot is located

- Have permissions to view server state on the subscriber (This only applies if you plan to use multiple subscription streams.)

In the first section of the dialog box, you select if you want to impersonate the SQL Server service account or specify a different account on which to run the agent. To enforce the principle of least privilege, you should use a different account. In the second section of the dialog box, you specify how the Distribution Agent connects to the distributor. If you are using push subscriptions, then the agent must use the account that runs the Distribution Agent. In the third section of the dialog box, you specify how the Distribution Agent connects to the subscriber. If you are using pull subscriptions, then you must use the same account that is running the Distribution Agent.

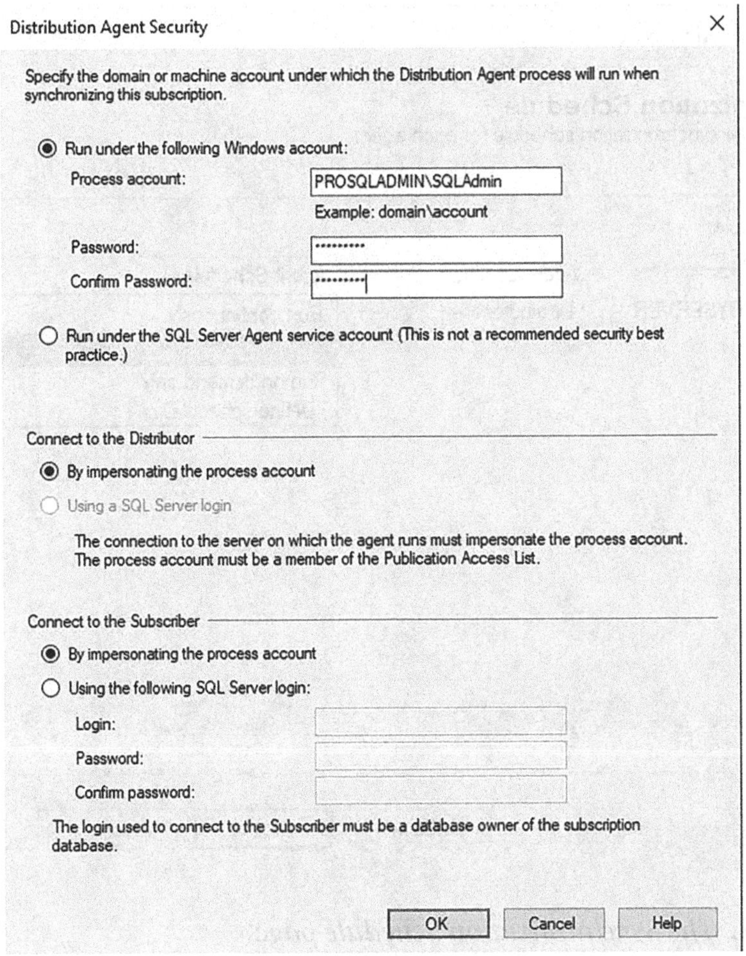

Figure 17-23. *The Distribution Agent Security dialog box*

On the Synchronization Schedule page, you define a schedule for the Distribution Agent to run. You can choose to run the agent continuously, run the agent only on demand, or define a new server agent schedule on which to run the Distribution Agent, as illustrated in Figure 17-24. We choose to run the agent continuously.

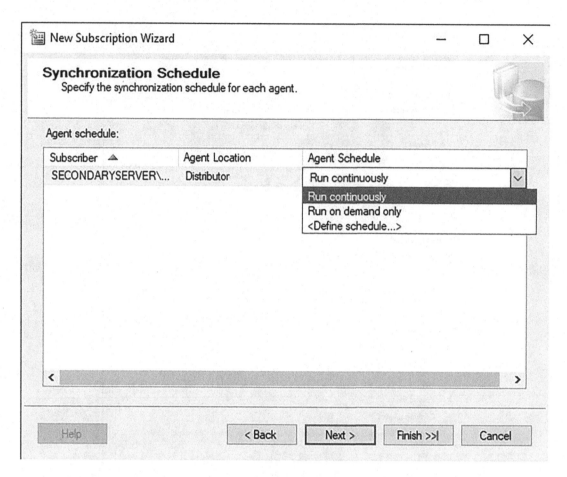

Figure 17-24. *The Synchronization Schedule page*

On the Initialize Subscriptions page, depicted in Figure 17-25, you choose if you want the subscription to be initialized immediately, or if you want to wait for the first synchronization, and then initialize it from the snapshot at that point. For this demonstration, we initialize the subscription immediately. If you select the Memory Optimized check box, then the tables will be replicated into memory-optimized tables on the Subscriber. To select this option, you must have already created the memory-optimized file group. You must also have configured the Enable Memory Optimization property of the Article to True.

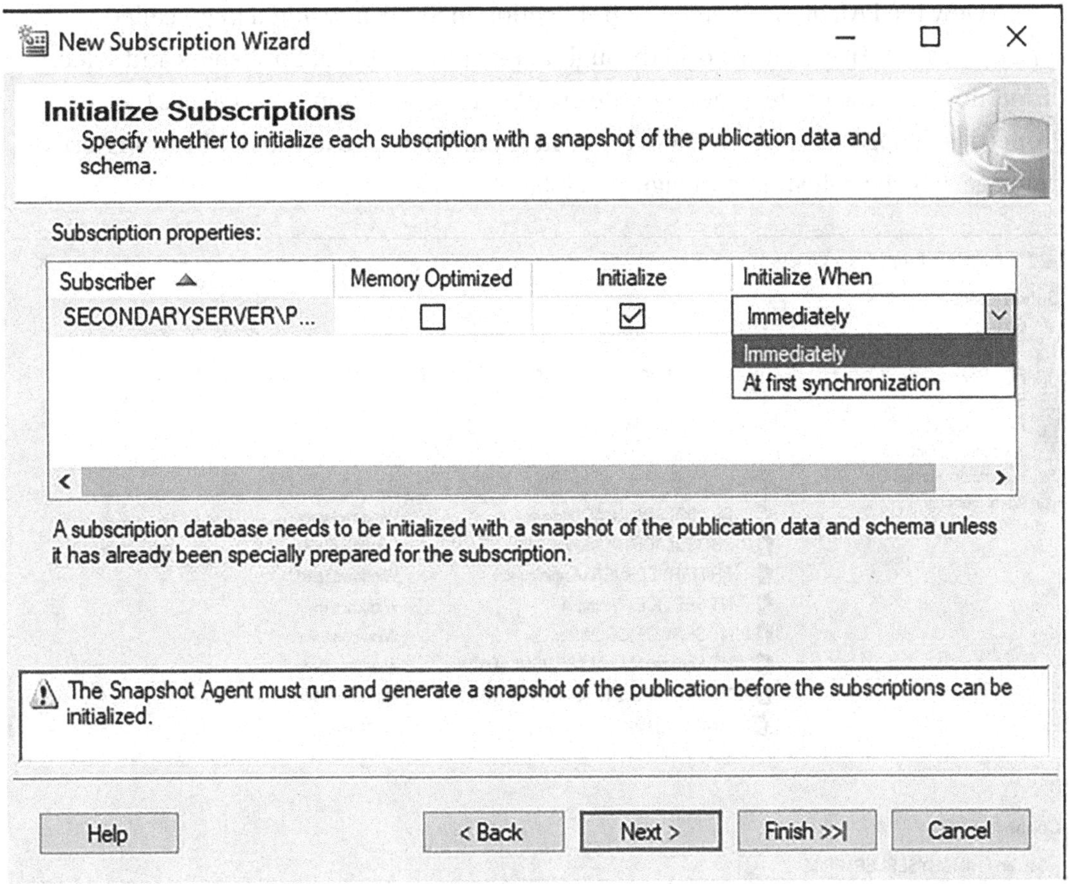

Figure 17-25. *The Initialize Subscriptions page*

On the Wizard Actions page, you need to choose between whether you want to create the subscription immediately or if you want to script the process. We choose to create the subscription immediately. Finally, on the Complete the Wizard page, you are given a summary of the actions that the wizard performs.

Modifying the PAL

The PAL (Publication Access List) is used to control access security to the publication. When agents connect to the publication, their credentials are compared to the PAL to ensure they have the correct permissions. The benefit of the PAL is that it abstracts security from the publication database and prevents client applications from needing to modify it directly.

To view the PAL of the Chapter17 publication in SSMS and add a login called ReplicationAdmin, you must drill through Replication ➤ Local Publishers and select Properties from the context menu of the Chapter17 publication. This causes the Properties dialog box to be invoked, and you should navigate to the Publication Access List page, which is illustrated in Figure 17-26.

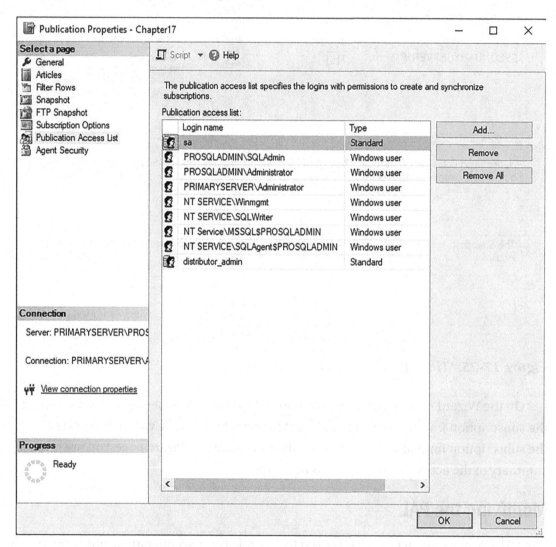

Figure 17-26. *The Publication Access List page*

You can now use the Add button to display a list of logins that do not have current access to the publication. You should select the appropriate login from the list to add it to the PAL, as shown in Figure 17-27.

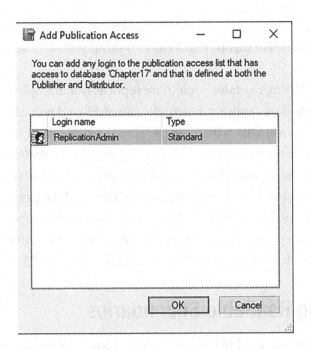

Figure 17-27. *Add Publication Access*

AlwaysOn Readable Secondary Replicas

It can be very useful to add readable secondary replicas to an AlwaysOn Availability Group topology in order to implement horizontal scaled reporting. When you use this strategy, the databases are kept synchronized, with variable, but typically low latency, using log streaming. The additional advantage of readable secondary replicas is that they stay online, even if the primary replica is offline. Readable secondary replicas can be added to an existing Availability Group, which is configured for HA and/or DR. Alternatively, if there is no HA or DR requirement for a database, but read scaling would be advantageous, an Availability Group can be created, specifically for the purpose of read scaling.

Benefits and Considerations

Over and above pure horizontal scaling, readable secondary replicas offer other advantages, such as temporary statistics, which you can also use to optimize read-only workloads. Also, snapshot isolation is also used exclusively on readable secondary replicas, even if other isolation levels or locking hints are explicitly requested. This helps avoid contention, but it also means that TempDB should be suitably scaled and on a fast disk array.

The main risk of using readable secondary replicas is that implementing snapshot isolation on the secondary replica can actually cause deleted records not to be cleaned up on the primary replica. This is because the ghost record cleanup task only removes rows from the primary once they are no longer required at the secondary. In this scenario, log truncation is also delayed on the primary replica. This means that you potentially risk having to kill long-running queries that are being satisfied against the readable secondary. This issue can also occur if the secondary replica becomes disconnected from the primary. Therefore, there is a risk that you may need to remove the secondary replica from the Availability Group and subsequently read it.

Implementing Readable Secondaries

In this section, we will use the PROSQLADMIN-C cluster that we also used in Chapter 15. This time, however, an additional node has been added to the Cluster, in Site 1. The server is called CLUSTERNODE4 and hosts an instance called READABLE. This instance has had AlwaysOn Availability Groups enabled on the service.

Tip   In this section, we will touch upon the generic configuration of Availability Groups, but further details can be found in Chapter 15, as the primary focus here will be configuring a readable secondary.

Before we create an Availability Group, we will first create a database called Chapter17ReadScale, by using the script in Listing 17-6.

Listing 17-6. Create the Chapter17ReadScale Database

```
CREATE DATABASE Chapter17ReadScale ;
GO

USE Chapter17ReadScale
GO
```

```
CREATE TABLE Customers
(
ID                      INT              PRIMARY KEY          IDENTITY,
FirstName               NVARCHAR(30),
LastName                NVARCHAR(30),
CreditCardNumber        VARBINARY(8000)
) ;
GO

--Populate the table
DECLARE @Numbers TABLE
(
        Number           INT
)
;WITH CTE(Number)
AS
(
        SELECT 1 Number
        UNION ALL
        SELECT Number + 1
        FROM CTE
        WHERE Number < 100
)
INSERT INTO @Numbers
SELECT Number FROM CTE ;

DECLARE @Names TABLE
(
        FirstName        VARCHAR(30),
        LastName         VARCHAR(30)
) ;

INSERT INTO @Names
VALUES('Peter', 'Carter'),
                ('Michael', 'Smith'),
                ('Danielle', 'Mead'),
```

```
                    ('Reuben', 'Roberts'),
                    ('Iris', 'Jones'),
                    ('Sylvia', 'Davies'),
                    ('Finola', 'Wright'),
                    ('Edward', 'James'),
                    ('Marie', 'Andrews'),
                    ('Jennifer', 'Abraham'),
                    ('Margaret', 'Jones') ;

INSERT INTO Customers(Firstname, LastName, CreditCardNumber)
SELECT   FirstName, LastName, CreditCardNumber FROM
        (SELECT
                (SELECT TOP 1 FirstName FROM @Names ORDER BY NEWID())
FirstName
                ,(SELECT TOP 1 LastName FROM @Names ORDER BY NEWID())
LastName
                ,(SELECT CONVERT(VARBINARY(8000)
                ,(SELECT TOP 1 CAST(Number * 100 AS CHAR(4))
                  FROM @Numbers
                  WHERE Number BETWEEN 10 AND 99
                  ORDER BY NEWID()) + '-' +
                        (SELECT TOP 1 CAST(Number * 100 AS CHAR(4))
                         FROM @Numbers
                         WHERE Number BETWEEN 10 AND 99
                         ORDER BY NEWID()) + '-' +
                        (SELECT TOP 1 CAST(Number * 100 AS CHAR(4))
                         FROM @Numbers
                         WHERE Number BETWEEN 10 AND 99
                         ORDER BY NEWID()) + '-' +
                        (SELECT TOP 1 CAST(Number * 100 AS CHAR(4))
                         FROM @Numbers
                         WHERE Number BETWEEN 10 AND 99
                         ORDER BY NEWID())))) CreditCardNumber
FROM @Numbers a
CROSS JOIN @Numbers b
) d
```

Next, we will create an Availability Group, using the Availability Group Wizard. On the first page of the wizard (Figure 17-28), we will provide a name for our new Availability Group. In our case, we will call it Chapter17. We will also specify the cluster type as a Windows Failover Cluster.

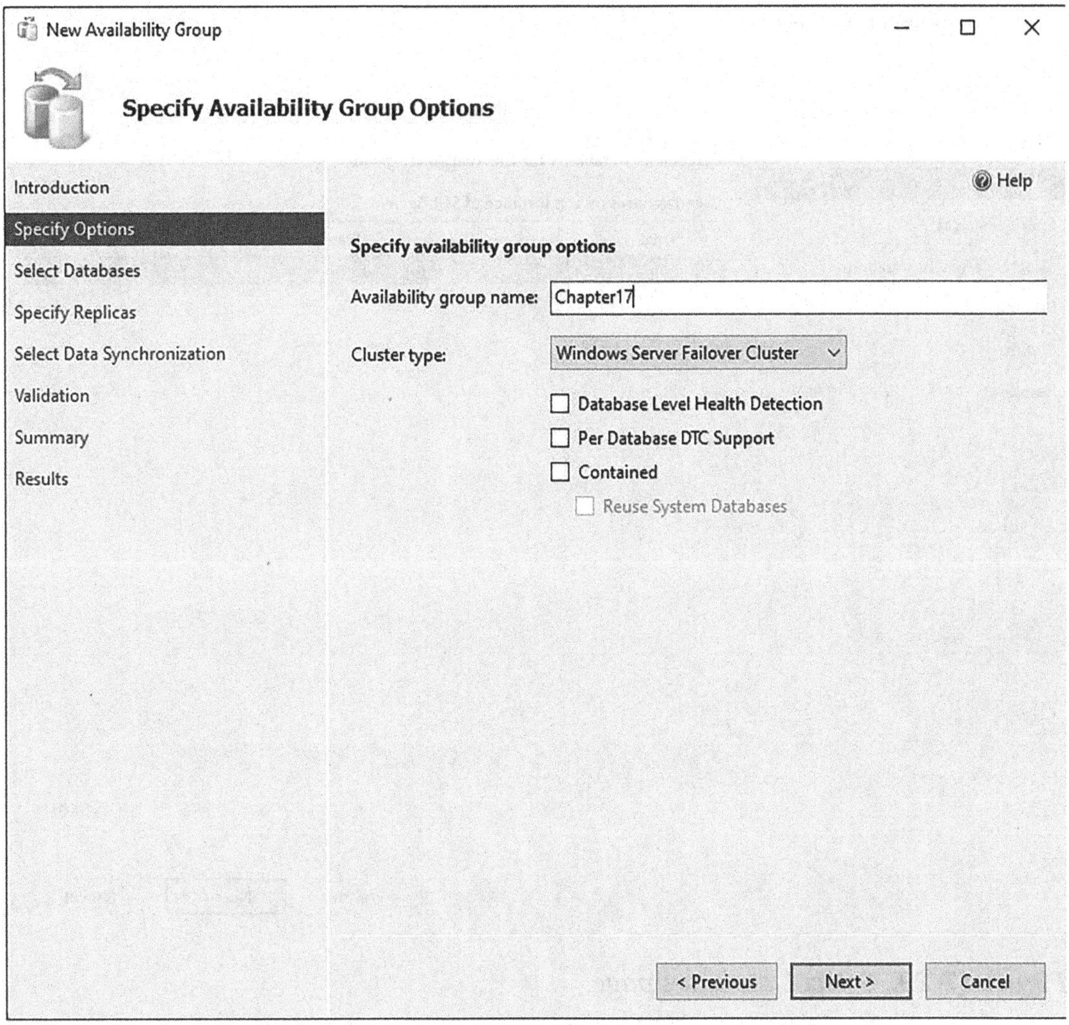

Figure 17-28. *Specify Availability Group Options page*

On the Select Databases page of the wizard, illustrated in Figure 17-29, we will select the database that we want to add to the Availability Group.

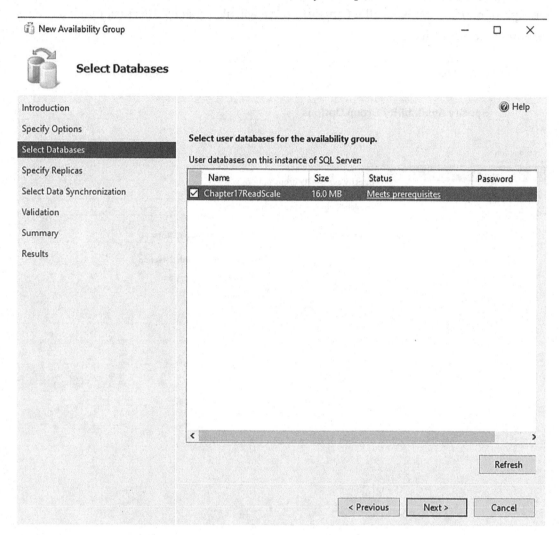

Figure 17-29. *Select Databases page*

The Replicas tab of the Specify Replicas page is shown in Figure 17-30. Here, we have added CLUSTERNODE1, CLUSTERNODE2, and CLUSTERNODE3 as the initial Primary Replica, HA Replica, and DR Replica, respectively. You will notice, however, that we have also added CLUSTERNODE4 as an asynchronous Replica and marked it as a Readable Secondary.

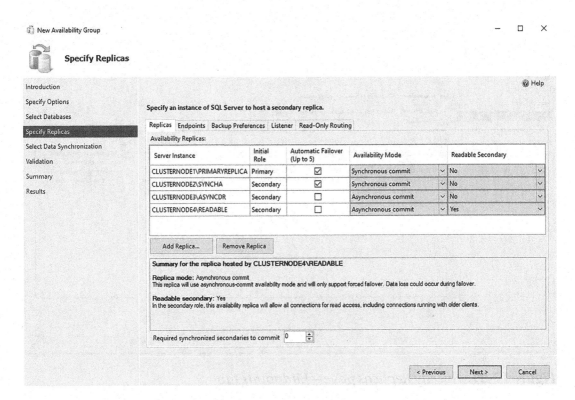

Figure 17-30. *Specify Replicas page—Replicas tab*

On the Endpoints tab, shown in Figure 17-31, you will see that the endpoints for
CLUSTERNODE1, CLUSTERNODE2, and CLUSTERNODE3 are grayed out. This is because you can
only have one database mirroring endpoint per instance, and on these instances, the
endpoints already exist, due to our work in Chapter 15.

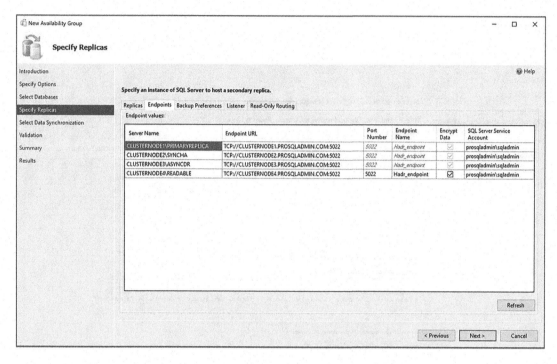

Figure 17-31. *Specify Replicas page—Endpoints tab*

On the Backup Preferences tab, illustrated in Figure 17-32, we have configured the replicas, so that backups will only occur on the Primary Replica, if Secondary Replicas are not available. We have excluded our synchronous Replica on CLUSTERNODE2 and set a higher priority to our Readable Secondary Replica. This means that backups will occur on the Readable Secondary, if it is available. If it is not, then the backups will be taken on the DR Replica. Only if neither of these are available will the backup be taken against the Primary Replica. Backups will never occur against the HA synchronous Replica.

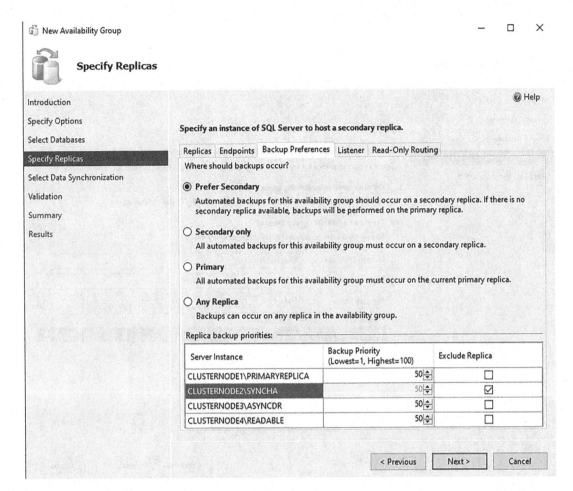

Figure 17-32. *Specify Replicas—Backup Preferences tab*

On the Listener tab, which is shown in Figure 17-33, we have specified a name and a port for the Listener. We have also added two IP addresses, one for each subnet, that the Listener spans.

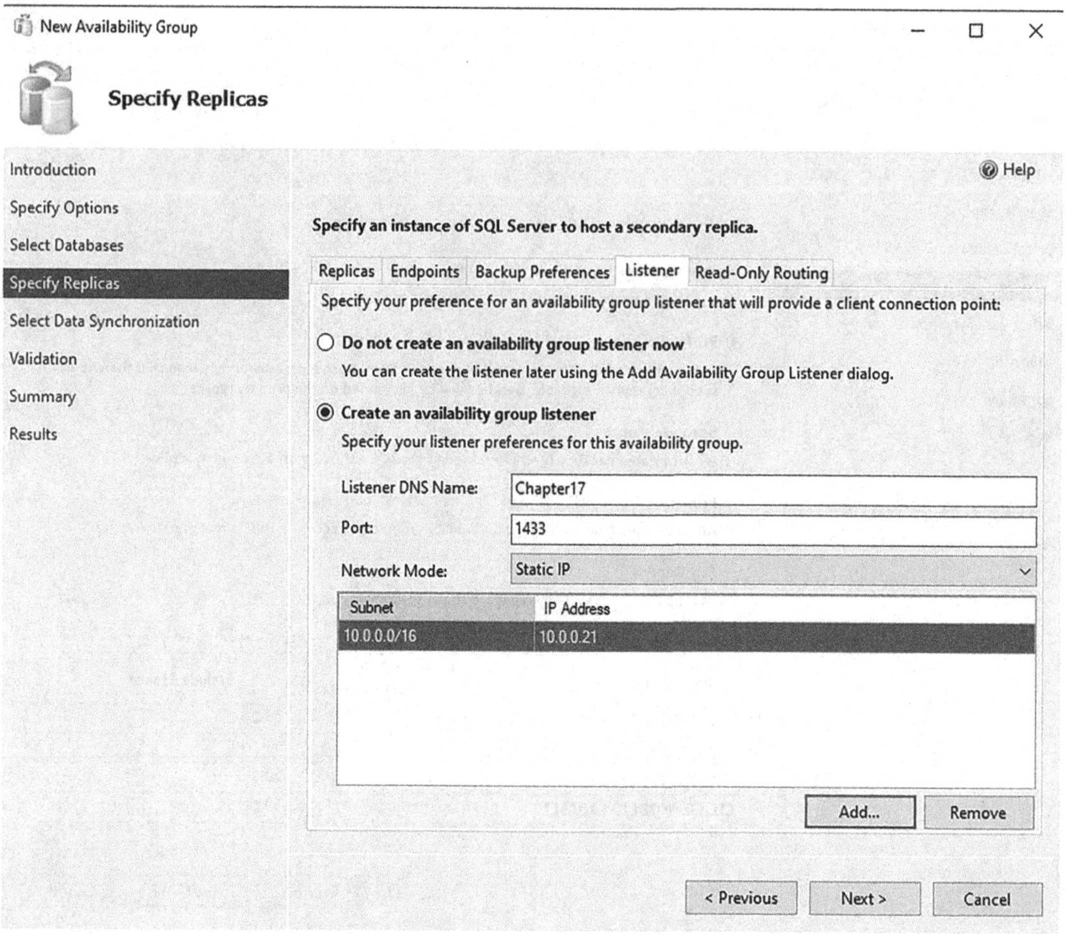

Figure 17-33. *Specify Replicas page—Listener tab*

Tip   If you followed the example in Chapter 15, you should add both cluster subnets.

The Read-Only Routing tab is where things get interesting, from the perspective of Readable Secondaries. Each Readable Secondary Replica must be given a Read-Only Routing URL. This is the path to which read-only requests will be sent and consists of the protocol (TCP), followed by the fully qualified address of the server hosting the readable secondary, including the port number.

After this Read-Only URL has been specified, we can then add the Read-Only Routing List. This specifies the Replica(s) that read-only requests will be routed to. The routing list only applies to a node, when it has the Primary role, within the Availability Group. Therefore, different routing lists can be supplied for each node. This is useful when you have multiple readable secondaries in different sites. If we had a second readable secondary replica in Site 2, for example, then we could configure the Replica on CLUSTERNODE3 to route read-only requests to this readable secondary, when it holds the Primary role.

You can also specify multiple readable secondary Replicas in each routing list, if more than one readable secondary exists. Read-only requests will be routed to the first server in the list. If this server is not available, however, then requests will be routed to the second server in the list, and so on. If you wish to use this feature, then the servers should be separated by a comma.

It is also possible to load balance read-only requests. In this scenario, requests will be routed between each load balanced server, alternately. If you wish to use this feature, then the servers that form part of the load balancing group should be wrapped in parentheses. For example, imagine that we had six cluster nodes in our configuration. CLUSTERNODE1 has the Primary role. CLUSTERNODE2 is a synchronous HA server, CLUSTERNODE3 is a DR server, and CLUSTERNODE4, CLUSTERNODE5, and CLUSTERNODE6 are all readable secondaries. The read-only routing list in Listing 17-7 would alternate read-only requests between CLUSTERNODE4 and CLUSTERNODE5. If neither of these servers were available, then read-only requests would be routed to CLUSTERNODE6.

Listing 17-7. Complex Read-Only Routing List

```
(CLUSTERNODE4\READABLE, CLUSTERNODE5\READABLE2), CLUSTERNODE6\READABLE3
```

In our scenario, however, we only have a single Readable Secondary Replica, so we can add the Replica to each node, using the Add button, as shown in Figure 17-34.

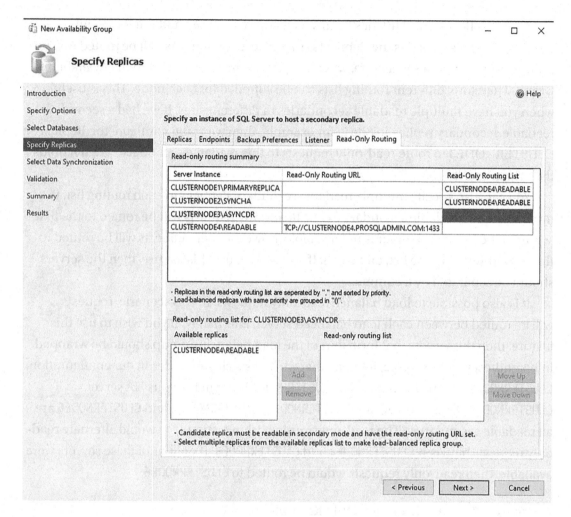

Figure 17-34. *Specify Replicas page—Read-Only Routing tab*

We can now specify how we want to synchronize the Availability Group, using the Select Initial Data Synchronization page of the wizard, shown in Figure 17-35.

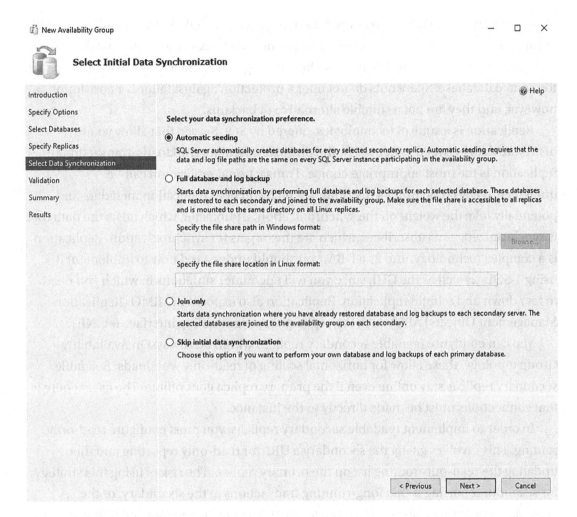

Figure 17-35. *Select Initial Data Synchronization page*

After the wizard has run validation tests, you can now create and synchronize the Availability Group.

Summary

Database snapshots use copy-on-write technology to create a point-in-time copy of a database. The snapshot must exist on the same instance as the source database, so although you cannot use them to distribute load between servers, you can use them to reduce contention between read and write operations.

Snapshots can be used to recover data that has been lost due to human error as well as for reporting purposes. You can either copy the data back to the source database or restore the source database from a snapshot, as long as it is the only snapshot linked with the source database. Snapshots do not offer a protection against failure or corruption, however, and they are not a suitable alternative to backups.

Replication is a suite of technologies, offered by SQL Server, that allow you to distribute data between systems. For the purpose of scaling workloads, transactional replication is the most appropriate choice. Transactional replication can be implemented by configuring a distributor, which will hold replication metadata and potentially take the weight off the synchronization; a publisher, which hosts the data that is synchronized; and subscribers, which are the targets for synchronization. Replication is a complex technology, and as a DBA, you should understand how to implement it using T-SQL, as well as the GUI, since you will encounter situations in which you need to tear down and rebuild replication. Replication also exposes the RMO (Replication Management Objects) API, which is a replication programming interface for .NET.

You can configure readable secondary replicas within an AlwaysOn Availability Group topology; these allow for horizontal scaling of read-only workloads. Readable secondary replicas stay online even if the primary replica goes offline. The caveat here is that connections must be made directly to the instance.

In order to implement readable secondary replicas, you must configure read-only routing. This involves giving the secondary a URL for read-only reporting and then updating the read-only routing list on the primary replica. The risk of using this strategy for scale-out reporting is that long-running transactions at the secondary, or the secondary becoming disconnected, can lead to log truncation delays and delays in ghost records being cleaned up.

PART IV

Performance and Maintenance

CHAPTER 18

SQL Server Metadata

Metadata is data that describes other data. SQL Server exposes a vast array of metadata including structural metadata, which describes every object, and descriptive metadata, which described the data itself. Metadata is exposed through a series of

- Catalog views

- Information schema views

- Dynamic management views and functions

- System functions

- System stored procedures

In this chapter, we will discuss how metadata can be used to perform actions at the instance level, such as expose registry values, examine how metadata can assist in capacity planning, and discuss how metadata can be used for troubleshooting and performance tuning. Finally, we will see how metadata can be used to drive automated maintenance.

Tip   Metadata is a huge topic, worthy of a book in its own right. I therefore encourage you to play with other metadata objects, which may not be covered in this chapter.

Introducing Metadata Objects

Catalog views reside in the sys schema. There are many catalog views; some of the most useful of which, such as sys.master_files, are explored in this chapter. Listing 18-1 shows an example of how to use a catalog view to produce a list of databases that are in FULL recovery model.

© Peter A. Carter 2023
P. A. Carter, *Pro SQL Server 2022 Administration*, https://doi.org/10.1007/978-1-4842-8864-1_18

Listing 18-1. Using Catalog Views

```
SELECT name
FROM sys.databases
WHERE recovery_model_desc = 'FULL' ;
```

Information schema views reside in the `INFORMATION_SCHEMA` schema. They return less detail than catalog views but are based on the ISO standards. This means that you can port your queries between RDBMS (relational database management systems). Listing 18-2 shows an example of using information schema views to produce a list of principals that have been granted `SELECT` access to the `Chapter10.dbo.SensitiveData` table.

Tip   A script for creating the Chapter10 database can be found in Chapter 10.

Listing 18-2. Using Information Schema Views

```
USE Chapter10
GO

SELECT GRANTEE, PRIVILEGE_TYPE
FROM INFORMATION_SCHEMA.TABLE_PRIVILEGES
WHERE TABLE_SCHEMA = 'dbo'
        AND TABLE_NAME = 'SensitiveData'
        AND PRIVILEGE_TYPE = 'SELECT' ;
```

Many dynamic management views and functions are available in SQL Server. Collectively, they are known as DMVs and they provide information about the current state of the instance, which you can use for troubleshooting and tuning performance. The following categories of DMV are exposed in SQL Server 2022:

- AlwaysOn Availability Groups

- Big Data Clusters

- Change data capture

- Change tracking

- Common language runtime (CLR)

- Database mirroring

- Databases

- Execution

- Extended events

- FILESTREAM and FileTable

- Full-text search and semantic search

- Indexes

- I/O

- Memory-optimized tables

- Objects

- Query notifications

- Replication

- Resource Governor

- Security

- Server

- Service broker

- Spatial

- SQL Server operating system

- Stretch Databases

- Transactions

We demonstrate and discuss how to use DMVs many times throughout this chapter. DMVs always begin with a dm_ prefix, followed by two to four characters that describe the category of the object—for example, os_ for operating system, db_ for database, and exec_ for execution. This is followed by the name of the object. In Listing 18-3, you can see three things: an example of how to retrieve a full list of dynamic management views and functions, an example of how to use a dynamic management view to find a list of logins that are currently connected to the Chapter16 database, and a dynamic management function you can use to produce details of the pages that store the data relating to the Chapter17.dbo.Customers table.

Tip   A full list of DMVs and DMFs can be exposed by querying `sys.all_objects` demonstrated in Listing 18-3. I strongly encourage you to explore the full range of dynamic management objects available.

Listing 18-3. Using Dynamic Management Views and Functions

```
--Retrieve a list of all DMVs and DMFs

SELECT *
FROM sys.all_objects
WHERE name LIKE 'dm%'
ORDER BY name

USE Chapter17 -This database will exist if you followed the examples in
Chapter17 of this book
GO

--Find logins connected to the Chapter16 database

SELECT login_name
FROM sys.dm_exec_sessions
WHERE database_id = DB_ID('Chapter17') ;

--Return details of the data pages storing the Chapter17.dbo.
Customers table

SELECT *
FROM sys.dm_db_database_page_allocations(DB_ID('Chapter17'),
                                         OBJECT_ID('dbo.Customers'),
                                         NULL,
                                         NULL,
                                         'DETAILED') ;
```

SQL Server also offers many metadata-related system functions, such as `DB_ID()` and `OBJET_ID()`, which we used in Listing 18-3. Another example of a metadata-related system function is `DATALENGTH`, which we used in Listing 18-4 to return the length of each value in the `LastName` column of the `Chapter17.dbo.Customers` table.

Listing 18-4. Using System Functions

```
USE Chapter17
GO

SELECT DATALENGTH(LastName)
FROM dbo.Customers ;
```

Server-Level and Instance-Level Metadata

Many forms of metadata are available for the server and instance. Server-level metadata can be very useful for DBAs who need to find configuration information or troubleshoot an issue when they do not have access to the underlying operating system. For example, the dm_server category of DMVs offers views that allow you to check the status of server audits, view SQL Server's Registry keys, find the location of memory dump files, and find details of the instance's services. In the following sections, we discuss how to view the Registry keys associated with the instance, expose details of SQL Server's services, and view the contents of the buffer cache.

Exposing Registry Values

The sys.dm_server_registry DMV exposes key registry entries pertaining to the instance. The view returns three columns, which are detailed in Table 18-1.

Table 18-1. *sys.dm_server_registry Columns*

Column	Description
Registry_key	The name of the Registry key
Value_name	The name of the key's value
Value_data	The data contained within the value

A very useful piece of information that you can find in the sys.dm_server_registry DMV is the port number on which SQL Server is currently listening. The query in Listing 18-5 uses the sys.dm_server_registry DMV to return the port on which the instance is listening, assuming the instance is configured to listen on all IP addresses.

Listing 18-5. Finding the Port Number

```
SELECT *
FROM (
        SELECT
        CASE
                WHEN value_name = 'tcpport' AND value_data <> ''
                        THEN value_data
                WHEN value_name = 'tcpport' AND value_data = ''
                        THEN (
                                SELECT value_data
                                FROM sys.dm_server_registry
                                WHERE registry_key LIKE '%ipall'
                                        AND value_name = 'tcpdynamicports' )
        END PortNumber
        FROM sys.dm_server_registry
        WHERE registry_key LIKE '%IPAll' ) a
WHERE a.PortNumber IS NOT NULL ;
```

Another useful feature of this DMV is its ability to return the startup parameters of
the SQL Server service. This is particularly useful if you want to find out if switches such
as -E have been configured for the instance. The -E switch increases the number of
extents that are allocated to each file in the round-robin algorithm. The query in
Listing 18-6 displays the startup parameters configured for the instance.

Listing 18-6. Finding Startup Parameters

```
SELECT *
FROM sys.dm_server_registry
WHERE value_name LIKE 'SQLArg%' ;
```

Exposing Service Details

Another useful DMV within the dm_server category is sys.dm_server_services, which
exposes details of the services the instance is using. Table 18-2 describes the columns
returned.

Table 18-2. *sys.dm_server_services Columns*

Column	Description
Servicename	The name of the service.
Startup_type	An integer representing the startup type of the service.
Startup_desc	A textual description of the startup type of the service.
Status	An integer representing the current status of the service.
Status_desc	A textual description of the current service state.
Process_id	The process ID of the service.
Last_startup_time	The date and time that the service last started.
Service_account	The account used to run the service.
Filename	The file name of the service, including the full file path.
Is_clustered	1 indicates that the service is clustered; 0 indicates that it is stand-alone.
Clusternodename	If the service is clustered, this column indicates the name of the node on which the service is running.

The query in Listing 18-7 returns the name of each service, its startup type, its current status, and the name of the service account that runs the service.

Listing 18-7. Exposing Service Details

```
SELECT servicename
       ,startup_type_desc
       ,status_desc
       ,service_account
FROM sys.dm_server_services ;
```

Analyzing Buffer Cache Usage

The dm_os category of DMV exposes 41 objects that contain information about the current status of SQLOS, although only 31 of these are documented. A particularly useful DMV in the dm_os category, which exposes the contents of the buffer cache, is sys.dm_os_buffer_descriptors. When queried, this object returns the columns detailed in Table 18-3.

Table 18-3. *sys.dm_os_buffer_descriptors Columns*

Column	Description
Database_id	The ID of the database that the page is from
File_id	The ID of the file that the page is from
Page_id	The ID of the page
Page_level	The index level of the page
Allocation_unit_id	The ID of the allocation unit that the page is from
Page_type	The type of page, for example, DATA_PAGE, INDEX_PAGE, IAM_PAGE, or PFS_PAGE
Row_count	The number of rows stored on the page
Free_space_in_bytes	The amount of free space on the page
Is_modified	A flag that indicates if the page is dirty
Numa_node	The NUMA node for the buffer
Read_microset	The amount of time taken to read the page into cache, specified in microseconds

The script in Listing 18-8 demonstrates how we can use the sys.dm_os_buffer_descriptors DMV to determine the percentage of the buffer cache each database is using on the instance. This can help you during performance tuning as well as give you valuable insights that you can use during capacity planning or consolidation planning.

Listing 18-8. Determining Buffer Cache Usage per Database

```
DECLARE @DB_PageTotals TABLE
(
CachedPages INT,
Database_name NVARCHAR(128),
database_id INT
) ;

INSERT INTO @DB_PageTotals
SELECT COUNT(*) CachedPages
        ,CASE
```

```
                WHEN database_id = 32767
                        THEN 'ResourceDb'
                ELSE DB_NAME(database_id)
        END Database_name
        ,database_id
FROM sys.dm_os_buffer_descriptors a
GROUP BY DB_NAME(database_id)
                ,database_id ;

DECLARE @Total FLOAT = (SELECT SUM(CachedPages) FROM @DB_PageTotals) ;


SELECT      Database_name,
            CachedPages,
            SUM(cachedpages) over(partition by database_name)
                    / @total * 100 AS RunningPercentage
FROM        @DB_PageTotals a
ORDER BY    CachedPages DESC ;
```

Note   More DMVs within the dm_os category are discussed in the "Metadata for Troubleshooting and Performance Tuning" section of this chapter.

Metadata for Capacity Planning

One of the most useful ways you can use metadata is during your pursuit of proactive capacity management. SQL Server exposes metadata that provides you with information about the current size and usage of your database files, and you can use this information to plan ahead and arrange additional capacity, before your enterprise monitoring software starts generating critical alerts.

Exposing File Stats

The sys.dm_db_file_space_usage DMV returns details of the space used within each data file of the database in which it is run. The columns returned by this object are detailed in Table 18-4.

Table 18-4. *sys.dm_db_file_space_usage Columns*

Column	Description
database_id	The ID of the database to which the file belongs.
file_id	The ID of the file within the database. These IDs are repeated between databases. For example, the primary file always has an ID of 1, and the first log file always has an ID of 2.
filegroup_id	The ID of the filegroup in which the file resides.
total_page_count	The total number of pages within the file.
allocated_extent_page_count	The number of pages within the file that are in extents that have been allocated.
unallocated_extent_page_count	The number of pages within the file that are in extents that have not been allocated.
version_store_reserved_page_count	The number of pages reserved to support transactions using snapshot isolation. Only applicable to TempDB.
user_object_reserved_page_count	The number of pages reserved for user objects. Only applicable to TempDB.
internal_object_reserved_page_count	The number of pages reserved for internal objects. Only applicable to TempDB.
mixed_extent_page_count	The number of extents that have pages allocated to different objects.
modified_extend_page_count	The total number of modified pages since the last time a full database backup was taken

The sys.dm_io_virtual_file_stats DMV returns I/O statistics for the database and log files of the database. This can help you determine the amount of data being written to each file and warn you of high I/O stalls. The object accepts database_id and file_id as parameters and returns the columns detailed in Table 18-5.

Table 18-5. *sys.dm_io_virtual_file_stats Columns*

Column	Description
database_id	The ID of the database to which the file belongs.
file_id	The ID of the file within the database. These IDs are repeated between databases. For example, the primary file always has an ID of 1 and the first log file always has an ID of 2.
sample_ms	The number of milliseconds since the computer started.
num_of_reads	The total number of reads against the file.
num_of_bytes_read	The total number of bytes read from the file.
io_stall_read_ms	The total time waiting for reads to be issued against the file, specified in milliseconds.
num_of_writes	The total number of write operations performed against the file.
num_of_bytes_written	The total number of bytes written to the file.
io_stall_write_ms	The total time waiting for writes to complete against the file, specified in milliseconds.
io_stall	The total time waiting for all I/O requests against the file to be completed, specified in milliseconds.
size_on_disk_bytes	The total space used by the file on disk, specified in bytes.
file_handle	The Windows file handle.
io_stall_queued_read_ms	Total I/O latency for read operations against the file, caused by Resource Governor.
io_stall_queued_write_ms	Total I/O latency for write operations against the file, caused by Resource Governor.

Tip   *I/O stalls* are the amount of time it takes the I/O subsystem to respond to SQL Server.

Unlike the previous two DMVs discussed in this section, the sys.master_files catalog view is a system-wide view, meaning that it returns a record for every file within every database on the instance. The columns returned by this view are described in Table 18-6.

Table 18-6. *sys.master_files Columns*

Column	Description
database_id	The ID of the database to which the file belongs.
file_id	The ID of the file within the database. These IDs are repeated between databases. For example, the primary file always has an ID of 1 and the first log file always has an ID of 2.
file_guid	The GUID of the file.
type	An integer representing the file type.
type_desc	A textual description of the file type.
data_space_id	The ID of the filegroup in which the file resides.
name	The logical name of the file.
physical_name	The physical path and name of the file.
state	An integer indicating the current state of the file.
state_desc	A textual description of the current state of the file.
size	The current size of the file, specified as a count of pages.
max_size	The maximum size of the file, specified as a count of pages.
growth	The growth setting of the file. 0 indicates autogrowth is disabled. If is_percent_growth is 0, then the value indicates the growth increment as a count of pages. If is_percent_growth is 1, then the value indicates a whole number percentage increment.
is_media_read_only	Specifies if the media on which the file resides is read only.
is_read_only	Specifies if the file is in a read-only filegroup.
is_sparse	Specifies that the file belongs to a database snapshot.
is_percent_growth	Indicates if the growth output is a percentage or a fixed rate.

(continued)

Table 18-6. (*continued*)

Column	Description
is_name_reserved	Specifies if the filename is reusable.
create_lsn	The LSN (log sequence number) at which the file was created.
drop_lsn	The LSN at which the file was dropped (if applicable).
read_only_lsn	The most recent LSN at which the filegroup was marked read only.
read_write_lsn	The most recent LSN at which the filegroup was marked read/write.
differential_base_lsn	The LSN at which changes in the file started being marked in the DIFF pages.
differential_base_guid	The GUID of the full backup on which differential backups for the file are made.
differential_base_time	The time of the full backup on which differential backups for the file are made.
redo_start_lsn	The LSN at which the next roll forward will start.
redo_start_fork_guid	The GUID of the recovery fork.
redo_target_lsn	The LSN at which an online roll forward for the file can stop.
redo_target_fork_guid	The GUID of the recovery fork.
backup_lsn	The most recent LSN at which a full or differential backup was taken.

Using File Stats for Capacity Analysis

When combined together, you can use the three metadata objects described in the previous section to produce powerful reports that can help you with capacity planning and diagnosing performance issues. For example, the query in Listing 18-9 provides the file size, amount of free space remaining, and I/O stalls for each file in the database. Because sys.dm_io_virtual_file_stats is a function as opposed to a view, we CROSS APPLY the function to the results set, passing in the database_id and the file_id of each row as parameters.

Listing 18-9. File Capacity Details

```
SELECT m.name
        ,m.physical_name
        ,CAST(fsu.total_page_count / 128. AS NUMERIC(12,4)) [Fie Size (MB)]
        ,CAST(fsu.unallocated_extent_page_count / 128. AS NUMERIC(12,4))
        [Free Space (MB)]
        ,vfs.io_stall_read_ms
        ,vfs.io_stall_write_ms
FROM sys.dm_db_file_space_usage fsu
CROSS APPLY sys.dm_io_virtual_file_stats(fsu.database_id, fsu.file_id) vfs
INNER JOIN sys.master_files m
        ON fsu.database_id = m.database_id
                AND fsu.file_id = m.file_id ;
```

The script in Listing 18-10 demonstrates how you can use `sys.master_files` to analyze drive capacity for each volume by detailing the current size of each file, the amount each file will grow by the next time it grows, and the current free capacity of the drive. You can obtain the free space on the drive by using the `xp_fixeddrives` stored procedure.

Listing 18-10. Analyzing Drive Space with xp_fixeddrives

```
DECLARE @fixeddrives TABLE
(
    Drive           CHAR(1),
    MBFree          BIGINT
) ;

INSERT INTO @fixeddrives
EXEC xp_fixeddrives ;

SELECT
    Drive
    ,SUM([File Space Used (MB)]) TotalSpaceUsed
    , SUM([Next Growth Amount (MB)]) TotalNextGrowth
    , SpaceLeftOnVolume
FROM (
SELECT Drive
        ,size * 1.0 / 128 [File Space Used (MB)]
```

```
        ,CASE
                WHEN is_percent_growth = 0
                        THEN growth * 1.0 / 128
                WHEN is_percent_growth = 1
                        THEN (size * 1.0 / 128 * growth / 100)
                END [Next Growth Amount (MB)]
        ,f.MBFree SpaceLeftOnVolume
FROM sys.master_files m
INNER JOIN @fixeddrives f
        ON LEFT(m.physical_name, 1) = f.Drive ) a
GROUP BY Drive, SpaceLeftOnVolume
ORDER BY drive ;
```

The issue with xp_fixeddrives is that it cannot see mapped drives. Therefore, as an alternative, you can employ the script in Listing 18-11, which uses PowerShell to return the information.

Caution   The drawback of this approach is that it requires xp_cmdshell to be enabled, which is against security best practice.

Listing 18-11. Analyzing Drive Space with PowerShell

```
USE [master];

DECLARE @t TABLE
(
        name varchar(150),
        minimum tinyint,
        maximum tinyint ,
        config_value tinyint ,
        run_value tinyint
)

DECLARE @psinfo TABLE(data  NVARCHAR(100)) ;

INSERT INTO @psinfo
```

```
EXEC xp_cmdshell 'Powershell.exe "Get-WMIObject Win32_LogicalDisk -filter
"DriveType=3"| Format-Table DeviceID, FreeSpace, Size"'  ;

DELETE FROM @psinfo WHERE data IS NULL  OR data LIKE '%DeviceID%' OR data
LIKE '%----%';
UPDATE @psinfo SET data = REPLACE(data,' ',',');

;WITH DriveSpace AS
(
        SELECT LEFT(data,2)  as [Drive],
        REPLACE((LEFT((SUBSTRING(data,(PATINDEX('%[0-9]%',data))
               , LEN(data))),CHARINDEX(',',
         (SUBSTRING(data,(PATINDEX('%[0-9]%',data))
               , LEN(data))))-1)),',',',') AS FreeSpace
        ,
        REPLACE(RIGHT((SUBSTRING(data,(PATINDEX('%[0-9]%',data))
               , LEN(data))),PATINDEX('%,%',
         (SUBSTRING(data,(PATINDEX('%[0-9]%',data)) , LEN(data)))))
        ,',',',')
        AS [Size]
        FROM @psinfo
)
SELECT
    mf.Drive
    ,CAST(sizeMB as numeric(18,2)) as [File Space Used (MB)]
    ,CAST(growth as numeric(18,2)) as [Next Growth Amount (MB)]
    ,CAST((CAST(FreeSpace as numeric(18,2))
                /(POWER(1024., 3))) as numeric(6,2)) AS FreeSpaceGB
    ,CAST((CAST(size as numeric(18,2))/(POWER(1024., 3))) as numeric(6,2))
    AS TotalSizeGB
    ,CAST(CAST((CAST(FreeSpace as numeric(18,2))/(POWER(1024., 3))) as
    numeric(6,2))
                / CAST((CAST(size as numeric(18,2))/(POWER(1024., 3)))
                  as numeric(6,2))
                * 100 AS numeric(5,2)) [Percent Remaining]
FROM DriveSpace
        JOIN
```

```
(          SELECT DISTINCT  LEFT(physical_name, 2) Drive, SUM(size /
           128.0) sizeMB
        ,SUM(CASE
                WHEN is_percent_growth = 0
                        THEN growth / 128.
                WHEN is_percent_growth = 1
                        THEN (size / 128. * growth / 100)
                END) growth
        FROM master.sys.master_files
        WHERE db_name(database_id) NOT IN('master','model','msdb')
        GROUP BY LEFT(physical_name, 2)
)              mf ON DriveSpace.Drive = mf.drive ;
```

A third way of working with drive information is the sys.dm_os_enumerate_fixed_ drives DMV. This DMV returns the path of the drive, for example, C:\ as well as the free space on the drive, expressed in bytes. Additionally, columns are returned for a drive type ID and description.

Metadata for Troubleshooting and Performance Tuning

You can use many metadata objects to tune performance and troubleshoot issues within SQL Server. In the following sections, we explore how to capture performance counters from within SQL Server, how to analyze waits, and how to use DMVs to troubleshoot issues with expensive queries.

Retrieving Perfmon Counters

Perfmon is a Windows tool that captures performance counters for the operating system, plus many SQL Server–specific counters. DBAs who are trying to diagnose performance issues find this very useful. The problem is that many DBAs do not have administrative access to the underlying operating system, which makes them reliant on Windows Administrators to assist with the troubleshooting process. A workaround for this issue is the sys_dm_os_performance_counters DMV, which exposes the SQL Server Perfmon counters within SQL Server. The columns returned by sys.dm_os_performance_ counters are described in Table 18-7.

Table 18-7. *sys.dm_os_performance_counters Columns*

Column	Description
object_name	The category of the counter.
counter_name	The name of the counter.
instance_name	The instance of the counter. For example, database-related counters have an instance for each database.
cntr_value	The value of the counter.
cntr_type	The type of counter. Counter types are described in Table 18-8.

The sys.dm_os_performance_counters DMV exposes different types of counters that can be identified by the cntr_type column, which relates to the underlying WMI performance counter type. You need to handle different counter types in different ways. The counter types exposed are described in Table 18-8.

Table 18-8. *Counter Types*

Counter Type	Description
1073939712	You will use PERF_LARGE_RAW_BASE as a base value in conjunction with the PERF_LARGE_RAW_FRACTION type to calculate a counter percentage, or with PERF_AVERAGE_BULK to calculate an average.
537003264	Use PERF_LARGE_RAW_FRACTION as a fractional value in conjunction with PERF_LARGE_RAW_BASE to calculate a counter percentage.
1073874176	PERF_AVERAGE_BULK is a cumulative average that you use in conjunction with PERF_LARGE_RAW_BASE to calculate a counter average. The counter, along with the base, is sampled twice to calculate the metric over a period of time.
272696320	PERF_COUNTER_COUNTER is a 32-bit cumulative rate counter. The value should be sampled twice to calculate the metric over a period of time.
272696576	PERF_COUNTER_BULK_COUNT is a 64-bit cumulative rate counter. The value should be sampled twice to calculate the metric over a period of time.
65792	PERF_COUNTER_LARGE_RAWCOUNT returns the last sampled result for the counter.

The query in Listing 18-12 demonstrates how to use `sys.dm_os_performance_`
`counters` to capture metrics of the `PERF_COUNTER_LARGE_RAWCOUNT` type, which is the
simplest form of counter to capture. The query returns the number of memory grants
that are currently pending.

Listing 18-12. Using Counter Type 65792

```
SELECT *
FROM sys.dm_os_performance_counters
WHERE counter_name = 'Memory Grants Pending' ;
```

The script in Listing 18-13 demonstrates capturing the number of lock requests that
are occurring per second over the space of one minute. The lock requests/sec counter
uses the `PERF_COUNTER_BULK_COUNT` counter type, but the same method applies to
capturing counters relating to In-Memory OLTP, which uses the `PERF_COUNTER_COUNTER`
counter type.

Listing 18-13. Using Counter Types 272696576 and 272696320

```
DECLARE @cntr_value1 BIGINT = (
SELECT cntr_value
FROM sys.dm_os_performance_counters
WHERE counter_name = 'Lock Requests/sec'
        AND instance_name = '_Total') ;

WAITFOR DELAY '00:01:00'

DECLARE @cntr_value2 BIGINT = (
SELECT cntr_value
FROM sys.dm_os_performance_counters
WHERE counter_name = 'Lock Requests/sec'
        AND instance_name = '_Total') ;

SELECT (@cntr_value2 - @cntr_value1) / 60 'Lock Requests/sec' ;
```

The script in Listing 18-14 demonstrates capturing the plan cache hit ratio for the
instance. The Plan Cache Hit Ratio counter is counter type 537003264. Therefore, we
need to multiply the value by 100 and then divide by the base counter to calculate the
percentage.

> **Tip**   Before running the script, you should change the instance name to match your own.

Listing 18-14. Using Counter Type 537003264

```
SELECT
        100 *
        (
        SELECT cntr_value
        FROM sys.dm_os_performance_counters
        WHERE object_name = 'MSSQL$PROSQLADMIN:Plan Cache'
                AND counter_name = 'Cache hit ratio'
                AND instance_name = '_Total')
        /
        (
        SELECT cntr_value
        FROM sys.dm_os_performance_counters
        WHERE object_name = 'MSSQL$PROSQLADMIN:Plan Cache'
                AND counter_name = 'Cache hit ratio base'
                AND instance_name = '_Total') [Plan cache hit ratio %] ;
```

The script in Listing 18-15 demonstrates how to capture the Average Latch Wait Time (ms) counter. Because this counter is of type PERF_AVERAGE_BULK, we need to capture the value and its corresponding base counter twice. We then need to deduct the first capture of the counter from the second capture, deduct the first capture of the base counter from the second capture, and then divide the fractional counter value by its base value to calculate the average over the time period. Because it is possible that no latches will be requested within the time period, we have wrapped the SELECT statement in an IF/ELSE block to avoid the possibility of a divide-by-0 error being thrown.

Listing 18-15. Using Counter Type 1073874176

```
DECLARE @cntr TABLE
(
ID          INT          IDENTITY,
counter_name NVARCHAR(256),
```

```
counter_value BIGINT,
[Time] DATETIME
) ;

INSERT INTO @cntr
SELECT
        counter_name
        ,cntr_value
        ,GETDATE()
        FROM sys.dm_os_performance_counters
        WHERE counter_name IN('Average Latch Wait Time (ms)',
                            'Average Latch Wait Time base') ;

--Adds an artificial delay
WAITFOR DELAY '00:01:00' ;

INSERT INTO @cntr
SELECT
        counter_name
        ,cntr_value
        ,GETDATE()
        FROM sys.dm_os_performance_counters
        WHERE counter_name IN('Average Latch Wait Time (ms)',
                            'Average Latch Wait Time base') ;

IF (SELECT COUNT(DISTINCT counter_value)
    FROM @cntr
    WHERE counter_name = 'Average Latch Wait Time (ms)') > 2
BEGIN
SELECT
        (
            (
            SELECT TOP 1 counter_value
            FROM @cntr
            WHERE counter_name = 'Average Latch Wait Time (ms)'
            ORDER BY [Time] DESC
            )
            -
```

```
                (
                SELECT TOP 1 counter_value
                FROM @cntr
                WHERE counter_name = 'Average Latch Wait Time (ms)'
                ORDER BY [Time] ASC
                )
        )
        /
         (

                (
                SELECT TOP 1 counter_value
                FROM @cntr
                WHERE counter_name = 'Average Latch Wait Time base'
                ORDER BY [Time] DESC
                )
                -
                (
                SELECT TOP 1 counter_value
                FROM @cntr
                WHERE counter_name = 'Average Latch Wait Time base'
                ORDER BY [Time] ASC
                )
        ) [Average Latch Wait Time (ms)] ;
END
ELSE
BEGIN
        SELECT 0 [Average Latch Wait Time (ms)] ;
END
```

Analyzing Waits

Waits are a natural aspect of any RDBMS, but they can also indicate a performance bottleneck. Analyzing these waits, with a view to reducing them, often improve performance. A full explanation of all wait types can be found at msdn.microsoft.com, but all wait types break down into three categories: resource waits, queue waits, and external waits.

Note   A query in SQL Server is either running, waiting for its turn on the processor (runnable), or waiting for another resource (suspended). If it is waiting for another resource, SQL Server records the reason why it is waiting and the duration of this wait.

Resource waits occur when a thread requires access to an object, but that object is already in use, and therefore, the thread has to wait. This can include the thread waiting to take a lock out on an object or waiting for a disk resource to respond. *Queue waits* occur when a thread is idle and is waiting for a task to be assigned. This does not necessarily indicate a performance bottleneck, since it is often a background task, such as the Deadlock Monitor or Lazy Writer waiting until it is needed. *External waits* occur when a thread is waiting for an external resource, such as a linked server. The hidden gotcha here is that an external wait does not always mean that the thread is actually waiting. It could be performing an operation external to SQL Server, such as an extended stored procedure running external code.

Any task that has been issued is in one of three states: running, runnable, or suspended. If a task is in the running state, then it is actually being executed on a processor. When a task is in the runnable state, it sits on the processor queue, awaiting its turn to run. This is known as a *signal wait*. When a task is suspended, it means that the task is waiting for any reason other than a signal wait. In other words, it is experiencing a resource wait, a queue wait, or an external wait. Each query is likely to alternate between the three states as it progresses.

The sys.dm_os_wait_stats returns details of the cumulative waits for each wait type, since the instance started, or since the statistics exposed by the DMV were reset. This is important, as it gives a holistic view, as to the source of bottlenecks. You can reset the statistics by running the command in Listing 18-16.

Listing 18-16.   Resetting Wait Stats

```
DBCC SQLPERF ('sys.dm_os_wait_stats', CLEAR) ;
```

The columns returned by sys.dm_os_wait_stats are detailed in Table 18-9.

Table 18-9. *sys.dm_os_wait_stats Columns*

Column	Description
wait_type	The name of the wait type that has occurred.
waiting_tasks_count	The number of tasks that have occurred on this wait type.
wait_time_ms	The cumulative time of all waits against this wait type, displayed in milliseconds. This includes signal wait times.
max_wait_time_ms	The maximum duration of a single wait against this wait type.
signal_wait_time_ms	The cumulative time for all signal waits against this wait type.

To find the wait types that are responsible for the highest cumulative wait time, run the query in Listing 18-17. This query adds a calculated column to the result set, which deducts the signal wait time from the overall wait time to avoid CPU pressure from skewing the results.

Listing 18-17. Finding the Highest Waits

```
SELECT *
        , wait_time_ms - signal_wait_time_ms ResourceWaits
FROM sys.dm_os_wait_stats
ORDER BY wait_time_ms - signal_wait_time_ms DESC ;
```

Of course, signal wait time can be a cause for concern in its own right, potentially identifying the processor as a bottleneck, and you should analyze it. Therefore, use the query in Listing 18-18 to calculate the percentage of overall waits, which are due to a task waiting for its turn on the processor. The value is displayed for each wait type and it is followed by a row that displays the overall percentage for all wait types.

Listing 18-18. Calculating Signal Waits

```
SELECT ISNULL(wait_type, 'Overall Percentage:') wait_type
        ,PercentageSignalWait
FROM (
                SELECT wait_type
                        ,CAST(100. * SUM(signal_wait_time_ms)
```

```
                          / SUM(wait_time_ms) AS NUMERIC(20,2))
                       PercentageSignalWait
           FROM sys.dm_os_wait_stats
           WHERE wait_time_ms > 0
           GROUP BY wait_type WITH ROLLUP
    ) a
ORDER BY PercentageSignalWait DESC ;
```

To find the highest waits over a defined period, you need to sample the data twice and then deduct the first sample from the second sample. The script in Listing 18-19 samples the data twice with a ten-minute interval and then displays the details of the five highest waits within that interval.

Listing 18-19. Calculating the Highest Waits over a Defined Period

```
DECLARE @Waits1 TABLE
(
wait_type NVARCHAR(128),
wait_time_ms BIGINT
) ;

DECLARE @Waits2 TABLE
(
wait_type NVARCHAR(128),
wait_time_ms BIGINT
) ;

INSERT INTO @waits1
SELECT wait_type
        ,wait_time_ms
FROM sys.dm_os_wait_stats ;

WAITFOR DELAY '00:10:00' ;

INSERT INTO @Waits2
SELECT wait_type
        ,wait_time_ms
FROM sys.dm_os_wait_stats ;
```

```
SELECT TOP 5
        w2.wait_type
        ,w2.wait_time_ms - w1.wait_time_ms
FROM @Waits1 w1
INNER JOIN @Waits2 w2
        ON w1.wait_type = w2.wait_type
ORDER BY w2.wait_time_ms - w1.wait_time_ms DESC ;
```

Database Metadata

In previous versions of SQL Server, if DBAs needed to discover information about specific pages within a database, they had no choice but to use the well-known, but undocumented DBCC command, DBCC PAGE. SQL Server addresses this issue, by adding a new dynamic management view, called sys.dm_db_page_info. It is fully documented and supported by Microsoft, and provides the ability to return a page header, in a table-valued format. The function accepts the parameters detailed in Table 18-10.

Table 18-10. *Parameters Accepted by sys.dm_db_page_info*

Parameter	Description
Database_id	The database_id of the database that you wish to return details for.
File_id	The file_id of the file that you wish to return details for.
Page_id	The page_id of the page that you are interested in.
Mode	Mode can be set to either LIMITED or DETAILED. The only difference between the modes is that when LIMITED is used, the description columns are not populated. This can improve performance against large tables.

In order to populate these parameters, an additional system function has been added, called sys.fn_PageResCracker. This function can be cross applied to a table, passing %%physloc%% as a parameter. Alternatively, if cross applied to the sys.dm_exec_requests DMV, or sys.sysprocesses, a deprecated system view, an additional column has been added, called page_resource, which can be passed as a parameter to the function. This is helpful if you are diagnosing an issue with page waits. When passed a page resource/physical location object, the function will return the database_id, file_id, and page_id of each row in a result set.

Caution   When used with %%physloc%% as opposed to a page_resource object, the sys.fn_PageResCracker function returns a slot_id, as opposed to a database_id. Therefore, when used with %%physloc%%, the DB_ID() function should be used to obtain the database_id and the database_id column returned by the function should be discarded.

Table 18-11 details the columns that are returned by the sys.dm_db_page_info DMF.

Table 18-11. *Columns Returned by sys.db_db_page_info*

Column	Description
Database_id	The ID of the database
File_id	The ID of the file
Page_id	The ID of the page
page_type	The internal ID associated with the page type description
Page_type_desc page_flag_bits page_flag_bits_desc	The type of page. For example, data page, index page, IAM page, PFS page, etc.
page_type_flag_bits	Hexadecimal value representing the page flags
page_type_flag_bits_desc	A description of the page flags
object_id	The ID of the object that the page is a part of
index_id	The ID of the index that the page is part of
partition_id	The partition ID of the partition that the page is part of
alloc_unit_id	The ID of the allocation unit where the page is stored
page_level	The level of the page within a B-Tree structure
slot_count	The number of slots within the page
ghost_rec_count	The number of records of the page that have been marked for deletion, but have not yet been physically removed

(continued)

Table 18-11. (*continued*)

Column	Description
torn_bits	Used to detect data corruption, by storing 1 bit for every torn write detected
is_iam_pg	Indicates if the page is an IAM page
is_mixed_ext	Indicates if the page is part of a mixed extent (an extent allocated to multiple objects)
pfs_file_id	The file ID of the file where the page's associated PFS (Page Free Space) page is stored
pfs_page_id	The page ID of the PFS page that is associated with the page
pfs_alloc_percent	The amount of free space on the page
pfs_status	The value of the page's PFS byte
pfs_status_desc	A description of the page's PFS byte
gam_file_id	The file ID of the file where the page's associated GAM (global allocation map) page is stored
gam_page_id	The page ID of the GAM page, which is associated with the page
gam_status	Indicates if the page is allocated in GAM
gam_status_desc	Describes the GAM status marker
sgam_file_id	The file ID of the file where the page's associated SGAM (shared global allocation map) page is stored
sgam_page_id	The page ID of the SGAM page, which is associated with the page
sgam_status	Indicates if the page is allocated in SGAM
sgam_status_desc	Describes the SGAM status marker
diff_map_file_id	The file ID of the file containing the page's associated differential bitmap page
diff_map_page_id	The page ID of the differential bitmap page associated with the page
diff_status	Indicates if the page has changed since the last differential backup
diff_status_desc	Describes the differential status marker

(*continued*)

Table 18-11. (*continued*)

Column	Description
ml_file_id	The file ID of the file that stores the page's associated minimally logged bitmap page
ml_page_id	The page ID of the minimally logged bitmap page, associated with the page
ml_status	Indicates if the page is minimally logged
ml_status_desc	Describes the minimally logged status marker
free_bytes	The amount of free space on the page (in bytes)
free_data_offset	The page offset, to the start of the free space on the page
reserved_bytes	If the page is a leaf-level index page, indicates the amount of rows awaiting ghost cleanup. If the page is on a heap, then indicates the number of free bytes reserved by all transactions
reserved_xdes_id	Used for MSFT support for debugging
xdes_id	Used for MSFT support for debugging
prev_page_file_id	The file ID of the previous page in the IAM chain
prev_page_page_id	The page ID of the previous page in the IAM chain
next_page_file_id	The file ID of the next page in the IAM chain
next_page_page_id	The page ID of the next page in the IAM chain
min_len	The length of fixed width rows
Page_lsn	The last LSN (log sequence number) to modify the page
header_version	The version of the page header

The potential occasions where this data may prove invaluable are almost limitless. The script in Listing 18-20 demonstrates how this data could be used to determine the maximum log sequence number in a critical table, in preparation for a restore activity. The DBA can then use the maximum LSN to ensure that a point-in-time restore captures the latest modifications to the critical data.

Listing 18-20. Find the Most Recent LSN to Modify a Table

```
CREATE DATABASE Chapter18
GO

ALTER DATABASE Chapter18
SET RECOVERY FULL
GO

USE Chapter18
GO

CREATE TABLE dbo.CriticalData (
    ID              INT     IDENTITY    PRIMARY KEY     NOT NULL,
    ImportantData                       NVARCHAR(128)   NOT NULL
)

INSERT INTO dbo.CriticalData(ImportantData)
VALUES('My Very Important Value')
GO

SELECT MAX(page_info.page_lsn)
FROM dbo.CriticalData c
CROSS APPLY sys.fn_PageResCracker(%%physloc%%) AS r
CROSS APPLY sys.dm_db_page_info(DB_ID(), r.file_id, r.page_id, 'DETAILED')
AS page_info
```

Metadata-Driven Automation

You can use metadata to drive intelligent scripts that you can use to automate routine
DBA maintenance tasks while at the same time incorporating business logic. In the
following sections, you see how you can use metadata to generate rolling database
snapshots and also to rebuild only those indexes that are fragmented.

Dynamically Cycling Database Snapshots

As discussed in Chapter 16, we can use database snapshots to create a read-only copy of the database that can reduce contention for read-only reporting. The issue is that the data becomes stale, as data in the source database is modified. For this reason, a useful tool for managing snapshots is a stored procedure, which dynamically creates a new snapshot and drops the oldest existing snapshot. You can then schedule this procedure to run periodically, using SQL Server Agent. (SQL Server Agent is discussed in Chapter 21.) The script in Listing 18-21 creates a stored procedure that, when passed the name of the source database, drops the oldest snapshot and creates a new one.

The procedure accepts two parameters. The first specifies the name of the database that should be used to generate the snapshot. The second parameter specifies how many snapshots you should have at any one time. For example, if you pass in a value of Chapter18 to the @DBName parameter and a value of 2 to the @RequiredSnapshots parameter, the procedure creates a snapshot against the Chapter18 database but only removes the oldest snapshot if at least two snapshots already exist against the Chapter18 database.

The procedure builds up the CREATE DATABASE script in three parts (see Listing 18-21). The first part contains the initial CREATE DATABASE statement. The second part creates the file list, based on the files that are recorded as being part of the database in sys.master_files. The third part contains the AS SNAPSHOT OF statement. The three strings are then concatenated together before being executed. The script appends a sequence number to the name of the snapshot, and the name of each file within the snapshot, to ensure uniqueness.

Listing 18-21. Dynamically Cycling Database Snapshots

```
CREATE PROCEDURE dbo.DynamicSnapshot @DBName NVARCHAR(128),
@RequiredSnapshots INT
AS
BEGIN

        DECLARE @SQL NVARCHAR(MAX)
        DECLARE @SQLStart NVARCHAR(MAX)
        DECLARE @SQLEnd NVARCHAR(MAX)
        DECLARE @SQLFileList NVARCHAR(MAX)
```

```
DECLARE @DBID INT
DECLARE @SS_Seq_No INT
DECLARE @SQLDrop NVARCHAR(MAX)

SET @DBID = (SELECT DB_ID(@DBName)) ;

--Generate sequence number

IF (SELECT COUNT(*) FROM sys.databases WHERE source_database_id =
@DBID) > 0
        SET @SS_Seq_No = (SELECT TOP 1 CAST(SUBSTRING(name,
        LEN(Name), 1) AS INT)
                          FROM sys.databases
                          WHERE source_database_id = @DBID
                          ORDER BY create_date DESC) + 1
ELSE
        SET @SS_Seq_No = 1
        --Generate the first part of the CREATE DATABASE statement

SET @SQLStart = 'CREATE DATABASE '
                + QUOTENAME(@DBName + CAST(CAST(GETDATE() AS DATE)
                AS NCHAR(10))
                + '_ss' + CAST(@SS_Seq_No AS NVARCHAR(4))) +
                ' ON ' ;

--Generate the file list for the CREATE DATABASE statement

SELECT @SQLFileList =
 (
        SELECT
                '(NAME = N''' + mf.name + ''', FILENAME = N'''
                + SUBSTRING(mf.physical_name, 1, LEN(mf.physical_
                name) - 4)
                + CAST(@SS_Seq_No AS NVARCHAR(4)) + '.ss' +
                '''),' AS [data()]
        FROM  sys.master_files mf
        WHERE mf.database_id = @DBID
                AND mf.type = 0
```

```
        FOR XML PATH ('')
) ;

--Remove the extra comma from the end of the file list

SET @SQLFileList = SUBSTRING(@SQLFileList, 1, LEN(@
SQLFileList) - 2) ;

--Generate the final part of the CREATE DATABASE statement

SET @SQLEnd = ') AS SNAPSHOT OF ' + @DBName ;

--Concatenate the strings and run the completed statement

SET @SQL = @SQLStart + @SQLFileList + @SQLEnd ;

EXEC(@SQL) ;

--Check to see if the required number of snapshots exists for the
database,
--and if so, delete the oldest

IF (SELECT COUNT(*)
        FROM sys.databases
        WHERE source_database_id = @DBID) > @RequiredSnapshots
BEGIN
        SET @SQLDrop = 'DROP DATABASE ' + (
        SELECT TOP 1
                QUOTENAME(name)
        FROM sys.databases
        WHERE source_database_id = @DBID
        ORDER BY create_date ASC )
                EXEC(@SQLDrop)
    END ;

END
```

The command in Listing 18-22 runs the DynamicSnapshot procedure against the Chapter18 database specifying that two snapshots should exist at any one time.

Listing 18-22. Running the DynamicSnapshot Procedure

```
EXEC dbo.DynamicSnapshot 'Chapter18', 2 ;
```

Rebuilding Only Fragmented Indexes

When you rebuild all indexes with a maintenance plan, which we discuss in Chapter 21, SQL Server supplies no intelligent logic out of the box. Therefore, all indexes are rebuilt, regardless of their fragmentation level, which requires unnecessary time and resource utilization. A workaround for this issue is to write a custom script that rebuilds indexes only if they are fragmented.

The script in Listing 18-23 demonstrates how you can use SQLCMD to identify indexes that have more than 25% fragmentation and then rebuild them dynamically. The reason that the code is in a SQLCMD script, as opposed to a stored procedure, is because `sys.dm_db_index_physical_stats` must be called from within the database that you wish to run it against. Therefore, when you run it via SQLCMD, you can use a scripting variable to specify the database you require; doing so makes the script reusable for all databases. When you run the script from the command line, you can simply pass in the name of the database as a variable.

Listing 18-23. Rebuilding Only Required Indexes

```
USE $(DBName)
GO

DECLARE @SQL NVARCHAR(MAX)

SET @SQL =
(
        SELECT 'ALTER INDEX '
                + i.name
                + ' ON ' + s.name
                + '.'
                + OBJECT_NAME(i.object_id)
                + ' REBUILD ; '
        FROM sys.dm_db_index_physical_stats(DB_ID('$(DBName)'),NULL,NULL,NU
        LL,'DETAILED') ps
        INNER JOIN sys.indexes i
```

```
            ON ps.object_id = i.object_id
                    AND ps.index_id = i.index_id
    INNER JOIN sys.objects o
            ON ps.object_id = o.object_id
            INNER JOIN sys.schemas s
                    ON o.schema_id = s.schema_id
    WHERE index_level = 0
            AND avg_fragmentation_in_percent > 25
            FOR XML PATH('')
) ;

EXEC(@SQL) ;
```

When this script is saved as in the root of C:\ as RebuildIndexes.sql, it can be run
from the command line. The command in Listing 18-24 demonstrates running it against
the Chapter18 database.

Listing 18-24. Running RebuildIndexes.sql

```
Sqlcmd -v DBName="Chapter18" -I c:\RebuildIndexes.sql -S ./PROSQLADMIN
```

Summary

SQL Server exposes a vast array of metadata, which describes the data structures
within SQL Server as well as the data itself. Metadata is exposed through a series of
catalog views, dynamic management views and functions, system functions, and the
INFORMATION_SCHEMA. Normally you only use the INFORMATION_SCHEMA if you need your
scripts to be transferable to other RDBMS products. This is because it provides less detail
than SQL Server–specific metadata but conforms to ISO standards, and therefore, it
works on all major RDBMS.

This chapter also covered much useful information about the underlying operating
system, as well as SQLOS. For example, you can use the dm_server category of DMV to
find details of the instance's Registry keys and expose details of the instance's services.
You can use the dm_os category of DMV to expose many internal details regarding the
SQLOS, including the current contents of the buffer cache.

SQL Server also exposes metadata that you can use for capacity planning, such as the usage statistics for all files within a database (e.g., I/O stalls) and the amount of free space remaining. You can use this information to proactively plan additional capacity requirements before alerts start being triggered and applications are put at risk.

Metadata can also help in the pursuit of troubleshooting and performance tuning. The `sys.dm_os_performance_counters` DMV allows DBAs to retrieve Perfmon counters, even if they do not have access to the operating system. This can remove inter-team dependencies. You can use `sys.dm_os_wait_stats` to identify the most common cause of waits within the instance, which can in turn help diagnose hardware bottlenecks, such as memory or CPU pressure. The `dm_exec` category of DMV can help identify expensive queries, which may be tuned, to improve performance.

DBAs can also use metadata to create intelligent scripts, which can reduce their workload by adding business rules to common maintenance tasks. For example, a DBA can use metadata for tasks such as dynamically rebuilding only indexes that have become fragmented, or dynamically managing the cycling of database snapshots. I encourage you to explore the possibilities of metadata-driven automation further; the possibilities are endless.

## CHAPTER 19

Locking and Blocking

Locking is an essential aspect of any RDBMS, because it allows concurrent users to access the same data, without the risk of their updates conflicting and causing data integrity issues. This chapter discusses how locking, deadlocks, and transactions work in SQL Server; it then moves on to discuss how transactions impact In-Memory transaction functionality and how the DBA can observe lock metadata regarding transactions and contention.

Understanding Locking

The following sections discuss how processes can take locks at various levels of granularity, which types of lock are compatible with others and features for controlling lock behavior during online maintenance operations and lock partitioning, which can improve performance on large systems.

Lock Granularity

Processes can take out locks at many different levels of granularity, depending on the nature of the operation requesting the lock. To reduce the impact of operations blocking each other, it is sensible to take out a lock at the lowest possible level of granularity. The trade-off, however, is that taking out locks uses system resources, so if an operation requires acquiring millions of locks at the lowest level of granularity, then this is highly inefficient, and locking at a higher level is a more suitable choice. Table 19-1 describes the levels of granularity at which locks can be taken out.

© Peter A. Carter 2023
P. A. Carter, *Pro SQL Server 2022 Administration*, https://doi.org/10.1007/978-1-4842-8864-1_19

Table 19-1. *Locking Granularity*

Level	Description
RID/KEY	A row identifier on a heap or an index key. Use locks on index keys in serializable transactions to lock ranges of rows. Serializable transactions are discussed later in this chapter.
PAGE	A data or index page.
EXTENT	Eight continuous pages.
HoBT (Heap or B-Tree)	A heap of a single index (B-Tree).
TABLE	An entire table, including all indexes.
FILE	A file within a database.
METADATA	A metadata resource.
ALLOCTION_UNIT	Tables are split into three allocation units: row data, row overflow data, and LOB (Large Object Block) data. A lock on an allocation unit locks one of the three allocation units of a table.
DATABASE	The entire database.

When SQL Server locks a resource within a table, it takes out what is known as an *intent lock* on the resource directly above it in the hierarchy. For example, if SQL Server needs to lock a RID or KEY, it also takes out an intent lock on the page containing the row. If the Lock Manager decides that it is more efficient to lock at a higher level of the hierarchy, then it escalates the lock to a higher level. It is worth noting, however, that row locks are not escalated to page locks; they are escalated directly to table locks. If the table is partitioned, then SQL Server can lock the partition as opposed to the whole table. The thresholds that SQL Server uses for lock escalation are as follows:

- An operation requires more than 5000 locks on a table, or a partition, if the table is partitioned.

- The number of locks acquired within the instance causes memory thresholds to be exceeded.

You can change this behavior for specific tables, however, by using the LOCK_ESCALATION option of a table. This option has three possible values, as described in Table 19-2.

Table 19-2. *LOCK_ESCALATION Values*

Value	Description
TABLE	Locks escalate to the table level, even when you are using partitioned tables.
AUTO	This value allows locks to escalate to a partition, rather than the table, on partitioned tables.
DISABLE	The value disables locks being escalated to the table level except when a table lock is required to protect data integrity.

Locking Behaviors for Online Maintenance

In SQL Server, you can also control the behavior of locking for online index rebuilds and partition SWITCH operations. The available options are described in Table 19-3.

Table 19-3. *Blocking Behaviors*

Option	Description
MAX_DURATION	The duration, specified in minutes, that an online index rebuild or SWITCH operation waits before the ABORT_AFTER_WAIT action is triggered.
ABORT_AFTER_WAIT	These are the available actions: • NONE specifies that the operation will continue to wait, with normal priority. • SELF means that the operation will be terminated. • BLOCKERS means that all user transactions that are currently blocking the operation will be killed.
WAIT_AT_LOW_PRIORITY	Functionally equivalent to MAX_DURATION = 0, ABORT_AFTER_WAIT = NONE.

The script in Listing 19-1 creates the Chapter19 database, which includes a table called Customers that is populated with data. The script then demonstrates configuring LOCK_ESCALATION before rebuilding the nonclustered index on dbo.customers, specifying that any operations should be killed if they are blocking the rebuild for more than one minute. Note that the script requires either Enterprise or Developer edition to run.

Tip   Be sure to change the file paths to match your own configuration, before
running the script.

Listing 19-1. Configuring Table Locking Options

```
--Create the database

CREATE DATABASE Chapter19
ON  PRIMARY
( NAME = N'Chapter19', FILENAME = 'F:\MSSQL\DATA\Chapter19.mdf' ),
 FILEGROUP MemOpt CONTAINS MEMORY_OPTIMIZED_DATA  DEFAULT
( NAME = N'MemOpt', FILENAME = 'F:\MSSQL\DATA\MemOpt' )
 LOG ON
( NAME = N'Chapter19_log', FILENAME = 'E:\MSSQL\DATA\Chapter19_log.ldf' ) ;
GO

USE Chapter19
GO

--Create and populate numbers table

DECLARE @Numbers TABLE
(
        Number          INT
)

;WITH CTE(Number)
AS
(
        SELECT 1 Number
        UNION ALL
        SELECT Number + 1
        FROM CTE
        WHERE Number < 100
)
```

```
INSERT INTO @Numbers
SELECT Number FROM CTE;

--Create and populate name pieces

DECLARE @Names TABLE
(
        FirstName           VARCHAR(30),
        LastName            VARCHAR(30)
);

INSERT INTO @Names
VALUES('Peter', 'Carter'),
                ('Michael', 'Smith'),
                ('Danielle', 'Mead'),
                ('Reuben', 'Roberts'),
                ('Iris', 'Jones'),
                ('Sylvia', 'Davies'),
                ('Finola', 'Wright'),
                ('Edward', 'James'),
                ('Marie', 'Andrews'),
                ('Jennifer', 'Abraham');

--Create and populate Addresses table

CREATE TABLE dbo.Addresses
(
AddressID           INT             NOT NULL        IDENTITY        PRIMARY KEY,
AddressLine1        NVARCHAR(50),
AddressLine2        NVARCHAR(50),
AddressLine3        NVARCHAR(50),
PostCode            NCHAR(8)
) ;

INSERT INTO dbo.Addresses
VALUES('1 Carter Drive', 'Hedge End', 'Southampton', 'SO32 6GH')
        ,('10 Apress Way', NULL, 'London', 'WC10 2FG')
        ,('12 SQL Street', 'Botley', 'Southampton', 'SO32 8RT')
        ,('19 Springer Way', NULL, 'London', 'EC1 5GG') ;
```

```
--Create and populate Customers table
CREATE TABLE dbo.Customers
(
        CustomerID              INT           NOT NULL    IDENTITY    PRIMARY KEY,
        FirstName               VARCHAR(30)   NOT NULL,
        LastName                VARCHAR(30)   NOT NULL,
        BillingAddressID        INT           NOT NULL,
        DeliveryAddressID       INT           NOT NULL,
        CreditLimit             MONEY         NOT NULL,
        Balance                 MONEY         NOT NULL
);
SELECT * INTO #Customers
FROM
        (SELECT
                (SELECT TOP 1 FirstName FROM @Names ORDER BY NEWID())
                FirstName,
                (SELECT TOP 1 LastName FROM @Names ORDER BY NEWID())
                LastName,
                (SELECT TOP 1 Number FROM @Numbers ORDER BY NEWID())
                BillingAddressID,
                (SELECT TOP 1 Number FROM @Numbers ORDER BY NEWID())
                DeliveryAddressID,
                (SELECT TOP 1 CAST(RAND() * Number AS INT) * 10000
                   FROM @Numbers
                   ORDER BY NEWID()) CreditLimit,
                (SELECT TOP 1 CAST(RAND() * Number AS INT) * 9000
                   FROM @Numbers
                   ORDER BY NEWID()) Balance
        FROM @Numbers a
        CROSS JOIN @Numbers b
) a;

INSERT INTO dbo.Customers
SELECT * FROM #Customers;
GO
```

```
--This table will be used later in the chapter
CREATE TABLE dbo.CustomersMem
(
        CustomerID              INT             NOT NULL    IDENTITY
                                PRIMARY KEY NONCLUSTERED HASH WITH
                                (BUCKET_COUNT = 20000),
        FirstName               VARCHAR(30)     NOT NULL,
        LastName                VARCHAR(30)     NOT NULL,
        BillingAddressID        INT             NOT NULL,
        DeliveryAddressID       INT             NOT NULL,
        CreditLimit             MONEY           NOT NULL,
        Balance                 MONEY           NOT NULL
) WITH(MEMORY_OPTIMIZED = ON) ;

INSERT INTO dbo.CustomersMem
SELECT
        FirstName
        , LastName
        , BillingAddressID
        , DeliveryAddressID
        , CreditLimit
        , Balance
FROM dbo.Customers ;
GO

CREATE INDEX idx_LastName ON dbo.Customers(LastName)

--Set LOCK_ESCALATION to AUTO

ALTER TABLE dbo.Customers SET (LOCK_ESCALATION = AUTO) ;

--Set WAIT_AT_LOW_PRIORITY

ALTER INDEX idx_LastName ON dbo.Customers REBUILD
WITH
(ONLINE = ON (WAIT_AT_LOW_PRIORITY (MAX_DURATION = 1 MINUTES, ABORT_AFTER_
WAIT = BLOCKERS))) ;
```

Lock Compatibility

A process can acquire different types of locks. These lock types are described in Table 19-4.

Table 19-4. Lock Types

Type	Description
Shared (S)	Used for read operations.
Update (U)	Taken out on resources that may be updated.
Exclusive (X)	Used when data is modified.
Schema Modification (Sch-M)/Schema Stability (Sch-S)	Schema modification locks are taken out when DDL statements are being run against a table. Schema stability locks are taken out while queries are being compiled and executed. Stability locks only block operations that require a schema modification lock, whereas schema modification locks block all access to a table.
Bulk Update (BU)	Bulk update locks are used during bulk load operations to allow multiple threads to parallel load data to a table while blocking other processes.
Key-range	Key-range locks are taken on a range of rows when using pessimistic isolation levels. Isolation levels are discussed later in this chapter.
Intent	Intent locks are used to protect resources lower in the lock hierarchy by signaling their intent to acquire a shared or exclusive lock.

Intent locks improve performance, because they are only examined at the table level, which negates the need to examine every row or page before another operation acquires a lock. The types of intent lock that can be acquired are described in Table 19-5.

Table 19-5. *Intent Lock Types*

Type	Description
Intent shared (IS)	Protects shared locks on some resources at the lower level of the hierarchy
Intent exclusive (IX)	Protects shared and exclusive locks on some resources at the lower level of the hierarchy
Shared with intent exclusive (SIX)	Protects shared locks on all resources and exclusive locks on some resources at the lower level of the hierarchy
Intent update (IU)	Protects update locks on all resources at the lower level of the hierarchy
Shared intent update (SIU)	The resultant set of S and IU locks
Update intent exclusive (UIX)	The resultant set of X and IU locks

The matrix in Figure 19-1 shows basic lock compatibility. You can find a complete matrix of lock compatibility at `msdn.micrososft.com`.

	Shared	Update	Exclusive
Shared	Yes	Yes	No
Update	Yes	No	No
Exclusive	No	No	No

Figure 19-1. *Lock compatibility matrix*

Lock Partitioning

It is possible for locks on frequently accessed resources to become a bottleneck. For this reason, SQL Server automatically applies a feature called *lock partitioning* for any instance that has affinity with more than 16 cores. Lock partitioning reduces contention by dividing a single lock resource into multiple resources. This means that contention is reduced on shared resources such as the memory used by the lock resource structure.

Understanding Deadlocks

Because of the very nature of locking, operations need to wait until a lock has been released before they can acquire their own lock on a resource. A problem can occur, however, if two separate processes have taken out locks on different resources, but both are blocked, waiting for the other to complete. This is known as a *deadlock*. Most blocks are resolved automatically with time, so that both queries complete. With deadlocks, however, only one of the queries can complete.

How Deadlocks Occur

To see how this issue can arise, examine Table 19-6.

Table 19-6. *Deadlock Chronology*

Process A	Process B
Acquires an exclusive lock on Row1 in Table1	
	Acquires an exclusive lock on Row2 in Table2
Attempts to acquire a lock on Row2 in Table2 but is blocked by Process B	
	Attempts to acquire a lock on Row1 in Table1 but is blocked by Process A

In the sequence described here, neither Process A nor Process B can continue, which means a deadlock has occurred. SQL Server detects deadlocks via an internal process called the deadlock monitor. When the deadlock monitor encounters a deadlock, it checks to see if the processes have been assigned a transaction priority. If the processes have different transaction priorities, it kills the process with the lowest priority. If they have the same priority, then it kills the least expensive process in terms of resource utilization. If both processes have the same cost, it picks a process at random and kills it.

The script in Listing 19-2 generates a deadlock. You must run the first and third parts of the script in a different query window than the second and fourth parts. You must run each section of the script in sequence.

Listing 19-2. Generating a Deadlock

```
--Part 1 - Run in 1st query window

BEGIN TRANSACTION

UPDATE dbo.Customers
SET LastName = 'Andrews'
WHERE CustomerID = 1

--Part 2 - Run in 2nd query window

BEGIN TRANSACTION

UPDATE dbo.Addresses
SET PostCode = 'SA12 9BD'
WHERE AddressID = 2

--Part 3 - Run in 1st query window

UPDATE dbo.Addresses
SET PostCode = 'SA12 9BD'
WHERE AddressID = 2

--Part 4 - Run in 2nd query window

UPDATE dbo.Customers
SET LastName = 'Colins'
WHERE CustomerID = 1
```

SQL Server chooses one of the processes as a deadlock victim and kills it. This leads to an error message being thrown in the victim's query window, as illustrated in Figure 19-2.

```
Messages
Msg 1205, Level 13, State 51, Line 13
Transaction (Process ID 54) was deadlocked on lock resources with another process and has been chosen as the deadlock victim. Rerun the transaction.
```

Figure 19-2. *Deadlock victim error*

Minimizing Deadlocks

Your developers can take various steps to minimize the risk of deadlocks. Because it is you (the DBA) who is responsible for supporting the instance in production, it is prudent to check to make sure the development team's code meets standards for minimizing deadlocks before you release the code to production.

When reviewing code, prior to code release, you should look to ensure that the following guidelines are being followed:

- Optimistic isolation levels are being used where appropriate (you should also consider the trade-offs regarding TempDB usage, disk overhead, etc.).

- There should be no user interaction within transactions (this can avoid locks being held for extended periods).

- Transactions are as short as possible and within the same batch (this can avoid long-running transactions, which hold locks for longer than necessary).

- All programmable objects access objects in the same order (this can offset the likelihood of deadlocks and replace at the expense of contention on the first table).

Understanding Transactions

Every action that causes data or objects to be modified happens within the context of a transaction. SQL Server supports three types of transaction: autocommit, explicit, and implicit. *Autocommit transactions* are the default behavior and mean that each statement is performed in the context of its own transaction. *Explicit transactions* are started and ended manually. They start with a BEGIN TRANSACTION statement and end with either a COMMIT TRANSACTION statement, which causes the associated log records to be hardened to disk, or a ROLLBACK statement, which causes all actions within the transaction to be undone. If *implicit transactions* are turned on for a connection, then the default autocommit behavior no longer works for that connection. Instead, transactions are started automatically, and then committed manually, using a COMMIT TRANSACTION statement.

Transactional Properties

Transactions exhibit properties known as ACID (atomic, consistent, isolated, and durable). Each of these is discussed in the following sections.

Atomic

For a transaction to be atomic, all actions within a transaction must either commit together or roll back together. It is not possible for only part of a transaction to commit. SQL Server's implementation of this property is slightly more flexible, however, through the implementation of save points.

A *Save point* is a marker within a transaction where, in the event of a rollback, everything before the Save point is committed and everything after the Save point can be either committed or rolled back. This can be helpful in trapping occasional errors that may occur. For example, the script in Listing 19-3 performs a large insert into the Customers table before performing a small insert into the Addresses table. If the insert into the Addresses table fails, the large insert into the Customers table is still committed.

Listing 19-3. Save Points

```
SELECT COUNT(*) InitialCustomerCount FROM dbo.Customers ;

SELECT COUNT(*) InitialAddressesCount FROM dbo.Addresses ;

BEGIN TRANSACTION

DECLARE @Numbers TABLE
(
        Number          INT
)
```

```
;WITH CTE(Number)
AS
(
        SELECT 1 Number
        UNION ALL
        SELECT Number + 1
        FROM CTE
        WHERE Number < 100
)
INSERT INTO @Numbers
SELECT Number FROM CTE;

--Create and populate name pieces

DECLARE @Names TABLE
(
        FirstName        VARCHAR(30),
        LastName         VARCHAR(30)
);

INSERT INTO @Names
VALUES('Peter', 'Carter'),
                ('Michael', 'Smith'),
                ('Danielle', 'Mead'),
                ('Reuben', 'Roberts'),
                ('Iris', 'Jones'),
                ('Sylvia', 'Davies'),
                ('Finola', 'Wright'),
                ('Edward', 'James'),
                ('Marie', 'Andrews'),
                ('Jennifer', 'Abraham');

--Populate Customers table

SELECT * INTO #Customers
FROM
                (SELECT
```

```
        (SELECT TOP 1 FirstName FROM @Names ORDER BY NEWID()) FirstName,
        (SELECT TOP 1 LastName FROM @Names ORDER BY NEWID()) LastName,
        (SELECT TOP 1 Number FROM @Numbers ORDER BY NEWID())
        BillingAddressID,
         (SELECT TOP 1 Number FROM @Numbers ORDER BY NEWID())
         DeliveryAddressID,
         (SELECT TOP 1 CAST(RAND() * Number AS INT) * 10000
         FROM @Numbers
         ORDER BY NEWID()) CreditLimit,
         (SELECT TOP 1 CAST(RAND() * Number AS INT) * 9000
         FROM @Numbers
         ORDER BY NEWID()) Balance
     FROM @Numbers a
     CROSS JOIN @Numbers b
) a;

INSERT INTO dbo.Customers
SELECT * FROM #Customers;

SAVE TRANSACTION CustomerInsert

BEGIN TRY
--Populate Addresses table - Will fail, due to length of Post Code

INSERT INTO dbo.Addresses
VALUES('1 Apress Towers', 'Hedge End', 'Southampton', 'SA206 2BQ') ;
END TRY
BEGIN CATCH
        ROLLBACK TRANSACTION CustomerInsert
END CATCH

COMMIT TRANSACTION

SELECT COUNT(*) FinalCustomerCount FROM dbo.Customers ;

SELECT COUNT(*) FinalAddressesCount FROM dbo.Addresses ;
```

The results of the row counts, illustrated in Figure 19-3, show that the insert to the Customers table committed, while the insert to the Addresses table rolled back. It is also possible to create multiple save points within a single transaction and then roll back to the most appropriate point.

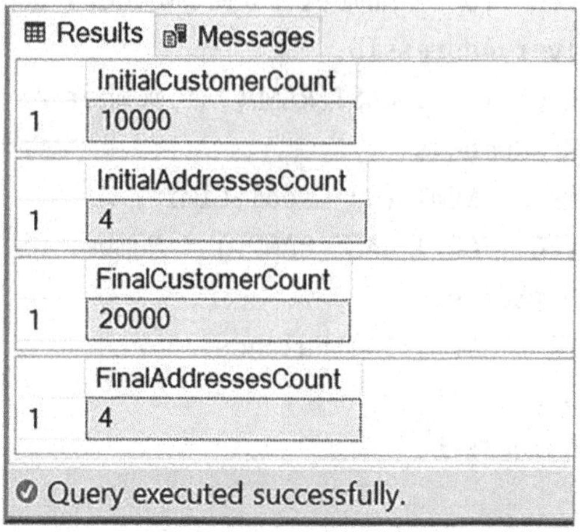

Figure 19-3. *Row counts*

Consistent

The consistent property means that the transaction moves the database from one consistent state to another; at the end of the transaction, all data must conform to all data rules, which are enforced with constraints, data types, and so on.

SQL Server fully enforces this property, but there are workarounds. For example, if you have a check constraint, or a foreign key on a table, and you wish to perform a large bulk insert, you can disable the constraint, insert the data, and then reenable the constraint with NOCHECK. When you use NOCHECK, the constraint enforces the rules for new data modification, but it does not enforce the rule for data that already exists in the table. When you do this, however, SQL Server marks the constraint as not trusted, and the Query Optimizer ignores the constraint until you have validated the existing data in the table using an ALTER TABLE MyTable WITH CHECK CHECK CONSTRAINT ALL command.

Isolated

Isolation refers to the concurrent transaction's ability to see data modifications made by a transaction before they are committed. Isolating transactions avoids transactional anomalies and is enforced by either acquiring locks or maintaining multiple versions of rows. Each transaction runs with a defined isolation level. Before we discuss available isolation levels, however, we first need to examine the transactional anomalies that can occur.

Transactional Anomalies

Transactional anomalies can cause queries to return unpredictable results. Three types of transaction anomalies are possible within SQL Server: dirty reads, nonrepeatable reads, and phantom reads. These are discussed in the following sections.

Dirty Reads

A *dirty read* occurs when a transaction reads data that never existed in the database. An example of how this anomaly can occur is outlined in Table 19-7.

Table 19-7. *A Dirty Read*

Transaction1	Transaction2
Inserts `row1` into `Table1`	
	Reads `row1` from `Table1`
Rolls back	

In this example, because `Transaction1` rolled back, `Transaction2` read a row that never existed in the database. This anomaly can occur if shared locks are not acquired for reads, since there is no lock to conflict with the exclusive lock taken out by `Transaction1`.

Nonrepeatable Read

A nonrepeatable read occurs when a transaction reads the same row twice but receives different results each time. An example of how this anomaly can occur is outlined in Table 19-8.

Table 19-8. *A Nonrepeatable Read*

Transaction1	Transaction2
Reads `row1` from `Table1`	
	Updates `row1` in `Table1`
	Commits
Reads `row1` from `Table1`	

In this example, you can see that `Transaction1` has read `row1` from `Table1` twice. The second time, however, it receives a different result, because `Transaction2` has updated the row. This anomaly can occur if `Transaction1` takes out shared locks but does not hold them for the duration of the transaction.

Phantom Read

A phantom read occurs when a transaction reads a range of rows twice but receives a different number of rows the second time it reads the range. An example of how this anomaly can occur is outlined in Table 19-9.

Table 19-9. *Phantom Reads*

Transaction1	Transaction2
Reads all rows from `Table1`	
	Inserts ten rows into `Table1`
	Commits
Reads all rows from `Table1`	

In this example, you can see that `Transaction1` has read all rows from `Table1` twice. The second time, however, it reads an extra ten rows, because `Transaction2` has inserted ten rows into the table. This anomaly can occur when `Transaction1` does not acquire a key-range lock and hold it for the duration of the transaction.

Isolation Levels

SQL Server provides four pessimistic and two optimistic transaction isolation levels for transactions that involve disk-based tables. Pessimistic isolation levels use locks to protect against transactional anomalies and optimistic isolation levels use row versioning.

Pessimistic Isolation Levels

Read Uncommitted is the least restrictive isolation level. It works by acquiring locks for write operations but not acquiring any locks for read operations. This means that under this isolation level, read operations do not block other readers or writers. The result is that all transactional anomalies described in the previous sections are possible.

Read Committed is the default isolation level. It works by acquiring shared locks for read operations as well as locks for write operations. The shared locks are only held during the read phase of a specific row, and the lock is released as soon as the record has been read. This results in protection against dirty reads, but nonrepeatable reads and phantom reads are still possible.

Tip   In some circumstances, shared locks may be held until the end of the statement. This occurs when a physical operator is required to spool data to disk.

In addition to acquiring locks for write operations, Repeatable Read acquires shared locks on all rows that it touches and then it holds these locks until the end of the transaction. The result is that dirty reads and nonrepeatable reads are not possible, although phantom reads can still occur. Because the reads are held for the duration of the transaction, deadlocks are more likely to occur than when you are using Read Committed or Read Uncommitted isolation levels.

Serializable is the most restrictive isolation level, and the level where deadlocks are most likely to occur. It works by not only acquiring locks for write operations, but also by acquiring key-range locks for read operations, and then holding them for the duration of the transaction. Because key-range locks are held in this manner, no transactional anomalies are possible, including phantom reads.

Optimistic Isolation Levels

Optimistic isolation levels work without acquiring any locks for either read or write operations. Instead, they use a technique called *row versioning*. Row versioning works by maintaining a new copy of a row in TempDB for uncommitted transactions every time the row is updated. This means that there is always a consistent copy of the data that transactions can refer to. This can dramatically reduce contention on highly concurrent systems. The trade-off is that you need to scale TempDB appropriately, in terms of both size and throughput capacity, since the extra I/O can have a negative impact on performance.

Snapshot isolation uses optimistic concurrency for both read and write operations. It works by assigning each transaction a transaction sequence number at the point the transaction begins. It is then able to read the version of the row from TempDB that was current at the start of the transaction by looking for the closest sequence number that is lower than the transaction's own sequence number. This means that although other versions of the row may exist with modifications, it cannot see them, since the sequence numbers are higher. If two transactions try to update the same row at the same time, instead of a deadlock occurring, the second transaction throws error 3960 and the transaction is rolled back. The result of this behavior is that dirty reads, nonrepeatable reads, and phantom reads are not possible.

The Read Committed Snapshot uses pessimistic concurrency for write operations and optimistic concurrency for read operations. For read operations, it uses the version of the row that is current at the beginning of each statement within the transaction, as opposed to the version that was current at the beginning of the transaction. This means that you achieve the same level of isolation as you would by using the pessimistic Read Committed isolation level.

Unlike the pessimistic isolation levels, you need to turn on optimistic isolation levels at the database level. When you turn on Read Committed Snapshot, this replaces the functionality of Read Committed. This is important to bear in mind, because Read Committed Snapshot becomes your default isolation level and is used for all transactions that do not specifically set an isolation level. The script in Listing 19-4 demonstrates how to turn on Snapshot isolation and Read Committed Snapshot isolation for the Chapter19 database. The script first checks to make sure that Read Committed and Read Committed Snapshot are not already enabled. If they are not, it kills any sessions that are currently connected to the Chapter19 database before finally running the ALTER DATABASE statements.

Listing 19-4. Turning On Optimistic Isolation

```
--Check if already enabled

IF EXISTS (
        SELECT name
                ,snapshot_isolation_state_desc
                ,is_read_committed_snapshot_on
        FROM sys.databases
        WHERE name = 'Chapter19'
                AND snapshot_isolation_state_desc = 'OFF'
                AND is_read_committed_snapshot_on = 0 )
BEGIN
        --Kill any existing sessions

        IF EXISTS(
        SELECT * FROM sys.dm_exec_sessions where database_id = DB_
        id('Chapter19')
        )
        BEGIN
                PRINT 'Killing Sessions to Chapter19 database'
                DECLARE @SQL NVARCHAR(MAX)
                SET @SQL = (SELECT 'KILL ' + CAST(Session_id AS
                NVARCHAR(3)) + '; ' [data()]
                                        FROM sys.dm_exec_sessions
                                        WHERE database_id = DB_id('Chapter19')
                                        FOR XML PATH('')
                                        )
                EXEC(@SQL)
        END

        PRINT 'Enabling Snapshot and Read Committed Snapshot Isolation'

        ALTER DATABASE Chapter19
        SET ALLOW_SNAPSHOT_ISOLATION ON ;

        ALTER DATABASE Chapter19
```

```
        SET READ_COMMITTED_SNAPSHOT ON ;
END
ELSE
        PRINT 'Snapshot Isolation already enabled'
```

Durable

For a transaction to be durable, after it has been committed, it stays committed, even in a catastrophic event. This means that the change must be written to disk, since the change within memory will not withstand a power failure, a restart of the instance, and so on. SQL Server achieves this by using a process called write-ahead logging (WAL). This process flushes the log cache to disk at the point the transaction commits, and the commit only completes once this flush finishes.

SQL Server relaxed these rules, however, by introducing a feature called delayed durability. This feature works by delaying the flush of the log cache to disk until one of the following events occurs:

- The log cache becomes full and automatically flushes to disk.

- A fully durable transaction in the same database commits.

- The sp_flush_log system stored procedure is run against the database.

When delayed durability is used, the data is visible to other transactions as soon as the transaction commits; however, the data committed within the transaction could potentially be lost, if the instance goes down or is restarted, until the log records have been flushed. This means that it can be useful in use cases such as rerunnable ETL loads. Support for delayed durability is configured at the database level, using one of the three options detailed in Table 19-10.

Table 19-10. *Support Levels for Delayed Durability*

Support Level	Description
ALLOWED	Delayed durability is supported within the database and specified on a transaction level basis.
FORCED	All transactions within the database will use delayed durability.
DISABLED	The default setting. No transactions within the database are permitted to use delayed durability.

The command in Listing 19-5 shows how to allow delayed durability in the Chapter19 database.

Listing 19-5. Allowing Delayed Durability

```
ALTER DATABASE Chapter19
SET DELAYED_DURABILITY  = ALLOWED ;
```

If a database is configured to allow delayed durability, then Full or Delayed durability is configured at the transaction level, in the COMMIT statement. The script in Listing 19-6 demonstrates how to commit a transaction with delayed durability.

Listing 19-6. Committing with Delayed Durability

```
USE Chapter19
GO

BEGIN TRANSACTION
        UPDATE dbo.Customers
        SET DeliveryAddressID = 1
        WHERE CustomerID = 10 ;
COMMIT WITH (DELAYED_DURABILITY = ON)
```

Caution   The most important thing to remember, when using delayed durability, is the potential for data loss. If any transactions have committed but the associated log records have not been flushed to disk when the instance goes down, this data is lost.

In the event of an issue, such as an I/O error, it is possible for uncommitted transactions to enter a state where they cannot be committed or rolled back. This occurs when you are bringing a database back online and it fails during both the redo phase and the undo phase. This is called a *deferred transaction.* Deferred transactions stop the VLF that they are in from being truncated, meaning that the transaction log continues to grow.

Resolving the issue depends on the cause of the problem. If the problem is caused by a corrupt page, then you may be able to restore this page from a backup. If the issue is caused because a filegroup was offline, then you must either restore the filegroup or mark the filegroup as defunct. If you mark a filegroup as defunct, you cannot recover it.

Transaction with In-Memory OLTP

Memory-optimized tables do not support locks to improve concurrency; this changes the way isolation levels can work, since pessimistic concurrency is no longer an option. We discuss isolation levels supported for In-Memory OLTP, along with considerations for cross-container queries, in the following sections.

Isolation Levels

Because all isolation levels used with In-Memory OLTP must be optimistic, each isolation level implements row versioning. Unlike row versi
oning for disk-based tables, however, row versions for memory-optimized tables are not maintained in TempDB. Instead, they are maintained in the memory-optimized table that they relate to.

Read Committed

The Read Committed isolation level is supported against memory-optimized tables, but only if you are using autocommit transactions. It is not possible to use Read Committed in explicit or implicit transactions. It is also not possible to use Read Committed in the ATOMIC block of a natively compiled stored procedure. Because Read Committed is the default isolation level for SQL Server, you must either ensure that all transactions involving memory-optimized tables explicitly state an isolation level, or you must set the MEMORY_OPTIMIZED_ELEVATE_TO_SNAPSHOT database property. This option elevates all transactions that involve memory-optimized tables but do not specify an isolation level to Snapshot isolation, the least restrictive isolation level, which is fully supported for In-Memory OLTP.

The command in Listing 19-7 shows how to set the MEMORY_OPTIMIZED_ELEVATE_TO_SNAPSHOT property for the Chapter19 database.

Listing 19-7. Elevating to Snapshot

```
ALTER DATABASE Chapter19
SET MEMORY_OPTIMIZED_ELEVATE_TO_SNAPSHOT = ON ;
```

Read Committed Snapshot

The Read Committed Snapshot isolation level is supported for memory-optimized tables, but only when you are using autocommit transactions. This isolation level is not supported when the transaction accesses disk-based tables.

Snapshot

The Snapshot isolation level uses row versioning to guarantee that a transaction always sees the data, as it was at the start of the transaction. Snapshot isolation is only supported against memory-optimized tables when you use interpreted SQL if it is specified as a query hint as opposed to at the transaction level. It is fully supported in the ATOMIC block of natively compiled stored procedures.

If a transaction attempts to modify a row that has already been updated by another transaction, then the conflict detection mechanism rolls back the transaction, and Error 41302 is thrown. If a transaction attempts to insert a row that has the same primary key value as a row that has been inserted by another transaction, then conflict detection rolls back the transaction and Error 41352 is thrown. If a transaction attempts to modify the data in a table that has been dropped by another transaction, then Error 41305 is thrown, and the transaction is rolled back.

Repeatable Read

The Repeatable Read isolation level provides the same protection as Snapshot, but additionally, it guarantees that rows read by the transaction have not been modified by other rows since the start of the transaction. If the transaction attempts to read a row that has been modified by another transaction, then Error 41305 is thrown and the transaction is rolled back. The Repeatable Read isolation is not supported against memory-optimized tables when using interpreted SQL, however. It is only supported in the ATOMIC block of natively compiled stored procedures.

Serializable

The Serializable isolation level offers the same protection that is offered by Repeatable Read, but in addition, it guarantees that no rows have been inserted within the range of rows being accessed by queries within the transaction. If a transaction using the Serializable isolation level cannot meet its guarantees, then the conflict detection mechanism rolls back the transaction and Error 41325 is thrown. Serializable isolation is not supported against memory-optimized tables when using interpreted SQL, however. It is only supported in the ATOMIC block of natively compiled stored procedures.

Cross-Container Transactions

Because isolations levels' use is restricted, when a transaction accesses both memory-optimized tables and disk-based tables, you may need to specify a combination of isolation levels and query hints. The query in Listing 19-8 joins together the Customers and CustomersMem tables. It succeeds only because we have turned on MEMORY_OPTIMIZED_ELEVATE_TO_SNAPSHOT. This means that the query uses the default Read Committed Snapshot isolation level to access the disk-based table and automatically upgrades the read of the CustomersMem table to use Snapshot isolation.

Listing 19-8. Joining Disk and Memory Tables with Automatic Elevation

```
BEGIN TRANSACTION
        SELECT *
        FROM dbo.Customers C
        INNER JOIN dbo.CustomersMem CM
                ON C.CustomerID = CM.CustomerID ;
COMMIT TRANSACTION
```

However, if we now turn off MEMORY_OPTIMIZED_ELEVATE_TO_SNAPSHOT, which you can do using the script in Listing 19-9, the same transaction now fails with the error message shown in Figure 19-4.

Listing 19-9. Turning Off MEMORY_OPTIMIZED_ELEVATE_TO_SNAPSHOT

```
ALTER DATABASE Chapter19
SET MEMORY_OPTIMIZED_ELEVATE_TO_SNAPSHOT=OFF
GO
```

Figure 19-4. *Join disk and memory tables without automatic elevation*

The query in Listing 19-10 demonstrates how we can join the Customers table with the CustomersMem table using the Snapshot isolation level for the memory-optimized table and the Serializable isolation level for the disk-based table. Because we are using interpreted SQL, the Snapshot isolation level is the only level we can use to access the memory-optimized table, and we must specify this as a query hint. If we specify it at the transaction level instead of at serializable, the transaction fails.

Listing 19-10. Joining Disk and Memory-Optimized Tables Using Query Hints

```
BEGIN TRANSACTION
SET TRANSACTION ISOLATION LEVEL SERIALIZABLE
        SELECT *
        FROM dbo.Customers C
        INNER JOIN dbo.CustomersMem CM (SNAPSHOT)
                ON C.CustomerID = CM.CustomerID ;
COMMIT TRANSACTION
```

If we use a natively compiled stored procedure, which can often be much faster than interpreted SQL, we need to add the required transaction isolation level to the ATOMIC block of the procedure definition. The script in Listing 19-11 demonstrates creating a natively compiled stored procedure that updates the CustomersMem table using the

Serializable isolation level. Because natively compiled stored procedures are not able to access disk-based tables, you do not need to be concerned with locking hints to support cross-container transactions.

Listing 19-11. Using Serializable Isolation in a Natively Compiled Stored Procedure

```
CREATE PROCEDURE dbo.UpdateCreditLimit
WITH native_compilation, schemabinding, execute as owner
AS
BEGIN ATOMIC
        WITH(TRANSACTION ISOLATION LEVEL = SERIALIZABLE, LANGUAGE = 'English')
                UPDATE dbo.CustomersMem
                SET CreditLimit = CreditLimit * 1.1
                WHERE Balance < CreditLimit / 4 ;

                UPDATE dbo.CustomersMem
                SET CreditLimit = CreditLimit * 1.05
                WHERE Balance < CreditLimit / 2 ;
END
```

Retry Logic

Whether you are using interpreted SQL or a natively compiled stored procedure, always ensure that you use retry logic when you are running transactions against memory-optimized tables. This is because of the optimistic concurrency model, which means that the conflict detection mechanism rolls transactions back, as opposed to managing concurrency with locking. It is also important to remember that SQL Server even rolls back read-only transactions if the required level of isolation cannot be guaranteed. For example, if you are using serializable isolation in a read-only transaction, and another transaction inserts rows that match your query filters, the transaction is rolled back.

The script in Listing 19-12 creates a wrapper-stored procedure for the UpdateCreditLimit procedure, which retries the procedure up to ten times should the procedure fail, with a one-second gap between each iteration. You should change this delay to match the average duration of conflicting transactions.

Listing 19-12. Retry Logic for Memory-Optimized Tables

```
CREATE PROCEDURE UpdateCreditLimitWrapper
AS
BEGIN
        DECLARE @Retries INT = 1 ;

        WHILE @Retries <= 10
        BEGIN
                BEGIN TRY
                        EXEC dbo.UpdateCreditLimit ;
                END TRY
                BEGIN CATCH
                        WAITFOR DELAY '00:00:01' ;
                        SET @Retries = @Retries + 1 ;
                END CATCH
        END
END
```

Observing Transactions, Locks, and Deadlocks

SQL Server provides a set of DMVs that expose information about current transactions and locks. The following sections explore the metadata available.

Observing Transactions

The sys.dm_tran_active_transactions DMV details the current transactions within the instance. This DMV returns the columns described in Table 19-11.

Table 19-11. *Columns Returned by sys.dm_tran_active_transactions*

Column	Description
transaction_id	The unique ID of the transaction.
name	The name of the transaction. If the transaction has not been marked with a name, then the default name is displayed—for example, "user_transaction".
transaction_begin_time	The date and time that the transaction started.
transaction_type	An integer value depicting the type of transaction. • 1 indicates a read/write transaction. • 2 indicates a read-only transaction. • 3 indicates a system transaction. • 4 indicates a distributed transaction.
transaction_uow	A unit of work ID that MSDTC (Microsoft Distributed Transaction Coordinator) uses to work with distributed transactions.
transaction_state	The current status of the transaction. • 0 indicates that the transaction is still initializing. • 1 indicates that the transaction is initialized but has not yet started. • 2 indicates that the transaction is active. • 3 indicates that the transaction has ended. This status is only applicable to read-only transactions. • 4 indicates that the commit has been initiated. This status is only applicable to distributed transactions. • 5 indicates that the transaction is prepared and awaiting resolution. • 6 indicates that the transaction has been committed. • 7 indicates that the transaction is being rolled back. • 8 indicates that the rollback of a transaction has finished.
dtc_state	Indicates the state of a transaction on an Azure database. • 1 indicates that the transaction is active. • 2 indicates that the transaction is prepared. • 3 indicates that the transaction is committed. • 4 indicates that the transaction is aborted. • 5 indicates that the transaction is recovered.

Note   Undocumented columns have been omitted from DVMs in this chapter.

The script in Listing 19-13 indicates how to use sys.dm_tran_active_transactions to find details of long-running transactions. The query looks for transactions that have been running for longer than ten minutes and returns information including their current state, the amount of resources they are consuming, and the login that is executing them.

Tip   In a test environment, begin a transaction but do not commit it ten minutes before running this query.

Listing 19-13. Long-Running Transactions

```
SELECT
        name
        ,transaction_begin_time
        ,CASE transaction_type
                WHEN 1 THEN 'Read/Write'
                WHEN 2 THEN 'Read-Only'
                WHEN 3 THEN 'System'
                WHEN 4 THEN 'Distributed'
        END TransactionType,
        CASE transaction_state
                WHEN 0 THEN 'Initializing'
                WHEN 1 THEN 'Initialized But Not Started'
                WHEN 2 THEN 'Active'
                WHEN 3 THEN 'Ended'
                WHEN 4 THEN 'Committing'
                WHEN 5 THEN 'Prepared'
                WHEN 6 THEN 'Committed'
                WHEN 7 THEN 'Rolling Back'
                WHEN 8 THEN 'Rolled Back'
        END State
, SUBSTRING(TXT.text, ( er.statement_start_offset / 2 ) + 1,
```

```
  ( ( CASE WHEN er.statement_end_offset = -1
   THEN LEN(CONVERT(NVARCHAR(MAX), TXT.text)) * 2
      ELSE er.statement_end_offset
END - er.statement_start_offset ) / 2 ) + 1) AS CurrentQuery
 , TXT.text AS ParentQuery
 , es.host_name
 , CASE tat.transaction_type
    WHEN 1 THEN 'Read/Write Transaction'
    WHEN 2 THEN 'Read-Only Transaction'
    WHEN 3 THEN 'System Transaction'
          WHEN 4 THEN 'Distributed Transaction'
          ELSE 'Unknown'
  END AS TransactionType
      ,SUSER_SNAME(es.security_id) LoginRunningTransaction
      ,es.memory_usage * 8 MemUsageKB
      ,es.reads
      ,es.writes
      ,es.cpu_time
FROM sys.dm_tran_active_transactions tat
INNER JOIN sys.dm_tran_session_transactions st
    ON tat.transaction_id = st.transaction_id
INNER JOIN sys.dm_exec_sessions es
    ON st.session_id = es.session_id
INNER JOIN sys.dm_exec_requests er
    ON er.session_id = es.session_id
CROSS APPLY sys.dm_exec_sql_text(er.sql_handle) TXT
WHERE st.is_user_transaction = 1
    AND tat.transaction_begin_time < DATEADD(MINUTE,-10,GETDATE()) ;
```

The query works by joining to sys.dm_exec_sessions via sys.dm_tran_session transactions. This DMV can be used to correlate transactions with sessions and it returns the columns described in Table 19-12.

Table 19-12. *sys.dm_tran_session_transactions Columns*

Column	Description
session_id	The ID of the session in which the transaction is running.
transaction_id	The unique ID of the transaction.
transaction_ descriptor	The ID used to communicate with the client driver.
enlist_count	The number of active requests in the session.
is_user_ transaction	Indicates if the transaction is a user or a system transaction. 0 indicates a system transaction and 1 indicates a user transaction.
is_local	Indicates if the transaction is distributed. 0 indicates a distributed transaction and 1 indicates a local transaction.
is_enlisted	Indicates that a distributed transaction is enlisted.
is_bound	Indicates if the transaction is running in a bound session.
open_ transaction_ count	A count of open transactions within the session.

Tip   Joining to sys.dm_exec_requests and cross applying sys.dm_exec_ sql_text will also provide you with the SQL statement that was executed.

Observing Locks and Contention

Details of current locks on the instance are exposed through a DMV called sys.dm_tran_ locks. This DMV returns the columns detailed in Table 19-13.

Table 19-13. *sys.dm_tran_locks*

Column	Description
resource_type	The resource type on which the lock has been placed.
resource_subtype	The subtype of the resource type that has a lock placed on it. For example, if you are updating the properties of a database, then the resource_type is METADATA and the resource_subtype is DATABASE.
resource_database_id	The ID of the database that contains the resource that has a lock placed on it.
resource_description	Additional information about the resource that is not contained in other columns.
resource_associated_entity_id	The ID of the database entity with which the resource is associated.
resource_lock_partition	The partition number of the lock, if lock partitioning is being used.
request_mode	The locking mode that has been requested or acquired. For example, S for a shared lock, or X for an exclusive lock.
request_type	The request_type is always LOCK.
request_status	The current status of the lock request. Possible values are ABORT_BLOCKERS, CONVERT, GRANTED, LOW_PRIORITY_CONVERT, LOW_PRIORITY_WAIT, and WAIT.
request_reference_count	The number of times that the requestor has requested a lock on the same resource.
request_session_id	The session ID that currently owns the request. It is possible for the session ID to change if the transaction is distributed.
request_exec_context_id	The execution ID of the process that requested the lock.
request_request_id	The Batch ID of the batch that currently owns the request. This ID can change if Multiple Active Result Sets (MARS) are being used by the application.

(continued)

Table 19-13. (*continued*)

Column	Description
request_owner_type	The type of the owner of the lock request. Possible vales are TRANSACTION, SESSION, and CURSOR for user operations. Values can also be SHARED_TRANSACTION_WORKSPACE and EXCLUSIVE_TRANSACTION_WORKSPACE, which are used internally to hold locks for enlisted transactions; or NOTIFICATION_OBJECT, which is used by internal SQL Server operations.
request_owner_id	The ID of the transaction that owns the lock request, unless the request was made by a FileTable, in which case -3 indicates a table lock, -4 indicates a database lock, and other values indicate the file handle of the file.
request_owner_guid	A GUID identifying the request owner. Only applicable to distributed transactions.
lock_owner_address	Memory address of the request's internal data structure.

The sys.dm_os_waiting_tasks DMV returns information about tasks that are waiting on resources, including locks. The columns returned by this DMV are detailed in Table 19-14. This DMV can be used with sys.dm_tran_locks to find the details of processes that are blocked and blocking, due to locks.

Table 19-14. *sys.dm_os_waiting_tasks Columns*

Column	Description
waiting_task_address	The address of the task that is waiting.
session_id	The ID of the session in which the waiting task is running.
exec_context_id	The ID of the thread and subthread that is running the task.
wait_duration_ms	The duration of the wait, specified in milliseconds.
wait_type	The type of wait that is being experienced. Waits are discussed in Chapter 18.
resource_address	The address of the resource the task is waiting for.
blocking_task_address	Indicates the address of the task that is currently consuming the resource.
blocking_session_id	The Session ID of the task that is currently consuming the resource.
blocking_exec_context_id	The ID of the thread and subthread of the task that is currently consuming the resource.
resource_description	Additional information about the resource, which is not contained in other columns, including the lock resource owner.

The script in Listing 19-14 demonstrates how to use sys.dm_tran_locks and sys.dm_os_waiting_tasks to identify blocking on the instance. The script contains three parts, each of which you should run in a separate query window. The first two parts of the script cause contention. The third part identifies the source of the contention.

Listing 19-14. Using sys.dm_tran_locks

```
--Part 1 - Run in 1st query window

BEGIN TRANSACTION
UPDATE Customers
SET CreditLimit = CreditLimit ;

--Part 2 - Run in 2nd query window
```

```
SELECT creditlimit
FROM dbo.Customers (SERIALIZABLE) ;

--Part 3 - Run in 3rd query window

SELECT
        DB_NAME(tl.resource_database_id) DatabaseName
        ,tl.resource_type
        ,tl.resource_subtype
        ,tl.resource_description
        ,tl.request_mode
        ,tl.request_status
        ,os.session_id BlockedSession
        ,os.blocking_session_id BlockingSession
        ,os.resource_description
        ,OBJECT_NAME(
                CAST(
                    SUBSTRING(os.resource_description,
                            CHARINDEX('objid=',os.resource_
                            description,0)+6,9)
                    AS INT)
            ) LockedTable
FROM sys.dm_os_waiting_tasks os
INNER JOIN sys.dm_tran_locks tl
        ON os.session_id = tl.request_session_id
WHERE tl.request_owner_type IN ('TRANSACTION', 'SESSION', 'CURSOR') ;
```

Tip   To stop the blocking, run ROLLBACK in the first query window.

The results in Figure 19-5 show that the second part of our script is being blocked by the first part of the script. The final column pulls the Object ID out of the resource_description column and identifies the table on which the contention is occurring.

	DatabaseName	resource_type	resource_subtype	resource_description	request_mode	request_status	BlockedSession	BlockingSession	resource_description	LockedTable
1	Chapter19	OBJECT			IS	WAIT	51	54	objectlock lockPartition=0 objid=933578364 subre...	Customers

Query executed successfully.   WIN-Q4G88VPDBIM (16.0 CTP2.0)   WIN-Q4G88VPDBIM\Admini...   Chapter19   00:00:00   1

Figure 19-5. sys.dm_tran_locks results

Observing Deadlocks

You can capture details of deadlocks and have them written to the error log by turning on trace flags 1204 and 1222. Trace flag 1204 captures details of the resources and types of lock involved in a deadlock. It contains a section for each node involved in the deadlock, followed by a section detailing the deadlock victim. Trace flag 1222 returns three sections. The first gives details of the deadlock victim; the second gives details of the processes involved in the deadlock; and the final section describes the resources that are involved in the deadlock.

In the modern world of SQL Server, it is often not necessary to turn on these trace flags, since you can find details of deadlocks retrospectively, by looking at the system health session, which is an extended event session enabled by default on every instance of SQL Server. Among other important details, the system health session captures details of any deadlocks that occur. You can access the System Health Session by drilling through Management ➤ Extended Events ➤ Sessions ➤ system_health in SQL Server Management Studio and then by selecting View Target Data from the context menu of Package0.eventfile. If you search for xml_deadlock_report in the name column, you will expose details of deadlock incidents that have occurred. The Details tab provides the full deadlock report, including information about the deadlock victim, and the processes, resources, and owners involved in the deadlock. The Deadlock tab displays the Deadlock Graph, as shown in Figure 19-6, for the deadlock that we generated in Listing 19-2.

Figure 19-6. Deadlock Graph

> **Caution**   If the system health session has a rollover size limit, then details of deadlock can be lost.

Summary

Locks can be taken at different levels of granularity. Locking at a lower level reduces contention but uses additional resources for internal lock memory structures. Locking at a higher level can increase the wait time of other processes and increase the likelihood of deadlocks. SQL Server supports features that give DBAs the ability to control locking behaviors for online maintenance operations, such as index rebuilds and partition switching operations. On large systems with 16 or more cores available to the instance, SQL Server automatically implements lock partitioning, which can reduce contention by splitting a single lock resource into multiple resources.

Transactions have ACID properties, making them atomic, consistent, isolated, and durable. SQL Server offers the functionality to relax some of these rules, however, in order to improve performance and make coding easier. Six isolation levels are available against disk tables, two of which are optimistic and the others are pessimistic. Pessimistic isolation levels work by acquiring locks to avoid transactional anomalies, whereas optimistic concurrency relies on row versioning.

Because memory-optimized tables do not support locks, all transactions against memory-optimized tables use optimistic concurrency. SQL Server has implemented optimistic isolation levels, which can only be used against memory-optimized tables. Because of the optimistic nature of the transactions, you should implement retry logic for both read-only and read/write transactions.

SQL Server offers a wide array of metadata that can help you, as a DBA, observe transactions, locks, contention, and deadlocks. Sys.dm_tran_active_transactions show details of transactions that are currently active on the instance. Sys.dm_tran_locks expose information about locks that have currently been requested or granted within the instance. You can capture deadlock information in the SQL Server error log by enabling trace flags 1204 and 1222, but the system health trace also captures deadlock information by default. This means that you can retrieve deadlock information after the fact, without having to perform upfront configuration or tracing.

## CHAPTER 20

Extended Events

Extended Events are a lightweight monitoring system offered by SQL Server. Because the architecture uses so few system resources, they scale very well and allow you to monitor their instances, with minimal impact on user activity. They are also highly configurable, which gives you in your role as a DBA a wide range of options for capturing details from a very fine grain, such as page splits, to higher-level detail, such as CPU utilization. You can also correlate Extended Events with operating system data to provide a holistic picture when troubleshooting issues. The predecessor to Extended Events was SQL Trace, and its GUI, called Profiler. This is now deprecated for use with the Database Engine, and it is recommended that you only use it for tracing Analysis Service activity.

In this chapter, we will discuss the concepts associated with Extended Events, before discussing how to implement the technology. Finally, we will discuss how to integrate them with operating system counters.

Extended Events Concepts

Extended Events have a rich architecture, which consists of events, targets, actions, types, predicates, and maps. These artifacts are stored within a package, which is, in turn, stored within a module, which can be either a `.dll` or an executable. We discuss these concepts in the following sections.

Packages

A *package* is a container for the objects used within Extended Events. Here are the four types of SQL Server package:

- `Package0`: The default package, used for Extended Events system objects.

- `Sqlserver`: Used for SQL Server–related objects.

755

P. A. Carter, *Pro SQL Server 2022 Administration*, https://doi.org/10.1007/978-1-4842-8864-1_20

- `Sqlos`: Used for SQLOS-related objects.

- `SecAudit`: Used by SQL Audit; however, its objects are not exposed.

Events

An *event* is an occurrence of interest that you can trace. It may be a SQL batch completing, a cache miss, or a page split, or virtually anything else that can happen within the Database Engine, depending on the nature of the trace that you are configuring. Each event is categorized by channel and keyword (also known as category). A *channel* is a high-level categorization, and all events in SQL Server fall into one of the channels described in Table 20-1.

Table 20-1. *Channels*

Channel	Description
Admin	Well-known events with well-known resolutions. For example, deadlocks, server starts, CPU thresholds being exceeded, and the use of deprecated features.
Operational	Used for troubleshooting issues. For example, bad memory being detected, an AlwaysOn Availability Group replica changing its state, and a long I/O being detected are all events that fall within the Operational channel.
Analytic	High-volume events that you can use for troubleshooting issues such as performance. For example, a transaction beginning, a lock being acquired, and a file read completing are all events that fall within the Analytic channel.
Debug	Used by developers to diagnose issues by returning internal data. The events in the Debug channel are subject to change in future versions of SQL Server, so you should avoid them when possible.

Keywords, also known as categories, are much more fine grain. There are 100 categories within SQL Server 2022. These categories can be listed, by running the query in Listing 20-1.

Listing 20-1. Return List of Categories

```
SELECT DISTINCT map_value AS Category
FROM sys.dm_xe_map_values map
WHERE map.name = 'keyword_map'
ORDER BY map.map_value
```

Targets

A *target* is the consumer of the events; essentially, it is the device to which the trace data will be written. The targets available within SQL Server 2022 are detailed in Table 20-2.

Table 20-2. *Targets*

Target	Synchronous/ Asynchronous	Description
Event counter	Synchronous	Counts the number of events that occur during a session
Event file	Asynchronous	Writes the event output to memory buffers and then flushes them to disk
Pair matching	Asynchronous	Determines if a paired event occurs without its matching event, for example, if a statement started but never completed
ETW*	Synchronous	Used to correlate Extended Events with operating system data
Histogram	Asynchronous	Counts the number of events that occur during a session, based on an action or event column
Ring buffer	Asynchronous	Stores data in a memory buffer, using first in first out (FIFO) methodology

Event Tracking for Windows

Actions

Actions are commands that allow additional information to be captured when an event fires. An action is fired synchronously when an event occurs and the event is unaware of the action. There are 67 actions available in SQL Server 2022, which allow you to capture a rich array of information, including the statement that caused the event to fire, the login that ran this statement, the transaction ID, the CPU ID, and the call stack.

Predicates

Predicates are filter conditions that you can apply before the system sends events to the target. It is possible to create simple predicates, such as filtering statements completing based on a database ID, but you can also create more complex predicates, such as only capturing a long I/O that has a duration greater than five seconds, or only capturing the role change of an AlwaysOn Availability Group replica if it happens more than twice.

Predicates also fully support short-circuiting. This means that if you use multiple conditions within a predicate, then the order of predicates is important, because if the evaluation of the first predicate fails, the second predicate will not be evaluated. Because predicates are evaluated synchronously, this can have an impact on performance. Therefore, it is prudent to design you predicates in such a way that predicates that are least likely to evaluate to `true` come before predicates that are very likely to evaluate to `true`. For example, imagine that you are planning to filter on a specific database (with a database ID of 6) that is the target of a high percentage of the activity on the instance, but you also plan to filter on a specific user ID (`MyUser`), which is responsible for a lower percentage of the activity. In this scenario, you would use the `WHERE (([sqlserver].[username]=N'MyUser')` `AND ([sqlserver].[database_id]=(6)))` predicate to first filter out activity that does not relate to `MyUser` and then filter out activity that does not relate to database ID 6.

Types and Maps

All objects within a package are assigned a type. This type is used to interpret the data stored within the byte collection of an object. Objects are assigned one of the following types:

- `Action`
- `Event`
- `Pred_compare` (retrieve data from events)
- `Pred_source` (compare data types)
- `Target`
- `Type`

You can find a list of predicate comparators and predicate sources by executing the queries in Listing 20-2.

Listing 20-2. Retrieving Predicate Comparators and Sources

```
--Retrieve list of predicate comparators

SELECT name
      ,description,
    (SELECT name
                FROM sys.dm_xe_packages
                WHERE guid = xo.package_guid) Package
FROM sys.dm_xe_objects xo
WHERE object_type = 'pred_compare'
ORDER BY name ;

--Retrieve list of predicate sources

SELECT name
      ,description,
    (SELECT name
                FROM sys.dm_xe_packages
                WHERE guid = xo.package_guid) Package
FROM sys.dm_xe_objects xo
WHERE object_type = 'pred_source'
ORDER BY name ;
```

A *map* is a dictionary that maps internal ID values to strings that DBAs can understand. Map keys are only unique within their context and are repeated between contexts. For example, within the statement_recompile_cause context, a map_key of 1 relates to a map_value of Schema Changed. Within the context of a database_sql_ statement type, however, a map_key of 1 relates to a map_value of CREATE DATABASE. You can find a complete list of mappings by using the sys.dm_xe_map_values DMV, as demonstrated in Listing 20-3. To check the mappings for a specific context, filter on the name column.

Listing 20-3. Sys.dm_xe_map_values

```
SELECT
        map_key
        , map_value
        , name
FROM sys.dm_xe_map_values ;
```

Sessions

A *session* is essentially a trace. It can contain events from multiple packages, actions, targets, and predicates. When you start or stop a session, you are turning the trace on or off. When a session starts, events are written to memory buffers and have predicates applied before they are sent to the target. Therefore, when creating a session, you need to configure properties, such as how much memory the session can use for buffering, what events can be dropped if the session experiences memory pressure, and the maximum latency before the events are sent to the target.

Creating an Event Session

You can create an event session using either the New Session Wizard, the New Session Dialog Box, or via T-SQL. We explore each of these options in the following sections. Before creating any event sessions, however, we first create the Chapter20 database, populate it with data, and create stored procedures, which we use in later examples. Listing 20-4 contains the script to do this.

Listing 20-4. Creating the Chapter20 Database

```
--Create the database

CREATE DATABASE Chapter20 ;
GO

USE Chapter20
GO

--Create and populate numbers table
```

```
DECLARE @Numbers TABLE
(
        Number          INT
)

;WITH CTE(Number)
AS
(
        SELECT 1 Number
        UNION ALL
        SELECT Number + 1
        FROM CTE
        WHERE Number < 100
)
INSERT INTO @Numbers
SELECT Number FROM CTE;

--Create and populate name pieces

DECLARE @Names TABLE
(
        FirstName         VARCHAR(30),
        LastName          VARCHAR(30)
);

INSERT INTO @Names
VALUES('Peter', 'Carter'),
                ('Michael', 'Smith'),
                ('Danielle', 'Mead'),
                ('Reuben', 'Roberts'),
                ('Iris', 'Jones'),
                ('Sylvia', 'Davies'),
                ('Finola', 'Wright'),
                ('Edward', 'James'),
                ('Marie', 'Andrews'),
                ('Jennifer', 'Abraham');
```

```
--Create and populate Customers table

CREATE TABLE dbo.Customers
(
        CustomerID              INT                     NOT
NULL        IDENTITY        PRIMARY KEY,
        FirstName               VARCHAR(30)     NOT NULL,
        LastName                VARCHAR(30)     NOT NULL,
        BillingAddressID        INT             NOT NULL,
        DeliveryAddressID       INT             NOT NULL,
        CreditLimit             MONEY           NOT NULL,
        Balance                 MONEY                   NOT NULL
);

SELECT * INTO #Customers
FROM
        (SELECT
                (SELECT TOP 1 FirstName FROM @Names ORDER BY NEWID())
                FirstName,
                (SELECT TOP 1 LastName FROM @Names ORDER BY NEWID())
                LastName,
                (SELECT TOP 1 Number FROM @Numbers ORDER BY NEWID())
                BillingAddressID,
                (SELECT TOP 1 Number FROM @Numbers ORDER BY NEWID())
                DeliveryAddressID,
                (SELECT TOP 1 CAST(RAND() * Number AS INT) * 10000
                FROM @Numbers
                ORDER BY NEWID()) CreditLimit,
                (SELECT TOP 1 CAST(RAND() * Number AS INT) * 9000
                FROM @Numbers
                ORDER BY NEWID()) Balance
        FROM @Numbers a
        CROSS JOIN @Numbers b
) a;

INSERT INTO dbo.Customers
SELECT * FROM #Customers;
```

```
GO

CREATE INDEX idx_LastName ON dbo.Customers(LastName)
GO

CREATE PROCEDURE UpdateCustomerWithPageSplits
AS
BEGIN
        UPDATE dbo.Customers
        SET FirstName = cast(FirstName + replicate(FirstName,10) as varchar(30))
        ,LastName = cast(LastName + replicate(LastName,10) as varchar(30)) ;
END ;
GO

CREATE PROCEDURE UpdateCustomersWithoutPageSplits
AS
BEGIN
        UPDATE dbo.Customers
        SET CreditLimit = CreditLimit * 1.5
        WHERE Balance < CreditLimit - 10000 ;
END ;
GO
```

Using the New Session Dialog Box

You can access the New Session dialog box from SQL Server Management Studio by first drilling through Management ➤ Extended Events in Object Explorer and then by selecting New Session from the Sessions context menu. We use the New Session dialog box to create a session that monitors page splits and correlates them with the stored procedures that caused them to occur. To allow this, we need to enable causality tracking, which gives each event an additional GUID value, called an ActivityID, and a sequence number; together, these allow the events to be correlated.

When you invoke the dialog box, the General page displays, as illustrated in Figure 20-1. On this page, you can specify a name for the session, choose whether or not it should start automatically after it is completed and automatically when the instance starts, whether the live data view launches after the session completes, and if causality tracking should be enabled.

763

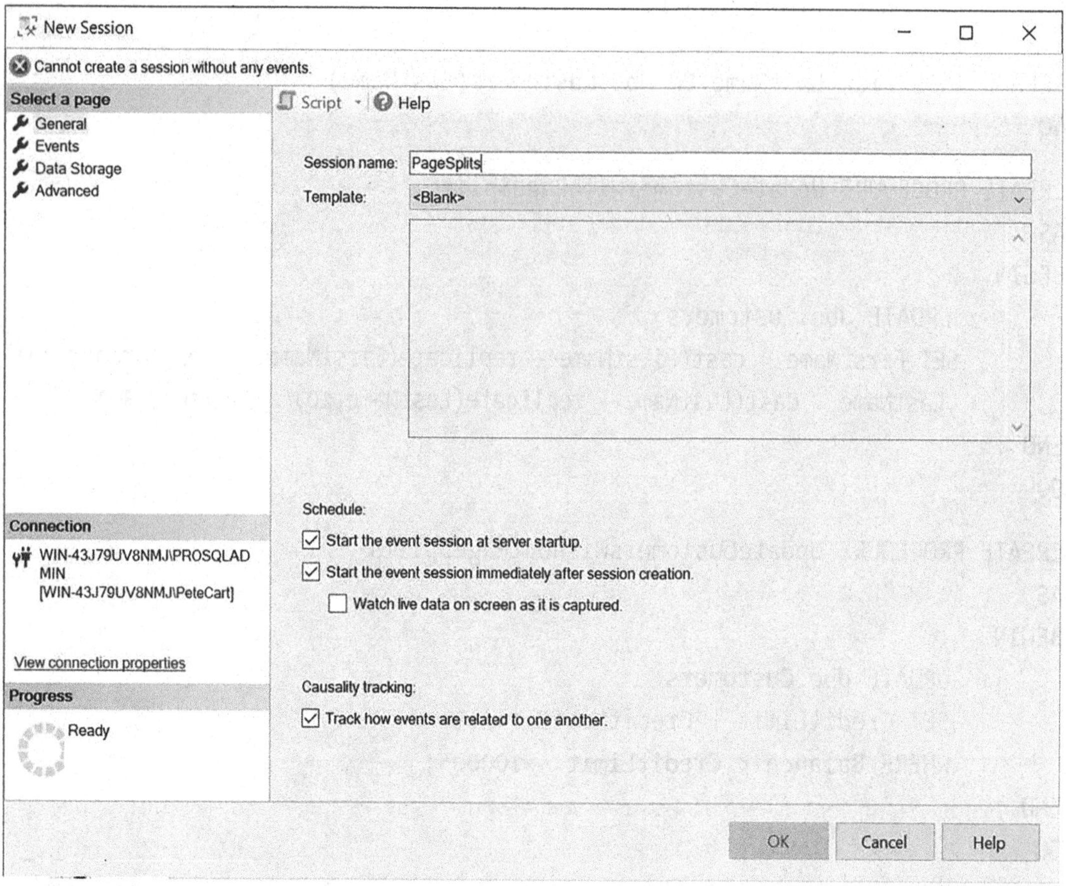

Figure 20-1. *The General page*

Because we are going to monitor page splits, we name the session PageSplits and specify that the session should start automatically, both after creation and also when the instance starts. We also turn on causality tracking.

On the Events page, we first search for and select the page_splits and module_start events, as shown in Figure 20-2. The module_start event is triggered every time a programmable object fires.

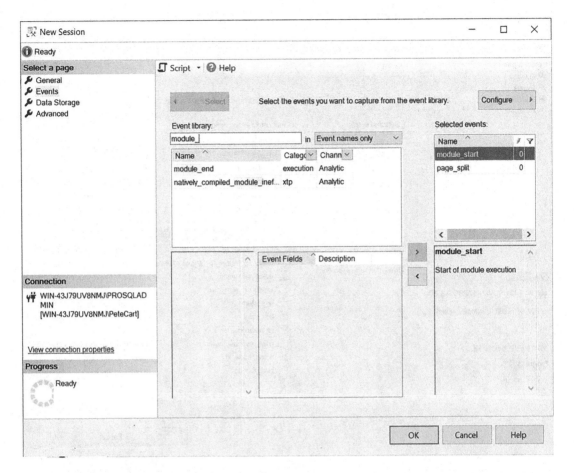

Figure 20-2. *The Events page*

We now need to use the Configure button to configure each of the events. In the Global Fields (Actions) tab of the Configure screen, we select the nt_username and database_name actions for the module_start event, as illustrated in Figure 20-3.

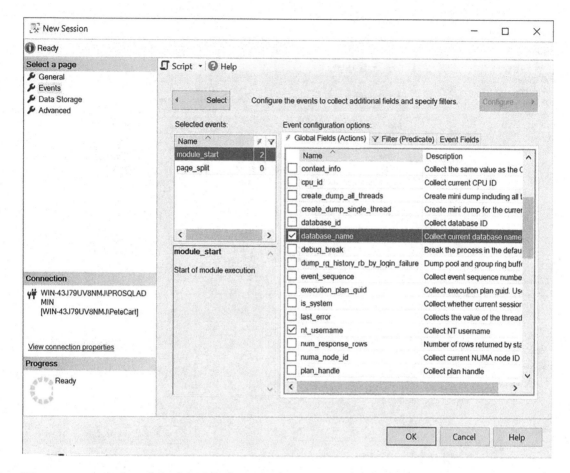

Figure 20-3. *The Global Fields (Actions) tab*

Tip   If you need to configure the same actions for multiple events, you can multiselect the events.

On the Filter (Predicate) tab, we configure the page_splits event to be filtered on the database_name, which is Chapter20 in this case, as show in Figure 20-4. This means that only page splits relating to this database are captured. We do not filter the module_ start event on the database_name, because the procedure that caused the page splits could, in theory, have been fired from any database.

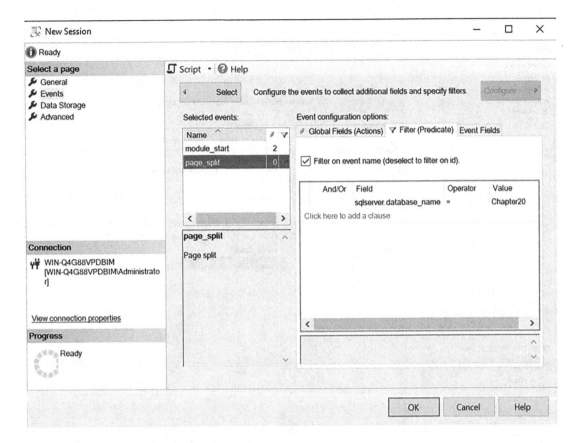

Figure 20-4. *The Filter (Predicate) tab*

In the Event Fields tab of the Configure screen, the fields that relate to the event are displayed. If there are any optional fields, then we are able to select them. Figure 20-5 shows that we have selected the statement field for the module_start event.

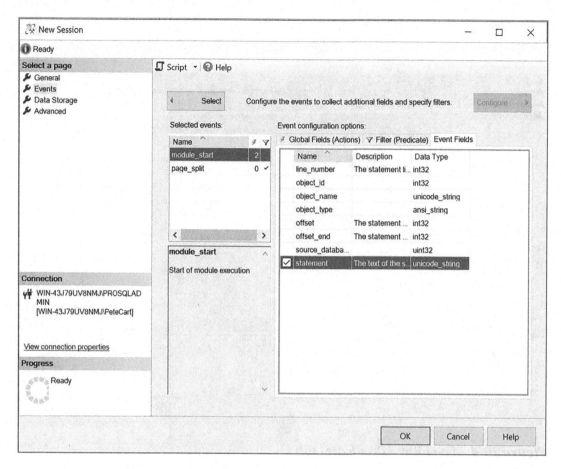

Figure 20-5. *The Event Fields tab*

On the Data Storage page of the New Session dialog box, we configure the target(s). For our scenario, we configure a single event file target, as demonstrated in Figure 20-6. The parameters are context sensitive, depending on the type of target that you select. Because we have selected a file target, we need to configure the location and maximum size of the file. We also need to specify if we want new files to be created if the initial file becomes full, and if so, how many times this should happen.

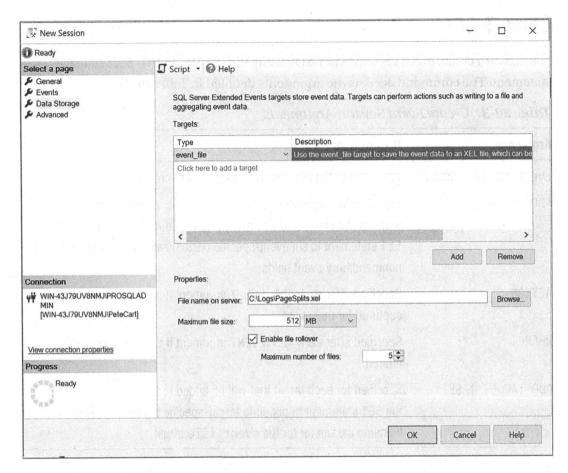

Figure 20-6. *The Data Storage page*

On the Advanced page, we can specify the desired behavior in the event of memory pressure: whether single-event loss is acceptable, whether multiple-event loss is acceptable, or whether there should be no event loss at all. We can also set the minimum and maximum size for events and how memory partitioning should be applied. This is discussed in more detail in the following section. Additionally, we can configure dispatch latency. This indicates the maximum amount of time that an event remains in the buffers before it is flushed to disk.

Using T-SQL

You can also create event sessions via T-SQL using the CREATE EVENT SESSION DDL statement. The command accepts the arguments detailed in Table 20-3.

Table 20-3. *Create Event Session Arguments*

Argument	Description
event_session_name	The name of the event session that you are creating.
ADD EVENT | SET	Specified for every event that is added to the session, followed by the name of the event, in the format package.event. You can use the SET statement to set event-specific customizations, such as including nonmandatory event fields.
ACTION	Specified after each ADD EVENT argument if global fields should be captured for that event.
WHERE	Specified after each ADD EVENT argument if the event should be filtered.
ADD TARGET | SET	Specified for each target that will be added to the session. You can use the SET statement to populate target-specific parameters, such as the filename parameter for the event_file target.

The statement also accepts the WITH options, detailed in Table 20-4. The WITH statement is specified once, at the end of the CREATE EVENT SESSION statement.

Table 20-4. *Create Event Session WITH Options*

Option	Description
MAX_MEMORY	The maximum amount of memory that the event session can use for buffering events before dispatching them to the target(s).
EVENT_RETENTION_MODE	Specifies the behavior if the buffers become full. Acceptable values are ALLOW_SINGLE_EVENT_LOSS, which indicates that a single event can be can be dropped if all buffers are full; ALLOW_MULTIPLE_EVENT_LOSS, which indicates that an entire buffer can be dropped if all buffers are full; and NO_EVENT_LOSS, which indicates that tasks that cause events to fire are to wait until there is space in the buffer.
MAX_DISPATCH_LATENCY	The maximum amount of time that events can reside in the session's buffers before being flushed to the target(s), specified in seconds.
MAX_EVENT_SIZE	The maximum possible size for event data from any single event. It can be specified in kilobytes or megabytes and should only be configured to allow events that are larger than the MAX_MEMORY setting.
MEMORY_PARTITION_MODE	Specifies where vent buffers are created. Acceptable values are NONE, which indicates that the buffers will be created within the instance; PER_NODE, which indicates that the buffers will be created for each NUMA node; and PER_CPU, which means that buffers will be created for each CPU.
TRACK_CAUSALITY	Specifies that an additional GUID and sequence number will be stored with each event so that events can be correlated.
STARTUP_STATE	Specifies if the session automatically starts when the instance starts. ON indicates it does, OFF indicates it does not.

Caution   Using the NO_EVENT_LOSS option for EVENT_RETENTION_MODE can cause performance issues on your instance, because tasks may have to wait to complete until there is space in the event session's buffers to hold the event data.

The script in Listing 20-5 demonstrates how you can use T-SQL to create a session called LogFileIO. This session is similar to the Database Log File IO Tracking template, provided through the GUI. The difference is that we are additionally capturing the sqlos.wait_completed event and the sqlserver.DatabaseName global field, and filtering on this, so that only details of the Chapter20 transaction log are tracked.

The results of the trace will be written to a file called LogFilIO.xel in the C:\Logs folder (which needs to be precreated). The STARTUP_SATATE option is used to start the session.

Listing 20-5. Creating an Event Session

```
CREATE EVENT SESSION [LogFileIO] ON SERVER
ADD EVENT sqlos.async_io_completed(
    ACTION(sqlserver.database_name)
    WHERE ([sqlserver].[database_name]=N'Chapter20')),
ADD EVENT sqlos.async_io_requested(
    ACTION(sqlserver.database_name)
    WHERE ([sqlserver].[database_name]=N'Chapter20')),
ADD EVENT sqlos.spinlock_backoff(
    ACTION(sqlserver.database_name,sqlserver.sql_text)
    WHERE ((([package0].[equal_uint64]([type],(85))) AND ([sqlserver].
[database_name]=N'Chapter20'))),
ADD EVENT sqlos.wait_completed(
    ACTION(sqlserver.database_name)
    WHERE ([sqlserver].[database_name]=N'Chapter20')),
ADD EVENT sqlos.wait_info(
ACTION(sqlserver.client_app_name,sqlserver.database_name,sqlserver.is_
system,sqlserver.session_id)
    WHERE (((([package0].[equal_uint64]([opcode],(1))) AND ([package0].
[equal_uint64]([wait_type],(182)))) AND ([sqlserver].[database_
name]=N'Chapter20'))),
ADD EVENT sqlserver.databases_log_flush(
    ACTION(sqlserver.database_name)
    WHERE ([sqlserver].[database_name]=N'Chapter20')),
ADD EVENT sqlserver.databases_log_flush_wait(
    ACTION(sqlserver.database_name)
```

```
    WHERE ([sqlserver].[database_name]=N'Chapter20')),
ADD EVENT sqlserver.file_write_completed(SET collect_path=(1)
    ACTION(sqlserver.database_name)
    WHERE (([package0].[equal_uint64]([file_id],(2))) AND ([sqlserver].
[database_name]=N'Chapter20'))),
ADD EVENT sqlserver.file_written(SET collect_path=(1)
    ACTION(sqlserver.database_name)
    WHERE (([package0].[equal_uint64]([file_id],(2))) AND ([sqlserver].
[database_name]=N'Chapter20')))
ADD TARGET package0.event_file(SET filename=N'C:\Logs\LogFileIO.xel',max_
file_size=(512)),
ADD TARGET package0.histogram(SET filtering_event_name=N'sqlos.spinlock_
backoff',source=N'sqlserver.sql_text'),
ADD TARGET package0.ring_buffer
WITH (MAX_MEMORY=4096 KB, EVENT_RETENTION_MODE=ALLOW_SINGLE_EVENT_LOSS,MAX_
DISPATCH_LATENCY=30 SECONDS,MAX_EVENT_SIZE=0 KB, MEMORY_PARTITION_
MODE=NONE,TRACK_CAUSALITY=OFF,STARTUP_STATE=ON)

GO
```

Note   This session will start automatically, due to the STARTUP_STATE begin configured as ON.

Viewing the Collected Data

SQL Server provides a data viewer that you can use for basic analysis of event data from a file or live data from the buffers. For more complex analysis, however, you can access and manipulate the event data via T-SQL. The following sections discuss each of these methods of analysis.

Analyzing Data with Data Viewer

You can use the data viewer to watch live data as it hits the buffers by drilling through Management ➤ Extended Events ➤ Sessions in Object Explorer and selecting Watch Live Data from the Session context menu. Alternatively, you can use it to view data in the target by drilling through the session and selecting View Target Data from the Target context menu.

Tip   The data viewer does not support the ring buffer or ETW target types.

The script in Listing 20-6 inserts data into the Customers table in the Chapter20 database, which causes I/O activity for the transaction log, which is captured by our LogFileIO session.

Listing 20-6. Inserting into Customers

```
USE Chapter20
GO

--Create and populate numbers table

DECLARE @Numbers TABLE
(
        Number          INT
)

;WITH CTE(Number)
AS
(
        SELECT 1 Number
        UNION ALL
        SELECT Number + 1
        FROM CTE
        WHERE Number < 100
)
INSERT INTO @Numbers
SELECT Number FROM CTE;
```

```
--Create and populate name pieces

DECLARE @Names TABLE
(
        FirstName           VARCHAR(30),
        LastName            VARCHAR(30)
);

INSERT INTO @Names
VALUES('Peter', 'Carter'),
                ('Michael', 'Smith'),
                ('Danielle', 'Mead'),
                ('Reuben', 'Roberts'),
                ('Iris', 'Jones'),
                ('Sylvia', 'Davies'),
                ('Finola', 'Wright'),
                ('Edward', 'James'),
                ('Marie', 'Andrews'),
                ('Jennifer', 'Abraham');

--Insert to Customers

SELECT * INTO #Customers
FROM
          (SELECT
                (SELECT TOP 1 FirstName FROM @Names ORDER BY NEWID()) FirstName,
                (SELECT TOP 1 LastName FROM @Names ORDER BY NEWID()) LastName,
                 (SELECT TOP 1 Number FROM @Numbers ORDER BY NEWID())
                 BillingAddressID,
                 (SELECT TOP 1 Number FROM @Numbers ORDER BY NEWID())
                 DeliveryAddressID,
                 (SELECT TOP 1 CAST(RAND() * Number AS INT) * 10000
                 FROM @Numbers
                 ORDER BY NEWID()) CreditLimit,
                 (SELECT TOP 1 CAST(RAND() * Number AS INT) * 9000
                 FROM @Numbers
                 ORDER BY NEWID()) Balance
```

```
        FROM @Numbers a
        CROSS JOIN @Numbers b
        CROSS JOIN @Numbers c
) a;

INSERT INTO dbo.Customers
SELECT * FROM #Customers;
GO
```

If we now open the data viewer for the event_file target under the LogFileIO session in Object Explorer, we see the results illustrated in Figure 20-7. The viewer shows each event and timestamp in a grid; selecting an event exposes the Details pane for that event.

Figure 20-7.   *Data view on event_file target*

Notice that a data viewer toolbar is displayed in SQL Server Management Studio, as illustrated in Figure 20-8. You can use this toolbar to add or remove columns from the grid, as well as to perform grouping and aggregation operations.

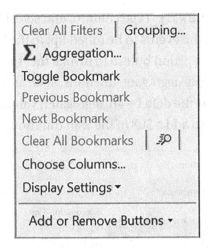

Figure 20-8. *Data viewer toolbar*

Clicking the Choose Columns button invokes the Choose Columns dialog box. We use this dialog box to add the `duration` and `wait_type` columns to the grid, as shown in Figure 20-9.

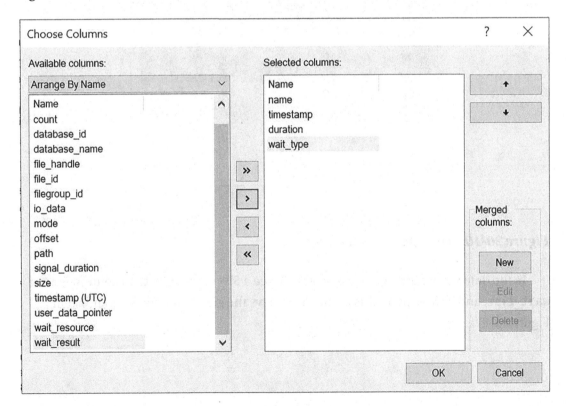

Figure 20-9. *The Choose Columns dialog box*

We can now right-click the wait_type column, and select the Group By This Column option. This will cause all of the events to be rolled up, to the level of Wait Type.

We can now use the Aggregation button to invoke the Aggregation dialog box. We can use this dialog box to apply aggregate functions, such as SUM, AVG, or COUNT, to the data. It is also possible to sort the data by an aggregated value. Figure 20-10 shows that we are using this dialog box to add a SUM of the wait durations.

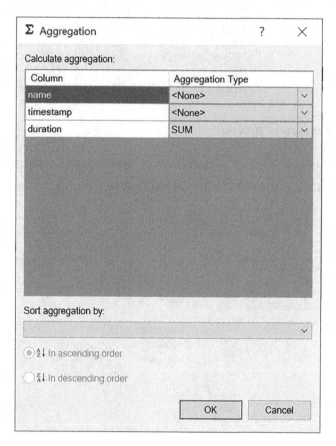

Figure 20-10. *The Aggregation dialog box*

In the data viewer grid, we are now able to see a SUM of the duration column for the wait_type, and if we expand this group, it displays the granular details, as shown in Figure 20-11.

name	timestamp	duration	wait_type
Displaying 54569 Events			
⊞ **wait_type: SOS_SCHEDULER_YIELD (2480)**			
		SUM: 3051	
⊞ **wait_type: WRITELOG (56)**			
		SUM: 72	
⊟ **wait_type: LATCH_SH (5)**			
		SUM: 108	
wait_completed	2019-05-10 10:42:01.5265554	0	LATCH_SH
wait_completed	2019-05-10 10:42:22.1092197	0	LATCH_SH
wait_completed	2019-05-10 10:42:22.1109300	1	LATCH_SH
wait_completed	2019-05-10 10:42:30.4776024	106	LATCH_SH
wait_completed	2019-05-10 10:42:55.0967626	1	LATCH_SH
⊞ **wait_type: PAGEIOLATCH_EX (97)**			
		SUM: 32	
⊞ **wait_type: CXCONSUMER (1159)**			

Figure 20-11.   *The data viewer grid*

Analyzing Data with T-SQL

If you require more complex analysis of the data, then you can achieve this via
T-SQL. The sys.fn_xe_file_target_read_file function makes this possible by reading
the target file and returning one row per event in XML format. The sys.fn_xe_file_
target_read_file accepts the parameters detailed in Table 20-5.

Table 20-5. *sys.fn_xe_file_target_read_file Parameters*

Parameter	Description
path	The file path and file name of the .XEL file. This can contain the * wildcard so that rollover files can be included.
mdpath	The file path and name of the metadata file. This is not required for SQL Server 2012 and above but is for backward compatibility only, so you should always pass NULL.
initial_file_name	The first file in the path to read. If this parameter is not NULL, then you must also specify initial_offset.
initial_offset	Specifies the last offset that was read so that all events prior are skipped. If specified, then you must also specify initial_file_name.

The sys.fn_xe_file_target_read_file procedure returns the columns detailed in Table 20-6.

Table 20-6. *sys.fn_xe_file_target_read_file Results*

Column	Description
module_guid	The GUID of the module that contains the package
package_guid	The GUID of the package that contains the event
object_name	The name of the event
event_data	The event data, in XML format
file_name	The name of the XEL file that contains the event
file_offset	The offset of the block within the file that contains the event

Because the event data is returned in XML format, we need to use XQuery to shred the nodes into relational data. A full description of XQuery is beyond the scope of this book, but Microsoft provides an XQuery language reference on msdn.microsoft.com.

The script in Listing 20-7 runs the UpdateCustomersWithPageSplits and UpdateCustomersWithoutPageSplits procedures in the Chapter20 database before extracting the event data using the sys.fn_xe_file_target_read_file. We then use the XQuery Value method to extract relational values from the XML results. Finally, because we have turned on causality tracking, we group the data by the correlation GUID to see how many page splits each stored procedure caused. UpdateWithoutPageSplits provides a contrast.

Tip   Remember to update filepaths to match your own configuration before running the query.

Listing 20-7. Analyzing Event Data with T-SQL

```
--Run the update procedures

EXEC UpdateCustomersWithoutPageSplits ;
GO

EXEC UpdateCustomerWithPageSplits ;
GO

--Wait 30 seconds to allow for the XE buffers to be flushed to the target

WAITFOR DELAY '00:00:30' ;

--Query the XE Target

SELECT c.procedurename, d.pagesplits
 FROM
 (
      SELECT
              correlationid,
              COUNT(*) -1 PageSplits -- -1 to remove the count of the
              module_start event
      FROM
      (
            SELECT CapturedEvent,
                    xml_data.value('(/event/data[@name=''object_name'']
                    /value)[1]', 'nvarchar(max)')
                    procedurename,  --extract procedure name
                    xml_data.value('(/event/action[@name=''attach_
                    activity_id'']/value)[1]', 'uniqueidentifier')
                    correlationid --extract Correlation ID
```

```
                FROM
                    (
--Query the fn_xe_file_target_read_file function, to extract the raw XML
                                SELECT
                                OBJECT_NAME CapturedEvent,
                                CAST(event_data AS XML) xml_data
                                FROM
sys.fn_xe_file_target_read_file('C:\mssql\pagesplits*.xel', NULL , NULL,
NULL) as XE ) a
                    ) b
                    GROUP BY correlationid
            ) d
INNER JOIN --Self join, to allow the count of page splits
(
        SELECT CapturedEvent,
                xml_data.value('(/event/data[@name=''object_name'']/value)
                [1]', 'nvarchar(max)') procedurename,
                xml_data.value('(/event/action[@name=''attach_activity_
                id'']/value)[1]', 'uniqueidentifier') correlationid
        FROM
        (
                SELECT object_name CapturedEvent,
                CAST(event_data AS XML) xml_data
                FROM
                sys.fn_xe_file_target_read_file('C:\mssql\pagesplits*.xel',
                NULL , NULL, NULL) as XE ) a
        ) c
ON c.correlationid = d.correlationid
        AND c.procedurename IS NOT NULL ;
```

Tip Using XQuery allows you to query on every event field and action that is
captured within your trace, so you can create very complex queries, providing rich
and powerful analysis of the activity within your instance.

Correlating Extended Events with Operating System Data

Extended Events offer the capability to integrate with operating system–level data. This gives useful insights, such as the queries that were running when CPU spiked, etc. The following sections discuss how to correlate SQL Server events with Perfmon data and other operating system–level events.

Correlating Events with Perfmon Data

Before Extended Events were introduced, DBAs used a tool called SQL Trace and its GUI, Profiler, to capture traces from SQL Server; it was possible to correlate this data with data from Perfmon. With Extended Events, you do not often need to make this correlation, because Extended Events include Perfmon counters for processor, logical disk, and system performance objects, such as context switches and file writes. Therefore, you can correlate SQL Server events with operating system counters by adding these objects to the session and by following the T-SQL analysis techniques discussed in the previous section.

Tip   Perfmon counters are in the Analytic channel but have no category.

The script in Listing 20-8 demonstrates creating an event session that captures statements executed within the instance, alongside processor counters. Processor counters are captured every 15 seconds for each processor in the system. The results are saved to an event file target and an ETW target.

Listing 20-8. Creating an Event Session with Perfmon Counters

```
CREATE EVENT SESSION Statements_with_Perf_Counters
ON SERVER
--Add the Events and Actions relating to each Event
ADD EVENT sqlserver.error_reported(
    ACTION(sqlserver.client_app_name,sqlserver.database_id,sqlserver.query_
    hash,sqlserver.session_id)
```

```
    WHERE ([package0].[greater_than_uint64]([sqlserver].[database_id],
    (4)) AND
[package0].[equal_boolean]([sqlserver].[is_system],(0)))),
ADD EVENT sqlserver.module_end(SET collect_statement=(1)
    ACTION(sqlserver.client_app_name,sqlserver.database_id,sqlserver.query_
    hash,sqlserver.session_id)
    WHERE ([package0].[greater_than_uint64]([sqlserver].[database_id],
    (4)) AND
[package0].[equal_boolean]([sqlserver].[is_system],(0)))),
ADD EVENT sqlserver.perfobject_processor,
ADD EVENT sqlserver.rpc_completed(
    ACTION(sqlserver.client_app_name,sqlserver.database_id,sqlserver.query_
    hash,sqlserver.session_id)
    WHERE ([package0].[greater_than_uint64]([sqlserver].[database_id],
    (4)) AND
[package0].[equal_boolean]([sqlserver].[is_system],(0)))),
ADD EVENT sqlserver.sp_statement_completed(SET collect_object_name=(1)
    ACTION(sqlserver.client_app_name,sqlserver.database_id,sqlserver.query_
    hash,sqlserver.query_plan_hash,sqlserver.session_id)
    WHERE ([package0].[greater_than_uint64]([sqlserver].[database_id],(4))
    AND [package0].[equal_boolean]([sqlserver].[is_system],(0)))),
ADD EVENT sqlserver.sql_batch_completed(
    ACTION(sqlserver.client_app_name,sqlserver.database_id,sqlserver.query_
    hash,sqlserver.session_id)
    WHERE ([package0].[greater_than_uint64]([sqlserver].[database_id],
    (4)) AND
[package0].[equal_boolean]([sqlserver].[is_system],(0)))),
ADD EVENT sqlserver.sql_statement_completed(
    ACTION(sqlserver.client_app_name,sqlserver.database_id,sqlserver.query_
    hash,sqlserver.query_plan_hash,sqlserver.session_id)
    WHERE ([package0].[greater_than_uint64]([sqlserver].[database_id],
    (4)) AND
[package0].[equal_boolean]([sqlserver].[is_system],(0))))
--Add the Targets
```

```
ADD TARGET package0.event_file(SET filename=N'C:\MSSQL\
StatementsAndProcessorUtilization.xel'),
ADD TARGET package0.etw_classic_sync_target(SET default_etw_session_
logfile_path=N'C:\MSSQL\StatementsWithPerfCounters.etl')
WITH (MAX_MEMORY=4096 KB,EVENT_RETENTION_MODE=ALLOW_SINGLE_EVENT_LOSS,MAX_
DISPATCH_LATENCY=30 SECONDS,MAX_EVENT_SIZE=0 KB,MEMORY_PARTITION_
MODE=NONE,TRACK_CAUSALITY=ON,STARTUP_STATE=OFF) ;
GO

--Start the instance
ALTER EVENT SESSION Statements_with_Perf_Counters
ON SERVER
STATE = start;
```

Tip   The SQL Server service account must be in the Performance Log Users group, or an error is thrown.

Integrating Event Sessions with Operating System–Level Events

---

Note   To follow the demonstrations in this section, you need to install Windows Performance Toolkit, which you can download from msdn.microsoft.com as part of the Windows Deployment and Assessment Toolkit.

There are instances in which you may need to integrate event session data with operating system data other than Perfmon counters that SQL Server provides. For example, imagine a scenario in which you have an application that exports SQL Server data to flat files in the operating system so that a middleware product, such as BizTalk, can pick them up. You are having trouble generating some files and you need to view the process flow—from SQL statement being run through to the WMI events being triggered in the operating system. For this, you need to merge event session data with a trace of WMI events. You can achieve this through the ETW (Event Tracking for Windows) architecture.

To demonstrate this, we first create an event trace session in Performance Monitor using the WMI provider, and then we integrate it with the event session that we created in the previous section. (You can find Performance Monitor in Administrative Tools in Windows.) After we open Performance Monitor, we select New ➤ Data Collector Set from the Event Trace Sessions context menu, which causes the Create New Data Collector Set wizard to be invoked. On the first page of the wizard, specify a name for the Collector Set, as illustrated in Figure 20-12, and specify if the Data Collector set should be configured manually or based on a template. In our scenario, we choose to configure it manually.

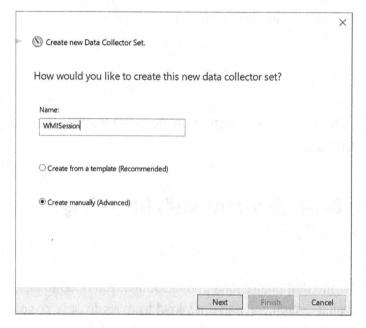

Figure 20-12. *The Create New Data Collector Set wizard*

On the page for enabling event trace providers, we can use the Add button to add the WMI-Activity provider, as illustrated in Figure 20-13.

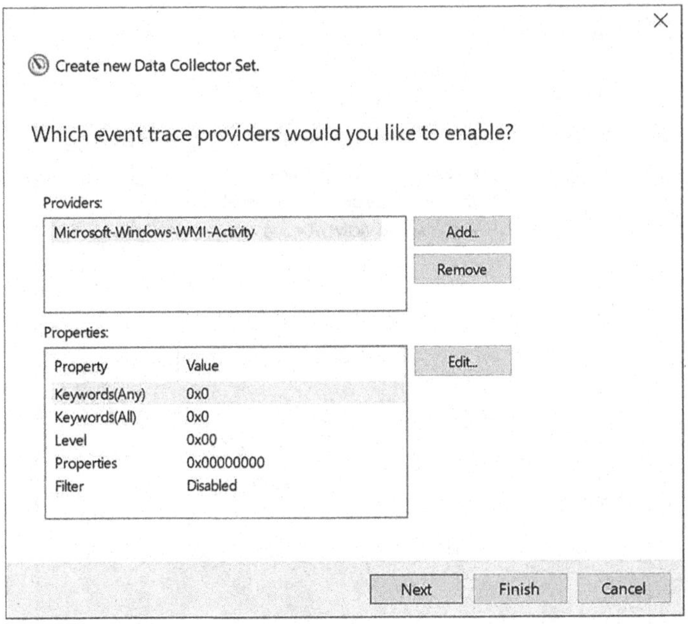

Figure 20-13. *Add the WMI provider*

We now use the Edit button to invoke the Properties dialog box. Here, we add the Trace and Operational categories by using the check boxes, as shown in Figure 20-14.

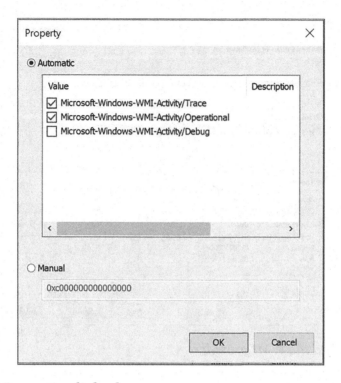

Figure 20-14. *Properties dialog box*

After exiting the Properties dialog box, we move to the next page of the wizard, where we can configure the location where the trace file is stored. We configure the trace file to be saved to the same location as our event session trace, as shown in Figure 20-15.

Figure 20-15. *Configure the trace file location*

On the final page of the wizard, we leave the default options of running the trace under the default account and then save and close the trace.

In Performance Monitor, our trace is now visible in the Event Trace Sessions folder, but showing as stopped. We can use the context menu of the trace to start the Data Collector Set, as shown in Figure 20-16. Also notice that there is a Data Collector Set called XE_DEFAULT_ETW_SESSION. Our extended event session created this because we created an ETW target. This session is required for integrating the data.

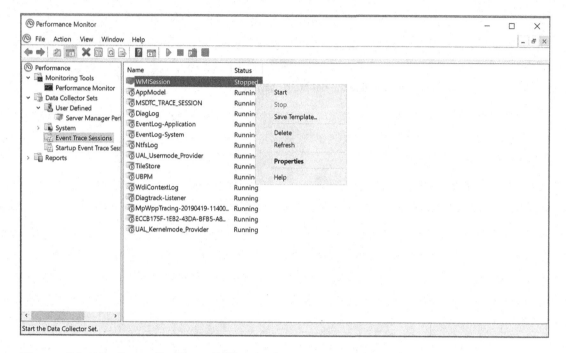

Figure 20-16. *Start the Data Collector Set*

Now that both the WMISession and Statements_with_Perf_Counters sessions are started, we use the BCP command in Listing 20-9 to generate activity, which causes events to fire in both sessions.

Listing 20-9. Generating Activity

```
bcp chapter20.dbo.customers out c:\mssql\dump.dat -S .\PROSQLADMIN -T -c
```

We now need to ensure that the buffers of both sessions are flushed to disk. We do this by stopping both sessions. After stopping the Statements_with_Perf_Counters session, we also need to stop the XE_DEFAULT_ETW_SESSION ETW session in Performance Monitor. You can stop the Statements_with_Perf_Counters session by using the T-SQL command in Listing 20-10.

Listing 20-10. Stopping the Event Session

```
ALTER EVENT SESSION Statements_with_Perf_Counters
ON SERVER
STATE = stop;
```

You can stop the WMISession and XE_DEFAULT_ETW_SESSION by selecting Stop from their respective context menus in Performance Monitor.

The next step is to merge the two trace files together. You can achieve this from the command line by using the XPERF utility with the -Merge switch (demonstrated in Listing 20-11). This command merges the files together, with StatementsWithPerf Counters.etl being the target file. You should navigate to the C:\Program Files (x86)\Windows Kits\8.1\Windows Performance Toolkit folder, before running the script.

Listing 20-11. Merging Trace Files

```
xperf -merge c:\mssql\wmisession.etl C:\MSSQL\
StatementsWithPerfCounters.etl
```

Now that all events are in the same file, you can open and analyze this .etl file with Windows Performance Analyzer, which is available as part of the Windows Performance Toolkit, as shown in Figure 20-17. Once installed, you can access Windows Performance Analyzer via the Windows Start menu. A full discussion of Windows Performance Analyzer is beyond the scope of this book, but you can find it in Administrative Tools in Windows after it's installed. You will find full documentation on msdn.microsoft.com.

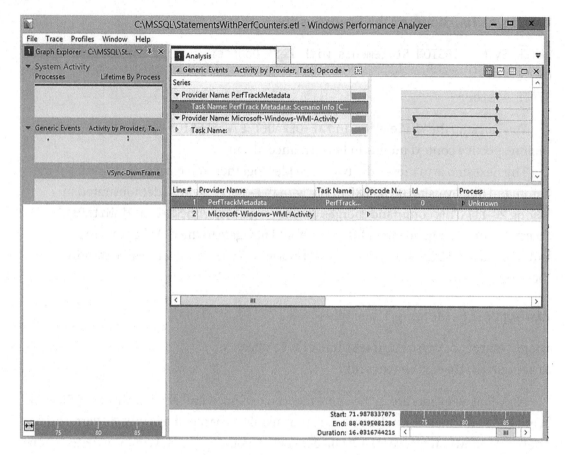

Figure 20-17. *Windows Performance Analyzer*

Summary

Extended Events introduce new concepts that you must understand in order to fully
harness their power. Events are points of interest that are captured in a trace, whereas
actions provide extended information, in addition to the event columns. Predicates allow
you to filter events in order to provide a more targeted trace, and targets define how
the data is stored. A session is the trace object itself, and it can be configured to include
multiple events, actions, predicates, and targets.

You can create an event session through the New Session Wizard, an easy and
quick method that exposes Templates; via the New Session dialog box; or of course, via
T-SQL. When creating a session via T-SQL, you use the CREATE EVENT SESSION DDL
statement to configure all aspects of the trace.

Each Extended Event artifact is contained within one of four packages: `Package0`, `Sqlserver`, `Sqlos`, and `SecAudit`. The contents of `SecAudit` are not exposed, however, since these are used internally to support SQL Audit functionality, which is discussed in *Chapter* 11.

You can view data using the data viewer. The data viewer allows you to watch live data in the session's buffers, and it also supports viewing target data from the Event File, Event Count, and Histogram Target types. The data viewer provides basic data analysis capability, including grouping and aggregating data.

For more complex data analysis, you can open targets in T-SQL. To open an Event File target, use the `sys. fn_xe_file_target_read_file` results system stored procedure. You then have the power of T-SQL at your disposal for complex analysis requirements.

You can correlate events by turning on causality tracking within the session. This adds a GUID and a sequence number to each event so that you can identify relationships. You can also easily correlate SQL events with Perfmon data, because Extended Events expose processor, logical disk, and system performance counters. To correlate events with other operating system–level events, event sessions can use the ETW target, which you can then merge with other data collector sets to map Extended Events to events from other providers in the ETW architecture.

Monitoring and Managing a Hybrid Environment

SQL Server 2022 has functionality, which helps you to manage your SQL Server estate in a hybrid environment, meaning that you can centralize administration and gain some of the benefits of cloud, even for your on-premises SQL Server estate.

In this chapter, we will explore hybrid features that become available, once we have registered a SQL Server instance with Azure ARC—a technology that allows you to view remote infrastructure resources, as if they were hosted in Azure. These features include environmental health/SQL Best Practice Assessment (SQL BPA) and Microsoft Defender for Cloud.

Tip Examples in this chapter require Log Analytics Workspace to be configured. Log Analytics Workspace is an Azure feature for collecting and analyzing metrics and logs. It is a large topic and a full discussion is beyond the scope of this book. A tutorial is supplied by Microsoft, however, and can be found at `https://learn.microsoft.com/en-us/azure/azure-monitor/logs/log-analytics-tutorial`.

Hybrid Management

Integrating a Server and a SQL Server instance with Azure Arc allows you to manage a resource as if it were natively in Azure. The server could actually be located on-premises, or even in another cloud provider. For example, the server that is used in the examples, within this chapter, is built in AWS.

© Peter A. Carter 2023
P. A. Carter, *Pro SQL Server 2022 Administration*, https://doi.org/10.1007/978-1-4842-8864-1_21

It is possible to generate a script, from Azure, that can be run on a server in a different environment, which will onboard a SQL Server instance into Azure Arc. If you are using SQL Server 2022, however, then Arc integration is embedded into the instance setup. This is discussed in Chapter 2.

Once a Server is onboarded, then it will appear in your chosen resource group, as if it were a native resource. For example, Figure 21-1 shows the AWS server, within an Azure resource group. The resource name is the instance name of the EC2 instance in AWS. The computer name is the machine name of the server, at the operating system level.

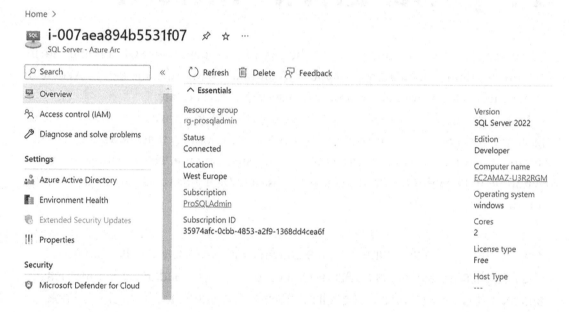

Figure 21-1. *SQL VM in Azure Arc*

The server will also become available in Log Analytics Workspace. A full discussion of this feature is beyond the scope of this book, mainly because the direction of travel is Azure Monitor. At the most basic level, however, to illustrate how Azure treats the AWS-based server as a native resource, consider Figure 21-2. You can see that Azure keeps a heartbeat with the server and treats it as an Azure resource.

Subscriptions	Workspaces		Time Range	
ProSQLAdmin ∨	DefaultWorkspace-35974afc-0cbb-4853-a2f9-1368dd4cea6f-WEU ∨		Last 4 hours ∨	

Top 100 Machines   Top 10 Machines

Computer Name Conta... ⓘ	Counter ⓘ	Aggregators ⓘ	TableTrend ⓘ
EC2AMAZ-U3R2RGM	Heartbeat ∨	Min ∨	Average ∨

ResourceName	↑↓	Type	↑↓	Min ↑↓	Average ↑↓	Trend (Average)	Properti...
EC2AMAZ-U3R2RGM.prosqladmin.com		Azure Virtual Machine		1	1	‖‖‖‖‖‖‖‖‖‖‖‖‖‖‖‖‖‖‖‖‖‖‖‖‖‖	ⓘ Info

Figure 21-2. *Azure Arc heartbeat*

Once onboarded, various Azure management options become available. Some of these options, such as Environmental Health and Defender for Cloud, are discussed in the following sections.

Environmental Health and SQL Best Practice Assessment

Note   At the time of writing, Environmental Health is in a period of transition. Azure SQL VMs have transitioned to SQL Best Practice Analyzer (SQL BPA), whereas VMs onboarded through Azure Arc still use the older Environment Health feature. The two features are very similar. They use the same agent and are configured in the same way. Because the focus of this chapter is on Azure Arc, I will discuss the setup process for Environment Health, as this will be transferable. The real difference between the features is that SQL BPA provides a much richer reporting experience. Therefore, when we look at using the report, I will switch to SQL BPA, as this is what you will most likely see at the time of reading.

Environmental Health/SQL BPA run hundreds of tests against a VM running SQL Server, the SQL Server instance, and the databases hosted within the instance to check for good practice configuration, throughout the stack.

Scrolling to the bottom of the resource will allow you to see compatible features, as shown in Figure 21-3. In this case, you can see that Microsoft Defender and Environmental Health are available.

Capabilities   Properties

 Microsoft Defender for Cloud
Continuously monitor for potential
security vulnerabilities and
recommendations.

 Environment Health
Environment Health provides a
mechanism to evaluate the
configuration of your SQL Server.

Figure 21-3. *Available Capabilities*

Selecting the Environmental Health option will open the configuration page. To be
able to continue, the Microsoft Monitoring Agent must be installed on the target server.
This can be achieved by using the PowerShell script in Listing 21-1.

Listing 21-1. Install the Microsoft Monitoring Agent

```
#Install the Azure PowerShell Module

Install-Module -Name Az -Repository PSGallery -Force

#Install the Connected Machine Module

Install-Module -Name Az.Connectedmachine

#Set Log Analytics Workspace Parameters

$Setting = @{ "workspaceId" = "8ca234da-dbf2-4ff4-bb3d-4b762f3248e1" }
$protectedSetting = @{ "workspaceKey" = "Cryr1AJbtzjIsW7i1LZx3lGX+15OXppi2
Q5X1D9ioB==" }

#Set Machine Parameters

$genericSettings = @{
    Name = "MicrosoftMonitoringAgent"
    ResourceGroupName = "rg-prosqladmin"
    MachineName = "i-007aea894b5531f07"
    Location = "westeurope"
    Publisher = "Microsoft.EnterpriseCloud.Monitoring"
    ExtensionType = "MicrosoftMonitoringAgent"
}
```

```
#Configure Agent

New-AzConnectedMachineExtension @genericSettings -Settings
$Setting -ProtectedSetting $protectedSetting
```

The configuration page is illustrated in Figure 21-4. If the Microsoft Monitoring Agent hasn't been installed, then there will be a warning stating that this must be completed. The Account Type can be configured as a Domain Account or a Managed Service Account, and the working directory that you specify should be prestaged.

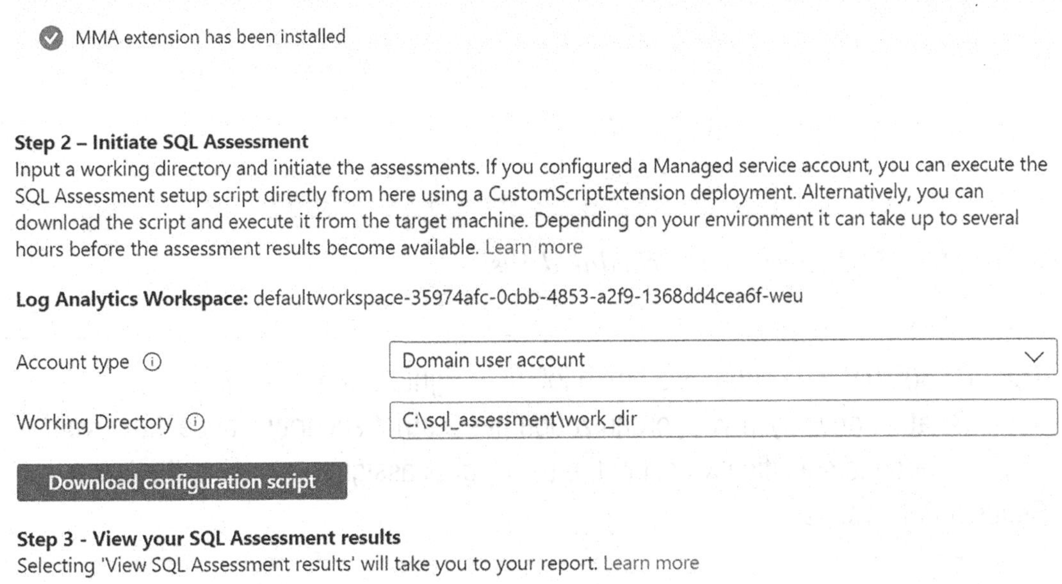

⊘ MMA extension has been installed

Step 2 – Initiate SQL Assessment
Input a working directory and initiate the assessments. If you configured a Managed service account, you can execute the SQL Assessment setup script directly from here using a CustomScriptExtension deployment. Alternatively, you can download the script and execute it from the target machine. Depending on your environment it can take up to several hours before the assessment results become available. Learn more

Log Analytics Workspace: defaultworkspace-35974afc-0cbb-4853-a2f9-1368dd4cea6f-weu

Account type ⓘ	Domain user account ⌄
Working Directory ⓘ	C:\sql_assessment\work_dir

Download configuration script

Step 3 - View your SQL Assessment results
Selecting 'View SQL Assessment results' will take you to your report. Learn more

***Figure 21-4.** Environmental health configuration*

Once this form is completed, you can use the button to download the configuration script, which must be run on the target server. When running this script, you will be prompted to enter the name of the account (and password, if it is a domain account). The script will then create a Windows Scheduled Task (Figure 21-5), which runs under the context of the specified account. The account needs to be a local administrator and needs to have the Logon as a batch job user rights assignment, and the Do not forcefully unload the user registry at user logoff setting must be enabled in group policy editor. It also needs to have sysadmin rights within the SQL Server instance.

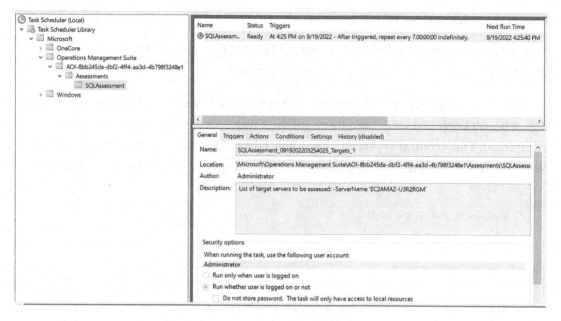

Figure 21-5. *SQL Assessment Scheduled Task*

Tip   By default, the Logon as a batch job user rights assignment is assigned to administrators anyway. If your organization has a strict security stance, however, you may need to specifically assign the user rights assignment, using the Local Security Policy console.

For reference, Listing 21-2 shows the script that can be downloaded from the Azure portal. If you are comfortable with PowerShell, then you can just use the commands manually, as opposed to downloading the script.

Tip   Both the Microsoft Management Agent and the sqlserver PowerShell module must be installed on the target server.

Listing 21-2. Script to Create Scheduled Task

```
[CmdletBinding()]
Param(
        [Parameter(Mandatory=$false)]
        [string]$ManagedServiceAccountName
)
if ($ManagedServiceAccountName)
{
        Add-SQLAssessmentTask -SQLServerName "EC2AMAZ-U3R2RGM" -Working
        Directory "C:\sql_assessment\work_dir" -RunWithManagedServiceAccount
        $True -ScheduledTaskUsername $ManagedServiceAccountName -Scheduled
        TaskPassword (new-object System.Security.SecureString)
}
else
{
        Add-SQLAssessmentTask -SQLServerName "EC2AMAZ-U3R2RGM" -WorkingDirectory
        "C:\sql_assessment\work_dir"
}
```

Figure 21-5 shows the Scheduled Task that is created.

Tip   Microsoft advise that it can take up to 24 hours for the assessment to register in Azure, but in my experience, it usually appears within an hour.

Once the Server has registered, then you are able to view the findings of the best practice analysis. Figure 21-6 illustrates the front page of the SQL BPA, which can be found by clicking the SQL Best Practice Assessment page (or Environment Health page) within the resource.

SQL best practices assessment

SQL best practices assessment provides a mechanism to evaluate the configuration of your Azure SQL VM for best practices like indexes, deprecated features, trace flag usage, statistics, etc. Assessment results are uploaded to your Log Analytics workspace using Microsoft Monitoring Agent (MMA). The run time depends on your environment (number of databases, objects). Learn more

| Run assessment | View latest successful assessment |

Assessment results

The latest in progress and completed results are shown below. Select any completed assessment to view recommendations in an Azure workbook. Once you are in the workbook, you can also select to view older results.

Assessments	Status
2022-09-25 12:00 AM UTC	⏱ Scheduled
2022-09-24 10:55 PM UTC	↻ In progress - uploading results
2022-09-24 09:12 PM UTC	✓ Completed
2022-09-24 09:26 AM UTC	✓ Completed

Figure 21-6. *SQL BPA front page*

Tip   Remember, we are now switching to SQL BPA, instead of Environmental Health, to discuss the reports.

The page shows the timestamp of each assessment and the current status of that assessment. You can change the scheduling of the assessment by using the configuration tab, which is shown in Figure 21-7.

SQL best practices assessment configuration   ✕

vm-prosqladmin

SQL best practices assessment results are uploaded to Log Analytics workspace. You can either
use the existing connection or configure MMA using this blade. Learn more

Enable SQL best practices assessments *

☑

Log Analytics workspace name

| DefaultWorkspace-35974afc-0cbb-4853-a2f9-1368dd4cea6f-WEU | ⌄ |

✔ Log Analytics workspace has been successfully configured for this VM.

Enable scheduling

☑

Frequency

◉ Weekly

◯ Monthly

Day of week

| Sunday | ⌄ |

Recurrence

| Every 1 week | ⌄ |

Assessment start (local VM time)

| 00:00 (12:00 midnight) | ⌄ |

Figure 21-7. *SQL BPA configuration*

Drilling through the timestamp will show the completed assessment. Every region
of the report is interactive. For example, hovering over a slice of a pie chart (at the
top of Figure 21-8) will display its category name and percentage. Clicking a section
of the pie chart will filter the findings below, by that issue severity or category. The
filters in blue, below, will allow you to filter the report further. The name filter allows
you to filter by either SQL Server instance or by database, in the format `sql server`
`instance:database`. For example, Figure 21-9 shows the report filtered by the Chapter21
database.

Figure 21-8. *SQL BPA report*

Figure 21-9. *SQL BPA report filtered for Chapter21 database*

You can also filter the instances of a "finding" in the bottom-right table, by clicking the overall "finding" in the bottom-left table. For example, clicking the DbIntegrity finding on the left filters the table on the right, so that only instances of that finding are displayed. This is demonstrated in Figure 21-10.

Severity ↑↓	Tags	Check Id ↑↓	Issues↑↓
High	DBConfiguration,Performance	InstantFileInitialization	1
High	Performance,Memory	LockedPagesInMemory	1
Medium	DBCC,Performance,DataIntegrity	DbIntegrity	4
Medium	Backup	FullBackup	3
Medium	Configuration,DBFileConfiguration	DbSpaceAvailable	2
Medium	Security,WeakPassword	WeakPassword	1
Medium	Configuration,Performance	AzErrorLogLocation	1
Medium	Backup	OutdatedTranLogBackup	1
Low	DBFileConfiguration,DBConfiguration	AzDataOnDataDisks	3
Low	DBConfiguration,Statistics,Performance	AutoCreateStatsIncremen...	2
Low	Deprecated,Security,UpdateIssues,Performance	DeprecatedFeatures	1
Low	Configuration	BrowserSvcStoped	1
Low	Memory,Performance,MaxMemory	MaxMemorySystem	1

Target ↑↓	Name	Severity ↑↓	Message
Database	vm-prosqladmin:Chapter21	Medium	Run 'DBCC CHECKDB' command checks
Database	vm-prosqladmin::master	Medium	Run 'DBCC CHECKDB' command checks
Database	vm-prosqladmin::model	Medium	Run 'DBCC CHECKDB' command checks
Database	vm-prosqladmin::msdb	Medium	Run 'DBCC CHECKDB' command checks

***Figure 21-10.** SQL BPA filtered by check*

The message column provides remediation advice and clicking the message will provide more verbose details. For example, clicking the link for the CHECKDB finding against the Chapter21 database shows the details in Figure 21-11.

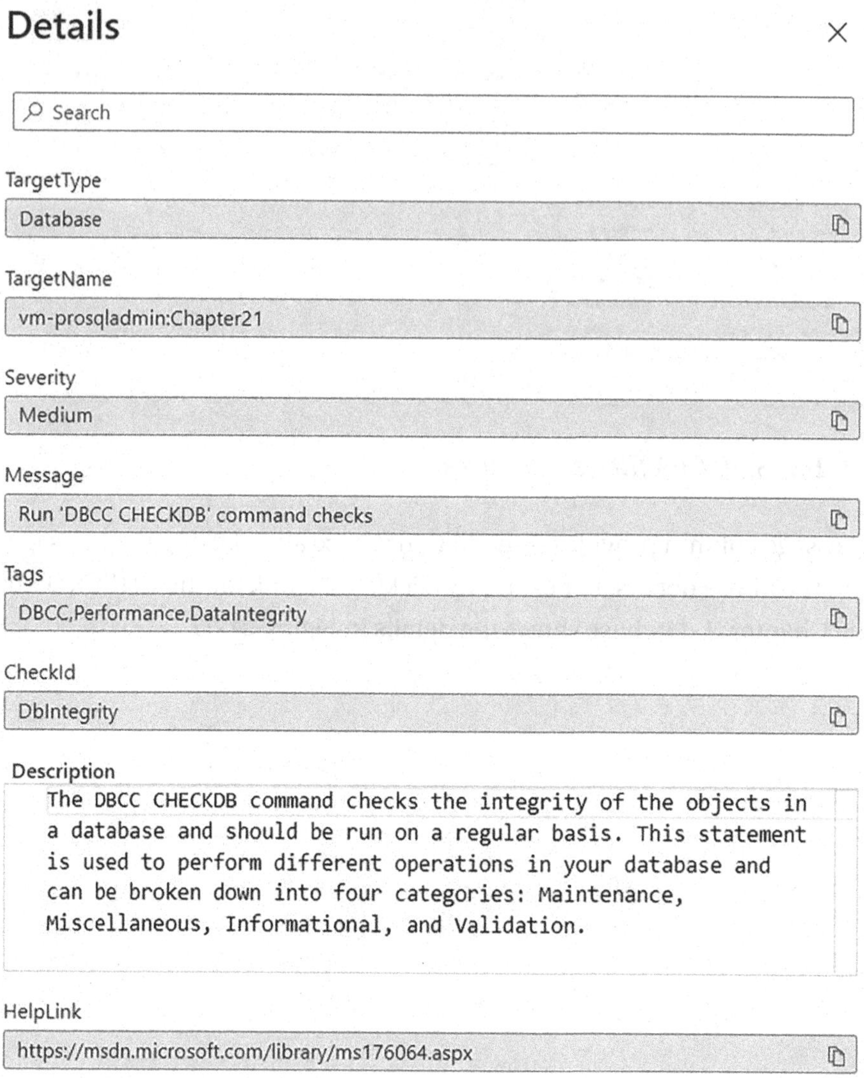

Details   ✕

> 🔍 Search

TargetType

> Database   ⧉

TargetName

> vm-prosqladmin:Chapter21   ⧉

Severity

> Medium   ⧉

Message

> Run 'DBCC CHECKDB' command checks   ⧉

Tags

> DBCC,Performance,DataIntegrity   ⧉

CheckId

> DbIntegrity   ⧉

Description

> The DBCC CHECKDB command checks the integrity of the objects in
> a database and should be run on a regular basis. This statement
> is used to perform different operations in your database and
> can be broken down into four categories: Maintenance,
> Miscellaneous, Informational, and Validation.

HelpLink

> https://msdn.microsoft.com/library/ms176064.aspx   ⧉

Figure 21-11. *Message details*

The New Issues tab of the report provides a filtered list of the findings that have appeared since the previous assessment was run, and the Resolved Issues tab provides details of the issues that have been resolved since the last time the assessment was run. The Insights tab (Figure 21-12) is particularly useful, giving you details of the most commonly reoccurring issues followed by a list of the databases that have the most issues.

Most recurring issues

Issues↑↓	CheckId	↑↓	Name	↑↓	TargetName	↑↓
1	FullBackup		Full backup is missed or outdated		vm-prosqladmin:Chapter21	
1	TF834		TF 834 enables large-page allocations		vm-prosqladmin	
1	OutdatedTranLogBackup		Transaction Log backup is missed or outdated		vm-prosqladmin:Chapter21	
1	TF1118		TF 1118 has no effect in SQL Server 2016 and higher		vm-prosqladmin	
1	DeprecatedFeatures		Deprecated or discontinued features should not be used		vm-prosqladmin	
1	WeakPassword		SQL logins have weak passwords		vm-prosqladmin	
1	AutoCreateStatsIncremental		Incremental option of auto stats should be ON		vm-prosqladmin:Chapter21	
1	BrowserSvcStoped		'SQL Server Browser' service is stopped		vm-prosqladmin	
1	MaxMemorySystem		Max server memory exceeds system memory		vm-prosqladmin	
1	DbIntegrity		Database Integrity Checks		vm-prosqladmin:Chapter21	

Top databases with issues

Issues↑↓	Database	↑↓
5	vm-prosqladmin:master	
4	vm-prosqladmin:Chapter21	
4	vm-prosqladmin:msdb	
3	vm-prosqladmin:model	

Figure 21-12. *SQL BPA Issues tab*

The Trends tab, shown in Figure 21-13, offers bar charts, tracking (at time of writing) the number of new issues, resolved issues, and issue severity over time, with each bar representing an assessment.

Total Issues

This chart shows the number of issues for all the assessment runs available in your Log Analytics workspace. Each bar represents a single assessment run. If there are multiple runs on a given day, it only shows the latest one. The legend shows the averages for each severity level. If you hover over each bar, you can see the number of issues for individual runs. Ideally you should see the number of issues going down over time, especially for high and medium severity issues.

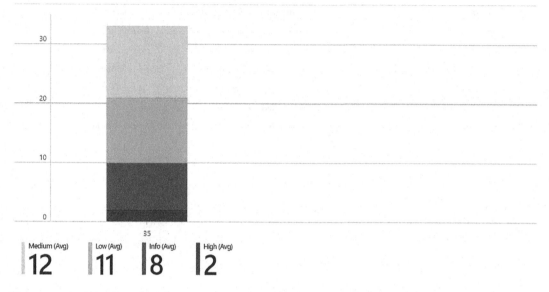

Figure 21-13. *Trends tab*

The Log button in the BPA report, shown in Figure 21-8 and Figure 21-9, will open the last query to be run in a Workspace Analytics Logs query window. This is shown in Figure 21-14. The query is written in the Kusto Query Language. You can modify the query, or write your own. A list of categorized functions, example queries, and data tables can be found in the left-hand pane, along with helpers, such as data preview for the tables. The results pane is split into Results and Chat tabs, allowing you to choose how you consume the query results.

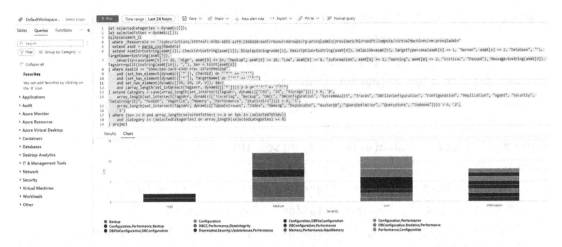

Figure 21-14. *Logs query window*

Tip   Kusto Query Language, or KQL, is a variation of SQL that can be used to search logs.

For reference, the query shown in Figure 21-14 can be found in Listing 21-3.

Listing 21-3. *Kusto Query*

```
let selectedCategories = dynamic([]);
let selectedTotSev = dynamic([]);
SqlAssessment_CL
| where _ResourceId =~ "/subscriptions/35974afc-0cbb-4623-
a2f9-1368dd4cea6f/resourceGroups/rg-prosqladmin/providers/Microsoft.
Compute/virtualMachines/vm-prosqladmin"
| extend asmt = parse_csv(RawData)
| extend AsmtId=tostring(asmt[1]), CheckId=tostring(asmt[2]),
DisplayString=asmt[3], Description=tostring(asmt[4]), HelpLink=asmt[5],
TargetType=case(asmt[6] == 1, "Server", asmt[6] == 2, "Database", ""),
TargetName=tostring(asmt[7]),
    Severity=case(asmt[8] == 30, "High", asmt[8] == 20, "Medium",
    asmt[8] == 10, "Low", asmt[8] == 0, "Information", asmt[8] == 1,
    "Warning", asmt[8] == 2, "Critical", "Passed"), Message=tostring
    (asmt[9]), TagsArr=split(tostring(asmt[10]), ","), Sev = toint(asmt[8])
```

```
| where AsmtId == "8b0ec946-2ac0-4340-97ec-197a590eb3b8"
    and (set_has_element(dynamic(['*']), CheckId) or "'*'" == "'*'")
    and (set_has_element(dynamic(['*']), TargetName) or "'*'" == "'*'")
    and set_has_element(dynamic([30, 20, 10, 0]), Sev)
    and (array_length(set_intersect(TagsArr, dynamic(['*']))) > 0 or "'*'"
    == "'*'")
| extend Category = case(array_length(set_intersect(TagsArr,
dynamic(["CPU", "IO", "Storage"]))) > 0, '0',
    array_length(set_intersect(TagsArr, dynamic(["TraceFlag",
    "Backup", "DBCC", "DBConfiguration", "SystemHealth", "Traces",
    "DBFileConfiguration", "Configuration", "Replication", "Agent",
    "Security", "DataIntegrity", "MaxDOP", "PageFile", "Memory",
    "Performance", "Statistics"]))) > 0, '1',
    array_length(set_intersect(TagsArr, dynamic(["UpdateIssues", "Index",
    "Naming", "Deprecated", "masterDB", "QueryOptimizer", "QueryStore",
    "Indexes"]))) > 0, '2',
    '3')
| where (Sev >= 0 and array_length(selectedTotSev) == 0 or Sev in
(selectedTotSev))
    and (Category in (selectedCategories) or array_
    length(selectedCategories) == 0)
| project
    TargetType,
    TargetName,
    Severity,
    Tags=strcat_array(array_slice(TagsArr, 1, -1), ','),
    CheckId,
    SeverityCode = toint(Sev),
    Message
| distinct *
| summarize Cnt = count() by SeverityCode, Severity, Tags, CheckId
| project Severity, Tags, CheckId, Cnt, SeverityCode
| order by SeverityCode desc, Cnt desc
```

> **Tip** A full discussion of how to use Kusto is beyond the scope of this book. A Microsoft tutorial, however, can be found at `https://learn.microsoft.com/en-us/azure/data-explorer/kusto/query/tutorial`.

Microsoft Defender

Microsoft Defender for Cloud is a rich, vulnerability assessment tool. A subset of this tool is Microsoft Defender for SQL, which can be used to discover and help remediate vulnerabilities in database settings, feature configuration, and permissions. It scans configuration against multiple benchmarks, including the CIS (Center for Information Security) benchmark.

It can not only be configured against native Azure components, such as SQL Server Managed Instances, Azure SQL Databases, and even CosmosDB, but it can also be configured to scan servers running SQL Server in a hybrid environment. The only requirement is that the SQL Server extension is installed and that there is a secure network path to Azure, such as a VPN or Express Route. This means that while Arc enabling a SQL Server instance is not a requirement in its own right, when you do this, the SQL extension is installed, meaning that you automatically have the ability to use Defender. Because this chapter focuses on the Arc use case, however, from this point, I will assume that the instance is Arc enabled.

Once a server has been registered in Azure Arc, you will be able to integrate the SQL Server instance with Azure Defender for Cloud. This gives you the ability to identify potential database vulnerabilities and also offers remediation advice. At the bottom of the resource, you will find a Microsoft Defender for Cloud option (see Figure 21-3). If you are not already consuming Azure Defender for Cloud, then the upgrade screen shown in Figure 21-15 will be displayed. This screen gives you a summary of costs and allows you to select the subscriptions that you want to protect.

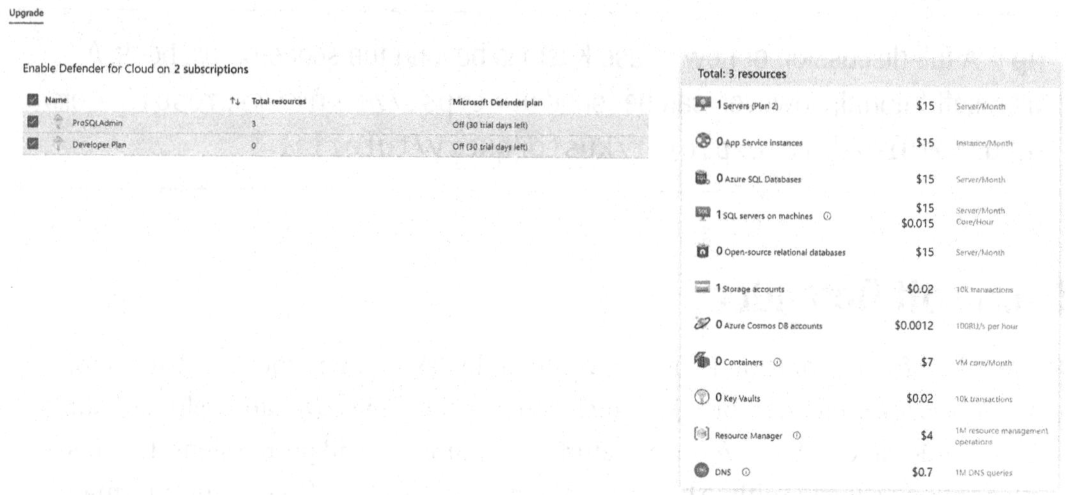

Upgrade

Figure 21-15. *Upgrade to Defender for Cloud*

After selecting the subscription(s) that you want to purchase Defender for, you will be able to specify the types of components that you want to protect with Defender. In this use case, we have selected Servers, Databases, and Storage, as shown in Figure 21-16.

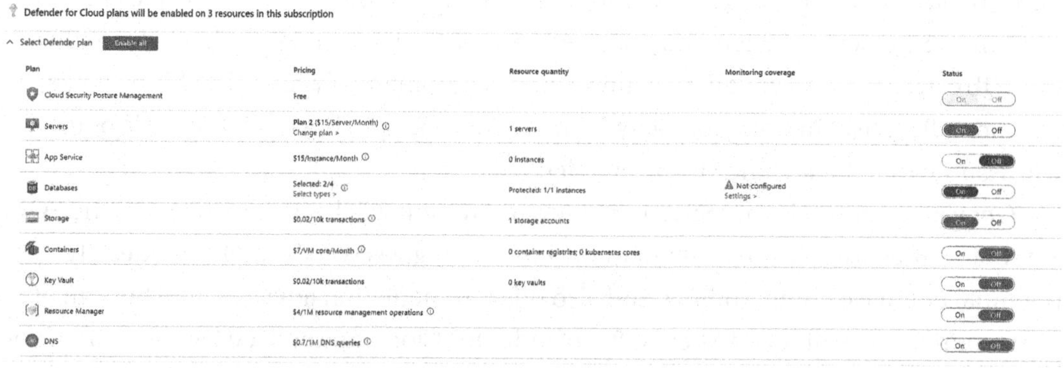

Figure 21-16. *Selecting Components to Protect*

The Databases category has an additional configuration menu in the pricing column, which allows you to choose the type of database(s) you wish to protect. For our use case, we will choose SQL Server on machines, as shown in Figure 21-17.

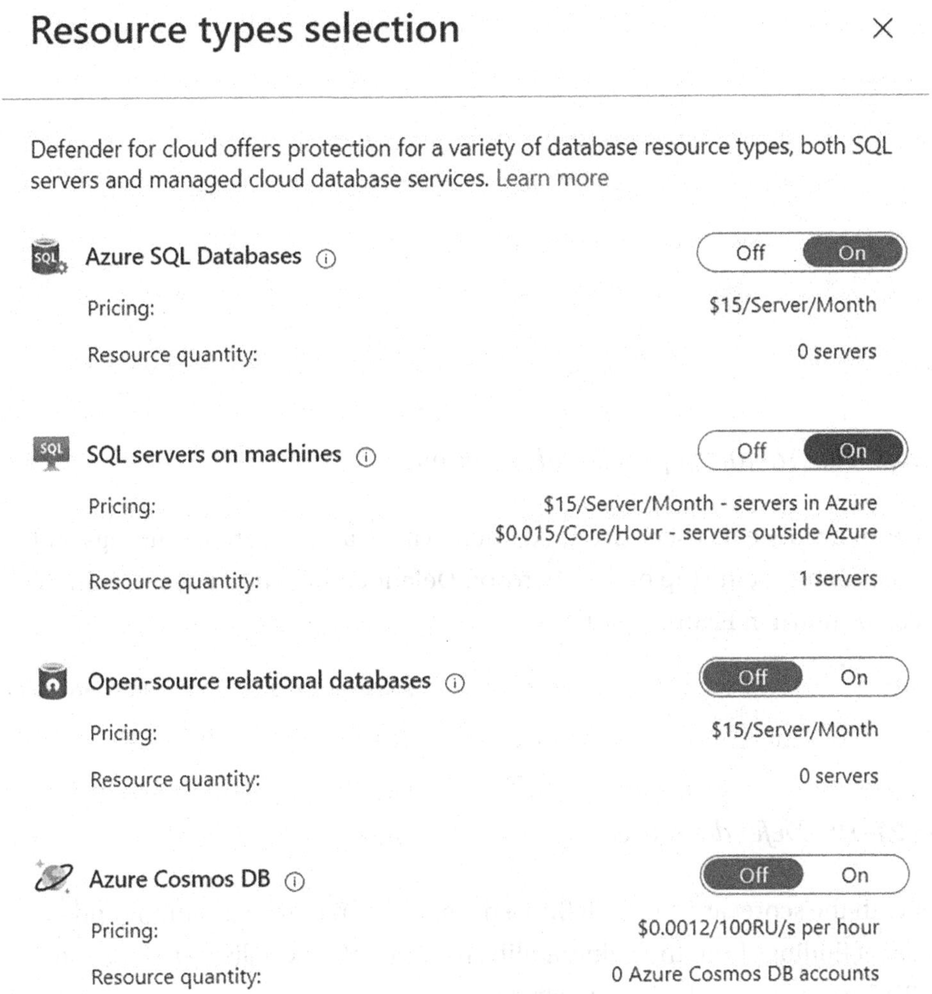

Resource types selection ✕

Defender for cloud offers protection for a variety of database resource types, both SQL servers and managed cloud database services. Learn more

Azure SQL Databases ⓘ

Off **On**

Pricing:	$15/Server/Month
Resource quantity:	0 servers

SQL servers on machines ⓘ

Off **On**

Pricing:	$15/Server/Month - servers in Azure
	$0.015/Core/Hour - servers outside Azure
Resource quantity:	1 servers

Open-source relational databases ⓘ

Off On

Pricing:	$15/Server/Month
Resource quantity:	0 servers

Azure Cosmos DB ⓘ

Off On

Pricing:	$0.0012/100RU/s per hour
Resource quantity:	0 Azure Cosmos DB accounts

***Figure 21-17.** Selecting database types*

In the Settings column, there is a link that will display a menu to configure provisioning. Figure 21-18 shows the advanced options menu, where we have selected to provision the Log Analytics agent.

Auto provisioning ···

🖫 Save

Auto provisioning - Extensions

Defender for Cloud collects security data and events from your resources and services to help you prevent, detect, and respond to threats.
When you enable an extension, it will be installed on any new or existing resource, by assigning a security policy. Learn more

Enable all extensions

Extension	Status	Resources missing extension	Description	Configuration
Log Analytics agent/Azure Monitor agent	On	-1 of 0 azure resources	Collects security-related configurations and event logs from the machine and stores the data in your Log Analytics workspace for analysis. Learn more	Agent Type: Azure Monitor Selected workspace: default workspace Security events: None Edit configuration
Vulnerability assessment for machines	Off	0 of 0 VMs & servers	Enables vulnerability assessment on your Azure and hybrid machines. Learn more	·
Guest Configuration agent (preview)	Off	0 of 0 virtual machines	Checks machines for security misconfigurations in the OS, applications, and environment settings. This deploys the agent to Azure virtual machines. Hybrid machines connected to Azure Arc already have this agent included in the Azure Connected Machine agent. Learn more about the Guest Configuration agent, in Understand Azure Policy's Guest Configuration.	·
Microsoft Defender for Containers components	Off	0 of 0 Kubernetes clusters	Deploys Defender for Containers components for environment hardening and run-time protections for your Azure, hybrid, and multi-cloud Kubernetes workloads. Learn more	·

Figure 21-18. *Advanced provisioning options*

Once an instance has been scanned, there will be a scorecard of findings and recommendations at the top of the Microsoft Defender for Cloud page, within the resource, as shown in Figure 21-19.

Recommendations	Security alerts	Findings	Enablement Status: **Enabled at the subscription-level** ⓘ
			Protection Status: **Protected** ✅ ⓘ
10 ❗	**0** ❗	**18** 🛡	

Figure 21-19. *Defender scorecard*

Beneath the scorecard, you will find a paged list of recommendations and a paged list of findings from the vulnerability assessment. These lists are illustrated in Figure 21-20 and Figure 21-21, respectively.

Recommendations

Defender for Cloud continuously monitors the configuration of your SQL Servers to identify potential security vulnerabilities and recommends actions to mitigate them.

Description	↑↓	Severity	↑↓
Machines should have a vulnerability assessment solution		⚠ Medium	
SQL servers on machines should have vulnerability findings resolved		❗ High	
File Integrity monitoring should be enabled on machines		❗ High	
Windows web servers should be configured to use secure communication protocols		❗ High	
Windows Defender Exploit Guard should be enabled on machines		⚠ Medium	

1   2   >

≔ View additional recommendations in Defender for Cloud >

Figure 21-20. *Defender recommendations*

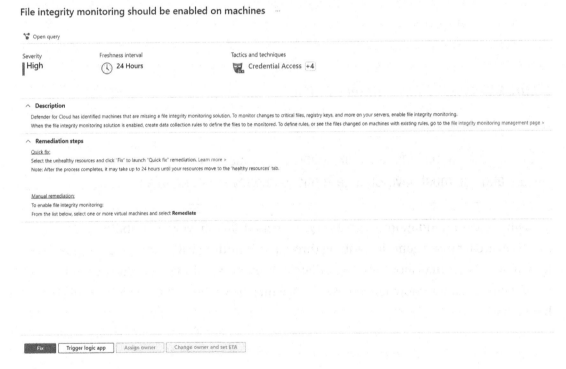

Vulnerability assessment findings

ID	Security Check	Applies to	Severity	
VA2108	Minimal set of principals should be members of fixed high impact database roles	3 of 5 resources	● High	
VA1058	'sa' login should be disabled	1 of 1 resources	● High	
VA1258	Database owners are as expected	1 of 1 resources	● High	
VA2120	Features that may affect security should be disabled	1 of 1 resources	● High	

Figure 21-21. *Defender findings*

Drilling through a recommendation will provide extra details, and in some cases, the ability to remediate. For example, drilling through the `File integrity monitoring should be enabled on machines` recommendation displays the full description and remediation steps, as shown in Figure 21-22.

File integrity monitoring should be enabled on machines   ⋯

👁 Open query

Severity	Freshness interval	Tactics and techniques
▌High	🕐 24 Hours	🦊 Credential Access +4

∧ **Description**

Defender for Cloud has identified machines that are missing a file integrity monitoring solution. To monitor changes to critical files, registry keys, and more on your servers, enable file integrity monitoring.

When the file integrity monitoring solution is enabled, create data collection rules to define the files to be monitored. To define rules, or see the files changed on machines with existing rules, go to the file integrity monitoring management page >

∧ **Remediation steps**

Quick fix:

Select the unhealthy resources and click "Fix" to launch "Quick fix" remediation. Learn more >

Note: After the process completes, it may take up to 24 hours until your resources move to the 'healthy resources' tab.

Manual remediation:

To enable file integrity monitoring:

From the list below, select one or more virtual machines and select **Remediate**

| Fix | Trigger logic app | Assign owner | Change owner and set ETA |

Figure 21-22. *File integrity monitoring recommendation*

You will note that this recommendation has a quick fix option. Clicking this button will display a confirmation window (Figure 21-23).

Fixing resources

Fix 1 resource

___

 This configures the change tracking extension for the Azure Monitor agent on the
selected machines. The change tracking extension is required for file integrity
monitoring. Learn more in Enable Change Tracking and Inventory .

Selected resources

  i-007aea894b5531f07

Figure 21-23. *Fix confirmation window*

___

Tip   In order to use the quick fix options, you must have an automation account in
Azure and you must have Change Tracking and Inventory enabled.

___

Other recommendations, such as SQL servers should have vulnerability findings
resolved, are far more generic. Drilling through this finding will display a subreport
for vulnerabilities that should be remediated. A filter that I find particularly useful is
the benchmark filter, shown in Figure 21-24, which gives the ability to filter results by
benchmark.

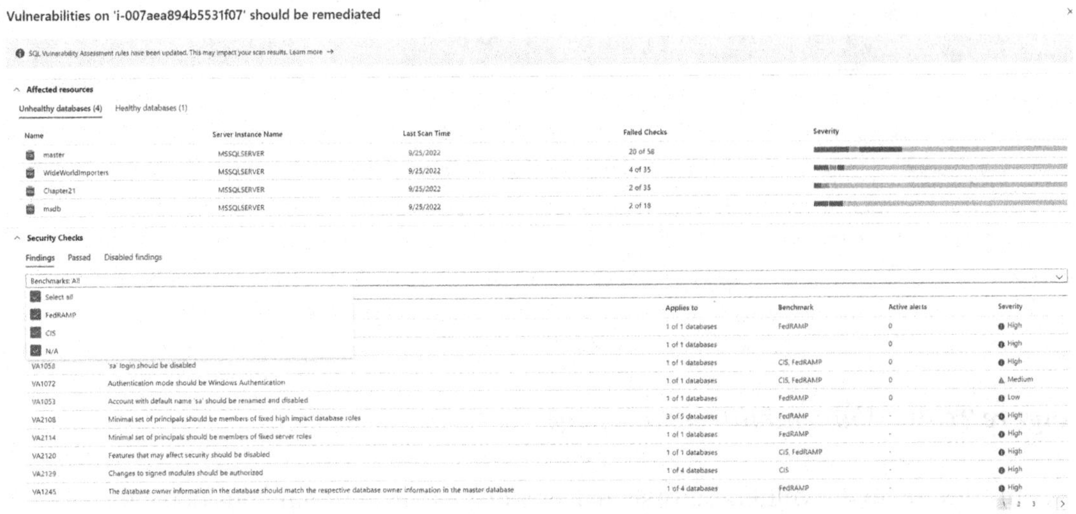

Figure 21-24. *Vulnerabilities that should be remediated subreport*

At the top of the report, you will see a list of databases, with a severity scorecard insight next to each. You can also filter the list of security checks, by clicking one of these databases. For example, the security checks in Figure 21-25 show the list filtered by the Chapter21 database.

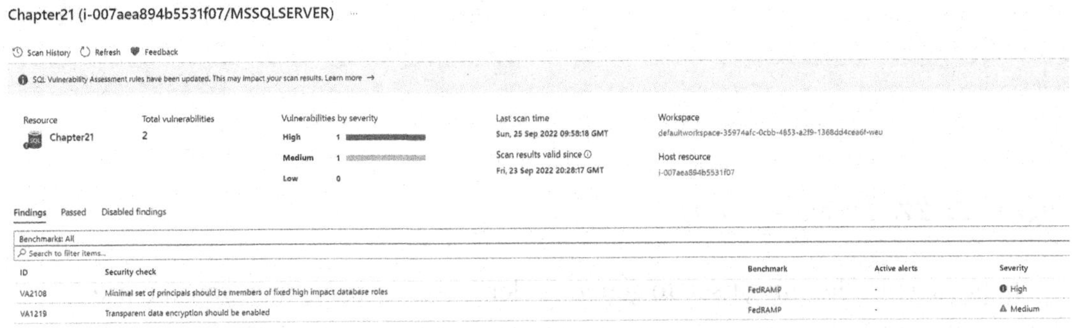

Figure 21-25. *Vulnerabilities filtered by database*

You can drill through a vulnerability to view additional information, including a description of the issue, the potential impact of the current configuration, the benchmark(s) which require the configuration, remediation instructions (although this is often a link to Microsoft Docs), and the query that is used to determine the result of the security check. This is shown in Figure 21-26 for the TDE not enabled vulnerability, which violates the FedRAMP benchmark.

VA1219 - Transparent data encryption should be enabled ···

Severity	Status	Scan time
⚠ Medium	⊗ Unhealthy	9/25/2022

Description

Transparent data encryption (TDE) helps to protect the database files against information disclosure by performing real-time encryption and decryption of the database, associated backups, and transaction log files 'at rest', without requiring changes to the application. This rule checks that TDE is enabled on the database.

Impact

Transparent Data Encryption (TDE) protects data 'at rest', meaning the data and log files are encrypted when stored on disk.

Benchmark

- FedRAMP

Remediation

Enable TDE on the affected database. Please follow the instructions on https://docs.microsoft.com/en-us/sql/relational-databases/security/encryption/transparent-data-encryption

There is no remediation script for this rule.

Query and results ⓘ

```
1   SELECT CASE WHEN EXISTS
2   ( SELECT *
3       FROM sys.databases
4       WHERE name = db_name()
5       AND is_encrypted = 0)
6   THEN 1
7   ELSE 0
8   END AS [Violation]
```

[Add all results as baseline]   [Remove all from baseline]

Status	Violation
⊗ Not in Baseline	True

Figure 21-26. *Vulnerability details page*

In addition to the vulnerability scan, Defender also uses anomalous behavior detection to alert you if there is suspicious activity on a server that could imply an attack, or preattack is in progress. Figure 21-27 uses sample alerts to demonstrate what these alerts may look like, if you are under attack.

🛡 8	☀ 8	⟳ 0	⊕ 1	Open alerts by severity
Open alerts	Active alerts	In progress alerts	Affected resources	▌High (6) ▌Medium (2)

	Severity ↓	Alert title ↑↓	Affected resource ↑↓	Resource Group ↑↓	Activity start time (UTC+1) ↑↓	MITRE ATT&CK® tactics	Status ↑↓
☐	High	🛡 Suspected successful brute force attack Sample alert	🖥 Sample-VM	Sample-RG	09/25/22, 11:48 AM	⬡ Pre-attack	Active
☐	High	🛡 Potential SQL Injection Sample alert	🖥 Sample-VM	Sample-RG	09/25/22, 11:48 AM	⬡ Pre-attack	Active
☐	High	🛡 Attempted logon by a potentially harmful appl... Sample alert	🖥 Sample-VM	Sample-RG	06/25/22, 11:48 AM	⬡ Pre-attack	Active
☐	High	🛡 Suspected successful brute force attack Sample alert	🖥 Sample-VM	Sample-RG	09/25/22, 11:43 AM	⬡ Pre-attack	Active
☐	High	🛡 Potential SQL Injection Sample alert	🖥 Sample-VM	Sample-RG	09/25/22, 11:43 AM	⬡ Pre-attack	Active
☐	High	🛡 Attempted logon by a potentially harmful appl... Sample alert	🖥 Sample-VM	Sample-RG	09/25/22, 11:43 AM	⬡ Pre-attack	Active
☐	Medium	🛡 Login from a suspicious IP Sample alert	🖥 Sample-VM	Sample-RG	09/25/22, 11:48 AM	⬡ Pre-attack	Active
☐	Medium	🛡 Login from a suspicious IP Sample alert	🖥 Sample-VM	Sample-RG	09/25/22, 11:43 AM	⬡ Pre-attack	Active

Figure 21-27. *Defender alerts*

If the machine learning used to generate alerts gets it wrong, then you can use the Suppression Rules screen to create suppression rules for the alerts. For example, Figure 21-28 shows a suppression rule which will suppress the `Login from a suspicious IP` alert, should the connection be made from the IP address 10.0.0.1, because we know this address to be safe.

New suppression rule   ✕

Create suppression rule in order to automatically dismiss alerts by pre-defined conditions. Learn more >

∧ **Rule Conditions**

Subscription *

| ProSQLAdmin   ∨ |

Alerts * ⓘ
◉ Custom   ○ All

| [SAMPLE ALERT] Login from a suspicious IP   ∨ |

Entities ⓘ

| IP   ∨ | Address ∨ | In   ∨ | 10.0.0.1   ∨ | 🗑 |

+

∧ **Rule details**

Rule name * ⓘ

| Allow_Connections_from_safe_IP   ✓ |

State *

| Enabled   ∨ |

Reason *

| The alert detecting normal activity on specific entity ∨ |

Comment

| This is a known IP Address   ✓ |

Rule expiration
Set an end date and time for this rule ⓘ

| 03/24/2023   📅 | 10:58:17 AM |

Test your rule | Simulate |

Figure 21-28. *Create a suppression rule*

Drilling through `Microsoft Defender for Cloud` ➤ `Environmental Settings` and choosing `Email notifications` allows you to configure e-mail notification for security alerts, as shown in Figure 21-29. Here, you can choose who should receive the notifications and what is the minimum level of severity, to which they should be notified.

🖫 Save

Email recipients

Select who'll get the email notifications from Defender for Cloud for the ProSQLAdmin subscription.

All users with the following roles

| Owner, AccountAdmin | ⌄ |

Additional email addresses (separated by commas)

| pete@prosqladmin.com | ✓ |

Notification types

Use the settings below to select the type of email notifications to be sent by Defender for Cloud.

☑ Notify about alerts with the following severity (or higher):

| Medium | ⌄ |

ℹ You'll receive a maximum of one email per 6 hours for high-severity alerts, one email per 12 hours for medium-severity alerts, and one email per 24 hours for low-severity alerts. Learn more >

Figure 21-29. *Configure e-mail notifications*

Summary

Registering a SQL Server instance with Azure Arc is possible with supported versions of SQL Server, but doing so is a manual process, which involves running scripts and installing agents on your server. SQL Server 2022 makes the process far more simple, by building Arc registration into the SQL Server setup.

Once registered in Arc, the resource appears as a resource in your designated Azure resource group. This opens up many possibilities, including using Environmental Health/SQL Best Practice Assessment and Azure Defender for Cloud.

Tip Although beyond the scope of this book, Arc-registered SQL Server instances can also be integrated with Azure Purview.

SQL BPA runs hundreds of checks against the full stack to ensure that your SQL Server environment is configured to best practices. SQL BPA provides a rich reporting interface, with drill-throughs that allow you to easily target the highest priority issues. It also provides trend analysis, so that you can keep track of the issues being addressed over time. This can feed into agile project methodology or BAU metrics.

Azure Defender for Cloud protects SQL Server workloads, both with vulnerability assessments and machine learning that alerts when anomalous activity is detected. The assessment provides drill-through reports, with the bottom level containing full details, including a description of the finding, the potential impact, and suggested remedial actions. In some instances, a quick fix feature is provided that allows you to resolve the issue directly from within Defender, although this does require addition agent installation and an Azure automation account.

The attack scanning provides alerts in situations such as brute-force attacks, SQL injection attacks, and access from unexpected IP addresses. These alerts appear in the Defender console, but can also be sent to members of Azure subscription roles, such as Owner or Contributor. Alerts can also be suppressed if the anomaly detection has made an error.

CHAPTER 22

Query Store

The Query Store captures the history of queries, their plans, and statistics. It allows DBAs to easily view the plans that were used by queries and troubleshoot performance issues. In this chapter, we will discuss how Query Store can be enabled and configured. We will also examine how the Query Store can be used to diagnose and resolve performance issues.

Enabling and Configuring Query Store

Query Store is enabled and configured at the database level, so the first thing we will do is create a database, called Chapter22. This can be achieved using the script in Listing 22-1.

Listing 22-1. Create the Chapter22 Database

```
--Create the database

CREATE DATABASE Chapter22 ;
GO

USE Chapter22
GO

--Create and populate numbers table

DECLARE @Numbers TABLE
(
        Number          INT
)

;WITH CTE(Number)
AS
```

© Peter A. Carter 2023
P. A. Carter, *Pro SQL Server 2022 Administration*, https://doi.org/10.1007/978-1-4842-8864-1_22

```
(
        SELECT 1 Number
        UNION ALL
        SELECT Number + 1
        FROM CTE
        WHERE Number < 100
)
INSERT INTO @Numbers
SELECT Number FROM CTE;

--Create and populate name pieces

DECLARE @Names TABLE
(
        FirstName        VARCHAR(30),
        LastName         VARCHAR(30)
);

INSERT INTO @Names
VALUES('Peter', 'Carter'),
                ('Michael', 'Smith'),
                ('Danielle', 'Mead'),
                ('Reuben', 'Roberts'),
                ('Iris', 'Jones'),
                ('Sylvia', 'Davies'),
                ('Finola', 'Wright'),
                ('Edward', 'James'),
                ('Marie', 'Andrews'),
                ('Jennifer', 'Abraham');

--Create and populate Customers table

CREATE TABLE dbo.Customers
(
    CustomerID           INT            NOT NULL     IDENTITY    PRIMARY KEY,
    FirstName            VARCHAR(30)    NOT NULL,
    LastName             VARCHAR(30)    NOT NULL,
    BillingAddressID     INT            NOT NULL,
```

```
    DeliveryAddressID INT              NOT NULL,
    CreditLimit       MONEY            NOT NULL,
    Balance           MONEY            NOT NULL
);

SELECT * INTO #Customers
FROM
        (SELECT
                (SELECT TOP 1 FirstName FROM @Names ORDER BY NEWID()) FirstName,
                (SELECT TOP 1 LastName FROM @Names ORDER BY NEWID()) LastName,
                 (SELECT TOP 1 Number FROM @Numbers ORDER BY NEWID())
                 BillingAddressID,
                 (SELECT TOP 1 Number FROM @Numbers ORDER BY NEWID())
                 DeliveryAddressID,
                 (SELECT TOP 1 CAST(RAND() * Number AS INT) * 10000
                 FROM @Numbers
                 ORDER BY NEWID()) CreditLimit,
                 (SELECT TOP 1 CAST(RAND() * Number AS INT) * 9000
                 FROM @Numbers
                 ORDER BY NEWID()) Balance
        FROM @Numbers a
        CROSS JOIN @Numbers b
) a;

INSERT INTO dbo.Customers
SELECT * FROM #Customers;
GO

CREATE INDEX idx_LastName ON dbo.Customers(LastName)
GO
```

In SQL Server 2022, Query Store is enabled, by default, for all new databases that are created. If you need to turn Query Store on, however, either because you have turned it off or because you have restored a database from an older version of SQL Server, you can do so, using the command in Listing 22-2.

Listing 22-2. Enable Query Store

```
ALTER DATABASE Chapter22 SET QUERY_STORE = ON
```

As well as enabling Query Store using an ALTER DATABASE command, this method is also used to configure Query Store properties. Table 22-1 details the Query Store-related SET options that are available.

Table 22-1. *Query Store SET Options*

SET Option	Description
ON	Enables the Query Store for the specified database.
OFF	Disables the Query Store for the specified database.
CLEAR	Clears the contents of the Query Store.
OPERATION_MODE	Can be configured as READ_ONLY, or the default of READ_WRITE. When configured as READ_WRITE, data is written to the Query Store and can be read from the Query Store. When set to READ_ONLY, data can still be read from the Query Store, but no further data will be written to it. The Query Store will automatically switch to READ_ONLY, if it runs out of space for storing new data.
CLEANUP_POLICY	Accepts STALE_QUERY_THRESHOLD_DAYS and a number of days. This determines how many days data for each query should be retained.
DATA_FLUSH_INTERVAL_SECONDS	Query Store data is flushed to disk asynchronously. DATA_FLUSH_INTERVAL_SECONDS specifies how frequently data should be flushed.
MAX_STORAGE_SIZE_MB	Specifies the maximum amount of space that can be used by Query Store data. If this value overflows, the Query Store will switch to READ_ONLY operational mode.
INTERVAL_LENGTH_MINUTES	Specifies the time interval at which runtime execution statistics data is aggregated.

(continued)

Table 22-1. (*continued*)

SET Option	Description
SIZE_BASED_CLEANUP_MODE	Specifies if an automatic cleanup is triggered, when the Query Store reaches 90% of its maximum size threshold. Can be set to AUTO or OFF. When set to AUTO, the oldest, least expensive queries will be removed, until the size drops to around 80% of the Query Store's maximum size threshold.
QUERY_CAPTURE_MODE	Specifies which queries data should be captured for. Can be configured as ALL, NONE, AUTO, or CUSTOM. When set to ALL, statistics will be captured for all queries. When set to NONE, statistics will only be captured for queries which already exist in the Query Store. When configured as AUTO, SQL Server will capture statistics for the most expensive queries, based on execution count and resource utilization. When configured as CUSTOM, then you will have more granular control over which queries have statistics captured. When CUSTOM is specified, QUERY_CAPTURE_POLICY should also be specified.
MAX_PLANS_PER_QUERY	Specifies the maximum number of plans that will be captured for each query, defaulting to 200.
WAIT_STATS_CAPTURE_MODE	Specifies if wait statistics should be captured for queries. This is, of course, very useful, but comes at the expense of extra disk space consumed.
QUERY_CAPTURE_POLICY	Can be used when QUERY_CAPTURE_MODE is set to CUSTOM. Please see Table 22-2 for details of the available options that can be passed.

Table 22-2 details the options that can be configured for QUERY_CAPTURE_POLICY.

Table 22-2. *QUERY_CAPTURE_POLICY Options*

Option	Description
STALE_CAPTURE_POLICY_THRESHOLD	Specifies an evaluation period, which is used by the other parameters, to determine if a query should have its statistics captured. Can be specified in hours, or days
EXECUTION_COUNT	Specifies the minimum number of executions within the evaluation period that should occur, for a query to be captured
TOTAL_COMPILE_CPU_TIME_MS	Specifies the total amount of CPU Compilation Time within the evaluation period that should occur, for a query to be captured
TOTAL_EXECUTION_CPU_TIME_MS	Specifies the total amount of CPU Execution Time within the evaluation period that should occur, for a query to be captured

Let's use the command in Listing 22-3 to configure the Query Store for the Chapter22 database. Here, we are configuring the Query Store to retain data for 30 days, persist data to disk every five minutes, capture wait statistics for queries, and run an automatic cleanup when 90% of a 2GB threshold is reached.

Listing 22-3. Configure the Query Store

```
ALTER DATABASE Chapter22
SET QUERY_STORE = ON (
        OPERATION_MODE = READ_WRITE,
        CLEANUP_POLICY = ( STALE_QUERY_THRESHOLD_DAYS = 30 ),
        DATA_FLUSH_INTERVAL_SECONDS = 300,
        MAX_STORAGE_SIZE_MB = 2048,
        SIZE_BASED_CLEANUP_MODE = AUTO,
        WAIT_STATS_CAPTURE_MODE = ON
) ;
```

The Query Store can also be configured using SSMS. To do this, drill through Databases in Object Explorer and select Properties from the context menu of the database, for which you wish to configure the Query Store. In the Properties page, you can select the Query Store tab, which is illustrated in Figure 22-1.

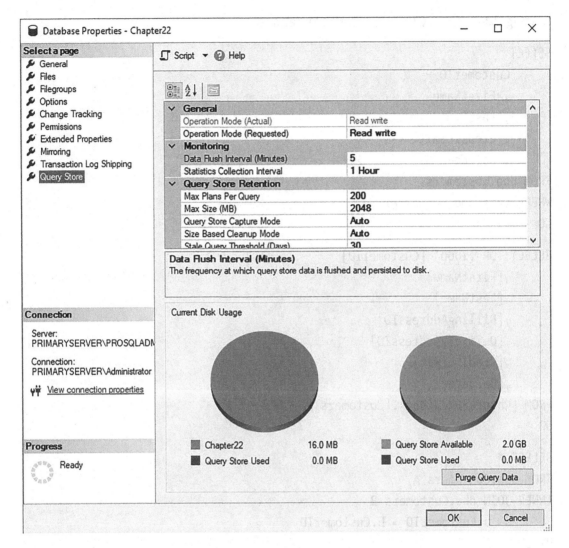

Figure 22-1. *Query Store Properties tab*

Working with Query Store Data

Before we can see how to work with Query Store data, we will first need to run some queries, so that the Query Store has some data to collect. The script in Listing 22-4 will run a number of queries against the Chapter22 database.

Listing 22-4. Query the Chapter22 Database

```
SELECT
      CustomerID
      , FirstName
      , LastName
      , CreditLimit
      , Balance
FROM dbo.Customers
WHERE LastName = 'Carter'
GO

SELECT TOP (1000) [CustomerID]
      ,[FirstName]
      ,[LastName]
      ,[BillingAddressID]
      ,[DeliveryAddressID]
      ,[CreditLimit]
      ,[Balance]
FROM [Chapter22].[dbo].[Customers]
GO

SELECT *
FROM dbo.Customers A
INNER JOIN dbo.Customers B
      ON a.CustomerID = b.CustomerID
UNION
SELECT *
FROM dbo.Customers A
INNER JOIN dbo.Customers B
      ON a.CustomerID = b.CustomerID
GO
```

Query Store Reports

Now we have run some queries, the Query Store will have captured data about those queries. We can view this data through a series of SSMS reports. The standard reports are

- View Regressed Queries

- View Overall Resource Consumption

- View Queries with Forced Plans

- View Queries with High Variation

- Query Wait Statistics

- View Tracked Queries

These reports can be accessed by drilling through Databases ➤ [Database Name] and then selecting the appropriate report from the context menu of the Query Store node. In this chapter, we will examine some of the reports that I find most useful, but I encourage you to experiment with all of them.

Tip   Because of the nature of the reports, when you first set up Query Store, there will be very little data. The data points will grow as time moves forward after Query Store is enabled.

The View Overall Resource Consumption report is illustrated in Figure 22-2. This report consists of four charts, representing execution duration, execution count, CPU Time, and Logical Reads, aggregated over time intervals.

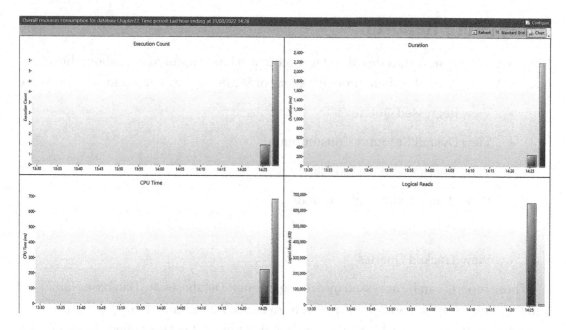

Figure 22-2. *Overall Resource Consumption*

Hovering your mouse over a bar will cause a box with further details to be displayed, as you can see in Figure 22-3.

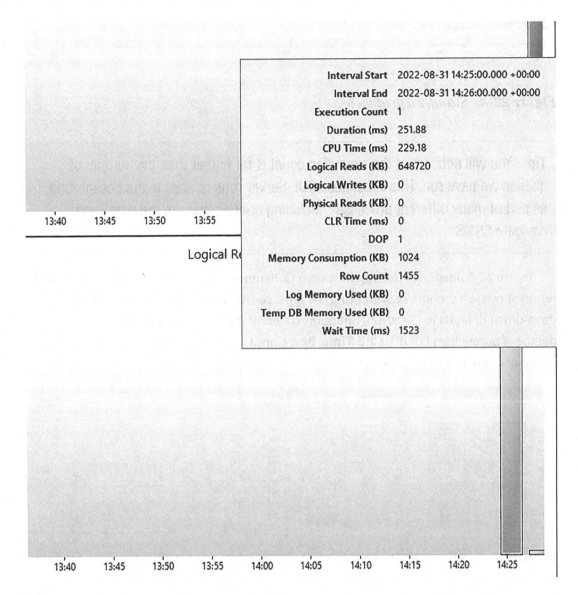

Interval Start	2022-08-31 14:25:00.000 +00:00
Interval End	2022-08-31 14:26:00.000 +00:00
Execution Count	1
Duration (ms)	251.88
CPU Time (ms)	229.18
Logical Reads (KB)	648720
Logical Writes (KB)	0
Physical Reads (KB)	0
CLR Time (ms)	0
DOP	1
Memory Consumption (KB)	1024
Row Count	1455
Log Memory Used (KB)	0
Temp DB Memory Used (KB)	0
Wait Time (ms)	1523

Figure 22-3. Viewing additional details

Clicking the Standard Grid button will replace the bar charts with a grid, with one row per time interval, showing aggregated runtime statistics. This grid can be copied to Excel for further analysis. The grid is illustrated in Figure 22-4.

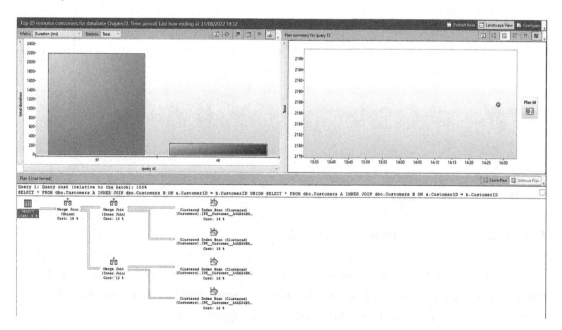

Figure 22-4. *Standard grid view*

Tip   You will notice that the execution count is far higher than the number of queries we have run. This is because SQL Server runs queries in the background, as part of many different processes, including queries that are run when you navigate SSMS.

Figure 22-5 illustrates the Top Resource Consumers report. The top-left corner of this report shows a bar chart, representing the most resource-intensive queries. The Metric drop-down defaults to Duration, but many different metrics can be selected, including degree of parallelism (DOP), CPU Time, Row Count, Wait Time even CLR Time, or Log Memory Used, to name but a few.

Figure 22-5. *Top Resource Consumers*

The top-right corner of the report shows a scatter chart, detailing resource utilization and execution time of each plan. This is helpful when a query has been executed using multiple plans, as you can easily assess the most efficient plans for a query.

The bottom half of the plan shows the accrual execution plan that was used. As with any other graphical query plan representation in SSMS, hovering over a physical operator will show cost information for that operator.

The front page of the Query Wait Statistics report can be seen in Figure 22-6. The bar chart at the top of the screen shows a summary of resources that the highest cumulative wait times have been against.

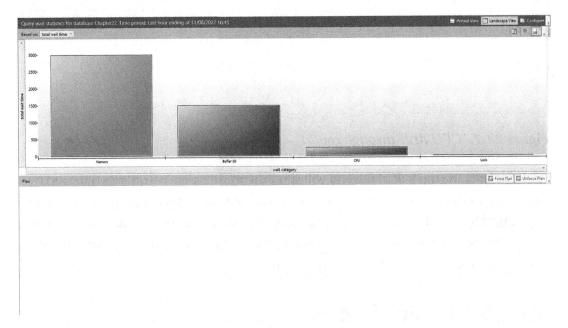

Figure 22-6. *Query Wait Statistics report*

Each bar in the bar chart is clickable. For example, if I were to click the CPU bar, then the drill-through report in Figure 22-7 would be displayed.

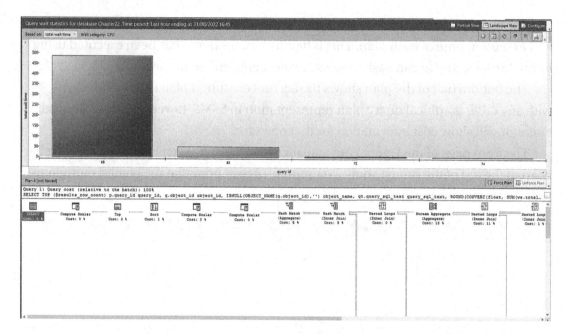

Figure 22-7. *CPU drill-through report*

By default, the top half of the grid will show the most expensive queries (labelled by Plan ID), based on Total Wait Time, but as you can see, the Based on drop-down list can be changed to base the results on average, min, max wait time, or the standard deviation.

The lower half of the report shows the graphical representation of the Query Plan that has been selected in the top half of the report.

Query Store T-SQL Objects

As well as graphical reports, SQL Server also exposes a number of catalog views which can be used to retrieve Query Store data. Table 22-3 details the catalog views which are exposed.

Table 22-3. *Query Store Catalog Views*

Catalog View	Description
Query_store_plan	Stores information about every query plan that is associated with a query.
Query_store_query	Stores query information and aggregated runtime statistics.
Query_store_wait_stats	Stores wait statistic details. Please see Table 22-4 for mappings of each wait type.
Query_store_query_text	Stores the SQL handle and SQL text of each query.
Query_store_runtime_ stats	Stores the runtime statistics for each query.

Table 22-4 details how each wait type category maps to underlying wait types.

Table 22-4. *Wait Statistics Mappings*

Wait Category	Wait Types
CPU	SOS_SCHEDULER_YIELD
Worker Thread	THREADPOOL
Lock	LCK_M_*
Latch	LATCH_*
Buffer Latch	PAGELATCH_*
Buffer IO	PAGEIOLATCH_*
SQL CLR	CLR*
	SQLCLR*
Mirroring	DBMIRROR*
Transaction	ACT*
	DTC*
	TRAN_MARKLATCH_*
	MSQL_XACT_*
	TRANSACTION_MUTEX

(continued)

Table 22-4. (*continued*)

Wait Category	Wait Types
Idle	SLEEP_*
	LAZYWRITER_SLEEP
	SQLTRACE_BUFFER_FLUSH
	SQLTRACE_INCREMENTAL_FLUSH_SLEEP
	SQLTRACE_WAIT_ENTRIES
	FT_IFTS_SCHEDULER_IDLE_WAIT
	XE_DISPATCHER_WAIT
	REQUEST_FOR_DEADLOCK_SEARCH
	LOGMGR_QUEUE
	ONDEMAND_TASK_QUEUE
	CHECKPOINT_QUEUE
	XE_TIMER_EVENT
Preemptive (Preemptive IO)	PREEMPTIVE_*
Service Broker	BROKER_*
Transaction Log IO	LOGMGR
	LOGBUFFER
	LOGMGR_RESERVE_APPEND
	LOGMGR_FLUSH
	LOGMGR_PMM_LOG
	CHKPT
	WRITELOG
Network IO	ASYNC_NETWORK_IO
	NET_WAITFOR_PACKET
	PROXY_NETWORK_IO
	EXTERNAL_SCRIPT_NETWORK_IOF
Parallelism	CXPACKET
	EXCHANGE

(*continued*)

Table 22-4. (*continued*)

Wait Category	Wait Types
Memory	RESOURCE_SEMAPHORE, CMEMTHREAD CMEMPARTITIONED, EE_PMOLOCK MEMORY_ALLOCATION_EXT RESERVED_MEMORY_ALLOCATION_EXT MEMORY_GRANT_UPDATE
User Wait	WAITFOR WAIT_FOR_RESULTS BROKER_RECEIVE_WAITFOR
Tracing	TRACEWRITE SQLTRACE_LOCK SQLTRACE_FILE_BUFFER SQLTRACE_FILE_WRITE_IO_COMPLETION SQLTRACE_FILE_READ_IO_COMPLETION SQLTRACE_PENDING_BUFFER_WRITERS, SQLTRACE_SHUTDOWN, QUERY_TRACEOUT TRACE_EVTNOTIFF
Full Text Search	FT_RESTART_CRAWL FULLTEXT GATHERER MSSEARCH FT_METADATA_MUTEX FT_IFTSHC_MUTEX FT_IFTSISM_MUTEX FT_IFTS_RWLOCK FT_COMPROWSET_RWLOCK FT_MASTER_MERGE FT_PROPERTYLIST_CACHE FT_MASTER_MERGE_COORDINATOR PWAIT_RESOURCE_SEMAPHORE_FT_PARALLEL_QUERY_SYNC

(*continued*)

Table 22-4. (*continued*)

Wait Category	Wait Types
Other IO	ASYNC_IO_COMPLETION, IO_COMPLETION BACKUPIO, WRITE_COMPLETION IO_QUEUE_LIMIT IO_RETRY
Replication	SE_REPL_* REPL_*, HADR_* PWAIT_HADR_*, REPLICA_WRITES FCB_REPLICA_WRITE, FCB_REPLICA_READ PWAIT_HADRSIM
Log Rate Governor	LOG_RATE_GOVERNOR POOL_LOG_RATE_GOVERNOR HADR_THROTTLE_LOG_RATE_GOVERNOR INSTANCE_LOG_RATE_GOVERNOR

*Denotes a wildcard, where all waits that match the portion to the left of the * are included*

Tip   Idle and User Wait are unlike other Wait Type Categories, in the respect that they are not waiting for a resource, they are waiting for work to do.

For example, the query in Listing 22-5 will return the three highest wait categories, by total wait time, excluding idle and user waits, which are "healthy" waits.

Listing 22-5. Return Top 3 Wait Types

```
SELECT TOP 3
        wait_category_desc
      , SUM(total_query_wait_time_ms) TotalWaitTime
FROM sys.query_store_wait_stats
WHERE wait_category_desc NOT IN ('Idle', 'User Wait')
GROUP BY wait_category_desc
ORDER BY SUM(total_query_wait_time_ms) DESC
```

Resolving Issues with Query Store

Figure 22-8 illustrates the Regressed Query report. This report displays queries, the impact of which, in terms of duration, or execution count have increased over time. These queries are illustrated with a bar chart in the top left of the report. The top right of the report illustrates the plans that have been used to execute the query, with their associated duration. At the bottom of the report, we can see the actual execution plan for the current selection of query, and plan in the top half of the screen.

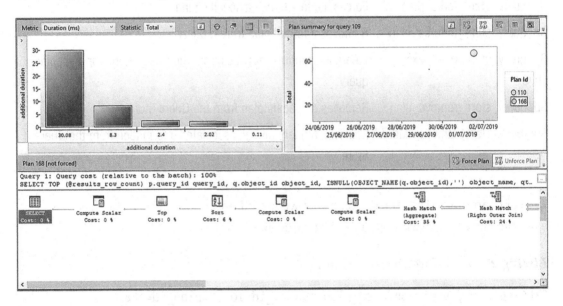

Figure 22-8. *Regressed Query report*

In this particular example, we can see that the query has run using two distinct plans and that the plan with an ID of 168 took significantly less time to execute than the plan with an ID of 110. Therefore, with the more efficient plan selected, we can use the Force Plan button, in the middle of the report, to ensure that the more efficient plan is always used to execute this query. Once we have used this feature, the Unforce Plan button will become active, allowing us to undo our action, if required.

Tip   The Force and Unforce buttons are available on all Query Store reports, where a specific plan is selectable.

As well as using the GUI to impart performance improvements on queries, there are also a number of system stored procedures exposed. These procedures are detailed in Table 22-5 and can be used to manage both plans and the Query Store itself.

Table 22-5. *Query Store Stored Procedures*

Procedure	Description
Sp_quey_store_flush_db	Flushes Query Store data to disk
Sp_query_store_force_plan	Forces a query to use a specific plan
Sp_query_store_unforce_plan	Removes a forced plan from a query
Sp_query_store_reset_exec_stats	Clears the runtime statistics from the Query Store, for a specific query
Sp_query_store_remove_plan	Removes a specific plan from the Query Store
Sp_query_store_remove_query	Removes a query and all associated information from the Query Store

For example, to Unforce the plan that we forced upon our query in the previous example, we could use the query in Listing 22-6.

Listing 22-6. Unforce a Query Plan

```
EXEC sp_query_store_unforce_plan @query_id=109, @plan_id=168
```

Query Store Hints

Unlike many other languages, T-SQL is a descriptive and declarative language. This means, when writing a query, that instead of telling the database engine exactly what to do, you describe the results that you want to receive and the query optimizer figures out the best way to deliver those results. The query optimizer is incredibly good at deciding the best way to do something, but if it does make a mistake, it can have a negative impact on query performance.

This is where query hints come in. A query hint allows you to force the optimizer down a specific route. For example, you might tell it that it should recompile the query every time it runs. Alternatively, you may tell it to always use a certain type of physical join operation, or to always use a specific MAXDOP.

The challenge with query hints is that you are not always able to modify the code, which means that you cannot add a query hint to the query. This may be because the code belongs to a third party and support agreements do not allow for code changes, or it could be because there is an urgent performance issue and code release procedures are simply too cumbersome to resolve the issue in a timely manner.

To address this, SQL Server introduced plan guides, where you could specify a statement and one or more query hints that should always be applied, whenever that query runs. You could even use plan freezing, where you specified the USE PLAN hint, and then pass a specific query plan that you wanted to be used. The problem with plan guides is that they are far from user friendly and generally required a highly experienced DBA to create them. SQL Server 2022 resolves this issue with query store hints, which give DBAs the opportunity to specify query hints in a much more friendly way.

If you are trying to address a performance issue with a query and need to specify a query hint, then you can use query store functionality to add a query hint. For example, imagine that your performance troubleshooting has uncovered that a Nested Loops join operator is not the ideal choice for the plan illustrated in Figure 22-9.

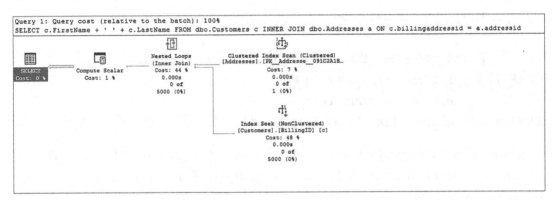

Figure 22-9. *Suboptimal hash match*

Tip I have used a simple example to illustrate the concept. In reality, this specific plan would be highly unlikely to need a query hint, as Intelligent Query Processing would alter the physical join operator dynamically, based on the inputs.

Because the optimizer is so good, I always advise working with the optimizer, rather than against it. Therefore, in this case, instead of using a query hint to force the optimizer to use a Merge Join, which is the natural inclination of many DBAs, I would advise using query hints to tell the optimizer to use either a Merge Join operation or a Hash Match operation. This translates to "Nested Loops is wrong. Use anything except this." The optimizer can then select the best option from its remaining choices.

We will then need to retrieve the Query ID from the query store. We can do this using the reports discussed earlier in this chapter, or we can use the query store catalog views to retrieve it. The query in Listing 22-7 will retrieve a list of queries and Query IDs for tracked queries that have been run against the dbo.Customers table. The query also returns useful compilation statistics.

Listing 22-7. Retrieve Query IDs

```
SELECT
        q.query_id
    , t.query_sql_text
    , q.avg_compile_duration
    , q.avg_optimize_duration
    , q.last_execution_timeFROM sys.query_store_query_text T
INNER JOIN sys.query_store_query q ON
    t.query_text_id = q.query_text_id
WHERE query_sql_text like '%dbo.Customers%'
```

Once we have the Query ID, we can use the sp_query_store_set_hints stored procedure, as shown in Listing 22-8, where the Query ID of the query with the suboptimal plan is 86.

Listing 22-8. Apply a Query Store Hint

```
EXEC sys.sp_query_store_set_hints
    @query_id= 86
    , @query_hints = N'OPTION(HASH JOIN, MERGE JOIN)'
```

A nice safety feature of query store hints is that it will ignore any hint that stops it from running, as opposed to blocking the query. Therefore, you cannot inadvertently break a query. The query store hints will also override any query hints or plan guides that conflict with it.

You can retrieve a list of query store hints, including any failures to apply hints, from the query_store_query_hints catalog view, as demonstrated in Listing 22-9.

Listing 22-9. Retrieve a List of Query Store Hints

```
SELECT
        query_id
      , query_hint_text
      , last_query_hint_failure_reason_desc
FROM sys.query_store_query_hints
```

The command in Listing 22-10 demonstrates how to remove the query store hint associated with our problematic query earlier.

Listing 22-10. Remove Query Store Hints

```
EXEC sys.sp_query_store_clear_hints @query_id = 86
```

Summary

The Query Store is a very powerful feature of SQL Server, which allows DBAs to monitor the performance of specific queries and their plans. Because the data is flushed to disk, this means that the data persists, even after an instance is restarted.

Six standard reports are available, which allow DBAs to view information such as regressed queries, the most resource-intensive queries, or even wait statistics, by query.

As well as viewing problematic queries, DBAs can also force the most performant plan to be used. This can be achieved through the interactive reports, or via automation, using T-SQL. The automated approach would examine the Query Store data through the catalog views and then pass the relevant data to the parameters of system stored procedures.

SQL Server gives DBAs granular control over which queries are captured by Query Store. This is implemented with custom capture policies, where details such as execution count and execution time can be used to capture only the queries with the highest performance impact. This not only saves disk space but also avoids "noise" when working with the captured data.

In SQL Server 2022, query store has been enhanced to include query store hints, which make it easy and safe for a DBA to use query hints to resolve performance issues, without the need to edit the code. SQL Server 2022 also introduces the ability to use query store on Secondary Availability Replicas, but at the time of writing, this feature was in preview, and not supported for production workloads. Further discussion of Availability Groups can be found in Chapter 15.

Tip   SQL Server 2022 introduces query store enhancements, which allow for feedback mechanisms which can automatically optimize query performance. These feedback mechanisms are discussed in various chapters throughout this book.

CHAPTER 23

Automating Maintenance Routines

Automation is a critical part of database administration because it reduces the total cost of ownership (TCO) of the enterprise by allowing repeatable tasks to be carried out with little or no human intervention. SQL Server provides a rich set of functionality for automating routine DBA activity, including a scheduling engine, decision-tree logic, and a comprehensive security model. In this chapter, we discuss how you can harness SQL Server Agent to reduce the maintenance burden on your time. We also look at how you can reduce effort by using multiserver jobs, which allow you to operate a consistent set of routines across the enterprise.

SQL Server Agent

SQL Server Agent is a service that provides the ability to create automated routines with decision-based logic and schedule them to run one time only, on a reoccurring basis, when the SQL Server Agent service starts or when a CPU idle condition occurs.

SQL Server Agent also controls alerts, which allow you to respond to a wide range of conditions, including errors, performance conditions, or WMI (Windows Management Instrumentation) events. Responses can include sending e-mails or running tasks.

After introducing you to the concepts surrounding SQL Server Agent, the following sections discuss the SQL Server Agent security model, how to create and manage jobs, and how to create alerts.

© Peter A. Carter 2023
P. A. Carter, *Pro SQL Server 2022 Administration*, https://doi.org/10.1007/978-1-4842-8864-1_23

SQL Server Agent Concepts

SQL Server Agent is implemented using jobs, which orchestrate the tasks that are run; schedules, which define when the tasks run; alerts, which can respond to events that occur within SQL Server; and operators, which are users (usually DBAs) who are notified of occurrences, such as job status or alerts that have been triggered. The following sections introduce you to each of these concepts.

Schedules

A *schedule* defines the time or condition that triggers a job to start running. A schedule can be defined as follows:

- One time: Allows you to specify a specific date and time.

- Start automatically when SQL Server Agent starts: Useful if a set of tasks should run when the instance starts, assuming that the SQL Server Agent service is configured to start automatically.

- Start when CPU becomes idle: Useful if you have resource-intensive jobs that you do not wish to impact user activity.

- Recurring: Allows you to define a complex schedule, with start and end dates, that can reoccur daily, weekly, or monthly. If you schedule a job to run weekly, then you can also define multiple days on which it should run. If you define the schedule as daily, you can opt to have the trigger occur once daily, on an hourly basis, every minute, or even as frequently as every ten seconds. If the schedule is reoccurring based on second, minute, or hour, then it is possible to define start and stop times within a day. This means that you can schedule a job to run every minute, between 18:00 and 20:00, for example.

Tip   A recurring daily schedule is actually used to define a schedule that runs daily, hourly, every minute, or every second.

You can create individual schedules for each job, or you can choose to define a schedule and use this to trigger multiple jobs that you need to run at the same times—for example, when you have multiple maintenance jobs you want to run when the CPU is idle. In this case, you use the same schedule for all of these jobs. Another example is when you have multiple ETL runs against different databases. If you have a small ETL window, you may want all of these jobs to run at the same time. Here again, you can define a single schedule and use it for all of the ETL jobs. This approach can reduce administration; if, for example, the ETL window moves, you can change a single schedule rather than many schedules.

Operators

An *operator* is an individual or team that is configured to receive a notification of job status or when an alert is triggered. You can confine operators to be notified via e-mail, NET SEND, or the pager. It is worth noting, however, that the pager and NET SEND options are deprecated and you should avoid using them.

If you choose to configure operators so they are notified through e-mail, then you must also configure Database Mail, discussed later in this chapter, specifying the address and port of the SMTP Replay server that delivers the messages. If you configure operators to be notified via NET SEND, then the SQL Server Agent Windows service is dependent on the NET SEND service, as well as the SQL Server service, in order to start. If you configure operators to be notified by pager, then you must use Database Mail to relay the messages to the e-mail to pager service.

Caution   You increase your operational risk by introducing reliance on the NET SEND service.

When using pager alerts, you can configure each operator with days and times that they are on duty. You can configure this in 24/7 organizations that run support shifts or "follow the sun" support models for operational support, which see shifts being passed to support teams in different global regions. This functionality also allows you to configure each operator with different shift patterns on weekdays, Saturdays, and Sundays.

Jobs

A job is comprised of a series of actions that you should perform. Each action is known as a *job step*. You can configure each job step to perform an action within one of the following categories:

- SSIS packages

- T-SQL commands

- PowerShell scripts

- Operating system commands

- Replication Distributor tasks

- Replication Merge Agent tasks

- Replication Queue Reader Agent tasks

- Replication Snapshot Agent tasks

- Replication Transaction Log Reader tasks

- Analysis Services commands

- Analysis Services queries

You can configure each job step, with the exception of T-SQL commands, to run under the context of the service account running the SQL Server Agent service or to run under a proxy account, which is linked to a credential. You can also configure each step to retry a specific number of times, with an interval between each retry.

Additionally, you can configure On Success and On Failure actions individually for each job step. This allows DBAs to implement decision-based logic and error handling, as outlined in Figure 23-1.

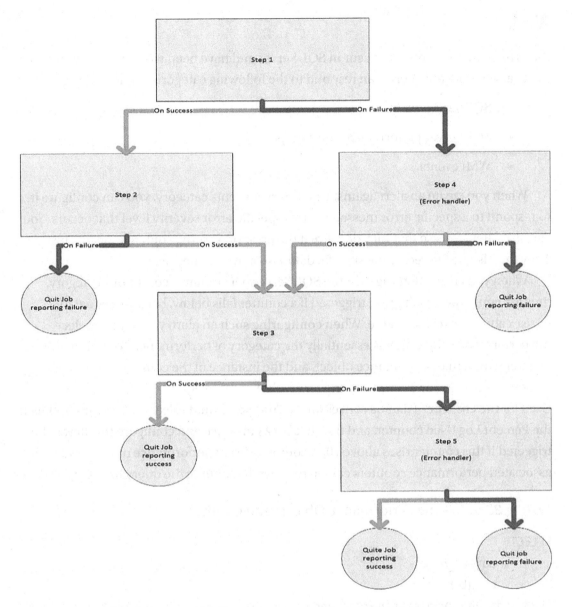

Figure 23-1. *Decision-tree logic*

You can run each job on a schedule that you can create specifically for the job that you are configuring, or share between multiple jobs, which should all run on the same schedule.

You can also configure notifications for each job. A notification alerts an operator to the success or failure of a job, but you can also configure it to write entries to the Windows application event log or even delete the job.

851

Alerts

Alerts respond to events that occur in SQL Server and have been written to the Windows application event log. Alerts can respond to the following categories of activity:

- SQL Server events

- SQL Server performance conditions

- WMI events

When you create an alert against a SQL Server events category, you can configure it to respond to a specific error message or to a specific error severity level that occurs. You can also filter alerts so that they only fire if the error or warning contains specific text. They can also be filtered by the specific database in which they occur.

When you create alerts against the SQL Server performance conditions category, they are configured so they are triggered if a counter falls below, becomes equal to, or rises above a specified value. When configuring such an alert, you need to select the performance object that is essentially the category of performance condition, the counter within that performance object, and the instance of the counter that you wish to alert against. So, for example, to trigger an alert in the event that the Percentage Log Used for the Chapter23 database rises above 70%, you would select the Databases object, the Percent Log Used counter, and the Chapter23 instance and configure the alert to be triggered if this counter rises above 70. A complete list of performance objects and their associated performance counters can be revealed by running the query in Listing 23-1.

Listing 23-1. Listing Performance Objects and Counters

```
SELECT
        object_name
      , counter_name
FROM msdb.dbo.sysalerts_performance_counters_view
ORDER BY object_name
```

SQL Server Agent Security

You control access to SQL Server Agent via database roles and you can run job steps under the context of the SQL Server Agent service account or by using separate proxy accounts that map to credentials. Both of these concepts are explored in the following sections.

SQL Server Agent Database Roles

Other than members of the sysadmin server role, who have full access to SQL Server Agent, access can be granted to SQL Server Agent using fixed database roles within the MSDB database. The following roles are provided:

- SQLAgentUserRole

- SQLAgentReaderRole

- SQLAgentOperatorRole

The permissions provided by the roles are detailed in Table 23-1. Members of the sysadmin role are granted all permissions to SQL Server Agent. This includes permissions that are not provided by any of the SQL Server Agent roles, such as editing multiserver job properties. Actions that are not possible through SQL Server Agent role membership can only be actioned by members of the sysadmin role.

Table 23-1. *SQL Server Agent Permissions Matrix*

Permission	SQLAgentUserRole	SQLAgentReaderRole	SQLAgentOperatorRole
CREATE/ALTER/DROP operator	No	No	No
CREATE/ALTER/DROP local job	Yes (Owned only)	Yes (Owned only)	Yes (Owned only)
CREATE/ALTER/DROP multiserver job	No	No	No
CREATE/ALTER/DROP schedule	Yes (Owned only)	Yes (Owned only)	Yes (Owned only)
CREATE/ALTER/DROP proxy	No	No	No
CREATE/ALTER/DROP alerts	No	No	No
View list of operators	Yes	Yes	Yes
View list of local jobs	Yes (Owned only)	Yes	Yes
View list of multiserver jobs	No	Yes	Yes
View list of schedules	Yes (Owned only)	Yes	Yes

(continued)

Table 23-1. (*continued*)

Permission	SQLAgentUserRole	SQLAgentReaderRole	SQLAgentOperatorRole
View list of proxies	Yes	Yes	Yes
View list of alerts	No	No	No
Enable/disable operators	No	No	No
Enable/disable local jobs	Yes (Owned only)	Yes (Owned only)	Yes
Enable/disable multiserver jobs	No	No	No
Enable/disable schedules	Yes (Owned only)	Yes (Owned only)	Yes
Enable/disable alerts	No	No	No
View operator properties	No	No	Yes
View local job properties	Yes (Owned only)	Yes	Yes
View multiserver job properties	No	Yes	Yes
View schedule properties	Yes (Owned only)	Yes	Yes
View proxy properties	No	No	Yes
View alert properties	No	No	Yes
Edit operator properties	No	No	No
Edit local job properties	No	Yes (Owned only)	Yes (Owned only)
Edit multiserver job properties	No	No	No
Edit schedule properties	No	Yes (Owned only)	Yes (Owned only)
Edit proxy properties	No	No	No
Edit alert properties	No	No	No
Start/stop local jobs	Yes (Owned only)	Yes (Owned only)	Yes
Start/stop multiserver jobs	No	No	No
View local job history	Yes (Owned only)	Yes	Yes
View multiserver job history	No	Yes	Yes

(*continued*)

Table 23-1. (*continued*)

Permission	SQLAgentUserRole	SQLAgentReaderRole	SQLAgentOperatorRole
Delete local job history	No	No	Yes
Delete multiserver job history	No	No	No
Attach/detach schedules	Yes (Owned only)	Yes (Owned only)	Yes (Owned only)

SQL Server Agent Proxy Accounts

By default, all job steps run under the context of the SQL Server Agent service account. Adopting this approach, however, can be a security risk, since you may need to grant the service account a large number of permissions to the instance and objects within the operating system. The amount of permissions you need to grant the service account is especially important for jobs that require cross-server access.

To mitigate this risk and follow the principle of least privilege, you should instead consider using proxy accounts. Proxies are mapped to credentials within the instance level and you can configure them to run only a subset of step types. For example, you can configure one proxy to be able to run operating system commands while configuring another to be able to run only PowerShell scripts. This means that you can reduce the permissions that each proxy requires.

For job steps with the Transact-SQL (T-SQL) script step type, it is not possible to select a proxy account. Instead, the Run As User option allows you to select a database user to use as the security context to run the script. This option uses the EXECUTE AS functionality in T-SQL to change the security context.

Creating SQL Server Agent Jobs

In the following sections, we create a simple SQL Server Agent job, which runs an operating system command to delete old backup files. We then create a more complex SQL Server Agent job, which backs up a database and runs a PowerShell script to ensure the SQL Server Browser service is running. Before creating the SQL Server Agent jobs, however, we first create the Chapter23 database, as well as security principles that we use in the following sections.

You can find the script to perform these tasks in Listing 23-2. The script uses PowerShell to create two domain users: SQLUser and WinUser. It then uses SQLCMD to create the Chapter23 database, before creating a login for SQLUser and mapping it to the Chapter23 database with backup permissions. You can run the script from the PowerShell ISE (Integrated Scripting Environment) or from the PowerShell command prompt. You should run the script on a Windows Server operating system; if you are running it on a different operating system, you need to prepare the environment manually.

Note   Be sure to change the server name in the following script to match your own.

Listing 23-2. Preparing the Environment

```
Set-ExecutionPolicy Unrestricted

import-module SQLPS
import-module servermanager

Add-WindowsFeature -Name "RSAT-AD-PowerShell" -IncludeAllSubFeature

New-ADUser SQLUser -AccountPassword (ConvertTo-SecureString -AsPlainText
"Pa$$w0rd" -Force) -Server "PROSQLADMIN.COM"
Enable-ADAccount -Identity SQLUser

New-ADUser WinUser -AccountPassword (ConvertTo-SecureString -AsPlainText
"Pa$$w0rd" -Force) -Server "PROSQLADMIN.COM"
Enable-ADAccount -Identity WinUser

$perm = [ADSI]"WinNT://SQLServer/Administrators,group"
$perm.psbase.Invoke("Add",([ADSI]"WinNT://PROSQLADMIN/WinUser").path)

invoke-sqlcmd -ServerInstance .\MasterServer -Query "--Create the database

CREATE DATABASE Chapter23 ;
GO

USE Chapter23
GO
```

```
--Create and populate numbers table

DECLARE @Numbers TABLE
(
        Number          INT
)

;WITH CTE(Number)
AS
(
        SELECT 1 Number
        UNION ALL
        SELECT Number + 1
        FROM CTE
        WHERE Number < 100
)
INSERT INTO @Numbers
SELECT Number FROM CTE;

--Create and populate name pieces

DECLARE @Names TABLE
(
        FirstName        VARCHAR(30),
        LastName         VARCHAR(30)
);

INSERT INTO @Names
VALUES('Peter', 'Carter'),
      ('Michael', 'Smith'),
      ('Danielle', 'Mead'),
      ('Reuben', 'Roberts'),
      ('Iris', 'Jones'),
      ('Sylvia', 'Davies'),
      ('Finola', 'Wright'),
      ('Edward', 'James'),
      ('Marie', 'Andrews'),
   ('Jennifer', 'Abraham');
```

```sql
--Create and populate Customers table

CREATE TABLE dbo.Customers
(
        CustomerID              INT             NOT
NULL    IDENTITY    PRIMARY KEY,
        FirstName               VARCHAR(30)     NOT NULL,
        LastName                VARCHAR(30)     NOT NULL,
        BillingAddressID        INT             NOT NULL,
        DeliveryAddressID       INT             NOT NULL,
        CreditLimit             MONEY           NOT NULL,
        Balance                 MONEY           NOT NULL
);

SELECT * INTO #Customers
FROM
        (SELECT
                (SELECT TOP 1 FirstName FROM @Names ORDER BY NEWID())
                FirstName,
                (SELECT TOP 1 LastName FROM @Names ORDER BY NEWID())
                LastName,
                (SELECT TOP 1 Number FROM @Numbers ORDER BY NEWID())
                BillingAddressID,
                (SELECT TOP 1 Number FROM @Numbers ORDER BY NEWID())
                DeliveryAddressID,
                (SELECT TOP 1 CAST(RAND() * Number AS INT) * 10000
                FROM @Numbers
                ORDER BY NEWID()) CreditLimit,
                (SELECT TOP 1 CAST(RAND() * Number AS INT) * 9000
                FROM @Numbers
                ORDER BY NEWID()) Balance
        FROM @Numbers a
) a;
```

```
--Create the SQLUser Login and DB User

USE Master
GO

CREATE LOGIN [PROSQLADMIN\sqluser] FROM WINDOWS WITH DEFAULT_
DATABASE=Chapter23 ;
GO

USE Chapter23
GO

CREATE USER [PROSQLADMIN\sqluser] FOR LOGIN [PROSQLADMIN\sqluser] ;
GO

--Add the SQLUser to the db_backupoperator group

ALTER ROLE db_backupoperator ADD MEMBER [PROSQLADMIN\sqluser] ;
GO"
```

Creating a Simple SQL Server Agent Job

We start by creating a simple Server Agent job, which uses an operating system command to delete backup files that are older than 30 days, and schedule this job to run on a monthly basis. We create the SQL Server Agent artifacts using the New Job dialog box. To invoke this dialog box, drill through SQL Server Agent in Object Explorer, and select New Job from the Jobs context menu. Figure 23-2 illustrates the General page of the New Job dialog box.

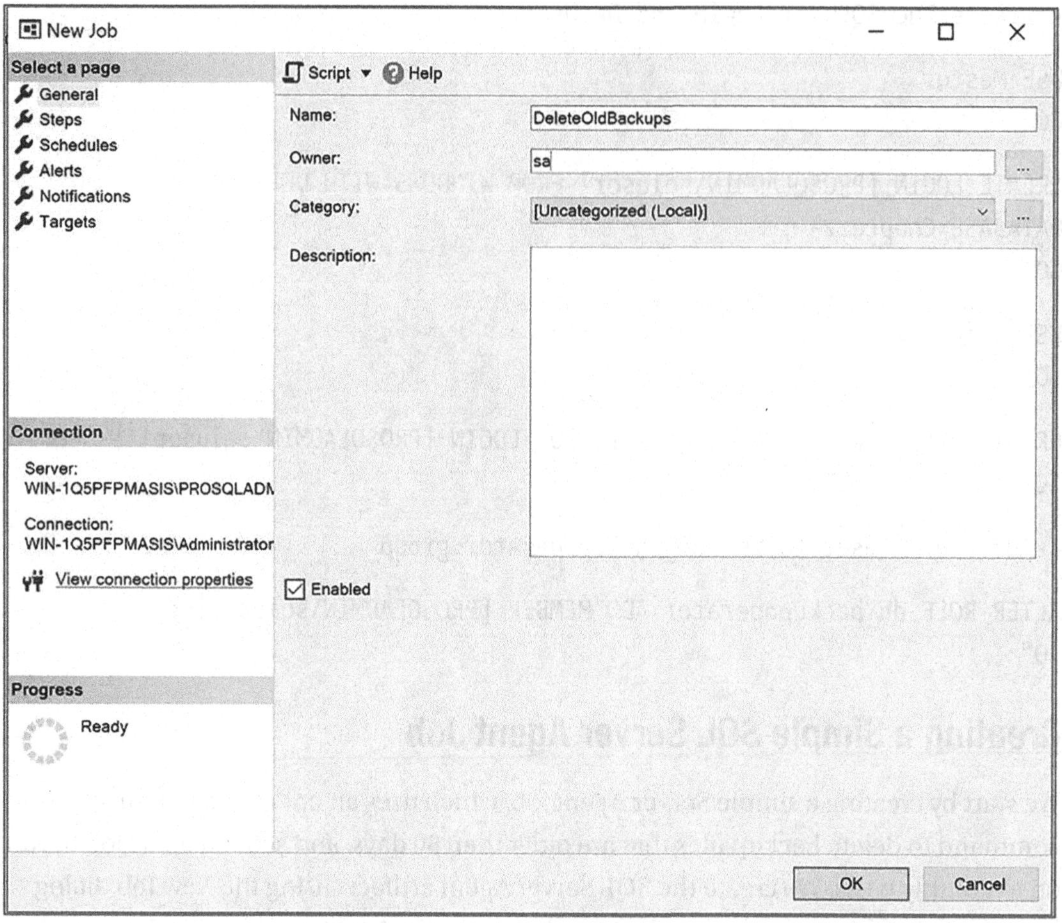

Figure 23-2. *The General page*

On this page, we name our job DeleteOldBackups and change the job owner to be the sa account. We can also optionally add a description for the job and choose a category.

On the Steps page, we use the New button to invoke the New Job Step dialog box. The General tab of this dialog box is illustrated in Figure 23-3.

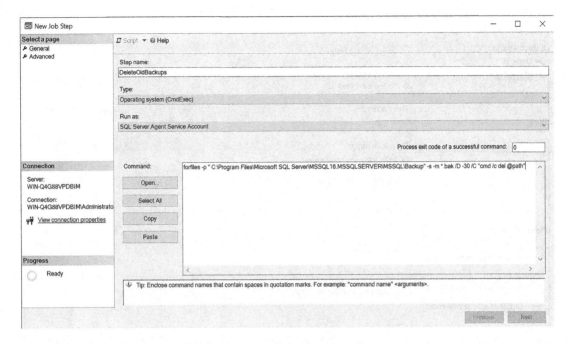

Figure 23-3. *The General tab*

On this page, we give our job step a name, specify that the step is an operating system command in the Type drop-down, and confirm in the Run As drop-down that the step runs under the security context of the SQL Server Agent service account. In the Command section, we enter a batch command, which deletes all files from our default backup location that are older than 30 days and have a file extension of .bak. You can find this batch command in Listing 23-3.

Listing 23-3. Removing Old Backups

```
forfiles -p " C:\Program Files\Microsoft SQL Server\MSSQL16.MSSQLSERVER\
MSSQL\Backup" -s -m *.bak /D -30 /C "cmd /c del @path"
```

On the Advanced page of the New Job Step dialog box, shown in Figure 23-4, we leave the default settings. We could use this page, however, in more complex scenarios, to configure logging and to control decision-tree logic. We discuss this in the next section.

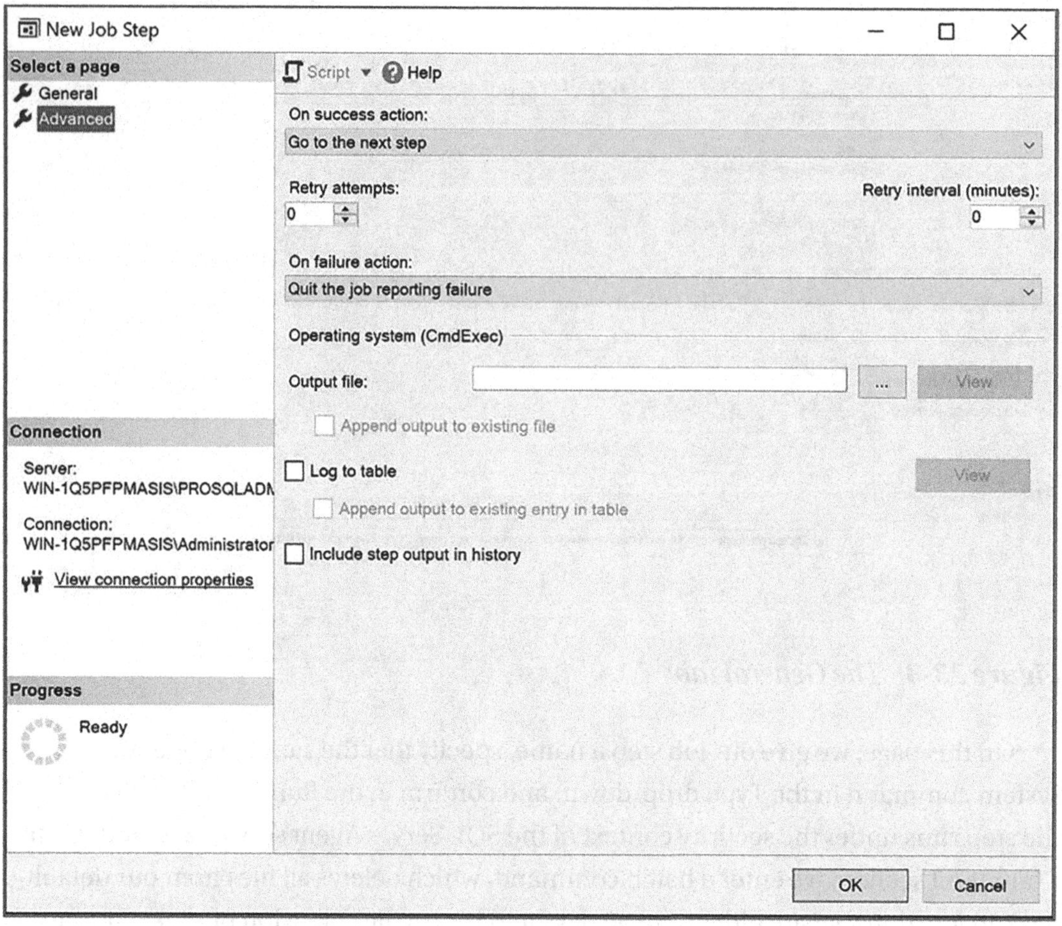

Figure 23-4. *The Advanced page*

Once we have configured our job step, we can exit out of the New Job Step dialog box and return to the New Job dialog box. Here, we now move to the Schedules page. On this page, we use the New button to invoke the New Job Schedule dialog box, illustrated in Figure 23-5.

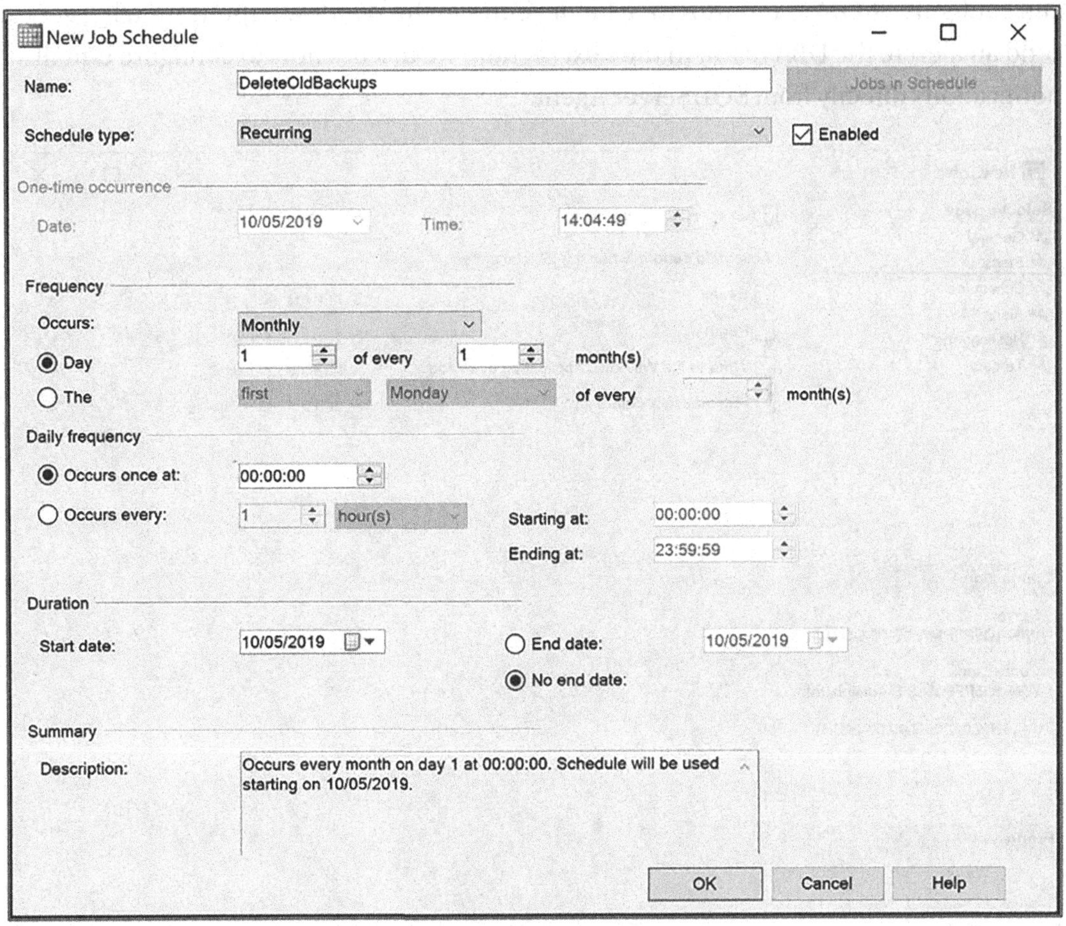

Figure 23-5. *The New Job Schedule dialog box*

In the New Job Schedule dialog box, we first enter a name for our schedule. The default schedule type is Recurring, but the screen changes dynamically if we choose other options. In the Frequency section of the screen, we select Monthly. Again, the screen changes dynamically if we select weekly or daily in this drop-down.

We can now configure the date and time that we would like the schedule to invoke job execution. In our scenario, we leave the default option of midnight, on the first day of each month.

On the Notifications page of the New Job dialog box, we configure any actions that we want to occur when the job completes. As illustrated in Figure 23-6, we configure an entry to write to the Windows Application Log if the job fails. This is an especially useful option if your enterprise is managed by a monitoring tool such as SCOM, because you can configure SCOM to monitor for a failure entry in the Windows Application log and send an alert to the DBA team. In the next section, we discuss how to configure e-mail notifications directly from SQL Server Agent.

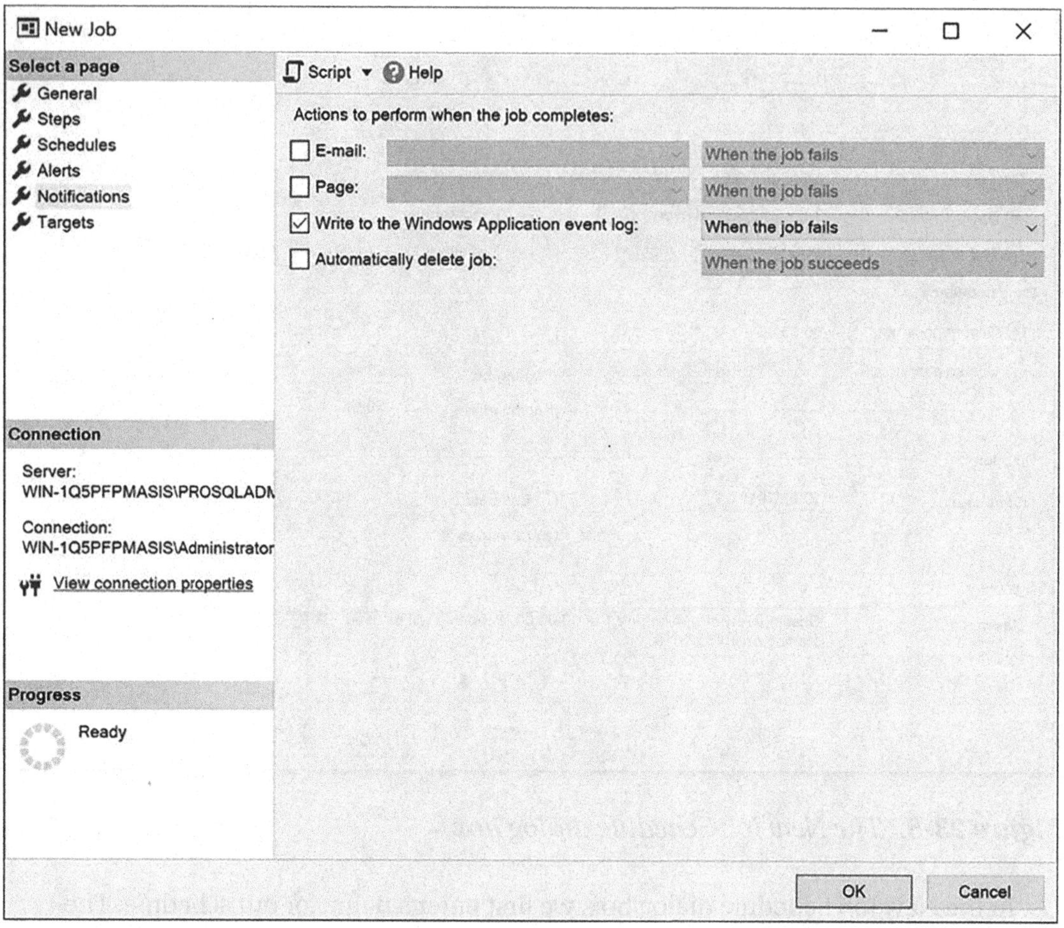

Figure 23-6. *The Notifications page*

Creating a Complex SQL Server Agent Job

In the following sections, we create a more complex SQL Server Agent job, which backs up the Chapter23 database. The job then checks that the SQL Server Browser service is running. We use Run As to set the context under which the T-SQL job step runs and a proxy to run the PowerShell job step. We also configure Database Mail so that an operator can be notified of the success or failure of the job and schedule the job to run periodically. You can also see how to create the SQL Server Agent artifacts using T-SQL, which may prove useful when you are working in Server Core environments.

Creating the Credential

Now that our environment is prepared, we create a SQL Server Agent job, which first backs up the Chapter23 database. The job then checks to ensure that the SQL Server Browser service is running. Checking that the browser service is running is a useful practice, because if it stops, then applications are only able to connect to the instance if they specify the port number of the instance in their connection strings. We run the backup as a T-SQL command under the context of SQL User, and we use PowerShell to check that the browser service is running by using the WinUser account. Therefore, our first step is to create a credential, which uses the WinUser account. We can achieve this in SQL Server Management Studio by drilling through Security and selecting New Credential from the Credentials context menu. This causes the New Credential dialog box to be invoked, as shown in Figure 23-7.

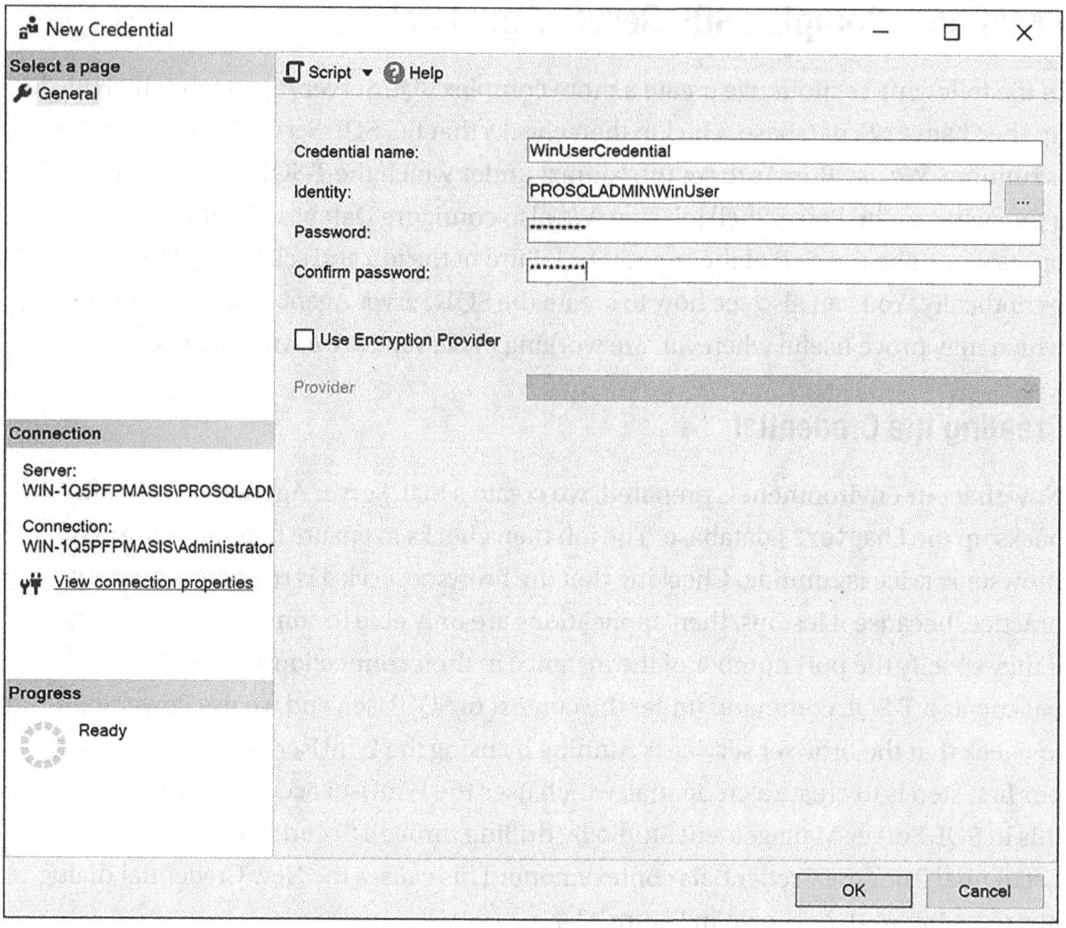

Figure 23-7. *The New Credential dialog box*

In this dialog box, use the Credential name field to specify a name for your new credential. In the Identity field, specify the name of the Windows security principle that you wish to use and then type the Windows password in the Password and Confirm password fields. You can also link the credential to an EKM provider. If you wish to do this, check Use Encryption Provider and select your provider from the drop-down list. EKM is discussed further in Chapter 12.

Creating the Proxy

Next, let's create a SQL Server Agent proxy account, which uses this credential. We configure this proxy account to be able to run PowerShell job steps. We can achieve this through SSMS by drilling through SQL Server Agent in Object Explorer and selecting New Proxy from the Proxies context menu. This causes the General page of the New Proxy Account dialog box to display, illustrated in Figure 23-8.

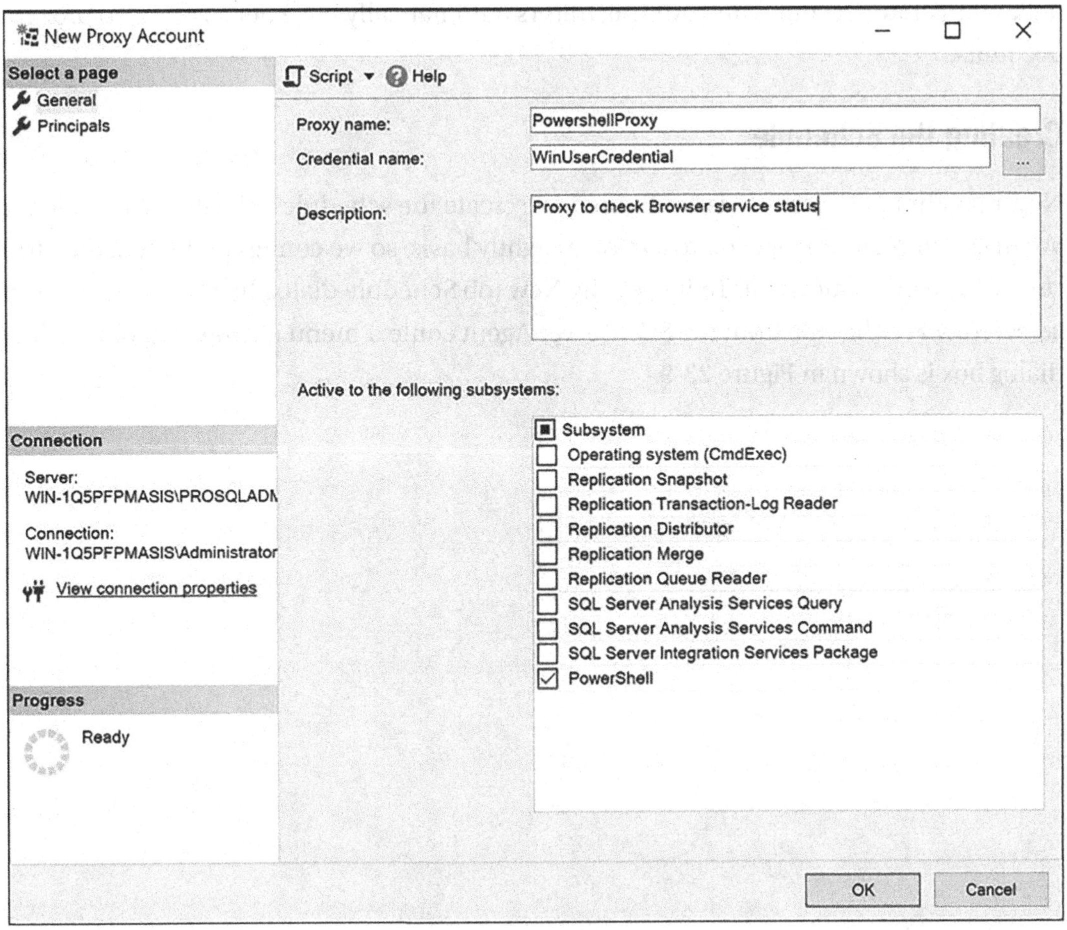

Figure 23-8. *The New Proxy Account dialog box*

On this page, we specify a name for our proxy account and give it a description. We use the Credential name field to select our WinUserCredential credential and then use the Active to the following subsystems section to authorize the proxy to run PowerShell job steps.

Tip   If you enter the new proxy account from the node of the relevant subsystem located under the Proxies node in Object Explorer, the relevant subsystem is automatically selected within the dialog box.

On the Principles page, we can add logins or server roles that have permissions to use the proxy. In our case, this is not required, because we are using SQL Server with an administrator account, and administrators automatically have permissions to proxy accounts.

Creating the Schedule

Now that our proxy account is configured, we create the schedule to be used by our job. We need our maintenance job to run on a nightly basis, so we configure the schedule to run at 1 AM every morning. To invoke the New Job Schedule dialog box from SSMS, we select New ➤ Schedule from the SQL Server Agent context menu in Object Explorer. This dialog box is shown in Figure 23-9.

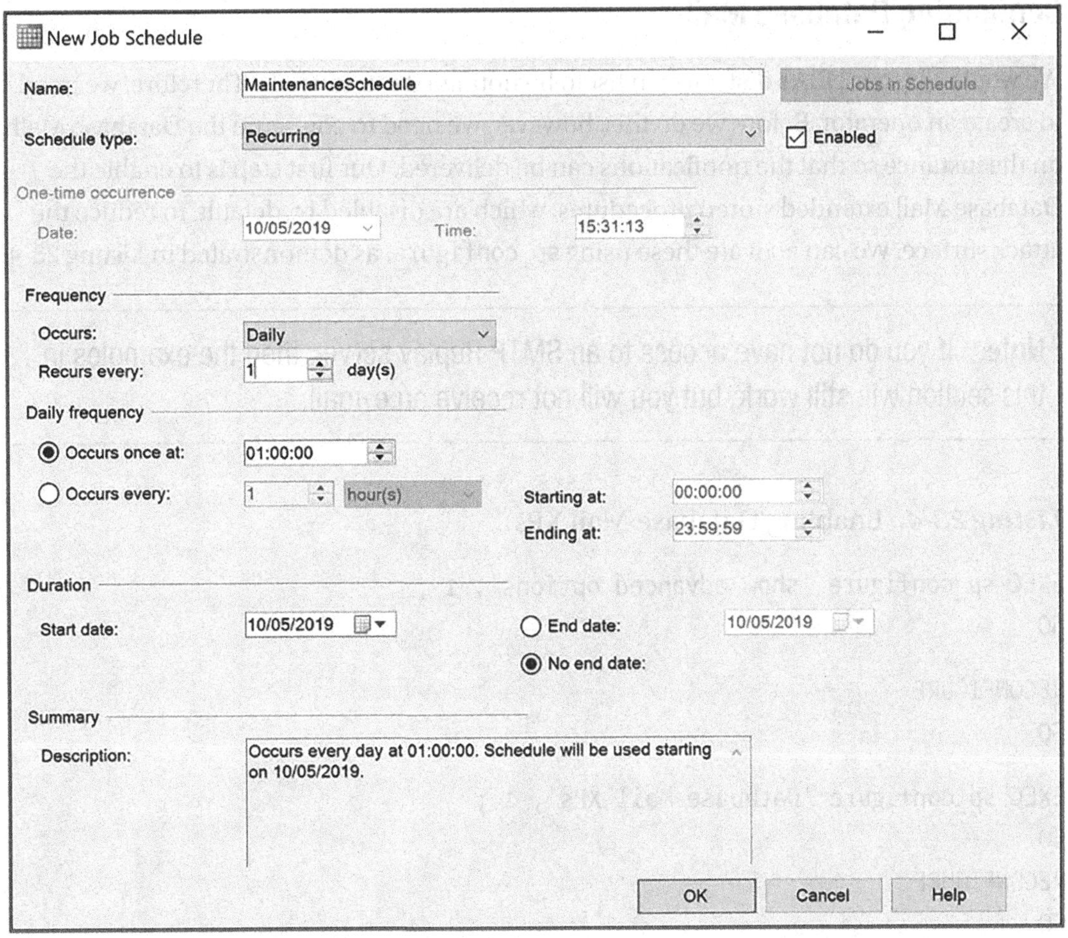

Figure 23-9. *The New Job Schedule dialog box*

In this dialog box, we specify a name for the schedule in the Name field and select the condition for the schedule in the Schedule type field. Selecting any condition other than Recurring causes the Frequency and Duration sections to become unavailable. Selecting any condition other than One Time causes the One-time occurrence section to become unavailable. We also ensure that the Enabled box is checked so that the schedule can be used.

In the Frequency section, we select Daily in the Occurs drop-down list. Our selection in this field causes the options within the Frequency and Daily frequency sections to be altered dynamically to suit our selection. Since we want our schedule to run daily at 1 AM, we ensure that 1 is specified in the Recurs every field and change the Occurs once at field to be 1 AM. Because we want our job to start running immediately and never expire, we do not need to edit the fields in the Duration section.

Configuring Database Mail

We would like our DBA's distribution list to be notified if our job fails. Therefore, we need to create an operator. Before we do this, however, we need to configure the Database Mail on the instance so that the notifications can be delivered. Our first step is to enable the Database Mail extended stored procedures, which are disabled by default, to reduce the attack surface. We can activate these using sp_configure, as demonstrated in Listing 23-4.

Note   If you do not have access to an SMTP Replay server, then the examples in this section will still work, but you will not receive an e-mail.

Listing 23-4. Enabling Database Mail XPs

```
EXEC sp_configure 'show advanced options', 1 ;
GO

RECONFIGURE
GO

EXEC sp_configure 'Database Mail XPs', 1 ;
GO
RECONFIGURE
GO
```

We can now launch the Database Mail Configuration Wizard by drilling through Management in Object Explorer and selecting Database Mail. After passing through the Welcome page, we see the Select Configuration Task page shown in Figure 23-10.

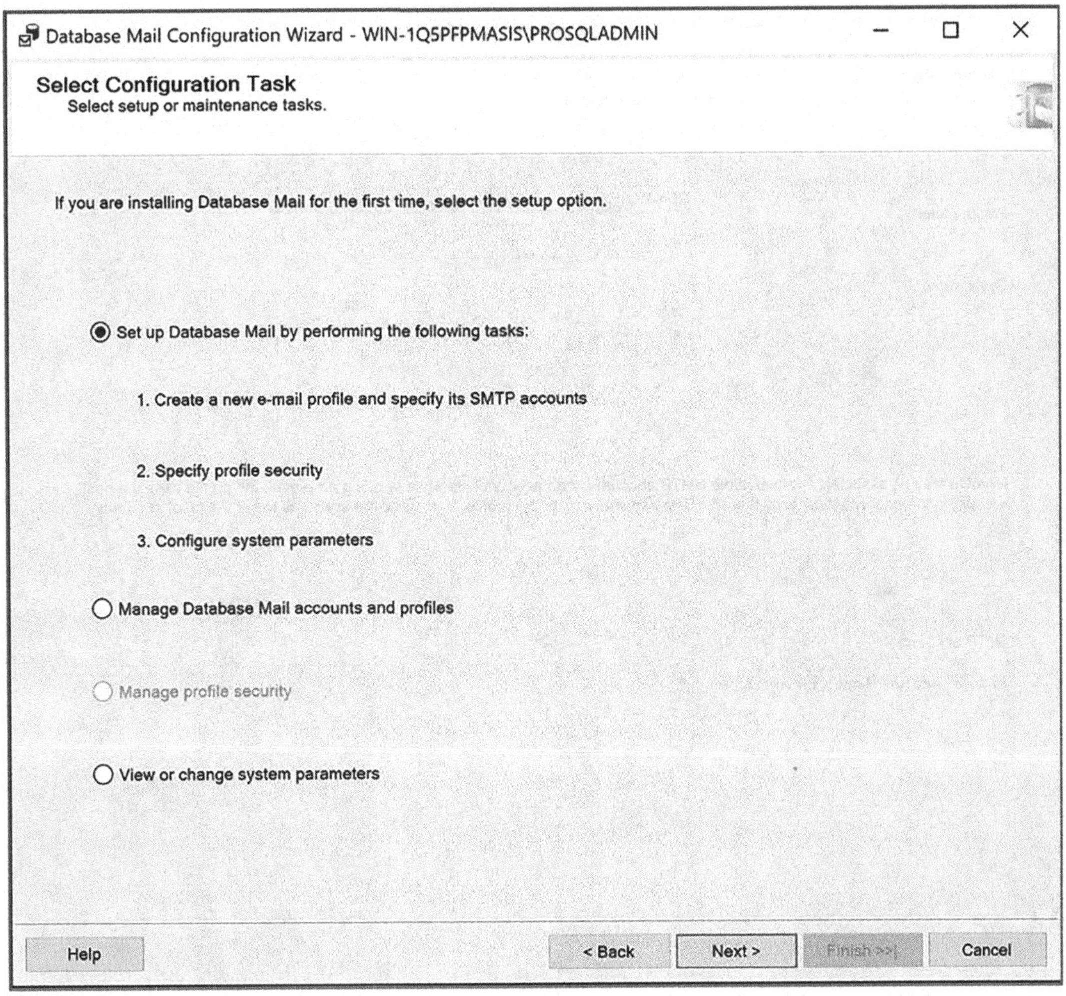

Figure 23-10. *The Select Configuration Task page*

On this page, we should ensure that the `Set Up Database Mail by performing the following tasks` option is selected. On the new Profile page, we specify a name for our profile. A profile is an alias for one or more mail accounts, which are used to send the notification to the operator. It is good practice to add multiple accounts to a profile; that way, if one account fails, you can use a different one. This page is illustrated in Figure 23-11.

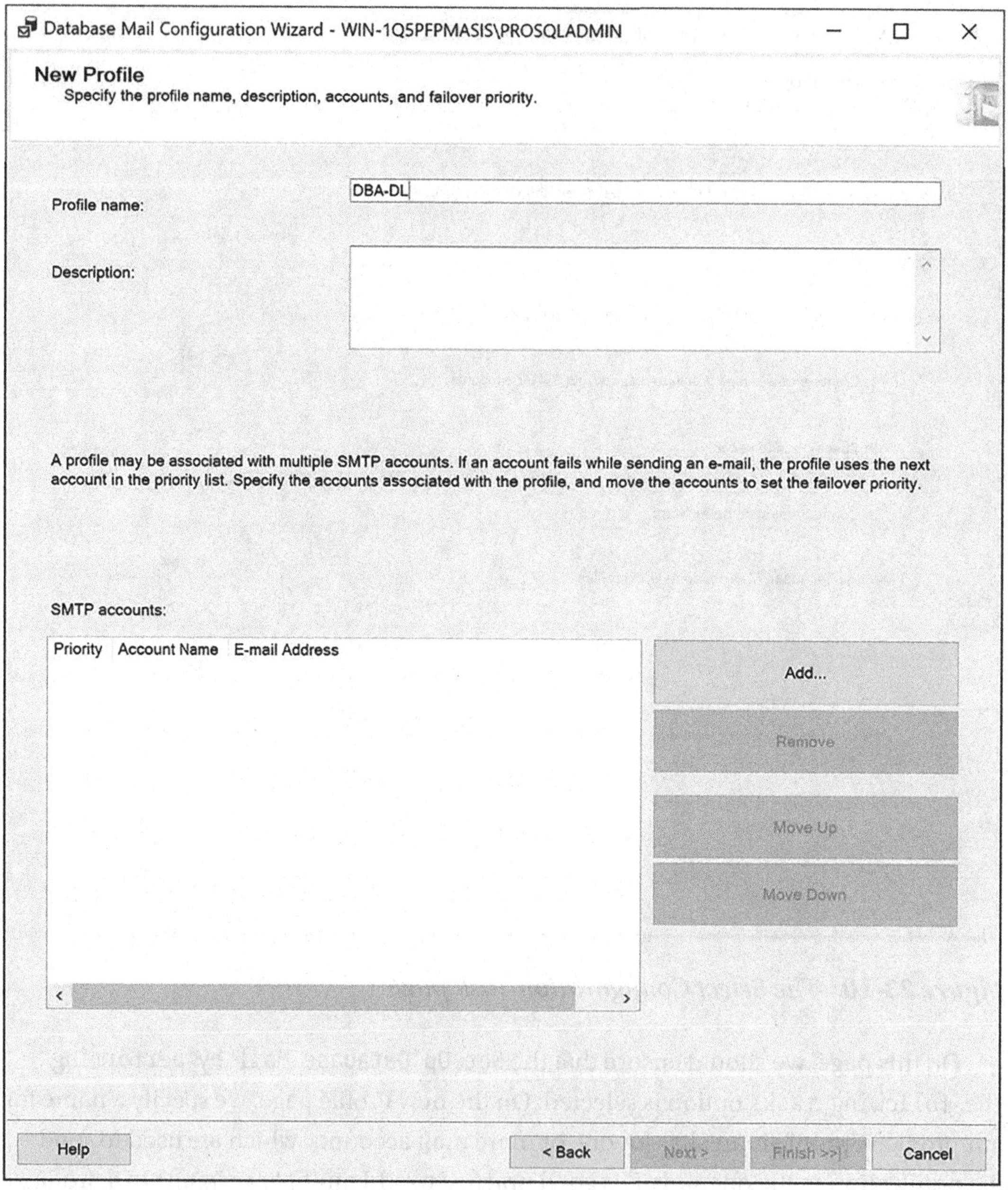

Figure 23-11. *The New Profile page*

Let's now use the Add button to add one or more SMTP (Simple Mail Transfer Protocol) e-mail accounts to the profile via the New Database Mail Account dialog box, show in Figure 23-12.

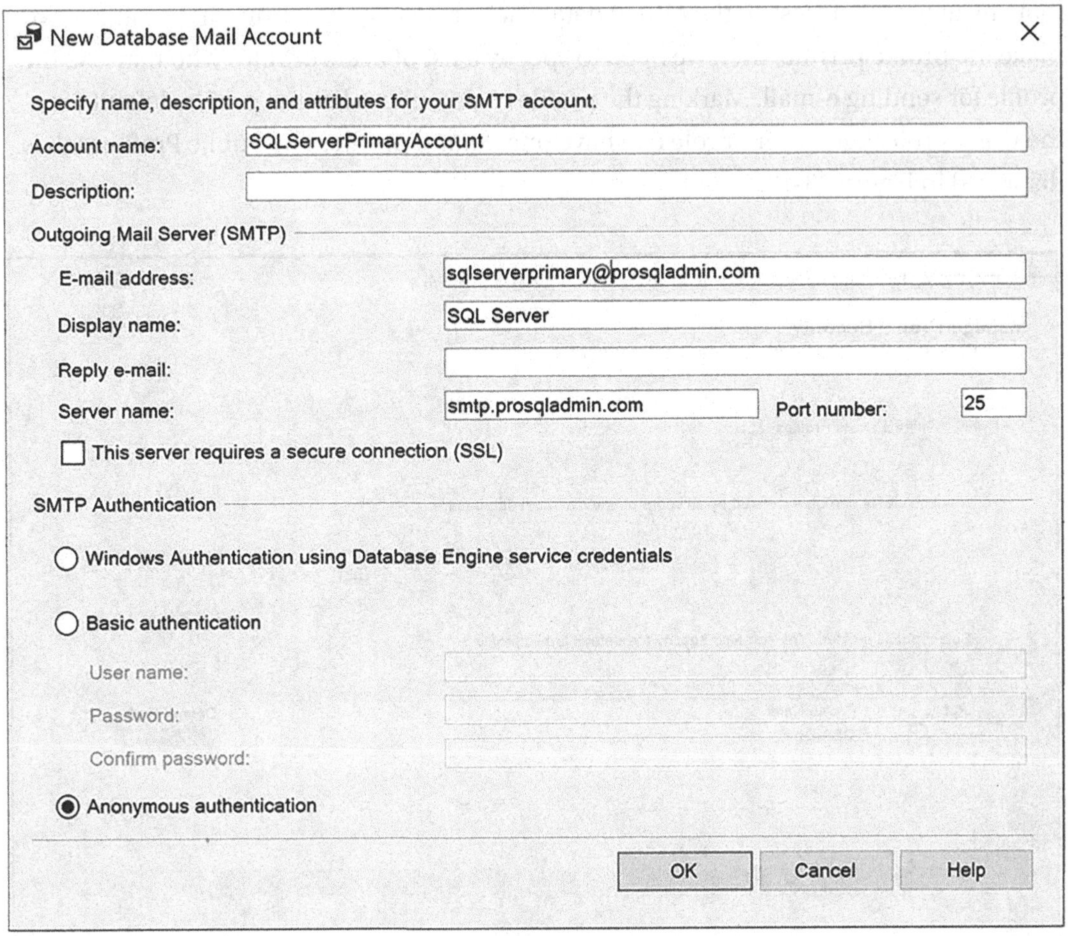

Figure 23-12. *The New Database Mail Account dialog box*

In this dialog box, we specify a name for the account and, optionally, a description. We then need to specify the e-mail address that we will use to send mails, along with the name and port of the SMTP server that will deliver the messages. You can also specify a display name for when the e-mails are received. For DBAs who receive the notification, it helps if the display name includes the server/instance from which the notification was generated. We have selected Anonymous authentication. This implies that access to the SMTP server is controlled with firewall rules, as opposed to authentication. This is a relatively common approach in enterprise environments.

After adding the account, we can move to the Manage Profile Security page of the wizard. This page has two tabs: Public Profiles and Private Profiles. We configure our profile as public and also mark it as the default profile. Making the profile public means that any user with access to the MSDB database can send e-mail from that profile. If we make the profile private, then we need to specify a list of users or roles who may use the profile for sending e-mail. Marking the profile as default makes the profile default for the user or role. Each user or role can have one default profile. The Public Profiles tab is displayed in Figure 23-13.

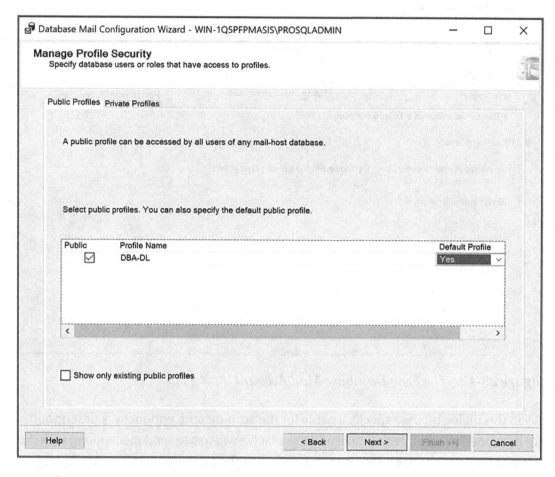

Figure 23-13. *The Public Profiles tab*

On the Configure System Parameters page of the wizard, illustrated in Figure 23-14, you can alter the default system properties, which control how mail is handled. This includes specifying the number of times an account should be retried and the time lapse between retries. It also involves setting the maximum allowable size of an e-mail and configuring a blacklist of extensions. The Database Mail Executable Minimum Lifetime

(Seconds) setting configures how long the Database Mail process should remain active when there are no e-mails in the queue waiting to be sent. The Logging Level can be configured with the following settings:

- Normal: Logs errors

- Extended: Logs errors, warnings, and informational messages

- Verbose: Logs errors, warnings, informational messages, success messages, and internal messages

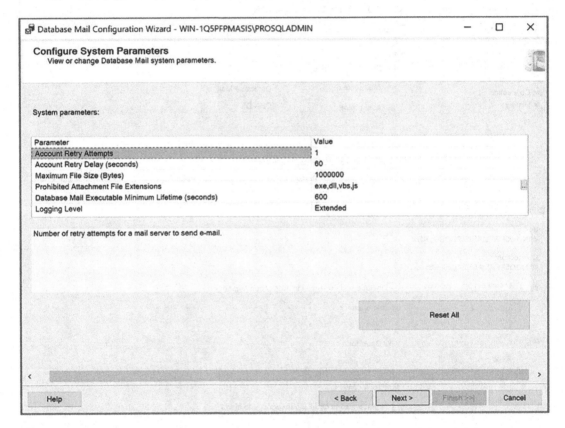

Figure 23-14. *The Configure System Parameters page*

Caution Unfortunately, attachment exclusions are implemented as a blacklist, as opposed to a whitelist. This means that to achieve the best balance of security and operational support, you should give time and thought to the file types that should be excluded.

On the Complete the Wizard page, you are provided with a summary of the tasks that will be performed. In our scenario, this includes creating a new account, creating a new profile, adding the account to the profile, and configuring the profile's security.

We now need to configure SQL Server Agent to use our mail profile. To do this, we select Properties from the SQL Server Agent context menu in Object Explorer to invoke the SQL Server Agent Properties dialog box and navigate to the Alert System page, shown in Figure 23-15.

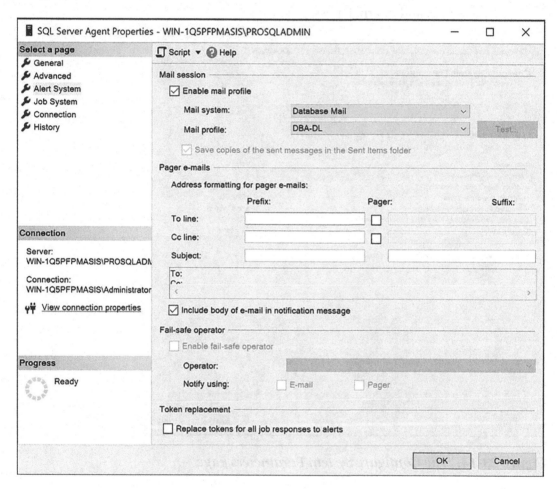

Figure 23-15.   *The Alert System page*

On this page, we check the Enable mail profile check box before selecting the DBA-DL profile from the drop-down list. After we exit the dialog box, operators are able to use Database Mail.

Creating the Operator

Now that Database Mail has been configured, we need to create an operator that will receive e-mails in the event that our job fails. We can access the New Operator dialog box by drilling through SQL Server Agent in Object Explorer and by selecting New Operator from the Operators context menu. The General page of the New Operator dialog box is shown in Figure 23-16.

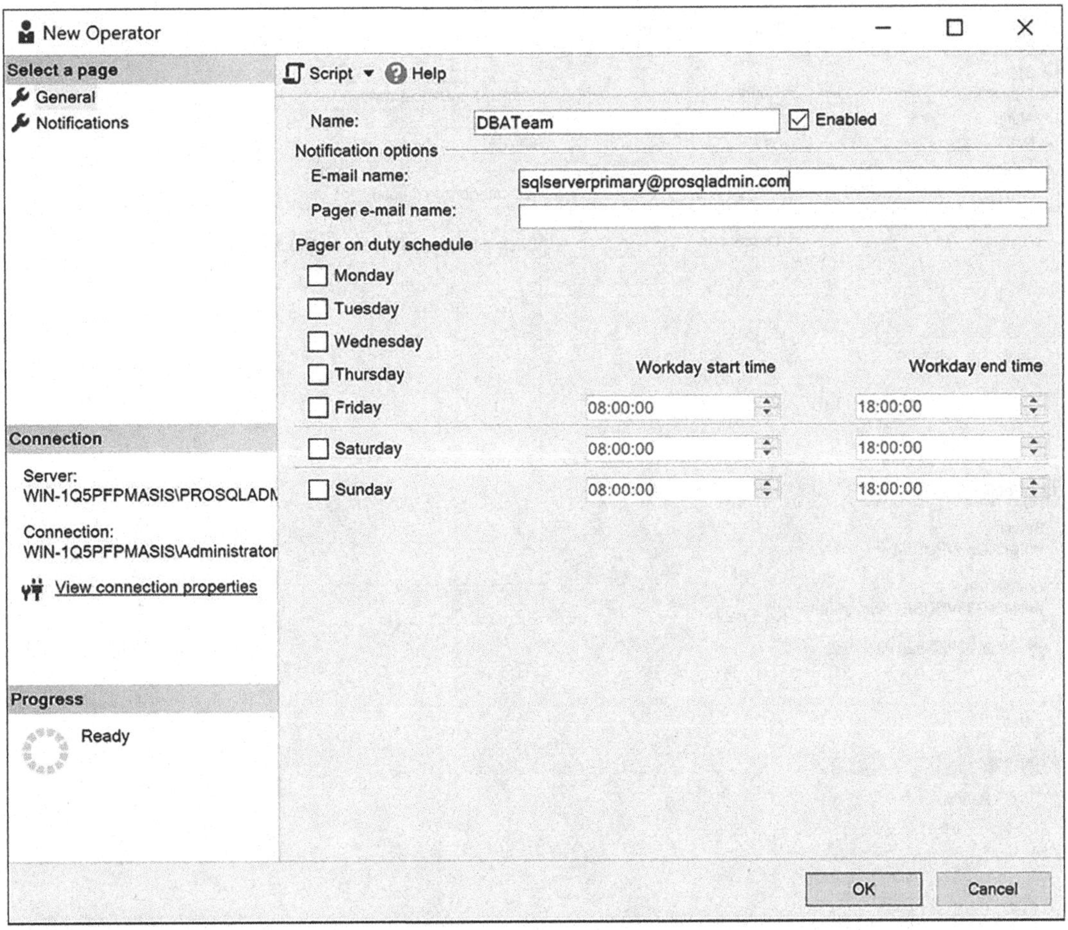

Figure 23-16. The General page

On this page, we specify a name for the operator and also add the e-mail address that the operator will be using. This must match the e-mail address that has been configured within Database Mail. The Notifications page displays details of the alerts and notifications that are already configured for the operator, so it is irrelevant to us at this point.

Creating the Job

Now that all of the prerequisites are in place, we can create the SQL Server Agent job. We can achieve this in SQL Server Management Studio by drilling through SQL Server Agent in Object Explorer and choosing New Job from the Jobs context menu. This causes the General page of the New Job dialog box to display, as illustrated in Figure 23-17.

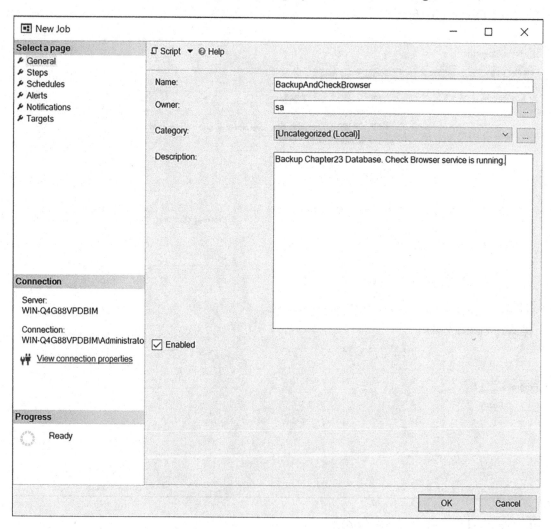

Figure 23-17. *The General page*

On this page, we use the Name field to specify a name for our job and, optionally, add a description in the Description field. It's also optional to add the job to a category; in our instance, we have added the job to the Database Maintenance category by selecting it from the drop-down list. We also check the Enabled box so that the job will be active as soon as it is created.

We also specify that the job owner will be sa. This is a controversial topic, but I generally recommend this approach for the following reason: job ownership does not matter much. No matter who owns the job, it functions in the same way. If the owner's account is dropped, however, then the job no longer functions. If you make sa the owner, then there is no chance of this situation occurring. If you are using the Windows authentication model as opposed to mixed-mode authentication, however, then it is reasonable to use the SQL Server Agent service account as an alternative. This is because, although it is possible that you will change the service account and drop the associated login, it is more unlikely than dropping other user's logins, such as DBAs' login, when they leaves the company.

On the Steps page of the dialog box, we use the New button to add our first step—backing up the Chapter23 database. The General page of the New Job Step dialog box is illustrated in Figure 23-18.

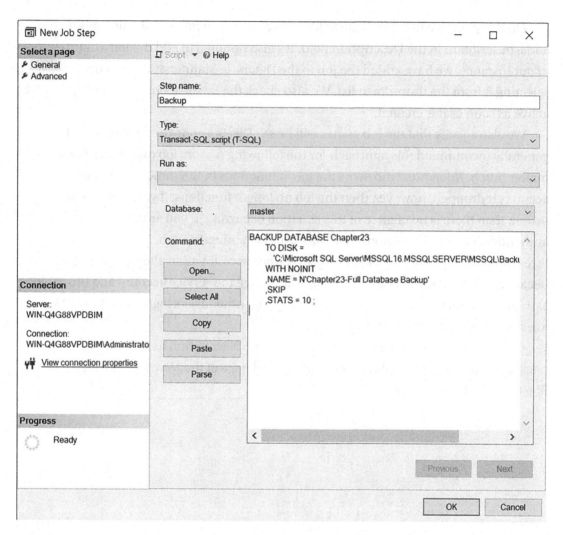

Figure 23-18. *The General page of the New Job Step dialog box*

On this page, we enter Backup as the name of the job step and type the BACKUP DATABASE command in the Command field. The Type field allows us to select the subsystem to use, but it defaults to T-SQL, so we do not need to alter this. Listing 23-5 contains the backup script.

Tip   Make sure to always test scripts before you add them to your jobs.

Listing 23-5. Backup Script

```
BACKUP DATABASE Chapter23
      TO DISK =
          'C:\Microsoft SQL Server\MSSQL16.MSSQLSERVER\MSSQL\Backup\
          Chapter23.bak'
      WITH NOINIT
      ,NAME = N'Chapter23-Full Database Backup'
      ,SKIP
      ,STATS = 10 ;
```

On the Advanced page of the dialog box, shown in Figure 23-19, we use the On success action and On failure action drop-down boxes to configure the step so that it moves to the next step, regardless of whether the step succeeds or fails. We do this because our two steps are unrelated. We also configure the step to retry three times, at one-minute intervals, before it fails.

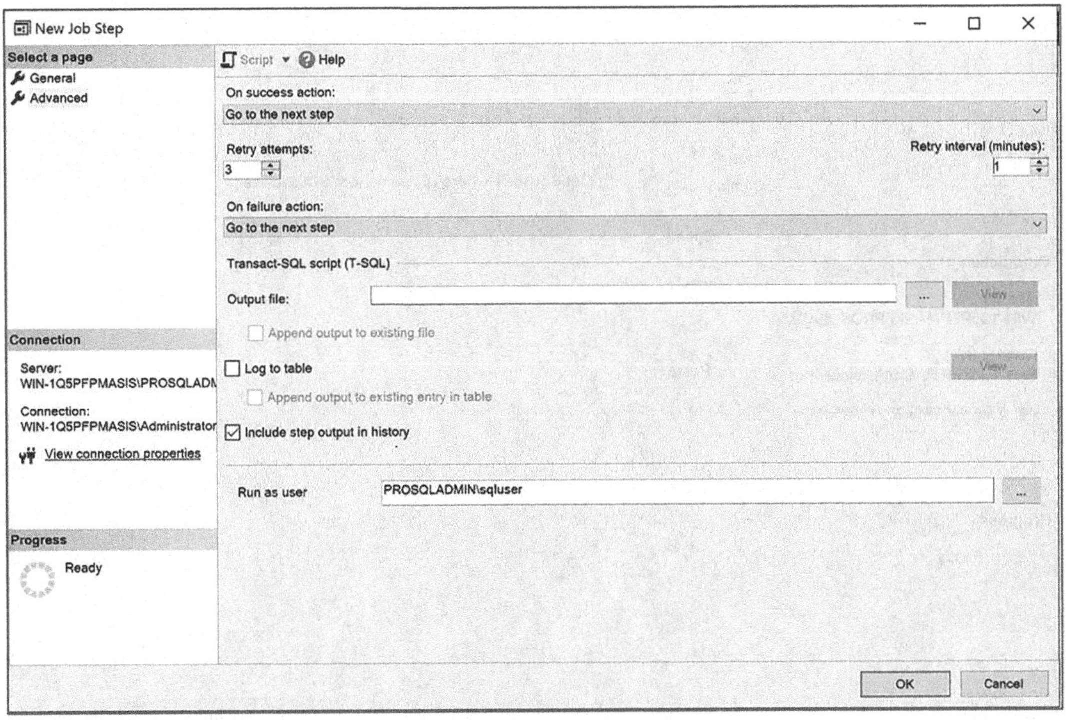

Figure 23-19. *The Advanced page*

We check the Include step output in history box so that the step output is included in the job history (doing so helps DBAs troubleshoot any issues) and configure the step to run as the SQLUser user. We configure the Run as user option because, as previously discussed, job steps of the T-SQL type use EXECUTE AS technology, instead of a proxy account to implement security.

Once we exit the dialog box, we need to use the New button on the Steps page of the New Job dialog box again to add our second job step. This time, on the General page, we specify the PowerShell type and enter the PowerShell script that checks the status of the SQL Server Browser service. We also use the Run as box to specify that the step runs under the context of the PowerShellProxy proxy. This is demonstrated in Figure 23-20. Listing 23-6 shows the command that we use.

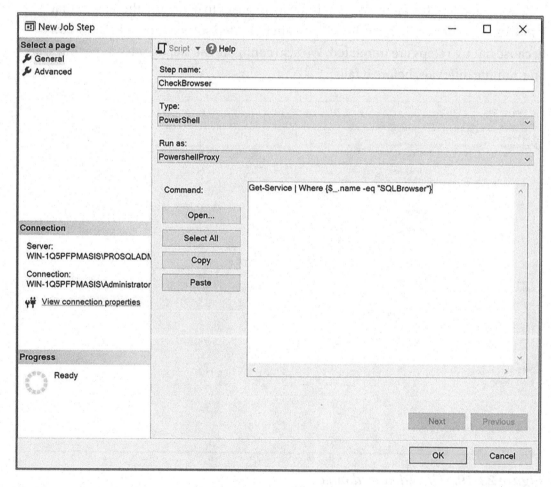

Figure 23-20. *The General page*

Listing 23-6. Checking Browser Service

```
Get-Service | Where {$_.name -eq "SQLBrowser"}
```

On the Advanced page, we choose to include the step output in the job history. We can leave all other options with their default values.

When we return to the Steps page of the New Job dialog box, we see both of our steps listed in the correct order, as shown in Figure 23-21. If we wish to change the order of the steps, however, we can use the up and down arrows in the Move step section. We can also bypass early steps by selecting to start the job at a later step using the Start step drop-down list.

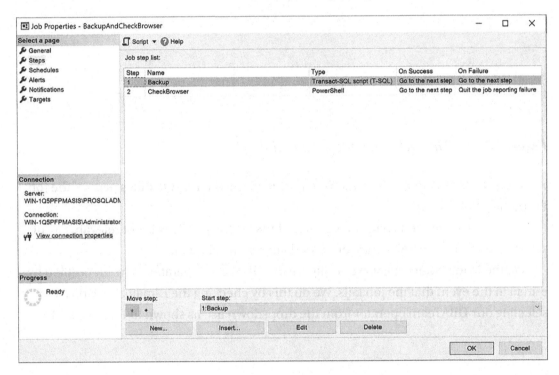

Figure 23-21. *The Steps page*

On the Schedules page of the wizard, we click the Pick button; doing so displays a list of existing schedules in the Pick Schedule for Job dialog box (see Figure 23-22). We use this dialog box to select our maintenance schedule.

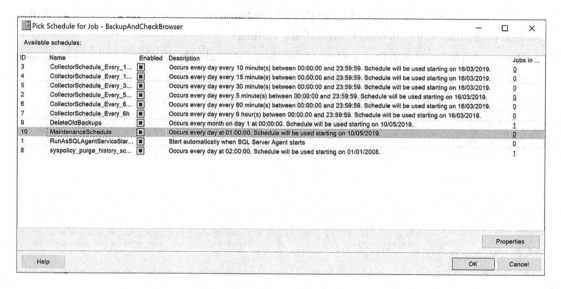

Figure 23-22. *The Pick Schedule for Job dialog box*

After we exit the dialog box, the Schedule displays on the Schedules page of the Job Properties dialog box.

You can use the Alerts page to organize alerts for the job. This is not relevant to our scenario right now, but alerts are discussed later in the chapter.

On the Notifications page, we configure the DBATeam operator we want notified by e-mail in the event that the job fails. We do this by checking the E-mail check box and selecting our DBATeam operator from the drop-down list, as shown in Figure 23-23.

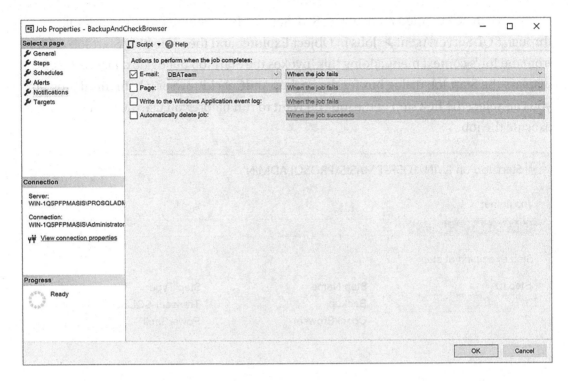

Figure 23-23. *The Notifications page*

You can use the Targets page to configure multiserver jobs, which are not relevant to our current scenario, but we do discuss them later in this chapter.

Monitoring and Managing Jobs

Although jobs are usually scheduled to run automatically, you still encounter monitoring and maintenance requirements, such as executing jobs manually and viewing job history. These tasks are discussed in the following sections.

Executing Jobs

Even if a job is scheduled to run automatically, at times you may wish to execute a job on an ad hoc basis. For example, if you have a job that is scheduled to run nightly to take full backups of the databases within your instance, you may wish to execute it manually just before a code release or software upgrade.

A job can be executed manually in SQL Server Management Studio by drilling through SQL Server Agent ➤ Jobs in Object Explorer and then selecting Start Job at Step from the Job's context menu; doing this invokes the Start Job dialog box. Figure 23-24 displays the Start Job dialog box for the BackupAndCheckBrowser job. In this dialog box, you can select the first step of the job you want to run before you use the Start button to execute the job.

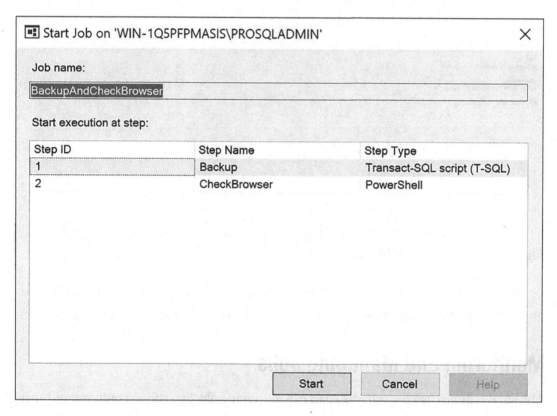

Figure 23-24. *Start Job dialog box*

To execute a job using T-SQL, you can use the sp_start_job system stored procedure. This procedure accepts the parameters detailed in Table 23-2.

Table 23-2. *sp_start_job Parameters*

Parameter	Description
@job_name	The name of the job to execute. If NULL, then the @job_name parameter must be specified.
@job_id	The ID of the job to execute. If NULL, then the @job_name parameter must be specified.
@server_name	Used for multiserver jobs. Specifies the target server on which to run the job.
@step_name	The name of the job step where execution should begin.

To run our BackupAndCheckBrowser job, we execute the command in Listing 23-7. Once a job has been executed, it cannot be executed again until it has completed.

Listing 23-7. Executing a Job

```
EXEC sp_start_job @job_name=N'BackupAndCheckBrowser' ;
```

If we wanted the job to start executing at a later step, we can use the @step_name parameter. For example, in our scenario, imagine that we want to execute our job in order to check that the SQL Server Browser service is running, but do not want the database backup to occur beforehand. To achieve this, we execute the command in Listing 23-8.

Listing 23-8. Starting a Job from a Specific Step

```
EXEC sp_start_job @job_name=N'BackupAndCheckBrowser', @step_name =
'CheckBrowser' ;
```

Viewing Job History

You can view the job history for a specific job by selecting View History from the Job context menu in SQL Server Agent ➤ Jobs within Object Explorer, or for all jobs by opening Job Activity Monitor, which you can find under the SQL Server Agent node in Object Explorer. Figure 23-25 shows what the job history of our BackupAndCheckBrowser job looks like after a single execution.

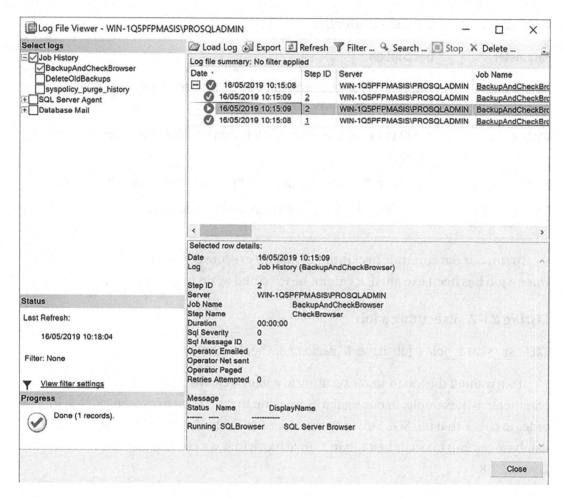

Figure 23-25. *The job history*

Here, you can see that we have drilled through Job History to see the history of each individual step. After highlighting the Step 2 progress entry, we can see that the results of the PowerShell script have been written to the step history and they show us that the SQL Server Browser service is running, as expected.

Creating Alerts

Creating an alert allows you to proactively respond to conditions that occur within your instance by either notifying an operator, running a job, or both. On our instance, we want to notify the DBATeam operator in the event that our Chapter23 log file becomes more than 75% full.

To create this alert in SQL Server Management Studio, we drill through SQL Server Agent in Object Explorer and select New Alert from the Alerts context menu. This causes the General page of the New Alert dialog box to display. This page is shown in Figure 23-26.

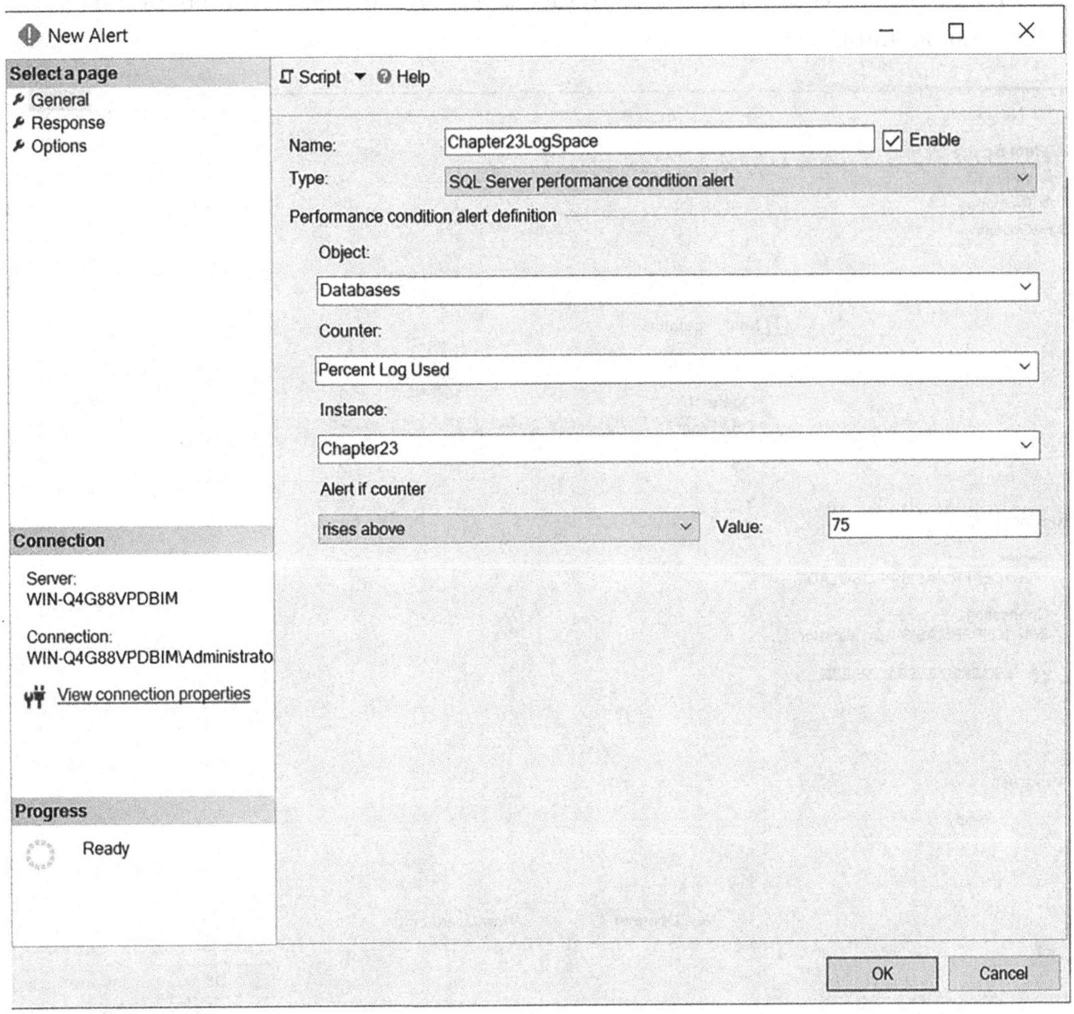

Figure 23-26. *The General page*

On this page of the dialog box, we use the Name field to specify a name for our alert and select SQL Server performance condition alert from the Type drop-down list. This causes the options within the page to dynamically update. We then select the Percent Log Used counter from the Databases object and specify that we are interested in the

Chapter23 instance of our object. (There is an instance of this counter for each database that resides on the instance.) Finally, we specify that the alert should be triggered if the value of this counter rises above 75 within the Alert if counter section of the page.

On the Response page of the dialog box, shown in Figure 23-27, we check the Notify operators box if the condition is met and then select an e-mail notification for our DBATeam operator.

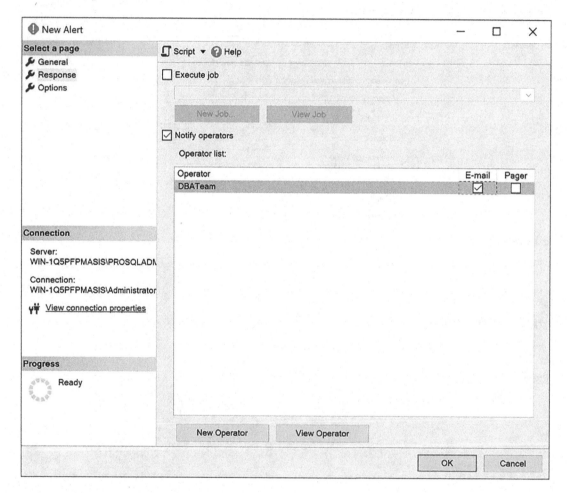

Figure 23-27. *Response page*

On the Options page of the dialog box, you can specify if alert error text should be included in the notification and also additional information to include. You can also configure a delay to occur between occurrences of the response being triggered. This can help you avoid duplicate notifications or needlessly running a job to fix an issue that is already being resolved. Figure 23-28 shows that we included the server/instance name in our notification to assist the DBAs in identifying the source of the alert.

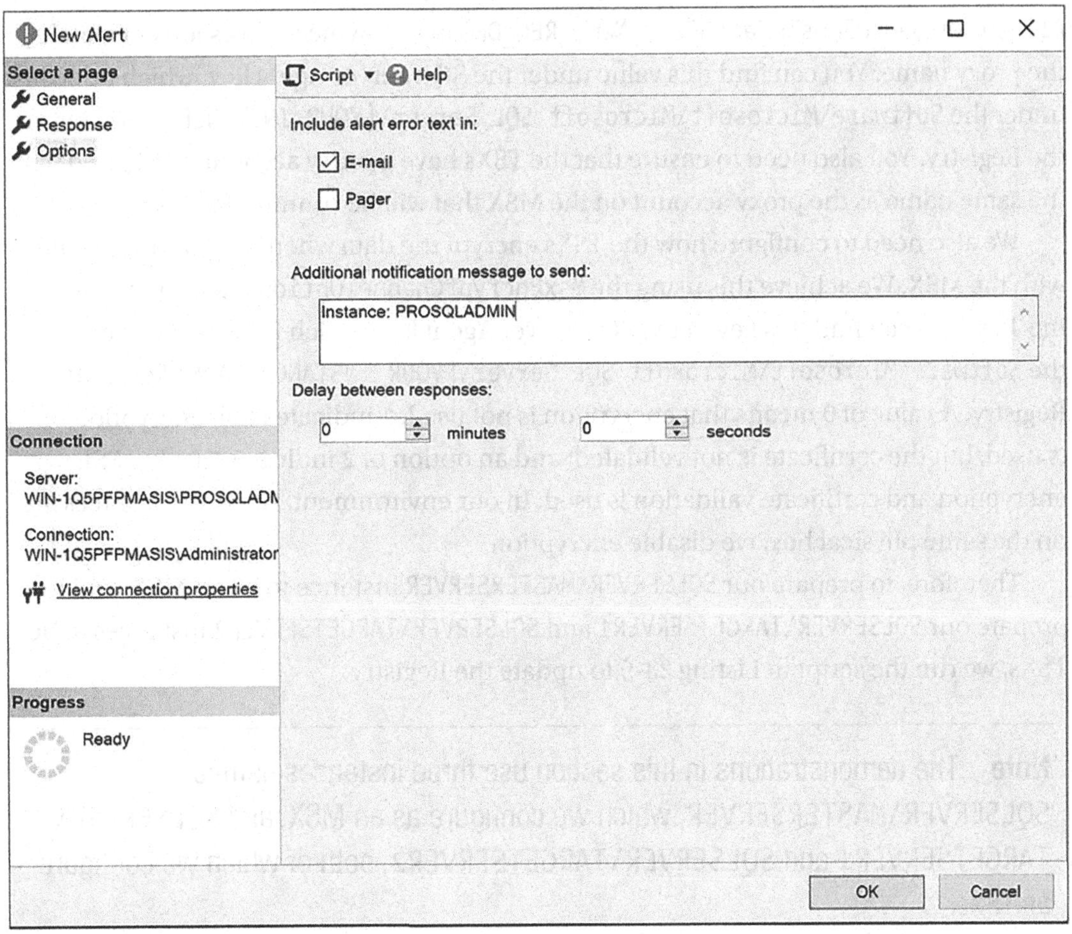

Figure 23-28. *The Options page*

Multiserver Jobs

Administration can be drastically simplified when you use multiserver administration. In a multiserver environment, you can configure one instance as a master server (MSX) and then other servers as target servers (TSX). You can then create a set of maintenance jobs on the MSX and configure them to run on the TSXs, or a subset of the TSXs.

Configuring the MSX and TSX Servers

Before creating multiserver jobs, you must first prepare the environment.
The first step is to edit the Registry on the MSX and set the value of the
AllowDownloadedJobsToMatchProxyName REG_DWORD to 1, which allows jobs to match
the proxy name. You can find this value under the SQL Server Agent key, which is located
under the Software\Microsoft\Microsoft SQL Server\[YOUR INSTANCE NAME] key in
the Registry. You also need to ensure that the TSXs have a proxy account configured with
the same name as the proxy account on the MSX that will be running the job.

We also need to configure how the TSXs encrypt the data when they communicate
with the MSX. We achieve this using the MsxEncryptChannelOptions Registry key for
the TSX. You can find this key in the SQL Server Agent key, which is located under
the Software\Microsoft\Microsoft SQL Server\[YOUR INSTANCE NAME] key in the
Registry. A value of 0 means that encryption is not used; 1 indicates that encryption
is used, but the certificate is not validated; and an option of 2 indicates that full SSL
encryption and certificate validation is used. In our environment, since all instances are
on the same physical box, we disable encryption.

Therefore, to prepare our SQLSERVER\MASTERSERVER instance to be an MSX, and to
prepare our SQLSERVER\TARGETSERVER1 and SQLSERVER\TARGETSERVER2 instances to be
TSXs, we run the script in Listing 23-9 to update the Registry.

Note   The demonstrations in this section use three instances named
SQLSERVER\MASTERSERVER, which we configure as an MSX, and SQLSERVER\
TARGETSERVER1 and SQLSERVER\TARGETSERVER2, both of which we configure
as TSXs.

Listing 23-9. Updating the Registry

```
USE Master
GO

EXEC xp_regwrite
  @rootkey = N'HKEY_LOCAL_MACHINE'
 ,@key = N'Software\Microsoft\Microsoft SQL Server\MSSQL16.MasterServer\SQL
 Server Agent'
```

```
 ,@value_name = N'AllowDownloadedJobsToMatchProxyName'
 ,@type = N'REG_DWORD'
 ,@value = 1 ;

EXEC xp_regwrite
  @rootkey='HKEY_LOCAL_MACHINE',
  @key='SOFTWARE\Microsoft\Microsoft SQL Server\MSSQL16.TARGETSERVER1\
  SQLServerAgent',
  @value_name='MsxEncryptChannelOptions',
  @type='REG_DWORD',
  @value=0 ;

EXEC xp_regwrite
  @rootkey='HKEY_LOCAL_MACHINE',
  @key='SOFTWARE\Microsoft\Microsoft SQL Server\MSSQL16.TARGETSERVER2\
  SQLServerAgent',
  @value_name='MsxEncryptChannelOptions',
  @type='REG_DWORD',
  @value=0 ;
GO
```

Tip   Because all of our instances reside on the same server, this script can be
run from any of the three instances. If your instances are on different servers, then
the first command will run on the MSX and the other two commands should run
against their corresponding TSX. You should also note that the service account
running the database engine will require permissions to the registry keys, for the
script to succeed.

We now use the SQLCMD script in Listing 23-10 to create the PowerShell proxy account
on TARGETSERVER1 and TARGETSERVER2. The script must be run in SQLCMD mode to
work because it connects to multiple instances.

Listing 23-10. Creating a Proxy

```
:connect sqlserver\targetserver1

CREATE CREDENTIAL WinUserCredential
        WITH IDENTITY = N'PROSQLADMIN\WinUser', SECRET = N'Pa$$w0rd' ;
GO

EXEC msdb.dbo.sp_add_proxy
                @proxy_name=N'PowerShellProxy',
                @credential_name=N'WinUserCredential',
                @enabled=1,
                @description=N'Proxy to check Browser Service status' ;
GO

EXEC msdb.dbo.sp_grant_proxy_to_subsystem
                @proxy_name=N'PowerShellProxy',
                @subsystem_id=12 ;
GO


:connect sqlserver\targetserver2

CREATE CREDENTIAL WinUserCredential
        WITH IDENTITY = N'PROSQLADMIN\WinUser', SECRET = N'Pa$$w0rd' ;
GO

EXEC msdb.dbo.sp_add_proxy
                @proxy_name=N'PowerShellProxy',
                @credential_name=N'WinUserCredential',
                @enabled=1,
                @description=N'Proxy to check Browser Service status' ;
GO

EXEC msdb.dbo.sp_grant_proxy_to_subsystem
                @proxy_name=N'PowerShellProxy',
                @subsystem_id=12 ;
GO
```

We can now begin to configure our SQLSERVER\MASTERSERVER instance as an MSX. To do this through SQL Server Management Studio, we invoke the Master Server Wizard by opening the SQL Server Agent context menu in Object Explorer and selecting Multi Server Administration ➤ Make This a Master.

After passing through the Welcome page of the wizard, we find the Master Server Operator page (see Figure 23-29). On this page, we enter the details of an operator who will be notified of the status of multiserver jobs.

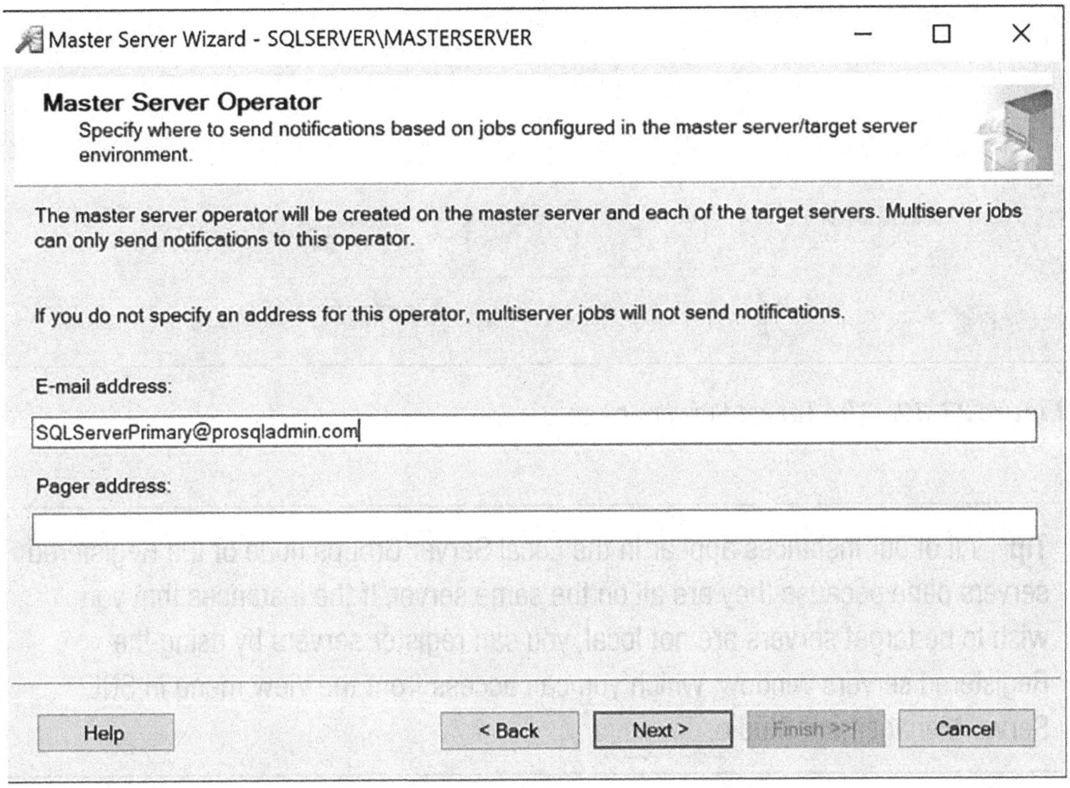

Figure 23-29. *The Master Server Operator page*

On the Target Servers page of the wizard, shown in Figure 23-30, we select our target servers from the list of registered servers in the Registered servers pane and move them to the Target servers pane using the arrows. After highlighting a server in the Target servers pane, we can use the Connection button to ensure connectivity.

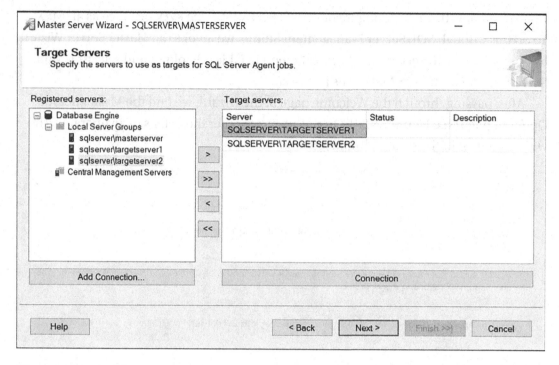

Figure 23-30. *The Target Servers page*

Tip   All of our instances appear in the Local Server Groups node of the Registered servers pane because they are all on the same server. If the instances that you wish to be target servers are not local, you can register servers by using the Registered servers window, which you can access from the View menu in SQL Server Management Studio.

On the Master Server Login Credentials page of the wizard, we are asked if a New Login should be created if required. This is the login that the TSXs use to connect to the MSX and download the jobs that they should run. If the instances of SQL Server Agent share the same service account as the MSX, then this is not required.

Now we see a summary of the actions that will be performed on the Completion page of the wizard before we are presented with a progress window, which informs us of the success or failure of each task.

Creating Master Jobs

You can create a master job in the same way as a local job, with the exception of specifying the target servers on which it should run. However, a limitation of using multiserver jobs is that T-SQL job steps cannot run under the context of another user; they must run under the context of the service account. Therefore, before we convert our BackupAndCheckBrowser job to be a multiserver job, we must edit it to remove the Run as Account. We can do this by using the sp_update_jobstep procedure, as demonstrated in Listing 23-11.

Listing 23-11. Updating Job Step

```
USE MSDB
GO

EXEC msdb.dbo.sp_update_jobstep
                @job_name=N'BackupAndCheckBrowser',
                @step_id=1 ,
                @database_user_name=N'' ;
GO
```

Another limitation of multiserver jobs is that the only allowable operator is the MSXOperator, who receives all notifications for multiserver jobs. Therefore, we also need to change the DBATeam operator to the MSXOperator operator before continuing. We can use the sp_update_job procedure to achieve this with the script in Listing 23-12.

Listing 23-12. Updating a Job

```
USE msdb
GO

EXEC msdb.dbo.sp_update_job
                @job_name=N'BackupAndCheckBrowser',
                @notify_email_operator_name=N'MSXOperator' ;
GO
```

We can now proceed to convert our BackupAndCheckBrowser job to a multiserver job from Management Studio by opening the Job Properties dialog box and navigating to the Targets page. As illustrated in Figure 23-31, we can use this page to change the job to a multiserver job and specify the target servers that it should run against from a list of target servers that have been enlisted using the sp_msx_enlist stored procedure. After closing the Properties dialog box, the job runs against the TargetServer1 and TargetServer2 instances instead of the MASTERSERVER instance.

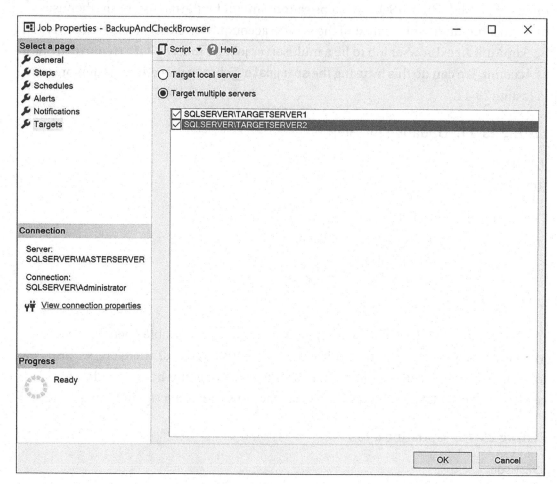

Figure 23-31.   *Convert to multiserver job*

To achieve the same results via T-SQL, we use the sp_delete_jobserver system stored procedure to stop the job from running against the MSX and the sp_add_jobserver system stored procedure to configure the job to run against the TSXs. Both of these procedures accept the parameters detailed in Table 23-3.

Table 23-3. *sp_delete_jobserver and sp_add_jobserver Parameters*

Parameter	Description
@job_id	The GUID of the job that you are converting to a multiserver job. If NULL, then the @job_name parameter must be specified.
@job_name	The name of the job that you are converting to a multiserver job. If NULL, then the @job_id parameter must be specified.
@server_name	The server/instance name that you want the job to run against.

In our scenario, we can use the script in Listing 23-13 to convert the job.

Listing 23-13. Converting to a Multiserver Job

```
EXEC msdb.dbo.sp_delete_jobserver
        @job_name=N'BackupAndCheckBrowser',
        @server_name = N'SQLSERVER\MASTERSERVER' ;
GO

EXEC msdb.dbo.sp_add_jobserver
        @job_name=N'BackupAndCheckBrowser',
        @server_name = N'SQLSERVER\TARGETSERVER1' ;
GO

EXEC msdb.dbo.sp_add_jobserver
        @job_name=N'BackupAndCheckBrowser',
        @server_name = N'SQLSERVER\TARGETSERVER2' ;
GO
```

Managing Target Servers

When you configure your MSX, make sure you consider various maintenance activities against the TSXs. These include polling the TSXs, synchronizing time across the servers, running ad hoc jobs, and defecting (delisting) TSXs.

We can achieve these tasks in the Target Server Status dialog box, which we can invoked from the context menu of SQL Server Agent on the MSX by selecting Multi Server Administration ➤ Manage Target Servers. The Target Server Status tab of this dialog box is shown in Figure 23-32.

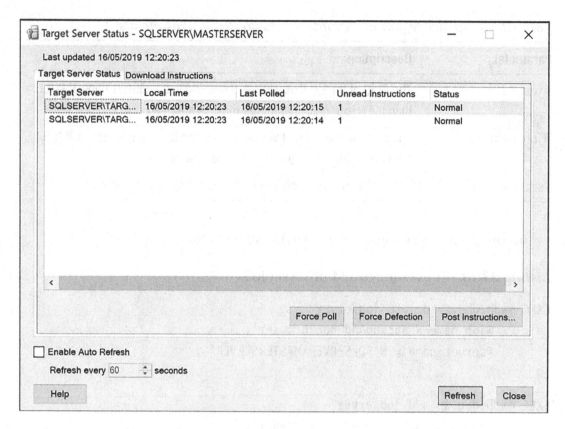

Figure 23-32. *The Target Server Status tab*

On this tab, we can use the Force Poll button to make the Target Servers poll the MSX. When a TSX polls the MSX, we are forcing it to download the latest copy of the jobs that it is configured to run. This is useful if you have updated the master job.

The Force Defection button causes the highlighted TSX to be delisted from the MSX. After it is delisted, the selected TSX no longer polls for or runs multiserver jobs.

The Post Instructions button invokes the Post Download Instructions dialog box, where you are able to send one of the following instructions to TSXs:

- Defect

- Set Polling Interval

- Synchronize Clocks

- Start Job

To synchronize the time on all servers, you would choose the Synchronize Clocks instruction type and ensure that All target servers is selected in the Recipients section, as illustrated in Figure 23-33. The clocks are then synchronized when the targets next poll the master.

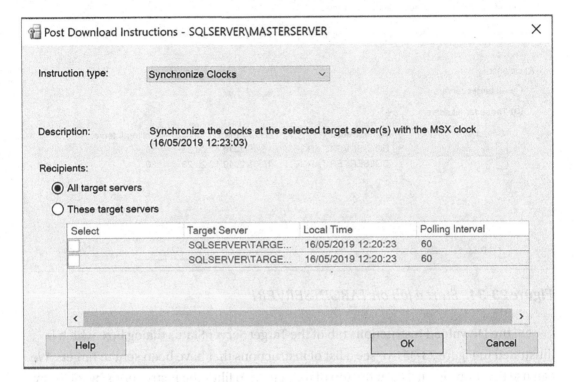

Figure 23-33. *Synchronize Clocks*

In another scenario, there may be a time when we wish to perform an ad hoc run of our BackupAndCheckBrowser job against TARGETSERVER1. We can do this by selecting Start Job as the Instruction type and then choosing our job from the Job name drop-down list. We then use the Recipients section of the screen to select TARGETSERVER1. This is illustrated in Figure 23-34.

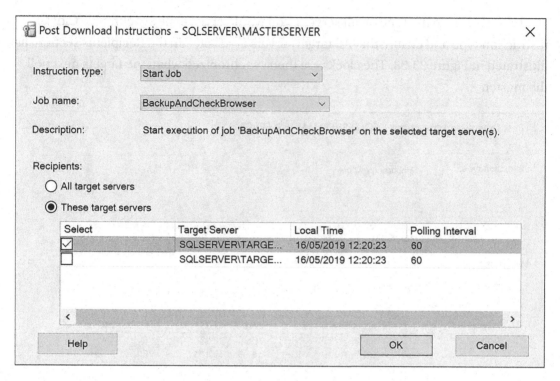

Figure 23-34. *Start a job on TARGETSERVER1*

On the Download Instructions tab of the Target Server Status dialog box, which is illustrated in Figure 23-35, we see a list of instructions that have been sent to targets. We can use the drop-down lists at the top of the screen to filter the instructions by job or by target server.

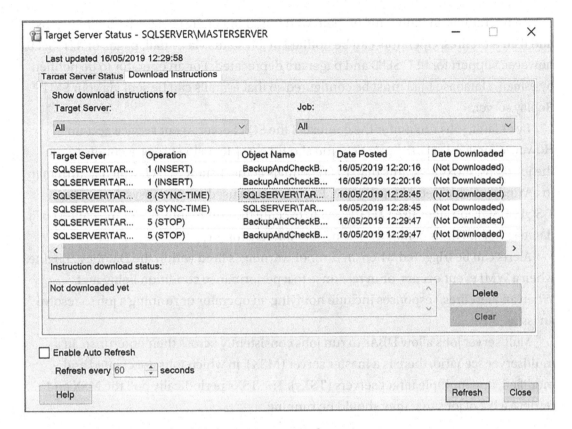

Figure 23-35. *The Download Instructions tab*

Summary

SQL Server Agent is a scheduling engine for SQL Server that allows you to create powerful maintenance jobs, with decision-based logic, on a variety of schedules. A job is the container for the tasks that should be performed, and each of these tasks is known as a step. Each job step can run under the context of a different account and can run tasks under different subsystems, or types, such as T-SQL, PowerShell, operating system command, or SSIS package.

A schedule is attached to a job and can be triggered at a specific date and time, when the CPU is idle, or on a reoccurring schedule, such as daily, weekly, or monthly. A schedule can also reoccur on an intraday basis, such as hourly, every minute, or even as frequently as every ten seconds.

An operator is an individual or team who is notified of the success or failure of jobs and if an alert fires. Operators can be notified of job status via e-mail, pager, or NET SEND; however, support for NET SEND and pager are deprecated. For an operator to be notified by e-mail, Database Mail must be configured so that e-mails can be sent via your SMTP Replay server.

By default, jobs run under the context of the SQL Server Agent service account. However, for good security practice, you should consider using proxy accounts to run the job steps. Proxy accounts map to credentials at the instance level, which in turn map to a Windows-level security principle. Proxies can be used for all subsystems, except T-SQL. T-SQL job steps use EXECUTE AS to execute the commands under the context of a database user. This is configured using the Run As property.

Alerts can be triggered when an error or warning is fired within the Database Engine, when a WMI event occurs, or in response to a performance condition being met. When an alert fires, responses include notifying an operator or running a job to resolve an issue.

Multiserver jobs allow DBAs to run jobs consistently across their enterprise. In a multiserver scenario, there is a master server (MSX), in which jobs are created and modified, and multiple target servers (TSXs). The TSXs periodically poll the MSX and retrieve a list of jobs that they should be running.

CHAPTER 24

Policy-Based Management

Policy-Based Management (PBM) is a system DBAs can use to report on or enforce standards across the enterprise, when used with a Central Management Server. This chapter first introduces you to the concepts used by PBM and then demonstrates how to use PBM to effectively manage an estate through the GUI and with PowerShell.

PBM Concepts

Policy-Based Management uses the concepts of targets, facets, conditions, and policies. *Targets* are entities PBM manages, such as databases or tables. *Facets* are collections of properties that relate to a target. For example, the database facet includes a property relating to the name of the database. *Conditions* are Boolean expressions that can be evaluated against a property. A binds conditions to targets. The following sections discuss each of these concepts.

Facets

A facet is a collection of properties that relate to a type of target, such as View, which has properties including `IsSchemaBound`, `HasIndex`, and `HasAfterTrigger`; Database Role, which has properties including `Name Owner` and `IsFixedRole`; and Index, which has properties including `IsClustered`, `IsPartitioned`, and `IsUnique`. The Index facet also exposes properties relating to geospatial indexes, memory-optimized indexes, XML indexes, and full-text indexes. Other notable facets include `Database`, `StoredProcedure`, `SurfaceAreaConfiguration`, `LinkedServer`, and `Audit`. SQL Server 2022 provides 96 facets in all, and you can find a complete list within the "Evaluation Modes" section of this chapter. You can also access a list of facets by running the command in Listing 24-1.

P. A. Carter, *Pro SQL Server 2022 Administration*, https://doi.org/10.1007/978-1-4842-8864-1_24

Listing 24-1. Finding a List of Facets

```
SELECT name
FROM msdb.dbo.syspolicy_management_facets ;
```

Conditions

A condition is a Boolean expression that is evaluated against an object property to determine whether or not it matches your requirement. Each facet contains multiple properties that you can create conditions against, but each condition can only access properties from a single facet. Conditions can be evaluated against the following operators:

- =

- !=

- LIKE

- NOT LIKE

- IN

- NOT IN

For example, you can use the LIKE operator to ensure that all database names begin with Chapter by using the following expression Database.Name LIKE 'Chapter%'.

Targets

A target is an entity to which a policy can be applied. This can be a table, a database, an entire instance, or most other objects within SQL Server. When adding targets to a policy, you can use conditions to limit the number of targets. This means, for example, if you create a policy to enforce database naming conventions on an instance, you can use a condition to avoid checking the policy against database names that contain the words "SharePoint," "bdc," or "wss," since these are your SharePoint databases and they may contain GUIDs that may be disallowed under your standard naming conventions.

Policies

A policy contains one condition and binds it to one or more targets (targets may also be filtered by separate conditions) and an evaluation mode. Depending on the evaluation mode you select, the policy may also contain a schedule on which you would like the policy to be checked. Policies support four evaluation modes, which are discussed in the following section.

Evaluation Modes

Policies support between one and four evaluation modes, depending on which facet you use within the condition. The following are the evaluation modes:

- On Demand
- On Schedule
- On Change: Log Only
- On Change: Prevent

If the evaluation mode is configured as On Demand, then the policies are only evaluated when you (the DBA) manually evaluate them. If the evaluation mode is configured as On Schedule, then you create a schedule when you create the policy; this causes the policy to be evaluated periodically.

Tip   A policy can be evaluated On Demand even if it has been configured with a different evaluation mode.

If you select the On Change: Log Only evaluation mode, then whenever the relevant property of a target changes, the result of the policy validation is logged to the SQL Server log. In the event that the policy is fired but not validated, a message is generated in the log. This occurs when a target has been configured in such a way that one of your policies is violated. If the policy is violated, then Error 34053 is thrown with a severity level of 16 (meaning the problem can be fixed by the user).

> **Tip**   When you create an object, this causes the properties to be evaluated in the same way that they are when an existing object's properties are altered.

If you choose On Change: Prevent as the evaluation mode, then when a property is changed, SQL Server evaluates the property, and if there is a violation, an error message is thrown and the statement that caused the policy violation is rolled back.

Because policies work based on DDL events being fired, depending on the properties within the facet, not all evaluation modes can be implemented for all facets. The rules for working out the evaluation modes supported by a specific facet are rather opaque, so you can discover them by running the query in Listing 24-2.

Listing 24-2. Listing Supported Execution Types per Facet

```
SELECT
      name ,
          'Yes' AS on_demand,
      CASE
          WHEN (CONVERT(BIT, execution_mode & 4)) = 1
          THEN 'Yes'
          ELSE 'No'
          END  AS on_schedule,
          CASE
          WHEN (CONVERT(BIT, execution_mode & 2)) = 1
          THEN 'Yes'
          ELSE 'No'
          END  AS on_change_log,
      CASE
          WHEN (CONVERT(BIT, execution_mode & 1)) = 1
          THEN 'Yes'
          ELSE 'No'
          END  AS on_change_prevent
FROM msdb.dbo.syspolicy_management_facets ;
```

Central Management Servers

SQL Server Management Studio provides a feature called a central management server. This feature allows you to register an instance as a central management server and then register other instances as registered servers of this central management server. Once you have registered servers under a central management server, you can run queries against all servers in the group or run policies against all servers within a group.

Tip   CMS is a great feature, when used with Policy Based Management, but also in its own right. I always implement CMS when I am looking after medium or large SQL Server estates, for purposes such as running ad hoc queries against multiple servers. This allows me to quickly answer management and capacity questions, such as "How many databases do we have in our estate?"

To register a central management server, select Registered Servers from the View menu in SQL Server Management Studio. This causes the Registered Servers window to appear, which is illustrated in Figure 24-1.

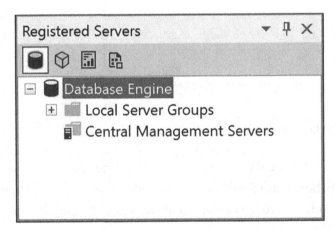

Figure 24-1. *The Registered Servers window*

Let's register our SQLSERVER\MASTERSERVER instance (which is the server/instance name we use in the demonstrations within this section) as a central management server by selecting Register Central Management Server from the context menu of Central Management Servers. This causes the General tab of the New Server Registration dialog box to display, as illustrated in Figure 24-2.

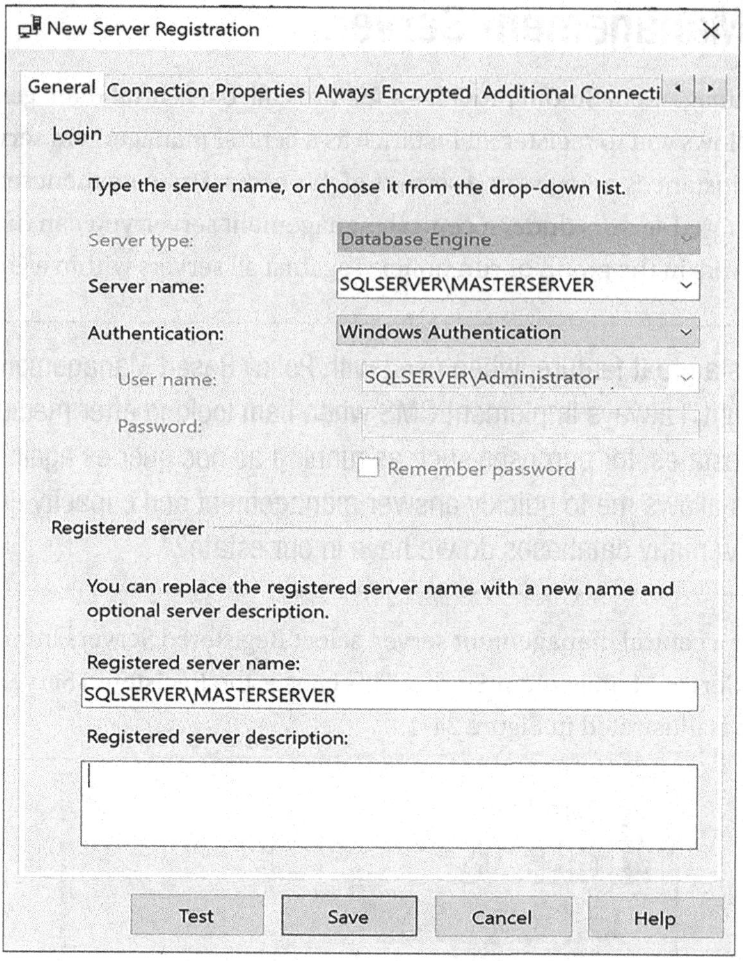

Figure 24-2. *The General tab*

On this tab, we enter the server/instance name of the central management server in the Server name box. This causes the Registered server name field to update, but you can edit this manually to give it a new name if you wish. Optionally, you can also add a description for the instance.

On the Connection Properties tab, displayed in Figure 24-3, we specify our preferences for connecting to the instance.

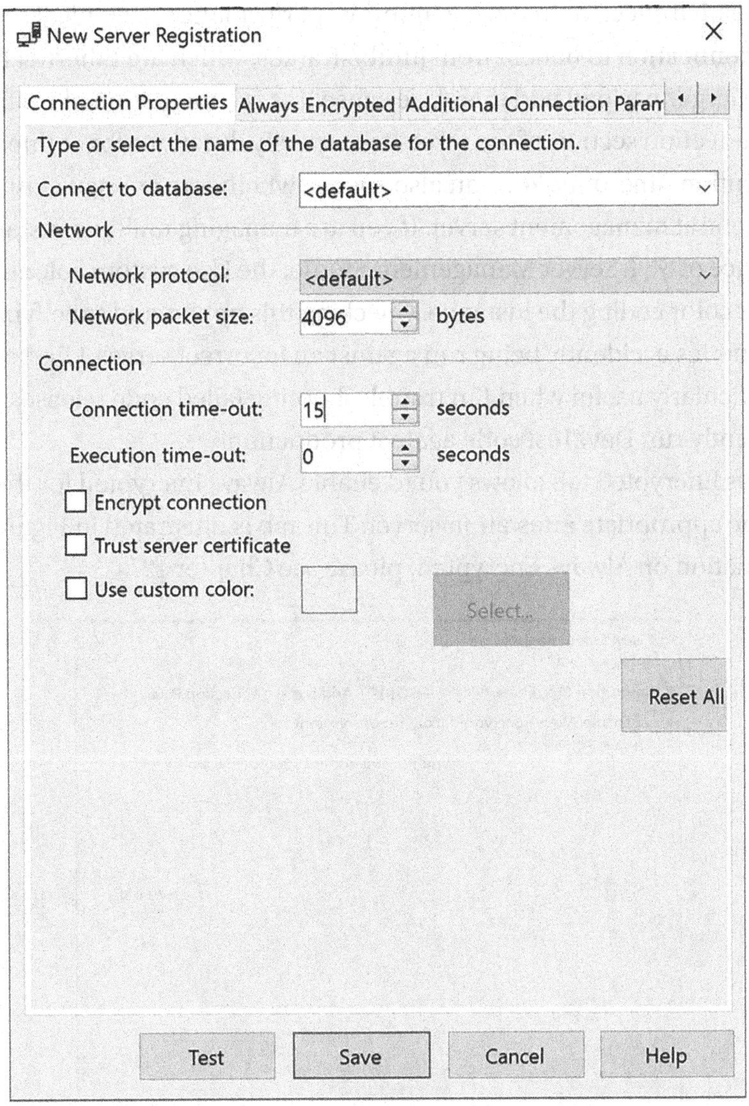

Figure 24-3. *The Connection Properties tab*

On this tab, we enter a database as a landing zone. If we leave the option as Default, then the connection is made to our default database. In the Network section of the tab, you can specify a specific network protocol to use, or leave the setting as Default, which is what we have done here. Leaving this as Default causes the connection to use the highest priority protocol specified in the instance's network configuration. Although changing the network packet size is not normally advised, because in most scenarios, it will have a negative effect, doing so can improve performance in atypical scenarios by allowing the connection to benefit from jumbo frames, which are Ethernet frames that can support a larger payload and therefore cause less fragmentation of traffic.

In the Connection section of the screen, we specify durations for connection time-outs and execution time-outs. You can also specify whether to encrypt connections made to the central management server. If you are managing multiple instances within a single instance of SQL Server Management Studio, the Use custom color option is very useful for color coding the instance. Checking this option and specifying a color helps avoid queries accidently being run against an incorrect server. I find color coding instances particularly useful when I'm troubleshooting failed code releases, since I don't want to accidently run Dev/Test code against production!

The Always Encrypted tab allows you to enable Always Encrypted for the connection and specify the appropriate attestation server. This tab is illustrated in Figure 24-4. For further information on Always Encrypted, please see Chapter 12.

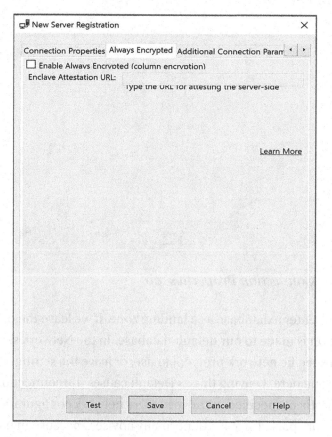

Figure 24-4. *Always Encrypted tab*

The Additional Connection Properties tab, shown in Figure 24-5, allows you to specify connection string properties manually. You should be aware, however, that if you enter connection properties that you have already specified on the other tabs, the manually specified properties will override your selections in the other tabs.

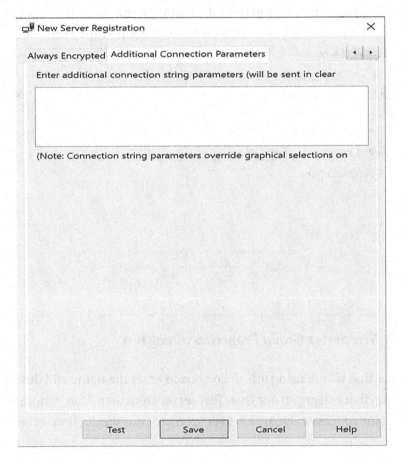

Figure 24-5. *Additional Connection Properties tab*

Clicking the Test button at the bottom of the New Server Registration window allows you to test the connection to the instance before you save it. This is always a good idea because it helps you avoid unnecessary troubleshooting at a later date.

Once we have registered the central management server, we can choose to either register servers directly below the central management server or create server groups below the central management server. Base the strategy you choose here on the requirements of your environment. For example, if all servers that the central management server manages should have the same policies applied, it is probably sufficient to register the servers directly below the central management server. If your central management server will manage servers from different environments, however, such as Prod and Dev/Test, then you probably want to enforce different sets of policies against different environments; in such cases, it makes sense to create different server groups. Selecting New Server Group from the context menu of your newly created central management server invokes the New Server Group Properties dialog box, as illustrated in Figure 24-6.

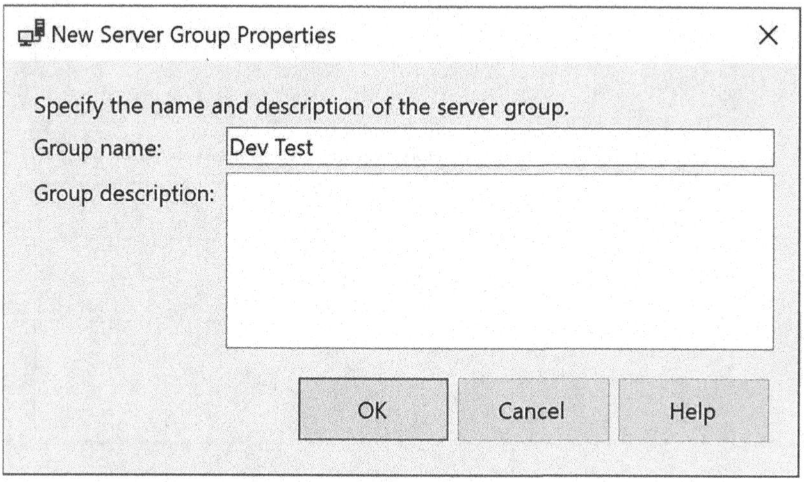

Figure 24-6. *New Server Group Properties dialog box*

You can see that we are using this dialog box to enter the name and description of the server group that will group our Dev/Test servers together. After exiting the dialog box, we repeat the process to create a server group for our production servers, which we name Prod.

Tip   You can also nest server groups. Therefore, in more complex topologies, you can have a server group for each geographical region, which contains a server group for each environment.

Now let's choose the New Server Registration option from the context menu of each server group to add our instances to the appropriate groups. We add SQLSERVER\ TARGETSERVER1 and SQLSERVER\TARGETSERVER2 to the Prod group and add the default instance of SQLSERVER to the DevTest group. You can add the servers using the same New

Server Registration dialog box that you used to register the central management server. Figure 24-7 shows the Registered Servers screen after the servers have been added.

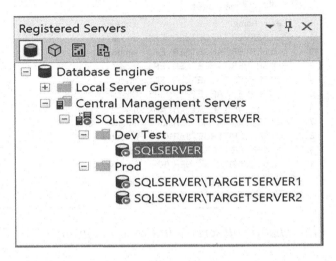

Figure 24-7. *The Registered Servers window*

One very useful feature of central management servers is their ability to run queries against all servers within a server group or against all servers they manage. For example, we can select New Query from the context menu of the Prod Server Group and run the query in Listing 24-3.

Listing 24-3. Listing All Database in the Server Group

```
SELECT name
FROM sys.Databases ;
```

This query returns the results displayed in Figure 24-8.

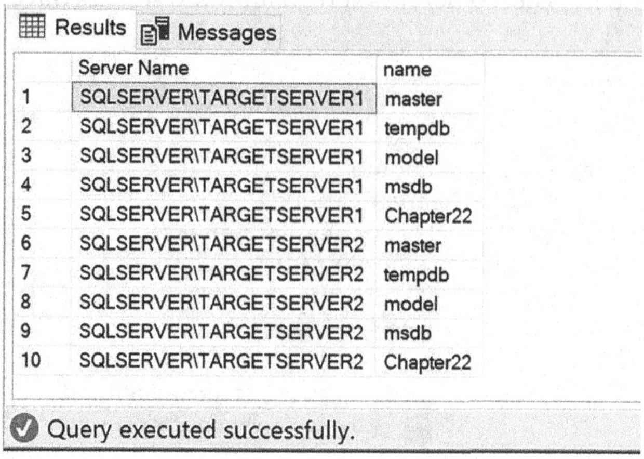

	Server Name	name
1	SQLSERVER\TARGETSERVER1	master
2	SQLSERVER\TARGETSERVER1	tempdb
3	SQLSERVER\TARGETSERVER1	model
4	SQLSERVER\TARGETSERVER1	msdb
5	SQLSERVER\TARGETSERVER1	Chapter22
6	SQLSERVER\TARGETSERVER2	master
7	SQLSERVER\TARGETSERVER2	tempdb
8	SQLSERVER\TARGETSERVER2	model
9	SQLSERVER\TARGETSERVER2	msdb
10	SQLSERVER\TARGETSERVER2	Chapter22

Query executed successfully.

Figure 24-8. Results of listing all servers in the server group

The first thing you notice is that the status bar below the query results is pink instead of yellow. This indicates that the query has been run against multiple servers. Second, instead of displaying an instance name, the status bar displays the server group that the query has been run against; in our case, this is Prod. Finally, notice that an additional column has been added to the result set. This column is called Server Name, and it indicates which instance within the server group the row returned from. Because no user databases exist on SQLSERVER\TARGETSERVER1 or SQLSERVER\TARGETSERVER2, the four system databases have been returned from each instance.

Creating Policies

You can create policies using either SQL Server Management Studio or T-SQL. The following sections discuss how to create a simple static policy, before they go on to discuss how to create advanced, dynamic policies.

Creating Simple Policies

PBM offers a great deal of flexibility within its predefined facets, properties, and conditions. You can use this flexibility to create a comprehensive set of policies for your enterprise. The following sections discuss how to use PBM's built-in functionality to create simple policies.

Creating a Policy That You Can Manually Evaluate

As you've probably noticed, example databases in this book use the name format of Chapter<ChapterNumber>. Therefore, here we create a policy that enforces this naming convention by causing any policy that violates this policy to roll back and generate an error. To do this, we invoke the Create New Policy dialog box by drilling through Management ➤ Policy Management in Object Explorer on the Master server and then selecting New Policy from the Policies context menu. Figure 24-9 displays the General page of the dialog box.

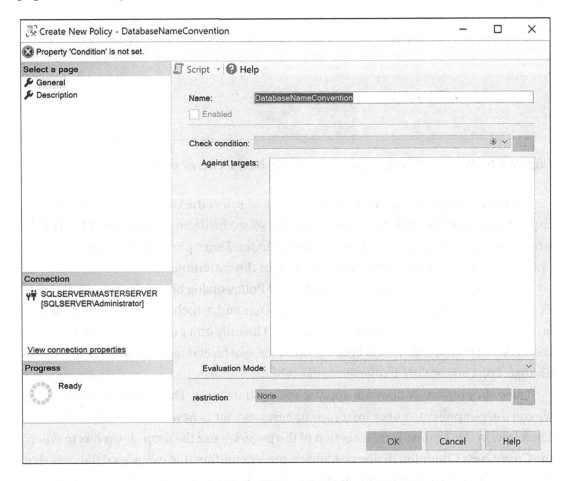

Figure 24-9. *New Policy dialog box, General page*

On this page, we give the policy a name but find that the Against targets and Evaluation Mode options are not accessible. This is because we have not yet created a condition. Therefore, our next step is to use the Check condition drop-down box to select New Condition. This causes the General page of the Create New Condition dialog box to display, illustrated in Figure 24-10.

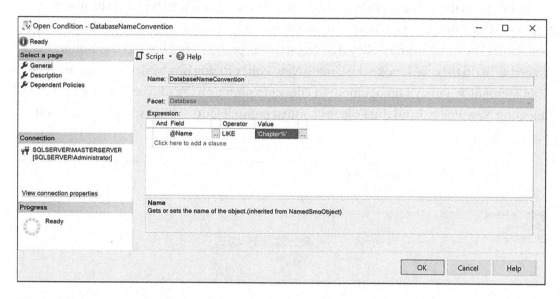

Figure 24-10. *Create New Condition dialog box, General page*

On this page, we give the condition a name and select the Database facet. In the Expression area of the screen, we select that the @Name field should be LIKE 'Chapter%', where % is a zero-or-more-character wildcard. On the Description page, we are optionally able to specify a textual description for the condition.

Back on the General page of the Create New Policy dialog box, we ensure that the Evaluation Mode drop-down is set to select On Demand, which means that the policy is not evaluated unless we explicitly evaluate it. The only other option available is to schedule the evaluation. This is because the Database facet does not support the On Change: Log Only or On Change: Prevent evaluation modes.

Our policy obviously does not apply to system databases. This matters because we can use our policy to check existing databases as well as new databases we create. Therefore, in the Against Targets section of the page, we use the drop-down box to enter the Create New Condition dialog box and create a condition that excludes databases that have a database ID of four or less, as shown in Figure 24-11.

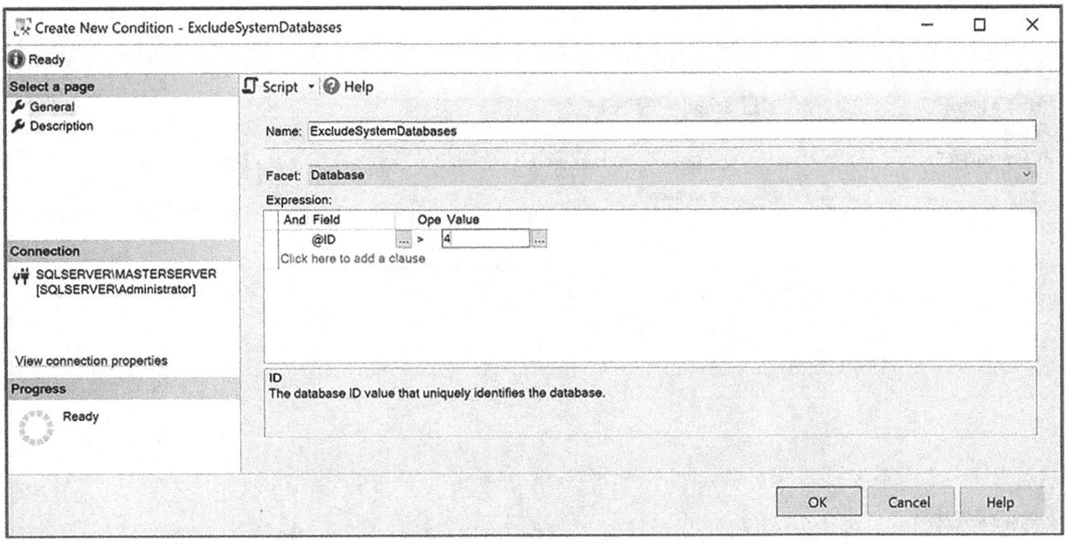

Figure 24-11. *Create an ExcludeSystemDatabases condition*

Back in the Create New Policy dialog box, we can create a condition to enforce a server restriction, which filters the instances that the policy is evaluated against. Because we are only evaluating the policy against our SQLSERVER\MASTERSERVER instance, however, we do not need to do this. Instead, we navigate to the Description page, illustrated in Figure 24-12.

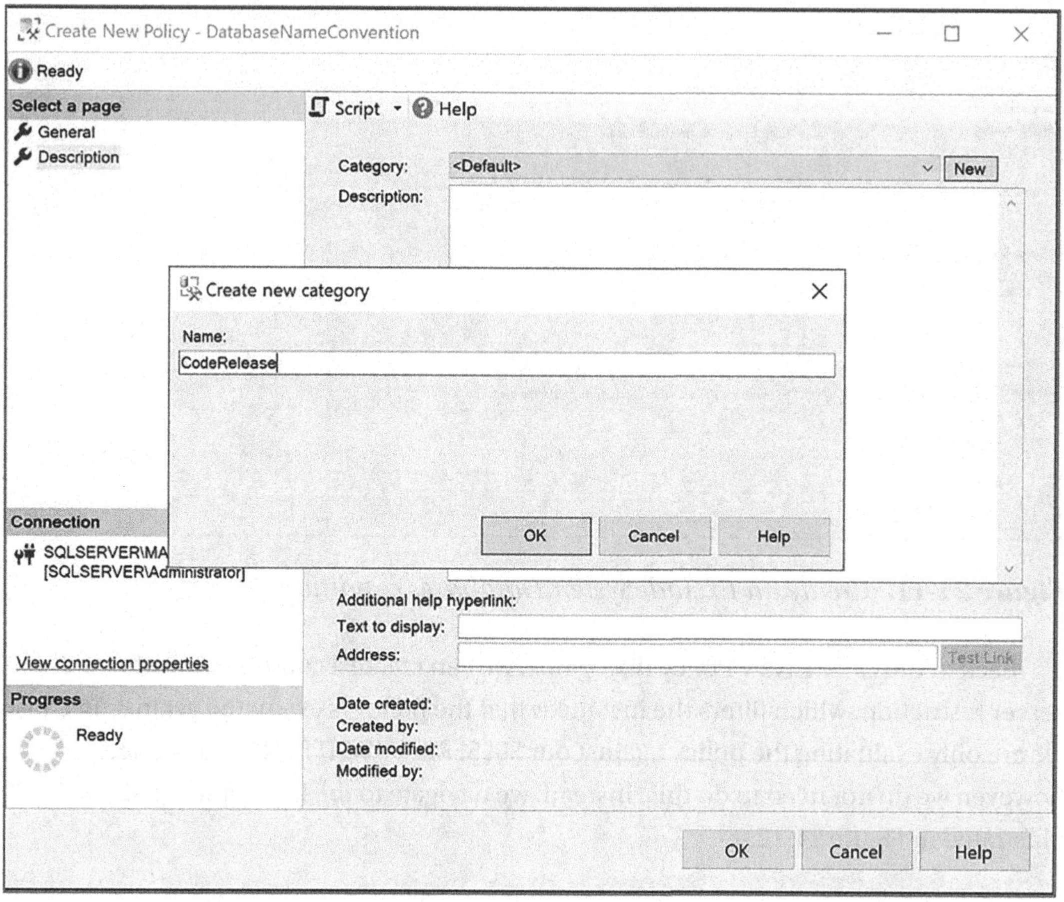

Figure 24-12. *The Description page*

On this page, we use the New button to create a new category, CodeRelease, which helps us check code quality in a UAT (user acceptance testing) or OAT (operational acceptance testing) environment before the code is promoted to production. Optionally, we can also add a free text description of the policy and a help hyperlink, alongside a website address or e-mail link.

Manually Evaluating a Policy

Before evaluating our policy, we first create a database that does not match our naming convention by executing the command in Listing 24-4.

Listing 24-4. Creating a BrokenPolicy Database

```
CREATE DATABASE BrokenPolicy ;
```

We can evaluate our new policy against our instance by using the Evaluate Policies dialog box, which we can invoke by drilling through Management ➤ Policy Management ➤ Policies and by selecting Evaluate from the context menu of our policy.

Tip   You can manually evaluate the policy even if it is disabled.

In the Evaluate Policies dialog box, shown in Figure 24-13, you see a list of policies that have been evaluated in the top half of the window; a status indicator informs you if any policies have been broken. In the bottom half of the window, you see a list of targets that the highlighted policy was evaluated against; here a status indicator informs you of the policy's status on a target-by-target basis.

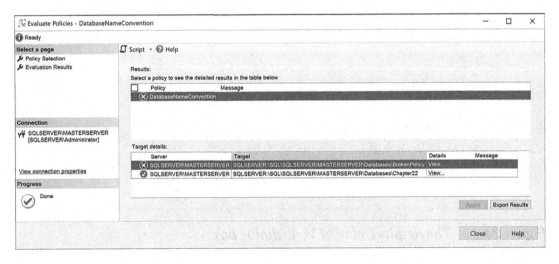

Figure 24-13. *The Evaluate Policies dialog box*

Tip   If you wish to evaluate multiple polices, select Evaluate from the context menu of the Policies folder in Object Explorer, and then select which policies you would like to evaluate. All selected policies are then evaluated and displayed in the Evaluation Results page.

Tip   We created the Chapter22 database in Chapter 22 of this book. If you do not have a Chapter22 database, you can create it using the statement CREATE DATABASE Chapter22 ;.

Click the View link in the Details column to invoke the Results Detailed View dialog box, as illustrated in Figure 24-14. This information is useful for failed policy evaluations because it provides the details of the actual value that did not meet the policy's condition.

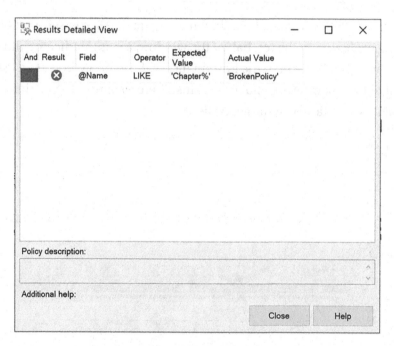

Figure 24-14.   *The Results Detailed View dialog box*

Creating a Policy That Prevents Unwanted Activity

Another very useful simple policy is one that helps you prevent developers from obfuscating their stored procedures. Procedure obfuscation arguably has a place in third-party software, in order to prevent the theft of intellectual property. For in-house applications, however, there is no need to use obfuscation, and doing so can lead to issues with diagnosing performance issues. Additionally, if the development teams are not using source control, it can lead to the loss of code, in the event of a disaster. In this instance, rather than just evaluating the policy on an ad hoc basis, we want to prevent stored procedures that are obfuscated from being created. This means that during code releases, you do not need to review every stored procedure for the WITH ENCRYPTION syntax. Instead, you can expect the policy to be evaluated and the CREATE PROCEDURE statement to be rolled back, preventing this from occurring.

Before we create this policy, we need to ensure that nested triggers are enabled on the instance. This is because the policy will be enforced using DDL triggers, and nested triggers are a hard technical requirement for the On Change:Prevent mode. You can enable nested triggers using sp_configure, with the script in Listing 24-5; however, they are turned on by default.

Listing 24-5. Enabling Nested Triggers

```
EXEC sp_configure 'nested triggers', 1 ;
RECONFIGURE
```

After creating the policy, you need to create a condition. When creating the condition, as illustrated in Figure 24-15, we use the @IsEncrypted property of the StoredProcedure facet.

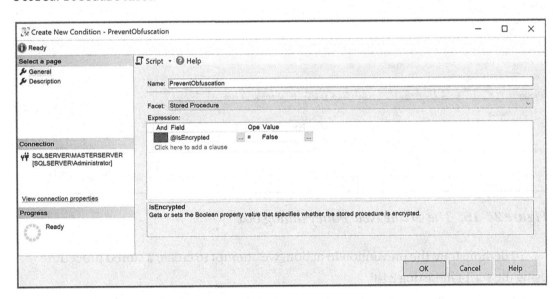

Figure 24-15. *The Create New Condition dialog box*

In the Create New Policy dialog box, illustrated in Figure 24-16, we could use the Against Targets area to configure which targets should be evaluated by the policy; the setting defaults to Every Stored Procedure in Every Database, however. This suits our needs, so we do not need to create a condition. In the Evaluation Mode drop-down, we select On Change: Prevent; this makes it, so it is not possible to create stored procedures on our SQLSERVER\MASTERSERVER instance if is obfuscated. We also make sure to check the Enabled box so that the policy is enabled when it is created.

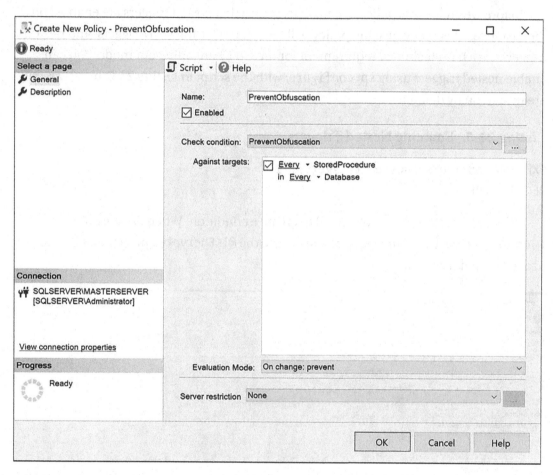

Figure 24-16. *The Create New Policy dialog box*

To demonstrate the prevention in action, we attempt to create a stored procedure using the script in Listing 24-6.

Listing 24-6. Creating a Stored Procedure with NOLOCK

```
CREATE PROCEDURE ObfuscatedProc
WITH ENCRYPTION
AS
BEGIN
        SELECT *
        FROM sys.tables
END
```

Figure 24-17 shows the error that is thrown when we attempt to run this `CREATE PROCEDURE` statement.

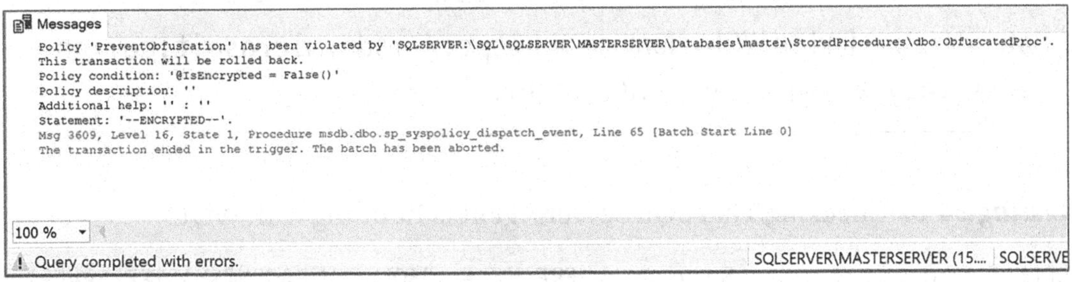

Figure 24-17. *The error thrown by the policy trigger*

Creating an Advanced Policy

PBM is extensible, and if you can't create the required condition using the built-in facet properties, the Expression Advanced Editor allows you to use a wide range of functions. These functions include `ExecuteSql()` and `ExecuteWql()`, which allow you to build your own SQL and WQL (Windows Query Language), respectively. The `ExecuteSql()` and `ExecuteWql()` functions are not T-SQL functions. They are part of the PBM framework.

You can use these functions to write queries against either the Database Engine or Windows and evaluate the result. The functions are called once for each target. So, for example, if they are used with the `Server` facet, they only run once, but if they are used against the `Table` facet, they are evaluated for every target table. If multiple columns are returned when you are using `ExecuteSql()`, then the first column of the first row is evaluated. If multiple columns are returned when you are using `ExecuteWql()`, then an error is thrown. For example, imagine that you want to ensure that the SQL Server Agent service starts. You can achieve this in T-SQL by running the query in Listing 24-7.

This query uses the LIKE operator because the servicename column also includes the name of the service, and the LIKE operator makes the query generic so that it can be run on any instance, without needing to be modified.

Listing 24-7. Checking to Make Sure SQL Server Agent Is Running with T-SQL

```
SELECT status_desc
FROM sys.dm_server_services
WHERE servicename LIKE 'SQL Server Agent%' ;
```

Or alternatively, you can achieve the same result by using the WQL query in Listing 24-8.

Note   You can find an WQL reference at https://msdn.microsoft.com/en-us/library/aa394606(v=vs.85).aspx.

Listing 24-8. Checking That SQL Server Agent Is Running with WQL

```
SELECT State FROM Win32_Service  WHERE Name ="SQLSERVERAGENT$MASTERSERVER"
```

To use the T-SQL version of the query, you need to use the ExecuteSql() function, which accepts the parameters in Table 24-1.

Table 24-1. *ExecuteSQL() Parameters*

Parameter	Description
returnType	Specifies the return type expected from the query. Acceptable values are Numeric, String, Bool, DateTime, Array, and GUID.
sqlQuery	Specifies the query that should run.

To use the WQL version of the query, you need to use ExecuteWql(), which accepts the parameters described in Table 24-2.

Table 24-2. *ExecuteWQL() Parameters*

Parameter	Description
returnType	Specifies the return type expected from the query. Acceptable values are Numeric, String, Bool, DateTime, Array, and GUID.
namespace	Specifies the WQL namespace that the query should be executed against.
wqlQuery	Specifies the query that should run.

Therefore, if you are using the T-SQL approach, your condition would use the script in Listing 24-9 in the Conditions editor of PBM (it will not work directly in SSMS).

Listing 24-9. ExecuteSQL()

```
ExecuteSql('string', 'SELECT status_desc FROM sys.dm_server_services WHERE
servicename LIKE ''SQL Server Agent%''')
```

Tip   It is important to note here that we had to escape the single quotes in our query, to ensure that they are recognized during execution.

If you use the WQL approach, your condition needs to use the script in Listing 24-10.

Listing 24-10. ExecuteWQL()

```
ExecuteWql('String', 'root\CIMV2', 'SELECT State FROM Win32_Service  WHERE
Name ="SQLSERVERAGENT$MASTERSERVER"')
```

Figure 24-18 shows how we would create the condition using the WQL approach.

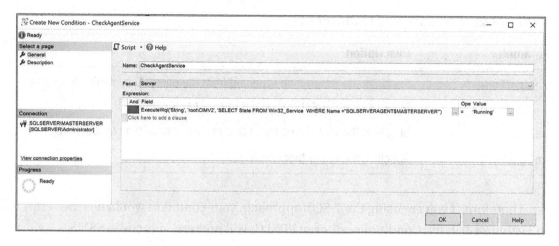

Figure 24-18. *Creating the condition with ExecuteWql()*

Caution   Because of the power and flexibility of the `ExecuteWql()` and `ExecuteSql()` functions, it is possible that they will be abused to create security holes. Therefore, make sure you carefully control who has permissions to create policies.

Managing Policies

Policies are installed on an instance of SQL Server, but you can export them to XML files, which in turn allows them to be ported to other servers or to central management servers so that they can be evaluated against multiple instances at the same time. The following sections discuss how to import and export policies, as well as how to use policies in conjunction with central management servers. We also discuss how to manage policies with PowerShell.

Importing and Exporting Policies

Policies can be exported to and imported from the file system, as XML files. To export our DatabaseNameConvention policy to the default file location, we select Export Policy from the context menu of the DatabaseNameConvention policy in Object Explorer, causing the Export Policy dialog box before to be invoked. Here, we can simply choose a name for the file and click Save, as shown in Figure 24-19.

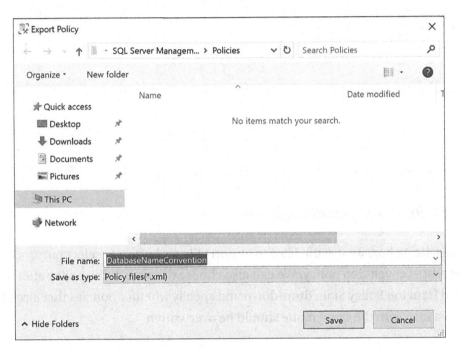

Figure 24-19. *The Export Policy dialog box*

We now import the policy into our SQLSERVER\TARGETSERVER1 instance. To do this, we connect to the TARGETSERVER1 instance in Object Explorer and then drill through Management ➤ Policy Based Management, before selecting Import Policy from the Policies context menu. This invokes the Import dialog box, as displayed in Figure 24-20.

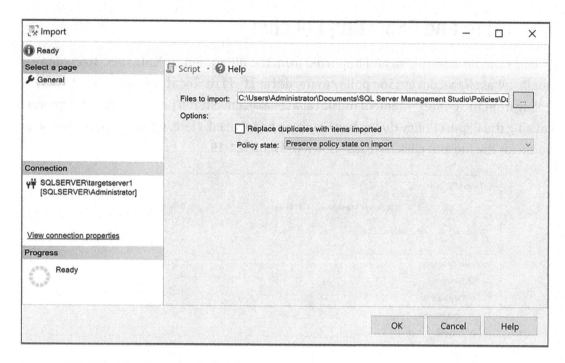

Figure 24-20. *The Import dialog box*

In this dialog box, we use the Files to import ellipses button to select our
DatabaseNameConvention policy. We can also choose the state of the policy after it is
imported from the Policy State drop-down and specify whether policies that already exist
on the instance with the same name should be overwritten.

Enterprise Management with Policies

Although being able to evaluate a policy against a single instance of SQL Server is useful,
to maximize the power of PBM, you can combine policies with central management
servers so that the policy can be evaluated against the SQL Server Enterprise in a single
execution.

For example, imagine that we want to evaluate the DatabaseNameConvention
policy against all servers within the Prod group that we created when we registered
the SQLSERVER\MASTERSERVER instance as a central management server. To do this,
we drill through Central Management Servers ➤ SQLSERVER\MASTERSERVER
in the Registered Servers window before we select Evaluate Policies from the Prod
context menu.

This invokes the Evaluate Policies dialog box. Here, you can use the Source ellipses button to invoke the Select Source dialog box and choose the policy or policies that you would like to evaluate against the group, as shown in Figure 24-21.

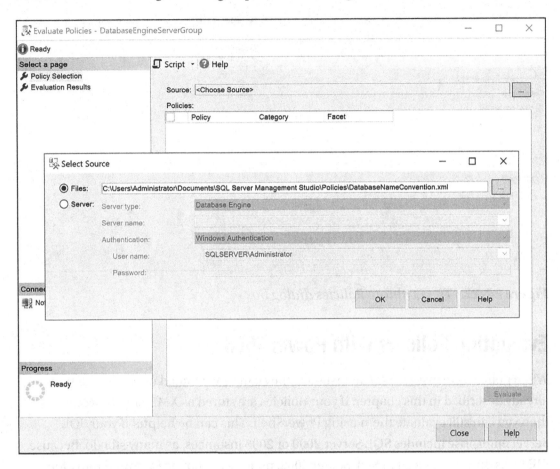

Figure 24-21. *The Evaluate Policies dialog box*

In the Select Source dialog box, either select policies stored as XML files from the file system or specify the connection details of an instance where the policy is installed. In our case, we select the DatabaseNameConvention by clicking the Files ellipses button.

Selected policies then display in the Policies section of the screen, as shown in Figure 24-22. If you selected a source with multiple policies, you can use the check boxes to define which policies to evaluate. Clicking the Evaluate button causes the selected policies to be evaluated against all servers in the group.

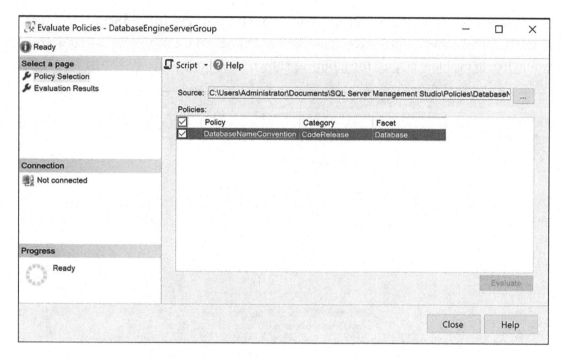

Figure 24-22. *The Evaluate Policies dialog box*

Evaluating Policies with PowerShell

When policies are installed on an instance, they can be evaluated using the methods already described in this chapter. If your policies are stored as XML files, however, then you can still evaluate them using PowerShell. This can be helpful if your SQL Server enterprise includes SQL Server 2000 or 2005 instances, as many still do. Because PBM was only introduced in SQL Server 2008, policies cannot be imported into older instances, but PowerShell offers a useful workaround for this issue.

To evaluate our DatabaseNameConvention policy against our SQLSERVER\ MASTERSERVER instance, from the XML file using PowerShell, we need to run the script in Listing 24-11. The first line of this script changes the path to the folder where the policy is stored. The second line actually evaluates the policy.

If the property we were configuring was settable and deterministic (which ours is not), then we could add the -AdHocPolicyExecutionMode parameter and set it to "Configure". This would cause the setting to change to fall in line with our policy.

Listing 24-11. Evaluating a Policy with PowerShell

```
sl "C:\Users\Administrator\Documents\SQL Server Management Studio\Policies"

Invoke-PolicyEvaluation -Policy "C:\Users\Administrator\Documents\
SQL Server Management Studio\Policies\DatabaseNameConvention.xml"
-TargetServerName ".\MASTERSERVER"
```

The output of this policy evaluation is shown in Figure 24-23.

```
PS C:\Users\Administrator\Documents\SQL Server Management Studio\Policies> sl "C:\Users\Administrator\Documents\SQL Server Management Studio\Policies"

Invoke-PolicyEvaluation -Policy "C:\Users\Administrator\Documents\SQL Server Management Studio\Policies\DatabaseNameConvention.xml" -TargetServerName ".\MASTERSERVER"

ID Policy Name            Result Start Date      End Date      Messages
-- -----------            ------ ----------      --------      --------
 1 DatabaseNameConvention False 17/05/2019 07:20 17/05/2019 07:20

PS C:\Users\Administrator\Documents\SQL Server Management Studio\Policies>
```

Figure 24-23. *Results of policy evaluation*

Tip   To evaluate multiple properties, provide a comma-separated list for the -Policy parameter.

Summary

Policy-Based Management (PBM) offers a powerful and flexible method for ensuring coding standards and hosting standards are met across your enterprise. A target is an entity managed by PBM. A condition is a Boolean expression that the policy evaluates against the targets, and a facet is a collection of properties that relate to a specific type of target.

Depending on the facet you use, a policy offers up to four policy evaluation modes: On Demand, On Schedule, On Change: Log Only, and On Change: Prevent. On Demand, On Schedule, and On Change: Log Only can be thought of as reactive, whereas On Change: Prevent can be thought of as proactive, since it actively stops a configuration from being made, which violates a policy. Because On Change modes rely on DDL triggers, you must enable nested triggers at the instance level, and they are not available for all facets.

933

Policies are extensible, through the use of the `ExecuteSql()` and `ExecuteWql()` functions, which allow you to evaluate the results of T-SQL or WQL queries. These functions offer massive flexibility, but their power can also cause security holes to be opened, so exercise caution when granting permissions to create policies.

An instance can be registered as a central management server, and other servers can be registered underneath it, either directly or in groups. This gives DBAs the ability to run a query across multiple instances at the same time, and it also offers them the ability to evaluate policies against multiple servers at the same time. This means that you can use Policy-Based Management at the Enterprise level to enforce standards.

You can evaluate policies from within SQL Server or using PowerShell with the `-InvokePolicyEvaluation` cmdlet. This offers you increased flexibility for managing estates that have older SQL Server instances, such as 2000 or 2005. This is because PowerShell allows DBAs to evaluate the policies from XML files, instead of only being able to evaluate them after importing them to MSDB.

CHAPTER 25

Resource Governor

Resource Governor provides a method for throttling applications at the SQL Server layer by imposing limits on CPU, memory, and physical I/O on different classifications of connection. This chapter discusses the concepts the Resource Governor uses before demonstrating how to implement them. We then look at how to monitor the effect that Resource Governor has on resource utilization.

Resource Governor Concepts

Resource Governor uses resource pools to define a subset of server resources, workload groups as logical containers for similar session requests, and a classifier function to determine to which workload group a specific request should be assigned. The following sections discuss each of these concepts.

Resource Pool

A *resource pool* defines a subset of server resources that sessions can utilize. When Resource Governor is enabled, three pools are automatically created: the internal pool, the default pool, and the default external pool. The *internal pool* represents the server resources the instance uses. This pool cannot be modified. The *default pool* is designed as a catchall pool and is used to assign resources to any session that is not assigned to a user-defined resource pool. You cannot remove this pool; however, you can modify its settings. The default external pool is used to govern resources used by the rterm.exe, BxlServer.exe, and python.exe processes, which are used by Machine Learning Services. The default external resource pool can be modified, but not removed, and new external resource pools can be added.

© Peter A. Carter 2023
P. A. Carter, *Pro SQL Server 2022 Administration*, https://doi.org/10.1007/978-1-4842-8864-1_25

Resource pools allow you to configure the minimum and maximum amount of resources (CPU, memory, and physical I/O) that will be available to sessions that are assigned to that pool. As you add additional pools, maximum values of existing pools are transparently adjusted so they do not conflict with the minimum resource percentages assigned to all pools. For example, imagine that you have configured the resource pools, which are represented in Table 25-1, to throttle CPU usage.

Table 25-1. *Resource Pools' Simple Effective Maximum Percentages*

Resource Pool*	Min CPU %	Max CPU %	Effective Max CPU %	Calculation
Default	0	100	75	Smallest(75,(100-0-25)) = 75
SalesApplication	25	75	75	Smallest(75,(100-0-0)) = 75
Default External	0	100	75	Smallest(75,(100-0-25)) = 75

*The internal resource pool is not mentioned here since it is not configurable either directly or implicitly. Instead, it can consume whatever resources it requires and has a minimum CPU of 0; therefore, it does not impact the effective maximum CPU calculation for other pools.

In this example, the actual Max CPU % settings will be as you configured them. However, imagine that you now add an additional resource pool, called AccountsApplication, which is configured with a Min CPU % of 50% and a Max CPU % of 80%. The sum of the minimum CPU percentages is now greater than the sum of the maximum CPU percentages. This means that the effective maximum CPU percentage for each resource pool is reduced accordingly. The formula for this calculation is Smallest(Default(Max), Default(Max) - SUM(Other Min CPU)), which is reflected in Table 25-2.

Table 25-2. *Resource Pools' Effective Maximum Percentages After Implicit Reductions*

Resource Pool*	Min CPU %	Max CPU %	Effective Max CPU %	Calculation
Default	0	100	25	Smallest((100,(100-sum(25,50,0)) = 25
SalesApplication	25	75	50	Smallest((75,(100-50-0)) = 50
AccountsApplication	50	80	75	Smallest((80,(100-25-0)) = 75
Default External	0	100	25	Smallest((100,(100-sum(25,50,0)) = 25

The internal resource pool is not mentioned here since it is not configurable either directly or implicitly. Instead, it can consume whatever resources it requires and has a minimum CPU of 0; therefore, it does not impact the effective maximum CPU calculation for other pools.

Workload Group

A resource pool can contain one or more workload groups. A *workload group* represents a logical container for similar sessions that have been classified as similar by executing a classifier function, which is covered in the next section. For example, in the SalesApplication resource pool mentioned earlier, we can create two workload groups. We can use one of these workload groups as a container for normal user sessions while using the second as a container for reporting sessions.

This approach allows us to monitor the groups of sessions separately. It also allows us to define separate policies for each set of sessions. For example, we may choose to specify that sessions used for reporting have a lower MAXDOP (maximum degree of parallelism) setting than the sessions used for standard users, or that sessions used for reporting should only be able to specify a limited number of concurrent requests. These settings are in addition to the settings we can configure at the resource pool level.

Classifier Function

A *classifier function* is a scalar function, created in the Master database. It is used to determine which workload group each session should be assigned to. Every new session is classified using a single classifier function, with the exception of DACs (dedicated administrator connections), which are not subject to Resource Governor. The classifier function can group sessions based on virtually any attribute that it is possible to code within interpreted SQL. For example, you may choose to classify requests based upon username, role membership, application name, host name, login property, connection property, or even time.

Implementing Resource Governor

To configure Resource Governor on an instance, you must create and configure one or more resource pools, each with one or more workload groups. In addition, you must also create a classifier function. Finally, you need to enable Resource Governor, which results in all subsequent sessions being classified. These topics are discussed in the following sections.

Creating Resource Pools

It is possible to create a maximum of 64 resource pools per instance. Let's create a resource pool through SQL Server Management Studio, drill through Management ➤ Resource Governor in Object Explorer, and then select New Resource Pool from the Resource Pools context menu. This causes the Resource Governor Properties dialog box to be invoked.

In the Resource Pools section of this dialog box, create a new row in the grid and populate it with the information we need to create our new resource pool. In our case, you should add the details for a resource pool named `SalesApplication`, which has a Minimum CPU % of 25, a Maximum CPU % of 75, a Minimum Memory % of 25, and a Maximum Memory % of 40.

Tip Highlighting a resource pool causes the workload groups associated with that resource pool to display in the Workload Groups for Resource Pool section of the screen. Here, you can add, amend, or remove resource pools at the same time. However, you can also access this dialog box by drilling through Management ➤ Resource Governor ➤ [*Resource Pool name*] and then selecting New Workload Group from the Workload Groups context menu.

In this scenario, the maximum memory limit is a hard limit. This means that no more than 40% of the memory available to this instance is ever allocated to this resource pool. Also, even if no sessions are using this resource pool, 25% of the memory available to the instance is still allocated to this resource pool and is unavailable to other resource pools.

In contrast, the maximum CPU limit is soft, or opportunistic. This means that if more CPU is available, the resource pool utilizes it. The cap only kicks in when there is contention on the processor.

Tip It is possible to configure a hard cap on CPU usage. This is helpful in PaaS (platform as a service) or DaaS (database as a service) environments where clients are charged based on CPU usage and you need to ensure consistent billing for their applications. A client can easily dispute a bill if they have agreed to pay for 40% of a core, but the soft cap allows them to reach 50%, resulting in a higher charge automatically being applied. Implementing this is discussed later in this section.

You can also create resource pools via T-SQL. When you do so, you have access to more functionality than you do through the GUI, which allows you to configure minimum and maximum IOPS (input/output per second), set hard caps on CPU usage, and affinitize a resource pool with specific CPUs or NUMA nodes. Creating an affinity between a resource pool and a subset of CPUs means that the resource pool will only use the CPUs, to which it is aligned. You can use the CREATE RESOURCE POOL DDL statement to create a resource pool in T-SQL. The settings you can configure on a resource pool are detailed in Table 25-3.

Table 25-3. *CREATE RESOURCE POOL Arguments*

Argument	Description
pool_name	The name that you assign to the resource pool.
MIN_CPU_PERCENT	Specifies the guaranteed average minimum CPU resource available to the resource pool as a percentage of the CPU bandwidth available to the instance.
MAX_CPU_PERCENT	Specifies the average maximum CPU resource available to the resource pool as a percentage of the CPU bandwidth available to the instance. This is a soft limit that applies when there is contention for the CPU resource.
CAP_CPU_PERCENT	Specifies a hard limit on the amount of CPU resource available to the resource pool as a percentage of the CPU bandwidth available to the instance.
MIN_MEMORY_PERCENT	Specifies the minimum amount of memory that is reserved for the resource pool as a percentage of the memory available to the instance.
MAX_MEMORY_PERCENT	Specifies the maximum amount of memory that the resource pool can use as a percentage of the memory available to the instance.
MIN_IOPS_PER_VOLUME	Specifies the number of IOPS per volume that is reserved for the resource pool. Unlike CPU and memory thresholds, IOPS are expressed as an absolute value, as opposed to a percentage.
MAX_IOPS_PER_VOLUME	Specifies the maximum number of IOPS per volume that the resource pool can use. Like the minimum IOPS threshold, this is expressed as an absolute number, as opposed to a percentage.
AFFINITY SCHEDULER*	Specifies that the resource pool should be bound to specific SQLOS (SQL operating system) schedulers, which in turn map to specific virtual cores within the server. Cannot be used with AFFINITY NUMANODE. Specify AUTO to allow SQL Server to manage the schedulers that are used by the resource pool. Specify the range of scheduler IDs. For example (0, 1, 32 TO 64).
AFFINITY NUMANODE*	Specifies that the resource pool should be bound to a specific range of NUMA nodes. For example (1 TO 4). Cannot be used with AFFINITY SCHEDULER.

For further details of CPU and NUMA affinity, refer to Chapter 5.

When we are working with minimum- and maximum-IOPS-per-volume thresholds, we need to take a few things into account. First, if we do not set a maximum IOPS limit, SQL Server does not govern the IOPS for the resource pool at all. This means that if you configure minimum IOPS limits for other resource pools, they are not respected. Therefore, if you want Resource Governor to govern I/O, always set a maximum IOPS threshold for every resource pool.

It is also worth noting that the majority of I/O that you can control through Resource Governor is read operations. This is because write operations, such as Lazy Writer and Log Flush operations, occur as system operations and fall inside the scope of the internal resource pool. Because you cannot alter the internal resource pool, you cannot govern the majority of write operations. This means that using Resource Governor to limit I/O operations is most appropriate when you have a reporting application or another application with a high ratio of reads to writes.

Finally, you should be aware that Resource Governor can only control the number of IOPS; it cannot control the size of the IOPS. This means that you cannot use Resource Governor to control the amount of bandwidth into a SAN an application is using.

To create an external resource pool, the CREATE EXTERNAL RESOURCE POOL DDL statement should be used. The settings that can be configured on an external resource pool are detailed in Table 25-4.

Table 25-4. *CREATE EXTERNAL RESOURCE POOL Arguments*

Argument	Description
pool_name	The name that you assign to the resource pool.
MAX_CPU_PERCENT	Specifies the average maximum CPU resource available to the resource pool as a percentage of the CPU bandwidth available to the instance. This is a soft limit that applies when there is contention for the CPU resource.
AFFINITY SCHEDULER	Specifies that the resource pool should be bound to specific SQLOS (SQL operating system) schedulers, which in turn map to specific virtual cores within the server. Cannot be used with AFFINITY NUMANODE. Specify AUTO to allow SQL Server to manage the schedulers that are used by the resource pool. Specify the range of scheduler IDs. For example (0, 1, 32 TO 64).

(continued)

Table 25-4. (*continued*)

Argument	Description
MAX_MEMORY_PERCENT	Specifies the maximum amount of memory that the resource pool can use as a percentage of the memory available to the instance.
MAX_PROCESSES	Specifies the maximum number of processes allowed within the pool at any given time. The default is 0, which limits the number of processes by server resources only

If you want to create a resource pool called ReportingApp that sets a minimum CPU percentage of 50, a maximum CPU percentage of 80, a minimum IOPS reservation of 20, and a maximum IOPS reservation of 100, you can use the script in Listing 25-1. The final statement of the script uses ALTER RESOURCE GOVERNOR to apply the new configuration. You should also run this statement after you create workload groups or apply a classifier function.

Listing 25-1. Creating a Resource Pool

```
CREATE RESOURCE POOL ReportingApp
    WITH(
        MIN_CPU_PERCENT=50,
        MAX_CPU_PERCENT=80,
        MIN_IOPS_PER_VOLUME = 20,
        MAX_IOPS_PER_VOLUME = 100
        ) ;
GO

ALTER RESOURCE GOVERNOR RECONFIGURE ;
GO
```

Creating Workload Groups

Each resource pool can contain multiple workload groups. To begin creating a workload group for our SalesApplication resource pool, we drill though Management ➤ Resource Governor | Resource Pools. We then drill through our SalesApplication resource pool and select New Workload Group from the Workload Groups context menu. This invokes the Resource Governor Properties dialog box, which is displayed in Figure 25-1.

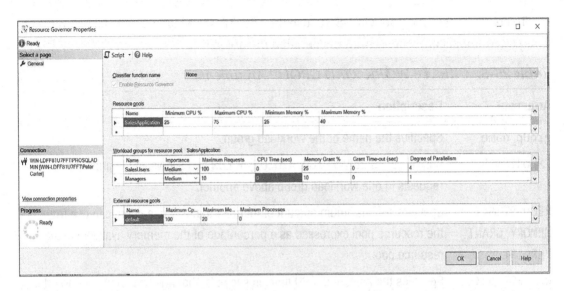

Figure 25-1. *The Resource Governor Properties dialog box*

You can see that with the SalesApplication resource pool highlighted in the
Resource Pools section of the dialog box, we have created two rows within the Workload
Groups section of the screen. Each of these rows represents a workload group that is
associated with the SalesApplication resource pool.

We have configured the SalesUsers workload group to allow a maximum of 100
simultaneous requests and a MAXDOP of 4, meaning that requests classified under this
workload group are able to use a maximum of four schedulers.

We have configured the Managers workload group to allow a maximum of ten
simultaneous requests and use a maximum of one scheduler. We have also configured
this workload group to be able to use a maximum of 10% of the memory that the
resource pool can reserve, as opposed to the default of 25%.

If the Memory Grant % setting is set to 0, then any requests classified under that
workload group are blocked from running any operations that require a SORT or HASH
JOIN physical operator. If queries need more than the specified amount of RAM,
then SQL Server reduces the DOP for that query in an attempt to reduce the memory
requirement. If the DOP reaches 1 and there is still not enough memory, then Error
8657 is thrown.

To create a resource pool via T-SQL, use the CREATE WORKLOAD GROUP DDL statement. This statement accepts the arguments detailed in Table 25-5.

Table 25-5. *CREATE WORKLOAD GROUP Arguments*

Argument	Description
group_name	Specifies the name of the workload group.
IMPORTANCE	Can be configured to HIGH, MEDIUM, or LOW and allows you to prioritize requests in one workload group above another.
REQUEST_MAX_ MEMORY_GRANT_ PERCENT	Specifies the maximum amount of memory that any one query can use from the resource pool expressed as a percentage of the memory available to the resource pool.
REQUEST_MAX_ CPU_TIME_SEC	Specifies the amount of CPU time, in seconds, that any one query can use. It is important to note that if the threshold is exceeded, then an event is generated that can be captured with Extended Events. The query is not cancelled, however.
REQUEST_ MEMORY_GRANT_ TIMEOUT_SEC	Specifies the maximum amount of time that a query can wait for a work buffer memory to become available before it times out. The query only times out under memory contention, however. Otherwise, the query receives the minimum memory grant. This results in performance degradation for the query. The maximum wait time is expressed in seconds.
MAX_DOP	The maximum number of processors that a single parallel query can use. The MAXDOP for a query can be further restrained by using query hints, by changing the MAXDOP setting for the instance, or when the relational engine chooses a serial plan.
GROUP_MAX_ REQUESTS	Specifies the maximum number of concurrent requests that can be executed within the workload group. If the number of concurrent requests reaches this value, then further queries are placed in a waiting state until the number of concurrent queries falls below the threshold.
USING	Specifies the resource pool with which the workload group is associated. If not specified, then the group is associated with the default pool.

Caution   Workload group names must be unique, even if they are associated with different pools. This is so they can be returned by the classifier function.

If we create two workload groups we want associated with our `ReportingApp` resource pool—one named `InternalReports` with a MAXDOP of 4 and a 25% maximum memory grant and the other named `ExternalReports` with a MAXDOP of 8 and a maximum memory grant percentage of 75%—we could use the script in Listing 25-2.

Listing 25-2. Creating Workload Groups

```
CREATE WORKLOAD GROUP InternalReports
    WITH(
        GROUP_MAX_REQUESTS=100,
        IMPORTANCE=Medium,
        REQUEST_MAX_CPU_TIME_SEC=0,
        REQUEST_MAX_MEMORY_GRANT_PERCENT=25,
        REQUEST_MEMORY_GRANT_TIMEOUT_SEC=0,
        MAX_DOP=4
                ) USING ReportingApp ;
GO

CREATE WORKLOAD GROUP ExternalReports
    WITH(
        GROUP_MAX_REQUESTS=100,
        IMPORTANCE=Medium,
        REQUEST_MAX_CPU_TIME_SEC=0,
        REQUEST_MAX_MEMORY_GRANT_PERCENT=75,
        REQUEST_MEMORY_GRANT_TIMEOUT_SEC=0,
        MAX_DOP=8
        ) USING ReportingApp ;
GO

ALTER RESOURCE GOVERNOR RECONFIGURE;
GO
```

Creating a Classifier Function

A classifier function is a scalar UDF (user-defined function) that resides in the Master database. It returns a value of type SYSNAME, which is a system-defined type equivalent to NVARCHAR(128). The value returned by the function corresponds to the name of the workload group into which each request should fall. The logic within the function determines which workload group name is returned. You only ever have one classifier function per instance, so you need to modify the function if you add additional workload groups.

Now let's create a classifier function using the Resource Governor environment that we have built in this chapter. This function will classify each request made against our instance using the following rules:

1. If the request is made under the context of the SalesUser login, then the request should fall under the SalesUsers workload group.

2. If the request is made by the SalesManager login, then requests should be placed in the Managers workload group.

3. If the request is made by the ReportsUser login and the request was made from a server named ReportsApp, then the request should fall into the InternalReports workload group.

4. If the request is made by the ReportsUser login but did not originate from the ReportsApp server, then it should fall into the ExternalReports workload group.

5. All other requests should be placed into the default workload group.

Before creating our classifier function, we prepare the instance. To do this, we first create the Chapter25 database. We then create the SalesUser, ReportsUser, and SalesManager logins, with Users mapped to the Chapter25 database. (Further detail on security principles can be found in Chapter 10.) Listing 25-3 contains the code we need to prepare the instance.

Note   The users are mapped to the Chapter25 database for the purpose of this example, but you can make the queries against any database in the instance.

Listing 25-3. Preparing the Instance

```
--Create the database

USE [master]
GO

CREATE DATABASE Chapter25 ;

--Create the Logins and Users

CREATE LOGIN SalesUser
    WITH PASSWORD=N'Pa$$w0rd', DEFAULT_DATABASE=Chapter25,
        CHECK_EXPIRATION=OFF, CHECK_POLICY=OFF ;
GO

CREATE LOGIN ReportsUser
    WITH PASSWORD=N'Pa$$w0rd', DEFAULT_DATABASE=Chapter25,
        CHECK_EXPIRATION=OFF, CHECK_POLICY=OFF ;
GO

CREATE LOGIN SalesManager
    WITH PASSWORD=N'Pa$$w0rd', DEFAULT_DATABASE=Chapter25,
        CHECK_EXPIRATION=OFF, CHECK_POLICY=OFF ;
GO

USE Chapter25
GO

CREATE USER SalesUser FOR LOGIN SalesUser ;
GO

CREATE USER ReportsUser FOR LOGIN ReportsUser ;
GO

CREATE USER SalesManager FOR LOGIN SalesManager ;
GO
```

In order to implement the business rules pertaining to which workload group each request should be placed into, we use the system functions detailed in Table 25-6.

Table 25-6. *System Functions for Implementing Business Rules*

Function	Description	Business Rule(s)
SUSER_SNAME()	Returns the name of a login	1, 2, 3, 4
HOST_NAME()	Returns the name of the host from which the request was issued	3, 4

When we create a classifier function, it must follow specific rules. First, the function must be *schema-bound*. This means that any underlying objects that are referenced by the function cannot be altered without the function first being dropped. The function must also return the SYSNAME data type and have no parameters.

It is worth noting that the requirement for the function to be schema-bound is significant, and it poses limitations on the flexibility of Resource Governor. For example, it would be very useful if you were able to delegate workloads based upon database role membership; however, this is not possible, because schema-bound functions cannot access objects in other databases, either directly or indirectly. Because the classifier function must reside in the Master database, you cannot access information regarding database roles in other databases.

As with all things, there are workarounds for this issue. For example, you can create a table in the Master database that maintains role membership from user databases. You can even keep this table updated automatically by using a combination of views and triggers in the user database. The view would be based on the sys.sysusers catalog view and the trigger would be based on the view that you created. This would be a complex design, however, which would pose operational challenges to maintain.

The script within Listing 25-4 creates the classifier function, which implements our business rules before associating the function with Resource Governor. As always, Resource Governor is then reconfigured so that our changes take effect.

Listing 25-4. Creating the Classifier Function

```
USE Master
GO

CREATE FUNCTION dbo.Classifier()
RETURNS SYSNAME
WITH SCHEMABINDING
```

```
AS
BEGIN

        --Declare variables

        DECLARE @WorkloadGroup          SYSNAME ;
        SET @WorkloadGroup = 'Not Assigned' ;

        --Implement business rule 1

        IF (SUSER_NAME() = 'SalesUser')
        BEGIN
                SET @WorkloadGroup = 'SalesUsers' ;
        END

        --Implement business rule 2

        ELSE IF (SUSER_NAME() = 'SalesManager')
        BEGIN
                SET @WorkloadGroup = 'Managers' ;
        END
                --Implement business rules 3 & 4
        ELSE IF (SUSER_SNAME() = 'ReportsUser')
        BEGIN
                IF (HOST_NAME() = 'ReportsApp')
                BEGIN
                        SET @WorkloadGroup = 'InternalReports'
                END
                ELSE
                BEGIN
                        SET @WorkloadGroup = 'ExternalReports'
                END
        END

        --Implement business rule 5 (Put all other requests into the
        default workload group)

        ELSE IF @WorkloadGroup = 'Not Assigned'
        BEGIN
                SET @WorkloadGroup = 'default'
```

```
        END

        --Return the apropriate Workload Group name

        RETURN @WorkloadGroup
END

GO

--Associate the Classifier Function with Resource Governor

ALTER RESOURCE GOVERNOR WITH (CLASSIFIER_FUNCTION = dbo.Classifier) ;

ALTER RESOURCE GOVERNOR RECONFIGURE ;
```

Testing the Classifier Function

After we create the classifier function, we want to test that it works. We can test business rules 1 and 2 by using the EXECUTE AS statement to change our system context and then call the classifier function. This is demonstrated in Listing 25-5. The script temporarily allows all logins to access the classifier function directly, which allows the queries to work. It implements this by granting the Public role the EXECUTE permission before revoking this permission at the end of the script.

Listing 25-5. Testing Business Rules 1 and 2

```
USE MASTER
GO

GRANT EXECUTE ON dbo.Classifier TO public ;
GO

EXECUTE AS LOGIN = 'SalesUser' ;
SELECT dbo.Classifier() AS 'Workload Group' ;
REVERT

EXECUTE AS LOGIN = 'SalesManager' ;
SELECT dbo.Classifier() as 'Workload Group' ;
REVERT

REVOKE EXECUTE ON dbo.Classifier TO public ;
GO
```

The result of running these two queries shows that business rules 1 and 2 are working as expected.

To test business rule 4, we can use the same process we used to validate business rules 1 and 2. The only difference is that we change the execution context to ReportsUser. In order to validate rule 3, we use the same process, but this time, we invoke the query from a server named ReportsApp.

Tip   If you do not have access to a server named ReportsApp, then update the function definition to use a server name that you do have access to.

Monitoring Resource Governor

SQL Server exposes dynamic management views (DMVs) that you can use to return statistics relating to resource pools and workload groups. You can also monitor Resource Governor's usage using Windows' Performance Monitor tool, however, and this gives you the advantage of a graphical representation. The following sections discuss both of these approaches to monitoring Resource Governor.

Monitoring with Performance Monitor

DBAs can monitor how resource pools and their associated workload groups are being utilized by using Performance Monitor, which is built into Windows. You can access Performance Monitor from Control Panel ➤ Administrative Tools or by searching for Perfmon in the Start menu.

Note   To follow the demonstrations in this section, you should be running a Windows Server operating system.

Two categories are available to Performance Monitor that relate to Resource Governor. The first is MSSQL$[INSTANCE NAME]:Resource Pool Stats. This contains counters that relate to the consumption of resources, which have been made available to resource groups. An instance of each counter is available for each resource group that has been configured on the instance.

The second category is MSSQL$[INSTANCE NAME]:Workload Group Stats, which contains counters that relate to the utilization of each workload group that has been configured on the instance. Figure 25-2 illustrates how we can add the InternalReports, ExternalReports, SalesUsers, and Managers instances of the CPU Usage % counter from within the Workload Group Stats category. After highlighting the instances, we will use the Add button to move them to the Added counters section. We can invoke the Add Counters dialog box by selecting Monitoring Tools ➤ Performance Monitor from the left pane and then using the Plus (+) symbol on the toolbar in the right-hand pane.

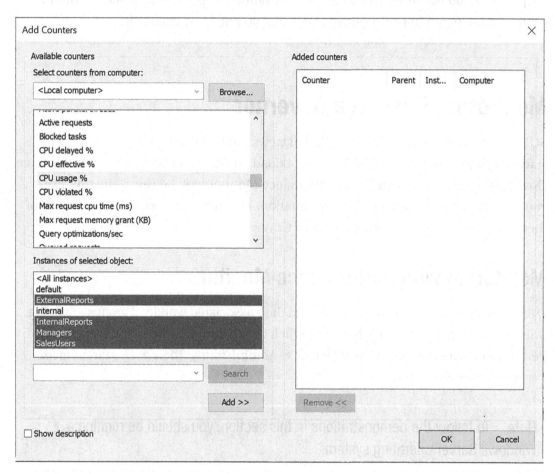

Figure 25-2. *Adding Workload Group Stats.*

Now that we have added this counter, we also need to add the ReportingApp and SalesApplication app instances of the Active memory grant amount (KB) counter from within the Resource Pool Stats category, as illustrated in Figure 25-3.

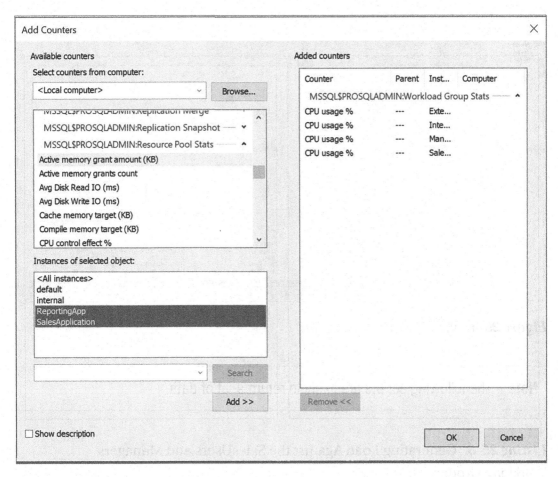

Figure 25-3. *Resource Pool Stats*

To test our Resource Governor configuration, we can use the script in Listing 25-6. This script is designed to run in two separate query windows. The first part of the script should run in a query window that is connected to your instance using the SalesUser login, and the second part of the script should run in a query window that is connected to your instance by using the SalesManager login. The two scripts should run simultaneously and cause Performance Monitor to generate a graph similar to the one Figure 25-4. Although the scripts do not cause the classifier function to be called, they act as an interactive way of testing our logic.

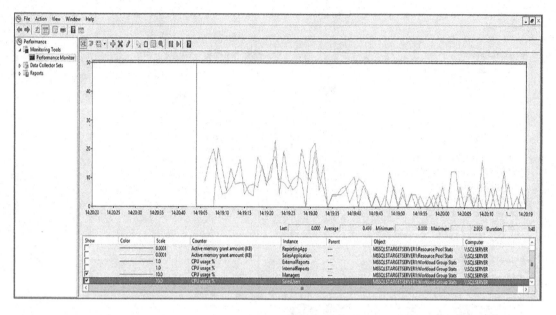

Figure 25-4. *Viewing CPU utilization*

Note   The following scripts are likely to return a lot of data.

Listing 25-6. Generating Load Against the SalesUsers and Managers
Workload Groups

```
--Script Part 1 - To be run in a query windows that is connected using the
SalesManager Login

EXECUTE AS LOGIN = 'SalesManager'

DECLARE @i INT = 0 ;

WHILE (@i < 10000)
BEGIN
SELECT DBName = (
        SELECT Name AS [data()]
        FROM sys.databases
        FOR XML PATH('')
) ;
```

```
SET @i = @i + 1 ;

END

--Script Part 2 - To be run in a query windows that is connected using the
SalesUser Login

EXECUTE AS LOGIN = 'SalesUser'

DECLARE @i INT = 0 ;

WHILE (@i < 10000)
BEGIN
SELECT DBName = (
        SELECT Name AS [data()]
        FROM sys.databases
        FOR XML PATH('')
) ;

SET @i = @i + 1 ;

END
```

You can see that the CPU usage for the SalesUsers and Managers workload groups is almost identical, which means that the Resource Governor implementation is working as expected.

Monitoring with DMVs

SQL Server provides the sys.dm_resource_governor_resource_pools and sys.dm_resource_governor_workload_groups DMVs that DBAs can use to examine Resource Governor statistics. The sys.dm_resource_governor_resource_pools DMV returns the columns detailed in Table 25-7.

Table 25-7. *Columns Returned by sys.dm_resource_governor_resource_pools*

Column	Description
pool_id	The unique ID of the resource pool
name	The name of the resource pool
statistics_start_time	The date/time of the last time the resource pool's statistics were reset
total_cpu_usage_ms	The total CPU time used by the resource pool since the statistics last reset
cache_memory_kb	The total cache memory currently being used by the resource pool
compile_memory_kb	The total memory the resource pool is currently using for compilation and optimization
used_memgrant_kb	The total memory the resource pool is using for memory grants
total_memgrant_count	A count of memory grants in the resource pool since the statistics were reset
total_memgrant_timeout_count	A count of memory grant time-outs in the resource pool since the statistics were last reset
active_memgrant_count	A count of current memory grants within the resource pool
active_memgrant_kb	The total amount of memory currently being used for memory grants in the resource pool
memgrant_waiter_count	A count of queries currently pending, waiting for memory grants within the resource pool
max_memory_kb	The maximum amount of memory the resource pool can reserve
used_memory_kb	The amount of memory the resource pool currently has reserved
target_memory_kb	The amount of memory that the resource pool is currently trying to maintain

(continued)

Table 25-7. (*continued*)

Column	Description
out_of_memory_count	A count of failed memory allocations for the resource pool
min_cpu_percent	The guaranteed average minimum CPU % for the resource pool
max_cpu_percent	The average maximum CPU % for the resource pool
min_memory_percent	The guaranteed minimum amount of memory that is available to the resource pool during periods of memory contention
max_memory_percent	The maximum percentage of server memory that can be allocated to the resource pool
cap_cpu_percent	The hard limit on the maximum CPU % available to the resource pool

The sys.dm_resource_governor_workload_groups DMV returns the columns detailed in Table 25-8.

Table 25-8. *Columns Returned by sys.dm_resource_governor_workload_groups*

Column	Description
group_id	The unique ID of the workload group.
name	The name of the workload group.
pool_id	The unique ID of the resource pool with which the workload group is associated.
statistics_start_time	The date/time of the last time the workload group's statistics were reset.
total_request_count	A count of the number of requests in the workload group since the statistics were last reset.

(*continued*)

Table 25-8. (*continued*)

Column	Description
total_queued_request_ count	The number of requests within the workload group that have been queued as a result of the GROUP_MAX_REQUESTS threshold being reached since the statistics were last reset.
active_request_count	A count of requests that are currently active within the workload group.
queued_request_count	The number of requests within the workload group that are currently queued as a result of the GROUP_MAX_REQUESTS threshold being reached.
total_cpu_limit_ violation_count	A count of requests in the workload group that have exceeded the CPU limit since the statistics were last reset.
total_cpu_usage_ms	The total CPU time used by requests within the workload group since the statistics were last reset.
max_request_cpu_time_ ms	The maximum CPU time used by any request within the workload group since the last time the statistics were reset.
blocked_task_count	A count of tasks within the workload group that are currently blocked.
total_lock_wait_count	A count of all lock waits that have occurred for requests within the workload group since the last time the statistics were reset.
total_lock_wait_time_ ms	A sum of time that locks have been held by requests within the workload group since statistics were last reset.
total_query_ optimization_count	A count of all query optimizations that have occurred within the workload group since the statistics were reset.
total_suboptimal_ plan_generation_count	A count of all suboptimal plans that have been generated within the workload group, since the last time the statistics were reset. These suboptimal plans indicate that the workload group was experiencing memory pressure.
total_reduced_ memgrant_count	A count of all memory grants that have reached the maximum size limit within the workload group since the last time the statistics were reset.

(continued)

Table 25-8. (*continued*)

Column	Description
max_request_grant_memory_kb	The size of the largest single memory grant that has occurred within the workload group since the last time the statistics were reset.
active_parallel_thread_count	A count of how many parallel threads are currently in use within the workload group.
importance	The current value specified for the workload group's importance setting.
request_max_memory_grant_percent	The current value specified for the workload group's maximum memory grant percentage.
request_max_cpu_time_sec	The current value specified for the workload group's CPU limit.
request_memory_grant_timeout_sec	The current value specified for the workload group's memory grant time-out.
group_max_requests	The current value specified for the workload group's maximum concurrent requests.
max_dop	The current value specified for the workload group's MAXDOP.

You can join the sys.dm_resource_governor_resource_pools and sys.dm_resource_governor_workload_groups DMVs using the pool_id column in each view. The script in Listing 25-7 demonstrates how you can achieve this so you can return a report of CPU usage across the workload groups as compared to the overall CPU usage of the resource pool.

Listing 25-7. Reporting on CPU Usage

```
SELECT
        rp.name ResourcePoolName
        ,wg.name WorkgroupName
        ,rp.total_cpu_usage_ms ResourcePoolCPUUsage
        ,wg.total_cpu_usage_ms WorkloadGroupCPUUsage
        ,CAST(ROUND(CASE
```

```
            WHEN rp.total_cpu_usage_ms = 0
                    THEN 100
            ELSE (wg.total_cpu_usage_ms * 1.)
                            / (rp.total_cpu_usage_ms * 1.) * 100
                        Percentage
            END, 3) AS FLOAT) WorkloadGroupPercentageOfResourcePool
FROM sys.dm_resource_governor_resource_pools rp
INNER JOIN sys.dm_resource_governor_workload_groups wg
        ON rp.pool_id = wg.pool_id
ORDER BY rp.pool_id ;
```

You can reset the cumulative statistics exposed by the sys.resource_governor_
resource_pools and sys.dm_resource_governor_workload_groups DMVs using the
command in Listing 25-8.

Listing 25-8. Resetting Resource Governor Statistics

```
ALTER RESOURCE GOVERNOR RESET STATISTICS ;
```

SQL Server exposes a third DMV named sys.dm_resource_governor_resource_
pool_affinity, which returns the columns detailed in Table 25-9.

Table 25-9. *Columns Returned by dm_resource_governor_resource_pool_affinity*

Column	Description
pool_id	The unique ID of the resource pool.
processor_group	The ID of the logical processor group.
scheduler_mask	The binary mask, which represents the schedulers that are affinitized with the resource pool. For further details on interpreting this binary mask, please refer to Chapter 5.

You can join the sys.dm_resource_governor_resource_pool_affinity DMV to the
sys.resource_governor_resource_pools DMV using the pool_id column in each view.
Listing 25-9 demonstrates this; it first alters the default resource pool so that it only uses
processor 0 before it displays the scheduler binary mask for each resource pool that has
processor affinity configured.

Listing 25-9. Scheduling a Binary Mask for Each Resource Pool

```
ALTER RESOURCE POOL [Default] WITH(AFFINITY SCHEDULER = (0)) ;


ALTER RESOURCE GOVERNOR RECONFIGURE ;


SELECT
        rp.name ResourcePoolName
        ,pa.scheduler_mask
FROM sys.dm_resource_governor_resource_pool_affinity pa
INNER JOIN sys.dm_resource_governor_resource_pools rp
        ON pa.pool_id = rp.pool_id ;
```

There is a DMV, called sys.dm_resource_governor_resource_pool_volumes, which returns details of the I/O statistics for each resource pool. This DMV's columns are described in Table 25-10.

Table 25-10. *Columns Returned by dm_resource_governor_resource_pool_volumes*

Column	Description
pool_id	The unique ID of the resource pool
volume_name	The name of the disk volume
min_iops_per_volume	The current configuration for the minimum number of IOPS per volume for the resource pool
max_iops_per_volume	The current configuration for the maximum number of IOPS per volume for the resource pool
read_ios_queued_total	The total read I/Os queued for the resource pool against this volume since the last time the statistics were reset
read_ios_issued_total	The total read I/Os issued for the resource pool against this volume since the last time the statistics were reset
read_ios_completed_ total	The total read I/Os completed for the resource pool against this volume since the last time the statistics were reset

(continued)

Table 25-10. (*continued*)

Column	Description
read_bytes_total	The total bytes read for the resource pool against this volume since the last time the statistics were reset
read_io_stall_total_ms	The cumulative time between read I/O operations being issued and completed for the resource pool against this volume since the last time the statistics were reset
read_io_stall_queued_ms	The cumulative time between read I/O operations arriving and being completed for the resource pool against this volume since the last time the statistics were reset
write_ios_queued_total	The total write I/Os queued for the resource pool against this volume since the last time the statistics were reset
write_ios_issued_total	The total write I/Os issued for the resource pool against this volume since the last time the statistics were reset
write_ios_completed_total	The total write I/Os completed for the resource pool against this volume since the last time the statistics were reset
write_bytes_total	The total bytes written for the resource pool against this volume since the last time the statistics were reset
write_io_stall_total_ms	The cumulative time between write I/O operations being issued and completed for the resource pool against this volume since the last time the statistics were reset
write_io_stall_queued_ms	The cumulative time between write I/O operations arriving and being completed for the resource pool against this volume since the last time the statistics were reset
io_issue_violations_total	The total number of times that more I/O operations were performed against the resource pool and volume than are allowed by the configuration
io_issue_delay_total_ms	The total time between when I/O operations were scheduled to be issued and when they were actually issued

You can use the sys.dm_resource_governor_resource_pool_volumes DMV to
determine if your resource pool configuration is causing latency by adding the read_io_
stall_queued_ms and write_io_stall_queued_ms and then subtracting this value from
the total of read_io_stall_total_ms added to write_io_stall_total_ms, as shown in
Listing 25-10. This script first alters the default resource pool so that IOPS are governed
before subsequently reporting on I/O stalls.

Tip   Remember that you are likely to see far fewer write operations than read
operations in user-defined resource pools. This is because the vast majority of
write operations are system operations, and therefore, they take place within the
internal resource pool.

Listing 25-10. Discovering If Resource Pool Configuration Is Causing
Disk Latency

```
ALTER RESOURCE POOL [default] WITH(
                min_iops_per_volume=50,
                max_iops_per_volume=100) ;

ALTER RESOURCE GOVERNOR RECONFIGURE ;

SELECT
        rp.name ResourcePoolName
        ,pv.volume_name
        ,pv.read_io_stall_total_ms
        ,pv.write_io_stall_total_ms
        ,pv.read_io_stall_queued_ms
        ,pv.write_io_stall_queued_ms
        ,(pv.read_io_stall_total_ms + pv.write_io_stall_total_ms)
           - (pv.read_io_stall_queued_ms + pv.write_io_stall_queued_ms)
           GovernorLatency
FROM sys.dm_resource_governor_resource_pool_volumes pv
RIGHT JOIN sys.dm_resource_governor_resource_pools rp
        ON pv.pool_id = rp.pool_id ;
```

Tip   If you do not see any I/O stalls, create a database on a low-performance drive and run some intensive queries against it before you rerun the query in Listing 25-10.

Summary

Resource Governor allows you to throttle applications at the SQL Server instance level. You can use it to limit a request's memory, CPU, and disk usage. You can also use it to affinitize a category of requests with specific scheduler or NUMA ranges, or to reduce the MAXDOP for a category of requests.

A resource pool represents a set of server resources and a workload group is a logical container for similar requests that have been classified in the same way. Resource Governor provides an internal resource pool and workload group for system requests and a default resource pool and workload group as a catchall for any requests that have not been classified. Although the internal resource pool cannot be modified, user-defined resource pools have a one-to-many relationship with workload groups.

Requests made to SQL Server are classified using a user-defined function, which the DBA must create. This function must be a scalar function that returns the sysname data type. It must also be schema-bound and reside in the Master database. DBAs can use system functions, such as USER_SNAME(), IS_MEMBER(), and HOST_NAME(), to assist them with the classification.

SQL Server provides four dynamic management views (DMVs) that DBAs can use to help monitor Resource Governor configuration and usage. DBAs can also monitor Resource Governor usage using Performance Monitor, however, and this gives them the advantage of a visual representation of the data. When taking this approach, you will find that Performance Monitor exposes counter categories for resource pools and workload groups for each instance that resides on the server. The counters within these categories have one instance for each resource pool or workload group, respectively, that is currently configured on the instance.

Index

A

Accelerated Database Recovery (ADR)
ALTER DATABASE command, 499
benefits, 499
filegroups, 499, 500
logical revert, 498
log stream, 498
Multithreaded Cleanup, 501
phases, 499
PVS, 498, 500, 502
Additional Connection Properties tab, 913
Advanced cluster preparation
wizard, 40, 41
Advanced Encryption Standard (AES), 546
Affinity mask, 138–140, 143, 170
ALTER SERVER CONFIGURATION,
143, 144
Always Encrypted
attestation service, 438
client key, 440, 441
configuration, 439, 440
configure client, 441
PowerShell script, 439
changes, 438
client driver, 437, 438
CreditCards table, 444
cryptographic objects, 441, 442
database engine, 437
definition, 437
deterministic encryption, 444
encryption types/feature
compatibility, 444

guarded host, 440
insert data, encrypted columns,
445, 446
keys, 437
Administrators, 449
Column Master Keys, 449–451
enclave enabled keys, 448
sys.column_encryption_keys, 447
sys.column_encryption_key_vales,
447, 448
sys.column_master_keys, 446, 447
key store values, 443
limitations, 438
randomized encryption, 444
secure enclaves, 438, 443
segregation of duties, 437
supported drivers, 437
AlwaysOn Availability Groups (AOAG),
533, 633, 664
administrative considerations, 583, 584
automatic page repair, 525, 526
contained availability group, 564–570
data-tier applications, 522
HA (*see* High availability (HA))
monitoring, 582
on Linux, 557–564
topology, 17, 524
synchronous failover, 573–576, 579–581
virtual machines (VMs), 521
AlwaysOn dashboard, 580–582
AlwaysOn Health Trace, 580, 582–583, 585
App3, 563, 565

965

B

C

D

I

M

Printed in the United States
by Baker & Taylor Publisher Services